24th EDITION

WRECKS & RELICS

KEN ELLIS

Crécy

Crécy Publishing Ltd

CONTENTS

Front Cover: Dornier Do 17Z 1160 emerges from the waters of the Goodwin Sands, 10th June 2013. It was shot down during the Battle of Britain on 26th August 1940. It is at the RAF Museum, Cosford, under an intensive stabilization and conservation programme.

Courtesy and copyright Trustees of the Royal Air Force Museum

Rear Cover: Main: Ferocious Sea Prince T.1 G-RACA at Long Marston, August 2013

Roger Richards

Sopwith Pup replica 'A7317', Stow Maries, May 2012 ***Phil Whalley***
Airliner 'graveyard' at Kent Airport, June 2013 ***Phil Whalley***
Gloster Meteor TT.20 WM167 at Newquay, June 2013 ***Tim R Badham***
Three-decade celebration line-up at Bruntingthorpe, November 2013

Steve Buckby

Title Page: A view of the fuselage of Hercules C.3 XV301 from the hold of another example, at Hixon, Staffs, April 2013. ***Phil Adkin***

This twenty-fourth edition published by
Crécy Publishing
1a Ringway Trading Estate, Shadowmoss Road
Manchester M22 5LH

www.crecy.co.uk

ISBN 978 085979 1779

Printed in Malta by Gutenberg Press Ltd

__Wrecks & Relics__ is put together using the best information available to the Author. Every effort is made to be as accurate as possible. However, neither the Author nor Crécy Publishing can be held responsible for any errors or changes that may occur in the location or status of aircraft or places listed.

PREFACE

I thought I'd bitten off more than I could chew and there are times when I *still* think that... In 1974, using a manual typewriter and 'Letraset' rub-down lettering, I put the fourth edition of *Wrecks & Relics* together - all 86 pages of it. (For younger readers, space prevents me from explaining just *what* a typewriter and rub-down lettering were.) That was *my* first edition and its been with me ever since - *four decades*!

Compiling this book is a rolling function and it is always being revised and amended. But *W&R24* has had a major refurbish and the long-held wish to include build and retirement dates has been largely achieved. (For more, see *Before You Start...* on page 5.) The build dates show an increasing number of centenarians, principally at Shuttleworth, Hendon and South Kensington. In November 2013 the Cody biplane clocked up *ten decades* with the Science Museum; the first machine to achieve this longevity of ownership in the UK. As our aviation heritage gains in years, so do the many exhibits and projects at museums and collections. A look at the retirement dates of some 'treasures' shows them to be into their *fifth decade* outdoors; and that does *not* include time in outside storage, or derelict on airfields, *before* they were 'preserved'. The clock is ticking...

The Cody centenary spurred another *W&R* 'special', *Great Aviation Collections of Britain*, and this appeared in 2013. Rampant commercialism compels me to say that it is still available and details can be found at the back of this volume!

-◆-

For a long while I've been using the phrase 'Grass Roots' to categorise the astonishing number of individuals who work as volunteers in museums; or toil in hangars, garages or sheds on their own projects, large or small. Turn the pages within and every line drips with their endeavours. These largely unsung preservationists frequently put the 'big boys' in the shadows with their achievements. Indeed without the vision and determination of this precious national resource, the rich heritage we bask in today wouldn't be half the size.

I decided to replace 'Grass Roots' with a catchier saying, but was worried I would come up with curator-speak and that people would be expecting me to establish a new paradigm and issue a 'mission statement'. I'd no sooner come up with something dynamic than John Craven started fronting *Heritage Heroes* on BBC - how'd he get to know?! So, back to the drawing board... A dive into a thesaurus came up with a good alternative - legacy. It's even got an aviation interpretation as it has become jargon for an earlier design that is still ploughing on. Then another term came to mind - enthusiast. This is often derided for its geekish interpretations, but is *perfect* in this case because passion is vital.

So, out goes 'Grass Roots', in comes Aviation Legacy Enthusiast - and the acronym is exquisite!

This edition is dedicated to the past and present unsung champions that have made our aeronautical heritage so vibrant, comprehensive and world-beating. Over those *four decades*, their friendship, co-operation, dedication and skill have never ceased to amaze and inspire me. I raise a glass to *real* ALEs. You know who you are!

Ken Ellis -
Overly soggy Rutland
28th February 2014

25th Edition deadlines

Images by **31st December 2015**. If you are new to contributing images to *W&R*, please get in touch beforehand for details of resolution required and how best to send.

Comments and notes by **1st February 2016**. Thank you for your support!

Myddle Cottage, 13 Mill Lane, Barrowden, Oakham, LE15 8EH

email: **wrecksandrelics@kenavhist.wanadoo.co.uk**
or, if all else fails: **sillenek@gmail.com**

Acknowledgements

This book relies on a broad spectrum of contributors, each making their mark in different ways. Without their efforts *Wrecks & Relics* would not be possible. Overseeing the draft, adding to it and refining it were: **Alan Allen** and **David J Burke**, both active and respected in the preservation movement; **Dave Allport,** backbone of news reporting and sleuthing at Key Publishing and long-term supporter of *W&R*; **Mick Boulanger** of the Wolverhampton Aviation Group and *Military Aviation Review's* UK guru; **John Coghill**, eagle-eyed wordsmith; **Andy Marden** of *Military Aviation Review's* excellent *Out of Service* feature; **Alistair Ness**, over-saw Scotland and via his column in the Central Scotland Aviation Group's superb *Scottish Air News*; **Nigel Price**, Editor of the flagship *FlyPast*; **David E Thompson**, for the north of England and other notes; **Ian Thompson**, Northern Ireland, Ireland, Isle of Man and more; **Andy Wood** looked after Humberside, Lincolnshire and Yorkshire, and via his column in the ever-brilliant *Humberside Air Review*.

The map is courtesy of **Pete West**, cover design by **Rob Taylor** and colour and page lay-outs by **Russell Strong**. Many, many thanks to **Gill Richardson** and **Jeremy Pratt** and their brilliant team at Crécy Publishing.

and there's much, much more...

A wide range of individuals from the heritage movement, subject and area specialists, and readers have helped with the the research. As ever, this section includes people that have provided *other* inspirations or diversions!

Phil Adkin, wide-ranging notes; **Mike Ager**, 95th BG Heritage Association; **Maggie Aggiss**, Wattisham Station Heritage; **Neil Airey** and **Heather Graham**, Lakes Lightnings; **Steve Allen; Dave Arkle**, and all of the team at **The Aeroplane Collection**; **Len Bachelor**; **Tim R Badham**, images and notes; **Nigel Bailey-Underwood**; **Alan Beattie**, Yorkshire Helicopter Preservation Group; **Philip Bedford**, South East Aviation Enthusiasts Group, Ireland; **Rowland Benbrook**, notes and images from his travels; **C J Bennett**; **David Bennett**; **John Berkeley**, sage-like observations; **Mike Biddulph**, Proctor restorer; **Roy Bonser**; **George Brigham**; **Ben Brown**, Sywell Aviation Museum and answers to many things!; **Steve Buckby**; **Trevor Buckley**; **Matthew Buddle**, Canberra and Lightning restorer, **Ian Burningham**; **Ray Burrows**, Ulster Aviation Society; **Mark Busby**; **Daniel Bygrave**, City of Norwich Aviation Museum; **Mike Cain**, extensive notes on Southend and elsewhere; **Chris Calvert**, Bamburgh Castle; **John Camp**, Boxted Airfield Historical Group; **Richard Capper**; **Russell Carter**; **Richard Cawsey**, notes on gliders; **Adrian Chadburn**; **David Chadwick**; **Simon Chamberlain**, North Weald Airfield Museum; **Richard Clarkson**, Vulcan Restoration Trust; **Theo Claassen**, Rugby Aviation Group; **Rebecca Clay**, Museum of Army Flying; **Pete Coe**; **Philip Cole**; **John D Coleman**, notes and images; **David Collins**, DH Hornet project; **Glyn Coney**, extensive notes; **Eric Cox**, Fenland and West Norfolk Aviation Museum; **David Coxon**, Tangmere Military Aviation Museum; **Roger Creed**, Auster restorer; **Paul Crellin** with a fine eye for details; **Charlie Croker**; **Ernie Cromie**, Ulster Aviation Society; **Tim Crumpton**; **Alan Curry**; **Andy Dann**; **Terry Dann**, extensive notes and images; **Mike Davey**, F-4PPS and much more!; **Clive Davies**, Gloster Aviation Club; **Jeremy Day**; **Paul Deacon**; **Martin Degg**; **Brian Downs**; **Ted Dwane; East Essex Aviation Museum**; **Geoff Eastham**; **Dylan Ecklund**; **Don Ellis**; **John Evans**, Pembroke Dock Sunderland Trust; **Mark Evans**, Midland Aircraft Recovery Group; **Neil Farley**, Imperial Airways Collection; **John Fawke**, Spitfire restorer; **Alf Fisher**, RAF Signals Museum; **Mike Fitch**, Yorkshire Helicopter Preservation Group; **Richard Flagg** and **Gemma Wilkinson**; **Nick Foden** and his light aircraft collection; **Daniel Ford**; **Ken Fostekew**, Museum of Berkshire Aviation; **Graham Francis**; **Keith Freeman**, Museum of Berkshire Aviation; **Ron Fulton**, Boscombe Down Aviation Collection; **Graham Gaff** - East London Aviation Society and UK military guru; **Jonathan Garraway**; **Richard Gibson**, 100th Bomb Group Memorial Museum; **John Golder**, Gnats and Dominies; **Pete Gosden; Gilmar Green**; **Stewart Gilligan Griffin**; **Richard Hall**, notes, images and a two-seat Lightning!; **Neil Hallett**, Hallett Collection/MCA Aviation; **Ian Hancock**, Norfolk and Suffolk Aviation Museum; **Dave Harding**; **Roger Hargreaves**, Britannia Aircraft Preservation Trust; **Mark Harris**; **Ian Haskell**, extensive notes and photography; **Andrew Hawkins**, Firefly restorer; **Graham Haynes**, Bentwaters Cold War Museum; **Ken Haynes**; **Richard Head**, Assault Glider Trust; **Howard Heeley**, Newark Air Museum; **Phil** and **Lynn Hewitt**; **Norman Hibberd**, Boscombe guru; **Mike Higginbottom**; **Dave Hills**, Auster restorer; **Pete Hobson**; **Mike Hodgson**, Thorpe Camp; **Trevor Hope**; **Jon Horswell**; **Jonathan Howard**, cockpit restorer; **Nigel Howarth**; **Ian Humphreys**, images from far and wide; **Daniel** and **Kevin Hunt**, Wings Museum; **Tony Hyatt**; **Mike Ingham**; **Barry James**, Midland Air Museum; **Alf Jenks**, notes and images from his travels; **David S Johnstone** for images from Scotland and raids south of the border!; **Milton Jones**; **Bob Kent**, Shoreham Airport Visitor Centre; **Tim Kershaw**, Jet Age Museum; **Peter Kindred**, Parham Airfield Museum; **Howard King**, Martlesham Heath Control Tower Museum; **David Kinsey**; **Max** and **Ritch La Rue-Blood**; **David Lane**, Caernarfon Airport Airworld Museum; **Andrew Lee**, Lee Air Services, Trident G-AWZI and 'Grippers' in general; **Darren Lewington**; **Andrew Lewis**, Brooklands Museum; **Anthony Livingstone**; **Martin Locke**, Assault Glider Trust; **Jonathan Longbottom**; **Ben Lovett**; **Chris Lowe**, Lakeland Motor Museum; **Brian Luff**, Farnborough Air Sciences Trust; **Doug MacDonald**; **Norman B Male**, rotorcraft; **Roger Marley**, Hawker Typhoon and other projects; **Winston Marshall**; **Trevor Matthews**, Lashenden Air Warfare Museum and 'Doddlebug' maestro; **Sarah Maughan**, Stanford Hall; **Tony** and **Brenda McCarthy**, notes and images from their travels; **Chris Michell**, Isle of Wight; **Anthony Mills**, extensive notes and images, above and below the water!; **Naylan Moore**, People's Front of Doncaster and South Yorkshire Aircraft Museum; **John S Morgan**, cockpit and glider collector; **Dave Morris**, Fleet Air Arm Museum; **Chris Morshead**, RAF Air Defence Radar Museum; **Marcus Mumford**; **163 ELT**; **David O'Mahony**, notes from Ireland; **Margaret O'Shaughnessy**, Foynes Flying-Boat and Maritime Museum; **Andrew Panton**, Lincolnshire Aviation Heritage Centre; **Steve Perry**, Davidstow Airfield and Cornwall at War Museum; **Dr Ian Pertbottom**; **John Phillips**, Skeeter owner, rotorcraft and others; **Mike Phipp**, Bournemouth and area; **Roger Pickett**, Thameside Aviation Museum; **Darren J Pitcher**, extensive reports, particularly Booker; **Cyril Plimmer**, Boulton Paul Association; **Nigel** and **Anne Ponsford**, Ponsford Collection; **Geoffrey Pool**, Bruntingthorpe, his Hunter and more!, **Col Pope**, Duxford, other warbirds and fine images; **David Potter**; **Mark Presswood**; **Simon Pulford**, Air Pulford and the Tornado collection; **Richard Pymar**, Halesworth Airfield Memorial Museum; **Ivor Ramsden**, Manx Aviation and Military Museum; **Elfan ap Rees**, The Helicopter Museum; **Roger Richards**, extensive notes and images; **Ian Richardson**, Yorkshire Air Museum; **Paco Rivas** - sage-like warbird studies, from Madrid!; **Norman Roberson**, Buccaneer historian; **Mark Roberts - Aerobilia**; **Elfan Safteigh**, progress prevention consultant; **Chris Salter**; **Steve Screech**; **Guy Shear**; **Jim Simpson**, Nimrods and others; **Tom Singfield**, notes and images from his travels; **Roz Skellorn**, Tank Museum; **Bob Sloan**, Dumfries and Galloway Aviation Museum; **P F Sloan**; **Kelvin Sloper**, City of Norwich Aviation Museum; **Mike Smith**, Newark Air Museum; **Graham Sparkes**, The Aeroplane Collection, Hooton Park Trust and his own airframes; **Denise Spearman**, Cranwell Aviation Visitor Centre; **Peter Spooner**, constant notes from all over the country; **Ajay Srivastava**, Royal Air Force Museum; **Brian Stafford**, North Coates Heritage Collection and other destinations; **Mike Stannard**; **Ralph Steiner**, De Havilland Aircraft Heritage Centre; **Barry Taylor**; **Dave Taylor**, Cockpitmania; **Julian Temple**, Brooklands Museum; **Hugh Trevor**, Lightning historian and cockpit owner; **Gavin Troon**; **Bob Turner**, Fleet Air Arm Museum; **Peter Turner**, Miles aircraft restororer; **Richard Turner**, Boxted Airfield Historical Group; **Sam Tyler**; **David Underwood**, glider craftsman; **Graham Vale**, East Midlands Airport Volunteers Association; **Bob Vandereyt**; **Francis Wallace**, The Buccaneer Aviation Group and 'Buccs' in general; **Simon Wallwork**, assorted sleuthings; **Michael Westwood**; **Phil Whalley** - Avpics, Southend, Vulcan Restoration Trust and more!; **Jon Wickenden**, images and notes from extensive travels; **Keith Williams**; **Chris Wilson**, Jet Art Aviation; **Carol Woodland**, Charnwood Museum; **Les Woodward**, notes and images; **Dean Wright**; **Brian Yost**.

...and to Pam and our quadruped, Rex

BEFORE YOU START...

Many readers will be well familiar with the 'rules of engagement', but they *do* alter from time to time. **Major changes in this edition are highlighted in bold** to draw the eye.

Scope: *Wrecks & Relics* serves to outline, in as much detail as possible, the status of all known PRESERVED (ie in museum or other collections, under restoration etc); INSTRUCTIONAL (ie static airframes in use for training); and DERELICT (ie out of use for a long period of time, on a fire dump, scrapped or damaged etc) aircraft in the United Kingdom and Ireland and HM Forces aircraft based on Crown Territory. The following exceptions apply: airworthy aircraft not part of a specific collection; aircraft that fall into any of the above categories for only a short period of time - generally less than a year. As a rule, aircraft will only be considered if they are *at least* a cockpit. For this edition, **there has been a cull of long-in-the-tooth references**, particularly of less 'interesting' light aircraft and microlights. After requests from readers, and acknowledging the inevitable rise of drones (alright then, UAVs), *all* unmanned aircraft, providing that they fall into the scope given above and are not the size of a sparrow, are included. Current MoD/RAF thinking is to call these remotely piloted aircraft systems (RPAS) presumably as 'unmanned' gives the impression there is no pilot in charge... well, certainly not in-theatre...

Locations: Are listed by county/province and then alphabetically. County boundaries are as given by the Ordnance Survey and as defined by the Local Government Act and include the changes up to April 2012. Entries for Scotland, Wales, Northern Ireland and Ireland are purely alphabetic, primarily to help the English! From 1st April 1996 all of Scotland and Wales were wholly divided into 'Single Tier' Unitary Authorities, with their 'Counties' now having little meaning.

Directions are given after each place name. Readers should note that these are *to the town or village mentioned* and ***not*** necessarily to the actual site in question. Directions are *not* given in the following instances: where the location is a large city or town; where specific directions to the site are not fully known; or at the request of several aircraft owners - who have every right to preserve their peace and quiet - some locations have been 'generalised'.

In recent times, the 'rebranding' of airports has reached farcical levels with seemingly *everywhere* deciding to attach the magic label 'London'. If, for example, you find yourself frustrated that you cannot locate Robin Hood Airport, then turn to the Locations Index which includes alternative names. (To alleviate any unnecessary tension, *W&R* adopts the CAA-accepted Doncaster Sheffield Airport, while hankering for when it was Finningley!)

A form of notation relating to the status of an 'aerodrome' is given. Bearing in mind that in the Air Navigation Order *all* places where flying is conducted are known as aerodromes, a wider interpretation has been employed: 'Aerodrome' signifies a civilian flying ground used by aircraft up to King Air, 'biz-jet' etc size. 'Airfield' is used to signify a flying ground used by the armed forces, test establishments or manufacturers. 'Airport' is used to denote a flying ground that takes 'serious' sized airliners on a regular basis. International Civil Aviation Organisation four-letter location indicators are also included. For privacy and security purposes, private strips etc are frequently *not* denoted as such.

Unless otherwise stated, *all* locations in this work are PRIVATE and access to them *is strictly by prior permission, if at all.* A mention in this book does not imply *any* right of access. Visitor data, is given as follows: **Access**: In these increasingly litigious times, more often than not, this segment is used to draw attention to locations that particularly *do not* allow access or where prior permission is required. Also here can be found details about how to find the venue, eg is it 'brown signed', what road is the best etc. For those who crave GPS or Google references to venues, in many cases this is wholly impractical. Get a road atlas, arm yourself with *prior* permission to visit and keep your eyes on the traffic and the scenery! (Note also that post codes given in this section may *not* lead a sat-nav thingie to the venue!) **Open**: Opening times etc are given as a *guide only*; they can and do change. Readers should use the 'Contact' segment to satisfy themselves that the venue will be open when they visit. **Contact**: Postal address, *daytime* telephone number(s), email and web-sites are given, where known. **Note:** web-sites are given for information only; no recommendation of content is to be implied. Some of these sites may also include routings to 'anti-social media' domains, examples of which I believe are 'Off-Your-Face' or 'Twaddle'; again, no recommendation to go there is to be implied at all. **Thinx**: Random notes relating to other sites that may be of interest and/or relevance. The writer makes no apologies that more than a few of these relate to pubs!

Entries and Aircraft Listings: Generally, entries are all dealt with in a standard manner. As *W&R* covers a two-year period, in this case 2012 to 2014, beyond the location header there is a narrative explaining the current status of the entry and outlining any airframes that have moved since the last edition. Airframes moving on are given underlined forwarding references, including the county, or province, that reference can be found in. This allows the reader to follow the more energetic examples around the book! Any aircraft which fall out of any of the categories above, or are exported, will not have forwarding references. 'Ownership' or 'custodianship' of airframes within this work is not to be inferred as definitive.

The tables have been re-vamped *a little bit more* for this edition. **Column 1**: Aircraft are listed alpha-numerically, using the following rubric. British civil first (except in Ireland where EI- comes first), followed by British Gliding Association and 'B Condition' (or 'trade plate') markings. Then overseas civil registrations in alpha-numeric order. British military serials follow (with reversal again in Ireland) followed by overseas military listed by country – ie France before Netherlands before USA.

Anonymous airframes are inserted where it is thought most logical! No attempt has been made to note if an identity is worn or not on the airframe. Incorrect or fictitious registrations and serials are marked in quotes, eg 'VZ999' or 'G-BKEN'. Codes worn by aircraft are given in Column 1, eg 'AF-V' or '825'. A dash (-) is used to denote an airframe that has no confirmed primary identity. Entries new to a heading in this edition are marked *.

Column 2: Is devoted to codes, eg 'Z' or '109' allocated, but not necessarily worn, on the airframe.

Column 3: **Now includes aircraft design origin**, type/designation, sometimes abbreviated. Design *origin* has been chosen in favour of manufacturer, otherwise there would be references to Short Canberras or Westland Spitfires which some may find confusing. (Although Column 6 contains manufacturer details for major types; homebuilds do not get this treatment.) Reference to the *Index I Types* will provide a cross-reference. (Major rethinks of types, eg Short's morphing of the Tucano and Westland's re-engineering of the Whirlwind, Wessex and Sea King is, however, acknowledged, though not the latter company's 'badge engineering' on the Gazelle and Puma.) To acquaint readers with the nature of some of the types listed, some abbreviations and a symbol are used: ✈ Believed airworthy, at time of going to press. CIM: Purpose-built instructional airframe, not intended for flight: Classroom Instruction Model, or even Module. EMU: Purpose-built test and evaluation airframe, not intended for flight, in most cases using prototype or production jigs and tooling: Engineering Mock-up. FSM: Full-scale model. Faithful external reproduction of an aircraft, but using construction techniques completely unrelated to the original, frequently in fibreglass. PAX: Cockpit for crew emergency egress training, mostly (now retired) Chipmunk T.10s: Passenger (= PAX) Trainer. Replica or rep: Reproduction, ie a faithful, or near-faithful copy or a facsimile of an aircraft type. Occasionally built to a different scale, but using construction techniques and proportions in keeping with the original. For reasons best known to themselves, the UK MoD has dropped the full stop from its designations. Thus the Boeing Sentry these days is an AEW1 not AEW.1. *W&R* ignores this *pointless* (geddit?!) 'innovation' and remains consistent!

Column 4: After a little bit of experimentation in *W&R23*, this column is devoted to *current* civil registrations allocated, but not worn, on 'warbirds' and the like. Also here are *correct* identities when an incorrect or fictitious identity is presented in Column 1. Other identities are to be found in appropriate sequence in Column 6.

Column 5: **Now gives year manufactured**; in most cases when first flown. Dates from 1915 *onwards* are given as two digits, eg 67 = 1967, or 07 = 2007. Airframes pre-1914 have the year in full, eg 1896. In some cases, it has been possible only to give a 'stab' at the build date in which case they are given as follows: c36. With some aircraft that have never flown, if no other data is given, then the date first registered is used, eg r76. Where it is impossible to give a date a wavy dash ~ is given - perhaps *you* can help eradicate these in *W&R25*?

Column 6: Where possible, brief historical details of the aircraft listed are given, in a necessarily abbreviated form. In each case, units, operators, previous identities etc are listed in *reverse* order, ie the last user (or identity) is given *first*. Seasoned readers should have little trouble with these potted histories and the *Abbreviations* section lists the most-used alphanumeric soup. Also given here are other registrations, or maintenance serials applicable to the airframe.

Royal Navy maintenance serials - 'A' numbers - were re-allocated, creating a confusing vista. Second, third or even *fourth* allocations are known and are noted in square brackets eg A2664 [3]. Readers should refer to the masterful BARG/Air-Britain *Royal Navy Instructional Airframes* for the 'Full Monty'. 'A' and 'M' numbers are no longer allocated. Where it helps to note when an airframe was withdrawn, the date of allocation of an 'A' or an 'M' number is given.

Much work has gone into showing, as much as possible, **when an airframe stopped flying**. This is relatively easy with UK civil registered aircraft - see the next paragraph. With British military the abbreviation **SOC (struck off charge)** has been used as a wide *generic* term, to avoid endless abbreviations and definitions. The date given may well be when the airframe in question *was* SOC'd, but it may also apply to it being sold (either intact or as scrap), transferred to display purposes, or to a museum, or similar. Occasionally, last flown dates are given. Work on this is on-going...

Where a date is given prefixed 'CoA' (Certificate of Airworthiness), this is the date at which it lapsed and is given as an *indication* of how long the airframe has been flightless. The term 'CoA' is a catch-all and used for all levels of certification, eg Permit to Fly, Ferry Permit etc. Where an airframe has suffered an accident, this is given as 'Crashed' or 'Cr', no attempt has been made to try to delineate the severity, or nature, or blame (!) of the incident. '**De-reg**' (previously given as the somewhat clumsy 'canx') refers to the date when a registration was formally cancelled from the civil register. It should be born in mind that in some cases the 'paperwork' can lag behind the reality by decades!

Also from this edition with museum aircraft in particular an attempt has been made to show **how long a collection has had a particular airframe**. Mostly, this is noted as 'arrived', but in some cases 'acquired' is used to signify that the airframe was taken on while the collection was based elsewhere, or similar. Work on this feature is also on-going...

Column 7: Used for footnotes – eg [7] and explained at the base of the listing.

Column 8: 'Last noted' dates are given primarily to help historians to trace the status (or demise) of an airframe and perhaps to alert readers intending a visit as to the 'currency' of the information given.

PART ONE

ENGLAND

BEDFORDSHIRE

Includes the unitary authority of Luton

BEDFORD

Bedford College: Adjacent to Cauldwell Street - *Busy campus, prior arrangement* **only** | **www.bedford.ac.uk**

❑ XX495	'C'	HP Jetstream T.1	75	ex Shawbury, Cranwell, 45, 3 FTS, 45, 6 FTS, METS. Arr 2005		1-06

Also: A Skeeter has long been kept at a *private* location in the general area.

❑ XL809*		Saro Skeeter AOP.12 G-BLIX	58	ex PH-HOF, Moordrecht, XL809, 26 Rgt, 652, 22 Flt, 654, 652. SOC 12-12-68		1-14

BEDFORD AIRFIELD now listed under Thurleigh, see below.

CRANFIELD AERODROME east of Newport Pagnell

EGTC

Cranfield Institute of Technology / College of Aeronautics / Cranfield Aerospace Ltd: Last noted in January 2007, Twin Comanche 160 G-AWBT has been deleted.

◆ **Access:** *Very busy campus, much located on an active airfield. Access* **only** *by prior permission* | **www.cranfield.ac.uk**

❑ G-COAI		Cranfield A1 Eagle	76	ex G-BCIT. Stored		9-09
❑ 'G-DHEA'		HS.125-3B/RA G-OHEA	67	ex Hatfield, G-AVRG, G-5-12. CoA 7-8-92; de-reg 23-6-94	[1]	5-13
❑ G-RAVL		HP Jetstream 200	69	ex G-AWVK, N1035S, G-AWVK. CoA 26-2-94; de-reg 30-1-01		5-13
❑ XX387		Sud Gazelle AH.1	75	ex Arborfield TAD.014, Fleetlands, 651, 661, 657, 16/5 Lancers. Westland-built. Crashed 15-12-92		5-10
❑ XZ668		Westland Lynx AH.7	81	ex Middle Wallop, 63, 3 Rgt, 653. Ditched 18-8-95	[2]	5-10
❑ ZJ515		HS Nimrod MRA.4	10	ex Woodford, MR.2 XV258, St Mawgan W, Kinloss W, MR.1 42, Kinloss, 203. Arr 29-3-11. Cockpit plus sections	[3]	7-12

■ **[1]** The low-loader based HS.125 has had its registration doctored to read G-DHEA - De Havilland Executive Aircraft? **[2]** The Lynx was last heard of at "Wallop's Accident Investigation Unit in 3-97. **[3]** Study in asset management: ZJ515 first flew 8-3-10 and made its last flight *15 days* later. It beggars belief what the unit cost of this one airframe divided by its flight hours comes out at! As MR.1 XV258, it first flew in 1972 and was retired to become a MRA.4 1999. Now *that's* VFM!

T5 Alive: Russell Carpenter and friends keep this wonderful machine 'in steam' and it regularly taxis. From 23rd June 2012 XS458 became a truly 'electric' Lightning. With the help of gifted friends, the Lightning has been weaned off the increasingly expensive and elusive AVPIN starter 'juice' to ignition by a chain of batteries. Following an extensive period of maintenance XS458 got back into first gear and taxied again on 13th July 2013.

◆ **Access:** *Occasional 'thunder runs' and special events. Details via the web-site. Please note that the airfield is on an operational airfield and access is* **only** *by prior arrangement.* **Contact: email** *via web-site* | **www.lightningt5.com**

❑ XS458	'T'	EE Lightning T.5	65	ex Binbrook, LTF, 11, LTF, 5-11 pool, LTF, 5, 226 OCU. SOC 24-6-88		12-13

Also: A clear-out of long-in-the-tooth entries, with last noted dates: Cessna F.177 G-BCUW (Aug 2005); Motor Cadet G-BDUX (Jul 1990); Cherokee 180 G-NITA and Cessna F.150L G-SADE (both Jan 2006).

❑ G-BAUJ		Piper Aztec 250E	73	ex N14390. CoA 25-7-94; de-reg 31-10-02. Stored		9-11
❑ G-SHIV		American GA-7 Cougar	79	ex N713G. CoA 18-1-98; de-reg 16-9-04		9-11

DUNSTABLE AERODROME on the B489 south-east of Dunstable

Last recorded in May 2001 as in use for spares, off-site, Rallye Club PH-MSB has been deleted.

❑ G-BLGS		MS Rallye 180T	78	ex Lasham. CoA 21-5-99. Stripped out		10-12

EATON BRAY west of Dunstable

Peter and **David Underwood**: The *private* glider workshop continues to work its magic.

❑ G-ASEA		Luton Minor	66	CoA 16-8-89		2-14
❑ -		Slingsby Kirby Kite 1	35	BGA.236, ex G-ALUD, BGA.236, BGA.222	[1]	2-14
❑ -		Slingsby Kirby Kite	37	BGA.327, ex Ilkley Moor, Tibenham, RAFGSA.182, VD218, BGA.310	[2]	2-14
❑ ALZ		Hawkridge Dagling	47	BGA.492, BAPC.81, Dunstable, Duxford, Warton		2-14

■ **[1]** The prototype Kite is being restored to its guise when it first flew in August 1935. **[2]** BGA.310 was rebuilt using elements of BGA.327 which is now at Shuttleworth, Beds - qv. The *original* fuselage, tail feathers and an aileron, after a crash in 1970, are here hence the change of BGA identity.

FLITWICK north-west of Luton, north of J12 of the M1

Roger Creed: During June 2012 Roger acquired fire-damaged J/1N G-AHCN, which offered a better basis for a restoration project. J/1N G-AHAT was scrapped during 2012, with parts salvaged for re-use. Progress on *Charlie-November* has been swift. Roger has a 'shopping list' of non-flight rated parts he needs - get in touch if you can help | **roger.creed@tesco.net**

❑ G-AHCN*	Auster J/1N Alpha	46	CoA 6-12-11. Fuselage, arrived 6-12	[1]	12-13

■ **[1]** Wings destined for G-AHCN are from J/1 G-AJDW - see Spilsby, Lincs.

HATCH off the B658, south-west of Sandy

Skysport Engineering: The DH.2 has been mentioned in several *W&Rs*; it has made sufficient progress to be given a formal listing. The Avro 504K has been underway for about five years; it is also making good headway. The Swift was acquired from a motor fair at Beaulieu and is a 'pending' project. Composite Beaufighter I G-DINT was exported during 2012. Last recorded in December 2007, the Da Vinci TV series 'replica' has been deleted.

◆ **Access: Strictly** *by prior permission* **only | www.skysportengineering.co.uk**

❑ AXB	Slingsby Skylark 2	56	BGA.733, ex Lyveden. CoA 30-6-02	[1]	10-13
❑ F-ANHO*	Comper Swift	33	ex France, HB-OXE, CH-352. Fuselage		12-13
❑ N5595T	Douglas C-47A-85-DL Skytrain	43	ex Thruxton, Blackbushe, G-BGCG, Spanish AF T3-27, N49V, N50322, 43-15536. Stored		12-13
❑ E2977*	Avro 504K	18	Morgan & Co-built. Fuselage		12-13
❑ -*	Airco DH.2 replica	~	-		12-13
❑ –	Hawker Demon I	~	fuselage frame		12-13

■ **[1]** Prototype Skylark 2, flown by Flt Lt Douglas Bridson up to 30,000ft. **[2]** Skysport-built hang-glider for the Channel 4 TV documentary *Leonardo's Dream Machines* in 2003.

HENLOW AIRFIELD on the A6007 south-west of Biggleswade — EGWE

RAF Signals Museum: Located within the base, this took on much of the collection that was amassed by 1 Radio School at Locking, Somerset. The volunteer staff has created incredible displays that appeal to specialists and enthusiasts alike.

◆ **Open:** *First Sat of the month, Feb to Nov, 10:00 to 18:00 or by prior arrangement. Please see the web-site for what is required to visit what is an operational RAF station.* **Contact: 01462 851515 extension 7997** - *leave message, including contact number, for phone-back* | **alf_fisher@tiscali.co.uk** | **www.rafsignalsmuseum.org.uk**

RAF Henlow: The Gazelle and the Lynx are with the **Centre of Aviation Medicine**; the Gazelle is kept in a classroom. Last noted in April 209, the cockpit of Viking T.1 ZE592 moved to Halton, Bucks, by March 2013.

❑ WT612		Hawker Hunter F.1	54	ex Halton, Credenhill, Yatesbury 7496M (29-11-57), A&AEE. Gate	10-13
❑ XZ312		Sud Gazelle AH.1	76	ex Shawbury, Wattisham, 3 Regt. Westland-built. Pod	10-13
❑ ZD250*	'636'	Westland Lynx HAS.3S	82	ex 702, 815, 702, 815, 702, 815, 829, 702. Less boom. First noted 4-12	2-14

Civil Enclave:

❑ G-ARRZ	Druine Turbulent	62	crashed 21-7-90, CoA 21-12-90. Rollason-built	2-14
❑ G-BGBF	Druine Turbulent	80	ex Eaglescott. CoA 25-3-04	2-14
❑ G-BHNX	Jodel D.117	56	ex F-BHNX. SAN-built. CoA 12-1-87	2-14

LONDON LUTON AIRPORT — EGGW

❑ G-AOVS	Bristol Britannia 312	58	ex Redcoat, 'G-BRAC', Lloyd, BOAC. CoA 31-7-79, de-reg 7-5-81. Fuselage. Fire crews	8-13
❑ VP-BJW	Boeing 737-301	87	ex Kemble, KD Avia, N563AU, N348US, N328P *Mitropoht Kirvil*. Forward fuselage. Fire crews	8-13

LOWER STONDON west of the A600, north of Hitchin

Stondon Transport Museum: Hundreds of motor vehicles and other artefacts in five halls, plus a coffee shop. A full size replica of Cook's HM *Bark Endeavour* of 1768 is available for guided tours.

◆ **Access:** *South of Henlow and signed off the A600.* **Open:** *Sat to Thurs 10:00 to 16:00 -* ***Note*** *closed on Fridays - other than Good Friday.* **Contact:** *Station Road, Lower Stondon, Henlow, SG16 6JN* | **01462 850339** | **transportmuseum@supanet.com** | **www.transportmuseum.co.uk**

❑ 'G-ADRG'	Mignet HM.14 'Flea'	74	BAPC.77, ex Cheltenham, Long Marston, Innsworth, Ross-on-Wye, Staverton	4-13
❑ G-AXOM	Penn-Smith Gyroplane	70	de-reg 11-10-74	4-13
❑ XN341	Saro Skeeter AOP.12	60	ex Luton, St Athan 8022M, 4 SoTT, 3 RTR, 651. SOC 21-9-89	4-13

SHUTTLEWORTH AERODROME or Old Warden EGTH

Shuttleworth Collection: During the spring of 2012 the collection refurbished a building visible on the 'woods' side of the aerodrome. The garage-like construction was put up in 1932 as a home for Richard Shuttleworth's DH.60 G-EBWD and the very same biplane was used to 'christen' the restored structure on April 19. Mew Gull G-AEXF departed Old Warden for Breighton, E Yorks, on 15th June 2002, much to the chagrin of many enthusiasts who regarded it as being a quintessential Shuttleworth type. This was put to rights on 6th October 2013 when 'Taff' Smith brought it 'home'.

As *W&R* closed for press, news was to hand that the collection was busy finalising the acquisition from Australia of a Santos-Dumont Demoiselle built for the film *Those Magnificent Men in Their Flying Machines*. One of three built by Personal Plane Services at White Waltham in 1963, this one *should* be PPS/DEM/2. With the Avro and the Boxkite, it will make for a great movie set-piece.

Tragedy struck on 1st July 2012 in the run-up to a flying display. **Trevor Roche** was flying the DH.53 when a problem was encountered and the aircraft came to grief on the aerodrome. Trevor was killed. An incredibly warm and likeable character, Trevor was much respected by his fellow pilots and admired by the regulars at Shuttleworth events. During his time at Old Warden, Trevor had flown in almost every type in the fleet. A British Airways captain, Trevor had previously flown fast jets with the RAF and was a First Gulf War veteran, being involved in the early low-level raids, amongst others.

The arrival of the presently skeletal Sopwith Camel in August 2013 marked the winding up of **Northern Aeroplane Workshops**, lately based at Batley, West Yorks. Founded in 1973, NAW created three superb replicas in that time, all for Shuttleworth: NAW-1 was the Sopwith Triplane, powered by a 130hp Clerget rotary and first flown on 10th April 1992 - see also its footnote. NAW-2 was the Bristol M.1C, flown for the first time on 25th September 2000, with a 110hp Le Rhône. The Camel, NAW-3, is also fitted with a 130hp Clerget.

Supporting in many ways is the **Shuttleworth Veteran Aeroplane Society** (SVAS) which is a major fund-raiser, it publishes the excellent *Prop-Swing*, and welcomes new members. The tally of aircraft acquired for the collection by SVAS includes: Chipmunk, Jungmann, Lysander, Provost, Super Cub. (Contacts: PO Box 42, Old Warden Aerodrome, Biggleswade, Beds, SG18 9EP | **01767 627909** | **SVAS@shuttleworth.org** | **www.svasweb.org**)

W&R23 (p10) had Luftwaffe-schemed Grunau Baby 'S1+1-11' (DNB) as joining the collection by June 2011. Fresh from the Eaton Bray workshop of vintage glider maestros Peter and David Underwood, it test flew from Old Warden and carried out two air displays there before moving on to fly with a syndicate at Haddenham, Bucks. During the summer of 2013 Fauvel AV.36 BGA.2932 / ETE was on show within the main hangars, it moved to Wycombe Air Park, Bucks, for restoration. Blériot BAPC.9 in on loan to the Midland Air Museum at Coventry, Warks.

Departures: The following, privately owned, are no longer resident: Tipsy Trainer G-AFWT, Santos Dumont Demoiselle '91AEH', Ryan PT-22 854 (G-BTBH). Off-site, the anonymous Ryan PT-22 spares ship, turned out to be G-BPUD and had moved by early 2012, settling on Rayleigh, Essex. Also stored off-site, Prentice T.1 VS610 (G-AOKL) was disposed of to Neil Butler in March 2013 and moved to Montrose, Scotland. Last used for rescue training in mid-2007, the hulk of Tomahawk 112 D-EGLW has moved on, in one form or another. On loan from Skysport, of Hatch, Beds, the fuselage frame of the Westland Wallace replica moved to Leicester, Leics, in January 2013.

◆ **Access:** *'Brown signed' from the A1 - turn off at Biggleswade junction.* ***Please note****: Hangars 9 and 10 are located on the non-public side of the aerodrome and its contents are not available for inspection and are not listed here.* **Open:** *Daily, Apr to Oct 09:30 to 17:00, Nov to Mar 10:00 to 16:00. Separate charges for airshows, and for the different 'segments' of the site - value-for-money combination tickets also available.* **Contact:** *Old Warden Aerodrome, Biggleswade, Beds, SG18 9EP* | **01767 627927** | **marketingevents@shuttleworth.org** | **www.shuttleworth.org**

❑ G-EBHX		DH Humming Bird	23	ex Lympne No.8. Acquired 4-8-60. *L'Oiseau Mouche* Crashed 1-7-12. CoA 4-4-13. Stored, off-site		3-12
❑ G-EBIR		DH.51 ✈	24	ex VP-KAA, G-KAA, G-EBIR. Acquired 7-65. AT&T colours	[1]	1-14
❑ G-EBJI		Hawker Cygnet replica ✈	77	arrived 4-10, first test flight 4-12	[2]	1-14
❑ G-EBJO		ANEC II ✈	24	ex Radcliffe on Trent, Old Warden, West Malling, Lympne 1924, No.7. Acquired 1-37		1-14
❑ G-EBLV		DH.60 Moth ✈	25	ex Hatfield. Arrived 1993	[3]	1-14
❑ G-EBNV	'4'	English Electric Wren II	23	BAPC.11, ex Warton, Ashton, Samlesbury, Preston, Science Museum, Lympne No.4. Acquired 15-9-57	[4]	1-14
❑ G-EBWD		DH.60X Moth ✈	28	acquired 21-1-32	[5]	1-14

❑ G-AAIN		Parnall Elf II ✈		32	ex Southend, Fairoaks, Badminton. Acquired 7-51		1-14
❑ G-AANG		Blériot XI ✈		1910	No.13, BAPC.3, ex Ampthill, Blackfriars, Hendon. Acq 1935		1-14
❑ G-AANH		Deperdussin ✈		1910	No.43, BAPC.4, ex *Those Magnificent Men*, Ampthill. Acquired 1935		1-14
❑ G-AANI		Blackburn Monoplane ✈		1912	No.9, BAPC.5, ex Wittering, M F Glew, Cyril Foggin. Acquired 1937		1-14
❑ G-AAPZ		Desoutter I ✈		30	ex Higher Blagdon, Old Warden, Warden Aviation Co. Acquired 5-1-35		1-14
❑ G-AAYX		Southern Martlet ✈		30	ex Shoreham, Redhill, Staverton, Woodley. Acquired 1955		1-14
❑ G-ABAG*		DH Gipsy Moth ✈		30	'arrived' 1-04	[6]	1-14
❑ G-ABXL		Granger Archaeopteryx		30	ex Radcliffe on Trent, Old Warden, Chilwell. Arrived 28-4-67. CoA 22-9-82. Off-site	[7]	3-12
❑ G-ACSS	'34'	DH.88 Comet		34	ex Hatfield, Farnborough, Old Warden, Leavesden, Hatfield, London Colney, Gravesend, Australian Anniversary, *The Burberry*, *The Orphan*, G-ACSS, K5084 A&AEE, RAE, AA&EE, RAE, G-ACSS. *Grosvenor House*. CoA 2-6-94. Acquired 30-10-65. Ground-looped 28-10-02		1-14
❑ G-ACTF		Comper Swift ✈		32	ex Rhos, VT-ADO. Acquired 16-8-96. *The Scarlet Angel*.		1-14
❑ G-AEBB		Mignet HM.14 'Flea'		36	ex Southampton. Acquired 1968. CoA 31-5-39		1-14
❑ G-AEBJ		Blackburn B-2 ✈		36	ex Brough, Warton, Blackburn, 4 EFTS, Brough, Hanworth. Arrived 3-08	[3]	1-14
❑ G-AEEG		Miles Falcon Major ✈		36	ex SE-AFN, RSwAF Fv913, SE-AFN, G-AEEG, U-20	[8]	1-14
❑ G-AESZ*	'29'	Chilton DW.1 ✈		37	arrived 6-11	[9]	1-14
❑ G-AEXF*		Percival Mew Gull ✈		36	ex Breighton, Old Warden, Sudbury, Old Warden, ZS-AHM, G-AEXF. Arrived 6-10-13	[10]	1-14
❑ G-AGSH		DH Dragon Rapide 6 ✈		45	ex Bournemouth, Lower Upham, EI-AJO, G-AGSH, NR808 n/s. Brush-built. Arrived 27-2-09. BEA colours, *Gemma Meeson*	[11]	1-14
❑ G-AHKX		Avro XIX Srs 2 ✈		46	ex Woodford, Strathallan, Kemps, Treffield, Smiths. Arrived 29-6-02	[3]	1-14
❑ G-ARSG	'12'	Avro Triplane IV rep ✈		64	BAPC.1, ex *Those Magnificent Men...* Hampshire Aero Club-built. Acquired 1966	[12]	1-14
❑ G-ASPP	'12A'	Bristol Boxkite replica ✈		64	BAPC.2, ex *Those Magnificent Men...* F G Miles-built. Acquired 1966	[13]	1-14
❑ G-BZSC*		Sopwith Camel F1 replica		01	ex Batley. NAW-built. Will have 130hp Clerget. Arrived 28-8-13. Uncovered		1-14
❑ G-CAMM	'6'	Hawker Cygnet replica ✈		92	ex Hucknall, G-ERDB ntu. Arrived 1995	[14]	1-14
❑ G-CDXU		Chilton DW.1 replica ✈		09	arrived 2010	[15]	1-14
❑ G-IBRO*		Cessna 152 II		85	ex Leicester, EI-BRO. Crashed 3-3-05, de-reg 29-6-05. Rescue training. Arrived mid-2009		4-12
❑ G-SVAS		Piper Super Cub 150 ✈		61	ex G-BGWH, ST-ABR, G-ARSR, N10F. Acquired 13-10-08		1-14
❑ –		Abbott-Baynes Scud II		35	BGA.231, CoA 1-6-06		1-14
❑ ADJ		Slingsby Kirby Kite		37	BGA.310, ex Tibenham	[16]	1-14
❑ AQQ		EoN Primary ✈		c47	BGA.580, ex Hatch, Duxford, Henlow, Twinwood Farm, G-ALPS. Acquired late 1960s		1-14
❑ –		Dixon Ornithopter		c1912	BAPC.8, ex Dunstable. Acquired 1960s		3-12
❑ –		Lilienthal replica		06	ex St Albans. 'Standard Flying Apparatus No.11'. Arr 4-07	[17]	1-14
❑ –		Pilcher Bat Mk.3 replica		08	ex St Albans. Arrived 11-08	[17]	1-14
❑ –*		Pilcher Triplane replica		03	arrived 2006	[18]	1-14
❑ '9917'		Sopwith Pup ✈	G-EBKY	20	ex 'N6181', 'N5180', 'N5184', West Malling, Kingston. Acquired 1937	[19]	1-14
❑ 'A1742'		Bristol Scout replica		62	BAPC.38, ex Solihull, Norwich, Lowestoft, Duxford, Avon area, St Mawgan, St Athan, Colerne, Weeton. Arrived 17-5-2009	[20]	1-14
❑ 'C4918'		Bristol M.1C rep ✈	G-BWJM	81	ex Dewsbury. 'C' Flight, NAW-built. 110hp Le Rhône. Acquired 28-10-97. 72 Sqn colours		1-14
❑ D8096		Bristol F.2b ✈	G-AEPH	18	ex Filton, Watford, D8096, 208. Acquired 2-52		1-14
❑ 'E3273'		Avro 504K ✈	G-ADEV	18	ex G-ACNB, 'H5199', 'E3404', *Reach for the Sky*, Woodford, Boscombe Down, Portsmouth, Airspeed, Avro 504N. Acquired 1936. 77 Sqn c/s, red-blue roundels	[21]	1-14

❑	F904		RAF SE.5a ✈	G-EBIA	18	ex 'D7000', Farnborough, Whitley, G-EBIA, F904 84 Sqn. Wolseley-built. Acquired 8-59. 92 Sqn colours		1-14
❑	K1786		Hawker Tomtit ✈	G-AFTA	31	ex Dunsfold, Langley, Hawker, Alex Henshaw, Castle Bromwich, Braunstone, RAF 5 GCF, 23 GCF, 3 FTS. Acquired 5-60		1-14
❑	'K2585'	'19'	DH Tiger Moth ✈	G-ANKT	42	ex Mk.II T6818, Aston Down, 21 EFTS. Morris-built. Acquired 9-72. CFS 'sunburst' colours	[22]	1-14
❑	'K3241'		Avro Tutor ✈	G-AHSA	33	ex HSA, K3215, 61 OTU, 41 OTU, Hawarden SF, CFS. Acquired 1959. CFS 'sunburst' colours		1-14
❑	'K5414'		Hawker Hind (Afghan) ✈	G-AENP	37	BAPC.78. ex 'K5457', Kabul, R Aghan AF. Acquired 1970. 15 Sqn colours		1-14
❑	'K7985'		Gloster Gladiator I ✈	G-AMRK	37	ex '423' *and* '427', L8032, 'N2308', L8032, 'K8032', Gloster, Ansty, Hamble, 8 MU, 61 OTU, 1624F, 2 AACU. Acquired 7-11-60. 73 Sqn colours	[23]	1-14
❑	K8203		Hawker Demon I ✈	G-BTVE	37	ex Hatch, Cardington, 2292M, 9 BGS, 9 AOS, 64. Boulton Paul-built. Arrived 23-7-09. 64 Sqn colours	[24]	1-14
❑	N3788		Miles Magister I ✈	G-AKPF	41	ex 'V1075', Shoreham, Sandown, Shoreham, V1075, 16 EFTS. Arrived 9-01	[8] [25]	1-14
❑	'N6290'		Sopwith Triplane replica ✈	G-BOCK	80	ex Dewsbury. NAW-built. 130hp Clerget. Arrived 6-90 8 Sqn RNAS colours, *Dixie II*	[26]	1-14
❑	P6382		Miles Magister I ✈	G-AJRS	39	ex 'G-AJDR', P6382, 3 EFTS, 16 EFTS. Acquired 3-4-70		1-14
❑	'V9367'	'MA-B'	Westland Lysander III ✈	G-AZWT	42	ex 'V9441', Duxford, Strathallan, RCAF 2355. Acquired 1997. 161 Sqn colours		1-14
❑	Z7015	'7-L'	Hawker Sea Hurricane I ✈	G-BKTH	39	ex Duxford, Staverton, Old Warden, Loughborough, Yeovilton, 759, 880. Acquired 21-2-61. 880 Sqn colours		1-14
❑	AR501	'NN-A'	Supermarine Spitfire V	G-AWII	42	ex Duxford, Henlow, Loughborough, CGS, 61 OTU, 1 TEU, 58 OTU, 422, 312, 504, 310. SOC 21-3-46, CoA 20-5-06. Arrived 1961. 310 colours		1-14
❑	XA241	JJS	Slingsby Grasshopper TX.1		53	BGA.4556, ex Cambridge, Croydon. Arrived 12-95. Stored		1-14
❑	XF603		Percival Provost T.1 ✈	G-KAPW	55	ex Cranfield, Filton, Bristol, 27 MU, CAW, RAFC. Acquired 2-11-01. RAF grey / green camo	[27]	1-14
❑	'671'		DHC Chipmunk 22 ✈	G-BNZC	52	ex G-ROYS, 7438M, WP905 CFS, 664, RAFC. Acquired 3-00. RCAF colours		1-14
❑	2008	'GM+AI'	Fieseler Fi 156A-1 Storch ✈	G-STCH	44	ex Fairoaks, MS.502 F-BDHO. Arrived 5-12-06. Luftwaffe colours	[8]	1-14
❑	'4477'	'GD+EG'	Bücker Jungmann 2000	G-RETA	67	ex North Weald, Spanish AF E3B-305. CASA-built Acquired 23-10-03. Local forced-landing 3-7-11		3-12
❑	'191454'		Me 163B Komet FSM		99	BAPC.271, wingless	[28]	1-14
❑	-	'28'	Polikarpov Po-2 *Mule* ✈	G-BSSY	44	ex N588NB, ZK-POZ ntu, New Zealand, N588NB Seattle, G-BSSY, YU-CLB, Yugoslav AF 0094, Sov AF. Acquired 31-7-03. Soviet colours	[29]	1-14
❑	-	'001'	Ryan ST3-KR ✈	G-BYPY	41	ex F-AZAV, N18926. Arrived 2008	[30]	1-14
❑	86690	'2-F'	Grumman FM-2 Wildcat ✈	G-CHPN	43	N49JC, ex Seattle, Pensacola, N49JC, N70637, N20HA, N68760, USN 86690. General Motors-built. Arrived 23-2-12. *Hannah*	[31]	1-14

■ **[1]** DH.51 was repainted in Aircraft Transport and Travel colours (standing in for a DH.9B?) for a British Airways advert. **[2]** Cygnet *Juliet-India* is owned by Coventry-based Colin Essex. **[3]** Moth G-EBLV, B-2 and the Avro XIX on loan from BAE Systems, forming the **BAE Systems Heritage Flight**. **[4]** Wren G-EBNV is substantially the unregistered Lympne trials No.4, which had been with the Science Museum until 1945, with engine parts from the original G-EBNV (Lympne No.3). **[5]** Moth G-EBWD was bought by Richard Ormonde Shuttleworth for £300 from Brooklands School of Flying on 21-1-32. Originally fitted with a Cirrus I, it was given a Cirrus Hermes II in 1933. **[6]** *Alpha-Golf* is on loan from A and P A Wood; it was a Shuttleworth aircraft from 11-77 to 1-04, until sold on. **[7]** Granger Archaeopteryx on loan from John R Granger of Nottingham. **[8]** Falcon, Magister N3788 and Storch on loan from Peter Holloway; *Echo-Golf* also shares time at Leicester, Leics. **[9]** Chilton *Sierra-Zulu* on loan from Roy Nerou. **[10]** See under Hendon, Gtr Lon, and Tattershall Thorpe, Lincs, for *more* 'G-AEXFs'. **[11]** Rapide on loan from Philip Meeson. **[12]** Triplane built by Hampshire Aero Club (Viv Bellamy / Ray Hilbourne) and fitted with an ADC Cirrus 3. **[13]** Boxkite built by F G Miles Ltd at Ford, powered by a Continental O-200B. **[14]** G-CAMM, built by Don Cashmore and fitted with a 37hp Mosler MM CB-35 flat-twin. **[15]** Chilton *Xray-Uniform* built in 2009 and on loan from Michael Gibbs. **[16]** By far and away the largest elements of BGA.310 can be found at Eaton Bray, Beds, qv. *This* BGA.310 uses the fuselage of BGA.327 plus parts from BGA.310. **[17]** Lilienthal No.11 'Standard Flying Apparatus' circa 1894 and the Pilcher Bat Mk.3 built by Eric Littledike of St Albans, Herts. **[18]** At the time Percy Pilcher was killed at Stanford Hall, Leics, on 18-9-1899 (see Stanford, Leics and East Fortune, Scotland) he was working on a weight-shift powered triplane. A team from Cranfield University and Bill Brooks of Mainair Sports built a modern-day version for a TV film in 2003.

Powered by a 8hp Radne Raket 2-stroke powerchute engine, it was flown for the first time by Bill Brooks on 29-8-03 and on 5-9-03 succeeded in a ¼ mile flight. It was presented to Shuttleworth by the TV company. **[19]** G-EBKY first 'surfaces' as a two-seat version of the Pup, the Sopwith Dove, registered to D L Hollis Williams 3-25. This one was part of a cache of unfinished examples stored at Kingston, and acquired by DHW for £5. Stored at West Malling from 1933, it went to Richard Shuttleworth in 1937 and given Pup status. **[20]** Bristol Scout is a fine static replica on loan from Keith Williams and Mike Thorne; it is destined for Filton, Glos, eventually. **[21]** The 504's history prior to being discovered at Portsmouth where it had been kept by Airspeed is problematical. It was converted to 504K status from what is believed to have been a glider or banner-towing 504N. The 'accepted' identity is G-ADEV, but as this ended up with an ATC unit in Windermere (as 3118M) in 1942, this is doubted. It was registered as G-ACNB in 12-82, but took up G-ADEV in 4-84. Its latest guise is as a night-fighter with 77 Home Defence Sqn, based at Turnhouse, Scotland, 1918. **[22]** Tiger Moth is a composite of three acquired by the collection in 1966; making its first flight in 10-77. **[23]** Gladiator flies in the colours of Plt Off 'Cobber' Kain. **[24]** Demon was restored at Hatch, Beds (qv) and is on loan from Demon Displays Ltd. **[25]** N3788 is a composite, using the centre section of G-AIUA, rear fuselage of G-ANLT, wings of G-AHYL plus others. N3788 was 'demobbed' on 27-8-47 becoming G-ANLT; its RAF pedigree was ex 169 Sqn, 2 FIS, 2 FTS, 5 EFTS, 8 EFTS, 27 ERFTS. **[26]** Production of Triplanes came to 152 and as the late Sir Thomas Sopwith decreed that *Charlie-Kilo* should be considered as a late production example, it is known at Old Warden as c/n 153. **[27]** XF603 carries the markings of one delivered to the Sultan of Oman's Air Force.**[28]** Me 163B Komet full-scale model fuselage is built around an original Walter HWK 509A-2 bi-fuel rocket motor. **[29]** Off-the-wall factoid: The Po-2's US registration pays homage to the Soviet all-woman 588th Night Bombing Regiment which flew nuisance raids against the Germans, earning the pilots the nickname 'Night Witches'. **[30]** Ryan '001' on loan from Tracey Curtis-Taylor. **[31]** General Motors-built FM-2, served in California in the 1950s in the USA as a Hardwick Special HG.1 'bug-bomber'. Restoration should see it put into Fleet Air Arm colours.

THURLEIGH, north of Bedford, east of the A6

Previously listed under 'Bedford Airfield': the site of the former Royal Aircraft Establishment. The **306th Bomb Group Museum** in the wartime Small Arms and Ammunition Store is well worth a visit in its own right and also because it affords excellent views of what was an astounding airfield. The memorial to the 306th that was in Thurleigh village was moved to adjacent the museum and rededicated on 8th July 2012.

◆ **Access:** *Follow 'Bedford Autodrome' and Technology Park signs from A6.* **Open:** *Weekends and Bank Holidays, Mar to Oct 10:00 to 16:00, or by prior arrangement.* **Contact:** *c/o Bedford Autodrome, Thurleigh Airfield Business Park, Bedford, MK44 2YP* | **01234 708715** | **306museum@nscmh.fsnet.co.uk** | **www.306bg.co.uk**

TWINWOOD FARM near Clapham, off the A6 north of Bedford

Glenn Miller Museum and **Twinwood Aviation Museum**: The tower has been turned into a Miller era 'shrine'. Other buildings have been refurbished, including Hut 37 which includes a collection of wartime fire fighting vehicles. This is open *most* weekends. A series of regular events are staged on the site, including concerts and festivals.

◆ **Access:** *Signed from within Clapham village.* **Open:** *Sat by prior arrangement* only; *Sun 10:30 to 16:00,* **Not** *open mid-week; Apr to mid-Oct - except during large events - check ahead for these.* **Contact:** *Twinwood Events, Twinwood Road, Clapham, Beds, MK41 6AB* | **01923 282725** | **info@twinwoodevents.com** | **www.twinwoodevents.co.uk**

BERKSHIRE

Includes the unitary authorities of Bracknell Forest, Reading, Slough, Windsor and Maidenhead, Wokingham

ARBORFIELD on the A327 south of Reading

REME Museum of Technology: The Corps of the Royal Electrical and Mechanical Engineers was formed in 1942 and its fascinating history is charted here, including vehicles, armament, a locomotive and much more. The Scout is within the Prince Philip Vehicle Exhibition Hall. There is also a shop and cafe. See below regarding the future of the facility.

◆ **Open:** *Mon to Thu 09:00 to 16:30, Fri 09:00 to 16:00 and Sun 11:00 to 16:00 - note* ***not*** *open Sat. Open* some *bank holidays - please check beforehand.* **Contact:** *Isaac Newton Road, Arborfield, Berks, RG2 9NJ* | **0118 9763375** | **enquiries@rememuseum.org.uk** | **www.rememuseum.org.uk**

❑ XV141	Westland Scout AH.1	68	ex Wroughton, 657, 659, 654, 661	6-13
❑ ZJ449	GEC Phoenix UAV	~	plinth mounted	6-13

Princess Marina College / Defence School of Electro-Mechanical Engineering (DSEME): Previously the **School of Electrical and Aeronautical Engineering**, within **Hazebrouck Barracks**, changed its name on 1st October 2012. This facility and another at Borden, Hampshire, is scheduled to close by 2014-2015 at the latest and will be the first to settle in at the tri-service technical training 'campus' at Lyneham, Wilts - which see.

TAD stands for Technical Aid and Demonstrator - but there are other interpretations! Purpose-built instructional airframes and teaching aids are also known as 'CIMs' - Classroom Instructional Models. Most TAD-numbered airframes proudly wear their identities. SEAE maintain a detachment at Middle Wallop, Hants.

❑ XP848		Westland Scout AH.1	62	ex Middle Wallop, Wroughton, 659, 669. Gate		6-13
❑ XP855		Westland Scout AH.1	63	ex Wroughton, 652, 651, 655		6-13
❑ XP899	'D'	Westland Scout AH.1	63	ex Middle Wallop, ARWF. Crashed 1-11-79		6-13
❑ XT623		Westland Scout AH.1	66	ex Wroughton, 655, 659, 655		6-13
❑ XT633		Westland Scout AH.1	66	ex Wroughton, 659, 653, 661, 660, Wroughton		6-13
❑ XZ170		Westland Lynx AH.9	77	ex Yeovil, A&AEE		6-13
❑ XZ172		Westland Lynx AH.7	77	ex 653, 655, Yeovil, LCF/671, IPTU		6-13
❑ XZ187		Westland Lynx AH.7	78	ex Fleetlands, 655, 667, 655, 667, 655, 651, 654		6-13
❑ XZ188		Westland Lynx AH.7	78	ex Fleetlands, 4 Rgt, 654, 662, 655, 665, 655, LCF, 651		6-13
❑ XZ207		Westland Lynx AH.7	79	ex Fleetlands, 652, 9 Rgt, 669, 4 Rgt, 669, 655, 654. Crashed 17-4-00. Cabin		6-13
❑ XZ216*		Westland Lynx AH.7	77	ex Fleetlands, 1 Rgt, 9 Rgt, 4 Rgt, 1 Rgt, 4 Rgt, 654, 663, 656, 671, 663, 662. Cabin, first noted 3-12		3-13
❑ XZ316	'B'	Sud Gazelle AH.1	77	ex Cosford, Shawbury, 666, 670, ARWS, ARWF	[1]	6-13
❑ XZ325	'T'	Sud Gazelle AH.1	77	ex Middle Wallop, 670, 655, 3 Regt		6-13
❑ XZ332		Sud Gazelle AH.1	77	ex Middle Wallop, 670, ARWF, 656, 664. BDR		6-13
❑ XZ333		Sud Gazelle AH.1	77	ex Middle Wallop, 670, ARWF		6-13
❑ XZ607*		Westland Lynx AH.7	81	ex Fleetlands, 657, 1 Rgt, 847, 657, 672, 3/4 Rgt, 9 Rgt, 672, 4 Rgt, 3 Rgt, 9 Rgt, 662, 663, 3 Rgt, 671, 653, 654. Cabin, first noted 3-12		6-13
❑ XZ666		Westland Lynx AH.7	81	ex 669, 655, 665, 655, LCF, 651		6-13
❑ XZ935		Sud Gazelle HCC.4	78	ex Cosford, 9332M, St Athan, Fleetlands, 32, CFS		6-13
❑ ZA735		Sud Gazelle AH.1	80	ex 25 Flt		6-13
❑ ZA769	'K'	Sud Gazelle AH.1	80	ex Middle Wallop, 670, ARWF		6-13
❑ ZE381	'X'	Westland Lynx AH.7	84	ex Yeovil, 671, 25 Flt, 657, 655, 659, 655, 665		6-13
❑ ZE412		Agusta A.109A	88	ex 8 Flt. Withdrawn from use 12-6-09		6-13
❑ TAD.001		Sud Gazelle CIM	~	ex Middle Wallop. Cabin only		6-12
❑ TAD.007		Westland Lynx CIM	~	ex Middle Wallop. Fuselage number TO.42		6-12
❑ TAD.009		W'land Lynx 1-03 XW838	72	ex Middle Wallop, Yeovil		6-13
❑ TAD.011		Westland Lynx CIM	~	ex Middle Wallop		6-12
❑ TAD.012		Westland Lynx CIM	~	ex Middle Wallop		6-12
❑ TAD.013	'A'	Westland Lynx HC.28	77	ex Fleetlands, Almondbank, Wroughton, Qatar Police QP-30, G-BFDV, de-reg 18-7-78		6-12
❑ TAD.015		Sud Gazelle AH.1 ZB668	92	ex Middle Wallop, Arborfield, Fleetlands, UNFICYP. Crashed 30-11-92		6-13
❑ TAD.016A		Westland Lynx HC.28	77	ex M' Wallop, Almondbank, Wroughton, Qatar Police QP-32		6-12
❑ TAD.017		Sud Gazelle AH.1 XW888	73	ex Middle Wallop, ARWF, GCF		6-13
❑ TAD.018		Sud Gazelle AH.1 XW889	74	ex Middle Wallop, ARWF, GCF		6-13
❑ TAD.019		Sud Gazelle AH.1 XW912	74	ex Fleetlands, 655, 3 CBAS, 656, 655, 3 CBAS		6-13
❑ TAD.021		Sud Gazelle HT.2 XW860	75	ex Middle Wallop, Fleetlands, Wroughton, 705. BDR		3-13
❑ TAD.023		Sud Gazelle AH.1 XX454	76	ex Waddington, M' Wallop, 663, 1 Rgt, 662, 656,657, 4 Rgt, 3 Rgt, 4 Rgt, 659, 669, 664, 654, 4 Rgt, 669, 659		6-13

■ **[1]** All of the Gazelles are Westland-built.

BINFIELD north of the B3034, north-west of Bracknell

Two rotorcraft, Airmaster H2-B1 GAYNS and Hollman HA-2M, last noted in October 2008, have been deleted.

❑ G-ASXF	Brantly 305	r64	ex Thruxton, Biggin Hill, CoA 16-2-79, de-reg 24-5-82	4-11
❑ G-BPCJ	Cessna 150J	69	ex Solihull, Tattershall Thorpe, N61096. *Charlie*. Damaged 25-1-90; de-reg 4-7-90	4-11

GREENHAM COMMON north of the A339, south-east of Newbury

The warbird store is believed to have been emptied. SE.5E G-BLXT and Seafire III PP972 (G-BUAR) moved to a workshop in Suffolk for restoration. Spitfire IX NH238 (G-MKIX) also moved on, but with even less of a 'forwarding address'.

HUNGERFORD on the A4 east of Marlborough

Newbury Aeroplane Company: Stampe G-AZGC had moved on by 2011, perhaps to Wales.

◆ **Access:** ***Private*** *location, visits possible* **only** *by prior arrangement*

❑ G-ACMA*		DH Leopard Moth		34	ex BD148, DH, ACCCF, 7 AACU, 110 Wing, G-ACMA. CoA 3-2-94. First noted 12-11	3-12
❑ G-AFGH		Chilton DW.1		38	ex Billingshurst. CoA 7-7-83	3-12

LAMBOURN on the B4000 north of Hungerford

In the *general* area is a private strip and workshop. Former Spanish Bf 109E-1 C4E-88 moved to Bremgarten, Germany, for long-term restoration to flying condition by Meier Motors in December 2012.

◆ **Access:** ***Private*** *location, visits possible* **only** *by prior arrangement*

❑ LV-RIE		Nord Pingouin		~	ex North Weald, Duxford, Kersey, Argentina	3-06
❑ 'DR628'	'PB1'	Beech D.17S	N18V	44	ex North Weald, NC18, Bu32898, FT507, 44-67761	7-09
❑ KZ191		Hawker Hurricane IV		43	ex North Weald, Fowlmere, Israel, 351, 1695 Flt, AFDU. SOC 26-9-46	7-09

LANGLEY on the B470 north of the junction of the M4 and A4, east of Slough

Langley Academy: Langley Road. The Lord Foster-designed academy on the site of the former Hawker flight test airfield, has among its mission statements: a "museum learning school". Brooklands Museum is back this with the loan of a 'Flea'.

◆ **Access:** *By prior arrangement* ***only*** **| www.langleyacademy.org**

❑ 'G-ADRY'*		Mignet HM.14 'Flea'		c67	BAPC.29, ex Brooklands, Aberdare, Swansea. Suspended in foyer, on loan. Arrived 8-10	1-14

MAIDENHEAD

Maidenhead Heritage Centre: A long-overdue exhibition to the incredible contribution and gallantry of the men and women of the Air Transport Auxiliary was opened by Prince Michael of Kent in October 2011. Maidenhead, being just a stone's throw from the ATA's headquarters airfield, White Waltham, is an ideal choice. Easily the largest gathering of artefacts on the ATA anywhere, the exhibition is entitled 'Grandma Flew Spitfires!' and is very absorbing.

◆ **Access:** *At 18 Park Street, Maidenhead. Parking close by in Grove Road.* **Open:** *Tue to Sat, 10:00 to 16:00 - Visitors wishing specifically to fly the Spitfire simulator are advised to check in advance for availability.* **Contact:** *18 Park Street, Maidenhead, SL6 1SL* | **01628 780555** | **info@maidenheadheritage.org.uk** | **www.atamuseum.org**

MEMBURY close to the Membury services, east of Swindon on the M4

❑ G-AWHX		Rollason Beta B.2		71	ex G-ATEE ntu. *Vertigo*. CoA 14-6-87	10-09
❑ G-BAVA		Piper Super Cub 150		56	ex D-EFKC, ALAT 18-5391. Cr 20-11-77, de-reg 19-4-83. Frame	10-09
❑ 'Z7258'		DH Dragon Rapide	G-AHGD	45	ex Old Warden, NR786, n/s. *Women of the Empire*. Brush-built. Crashed 30-6-91, de-reg 26-7-13	10-09

READING

Last noted in August 2008, Tiger Moths G-AGNJ and G-BRHW have moved on, perhaps to an Oxfordshire workshop. Not recorded since June 2007, the anonymous Beagle Pup cockpit has been deleted.

THATCHAM or Brimpton, north of the A4, west of Newbury

Sylmar Aviation and Services Ltd / Provost Team: Alan House and team operate from a *private* strip in the area.

❑ G-HRLK		SAAB Safir		59	ex G-BRZY, PH-RLK. CoA 15-8-10	1-12
❑ G-SAFR		SAAB Safir		60	ex Cranfield, Coventry, Rugby, Bruntingthorpe, PH-RLR RLS	1-12
❑ NC16403		Cessna C34 Airmaster		c35	-	7-11
❑ XF545	'O-K'	Percival Provost T.1		55	ex Linton-on-Ouse, Swinderby, Finningley 7957M (16-6-67), Shawbury, 6 FTS, 2 FTS. Fuselage, off-site	7-12
❑ XF597	'AH'	Perc' Provost T.1	G-BKFW	55	ex CAW, RAFC. CoA 27-7-07	10-13
❑ XF836		Percival Provost T.1	G-AWRY	55	ex Popham, Old Warden, 8043M, 27 MU, CATCS, CNCS, RAFC, Man UAS. Damaged 28-7-87. CoA 22-8-88	7-12

WELFORD or Welford Park, north of the M4, west of junction 13 (A34)

Ridgeway Military and Aviation Research Group: Within the former World War Two airfield, now known as Welford Park, is an impressive *private* museum run by RM&AMG, formed in 1991.

◆ **Access:** *Visits are possible* **only** *by prior appointment* | **rmarg@hotmail.co.uk** | **www.rmarg.co.uk**

❑ 42-93510	'CM'	Douglas C-47A-25-DK Skytrain	43	ex ??, Kew, Ottershaw, Kew, Cranfield, 6W-SAE, F-GEFY, Senegal AF, French AF, CSA OK-WAR, 42-93510. Cockpit	4-08
❑ -		Airspeed Horsa replica	c76	ex *Bridge Too Far*	4-08

WHITE WALTHAM AERODROME south of the A4 south-west of Maidenhead EGLM

❑ G-AFLW	Miles Monarch	38	CoA 30-7-98; de-reg 3-5-01. Stored	8-13
❑ G-ASMF	Beech Travelair	64	CoA 11-8-06	8-13
❑ G-NIKE*	Piper Archer II	83	ex N4315N. CoA 24-1-09	8-13
❑ SE-GVH	Piper Tomahawk 112	~	ex Little Staughton, Chessington. Cockpit	8-13
❑ XA459	Fairey Gannet AS.4	56	ex Woodlands St Mary, Lambourn, Cirencester, Cardiff, Culdrose SAH-7 A2608, Lee-on-Solent, 831. SOC 18-11-70	8-13

WINDSOR

Sydney Camm Memorial: Alongside the Thames in Barry Avenue, a couple of hundred yards from what was 2 Bounty Terrace, but is now 10 Alma Road, is a Hurricane honouring the place of birth and youth of designer Sir Sydney Camm. The replica was commissioned and financed by the Sydney Camm Commemorative Society. The choice could have been legion, Hart, Fury, Tempest, Sea Fury, Sea Hawk, Hunter, P.1127; he spanned the generations with ground-breaking designs but the Hurricane is the one that most evokes the reverential mention of his name.

❑ 'R4229'*	'GN-J'	Hawker Hurricane FSM	12	249 Sqn colours. Pole-mounted, unveiled 3-6-12	[1]	6-12

■ **[1]** The Hurricane is in the colours of Sqn Ldr John Grandy, 249's CO during the Battle of Britain and later MRAF.

WOKINGHAM south of the M4 and A329(M) south-east of Reading

A1 Motor Spares: Highland Avenue

❑ G-BSGV	Rotorway Executive	90	de-reg 7-4-95	11-10

WOODLEY east of Reading

Museum of Berkshire Aviation (MBA): This museum is a delight in the scope and detail of its contents and the visitor has to be constantly reminded that all of this took place within boundaries of the county. Add to this delicious names such as Handley Page and Miles and you are set for an engaging visit. As *W&R* went to press, apart from a few minor details, the challenging restoration of the Student was complete.

The gondola of Cameron D-96 G-BAMK was returned to its owner during 2013.

◆ **Open:** *Nov to Mar, Sun 12:00 to 16:00 and Wed 10:30 to 16:00. Mar to Oct Sat, Sun, Bank Hols and Weds 10:30 to 17:00. Group visits at other times with plenty of notice.* **Contact:** *Mohawk Way (off Bader Way), Woodley, near Reading, RG5 4UF.* | **0118 944 8089** | **museumberksav@gmail.com** | **www.museumofberkshireaviation.co.uk**

❑ G-APWA		HP Herald 100	59	ex Southend, BAF, PP-SDM, PP-ASV, G-APWA. CoA 6-4-82, de-reg 29-1-87. Arrived 29-8-92. BEA colours		1-14
❑ G-MIOO		Miles Student 2	57	ex North Weald, Bruntingthorpe, G-APLK, Cranfield, G-MIOO, Duxford, G-APLK, Glasgow, Shoreham, XS941, G-35-4. Crashed 24-8-85, de-reg 1-11-96. Arrived 1997	[1]	1-14
❑ AQZ		EoN Primary	c48	BGA.589, ex Farnborough, G-ALMN, BGA.589. Last flown 7-5-50, CoA 4-51. Arrived 2004	[2]	1-14
❑ '465'	BWG	EoN 460-1	65	BGA.1288, CoA 27-4-97. Arrived 27-5-09		1-14
❑ –		Broburn Wanderlust	46	BAPC.233, ex Farnborough. Arrived 28-11-92	[3]	1-14
❑ –		McBroom hang-glider	73	BAPC.248, built 1974, arrived 1993		1-14
❑ TF-SHC		Miles Martinet TT.1	43	ex Reykjavik, Akuereyi, MS902, Reykjavik SF, 251. Crashed 18-7-51, arrived 3-96		1-14
❑ 'L6906'		Miles Magister I G-AKKY	40	BAPC.44, ex Brooklands, Woodley, Wroughton, Frenchay, G-AKKY (de-reg 12-4-73), T9841, 11 EFTS, 16 EFTS. Arrived 26-4-91		1-14
❑ XG883	'773'	Fairey Gannet T.5	57	ex Cardiff, Yeovilton, 849, Culdrose SF. SOC 8-6-70. Arrived 24-3-96	[4]	1-14

❑ XJ389		Fairey Jet Gyrodyne	49	ex Cosford, Southampton, G-AJJP, XD759, Fairey. De-reg 9-11-50. Arrived 6-94	[5]	1-14
❑ 'XP849'		Westland Scout AH.1	63	ex Boscombe Down, Middle Wallop. Arrived 13-10-10. ETPS colours	[6]	1-14
❑ -		ML Sprite EMU	~	drone helicopter	[7]	1-14

■ **[1]** Student on loan from Aces High's Mike Woodley. **[2]** EoN Primary donated by Pat Pottinger. **[3]** On loan from Pat Pottinger. **[4]** Gannet on loan from the Fleet Air Arm Museum. **[5]** Gyrodyne is on loan from the RAF Museum. **[6]** Scout is *largely* XP895, last at Middle Wallop and crashed 10-11-66. It has the boom of XP854 - for the latter see Abridge, Essex. That said, it carries a plate giving 'F8-4256' which would make it XT619 which crashed 10-3-66. It is on loan from the Hallett Collection/MCA Aviation USA. **[7]** Sprite, of course, stands for Surveillance Patrol Reconnaissance Intelligence Target Designation, Electronic Warfare.

BUCKINGHAMSHIRE

Includes the unitary authority of Milton Keynes

AYLESBURY

Last noted in December 2007, Minor G-AFIR moved on, perhaps to Hampshire. By July 2012, Chipmunk T.10 PAX WB626 had moved to Halton, Bucks. The Hunter is kept by **Dan Lander**, who also owns Harrier XW268 - see Norwich, Norfolk.

❑ XL564*		Hawker Hunter T.7	58	ex South Molton, Yarmouth, Boscombe Down, ETPS, 229 OCU. Crashed 6-8-98. Cockpit		2-12

BLETCHLEY south of the A5, near Milton Keynes

The Blue Lagoon: Diving centre in Drayton Road. Cessna 150E G-ASVF was sunk here in 1984 | **www.mksac.co.uk**

HALTON AIRFIELD on the A4011 (camp) and east of the B4544 (airfield), north of Wendover — EGWN

RAF Halton: Within is the exceptional **Trenchard Museum**.

◆ **Open:** *Open Tue 10:00 to 16:00 or by prior arrangement.* **Contact:** *Trenchard Museum, RAF Halton, Halton Camp, Bucks, HP22 5PG* | **01296 624095** | **info@trenchardmuseum.org.uk** | **www.trenchardmuseum.org.uk**

❑ G-LOTI*	'2'	Blériot XI replica	82	ex Brooklands. CoA 19-7-82, de-reg 6-3-09. Arrived 30-4-13	[1]	12-13
❑ RA905		Slingsby Cadet TX.1	c45	BGA.1143. ex RAFGSA.273, RA905. CoA 14-3-00		12-13
❑ WB626*		DHC Chipmunk T.10 PAX	50	ex Aylesbury area, South Molton, Fownhope, Firbeck, Houghton-on-the-Hill, Southampton, Swanton Morley, Bicester, Kemble, Hendon SF, 5 FTS, 18 RFS. SOC 12-9-73		12-13
❑ WZ772		Slingsby Grasshopper TX.1	52	ex Middle Wallop, Halton, 1 MGSP, Brentwood		12-13
❑ XR574	'72'	Folland Gnat T.1	63	ex Cosford, Halton, Cosford 8631M (8-10-79), Kemble, 4 FTS, CFS, 4 FTS, CFS, 4 FTS, CFS, 4 FTS		12-13

■ **[1]** Blériot was built by Mike Beach and fitted with an ABC Scorpion II; it is on loan from the Brooklands Museum.

Also: The Bulldog and Hunter are with **2409 Squadron ATC** (Herts & Bucks Wing).

❑ XF522		Hawker Hunter F.6	56	ex Bletchley, Milton Keynes, Aylesbury, Halton, 92, 66, 92. SOC 8-1-63. Cockpit, trailer-mounted. 92 Sqn colours		6-11
❑ XF527		Hawker Hunter F.6	56	ex 1 SoTT 8680M (2-4-81), Laarbruch SF, 4 FTS, CFE, 19, Church Fenton SF, Linton SF. Gate		11-13
❑ XW303	'127'	BAC Jet Provost T.5A	70	ex Cosford, Halton 9119M (16-9-91), 7 FTS, 1 FTS. Fuselage	[1]	4-13
❑ XW364*	'MN'	BAC Jet Provost T.5A	71	ex Cosford 9188M (5-5-93), Shawbury, 3 FTS, RAFC, CFS, 1 FTS. Arrived 22-10-12, rescue training		6-13
❑ XX665		SAL Bulldog T.1	74	ex Newton 9289M, E Lowlands UAS, Abn UAS, ELow UAS. Crashed 20-9-97		9-06
❑ XZ630		Panavia Tornado GR.1	77	ex St Athan, Brüggen 8976M (24-8-88), BAe, A&AEE. Parade ground		11-13
❑ ZE592*	'WV'	Grob Viking T.1	89	ex Henlow, Syerston, 621, 662, 615, 626, 661, 625, 615, 614, BGA.3048. Damaged 2-06. Cockpit. First noted 3-13		3-13

■ **[1]** 'JP' XW303 serves as a jump on the equestrian course!

HIGH WYCOMBE or Walter's Ash, north-west of Naphill, north of the town

RAF High Wycombe: Headquarters, Air Command.

❑	'P7666'	'EB-Z'	Supermarine Spitfire FSM	~	41 Sqn colours	[1] 10-10
❑	'V7467'	'LE-D'	Hawker Hurricane FSM	89	BAPC.223, ex Coltishall. 242 Sqn colours	[2] 10-10

■ **[1]** The Spitfire was built by Gateguards (UK) Ltd. **[2]** The Hurricane is not to be confused with that at Farnsfield, Notts!

IVER HEATH on the A412 west of Uxbridge

Pinewood Film Studios: *W&R23*, p17, recorded the fuselage of Jetstream 31 G-UIST arriving by June 2011; part of the 'fleet' used in the making of *Batman - The Dark Knight Returns*. The cockpit moved to Inverness, Scotland.

◆ **Access:** ***Private*** *location, visits possible* ***only*** *by prior arrangement*

❑	G-EDAY		BAe Jetstream 3101	84	ex Inverness, Highland Airways, SE-LGB, N639LX, N409MX, G-31-639. Fuselage	6-11
❑	XX500	'H'	HP Jetstream T.1	76	ex Ipswich, Culdrose, Cranwell, 45, 3 FTS, 45, 6 FTS, METS. SOC 29-7-05. SAL-built	6-11

LAVENDON on the A428 west of Bedford

Tony Collins: Tony is an award-winning cockpit restorer, clinching another Grand Champion award at the 2013 *CockpitFest* with his exceptional Scimitar. But that is not the end of his talents. He also owns and operates the **Lavendon Narrow Gauge Railway**. There are regular open days, when the cockpit collection can also be inspected.

◆ **Access:** *Visits possible by prior arrangement or on railway open days* | **www.lavendonconnection.com/LNGR.htm**

❑	WT319		EE Canberra B(I).6	55	ex Castle Carey, Filton, Samlesbury, 213, Laarbruch SF, 213. SOC 8-12-69. Cockpit	9-13
❑	WT684		Hawker Hunter F.1	54	ex Doncaster, Firbeck, Long Marston, Brize Norton, Reading, Halton 7422M (8-4-57), 229 OCU, DFLS. Cockpit	9-13
❑	XD235	'148'	Supermarine Scimitar F.1	58	ex Ingatestone, Welshpool, Southampton, Ottershaw, Foulness, FRU, 803. SOC 20-3-70. 803 Sqn colours. Cockpit	9-13
❑	XN651	'705'	DH Sea Vixen FAW.2	61	ex Bletchley, Bristol, Culdrose A2616 (29-7-71), SAH, 766, FAW.1, 893. 890 Sqn colours. Cockpit	9-13
❑	XS898	'BD'	EE Lightning F.6	66	ex Bruntingthorpe, Cranfield, Binbrook, 11, 5. SOC (24-6-88). Cockpit	9-13
❑	XW541		HS Buccaneer S.2B	71	ex Welshpool, Ingatestone, Stock, Foulness, Honington 8858M (21-5-85), St Athan, 12, 16, 15. Cockpit	9-13

MILTON KEYNES

A *private* collector in the *general* area has a Vampire T.11.

❑	XH330	'76'	DH Vampire T.11	56	ex Abingdon, Camberley, Bridgnorth, Bushey, London Colney, Chester, Woodford, Chester, Shawbury, RAFC. SOC 20-2-64	9-10

PITSTONE between the B489 and B488 north of Tring

Pitstone Green Museum: Run Pitstone and Ivinghoe Museum Society volunteers, this is a rural life centre, including a World War Two aviation room. 'Star' of the latter is a Lancaster cockpit built by Norman Groom using many original fittings.

◆ **Open:** *Bank hols and Sun, 11:00 to 17:00. Other times by prior arrangement.* **Contact:** *Pitstone Green Farm, Pitstone, LU7 9EY* | **01582 605464** | **norman.groom@lineone.net** | **www.pitstonemuseum.co.uk**

❑	-		Avro Lancaster FSM	10	forward fuselage	12-13

TURWESTON AERODROME north of the A422, east of Brackley — EGBT

Last noted in August 2007, Jodel G-ARUH has been deleted.

❑	G-PADD		American AA-5 Cheetah	78	ex G-ESTE, G-GHNC, N26877. CoA 8-12-04	1-12

TWYFORD east of Bicester

A ***private*** workshop in the general area is thought still to have its Spitfire and Chipmunk.

❑	AD540		Supermarine Spitfire V	41	ex Dumfries, Carsphairn, 242, 122. *Blue Peter*. Crashed 23-5-42	3-06

❑ WK620	'T'	DHC Chipmunk T.10	52	ex Tattershall Thorpe, Middle Wallop, BFWF, Hull UAS, Mcr UAS, QUAS, Bri UAS, 22 RFS. Damaged 19-5-93. Stored		10-13

WYCOMBE AIR PARK or Booker, on the B482 south-west of High Wycombe EGTB

Personal Plane Services: Paul Andrews (the G2 Trust) holds several Spitfire projects at the aerodrome, and locally. (See also Sandown, Isle of Wight.) Spitfire IX TE517 (G-JGCA) moved to Biggin Hill, Gtr London, on 10th December 2012.

◆ **Access**: *Visits possible* **only** *by prior arrangement* | **www.bianchiaviation.com**

❑ G-BYDK		Stampe SV-4C		46	ex F-BCXY, FAF. Nord-built. Fuselage, stored		5-13
❑ G-BAAF		Manning-Flanders MF.1 replica		75	ex Compton Abbas, Wycombe AP, Old Warden, Wycombe AP. CoA 6-8-96. Stored		
❑ G-BPVE	'10'	Blériot XI replica	G-BPVE	99	ex Compton Abbas, Wycombe AP, N1197. CoA 29-6-01		2-11
❑ 'B2458'	'R'	Sopwith Camel replica	G-BPOB	73	ex Old Sarum, Wycombe AP, USA N8997, Tallmantz Av CoA 6-6-10		8-13
❑ 'B5539'		Stampe SV-4 FSM		~	ex Compton Abbas, Wycombe AP. *The Mummy, Indiana Jones and the Lost Crusade.* Gun position in rear cockpit		2-11
❑ EJ693		Hawker Tempest V	N7027E	44	ex Norfolk (?), USA, Chichester, Henlow, Delft, 486. Crashed 1-10-44	[1]	2-11
❑ 'MS824'		MS 'N' replica	G-AWBU	70	ex Compton Abbas, Wycombe AP. CoA 28-4-04. Stored		8-13
❑ MT818		Supermarine Spitfire Tr.VIII	G-AIDN	44	ex Kemble, USA N818MT, Tillamook N58JE, G-AIDN, Supermarine 'B' condition N32, MT818, RAE	[2]	9-13
❑ RM694		Supermarine Spitfire XIV	G-DBKL	44	ex High Wycombe area, USA, Bitteswell, Southend, Henlow, Charnock Richard, Hoylake, Dishforth, Bicester, Hornchurch, Locking 6640M (28-2-49), 6629M ntu, CFE, 402, 91. Off-site	[2]	7-11
❑ UB441		Supermarine Spitfire IX	G-SDNI	44	ex Sedlescombe, Rochester, USA N94149, Burmese AF, Israeli DF/AF 2020 Czech AF, RAF ML119, 1. Off-site	[2]	3-09
❑ '422/15'		Fokker E.III replica	G-AVJO	67	ex Compton Abbas, Wycombe AP. CoA 5-4-04		8-13
❑ '626/8'		Travel Air 2000	N6268	38	ex USA, NC6268. Stored, dismantled	[3]	2-11
❑ –		Pilatus P.2 replica		~	fuselage. Film mock-up. Luftwaffe colours		1-14
❑ –		Hulton hang-glider		69	BAPC.103, crashed 6-4-69. Stored	[4]	2-11
❑ -	'8'	Waxflatter Ornithopter		84	BAPC.238, ex Compton Abbas, Wycombe AP, *Young Sherlock Holmes*. Stored, dismantled	[5]	2-11

■ **[1]** The Tempest and Spitfire XIV are held for US collector/operator Kermit Weeks. **[2]** Registered to Paul M Andrews. **[3]** Painted to play the part of a Fokker D.VIII. **[4]** Built by E A S Hulton and based on the Ferris of 1906 and Anderson and Singer of 1911 biplane hang-gliders. Two flights only. **[5]** Built by PPS for the 1985 film *Young Sherlock Holmes*.

Parkhouse Aviation: See also Camberley, Surrey. By May 2012 one, possibly two, Tempest firewall/windscreen/cockpit elements had arrived from Wickenby, Lincs, to form a restoration project. It is too early to give this a formal listing, but a plate carries 41H-159182, if that helps Hawker sleuths. The Meteor T.7's cockpit was dispatched to the superb museum at Ta Qali on Malta, where it will be mated to T.7 WL360. (That machine was last mentioned in *W&R21*, p261, Mediterranean-bound from Yatesbury, Wilts.) The cockpit of WL360 is due to return and make WL345 whole.

Departures: Drover II 'VH-FDT' to St Athan, Wales, 5-8-13; Tiger Moth T7793 to Wickenby, Lincs, by 6-12; Sea Prince C.1 WF137 to St Athan, Wales, 11-7-13; Sea Hawk FGA.6 WV798 to Newquay, Cornwall, by 7-12; Tempest HA557 was exported to Houston, Texas, USA by 4-12.

◆ **Access:** *Visits possible* **only** *by prior arrangement.*

❑ G-BEYF		HP Herald 401	63	ex Bournemouth, Channel Express, RMAF FM1022. CoA 17-3-00, de-reg 18-11-99. Cockpit		1-14
❑ EC-JCC*		Cessna 421	~	Nord-jet titles. Fuselage, first noted 7-13		1-14
❑ -*		Hawker Typhoon	~	ex Wickenby. Cockpit/firewall. First noted 5-12	[1]	6-13
❑ WL345*		Gloster Meteor T.7	52	ex Hollington, Hastings, Kemble, CAW, 8 FTS, 5 FTS, CFE, 229 OCU. SOC 1-11-74. Arrived by 12-12. See notes above		1-14
❑ XL592	'Y'	Hawker Hunter T.7	58	ex Kemble, Exeter, Scampton 8836M (31-8-84), 1 TWU, TWU, 229 OCU		1-14
❑ 430861		NAA VB-25N-NC Mitchell	45	ex North Weald, Duxford, 'HD368', G-BKXW ntu, Southend, Biggin Hill, N9089Z, 44-30861. *Bedsheet Bomber*		1-14

■ **[1]** The Typhoon carries a plate marked 41H-159182, if that helps Hawker sleuths.

Also: Booker Gliding Club are restoring a Fauvel for the Shuttleworth Collection, Beds. Messenger 2A G-AJOE was off-site by February 2013 and was due to fly again as *W&R24* went to press.

❑ G-DYOU	Piper Tomahawk 112	81	fuselage. Crashed 23-7-92, de-reg 24-5-95. Hulk, dumped	5-13
❑ G-HALP	SOCATA Tobago	78	ex G-BITD. CoA 25-9-06	5-13
❑ ETE*	Fauvel AV.36CR	~	BGA.2932, ex Old Warden, RAFGSA R53, D-5353, D-8259. CoA 7-6-98	1-14
❑ C-GVXN	Piper Tomahawk 112	~	de-reg 10-5-91. Hulk, dumped	5-13
❑ FAB-184*	SIAI-Marchetti SF.260W G-SIAI	78	ex F-GVAB, OO-XCP, Bolivian Air Force FAB-184. CoA 3-9-10 Stored, first noted 8-12	10-13

CAMBRIDGESHIRE

Includes the unitary authority of Peterborough

ALCONBURY north-west of Huntingdon at the A1/A14 junction

USAF Alconbury, 423rd ABG / 501st CSW: Much of the former airfield is used for civilian storage/industrial purposes but there is still an extensive USAF enclave, with two display airframes.

❑ '01532'	Northrop F-5E Tiger II FSM	~	'outer' gate, 527 TFTAS colours	4-12
❑ 80-0219	Fairchild A-10A Thunderbolt II	80	ex 509th TFS, Bentwaters. Accident 4-4-89. 10th TFW, 509th TFS-511th TFS colours. *Phoenix*. 'Gate'	4-12

BASSINGBOURN on the A1198 north of Royston

Tower Museum Bassingbourn: The original tower is the basis for a superb museum dedicated to the history of the once resident 91st BG, 11 OTU, 231 OCU, the Army and others. There is a special exhibition dedicated to Bassingbourn's most famous USAAF resident, when it was USAAF Station 121, B-17F *Memphis Belle*.

◆ **Open:** *Second and fourth Sun in Mar through to Oct, 10:00 to 16:00, check website for more details.* ***NB*** *Photo ID essential as museum is on an active military establishment.* **Contact:** *Hangar 3, Bassingbourn Barracks, Royston, SG8 5LX* | **01763 243500** | **towermuseum.121@btinternet.com** | **www.towermuseumbassingbourn.co.uk**

Army Training Regiment, Bassingbourn: ATR staged its last parade in June 2012 and the base is in the process of being vacated. Part and parcel of this was the scrapping of Canberra PR.7 WJ821 by mid-2013.

BOTTISHAM north of the A14 east of Cambridge

Bottisham Airfield Museum Group: As you scream along the A14, take a look south as you are abeam Stow cum Quy and Bottisham and to the west of Little Wilbraham you will see what little remains of the former USAAF Station 374. The fighter base's northern edge was consumed in the making of the dual carriageway. Since 2010, a small group is working towards a permanent museum in tribute to all who flew from Bottisham. A team are building an impressive P-51D Mustang cockpit section, which will be painted as *Lou IV* as flown by Colonel Thomas J Christian of the 361st Fighter Group. At present the Royal British Legion in Bottisham is used as a display venue; but keep an eye on the website.

◆ **Open:** *By appointment only, occasional special events.* **Contact: jasonwebb@bottishamairfieldmuseum.org.uk** | **www.bottishamairfieldmuseum.org.uk**

BOURN AERODROME on the A428 west of Cambridge EGSN

Cessna 310B G-BPIL left by road in mid-2012; perhaps for Hungary. Three Cessnas have been deleted: FRA.150M G-BEKN (last noted Jun 2006), FR.172J G-BEZS (Feb 2002) and F.152 G-BNSV (Oct 2005).

❑ G-BCJH	Mooney M.20F	66	ex N9549M. CoA 30-6-91, de-reg 26-9-00	5-13
❑ G-BKNI	Gardan Horizon 160D	69	ex F-BRJN. CoA 13-5-02, de-reg 14-1-10. *Blue Lady*	5-13
❑ G-BKOT	Wassmer WA.81 Piranha	77	ex Little Gransden, Glatton, Eversden, F-GAIP	9-10
❑ G-BNSU	Cessna 152 II	78	ex N49410.CoA 13-10-07. Fuselage	9-10
❑ N420DD	Cessna 310D	~	store	8-10

CAMBRIDGE

Two restoration projects, at two separate venues, are in the *general* area.

❑ G-AANO	DH.60GMW Moth	30	ex Southampton, N590N, NC590N. Moth Corp-built	6-08

❑ WP977	DHC Chipmunk T.10 G-BHRD	52	ex Yateley, Crowland, Doncaster, Stamford, Burford, 9M-ANA, VR-SEK, WP977, Malayan Aux AF, Rufforth SF, Man UAS, Liv UAS,63 GCF, QUAS, Man UAS. Crashed 21-1-97, de-reg 19-1-98		4-08

CAMBRIDGE AIRPORT or Teversham

EGSC

Marshall Aerospace: Hercules C.3 XV307 was scrapped on 26th March 2012, followed by C.3 XV212 on 2nd May 2012. Cessna 421C G-FTAX (last noted Jan 2006) has been deleted. Active 'first generation' Hercules are now a thing of the past with the RAF - see under St Athan, Wales - for a Marshall 'sub-site'. The Tristar is now also in the last throes of its RAF service, with 214 Squadron due to disband On 31st March 2014. KC.1 ZD950 was only briefly in storage here, returning to service by 2013. A contract for the scrapping of ZD949 and ZE706 was announced in September 2013; the work should have started by April 2014. Parting out of the rest of the fleet will take place at Cotswold, Glos.

❑ -	Robinson R22	~	'Aeromega', training aid		5-13
❑ XV208	Lockheed Hercules W.2(m)	67	ex TP400 test-bed, Met Res Flt, A&AEE, 48, USAF 66-8558. Arrived 27-4-05. Last flown 30-9-09. Stored, minus wings	[1]	2-14
❑ XV302	Lockheed Hercules C.3	67	ex LTW, Fairford Wing, 30/47 Sqns, USAF 66-13538. Arrived 5-7-02. Fatigue rig		5-13
❑ ZD949	Lockheed Tristar K.1	79	ex Brize Norton, 216, G-BFCB British Airways. Arrived 17-11-07, last flown 5-11-10. See above		10-13
❑ ZE706*	Lockheed Tristar C.2A	80	ex Brize Norton, 216, N503PA PanAm. Arrived 7-8-13. See above		10-13

■ **[1]** XV208 was the test-bed for the Europrop International TP400 turboprop, the powerplant for the Airbus A400 Tottenham Court Road (sorry, Atlas) transport. The engine was mounted in the port inner position and it last flew 30-9-09. (Take a look at your road atlas - the A400 *really* is the Tottenham Court Road!)

DUXFORD AERODROME south of Cambridge, Junction 10 M11

EGSU

Imperial War Museum (IWM): In December 2013 the first delivery to the newly re-vamped IWM at South Lambeth, Gtr London, took place with the migration of the Harrier GR.9; to be positioned ready for the opening in July 2014. As *W&R* closed for press, just which airframes were due to follow it down the M11 had yet to be confirmed and most are listed, for this edition only, in a special section below.

Essentially, the first listing is devoted to Hangar 4, which contains the 'Air Defence Collection' of fighter types, Hangar 5 the main restoration hangar and miscellaneous IWM airframes. Nos.2 and 3 continue their traditional role of housing the 'flyers' – see below. Beyond that come the IWM's 'flying partners'. See under the Aircraft Restoration Company - below - for the IWM's long-term 'Blenheim' project.

IWM also has the following airframes out on loan: Sea Harrier FA.2 ZA175 (Flixton, Suffolk); F-86A Sabre 0242 (Coventry, Warks). As noted in *W&R23*, during September 2011, IWM undertook a major review of the collection and initiated a disposal plan. Several airframes out on loan to other museums were handed on: Sherpa G-36-1 at Long Kesh, N Ireland; Colditz Cock and and MiG-15 at Flixton, Suffolk; Draken at Dumfries, Scotland. Most of the machines leaving the inventory were at best peripheral to the overall 'message' of the IWM; others are of greater concern, either to aerial warfare, or the UK's heritage 'font'. Letting the French-built Ju 52 go was a major oversight. There is, of course, the CASA-built machine at the RAF Museum Cosford, but it is a fish-out-of-water in that collection. (Perhaps it could move to Duxford?) *The* place for an icon like the Ju 52 is Duxford. As to the import of the type, I quote none other than Captain Eric 'Winkle' Brown, from *Wings of the Luftwaffe*, published by Crécy under its Hikoki imprint: "I discovered the very real affection for the 'Tante Ju' (Auntie Ju) possessed by the Wehrmacht as a whole, and began to appreciate the fact that this transport had probably played a greater role in shaping the course of World War Two than any combat aeroplane."

Departures: Varsity T.1 WJ945 to Newquay, Cornwall, 9-1-13; Sea Venom FAW.21 XG613 left 5-13 bound for Krakow, Poland; Sea Vampire T.22 XG743 was initially thought bound for Greece, but instead moved to Pickhill, N Yorks, by 5-13; Harrier GR.9 ZD461 to South Lambeth, Gtr Lon, 2-12-13; Ju 52 (AAC.1) 63316 '4V+GH' joined the disapora to Poland 5-13; MS Criquet 'CF+HF' (EI-AUY) departed by road 8-10-12 to a private owner in Germany; Mil Mi-24D *Hind* 96+21, reportedly only ever on loan to the collection, left by road on 21-9-12, bound for the Pima Air and Space Museum, Arizona; F-105D 59-1822 departed by road on 17-6-10 bound for the museum at Krakow, Poland.

◆ **Open:** *Winter (Oct to Mar) daily 10:00 to 16:00, last admission 15:00; Closed New Year's Day and Dec 24-26. Summer (Mar to Oct) 10:00 to 18:00, last admission 17:00.* ***NB****: Additional charges for special events or airshows.* **Contact:** *IWM, Duxford Airfield, Cambs, CB2 4QR* | **01223 835000** | **duxford@iwm.org.uk** | **www.iwm.org.uk Thinx:** *See also the 'HQ', IWM South Lambeth, London, IWM North at Manchester, Gtr Man and two other London-based (but non-*W&R*) venues: HMS* Belfast *and the Churchill War Rooms - details via* **www.iwm.org.uk**

❑ E2581	'13'	Bristol F.2b	18	ex South Lambeth, Cardington, South Kensington, Crystal Palace, 2 GCF, 30 TDS, SE Area HQ Flt, 1 Comm Sqn, 39. SOC 22-4-20, acquired 16-12-22		2-14
❑ 'P2954'	'WX-E'	Hawker Hurricane FSM	00	BAPC.267, ex 'R4115', South Lambeth. 242 Sqn c/s. 'Gate'		2-14
❑ 'X4178'	'EB-K'	Supermarine Spitfire I FSM	06	ex 'DU-X' *and* 'IW-M'. 41 Sqn colours		2-14
❑ 'Z2315'	'JU-E'	Hawker Hurricane IIb	c40	ex TFC, Russia. Arrived 9-97. 111 Sqn colours	[1]	2-14
❑ HM580	'KX-K'	Cierva C.30A G-ACUU	34	ex Staverton, Elmdon, G-AIXE, HM580, 529, 1448 Flt, G-ACUU, AST Hamble. CoA 30-4-60, de-reg 14-11-88. Acquired 1978. 529 Sqn colours		2-14
❑ LZ766		Percival Proctor III G-ALCK	44	ex Staverton, Tamworth, G-ALCK, HQBC, 21 EFTS. CoA 19-6-63, de-reg 19-8-65. Arrived 1978		2-14
❑ WK991		Gloster Meteor F.8	53	ex South Lambeth, Kemble, 7825M, 56, 46, 13 Gp Comm Flt, Northern Sector Flt. Arrived 10-12-63		2-14
❑ WM969	'10'	Hawker Sea Hawk FB.5	54	ex Culdrose A2530 (14-5-64), FRU, 806, FB.3, 811, 898. Arrived 20-1-77		2-14
❑ WZ590	'49'	DH Vampire T.11	53	ex Woodford, Chester, St Athan, 8 FTS, 5 FTS, 228 OCU. SOC 9-12-68, arrived 4-5-73. 5 FTS colours		2-14
❑ XE627	'T'	Hawker Hunter F.6A	56	ex Brawdy, 1 TWU, TWU, 229 OCU, 1, 229 OCU, 54, 1, 54, Horsham St Faith SF, 54, 229 OCU, 92, 65. Arrived 14-11-86. 65 Sqn colours		2-14
❑ XG797	'277'	Fairey Gannet ECM.6	57	ex Arbroath, 831, AS.4, 700, 810. SOC 7-8-68, arrived 21-5-72. 831 Sqn colours, 'Flook' logo		2-14
❑ XH897		Gloster Javelin FAW.9	58	ex A&AEE, Bristol Siddeley, 5, 33, FAW.7, 25. Flew in 24-1-75		2-14
❑ XN239	'G'	Slingsby Cadet TX.3	59	ex Henlow 8889M (3-3-86), ACCGS, 644 GS, CGS, 2 GC, 644 GS. Stored, dismantled		9-11
❑ XP281		Auster AOP.9	61	ex St Athan, AFWF, Middle Wallop. NEA 8-11-68. Acquired 10-3-70. Stored, dismantled	[2]	9-11
❑ XS567	'434'	Westland Wasp HAS.1	64	ex Lee-on-Solent, A2719[2] (5-6-86), 829, 703, 829. Arrived 8-92. *Endurance* Flt colours		2-14
❑ XS576	'125'	DH Sea Vixen FAW.2	64	ex Sydenham, 899, 893, 899. Arrived 17-3-72. 899 Sqn c/s		2-14
❑ XV712	'66'	Westland Sea King HAS.6	72	ex Gosport, 814, 820, 814, 820, 810, 820, 706, 826, 706, 814. Arrived 27-5-10. 'Tiger' colours		2-14
❑ XV865		HS Buccaneer S.2B	68	ex Coningsby 9226M, Lossiemouth, 208, 12, 237 OCU, 208, 12, 208, 237 OCU, FAA, 809, 736. Arrived 21-1-99. 208 Sqn colours		2-14
❑ XZ194*	'V'	Westland Lynx AH.7	78	ex Middle Wallop, 671 Sqn, 7 Regt, AH.1. Arrived 15-4-13		2-14
❑ –		GAL Hotspur II	~	ex Aldershot. Cockpit, stored		4-10
❑ A-549		FMA Pucará	c81	ex ZD487 ntu, ex Boscombe Down, Yeovilton, Stanley, Arg AF. Arrived 10-83		2-14
❑ 1190	'4'	Messerschmitt Bf 109E-3	40	ex Bournemouth, Buckfastleigh, Canada, USA, Canada, 'White-4' of 4/JG.26, II/JG26. Force-landed 30-9-40, arrived 17-3-98		2-14
❑ 100143		Focke-Achgelis Fa 330A-1	43	ex Farnborough. Arrived 16-1-77		2-14
❑ –		Fieseler Fi 103 (V-1)	45	BAPC.93, ex Cosford	[3]	2-14
❑ –		Fieseler Fi 103 (V-1) rep	~	on original launch ramp, near American Air Museum		2-14
❑ 501		MiG-21PF *Fishbed*	c70	ex St Athan, Farnborough, Hungarian AF. Arrived 11-97		2-14
❑ 3685	'Y2-176'	Mitsubishi A6M3 *Zeke*	c43	ex Boise, USA, Taroa, Marshall Islands. Arrived 1986. Stored		2-14
❑ –		Yokosuka Ohka 11	45	BAPC.159, ex Chattenden. Arrived 4-11. Stored		2-14
❑ B2I-27		Heinkel He 111	c50	ex OFMC, Seville, Spanish AF. CASA-built 2-111. Acq 2002		2-14
❑ 252983		Schweizer TG-3A	45	ex AAM, N66630. Arrived 8-96. Stored, for disposal		7-12

■ **[1]** Hurricane II 'Z2315' could be BE146 if its upper cowling is anything to go by. BE146 was despatched to Russia on 2-10-41. **[2]** Auster XP281 is on loan from the Museum of Army Flying at Middle Wallop, Hants. **[3]** The Fi 103 is on loan from the RAF Museum.

'AirSpace': Within is 'Airborne Assault', an initial display of some of the contents of the Parachute Regiment and Airborne Forces Museum, previously at Aldershot, Hants.

❑ G-AFBS	Miles Magister I	39	ex Staverton, Bristol, G-AKKU, BB661, 10 FIS, 8 EFTS, G-AFBS. CoA 25-2-63, de-reg 22-12-95. Arrived 1978		2-14
❑ G-ALDG	HP Hermes 4	50	ex Gatwick, Silver City, Britavia, Airwork, BOAC. CoA 9-1-63, de-reg 12-10-68. BOAC c/s, *Horsa*. Fuselage	[1]	2-14
❑ G-ALFU	DH Dove 6	49	ex CAFU Stansted. CoA 4-6-71, de-reg 14-11-72	[1]	2-14

❑ G-ANTK		Avro York	45	ex Lasham, Dan-Air, MW232, Fairey, 511, 242. Last flight 30-4-64, de-reg 27-10-64. Dan-Air colours	[1]	2-14
❑ G-APDB		DH Comet 4	58	ex Dan-Air, MSA 9M-AOB, BOAC G-APDB. Flew in 12-2-74, de-reg 18-2-74. BOAC colours	[2]	2-14
❑ G-AXDN		BAC/Sud Concorde 101	68	ex BAC. CoA 30-9-77, de-reg 10-11-86	[1] [3]	2-14
❑ G-USUK		Colt 2500A gondola	87	CoA 19-8-87, de-reg 21-8-90. *Virgin Atlantic Flyer*.		2-14
❑ –		Airspeed Horsa II	~	ex Aldershot. Cockpit	[1]	2-14
❑ –		Hawker Hunter F.6	57	ex Wroughton, S' Kensington, Kingston G-9-185 (9-2-64), Dutch AF N-250. Fokker-Aviolander-built. Cockpit	[4]	2-14
❑ –		Pilcher Hawk replica	30	BAPC.57, ex St Albans, Wroughton, Hayes, South Lambeth. Arrived 11-04. In foyer	[5]	2-14
❑ D5649		Airco DH.9	17	ex St Leonards-on-Sea, Hatch, Bikaner, India, RAF/RFC. Waring & Gillow-built. Arrived 19-4-07		2-14
❑ F3556		RAF RE.8	18	ex South Lambeth, Cardington, Crystal Palace, Tadcaster, Radford, no service. Daimler-built. Acquired 20-2-20	[6]	2-14
❑ N4877	'MK-V'	Avro Anson I G-AMDA	38	ex Staverton, Elstree, London School of Flying, Derby AW G-AMDA, Watchfield SF, 3 FP, ATA, 3 FPP. CoA 14-12-62, accident 7-11-72, de-reg 9-9-81. Acquired 1978. 500 Sqn colours		2-14
❑ 'N6635'	'25'	DH Tiger Moth	c42	ex 'DE998', ARC, Stamford, Hooton, Warmingham, 'K2572', Hereford, Lutterworth, Holme-on-Spalding Moor. Arrived 5-3-02. 22 EFTS colours		2-14
❑ V3388		Airspeed Oxford I G-AHTW	40	ex Staverton, Elstree, Boulton Paul G-AHTW, V3388 n/s. CoA 15-12-60, de-reg 3-4-89. Arrived 1978		2-14
❑ 'V9673'	'MA-J'	Westland Lysander III G-LIZY	40	ex RCAF 1558, V9300. De-reg 18-4-89. Acquired 1991 161 Sqn colours		2-14
❑ KB889	'NA-I'	Avro Lancaster X G-LANC	44	ex Bitteswell, Blackbushe, RCAF 107 MRU, 428. Victory Aircraft, Canada-built. De-reg 2-9-91. Arrived 14-5-86. 428 Sqn colours		2-14
❑ ML796		Short Sunderland MR.5	44	ex La Baule, Maisden-le-Riviere, Aéronavale, 27F, 7FE, RAF 230, 4 OTU, 228. Arrived 9-7-76		2-14
❑ NF370	'NH-L'	Fairey Swordfish III	44	ex South Lambeth, Gosport, Stretton, RAF n/s. Blackburn-built. Acquired 30-6-52. 119 Sqn colours		2-14
❑ TA719		DH Mosquito TT.35 G-ASKC	45	ex Staverton, G-ASKC, Shawbury, 3/4 CAACU, 4 CAACU, Shawbury. Crashed 27-7-64, acquired 1978		2-14
❑ –		Hawker Typhoon	~	ex South Lambeth. Cockpit, in education area		2-14
❑ TG528		HP Hastings C.1A	48	ex Staverton, 24, 24-36, 242 OCU, 53-99 pool, 47. Last flight 24-1-68, arrived 1-4-79. 24 Sqn colours		2-14
❑ VN485		Supermarine Spitfire F.24	47	ex Kai Tak 7326M, Hong Kong Aux AF, 80. South Marston-built. Last flown 21-4-55, arrived 18-7-89		2-14
❑ WH725		EE Canberra B.2	53	ex Wroughton, 50, 44. Arrived 8-3-72. 50 Sqn colours	[7]	2-14
❑ XJ824		Avro Vulcan B.2	61	ex 101, 9-35, 9, 230 OCU, 27. Arrived 13-3-82		2-14
❑ XK936	'62'	Westland Whirlwind HAS.7	57	ex Wroughton, 705, 847, 848, 701, 820, 845. Arrived 28-10-75		2-14
❑ XM135	'B'	EE Lightning F.1	59	ex Leconfield, Leuchars TFF, 226 OCU, 74, AFDS. Flew in 20-11-74. 74 Sqn colours	[8]	2-14
❑ XR222		BAC TSR-2 XO-4	64	ex Cranfield, Weybridge. Unflown, arrived 21-3-78		2-14
❑ XS863	'304'	Westland Wessex HAS.1	65	ex A&AEE, ETPS, 826, 706, 815. Arrived 8-10-81. Royal Navy colours		2-14
❑ XT581		Northrop Shelduck D.1	~	drone		2-14
❑ XX108		SEPECAT Jaguar GR.1<u>B</u>	72	ex St Athan, BAe Warton, G-27-313 ntu, DERA, A&AEE. Last flown 28-5-02, arrived 29-10-03		2-14
❑ XZ133	'10'	HS Harrier GR.3	76	ex South Lambeth, St Athan, 4, 1, 1417 Flt, 233 OCU. Arrived 2-9-93		2-14
❑ ZA465	'FF'	Panavia Tornado GR.1B	83	ex Lossiemouth, 12, 617, 17, 16. Arrived 25-10-01		2-14
❑ 18393		Avro Canada CF-100 Canuck Mk.4B	55	ex Cranfield, G-BCYK, RCAF, 440, 419, 409. Flew in 29-3-75, de-reg 15-9-81		2-14
❑ 1133		BAC Strikemaster Mk.80<u>A</u> G-BESY	76	ex Warton, R Saudi AF, G-BESY, G-27-29<u>9</u>. De-reg 18-4-83, arrived 22-3-00		2-14

'AirSpace' Restoration / Storage Bay:

❑	XF708	'C'	Avro Shackleton MR.3/3		59	ex Kemble, 203, 120, 201. Arrived 22-8-72. 203 Sqn colours		2-14
❑	XH648		HP Victor B.1A (K2P)		59	ex 57, 55, Honington Wing, 15, 57. Arrived 2-6-76. 57 Sqn colours		2-14
❑	ZH590		Eurofighter Typhoon DA4		97	ex Coningsby, Warton, Eurofighter. Arrived 22-4-09	[9]	2-14

■ **[1]** Duxford Aviation Society airframes - see below for more. **[2]** *Delta-Bravo* operated the first ever scheduled service New York to London 4-10-58. Total time 36,269 hours, 15,733 landings. **[3]** *Delta-November* factoids: total hours 632, landings 273. **[4]** Fokker-Avioland built, repurchased by HSA and the rest of N-250 was re-worked as Indian T.66D S-581 in 1967. **[5]** The Pilcher Hawk is on loan from Eric Littledike - see also Old Warden, Beds. **[6]** The RE.8 is a presentation aircraft: *A Paddy Bird from Ceylon,* but this is not carried on the airframe. It very likely flew for no more than 2 hours in total. **[7]** The Canberra B.2 is on loan from the RAF Museum. **[8]** XM135 made famous 'unpiloted' circuits of Lyneham in 1965 with engineer W/C Walter Holden at the controls. It has a total time of 1,343 hours. **[9]** DA4 made its first flight on 3-3-97 and its last on 13-12-06.

American Air Museum (AAM): Heritage Lottery Fund (HLF) granted £980.000 for a redevelopment project centred on the AAM. The first stage is to create an 'interactive' website of the Roger A Freeman collection of USAAF images; a superb resource gifted to the IWM by the mild-mannered, inspiring historian and writer, who died on 7th October 2005.

Opened on 1st August 1997, the AAM will be significantly revised to take into account US-inspired conflicts since that time. Of the airframes, several will undergo extensive conservation work and there will be a 'review' of the airframes suspended from the ceiling. All of this will mean that the massive glass 'wall' will need to be brought down and a temporary closure of the building to the public... another reminder that this is the most impractical aircraft display hall in the UK. No timeline has been announced for this work, so keep an eye on the website. See under 'South Lambeth airframes' below for a new inmate.

Around the A505 end of the building is a series of plate glass monoliths, each of which poignantly depict the losses of 'Mighty Eighth' aircraft - and of course crews. While on the subject of remembrance...

◆ **Thinx:** *At some point, a visit to Duxford should include a short trip northwards up the M11 to Junction 13 and then the A1303 westbound to the* **American Forces Cemetery at Madingley** *and walk through the beautifully kept grounds, amid row after row of graves and impressive memorials.* | **www.madingleyamericancemetery.info**

❑	'S4513'	'1'	SPAD XIII replica	G-BFYO	78	ex 'S3398', Yeovilton, Land's End, Chertsey, G-BFYO, D-EOWM. CoA 21-6-82, de-reg 14-10-86, arrived 17-6-96		2-14
❑	31171		NAA TB-25J-30-NC Mitchell		45	ex Shoreham, Dublin, Prestwick, Luton,N7614C, USAF, 4000th ABU Wright Patterson JTB-25J / ETB-25J / EB-25J, USAAF B-25J 44-31171. Arrived 29-11-76. USMC PBJ-1J c/s		2-14
❑	'46214'	'X-3'	Grumman TBM-3E Avenger		44	ex CF-KCG, RCN 326, USN 69327. General Motors-built. Arrived 11-77. 'Lt George Bush' titling. *Ginny*		2-14
❑	155529	'114'	McD F-4J(UK) Phantom	ZE359	67	ex Wattisham, 74, US Navy 155529, VF-171, VF-31, VF-74, VF-33. Flew in 10-7-91. USN VF-74, *America* colours		2-14
❑	'217786'	'25'	Boeing PT-17 Kaydet		42	ex Swanton Morley, Duxford, CF-EQS, Evergreen, New Brunswick, Canada, 41-8169. Arrived 11-77	[1]	2-14
❑	'226413'	'UN-Z'	Republic P-47D-30-RA Thunderbolt		45	ex USA, Chino, N47DD, Harlingen, Peru AF FAP 119 and 545, USAAF 45-49192. Crashed 9-2-80. Acquired 11-85. 56th FG c/s as 'Hub' Zemke's a/c, *Oregon's Britannia*	[2]	2-14
❑	315509	'W7-S'	Douglas C-47A-85-DL Skytrain	G-BHUB	44	ex Aces High G-BHUB, *Airline* : 'G-AGIV', 'FD988',and 'KG418', Spanish AF T3-29, N51V, N9985F, SAS SE-BBH, 315 TCG, 316 TCG, 43-15509. De-reg 19-10-81. Acquired 7-80. 37th TCS / 316th TCG colours		2-14
❑	'450493'		Cons' B-24M-25-FO Liberator		44	ex Lackland, EZB-24M. Ford-built. Arrived 29-6-99. *Dugan*		2-14
❑	461748	'Y'	Boeing TB-29A-45-BN Superfortress	G-BHDK	45	ex G-BHDK, China Lake, 307th BG, Okinawa. Flew in 2-3-80,de-reg 29-3-84. *It's Hawg Wild* (stb). 307th BG colours		2-14
❑	'463209'	'WZ-S'	NAA P-51D Mustang FSM		91	BAPC.255, ex OFMC, London. Acquired1996. 78th FG, 84th FS colours, *Sherman Was Right!*		2-14
❑	483735		Boeing B-17G-95-DL Flying Fortress		44	ex *Mary Alice*, Creil, IGN F-BDRS, N68269, 44-83735. Douglas-built. Last flown 1971, arrived 1975, acquired 1978		2-14
❑	–		NAA Harvard II		42	ex North Weald, Dutch AF B-168, FE984, RCAF, 2 FIS, 42-2471. Acquired 1988		2-14
❑	51-4286		Lockheed T-33A-1-LO		52	ex Sculthorpe, FAF CIFAS 328. Last flown 25-1-78, arrived 8-4-79. USAF colours		2-14
❑	54-2165	'VM'	NAA F-100D-11-NA Super Sabre		56	ex Sculthorpe, FAF Esc 2/11, Esc 1/3, 48th TFW, USAF. Last flown 24-11-75, arrived 17-5-76, 352nd TFS, 35th TFW colours		2-14

❑ 56-0689		Boeing B-52D-40-BW Superfortress	57	ex 7th BW Carswell, 96th BW, 7th BW, 99th BW, 7th BW, 96th BW, 99th BW, U-Tapao, 509th BW, 454th BW, 306th BW, 99th BW, 91st BW, 509th BW, 494th BW, 95th BW, 28th BW. Wichita-built. Flew in 8-10-83		2-14
❑ 56-6692		Lockheed U-2CT-LO	56	ex Alconbury, 9th SRW, 100th SRW, U-2C, 6515th TS, U-2F, 6515th TS, CIA, U-2C, 4080th SRW, CIA. Last flown 28-12-87, arrived 26-6-92. Modded to single-seat configuration		2-14
❑ 61-17962		Lockheed SR-71A Blackbird	66	ex Palmdale, 9th SRW, 9th SRW Det 4 Mildenhall, 9th SRW. Arrived 5-4-01	[3]	2-14
❑ 67-0120		GD F-111E-CF Aardvark	69	ex Upper Heyford, 20th TFW, 57th TTW, 442nd TFTS, 27th TFW. Arr 19-10-93. *The Chief*, 78th TFS, 20th TFW c/s	[4]	2-14
❑ 72-21605		Bell UH-1H Iroquois	72	ex Coleman Barracks, ATCOM, 158th Av Regt. Arr 15-7-97		2-14
❑ 76-0020		McDD F-15A-15-MC Eagle	76	ex AMARC Davis-Monthan, 102nd FIW, 5th FIS, 33rd TFW, 36th TFW. Last flown 25-10-93, arrived 4-01. 5th FIS colours		2-14
❑ 77-0259	'AR'	Fairchild A-10A-FA ...Thunderbolt II	79	ex Alconbury, 10th TFW, 128th TFW, 111th TASG, 128th TFW, 81st TFW. Flew in 6-2-92		2-14
❑ -		GD F-111F-CF Aadvark	~	escape module	[5]	2-14
❑ -		McDD F-15 Eagle	~	ex 48th TFW, Lakenheath. Cockpit simulator, *Eagle Drivers*		2-14

■ **[1]** The PT-17 is a composite, having used elements of 42-17786 during its restoration (which was carried out by Eastern Stearman). **[2]** P-47 *Oregon's Britannia* was a major reconstruction based upon large elements of P-47D 45-49192 not used in the composite that created The Fighter Collection's machine *No Guts, No Glory* (now exported). **[3]** Achieved world altitude record 28-7-76 of 85,068ft. **[4]** *The Chief* carried out 19 operational missions during DESERT STORM, 1995. **[5]** Previously quoted as coming from 72-1447 but this is in private hands with Robert N Soek at Eindhoven in The Netherlands.

South Lambeth airframes: As these words hit the screen, the IWM in London was deep in the throes of its £35 million re-vamp and closed to the public; due to re-open in July 2014. From late 2012 to January 2013, all of the airframe exhibits came to Duxford. Just *which* (and others from the Duxford 'stock') will 'go south' was then yet to be confirmed. Accordingly, the Lambeth refugees are listed here, as a port of convenience, all to be settled in *W&R25*!

That said, Spitfire I R6915 (which arrived 13th December 2012) returned to South Lambeth, Gtr Lon, on 15th January 2014. The Mustang will *not* be returning; it is destined for the American Air Museum.

❑ 2699*		RAF BE.2c	16	ex South Lambeth, Duxford, South Lambeth, 192, 51, 50. Ruston, Proctor & Co-built. Acquired 1920, arr 10-12		2-14
❑ N6812*		Sopwith 2F1 Camel	18	ex South Lambeth, 'F3043', Yeovilton, Honington, Cardington, South Kensington (store), South Lambeth. William Beardmore-built. Acquired 1920, arr by 10-12	[1]	2-14
❑ DV372*		Avro Lancaster I	43	ex South Lambeth, 1651 CU, 467. SOC 4-1-45. Acquired 1960. Metropolitan-Vickers built. *Old Fred*. Cockpit. Arr 9-12		2-14
❑ PN323*		HP Halifax A.VII	45	ex South Lambeth, Duxford, South Lambeth, Duxford, Staverton, Radlett, Standard Telephones & Cables, 29 MU. Fairey-built. SOC 28-5-48. Acquired 1979. Cockpit. Arr 9-12		2-14
❑ 120235*	'6'	Heinkel He 162A-1	45	ex South Lambeth, Duxford, South Lambeth, Cranwell, Brize Norton, Farnborough AM.68, JG.1, Leck. Acquired 1960, arrived 1-13		2-14
❑ '472218'*	'WZ-I'	NAA P-51D-25-NA Mustang	44	ex South Lambeth, Duxford, RCAF 9246, USAAF 44-73979. Acquired 12-71. *Big, Beautiful Doll*, 78th FG colours Arrived 21-12-12. See note above		2-14
❑ –*		Mitsubishi A6M5 *Zeke*	c44	ex South Lambeth, Duxford, South Lambeth, ATIAU-SEA. Cockpit. Acquired 1955, arrived 10-12		2-14
❑ 477663*		Fieseler Fi 103F-1 (V-1)	44	BAPC.198, ex South Lambeth. Arrived 10-12		2-14

■ **[1]** Flown by Lt S D Culley, this William Beardmore-built Camel was flown off a lighter towed by HMS *Redoubt* on 11-8-18 to intercept, and shoot down, the Zeppelin L53.

Duxford Aviation Society - The British Airliner Collection: The following DAS airframes are within 'AirSpace' (see above). Hermes G-ALDG, Dove G-ALFU, York G-ANTK, Comet 4 G-APDB, Concorde G-AXDN. The cockpit of Viscount G-OPAS is on loan to the Bournemouth Aviation Museum, see Bournemouth Dorset.

◆ **Contact:** *Duxford Airfield, Duxford, Cambridge, CB2 4QR* | **01223 835000** | **www.das.org.uk**

❑ G-ALWF	Vickers Viscount 701	52	ex Liverpool, Cambrian, British Eagle, Channel, BEA. Last flown 12-4-72, de-reg 18-4-72, arr 21-2-76. BEA colours, *Sir John Franklin*	[1]	3-12
❑ G-ALZO	Airspeed Ambassador 2	52	ex Lasham, Dan-Air, Handley Page, Jordan AF 108, BEA. CoA 14-5-72, de-reg 10-9-81. Dan-Air colours	[2]	3-12

❑	G-AOVT	Bristol Britannia 312	58	ex Luton, Monarch, British Eagle, BOAC. Flew in 29-6-75, de-reg 21-9-81. Monarch colours	[3]	3-12
❑	G-APWJ	HP Herald 201	63	ex Norwich, Air UK, BIA, BUIA. Flew in 7-7-85, de-reg 10-7-85. Air UK colours		3-12
❑	G-ASGC	Vickers Super VC-10	65	ex BA, BOAC, BOAC-Cunard, BOAC. Flew in 15-4-80, de-reg 22-4-80. BOAC-Cunard c/s	[4]	3-12
❑	G-AVFB	HS Trident 2E	67	ex BA, Nicosia, Cyprus 5B-DAC, BEA. Flew in 13-6-82, de-reg 9-7-82. BEA colours	[5]	3-12
❑	G-AVMU	BAC 111-510ED	68	ex Bournemouth, BA, BEA. Last flight 4-3-93, de-reg 12-7-93. BA colours. *County of Dorset*	[6]	3-12

■ **[1]** *Zulu-Oscar* made the last-ever flight by the type in 10-71. **[2]** *Whisky-Fox* completed 28,299 flight hours and 25,398 landings. **[3]** *Victor-Tango* factoids: completed 35,739 flight hours and 10,760 landings. **[4]** *Golf-Charlie* totted up 54,623 flight hours and 16,415 landings. **[5]** *Fox-Bravo* was damaged by ground fire at Nicosia during the Turkish invasion of Cyprus, 7-74 and remained grounded until 5-77. It completed 21,642 flying hours and 11,726 landings in 1982. **[6]** *Mike-Uniform*'s stats: 45,541 landings, 40,280 hours.

Aircraft Restoration Company (ARC) / **Historic Flying Ltd** (HFL): ARC operates and/or maintains several aircraft on behalf of other organisations. Only long-term restoration projects, the ARC/HFL 'fleet' and is associates are given here. ARC has a contract to carry out major maintenance on the Battle of Britain Memorial Flight, all the way up to the Lancaster.

Blenheim (Duxford) Ltd, was set up for the restoration of G-BPIV. It was rolled out at Duxford on August 12, 2013 engineless, but in its 23 Squadron camouflage. The nose of Battle of Britain veteran Mk.I L6739 (a former 23 Squadron night-fighter) is fitted to make the project a *representative* Mk.I. This nose was previously an electric-driven car conversion! By January 2014, the engines had been installed. The **Blenheim Society** works tirelessly to support the restoration of *India-Victor*. **Contact:** *Ron Scott, 25 Herongate Road, Cheshunt, EN8 0TU* | **www.blenheimsociety.org.uk**

Spitfire XVIII SM845 was last mentioned in *W&R22* (p25), departing on 7th May 2009 for a new owner in Sweden. Sadly it crashed while attending a display in Norway on 10th August 2010. Acquired by Spitfire Ltd, the fuselage was worked on by Airframe Assemblies at Sandown and restoration came to fruition on 17th December 2013 with its return to the air. It will be based at Humberside Airport, Lincs, when the flight test regime is complete.

The Rolls-Royce Spitfire PR.XIX PS853 (G-RRGN) flew again on 24th August 2012. Sadly, it suffered an undercarriage collapse at its East Midlands Airport base on 2nd January 2013, but ARC had it back where it belongs by July 2013.

Airworthy Chipmunk 22 G-AOTR was based at Goodwood by the spring of 2012. Beech 18 3TM '1164' (G-BKGL) was acquired by Tim Darrah and flew out to Bruntingthorpe, Leics, in late 2012. Albatros G-OTAF was exported to South Africa in September 2013. Pilatus P.2-05 A-125 (G-BLKZ) was roaded out on 31st October 2013, perhaps bound for Cornwall.

◆ **Access: Please note** *that the ARC/HFL building is* **not** *open to public inspection.* Some *ARC aircraft can be viewed in other hangars during normal opening hours and during airshows* | **www.arc-duxford.co.uk**

❑	G-BZGL	NAA OV-10B Bronco	71	ex Luftwaffe 99+26, D-9555, 158302. Arrived 13-9-01	[1]	1-14
❑	G-DHCZ	DHC Beaver AL.1 ✈	60	ex G-BUCJ, XP772, Middle Wallop, Beverley, Leconfield, Middle Wallop, 15 Flt, 667, 132 Flt, AFWF	[2]	1-14
❑	SE-BRG	Fairey Firefly TT.1 G-CGYD	44	ex Sweden, Svensk Flygtjanst, FAA Mk.I DT989, 767, 766, Arrived 10-2-04	[2]	1-14
❑	–	Bristol Bolingbroke IVT G-BPIV	43	ex 'R3821', 'L8841', 'Z5722', G-BPIV, Strathallan, Canada, RCAF 10201. Fairchild Canada-built. Crashed 18-8-03. See note above		1-14
❑	–	Bristol Bolingbroke IVT	42	ex G-MKIV, G-BLHM ntu, RCAF 10038. Fairchild Canada-built. Crashed 21-6-87, de-reg 1-11-88. Stored	[3]	1-14
❑	N3200	Supermarine Spitfire Ia G-CFGJ	39	ex Sandown, Duxford, Braintree, Calais, 19. Shot down 27-5-40	[4] [5]	1-14
❑	'P7308'*	Supermarine Spitfire Ia ✈ G-AIST	41	ex Cotswold, Duxford, Booker, Old Warden, *Battle of Britain*, AR213, 8 MU, 53 OTU, 57 OTU. 71 Sqn colours and serial by 5-13	[6]	1-14
❑	P9374 'J'	Supermarine Spitfire Ia ✈ G-MKIA	39	ex Sandown, Duxford, Braintree, Calais, 92. Shot down 24-5-40. 92 Sqn colours	[4]	1-14
❑	V9312	Westland Lysander TT.IIIA G-CCOM	39	ex N9309K, Canada, RCAF, RAF, 4, 613, 225. SOC 1-10-46. Arrived 4-6-03	[2]	1-14
❑	'W3632'	Supermarine Spitfire Tr.9 ✈ G-CCCA	44	ex 'QV-I', 'AI-E', 'H-98','161', G-TRIX, Goodwood, G-BHGH, IAC 161, G-15-174, PV202, 412, 33. *Bahrain* by 1-14	[7] [8]	1-14
❑	MB293	Sup' Seafire IIc G-CFGI	42	ex Braintree, Malta, 879, 887, A&AEE. Stored	[4]	1-14
❑	'MH424'	Supermarine Spitfire IX MJ271	43	ex Lelystad, Schiphol, De Haag, Delfzijl, Volkel, RNethAF H-8, MJ271, 401, 132, 118. Stored		1-14

❑ PL983		Supermarine Spitfire PR.XI	G-PRXI	44	ex Sandown, Duxford, Goudhurst, North Weald, Biggin Hill, Duxford, East Midlands, Stonebroom, Duxford, Old Warden, Vickers G-15-109, NC74138, PL983, 2, 4, 1 PP. Crashed 4-6-01, CoA 11-6-01	[2]	1-14
❑ RK858		Supermarine Spitfire IX	G-CGJE	43	ex TFC, CIS, USSR, Sov AF, RK858 no RAF service. Went missing, Archangel region, 1947. Stored	[7]	1-14
❑ RX168		Supermarine Seafire III	G-BWEM	45	ex Swindon, Exeter, Andover, Norwich, Battle, Dublin, IAC 157, RX168. Stored	[4]	1-14
❑ SM845*	'R'	Supermarine Spitfire XVIII ✈	G-BUOS	45	ex Sandown, Humberside, Sweden SE-BIN, Duxford, G-BUOS, Audley End, Witney, USA, Ind AF HS687, RAF SM845, n/s. 28 Sqn c/s. See above		1-14
❑ WK522		DHC Chipmunk T.10	G-BCOU	52	ex Audley End, Abn AUS, Liv UAS, Man UAS, Gla UAS, Stn UAS, Bri UAS, 3 RFS, 5 BFTS. CoA 30-3-95	[9]	9-13
❑ WP929	'F'	DHC Chipmunk T.10 ✈	G-BXCV	52	ex Shawbury, 8 AEF, Liv UAS, Cam UAS, Wittering SF, RAFTTC, Coningsby SF, 61 GCF, 661	[10]	3-12
❑ XX543	'U'	SAL Bulldog T.1 ✈	G-CBAB	73	ex Shawbury, York UAS, 6 FTS, York UAS, RNEFTS, CFS. *Donna*	[7]	3-12
❑ 3349		NAA Yale ✈	G-BYNF	40	ex N55904, Canada, RCAF, 3349. Arrived 16-9-99	[11]	3-12
❑ 119		NAA T-28A Fennec ✈	N14113	51	ex USA, Haiti AF 1236, N14113, FAF (No.119), USAF 51-7545. *Little Rascal*	[12]	8-13
❑ 517692		NAA T-28A Fennec ✈	G-TROY	51	ex F-AZFR, AdA Fennec No.142, 51-7692. French AF EALA 09/72 colours	[13]	3-12
❑ '10'		Hispano Buchón ✈ (Bf 109)	G-BWUE	49	ex Spitfire Ltd, Breighton, Sandown, Breighton, Duxford, N9938, *Battle of Britain*, G-AWHK, SpanAF C4K-154	[7] [14]	3-12
❑ 1747		NAA Harvard IV ✈	G-BGPB	53	ex '20385' North Weald, Port AF 1747, WGAF BF+050, AA+050, 53-4619. CCF-built. PortAF colours. *Taz*	[15]	3-12
❑ '44'		Boeing PT-27 Kaydet ✈		42	G-RJAH - ex N75957, RCAF FJ991, 42-15852	[16]	3-12
❑ 8178	'FU-178'	NAA F-86A-5-NA Sabre ✈	G-SABR	48	ex Bournemouth, N178, N68388, 48-0178. 4th FW colours	[17]	3-12

■ **[1]** The Bronco is registered to Invicta Aviation. **[2]** Registered to Propshop Ltd. **[3]** Bolingbroke G-MKIV is stored for the IWM, which acquired it in 1974, and it will have the nose of 9893 - all of the latter airframe is also held. **[4]** N3200, P9374, MB293, and RX168 are with Mark One Partners LLC. **[5]** When Spitfire N3200 was shot down, 19 Sqn had gotten around to applying the unit code 'QV-' but no individual letter, it is likely that it will fly in this guise. **[6]** G-AIST registered to Spitfire The One Ltd. **[7]** Registered to HFL. **[8]** Painted in the guise of a Spitfire acquired by the Persian Gulf Fighter Fund in 1941, for participation at the Bahrain Airshow in late January 2014. **[9]** *Oscar-Uniform* is being painstakingly and lovingly restored by John and Peter Loweth. **[10]** WP929 registered to Ardmore Aviation Services. **[11]** Yale owned by Robert van Dijk. **[12]** *Little Rascal* operated by Radial Revelations - a consortium of owners including Martin Willing. **[13]** G-TROY is registered to Groupe Fennec. **[14]** G-BWUE has the fuselage of C4K-154 - a *Battle of Britain* non-flyer. It was originally C4K-102 which more properly relates to G-AWHK. It is *believed* that the rest of the airframe comes from C4K-102. It carries *Battle of Britain* colours as *Yellow 10*. **[15]** 1747 is registered to Aircraft Spares and Materials. **[16]** 'Stearman' is registered to Robert J A Horne. **[17]** Sabre is registered to Golden Apple Operations.

B-17 Preservation Ltd: Determination keeps this icon going; no lottery grants, government hand-outs or other funding. Its lifeblood is the ***Sally B*** **Supporters Club**, donations from the public, the grit of its engineering team and the expertise of its operator, Elly Sallingboe.

◆ **Contact:** *PO Box 92, Bury St Edmunds, IP28 8RR* | **01638 721304** | **sallyb@B-17preservation.demon.co.uk** | **www.sallyb.org.uk**

❑ '124485'	'DF-A'	Boeing B-17G-105-VE ✈ Flying Fortress	G-BEDF	44	ex N17TE, IGN F-BGSR, 44-85784. *Sally B* (port), *Memphis Belle* (stb)	2-14

The Fighter Collection (TFC): At 'Flying Legends' in July 2013, TFC founder, Stephen Grey bowed out of display flying in fine style by opening the show each day in the Bearcat. He continues at the helm of the incredible warbird collection.

Curtiss-built 'razorback' P-47G 225068 (G-CDVX) *Snafu* first flew on 21st April 2012 and had its public debut at Flying Legends that July. It was crated and exported to the USA 27th December 2013. Sea Fury VX653 (G-BUCM) has been shipped to New Zealand for restoration; it will return. The crated, former Soviet, Curtiss P-40 was disposed off and has gone to the USA. In December 2013 P-40B Warhawk '284' (G-CDWH) was acquired on behalf of the Collings Foundation and was due to depart to the USA in the spring.

◆ **Access:** *Open to the public during normal museum hours. TFC stages the 'Flying Legends' airshow and operates the* ***Friends of the Fighter Collection*** *support group* | **www.fighter-collection.com**

❑ G-ARUL	Le Vier Cosmic Wind ✈	73	ex N22C. *Ballerina II*	[1]	1-14
❑ G-BRVE	Beech D.17S ✈	45	ex North Weald, N1139V, NC1139V, FT475, 44-67724, 23689 ntu. Acquired 2005		1-14

❑ N5903		Gloster Gladiator II ✈	G-GLAD	39	ex Yeovilton, 'N2276', 'N5226', Old Warden, Eastleigh, Ansty, Gloster 61 OTU. Arrived 30-11-94. 72 Sqn colours		1-14
❑ S1581	'573'	Hawker Nimrod I ✈	G-BWWK	32	ex St Leonards-on-Sea, St Just, Henlow, 802. Acquired 2004. 802 Sqn colours		1-14
❑ EP120	'AE-A'	Supermarine Spitfire V ✈	G-LFVB	42	ex Audley End, Duxford, St Athan 8070M, Wattisham, Boulmer, Wilmslow, St Athan, 5377M,53 OTU, 402, 19, 501. Arrived 1-93. *City of Winnipeg* , 402 Sqn colours	[2]	1-14
❑ FE695	'94'	NAA Harvard IIB ✈	G-BTXI	42	ex RSwAF Fv16105, RCAF, 6 SFTS, RAF FE695, 42-892. Noorduyn-built. Arrived 25-10-91		1-14
❑ 'JV579'	'F'	Grumman FM-2 Wildcat ✈	G-RUMW	44	ex Monroe, USA N4845V, 86711. Arrived 25-4-93 846 Sqn colours		1-14
❑ 'KD345'	'A-130'	Vought FG-1D✈ Corsair ✈	G-FGID	45	ex N8297, N9154Z, USN 88297. Arrived 4-86 1850 Sqn, SEAC colours		1-14
❑ 'MV268'	'JE-J'	Supermarine Spitfire XIV ✈	G-SPIT	45	ex Sleaford, Blackbushe, G-BGHB ntu, Bangalore, Indian inst T20, IAF, MV293 ACSEA. Arrived 7-10-85. 'Johnnie' Johnson c/s		1-14
❑ PK624		Supermarine Spitfire F.22		45	ex St Athan, Abingdon 8072M, Northolt, Uxbridge, North Weald, 'WP916', 9 MU, 614. SOC 4-2-54. Arrived 1994. Stored		1-14
❑ WG655	'910'	Hawker Sea Fury ...T.20S	G-CHFP	51	ex N20MD, USA, RNHF Yeovilton (crashed 14-7-90), Colerne, DLB D-CACU, G-9-65, Dunsfold, Chilbolton, FAA WG655, Eglinton SF, 781. Arrived 2008	[3]	1-14
❑ 'A19-144'		Bristol Beaufighter XI		45	ex Melbourne, Sydney, Drysdale, RAAF A8-324. DAP-built. SOC 8-8-49. Arrived 1991	[4]	1-14
❑ No.82		Curtiss Hawk 75A-1 ✈	G-CCVH	39	ex NX80FR, Chino, France, Cazaux, GC 11/5. Acquired 1990. French AF colours	[5]	1-14
❑ –		Fiat CR-42 Falco	G-CBLS	41	ex Italy, Sweden, RSweAF (as a J11) Fv 2524. Acquired 1995, arrived 23-2-06. Off-site		1-14
❑ –		Nakajima Ki-43 Hyabusa		c44	ex Australia. Stored		1-14
❑ '20'		Lavochkin La-11		c45	ex Monino, CIS, USSR. Arrived 5-93. Stored		1-14
❑ –	'284'	Curtiss P-40B Warhawk ✈	G-CDWH	41	ex Chino, N80FR, Hawaii, 18th PG, 6th PS, 41-13297. Crashed 24-1-42. Acquired 2004, arrived 17-4-07. See notes above		1-14
❑ –	'X-17'	Curtiss P-40F-15-CU Warhawk ✈	G-CGZP	41	ex VH-PIV, Wangaratta, Espiritu Santo, 44th FG, 347th FG, 41-19841. Arrived 7-11. USAAF colours, 85th FS, 79th FG, *Lee's Hope*		1-14
❑ '40467'	'19'	Grumman F6F-5K Hellcat ✈	G-BTCC	44	ex N10CN ntu, N100TF, Yankee Air Corps,N80142, USMC Museum, 80141. Arrived 1-8-90		1-14
❑ 21714	'201'	Grumman F8F-2P Bearcat ✈	G-RUMM	48	ex NX700HL, N1YY, N4995V, 121714. Acquired 3-6-81 VF-20 colours, Lt Cdr 'Whiff' Caldwell's aircraft		1-14
❑ 484847	'CY-D'	NAA TF-51D Mustang✈	N251RJ	44	ex USA, USAAF 44-84847. Arrived 4-6-07. *Miss Velma,* 55th FG colours	[6]	3-12

■ All are British registered to Patina Ltd, unless noted. **[1]** Registered to Pete Kynsey - see under King's Cliffe, Northants, for the *original* G-ARUL. **[2]** Spitfire EP120 wears the colours of 402 'City of Winnipeg' Sqn RCAF as flown mostly by its CO, Sqn Ldr Geoffrey W Northcott; between Jun and Oct 1943 he chalked up the bulk of his 8 'kills' in EP120, 3 x Bf 109 and 3 x Fw 190. **[3]** During rebuild in the USA 2002-2005, Sea Fury WG655 became a composite with the centre section and wing from an Iraqi example and the rear fuselage from an FB.11. *Fox-Papa* is registered to Nick Grey. **[4]** Beaufighter is a composite, using large elements reputed to be from Mk.XIs A19-144 (ex RAF JM135) and A-19-148 (JL946) with the cockpit from an Australian-built Department of Aircraft Production example. **[5]** G-CCVH wears GC II/5 colours to port and Lafayette Esc 'chief's head' colours to starboard; the latter also being TFC's logo. **[6]** *Miss Velma* is registered to Steve Hinton.

Historic Aircraft Collection of Jersey (HAC): See under St Leonards-on-Sea, East Sussex, for HAC's closely-related **Retrotec**. Flt Lt Charlie Brown lifted Fury I K5674 off the turf at glorious Goodwood on 30th July 2012 for a spotless first flight. It did not return - see under St Leonards-on-Sea, East Sussex.

◆ **Access:** *Viewable during normal museum opening hours and at airshows* | **www.historicaircraftcollection.ltd.uk**

❑ K3661	'562'	Hawker Nimrod II ✈	G-BURZ	34	ex St Leonards-on-Sea, Henlow, Ashford, 802. 802 Sqn colours		1-14
❑ L7181		Hawker Hind I	G-CBLK	37	ex St Leonards on Sea, Rockliffe, Canada, Kabul, Afghanistan AF, RAF, 211	[1]	1-14
❑ 'Z5140'	'HA-C'	Hawker Hurricane XII ✈	G-HURI	42	ex 'Z7381', TFC, Coningsby, Coventry, Canada, 71. 126 Sqn colours		1-14

❑ BM597	'JH-C'	Supermarine Spitfire Vb ✈ G-MKVB	42	ex Audley End, Fulbourne, Church Fenton, Linton-on Ouse, Church Fenton, St Athan, 5718M, 58 OTU, 317. 317 Sqn c/s		1-14
❑ 'DM+BK'		MS Criquet G-BPHZ	60	ex 'TA+RC', F-BJQC, French mil. Luftwaffe colours. CoA 29-4-09. Off-site	[1] [2]	9-11

■ **[1]** Registered to Aero Vintage, all others to HAC. **[2]** MS.505 started life as a German-built airframe (No.1827), before completion as a Criquet with a Jacobs R-755A2 radial.

Old Flying Machine Company / Classic Aviation: The A6M may well be bound for South Lambeth.

◆ **Access:** *Viewable during normal museum opening hours and at airshows* | **www.ofmc.co.uk**

❑ MH434	'ZD-B'	Supermarine Spitfire IX ✈ G-ASJV	43	ex Booker, COGEA Nouvelle OO-ARA, Belgian AF SM-41, Fokker B-13, Netherlands H-68, H-105 322, MH434, 349, 84 GSU, 222, 350, 222. 222 Sqn colours, *Mylcraine*	1-14
❑ XV474	'T'	McD Phantom FGR.2	69	ex Wattisham, 74, 56, 23, 29, 56, 23, 19, 2, 31, 17, 14, 17 Flew in 13-10-92. 74 Sqn colours	1-14
❑ –		Mitsubishi A6M *Zeke*	c44	ex Russia (?), USA, Pacific. Stored - see note above	1-14
❑ '463221'	'B7-H'	NAA P-51D-25-NA Mustang ✈ G-BTCD	44	ex TFC, N51JJ, N6340T, RCAF 9568, USAAF 44-73149. *Ferocious Frankie*, 361st FG, 374th FS colours	1-14

Plane Sailing Ltd: Acting in support of the Canso (PBY-5A equivalent) and uniting those interested in Catalinas wherever they may be is the **Catalina Society**, which publishes the excellent *Catalina News*.

◆ **Access:** *Viewable frequently during normal museum opening hours and at airshows* | **www.ofmc.co.uk**

❑ '433915'	Consolidated Canso A ✈ G-PBYA	44	ex C-FNJF, CF-NJF, F-ZBBD, CF-NJF, F-ZBAY, CF-NJF, RCAF 11005. Canadian-Vickers built. 5th ERS colours, *Miss Pick Up*	2-14

Also: The pleasure flying fleet of **Classic Wings** shares bases here and at Clacton, Essex (which see). Accordingly, the Dragon Rapides and Tiger Moths here vary and, from this edition, they do not appear in the listing. Andreasson BA-4B G-AWPZ had moved on by late 2010. Albatros G-CCWB was exported to South Africa during September 2013.

❑ G-ACMN		DH Leopard Moth ✈	34	ex X9381, 9 GCF, Netheravon SF, 297, 7 AACU, 6 AACU, 24, G-ACMN	[1]	1-14
❑ G-AGJG		DH Dragon Rapide ✈	41	ex X7344, 1 Cam Flt. Scottish Airways wartime colours	[2]	1-14
❑ G-AGTO		Auster J/1 Autocrat ✈	45	–	[3]	1-14
❑ G-AYGE*		Stampe SV-4C ✈	46	ex F-BCGM. Nord-built	[4]	1-14
❑ WF877		Gloster Meteor T.7 (mod) G-BPOA	51	ex Washington, Kemble, North Weald G-BPOA, Higher Blagdon (arr 1-2-74), Tarrant Rushton, Chilbolton, 96, Meteor Flt Wunstorf, 11. De-reg 5-6-96. Stored	[5]	1-14
❑ 8*		Nieuport 17 rep ✈	97	French colours, Warner Scarab-powered. F/n 9-11	[6]	1-14
❑ 52-8543*	'66'	NAA T-6J Texan ✈ G-BUKY	53	ex Breighton, N455V, Breighton, FAP 1766, WGAF 'BF+063', 'AA+063', 52-8543. CCF-built. US Navy colours	[7]	1-14
❑ –	'57-H'	Piper L-4A-PI Cub ✈ G-AKAZ	44	ex F-BFYL, ALAT, 42-36375. USAAF colours	[8]	1-14

■ **[1]** Registered to M and R Slack. **[2]** Registered to David and Mark Miller. **[3]** Registered to David Miller and Mike Barnett. **[4]** Registered to Ian, Susan and Lee Proudfoot. **[5]** Meteor T.7 is stored for a US owner. **[6]** Registered to R Gauld-Galliers. **[7]** Registered to N T Oakman. **[8]** Registered to Frazerblades.

ELY on the A10 north-east of Cambridge

No.**1094 Squadron Air Cadets**: Located within the site of the former RAF Hospital.

❑ WG362	DHC Chipmunk T.10 PAX	51	ex Newton 8630M, Swinderby, Filton 8437M (30-1-75), Bir UAS, Wales UAS, Ox UAS, Swanton Morley SF, Carlisle SF, Mildenhall CF, 100, Edn UAS, 3 BFTS, 16 RFS, 3 BFTS, 7 RFS	4-10

EVERSDEN on the A603 west of Cambridge

A variety of airframes are *thought* to still be stored at a *private* location in the general area.

❑ G-AYBV	Chasle Tourbillon	r70	unfinished homebuild project. De-reg 11-7-91	4-06
❑ G-AZDY	DH Tiger Moth	44	ex F-BGDJ, French AF, Mk.II PG650 n/s. Morris-built. CoA 18-8-97	2-01
❑ G-BKKS	Mercury Dart	r82	unfinished homebuild project. De-reg 12-7-91	4-95

FOWLMERE AERODROME north of the A505, west of Duxford, on the B1368 EGMA

❑ G-IKAP*	Cessna T.303 Crusader	83	ex N63SA, D-IKAP, N9518C. CoA 23-9-05, de-reg 7-5-13	8-13

GAMLINGAY Last recorded as far back as February 2000, Hiller UH-12E G-BBAZ has been deleted.

HOUGHTON on the A1123 east of Huntingdon

Jon Wilson: Keeps his Canberra cockpit in the area.

❑ WJ567	EE Canberra B.2	53	ex Wyton, 100, 85, MinTech, 45, RNZAF, 45, 59, 149. HP-built. Cockpit	12-10

LITTLE GRANSDEN AERODROME south of the B1046, south of Great Gransden EGMJ

Access **Private** *aerodrome, access* **strictly** *by prior arrangement* **only**

❑ G-AIRI	DH Tiger Moth	40	ex Mk.II N5488, 29 EFTS, 14 EFTS, 20 ERFTS. CoA 9-11-81, de-reg 3-4-89	7-11

Cambridge Fighter and Bomber Society: The Hurricane makes progress - it is a complex composite - see below. The Fury likewise has an involved provenance and is being worked on in a *separate* workshop at another location.

◆ **Access:** *Visits by prior arrangement* only. *Annual workshop open day - check on web* | **www.cbfs.org.uk**

❑ 'K1928'	Hawker Fury I	31	fuselage, off-site	[1]	9-12
❑ L1639	Hawker Hurricane I	38	ex 504, 85. Shot down 14-5-40. Composite	[2]	9-12

■ **[1]** Being built up from a variety of sections. K1928 served mostly with 43 Sqn, suffering an accident at Tangmere 19-5-37. It later became instructional airframe 2196M. **[2]** Restoration takes identity from the cockpit area and other elements salvaged from the crash site of L1639. No.504's CO, Sqn Ldr J B Parnall was killed when L1639 was shot down operating from Marcq in France.

LITTLE STAUGHTON AERODROME south of the A45, west of Eaton Socon

Cessna F.150F G-ATMM was flying by 2012. Cessna F.172M G-BCPK departed circa 2011 to Spanhoe, Northants. Cessna 140 G-BTBV moved to Spanhoe, Northants, by late 2012. The hulk of Navajo B G-ISFC moved to Irthlingborough, Northants, by April 2013. While we are in the mood, some deletions; last noted dates in brackets: Cessna 150 G-ARAU (9-96); Cessna 175B G-ARRG (2-00); Cessna 150B G-ARSB (2-00); Aztec 250C G-BBVG (2-00).

❑ G-AXHA	Cessna 337A	66	ex EI-ATH, N5384S. CoA 30-8-02, de-reg 20-11-13	1-12
❑ G-BRCM	Cessna 172L Skyhawk	71	ex N3860Q. CoA 17-9-08	1-12
❑ G-BWYB	Piper Cherokee 160	61	ex N6374A, G-BWYB, 6Y-JLO, 6Y-JCH, VP-JCH. CoA 21-7-08	1-12

PETERBOROUGH

No.**115 Squadron Air Cadets**, Saville Road, Westwood - on the site of the former RAF Westwood. The Jetstream 41 cockpit was sold via a pixelated auction site circa 2010 - no 'forwarding addresses.

❑ WK127	'FO'	EE Canberra TT.18	54	ex Bassingbourn, Wyton 8985M, 100, 7, B.2, 10. Damaged 13-12-88. Avro-built. Cockpit	11-13

Also: Nord 1002 G-ASTG took to the air again on 6th October 2013 for the first time in at least four decades.

PETERBOROUGH (SIBSON) AERODROME west of the A1, south of Wansford EGSP

❑ G-ARBN	Piper Apache 160	58	ex EI-AKI, N3421P ntu. Damaged 8-86; de-reg 5-1-89	7-07
❑ G-ARMA	Piper Apache 160G	60	ex Oxford, N4448P. CoA 22-7-77, de-reg 3-3-11	7-07
❑ G-ATMU	Piper Apache 160G	65	ex Beccles, Southend, N4478P. CoA 14-4-90; de-reg 6-3-02. Fuselage	7-07
❑ G-AVIA	Cessna F.150G	67	Reims-built. CoA 5-5-08	12-13
❑ G-AZLH*	Cessna F.150L	71	Reims-built. CoA 30-11-03	12-13
❑ G-BBKF	Cessna FRA.150L	74	Reims-built. CoA 13-6-91; de-reg 15-2-07	7-07
❑ G-BDNR	Cessna FRA.150M	76	Reims-built. Damaged 22-1-92, de-reg 14-10-96	7-07
❑ G-BEIA	Cessna FRA.150M	76	Reims-built. CoA 27-10-03, de-reg 3-3-11	12-13
❑ G-BGEA	Cessna F.150M	77	ex OY-BJK. Reims-built. Crashed 20-7-04, de-reg 4-2-05	4-11
❑ G-BICY	Piper Apache 160	60	ex OO-AOL, 5N-ACL, VR-NDF, PH-ACL, N4010P. CoA 15-7-07; de-reg 1-8-06	12-13
❑ G-BIOJ	Rockwell C'der 112TC	77	ex N4662W. CoA 13-12-02	12-13
❑ G-BOFM*	Cessna 152	81	ex N6445M. De-reg 26-2-13	12-13
❑ G-BOVT	Cessna 150M	76	ex N8962U. CoA 13-4-07, de-reg 3-3-11	12-13
❑ G-BSYW	Cessna 150M	76	ex N9498U. CoA 27-11-09	12-13
❑ G-FAYE	Cessna F.150M	76	ex PH-VSK. Reims-built. CoA 29-7-07, de-reg 8-1-07	12-13

RAMSEY on the B1096 west of Chatteris

No.**511 Squadron Air Cadets**:

❑ WK584	DHC Chipmunk T.10 PAX	52	ex Bawtry, Church Fenton, Linton-on-Ouse, 7556M (28-2-58), Edzell SF, Ox UAS, Glas UAS, 11 RFS	8-09

ST IVES on the A1123 east of Huntingdon

The Stirling Project: Dedicated to the education of the public in all matters concerning the Short Stirling. Restoration of a flight deck plus turret and other elements continues at several sites.

◆ **Access:** *Visits by prior arrangement* **only | info@stirlingproject.co.uk | www.stirlingproject.co.uk**

Also: The B-2 is believed to still be extant in the *general* area.

❑ G-ADFV	Blackburn B-2	35	ex Breighton, East Kirkby, Tattershall, Wigan, Caterham 2893M (17-2-42) , 4 EFTS, Hanworth. CoA 26-6-41	7-01

UPWOOD south-east of Peterborough, west of Ramsey

Matt Buddle: Keeps his airframes in the *general* area. Always looking for a former RAF Lightning, Matt got his wish in November 2013. The cockpit of Lightning F.53 ZF590 moved to Gloucester, Glos, on 9th November 2013.

◆ **Access:** *Visitors welcome, by prior arrangement* **only | mbcornish@btinterent.com**

❑ WH887 '847'	EE Canberra TT.18	54	ex Basingstoke, Llanbedr St Athan, FRADU, B.2, Upwood SF, 21, 542, 1323 Flt. Short-built. Cockpit	1-14
❑ XR754*	EE Lightning F.6	65	ex Doncaster, Firbeck, Walpole, King's Lynn, Stock, Honington 8972M, Binbrook, 11, 5-11, 23, 5, A&AEE. Last flown 22-6-88. Cockpit. Arrived 17-11-13	1-14

Sean Edwards: Keeps his airframes in the *general* area.

◆ **Access**: *Visitors welcome, by prior arrangement* **only | rafupwood@hotmail.com | www.rafupwood.co.uk**

❑ WJ775	EE Canberra B.6RC	54	ex Bodney, St Athan, Swanton Morley 8581M (5-5-74), 51, 192. Cockpit	3-12
❑ WT534	EE Canberra PR.7	55	ex Doncaster, Boscombe Down, Solihull, Halton 8549M (10-7-78), St Athan, 17. Short-built. Cockpit	3-12

Others: A pair of former MEA Boeing 707 cockpits are stored on the Upwood Airpark industrial estate.

❑ OD-AHD	Boeing 707-323C	82	ex Beirut, MEA, American N7597A. Cockpit	11-11
❑ OD-AHE	Boeing 707-323C	82	ex Beirut, MEA, American N7596A. Cockpit	11-11

WATERBEACH on the A10 north of Cambridge

No.**39 Engineers Regiment | 12 (Air Support) Engineer Group**: The barracks is due to close in 2014-2015 with 12 Engineer Group moving to Wittering, Cambs. Hunter F.2 WN904 moved to Northampton, Northants, on 2nd August 2012.

WHITTLESEY on the A605 east of Peterborough

Dive In: At Gildenburgh Water, Eastrea Road, has two submerged airframes: Short 360 G-ROOM (last noted April 2008) and Jet Provost T.3 XM467 (January 2010). **www.divein.co.uk**

Others:

❑ G-AOGV	Auster J/5R Alpine	56	CoA 17-7-72	4-09

WINWICK AERODROME east of the B660 south of Great Gidding

❑ G-BAET	Piper L-4H Cub	43	ex OO-AJI, 43-30314. CoA 10-11-05	12-13

WITTERING AIRFIELD on the A1 south of Stamford EGXT

RAF Wittering: Launched in November 2011 was the **Harrier Heritage Centre**. A vast amount of artefacts has been amassed, included a series of BSE Pegasus vectored-thrust turbofans. Plans for this collection are in the early stages and no public access is anticipated on a regular basis. A Kestrel engineering test shell from Warton is also reported to be here. Harrier GR.9A ZD465 moved to Gosport, Hants, by March 2012.

❑ XV279		HS Harrier GR.1	67	ex 8566M (8-2-78), Farnborough, Culdrose, A&AEE		6-13
❑ XV779		HS Harrier GR.3	70	ex 8931M (23-1-87), 233 OCU, 3, Wittering SF, 3, 20, GR.1, 20, 4, 1. 20 Sqn colours		6-13
❑ XW923		HS Harrier GR.3	71	ex 8724M, 1417 Flt, 233 OCU, 1, GR.1, 1. Crashed 26-5-81. Cockpit		6-13
❑ XZ146	'S'	HS Harrier T.4	76	ex North Luffenham 9281M (17-12-97), Shawbury, 20, 233 OCU, Gütersloh SF, 233 OCU, 4. 20 Sqn colours		6-13
❑ ZD318		BAe Harrier GR.7A	85	ex Cottesmore, Warton, Boscombe Down, Warton. Last flown 11-7-07		6-13
❑ ZD469		BAe Harrier GR.7A	90	ex Cottesmore, Kandahar, 3. Crashed 14-10-05. On display from 28-4-11. Gate	[1]	2-14
❑ -		BAe Harrier GR.9	~	cockpit		1-12
❑ 162964		BAe AV-8B Harrier II	~	ex Peterborough, Wittering, Charlwood, St Athan, USMC. Cockpit in 20 Sqn colours		1-12

■ **[1]** ZD469 was damaged in a rocket attack 14-10-05 and declared Cat 5 2-5-08.

WYTON AIRFIELD on the B1090 north-west of St Ives EGUY

Pathfinder Collection: Within the base is an incredible volunteer-run museum, dedicated to the Path Finder Force; including material from crash sites and a vast array of artefacts, documentation and photographs.

◆ **Access:** *Visitors welcome, by prior arrangement* **only**. **Contact:** *The Curator, Pathfinder Museum, RAF Wyton, Huntingdon, PE28 2EA* | **01480 452451** | **WYT-pff-museumbookings@mod.uk**

RAF Wyton: Flying is due to stop at the airfield in mid-2014.

❑ XH170	EE Canberra PR.9	60	ex 8739M (27-1-82), 39, RAE, 58	1-14

Also: **John Lathwell** is working on the restoration of a Chipmunk cockpit.

❑ WP927	DHC Chipmunk T.10 PAX	52	ex South Molton, Ingatestone, London Colney, Ashton-under-Lyne, Woodvale, Ashton-under-Lyne, Crosby, 8216M 4-8-72), Hamble G-ATJK, MCS, Oxf UAS, Lon UAS, Detling SF, Lon UAS	6-09

CHESHIRE

BURTONWOOD south of the M62, west of Warrington

RAF Burtonwood Heritage Centre: Very little of the once huge USAF Burtonwood air base remains; cars that hurtle down the M62 are following the course of the main runway. The centre, to the south of the motorway and on the former domestic Site 4, part of the massive base, serves to set this to rights and has amassed an incredible amount of artefacts and images to tell the tale of this great airfield.

◆ **Access:** *Off the M62, Junction 8 or 9 and signed.* **Open:** *Wed to Sun 10:30 to 17:00. Other times by prior arrangement.* **Contact:** *RAF Burtonwood Heritage Centre, 'Gulliver's World', Shackleton Close, Bewsey Park, Warrington, WA5 9YZ* | **burtonwood@guliversfun.co.uk** | **www.burtonwoodbase.org**

CHESTER Note: All of the airframes listed under this heading are in the *general* location and at *separate* venues.

Air Pulford - Panavia Tornado Restorations: Simon Pulford's GR.1 cockpit will very likely be kept in an 'as is' condition. He also owns Tornado F.2 cockpit ZD938 at Doncaster, S Yorks, and a share in 'Twin Pin' cockpit G-AYFA at Dumfries, Scotland. Simon is always on the look out for Tornado parts and support material..

◆ **Access:** *Available for inspection* **only** *by prior arrangement* | **simonpulford@btinternet.com** | **www.airpulford.com**

❑ ZD710*	Panavia Tornado GR.1	83	ex Ruthin, South Molton, Welshpool, Robertsbridge, Stock, St Athan, Abingdon, 14. Crashed 14-9-89. Cockpit	1-14
❑ -	Panavia Tornado F.3 FSM	c85	ex Pant Glas, Hooton Park, Elvington, BBC *Fighter Pilot*	1-14
❑ -	Panavia Tornado ADV SIM	~	ex Millom	1-14

Andy Blair: Makes great progress with his 'JP', which has moved into a location in the area. Details of this aircraft can be found on the Air Pulford web-site - see above. **Access** *Available for inspection* **only** *by prior arrangement*

❑ XN549*	Hunting Jet Provost T.3	61	ex Warrington, South Molton, Book, Shawbury, Halton, '8235M'/8335M (21-3-73), Shawbury, 1 FTS, CFS. Cockpit	1-14

Nick Foden: The Cheetah is a working simulator and used by the **Disabled Flight Simulator Group**. The Pup fuselage is being turned into a trailer-based cockpit section. Pup 100 SE-FGV (G-CGHX) departed to France on 9th August 2012.

◆ **Access**: *Available for inspection* **only** *by prior arrangement* | **grummanaa5a@googlemail.com**

❑ G-AWCL	Cessna F.150H	68	ex Cheltenham, Doncaster, Firbeck, Tattershall. Reims-built. De-reg 2-2-88. Cockpit		1-14
❑ G-AXDW	Beagle Pup 100	69	ex Caterham, Cranfield. Crashed 26-2-09, CoA 31-3-09, de-reg 5-8-09		1-14
❑ OO-GCO	American AA-5A Cheetah	78	ex Skycraft, Belgium. Crashed 22-3-05. Fuselage, flight sim		1-14

Ian Starnes:

❑ XR654	Hunting Jet Provost T.4	63	ex Barton, Chelford, Macclesfield, Bournemouth, Coventry, Puckeridge, Hatfield, Shawbury, CAW, 3 FTS, 6 FTS. SOC 25-11-71. Cockpit		3-12

HOOTON PARK south of Junction 6 of the M53, near Eastham Locks

Hooton Park Trust (HPT): The trust manages the site, with other bodies basing themselves, including **The Aeroplane Collection** - see below. During early November 2013 HPT launched an appeal for funds to restore the Grade II*-listed Hangar 1. Former site owners Vauxhall Motors has pledged £272,000 in matching funds. Details of how to donate can be found on: **www.spacehive.com/hootonhangar1**

The cockpit of Twin Pioneer G-AYFA moved to Dumfries, Scotland, by October 2013. During July 2012, Meteor T.7 WL405 and the cockpit of F-4J(UK) ZE352 left for Liverpool, Merseyside.

◆ **Access:** *Off the M53, Junction 6 marked 'Eastham Oil Terminal'. Go north to a roundabout then right into South Road.* **Open:** *Guided tours are staged on the last Saturday of each month, other than December, starting at 1pm. Otherwise by prior arrangement, plus occasional special events.* **Contact:** *The Hangars, Airfield Way, Hooton Park Airfield, Ellesmere Port, CH65 1BQ.* **0151 327 3565** | **info@hootonparktrust.co.uk** | **www.hootonparktrust.co.uk**

The Aeroplane Collection (TAC): *W&R23* foretold the half-century anniversary of the founding of the pioneering Northern Aircraft Preservation Society - now named TAC - in June 2012, but this was such an important milestone that the author is very happy to emphasize it *again.* NAPS was the prototype of what became an explosion of part-time 'preservationists' in the 1960s and 1970s. Much of what the broader movement takes for granted today was initiated, encouraged or inspired by NAPS / TAC people. The organisation has proudly taken on the rider 'Preserving Aviation Heritage since 1962' to gently remind one and all of its unique status.

TAC is based at Hooton, although it has a strong presence at MOSI, Manchester, Gtr Man. With the Miles types, the aim is to create a static Gemini (to be 'labelled' G-AKHZ) and a static Messenger (likewise, G-AHUI) - both composites. TAC aircraft can also be found at Manchester, Gtr Man: Avian, Dragon Rapide, Bensen, 'Flea', Roe Triplane. Dragon 150s G-MJUZ and G-MMAI were disposed of and moved to Clacton, Essex, 16th October 2012.

◆ **Contact:** *Dave Arkle, 46 Sylvan Avenue, Altrincham, WA15 6AB* | **0161 9692697** | **d.arkle@ntlworld.com**

❑ G-AFIU	Luton Minor	c38	ex Barton, Wigan, Stoke, Hooton Park, Wigan, Peel Green, Pembroke. De-reg 31-3-99	[1]	1-14
❑ 'G-AHUI'	Miles Messenger	46	ex Pulborough. Composite	[2]	1-14
❑ G-AJEB	Auster J/1N Alpha	46	ex Manchester, Hooton, Warmingham, Brize Norton, Wigan, Cosford. CoA 27-3-69		1-14
❑ 'G-AKHZ'	Miles Gemini	47	ex Pulborough. Composite	[3]	1-14
❑ -*	Slingsby Tutor	47	BGA.473, ex Melton Mowbray, G-ALPU, BGA.473. CoA 12-87. Arrived 10-6-12	[4]	1-14
❑ 9G-ABD BMU	Slingsby T.21B (Powered)	62	ex North Coates, East Kirkby, 9G-ABD, BGA.1085. *Spruce Goose*. Crashed 22-9-97, CoA 27-9-97. Fuselage	[5]	1-14
❑ –	Mignet HM.14 'Flea'	36	BAPC.201, ex Millom, Caernarfon, Talysarn. Fuselage	[6]	1-14
❑ –	McBroom hang-glider	c77	BAPC.204, ex Winthorpe, Hooton Park, Warmingham		1-14
❑ XD624	DH Vampire T.11	55	ex Haverigg, Swinton, Manchester Airport, Macclesfield, CATCS, CNCS, Church Fenton SF, 19. SOC 15-12-70		1-14
❑ –*	Fairey Gannet T.2	c56	BAPC.309, ex Caernarfon, Buxton ATC, Sealand, Hooton Park, Tangmere, Fleetlands. Cockpit, travelling exhibit. Arrived 20-7-12	[7]	1-14

■ **[1]** G-AFIU is designated a Parker CA.4 from its builder, C F Parker of Pembroke. It differed little from the LA-4 except for the rear fuselage decking. Started in 1938, it was never finished. **[2]** The Messenger is centred upon Mk.2A G-AHUI, plus Mk.2 G-AILL (see also Stratford-upon-Avon, Warks), Mk.2A G-AJFF, Mk.2A G-AKDF (see also Stratford-upon-Avon, Warks), Mk.2A EI-AGB (G-AHFP) and Mk.4A VP-KJL (G-ALAR). *Uniform-India*, owned by E C Francis of Chester, was based at Hooton Park 1954 to 1957. **[3]** The Gemini is centred upon: Mk.1A G-AKHZ with the rear fuselage of Mk.1A G-ALUG and bits of Mk.1 G-AKGD. **[4]** Tutor G-ALPU was built by Martin Hearn at Hooton and so has come 'home'. It is on loan from Jonathan Howard, see also Warrington, Cheshire.

[5] This machine was regularly flown by former Luftwaffe test-pilot Hannah Reitsch when she was CFI of Ghana's Accra Gliding Club in the 1960s. **[6]** 'Flea' BAPC.201 was built by Idwal Jones at Talysarn, Wales, in 1936. Elements from this machine - undercarriage and other metal parts - are in 'Flea' 'G-EGCK' at Caernarfon, Wales. **[7]** Now confirmed as a T.2 trainer, TAC would like to hear of leads for the periscope structure used by the instructor to enhance forward vision. Thought moribund, the BAPC Register lurched into brief action to grant an identity to the Gannet - wholly beyond the original T&Cs of the register, but who needs consistency?!

Hawker Cockpits: Well-known TAC and Hooton Park stalwart, Graham Sparkes, bases his collection here.
◆ **Access:** *Available for inspection by prior arrangement* | **aeroplanecol@aol.com** | **www.hawkercockpits.com**

❑ WV903*	'128'	Hawker Sea Hawk FGA.4	55	ex Mold, Yeovilton, Dunsfold, Lee-on-Solent, Culdrose A2632, Halton 8153M, Sydenham, 801, 802, 897, 811, 804. SOC 17-3-71. Cockpit. Arrived 28-12-12	1-14
❑ XE584		Hawker Hunter FGA.9	56	ex Woodford, Barton, Chelford, Macclesfield, Bitteswell, G-9-450, 208, 8, 1. SOC 12-2-76. 111 Sqn c/s. Cockpit	1-14
❑ -		Hawker Sea Hawk	~	ex Peasedown St John, Cardiff-Wales. Cockpit, red scheme	1-14

Also:

❑ –	Slingsby Tutor	47	BGA.791, ex VM684, 26 GS, 49 GS. CoA 27-2-71. Off-site	[1]	3-12

■ **[1]** The Tutor is with the 610 Squadron Association.

KNUTSFORD on the A537 west of the M6

Oliver Valves: On the Parkgate Industrial Estate, has acquired a pair of 'guardians'.
◆ **Access:** *Available for inspection by prior arrangement* | **www.valves.co.uk**

❑ ZA399*	'AJC'	Panavia Tornado GR.1	82	ex Selby, Cosford 9316M, St Athan, 617, 15, 20, TWCU. *Plt Off Warner Ottley* DFC. Arrived 15-8-13	1-14
❑ ZD992*	'724'	HS Harrier T.8	87	ex Ipswich, Cranfield, Yeovilton, 899. Cr 16-11-00. Arr 11-12	1-14

A ***private*** collection of vehicles and aeronautica is located in the *general* area. The two 'warbird' projects may be at other workshops, but are listed here for convenience.
◆ **Access:** *Available for inspection by prior arrangement* **only**

❑ -*		Sopwith Camel rep	11	see notes	[1]	10-10
❑ P8088*		Supermarine Spitfire IIa G-CGRM	41	ex Brooklands, Oxford, Ibsley, 61 OTU, CGS, 61 OTU, 19, 152, 118, 66. Crashed 16-9-44. *Bette* and *Borough of Lambeth*. Cockpit, arrived 18-2-13	[2]	2-13
❑ 'W3850'	'PR-A'	Sup' Spitfire V FSM	08	BAPC.304, ex Leeming. 609 Sqn colours. *Irene*	[3]	10-10
❑ 13605*		Messerschmitt Bf 109G-2 G-JIMP	42	ex Lancing, North Russia, 6/JG5 Yellow 14. Shot down 21-6-43.	[2]	2-13

■ **[1]** Camel built by Peter Grieve's Flight Engineering of Carlisle, and to quote its website is an "aluminium-framed flying replica designed by Robert Baslee in the USA. It uses original instrumentation and fittings." **[2]** The Spitfire and Bf 109 registered to Michael Oliver. **[3]** Spitfire FSM built during 2008 by the Royal British Legion Ripon Branch; painted in the colours of P/O Joe Atkinson DFC.

MACCLESFIELD

Macclesfield College - European Centre for Aerospace Training, Park Lane
◆ **Access**: *Busy campus, by prior arrangement* **only** | **www.macclesfield.ac.uk**

❑ G-BLKP	BAe Jetstream 3102	84	ex Humberside, Eastern, G-BLEX ntu, G-31-364. CoA 19-4-03, de-reg 7-12-06	9-11

MARTHALL on the A537 west of Macclesfield

A long out-of-use P.149 is stored at a *private* location in the area.

❑ G-RORY*	Piaggio P.149D	58	ex G-TOWN, D-EFFY, Luftwaffe 90+06, BB+394. Focke-Wulf-built. CoA 7-1-08	9-13

NANTWICH west of Crewe

Hack Green Secret Nuclear Bunker:
◆ **Open:** *Daily mid-Mar to end of Oct, 10:30 to 17:30. Weekends Nov, Jan, Feb, Mar, 11:00 to 16:30. Closed all Dec.*
Contact: *PO Box 127, Nantwich, CW5 8BL*| **coldwar@hackgreen.co.uk** | **www.hackgreen.co.uk**

❑ XS179*	'20'	Hunting Jet Provost T.4	63	ex Manchester, Salford, Halton '8237M' (8337M - 9-8-3), Kemble, Shawbury, CAW, RAFC. Arrived 15-1-13	1-13

OLLERTON

Sometimes references need the occasional 'tweak'; once in a blue moon they need a seismic alteration. This is one of the latter. There was *no* paintball site here; it was at Brereton, Cheshire. But there has *never* been an Aztec there; for that you need to look at Hockley Heath, W Mids. Apart from that...

SANDBACH on the A534 north-east of Crewe

Sandbach Car and Commercial Ltd, The Yard, Moston Road: The Andover is a regular at the Glastonbury Festival!

❑ XS641	'Z'	HS Andover C.1(PR)	67	ex Cosford 9198M (10-1-94), Shawbury, 60, 115, 46, 84, SAR Flt, 84. Forward fuselage	12-13

STRETTON Last noted in March 2007, Jungmeister ES1-16 has been deleted.

WARRINGTON

Jonathan Howard: Jonathan keeps his Vampire project in the *general* area. He is keen to hear from anyone who can help with parts and/or information for the FB.5. See also his Slingsby Tutor at Hooton Park, Cheshire. He also has a part-share in 'Twin Pin' G-AYFA - see Dumfries, Scotland. (Andy Blair's 'JP' is now listed under Chester, Cheshire.)

◆ **Access:** *By prior arrangement* **only| email@jhoward.org.uk**

❑ VZ193		DH Vampire FB.5	49	ex Chelmsford, Doncaster, Firbeck, Malmesbury, Hullavington, 229 OCU, 247. SOC 29-5-59. Pod	2-14

WINSFORD on the A54 south of Northwich

Classic Autos: Woodford Park Industrial Estate

❑ ZE691	'710'	HS Sea Harrier FA.2	87	ex Queensbury, Ipswich, St Athan, Yeovilton, 899, 801, 899, 800, 899, 801, 800. Crashed 4-2-98	12-13

CORNWALL

BODMIN AERODROME east of the A30, north of Bodmin EGLA

Aeronca 7AC G-BRER was under air test by late 2013.

❑ G-ARUZ		Cessna 175C	61	ex Plymouth, N8380T. CoA 18-5-06	1-12
❑ G-AXDC		Piper Aztec 250D	69	ex N6829Y. CoA 24-8-98, de-reg 29-11-10	6-13
❑ G-BMFZ		Cessna F.152 II	85	Reims-built. CoA 27-5-10, de-reg 13-12-10. Fuselage	4-13

CALLINGTON on the A390 south-west of Tavistock

A Lightning is kept at a ***private*** location in the area.

❑ XR755	'BA'	EE Lightning F.6	65	ex Binbrook, 5, 5-11 pool. SOC 21-6-88	9-10

CUBERT on a minor road west of the A3075, south of Newquay

A *private* collector at this location has a Lightning cockpit.

❑ XR747		EE Lightning F.6	65	ex Plymouth, Rossington, Binbrook, 5, 11, 5, 11, 5, 111. 23. SOC 24-6-88. Cockpit	1-12

CULDROSE AIRFIELD on the A3083 south of Helston EGDR

HMS *Sea Hawk*: The **School of Flight Deck Operations** (SFDO) is the main 'user' of *W&R* airframes. The 'DD' codes relate to the 'dummy deck' that the trainees work on. The **Public Viewing Area** and **Merlin Cafe** is a popular vantage point, on the B3293 to the south of the base on the way to the village of Gweek is open weekdays April to October.

❑ G-ATUG*		Druine Condor	66	CoA 15-9-11. Rollason-built	4-13
❑ WF225		Hawker Sea Hawk F.1	53	ex A2623[2], A2645 (4-6-58), FRU, 738, 802. AWA-built. Gate	12-13

❑ XT761*		Westland Wessex HU.5	66	ex Gosport, Lee-on-Solent, A2678 [2], A2767 (12-4-88), Wroughton, 845, 771, 846, 848, 847, 848, 707. F/n 6-13		12-13
❑ XV280*	'31121RN'	HS Harrier GR.1	67	ex Yeovilton A2700[2] (1-11-90), Foulness, Boscombe Down, A&AEE, HSA. Cockpit, Sea Harrier style, trailer-mounted		12-13
❑ XV371	'DD261'	Sikorsky SH-3D Sea King	68	ex Gosport, A2699[2], Boscombe Down, RAE, RRE, RAE, A&AEE. SOC 30-4-95		12-13
❑ XV654	'DD705'	Westland Sea King HAS.6	69	ex Gosport, A2698[2], Fleetlands, 819, 820, 706, 824, 706. Crashed 21-7-93, stored		12-13
❑ XV657	' 'DD132	Westland Sea King HAS.5	70	ex A2600[4], ETS, Fleetlands, Wroughton, 826, 824, 706, 826, 824, 706, 824. Arrived 5-7-94	[1]	12-13
❑ XV706	'017'	Westland Sea King HAS.6	71	ex 8344M *and* A2656[3] (28-2-02), ex Culdrose, 810, 706, 810, 810, A&AEE, 706, 810, 706, 814, 819	[2]	12-13
❑ XV786	'123'	HS Harrier GR.3	70	ex A2611[3], A2615 (5-6-91), St Athan, 3, 4, 1, 4. Cockpit, in fire station		12-13
❑ XX510	'DD69'	Westland Lynx HAS.2	73	ex A2683[2], Gosport, Lee-on-S' A2772, A2601[2] (10-10-89), Foulness, Boscombe Down, A&AEE, RAE, A&AEE. SFDO		12-13
❑ XZ248	'DD02'	Westland Lynx HAS.3S	78	ex A2854 (18-8-10), Yeoviltton, 702, 815, 702, 815, 702, 815, 702, 815, 829, 815. SFDO		12-13
❑ XZ440	'DD40'	HS Sea Harrier FA.2	79	ex Yeovilton, 800, BAe, FRS.1, 801, 800, A&AEE. Arr 14-2-06		6-13
❑ ZA111	'565'	HP Jetstream T.2	81	ex 750, 9Q-CTC. SAL-built. Arr 15-3-11. Fire dump, engineless		12-13
❑ ZB603	'DDT03'	HS Harrier T.8	83	ex St Athan, 899, 233 OCU. Arrived 6-3-06. SFDO		12-13
❑ ZD579	'DD79'	HS Sea Harrier FA.2	85	ex Shawbury, Yeovilton, 800, 801, 800, 801, 899, FRS.1, 800, 801, 800, A&AEE, 801, 899, 800, 899. Arr 16-10-07. SFDO		12-13
❑ ZD611		HS Sea Harrier FA.2	85	ex St Athan, 899, 801, 899, 800, 899, 800, 899, 899, 800, 899, 801. Arrived 9-05. Displayed, 899 Sqn colours		12-13
❑ ZD990	'DDT90'	HS Harrier T.8	87	ex St Athan, 899. Arrived 15-3-06. SFDO		12-13
❑ ZE690	'DD90'	HS Sea Harrier FA.2	87	ex Yeovilton, 801, 899, 801, 800, 801, 800, 801, 899, FRS.1, 899. Arrived 29-3-06		12-13
❑ ZE692	'DD92'	HS Sea Harrier FA.2	87	ex Yeovilton, 899, 801, 899, 800, 801, 899, 801, 899, FRS.1, 801, 899. Arrived 23-3-06. SFDO		12-13
❑ ZF641		EHI EH-101 PP1	87	ex Fleetlands, Westland. Arrived 18-6-98. SFDO		12-13
❑ ZH796	'001'	HS Sea Harrier FA.2	95	ex Shawbury, Yeovilton, 801, 899. Arri 24-6-09. SFDO, stored		6-13
❑ ZH797	'DD97'	HS Sea Harrier FA.2	95	ex Yeovilton, 801, 899. Arrived 24-6-09		12-13
❑ ZH798	'DD98'	HS Sea Harrier FA.2	96	ex Shawbury, Yeovilton, 801, 800, 899, 801, 800. Arr 28-8-07		12-13
❑ ZH802	'DD02'	HS Sea Harrier FA.2	96	ex Yeovilton, 899, 800, 899, 800, 801. Arrived 21-2-06. SFDO		12-13
❑ ZH803	'DD03'	HS Sea Harrier FA.2	96	ex Shawbury, Yeovilton, 801, 800. Arrived 31-7-07		12-13
❑ ZH804	'003'	HS Sea Harrier FA.2	97	ex Shawbury, Yeovilton, 801, 899, 800, 899, 800. Arrived 25-8-09. SFDO, stored		12-13
❑ ZH811	'002'	HS Sea Harrier FA.2	98	ex Shawbury, Yeovilton, 801, 899. Arr 2-9-09. SFDO, stored		12-13
❑ ZH813	'DD13'	HS Sea Harrier FA.2	99	ex Culdrose, Shawbury, Yeovilton, 801, DERA. Arrived 18-1-09. SFDO		12-13
❑ 'AV511''DD511'		EHI Merlin EMU	~	ex Yeovil. Arrived 16-11-99. Avionics test-rig		6-13

■ **[1]** XV657 is fitted with the tail of ZA135. **[3]** XV706 is used by the **Engineering Training School** and has a rare distinction; its 'M' number was allocated on 2nd May 2003 and was the *last ever*. For good measure, it had been given an 'A' number a year earlier...

DAVIDSTOW MOOR on minor road west of the A39 and Camelford

Davidstow Airfield and Cornwall At War Museum: Occupying a range of former RAF buildings; the museum is dedicated to the three armed services and to life in the county during wartime.

◆ **Open:** *Easter to Nov. Daily Jul to Sep plus school hols 10:00 to 17:00. Apr to Jun and Oct Wed to Sat 10:00 to 17:00 (ie* closed *Sun, Mon, Tue), except school holidays.* **Contact:** *Nottles Park, Davidstow, Camelford, PL32 9YF* | **07799194918** | **hq@cornwallatwarmuseum.co.uk** | **www.cornwallatwarmuseum.co.uk**

❑ XG831	'396'	Fairey Gannet ECM.6	57	ex Helston, Culdrose SAH-8, A2539 (20-5-66), 831, AS.4	1-14
❑ XK627		DH Vampire T.11	56	ex Bournemouth, Felmersham, Lavendon, Barton, Bacup, Hazel Grove, Woodford, Chester, St Athan, 8 FTS, CFS. SOC 3-12-68. Pod	1-14
❑ XW999		Northrop Chukar D.1	~	ex Culdrose	1-14
❑ XZ791		Northrop Shelduck D.1	~	ex Culdrose	1-14
❑ ZG347		Northrop Chukar D.2	~	ex Culdrose	1-14
❑ -		Fieseler Fi 103 (V-1) FSM	~	-	1-14

Davidstow Moor RAF Memorial Museum: Housed in the former Sergeants' shower block; as the name implies, this specialises in the history of the airfield and its units.

◆ **Open:** *Daily 10:30 to 16:00, Easter to Oct.* **Contact:** *Davidstow, Camelford, PL32 9YF* | **01840 213266** | **www.davidstowmemorialmuseum.co.uk**

FALMOUTH at the end of the A39, south-east of Redruth

National Maritime Museum: With the sub-title 'Sea, Boats and Cornwall', the Sea King is in 'Search and Rescue' exhibition and carries RAF markings to starboard and Royal Navy to port.

◆ **Open:** *Daily 10:00 to 17:00, except for Xmas and New Year.* **Contact:** *Discovery Quay, Falmouth, Devon,TR11 3QY* | **01326 313588** | **via website** | **www.nmmc.co.uk**

❑	XV663 '18'	Westland Sea King HAS.6		70	ex Gosport A2807 (10-12-01), Fleetlands, 819, 810, 820, 819, 737, 706, 825, 706, 706, 826. Arrived 28-2-12	6-13

HELSTON on the A3083 north of Culdrose

The Flambards Experience: There are many attractions within, including 'Britain in the Blitz'. The Concorde cockpit is central to the 'Aviation Experience: A Century of Pioneering Flight' exhibit.

◆ **Access:** *'Brown signed' off the A3083 south of Helston, next to RNAS Culdrose.* **Open:** *Most days Easter to end of Oct 10:00 to 17:00. Check for winter opening and full details of opening times* **Contact:** *Clodgey Lane, Helston, TR13 0QA* | **01326 573404** | **info@flambards.co.uk** | **www.flambards.co.uk**

❑	WG511	Avro Shackleton T.4		52	ex Colerne, St Mawgan, MOTU, Kinloss Wing, MOTU, MR.1, 120, 42. SOC 3-8-66. Cockpit	11-12
❑	–	BAC/Sud Concorde EMU		~	ex Filton, cockpit, instrument layout trials	10-11

LAND'S END on the A30 south-west of Penzance

Land's End: The Bölkow 105 portrays the example flown by the Cornwall Air Ambulance and based at St Mawgan.

◆ **Open:** *From 10:30 daily, closing times vary.* **Contact:** *Sennen, Penzance, TR19 7AA* | **0871 7200044** | **info@landsend-landmark.co.uk** | **www.landsend-landmark.co.uk**

❑	'G-CDBS'	Bölkow Bö 105D	G-BCXO	73	ex 'G-BOND', D-HDCE. CoA 23-5-94, de-reg 4-3-92	6-12

LAND'S END AERODROME or St Just, on the B3306 south of St Just EGHC

In readiness for what was hoped to be the new base for the Scilly Islands helicopter schedule; residents of the Westward Airways hangar moved elsewhere by early 2012. The helicopter service passed into history and never made it to Land's End. The following have been deleted, last noted dates given: Rallye Club G-AWYX (Jan 2009), Islander G-BFNU (Jan 2007) and Fokker D.VIII replica G-BHCA (Jun 2005).

LISKEARD on the A38 north-west of Plymouth

Castle Motors / Castle Air: The dramatically-posed Lightning graces the car sales park.

◆ **Access:** *'Brown signed' on the* westbound *A38 at Trebrownbridge. Access to the heliport hangars possible* **only** *by* **prior** *permission, although a minor road gives a great view of the arrivals and departures* | **www.castleair.co.uk**

❑	XS936	EE Lightning F.6		67	ex Binbrook, 5, 11, LTF, 5/11, LTF, 5, 11, 23. SOC 21-6-88	9-13

NEWQUAY CORNWALL AIRPORT or St Mawgan, off the A3059, north-east of Newquay EGDG

Classic Air Force (CAF): Re-homed and re-branded from what was the much-loved Air Atlantique Classic Flight, and briefly AIRBASE: Festival of Flight, settling on the 'Classic Air Force' label. Sited within another 'buzz-word', the 'Aerohub', CAF uses the former 70,000ft^2 Nimrod hangar and opened to the public on 29th March 2013. Refer to Coventry Airport, Warwicks, for details of the on-going diaspora. During January 2014, CAF started a search of an airliner to turn into a clone of the 'DC-6 Diner' at Coventry; a plan to convert the VC-10 having fallen through.

See also under Coventry Airport, Warks, where - from 6th April 2014, AIRBASE was resurrected. See also Seaton Ross, East Yorks, for Classic's Miles Gemini restoration.

◆ **Access:** *Follow the brown signs and 'Airport' signage.* **Open:** *Daily Mar 1 to Oct 31, 10am to 6pm. Other times by appointment.* **Contact:** *Hangar 404, Aerohub 1, Newquay Cornwall Airport, TR8 4HP* | **01637 860717** | **email via the web** | **www.classicairforce.com**

❑ G-AGTM*		DH Dragon Rapide ✈		44	ex Coventry, JY-ACL, OD-ABP, G-AGTM, NF875. *Sybille.* Arrived 25-3-13	[1]	1-14
❑ G-AKIU*		Percival Proctor V ✈		48	ex Coventry, Seaton Ross, Coventry, Nottingham, Bedford, Houghton, North Weald, Southend, Edenbridge	[2]	1-14
❑ G-APLO*	'8'	DHC Chipmunk T.10 ✈		50	ex Coventry, 'WD379', EI-AHU, WB696, 11 RFS, Ab UAS, 11 RFS. Black RAF colours. Frist noted 4-13	[3]	1-14
❑ G-BWDS*		Hunting Jet Provost T.3A ✈		60	ex Coventry, XM424, Shawbury, 1 FTS, 3 FTS, RAFC, 6 FTS, CFS. Arrived 4-3-13	[1]	1-14
❑ G-JAYI*		Auster J/1 Autocrat ✈		46	ex Coventry, OY-ALU, D-EGYK, OO-ABF. Arrived 5-1-13	[1]	1-14
❑ TX310*		DH Dragon Rapide ✈	G-AIDL	46	ex Coventry, Biggin Hill, Allied Airways, TX310 - no service. Arrived 14-3-13	[2]	1-14
❑ 'VN799'*		EE Canberra T.4	G-CDSX	54	ex WJ874, Marham, 39,Gaydon SF, Binbrook SF, Coningsby SF, 231 OCU, FRADU, FRU, 231 OCU, Wyton, 231 OCU, 39. Prototype colours. Arrived by road 30-7-13	[1]	1-14
❑ VR259*	'M'	Percival Prentice T.1 ✈	G-APJB	48	ex Coventry, VR259, 1 ASS, 2 ASS, RAFC. 2 ASS colours Arrived 25-3-13	[2]	1-14
❑ WA591*	'FMK-Q'	Gloster Meteor T.7 ✈	G-BWMF	49	ex Coventry, Kemble, Yatesbury, Woodvale, St Athan 7917M, Kemble, CAW, 8 FTS, 5 FTS, CAW, 12 FTS, 215 AFS, 208 AFS, 203 AFS, 226 OCU, CFE. 203 AFS colours. Arrived 30-4-13	[1]	1-14
❑ 'WB188'*		Hawker Hunter GA.11	G-BZPB	54	ex Coventry, Kemble, Exeter, WV256, Shawbury, Yeovilton, FRADU, 738, 229 OCU, 26. CoA 17-7-03, de-reg 16-3-11. Prototype, green, colours. Arrived 13-7-12	[4]	1-14
❑ WD413*		Avro Anson C.21 ✈	G-VROE	50	ex Coventry, G-BFIR, Duxford, Lee-on-Solent, Enstone, Tees-side, Strathallan, Bournemouth, East Midlands, Aldergrove 7881M, TCCS, BCCS, 1 ANS. Arrived 20-3-13	[2]	1-14
❑ WE569*		Beagle Terrier 2 ✈	G-ASAJ	50	ex Auster T.7 WE569, 652, CFS, 2 FTS, CFS. AAC colours First noted 7-13	[5]	1-14
❑ WJ945*	'21'	Vickers Varsity T.1	G-BEDV	53	G-BEDV, ex Duxford, CFS, 5 FTS, AE&AEOS, CFS, 115, 116, 527. CoA 15-10-87, de-reg 15-6-89. Arrived 9-1-13		1-14
❑ 'WK436'*		DH Venom FB.50	G-VENM	55	ex Coventry, North Weald, Cranfield, J-1614, East Dereham, G-BLIE, Ipswich, Glasgow, Swiss AF. 11 Sqn colours First noted 4-13	[1]	1-14
❑ WM167*		Gloster Meteor TT.20 ✈	G-LOSM	52	ex Coventry, Bournemouth, Blackbushe, RAE Llanbedr, NF.11, 228 OCU, Colerne CS, 228 OCU. SOC 9-1-76. Arrived 18-5-13	[1]	1-14
❑ WT722*	'878'	Hawker Hunter T.8C	G-BWGN	55	ex Coventry, Kemble, Exeter, Shawbury, Yeovilton, FRADU, 764, 703, 26, 54. CoA 3-9-97, de-reg 16-3-11. Arr 9-7-12		1-14
❑ WV798*	'026'	Hawker Sea Hawk ...FGA.6		54	ex Wycombe, Lasham, Chertsey, Culdrose A2557, FRU, 801, 803, 787. SOC 25-5-67. Arrived 7-12		1-14
❑ XK895*		DH Sea Devon C.20	G-SDEV	56	ex Coventry, Kemble, Swansea, ex Bruntingthorpe, Cambridge, Culdrose SF, 781 Sqn. CoA 17-9-01. Arr 13-2-13		1-14
❑ 'XJ-771'*		DH Vampire T.55 ✈	G-HELV	58	ex Coventry, Bournemouth, '215' Sion, Swiss AF U-1215. RAF colours. Arrived 7-2-13	[1]	1-14
❑ XV753*	'53'	HS Harrier GR.3		69	ex Predannack, Culdrose A2691[2] (24-4-96), Halton, Abingdon 9075M, St Athan, 233 OCU, 1, 3, 233 OCU. Arrived 19-6-13		1-14
❑ XW433*		BAC Jet Provost T.5A ✈	G-JPRO	72	ex Coventry, Humberside, Shawbury, 7 FTS, 3 FTS, 7 FTS, 3 FTS. First noted 7-13	[2]	1-14
❑ ZA148*	'G'	Vickers VC-10 K.3		67	ex Brize Norton, 101 Sqn, Srs 1154, Filton, East African A/W 5Y-ADA. Flew in 28-8-13		1-14
❑ ZH763*		BAC 111-539GL		80	ex Boscombe Down, QinetiQ, DRA, Ferranti, G-BGKE British AW. Arrived 26-4-13	[6]	1-14
❑ J-1629*		DH Venom FB.50		56	ex Coventry Bournemouth, Dubendorf, Swiss AF. Stored		1-14
❑ J-1649*		DH Venom FB.50		56	ex Coventry, Market Drayton, Coventry, Bournemouth, Dubendorf, Swiss AF. Cockpit, first noted 4-13		1-14

■ **[1]** Registered to Aviation Heritage Ltd. **[2]** Registered to Air Atlantique Ltd. **[3]** *Lima-Oscar* registered to Lindholme Aircraft Ltd. **[4]** See under Melksham, Wilts, for *another* 'WB188' and Tangmere, W Sussex, for the *real* one. **[5]** Registered to Trevor Bailey. **[6]** Last 'military' flight at Boscombe 21-12-12.

The **Inter-Service Survival School** operates as an RAF enclave within the airport.

❑ WL795	'T'	Avro Shackleton AEW.2	53	ex 8753M (24-11-81), 8, 205, 38, 204, 210, 269, 204		7-13
❑ XV372		Sikorsky SH-3D Sea King	66	ex Culdrose, Predannack, St Mawgan, Trowbridge, Yeovil, Aston Down, Lee-on-Solent, Pyestock, BSE, Westland SOC 1-11-71, arrived 29-3-95		11-12

Gateguards (UK) Ltd: Manufacturers of Hurricane, Mustang, Spitfire and other full-scale models to commission and other specialised work. Included in the latter is a project for BAE Systems - see under Samlesbury, Lancs, for details. Hurricane FSM 'BN230' returned to Bentley Priory, Gtr Lon, by September 2012. Chipmunk T.10 WB763 (G-BBMR) moved to Bicester, Oxfordshire, by October 2012.

◆ **Access: Private** *workshop, visits by prior application* **only | www.gateguardsuk.com**

❑ XN198		Slingsby Cadet TX.3	59	ex Bodmin, Plymouth City, Challock, 661 GS, 645 GS, 632 GS		9-10
❑ ZF580*		EE Lightning F.53	67	ex Samlesbury, RSaudiAF 53-672, G-27-42. Last flown 14-1-86. Arrived 11-3-13. See above		3-13

Also: The VP-2 was written out of *W&R18* (p70) at Chilbolton. At some point it returned to the land of its birth.

❑ G-BTSC*		Evans VP-2	80	ex Chilbolton, Chacewater. *City of Truro*. CoA 18-7-84, de-reg 20-1-03		6-13

Spitfire Corner: Aviation artist Barry Wallond is based on the southern edge of the airfield. As well as the airframes there is a large collection of aviation archaeology artefacts and Barry's superb range of prints.

◆ **Access:** *On the A3059 on the southern edge of the airfield.* **Open:** *'Most weekends in the summer' and - best - by appointment.* **Contact:** *Middle Lodge, Carnanton, St Mawgan, TR8 4EA* | **01637 881126** | **spitfireman@supanet.com** | **www.wallond.com**

❑ 'N3290'	'AI-H'	Supermarine Spitfire I FSM	~	*Battle of Britain* colours, travelling exhibit	[1]	6-13
❑ 'PL279'	'ZF-F'	Supermarine Spitfire IX FSM	00	BAPC.268, ex 'OU-Z', 'MH978', 'N3317', Duxford, *Dark Blue World*. 485 Sqn colours		6-13
❑ WD954		EE Canberra B.2	51	ex Lumb, Hendon area, Rayleigh, East Kirkby, Tattershall, Bicester, 71 MU, Yatesbury, A&AEE. Cockpit	[2]	6-13
❑ WT525	'855'	EE Canberra T.22	55	ex Wyton, South Woodham Ferrers, Stock, St Athan, FRADU, 17, 80. Short-built. SOC 10-5-92. Cockpit		1-12
❑ XE921	'64'	DH Vampire T.11	55	ex Newbridge, Yarmouth, Welshpool, Stoke, Barton, Firbeck, Retford, Firbeck, Keevil, Exeter, 3/4 CAACU, 1 FTS, CFS. SOC 16-12-71. Pod		9-13
❑ -*		Panavia Tornado ADV FSM	~	ex -?-. Trailer-mounted		6-13

■ **[1]** 'N3290' built by Gateguards (UK) Ltd - see above. **[2]** WD954 converted to T.4 and majority, with new nose ended up in Australia and is extant. B.2 nose history as charted above.

PERRANPORTH AERODROME south-west of Newquay

❑ -*		Schleicher Ka-6CR	~	BGA.2348, ex D-5040. Crashed 13-4-02		6-13
❑ -*		Schleicher K-7	~	BGA.3111. Crashed 16-7-93		6-13
❑ 'BL924'*	'AZ-G'	Supermarine Spitfire Vb FSM	94	BAPC.242, ex Tangmere. *Valdemar Atterdag*, 234 Sqn c/s	[1]	6-13

■ **[1]** The Spitfire is owned by the Spitfire Society and may only be on 'temporary detachment'.

PREDANNACK AIRFIELD off the A3083 south of Helston

Fleet Air Arm School of Flight Deck Operations Fire School: There are also some complex purpose-built burning rigs here.

Departures: The following Harriers moved to Ipswich, Suffolk: GR.3 XV783 (10-12) T.4 XW271 (28-9-12); T.4 XZ145 (9-12 - and painted there as 'ZD993'); GR.3 XZ966 (12-12); GR.3 ZD667 (8-12-12); GR.3 XV753 to Newquay, Cornwall, 19-6-13.

❑ WT308		EE Canberra B(I).6	55	ex A2601, Culdrose, DRA Farnborough, A&AEE		6-13
❑ XP137	'711'	Westland Wessex HAS.3	62	ex Culdrose, A2634 [2], Culdrose, Lee-on-Solent A2710 [2] (27-9-83), Wroughton, 737, A&AEE, HAS.1, 737. On side		6-13
❑ XS520	'YF'	Westland Wessex HU.5	64	ex Gosport, A2659 [2], Lee-on-Solent A2749 (2-10-86), 845, 846, 845, 846, 845, 707. On side		6-13
❑ XS738	'U'	HS Dominie T.1	66	ex Cosford 9247M, Cranwell, 3 FTS, 6 FTS. Arrived 11-12-07		6-13
❑ XS885	'512'	Westland Wessex HAS.1	66	ex Culdrose A2631 [2], A2668 (3-11-78), Wroughton, 772, 771, 706, 819		6-13
❑ XX479	'563'	HP Jetstream T.2	69	ex A2611 [4] (19-2-97), St Athan, 750, CFS, 5 FTS, Sywell, Radlett, G-AXUR		6-13

❑ XX845	'EV'	SEPECAT Jaguar T.4	75	ex Cosford, St Athan, 6, T.2, 6, 226 OCU, 41, 226 OCU, 14, 17, 2, 20, 17. Last flown 1-6-05	6-13
❑ XZ570		Westland Sea King HAS.5(mod)	76	ex Culdrose, Gosport, A2672, A2686 (11-10-01), Boscombe Down, RAE Bedford, A&AEE	6-13
❑ XZ969		HS Harrier GR.3	80	ex Culdrose A2612 [3], Manadon A2610 (24-4-91), St Athan, 4, 1, 3	6-13
❑ ZD581	'124'	HS Sea Harrier F/A.2	85	ex St Athan,800, FRS.1, 800, 801, 899	6-13

REDRUTH on the A30 west of Truro

M Drew & Co: The yard may still have a pair of former Predannack inmates.

❑ XS516	'YQ'	Westland Wessex HU.5	64	ex Predannack A2652 [2], Gosport, A2739 (3-7-86), Lee-on-Solent, 845, 847, 846, 845, 848	7-10
❑ XS529	'461'	Westland Wasp HAS.1	63	ex Predannack A2696 [2], A2743 (22-9-86), Culdrose, Manadon, Lee-on-Solent, 829, A&AEE, 706, 829, 700W	7-10

ST AGNES on the B3277 south-west of Newquay

❑ G-ABTC		Comper Swift	32	ex Lelant. CoA 18-7-84, de-reg 22-2-99. *Spirit of Butler*	9-10

ST MERRYN AERODROME on the B3276 west of Padstow

A clear out in mid-2013 had all of the long-termers previously listed move on to unknown locations: McCandless G-ARTZ (last noted Aug 2009), Bensen G-ATLP (Sep 2008), McCandless G-AXVN (Aug 2009) and Bensen G-BNBU (Sep 2008).

TORPOINT on the A374, west of Plymouth, across the Tamar

HMS *Raleigh*: The large initial training base houses a Wessex.

❑ XR523	'M'	Westland Wessex HC.2	64	ex Fleetlands, Gosport, Shawbury, Fleetlands, 72	7-10

TRURO

Blackhawk Paintball: **Access:** *by prior arrangement* **only | www.blackhawkpaintball.co.uk**

❑ XS522	'ZL'	Westland Wessex HU.5	65	ex Redruth, Predannack, Culdrose, A2663 [2], A2753 (1-12-86), Lee-o-Solent, Wroughton, 707, 848, 772, 48, 707, 845, 707	4-11

CUMBRIA

BACKBARROW on the A590 north-east of Ulverston, near Newby Bridge

Lakeland Motor Museum: As well as the aeronautical exhibits, highlights include full-size replicas of Sir Malcolm Campbell's 1935 Bluebird car and his 1939 Bluebird K4 boat, plus the Bluebird K7 in which son Donald was killed in 1967.

◆ **Access:** *'Brown-signed' from Newby Bridge, A590/A592.* **Open:** *Daily 10:00 to 17:30 Feb to Oct, Nov to Jan 10:00 to 16:30; closed Xmas Day.* **Contact:** *Old Blue Mill, Backbarrow, Ulverston, LA12 8TA* | **015395 30400** | **info@lakelandmotormuseum.co.uk** | **www.lakelandmotormuseum.co.uk**

❑ 'G-ADYV'	Mignet HM.14 'Flea'	94	BAPC.243, ex Malvern Wells, 'A-FLEA', Leigh-on-Sea	12-13
❑ G-BNDV	Cameron N-77 HAB	87	CoA 9-5-93, *English Lake Hotels*. Basket, burner etc	12-13
❑ G-MBCG	Solar Wings Typhoon	r81	ex Blackburn. De-reg 6-9-94	12-13

BARROW-IN-FURNESS

❑ G-BMLC		Short 360-100	86	ex Market Drayton, Southend, SE-LDA, G-BMLC, G-14-3688. De-reg 6-6-07. Cockpit	2-13
❑ XE368	'200'	Hawker Sea Hawk FGA.6	55	ex Market Drayton, Bruntingthorpe, Helston, Culdrose SAH-3, Shotley A2534 (28-5-66), 738, 806, 803, 899. AWA-built. Stored	8-10

CARLISLE AIRPORT or Crosby-on-Eden

EGNC

Solway Aviation Museum: While the impressive airframe collection might draw the eye; the displays charting the incredible aviation heritage of the region are particularly impressive.

◆ **Open:** *Apr to end of Oct Sat Fri, Sat and Sun and Bank hols 10:30 to 17:00 - last entry 16:15. Other times by prior arrangement.* **Contact:** *'Aviation House', Carlisle Airport, Crosby-on-Eden, Carlisle, CA6 4NW* | **01228 573823** | **info@solway-aviation-museum.co.uk** | **www.solway-aviation-museum.co.uk**

❑ 'G-ADRX'		Mignet HM.14 'Flea'	c36	BAPC.231, ex Millom, Torver, Ulverston. Arrived 2102		1-14
❑ G-APLG		Auster J/5L Aiglet Tnr	58	ex Maryport, Bletchley, Romsey, Southend, Rettendon, Corringham, Felthorpe. CoA 26-10-68, de-reg 11-2-99		1-14
❑ G-ARPP		HS Trident 1C	65	ex Dumfries, Palnackie, Glasgow, Heathrow, BA, BEA. CoA 16-2-86, de-reg 10-3-83. Arrived 19-8-09. Cockpit		1-14
❑ G-BDTT		Bede BD-5 Micro	r76	ex Haverigg, Barrow, Tattershall Thorpe, Bourne. De-reg 2-2-87. Arrived 2012		1-14
❑ G-BNNR		Cessna 152 II	81	ex N40SX, N40SU, N6121Q. CoA 15-11-08, de-reg 8-9-11. Arrived 2011		1-14
❑ G-BRHL		Bensen B.8M	89	CoA 26-8-03, de-reg 19-10-10. Arrived 2012		1-14
❑ WB584		DHC Chipmunk T.10 PAX	50	ex Newcastle, Morpeth, East Fortune, Manston, Kilmarnock, Edinburgh 7706M (16-1-61), Shawbury, Debden CF, 11 GCF, Tangmere SF, Glas UAS, 8 FTS, Bri UAS, 12 RFS, 22 RFS	[1]	1-14
❑ WB670*		DHC Chipmunk T.10 PAX	50	ex Newcastle, Morpeth, East Fortune, Currie, Southend, London Colney, Welwyn Garden City, 8361M (22-8-73), Hatfield, MoS, 5 FTS, LAS, 12 RFS, 5 RFS. Arrived 13-12-12	[1]	1-14
❑ WE188		EE Canberra T.4	53	ex Samlesbury, 231 OCU, 360, 231 OCU, 360, 100, 56, 231 OCU, Upwood SF, 231 OCU, Upwood SF, Waddington SF, Hemswell SF. SOC 19-11-81. Arrived 4-88		1-14
❑ WP314	'573'	Percival Sea Prince T.1	53	ex Preston, Hull, Syerston, Halton 8634M (8-8-79), Kemble, 750, Sydenham SF, 750, Lossiemouth SF, Shorts FU, Brawdy SF, Lossiemouth SF, 750		1-14
❑ WS832	'W'	Gloster Meteor NF.14	54	ex Pershore, Llanbedr, 12 MU, 8 MU. AWA-built. SOC 24-4-69		1-14
❑ WV198	'K'	Sikorsky Whirlwind HAR.21 G-BJWY	52	ex Firbeck, Warmingham, Chorley, Blackpool, Heysham, Carnforth G-BJWY (de-reg 23-2-94), Gosport, Lee-on-Solent A2576, Arbroath, 781, 848, USN 130191. Last flown 9-56. Arrived 13-11-92. Arrived 1976		1-14
❑ WZ515		DH Vampire T.11	53	ex Duxford, Staverton, Woodford, Chester, St Athan, 4 FTS, 8 FTS, 56, 253, 16. SOC 4-12-68. Arrived 5-90		1-14
❑ 'WZ784'		Slingsby Grasshopper TX.1	52	arrived 2001. Displayed indoors	[3]	1-14
❑ 'XG190'		Hawker Hunter F.51	56	ex Coventry, Dunsfold, G-9-446, DanAF Esk.724, E-425. SOC 28-2-76. Arrived 26-11-08. ETPS colours		1-14
❑ XJ823		Avro Vulcan B.2	61	ex 50, Wadd Wing, 35, 27, 9/35, Wadd W, 230 OCU. Flew in 24-1-83	[4]	1-14
❑ XS209	'29'	Hunting Jet Provost T.4	64	ex Bruntingthorpe, Kemble, Staverton, Halton 8409M (7-10-74) St Athan, Kemble, Shawbury, CAW. Arrived 24-6-06. '5 MU' tail marking		1-14
❑ XV259		HS Nimrod AEW.3	71	ex Stock, Chattenden, Abingdon, Waddington, Woodford, MR.1, Kinloss Wing, St Mawgan Wing. SOC 10-10-91. Arrived 10-98. Cockpit	[5]	1-14
❑ XV406	'CK'	McD Phantom FGR.2	68	ex Longtown, Carlisle 9098M (14-11-91), St Athan, 228 OCU, 111, 43, 228 OCU, 56, 23, 111, 54, 41, 54, 228 OCU, HSA, A&AEE. Arrived 22-4-98		1-14
❑ ZF583		EE Lightning F.53	68	ex Warton, RSaudi AF 53-681, G-27-51. Last flown 14-1-86. Arrived 8-1-89. 11 Sqn colours		1-14

■ **[1]** WB584 is on loan from Phil Moore. It has the rear fuselage of WG303 - see also Stamford, Lincs. Phil has not been able to trace the background of the wings - can you help? Port: 'W645, Dr C1W 987 A/ND, DHB R DHB, Insp De Havilland 167, Mod 82'. Starboard: 'Dr C1W 1030 A/ND, MoD Chip STI 82 insp, O/H 1988'. **[2]** WB670 is also on loan from Phil Moore. It was used for life-extension trials at Hatfield and was SOC as tested to destruction 31-12-71. **[3]** The Grasshopper is composite, with the starboard wing of WZ824 – see Dirleton, Scotland *and* Southend, Essex! **[4]** Tom Stoddart co-owns Vulcan XJ823. **[5]** The Nimrod is on loan from a private collector.

HAVERIGG and MILLOM

Former **RAF Millom and Militaria Museum**: Tidying up the reference in *W&R23* (p37): Vampire T.11 XK637 to Stalybridge, Gtr Man; the cockpit of Jet Provost T.3 XN597 moved briefly to Blackpool, Lancs, before settling on Market Drayton, Shropshire, 17-2-12. Canberra PR.7 WT537 finally departed for Greece during mid-2012 having been stored locally.

HESKET NEWMARKET on minor roads south of the B5305, south-east of Wigton

At a ***private*** location, a Tomahawk has been turned into a simulator.

❑ G-OLFC	Piper Tomahawk 112	79	ex Millom, G-BGZG, N9658N. Damaged 24-6-07, CoA 21-4-08, de-reg 16-4-09. Cockpit, simulator	12-10

HOLMESCALES south of the B2654, west of the M6, south-east of Kendal

Holmescales Activity Centre: *Access by prior arrangement* **only | www.holmescales.com**

❑ TC-MBE	Fokker F.27-500 Friendship	81	ex Coventry, MNG Cargo, D-ACCT, G-JEAG, D-ADAP, G-JEAG. Damaged 18-1-07	2-11

KIRKBRIDE AERODROME south of the B5307, west of Carlisle

Home of some long flightless gyros and micros. Air Command 532 G-BOOJ, last noted November 2007, was cancelled as sold in Finland during January 2009. Gemini G-MMDP was flying by 2011.

❑ G-BHEM	Bensen B.8MV	85	CoA 5-10-00	6-11
❑ G-BHKE	Bensen B.8M5	80	de-reg 3-12-04	6-11
❑ G-BVIF	Bensen B.8MR	94	ex Blackwater Foot. CoA 21-8-95	6-11
❑ G-MVYF	Hornet RZ-A	89	de-reg 8-1-91	6-11
❑ G-MWHS	AMF Chevvron	90	CoA 21-8-95, de-reg 22-11-00	6-11
❑ G-MWNO	AMF Chevvron	90	CoA 30-4-05	6-11

SPADEADAM FOREST north of the B6318, north-east of Carlisle

RAF Spadeadam / Electronic Warfare Tactics Range: The ranges are a complex series of sites centred on the former ballistic missile test/launch facility. Location codes are as follows: Prior Lancey PL; the mock airfield (also known as 'Collinski') AF; the mock runway RW; revetment R7 RV; Wiley Sike bombing site and used as smoke bomb targets WS. The previously noted inventory numbers, prefixed 'SPA117-' appear to have been dropped, while some of the airframes now carry small white lettering such as 'AC6', or 'SU1' for the *Fitter*. The two T-33s removed from the 'live' weapons site in 2007 and taken to a local scrapyard are now confirmed as FT-01 and FT-29.

❑ FT-02	'12'	Lockheed T-33A-1-LO	52	ex Prestwick, Belgian AF, 51-4043. Arrived 13-3-80. Red stars	WS [1]	9-13
❑ FT-06	'10'	Lockheed T-33A-1-LO	52	ex Prestwick, Belgian AF, Neth AF M-44, 51-4231 Arrived 19-3-80	AF [1]	9-13
❑ FT-07	'70'	Lockheed T-33A-1-LO	52	ex Prestwick, Belgian AF, Neth AF M-45, 51-4233. Arrived 27-3-80	AF [1]	9-13
❑ FT-10	'11'	Lockheed T-33A-1-LO	52	ex Prestwick, Belgian AF, 51-6664. Arrived 7-3-80. Also wears '77', 'AC6' and red stars	AF [1]	9-13
❑ FT-11	'01'	Lockheed T-33A-1-LO	52	ex Prestwick, Belgian AF, Neth AF M-47, 51-6661. Arrived 3-80. Also wears '80', 'AC5' and red stars	AF [1]	9-13
❑ 61	'63'	Dassault Mystère IVA	c59	ex Sculthorpe, FAF. Last flown 27-7-81, arrived 28-2-82. Also carries '8-MI'	RW	9-13
❑ 64	'AC-1'	Dassault Mystère IVA	c59	ex Sculthorpe, FAF. Last flown 27-7-81, arrived 3-82. Also carries '8-NO'	RW	9-13
❑ 81	'8-NU'	Dassault Mystère IVA	c59	ex Sculthorpe, FAF. Last flown 19-1-82, arrived 17-3-82	AF	9-13
❑ 139	'8-MR'	Dassault Mystère IVA	c59	ex Sculthorpe, FAF. Last flown 1-7-81, arrived 3-82	AF	9-13
❑ 180	'8-NB'	Dassault Mystère IVA	c59	ex Sculthorpe, FAF. Last flown 1-7-81, arrived 28-2-82. Also carries '9'	AF	9-13
❑ 184	'8-NU'	Dassault Mystère IVA	c59	ex Sculthorpe, FAF. Last flown 19-1-82, arrived 17-3-82	AF	9-13
❑ 207	'8-NS'	Dassault Mystère IVA	c59	ex Sculthorpe, FAF. Also carries '6' and 'AC4'	AF	9-13
❑ 282	'8-MW'	Dassault Mystère IVA	c59	ex Sculthorpe, FAF. Also carries '6-NW' and 'AC3'	AF	9-13
❑ 98+10	'SU-1'	Sukhoi Su-22M-4 *Fitter*	c59	ex Farnborough, Boscombe Down, Luftwaffe, LSK-LV 820. Arrived 4-95	PL	9-13
❑ -	09559	Mil Mi-24 *Hind-D*	c59	ex Iraqi. Arrived by 5-08		9-13

SPARK BRIDGE on the A5092 north of Ulverston

Lakes Lightnings: Neil Airey, Heather Graham and team have a growing collection and at the 2013 *CockpitFest* were awarded a well-deserved 'Spirit' award. In July 2012 Lightning T.5 XS420 at Farnborough, Hants, was sold to Richard Hall. The cockpit of Lightning F.1 XM144 departed for Shannon, Ireland, on 12th February 2013. See also Lightning F.6 XS897 at Coningsby, Lincs.

◆ **Access:** *Available for inspection* **strictly** *by prior permission* | **lakeslightnings@hotmail.co.uk**

❑ WK122		EE Canberra TT.18	54	ex Chipperfield, Bruntingthorpe, Helston, Samlesbury, 7, 15, 61. SOC 10-11-81. Cockpit		1-14
❑ WT711	'833'	Hawker Hunter GA.11	55	ex Coventry, Culdrose A2645, A2731 (23-9-85), Shawbury, Kemble, FRADU, FRU, 764, 738, F.4, 14		1-14
❑ XL609*		Hawker Hunter T.7	58	ex South Molton, Yarmouth, Boscombe Down, Firbeck, Elgin, Lossiemouth 8866M (24-7-85), 12, 216, 237 OCU, 4 FTS, 56. Cockpit. 12 Sqn colours. Arrived 4-12		1-14
❑ XM172	'B'	EE Lightning F.1A	60	ex Wycombe AP, Coltishall 8427M (10-7-74), 226 OCU, 56		1-14
❑ XS181	'F'	Hunting Jet Provost T.4	63	ex Spanhoe, Bruntingthorpe, Market Harborough, North Weald, Bletchley, Desborough, Bruntingthorpe, Halton 9033M (15-2-90), Shawbury, CATCS, RAFC, 3 FTS. Cockpit		1-14
❑ XS922	'BJ'	EE Lightning F.6	66	ex Stansted, Salisbury, Stock, Wattisham 8973M (14-6-88), Binbrook, 5-11 pool, 56, 5. Cockpit		1-14
❑ XZ131		HS Harrier GR.3	76	ex Brierley Hill 9174M, St Athan, 1417 Flt, 233 OCU, 4, 1, 4. Cockpit		1-14
❑ ZF596		EE Lightning T.55	68	ex Haverigg, Swinton, Warton, Portsmouth, Stretton, Warton, R Saudi AF 233, 55-715, G-27-71. Last flown 22-1-86. Cockpit	[1]	1-14
❑ –		HS Harrier two-seater	~	ex Haddington, Long Marston, Dunsfold. Cockpit	[2]	1-14
❑ 7907		Sukhoi Su-7BMK *Fitter*	~	ex Robertsbridge, Farnborough, Egyptian AF. Cockpit		1-14

■ **[1]** See also under Bruntingthorpe, Leics, for other elements of ZF596. **[2]** The identification plate on the side of the Harrier cockpit declares it to be a Sea Harrier Mk.60 - that would be to the build spec for the Indian Navy T.60s.

WINDERMERE on the A592 north of Bowness on Windermere

Windermere Steamboats Museum: In July 2013 the Heritage Lottery Fund granted £9.4m towards the £13m new building, wharf and much more. All exhibits are currently in deep store. **info@steamboats.org.uk** | **www.steamboats.org.uk**

❑ –	Slingsby T.1 Falcon	36	BGA.266, stored	[1] 12-13

■ **[1]**. Modified by Capt T C Pattinson DFC as a flying-boat glider and first flown 3-2-43.

DERBYSHIRE

Includes the unitary authority of Derby City

CHESTERFIELD on the A61 south of Sheffield

M Walker Car Sales: On the Dronfield Road, have a former Finningley 'JP'.

❑ XM480	'02'	Hunting Jet Provost T.3	60	ex Finningley, Halton 8080M (21-4-70), 6 FTS, 1 FTS	8-11

DERBY

Derby Industrial Museum: Is **closed** for redevelopment; it could be as late as 2017 that it opens again.

◆ **Contacts:** *Silk Mill Lane, off Full Street, Derby, DE1 3AF* | **01332 642234** | **info@derbymuseums.org** | **www.derbymuseums.org**

Rolls-Royce Heritage Trust: Within the Rolls-Royce Learning and Development Centre in Willmore Road, the Trust has established an incredible heritage exhibition of aero engines and other memorabilia during the autumn of 2001 using engines, artefacts and input from all of the branches. The cockpit of Canberra B.15 WH960 moved to the RRHT workshops within Derby by November 2012 - see below.

◆ **Open:** *To groups by prior arrangement* **only**. **Contact:** *PO Box 31, Derby DE24 8BJ* | **01332 249118** | **heritage.trust@rolls-royce.com** | **www.rolls-royce.com/about/heritage**

Rolls-Royce Heritage Trust, Derby and Hucknall Branch and **Coventry Branch**: The Trust's extensive restoration workshops also include an incredible collection of engines (aero, vehicular and marine), rocketry, mock-ups, turbine blades, calibration and measuring equipment, archives and much more. By November 2013, MB.339AA 0767 had moved to Doncaster, S Yorks.

◆ **Access:** *By prior arrangement only and occasional open days – contacts as above*

❑ 'EN398'	Sup' Spitfire IX FSM	85	BAPC.184, ex North Weald, Duxford, Huntingdon	11-12
❑ WH960*	EE Canberra B.15	55	ex Willmore Road, Nottingham, Bruntingthorpe, Cosford 8344M (9-11-72), Akrotiri Wing, 32, 9, 12. Cockpit	11-13

Rolls-Royce: The Mk.XIV is stored in the general area. See under Duxford, Cambs, for the airworthy PR.XIX.

◆ **Access: Not** *available for inspection*

❑ RM689	Supermarine Spitfire XIV G-ALGT	44	ex Filton, Sandown, Filton, Hucknall, East Midlands, 'RM619',Hucknall, 443, 350. Crashed 27-6-92. Stored	1-13

DERBY AERODROME or Egginton, south of the A5132 between Egginton and Hilton EGBD

Comet Racer Project Group: With craftsman Ken Fern at the helm, the DH.88 project makes good progress. Since 2011, Ken has been building a from-scratch replica, G-RCSR, in parallel with *Black Magic*. Also here is Turbulent *November-Zulu* which is being restored to fly for/by a charitable trust. This is the only single-seater aircraft to have been flown by Prince Philip, who is supporting the project.

◆ **Access:** *Visits are possible* **only** *by prior arrangement*. **Contact:** *Derby Airfield, Hilton Road, Egginton, Derby, DE65 6GU* | **01283 733803** | **www.cometracer.co.uk**

❑ G-ACSP	DH.88 Comet	34	ex Stoke-on-Trent, Coventry / Staverton, Bodmin, Chirk, Portugal, CS-AAJ, E-1. *Black Magic*	[1]	8-13
❑ G-APNZ*	Druine Turbulent	59	ex Lashenden. Dam 2-7-95, CoA 13-12-95. Rollason-built	[2]	2-13

■ **[1]**. *Black Magic* was originally registered to James Allan Mollison 21-8-34 and was cancelled as sold in Portugal 12-34. **[2]** Registered to the Turbulent G-APNZ Preservation Society 9-13.

Also:

❑ G-AJPZ	Auster J/1 Autocrat	47	ex Bruntingthorpe, Stoke, Sopley, Bournemouth, Wimborne, New Milton, Thruxton, F-BFPE, G-AJPZ. Damaged 2-3-84. De-reg 18-11-88. Frame, off-site	8-09
❑ G-ASSF	Cessna 182G	64	ex N2492R. Crashed 26-12-07, CoA 10-4-08, de-reg 12-7-11	8-10
❑ G-AVDV	Piper Tri-Pacer 150	56	ex Tatenhill, N44231. Tail-dragger. CoA 23-10-03	7-11
❑ G-AVLM	Beagle Pup 160	67	ex Shenstone, Tatenhill, Tollerton, Chippenham. CoA 24-4-69	6-13
❑ G-AXSC	Beagle Pup 100	69	ex G-35-138. CoA 28-4-07, de-reg 2-12-10	6-13
❑ G-AYPH	Cessna F.177RG	71	Reims-built. CoA 27-5-07	6-13
❑ G-BDBF	Clutton FRED II	85	CoA 18-3-98. Off-site	1-13
❑ G-BHZS	SAL Bulldog 120	80	ex Botswana DF OD5, G-BHZS. CoA 20-2-06, de-reg 19-12-12	6-13
❑ G-BNMC	Cessna 152 II	78	ex N6921B. CoA 10-8-03, de-reg 19-1-09	6-13
❑ G-BNMD	Cessna 152 II	79	ex N5170B. Crashed 23-7-90, CoA 28-7-01. Fuselage	6-13
❑ G-BSWH	Cessna 152 II	78	ex N49861. CoA 14-3-02	6-13
❑ G-BUAO	Luscombe Silvaire 8A	46	ex Abbots Bromley, N1362K, NC1362K. Crashed 9-4-04. CoA 11-8-04, de-reg 18-10-10	7-11
❑ G-KWAX	Cessna 182E	62	ex N9902, YV-T-PTS, N2808Y. CoA 16-4-06, de-reg 27-4-10	7-11
❑ G-OFLG	SOCATA TB-10 Tobago	79	ex G-JMWT, F-GBHF. Crashed 23-7-05, CoA 29-5-06, de-reg 15-11-05	1-12
❑ G-SACF	Cessna 152 II	79	ex G-BHSZ, N47125. Crashed 21-3-97, de-reg 11-8-97	6-13
❑ D-EGEU	Piper Colt 108	~	ex Romsey, EL-AEU, 5N-AEH. Damaged 27-10-02. Fuselage	6-13

ILKESTON Not noted since December 2007, Quickie G-BUXM has been deleted.

DEVON

Includes the unitary authorities of Plymouth and Torbay

ABBOTSHAM on the A39 south-west of Bideford

The Big Sheep: This is a huge outdoor-and-indoor attraction with a 7-acre 'Battlefield Live' paintballing arena.

◆ **Access:** *Busy site, by prior application* **only | www.thebigsheep.co.uk**

❑ VR-BEU	Westland Whirlwind Srs 3	65	ex Weston-s-M, Redhill, VR-BEU, G-ATKV, EP-HAN, G-ATKV	1-12

BARNSTAPLE

Tim A Jones | *Access by prior appointment* **only** *via email* **timjones007@hotmail.com**

❑ XX888	HS Buccaneer S.2B	74	ex Dundonald, Ottershaw, Shawbury, St Athan, 16, 15. SOC 10-10-91. Cockpit	1-14

BERE ALSTON at the end of the B3257 north of Plymouth

Tony Thorne: Keeps his airframes in the general area. Last noted in February 2006, the following have been disposed of: Napier-Bensen G-ATWT, Bensen B.8M G-BIVL and Skycraft Scout II G-MBUZ.

◆ **Access: Access** *Viewing by prior appointment* **only | 01822 840515**

❑ G-STMP	Stampe SV-4A	49	ex St Merryn, F-BCKB. SAN-built	1-14
❑ –	Adams-Wilson Hobbycopter	~	ex 'Leicestershire'	1-14
❑ –*	Bensen B.7 Gyroglider	~	-	1-14
❑ –*	Brooklands Mosquito	~	dismantled	1-14

BRANSCOMBE on a minor road east of Sidmouth

Dragon Rapide G-AHAG returned to Membury, Berks, by May 2012 and flew again on 19th August 2013. Turbulent G-ASSY (last noted March 2006) is a 'live' project again within the county. Minicab G-BGKO (also March 2006) has moved to Sussex.

CHIVENOR AIRFIELD south of the A361 south of Braunton

Royal Marines: Last noted in July 2009, the anonymous Chipmunk T.10 PAX is believed to have moved to the Exeter area.

COBBATON north of the A377 / B3227 west of South Molton

Cobbaton Combat Collection: The sub-head to the website describes the collection as 'A hobby which got out of hand!' Many readers will associate with this! Within what is described as the largest private collection of military vehicles and wartime memorabilia in the south-west can be found a Horsa glider that was used in *A Bridge Too Far*.

◆ **Open:** *Apr, May, Jun, Sep and Oct, Sun to Fri; Jul and Aug all week, 10:00 to 17:00 - ie* **not** *open Sat. Open 'most weekdays' during the winter, check first.* **Contact:** Chittlehampton, Umberleigh, EX37 9RZ | **01769 540740** | **info@cobbatoncombat.co.uk | www.cobbatoncombat.co.uk**

❑ –	Airspeed Horsa replica	~	ex *A Bridge Too Far*	8-12

CREDITON Not noted since December 2008, the Wamria EMU has been deleted.

DUNKESWELL AERODROME north of Honiton EGTU

Aerodrome: Sadly, the **Dunkeswell Memorial Museum** closed its doors by March 2012. Not noted since December 2007, the anonymous Gannet cockpit section has been deleted.

❑ G-AFIN	Chrislea Airguard	38	ex Bury St Edmunds, Wigan, Stoke-on-Trent, Warmingham, Wigan, Finningley	[1]	7-13
❑ G-BJIG	Slingsby T.67A	82	CoA 15-4-04. Fuselage		3-13
❑ G-BJNG	Slingsby T.67AM	82	CoA 23-7-01		11-13
❑ G-BPRV	Piper Warrior II	83	ex N4292G. Crashed 29-3-97, de-reg 20-6-97. Cockpit		5-13
❑ G-BXYU	Cessna F.152 II	80	ex Exeter, Dunkeswell, OH-CKD, SE-IFY. Reims-built. Crashed 2-8-99, de-reg 16-10-99. Cockpit		11-13
❑ G-CBLP*	Raj Hamsa X'Air	02	CoA 17-5-06		11-13
❑ N21381	Piper Seneca 200	~	ex F-BUTM, F-ETAL		2-11

❑ OO-AJK*	Nord Norecrin		~	ex Exeter, F-BFJE, PT-ACF. First noted 7-11	1-13
❑ OY-AVW*	Piper Vagabond		~	ex D-EEMM, N4665H. First noted 2-12	11-13

■ **[1]** Airguard is under long-term restoration by Aerocrafting using original parts. It was withdrawn from use 2-6-45, was rescued by the Northern Aircraft Preservation Society in early 1970 and had a new - but non flight-rated - fuselage built at RAF Finningley.

EAGLESCOTT AERODROME west of the A377, north of Ashreigney EGHU

Last noted in July 2012, Cadet TX.3s WT867 and XA289 had moved to Eggesford, Devon, by June 2013.

❑ G-ARZW	Currie Wot	62	crashed 12-2-88	2-08
❑ N24730	Piper Tomahawk	80	ex G-BTIL	7-07

EGGESFORD AERODROME east of Winkleigh and west of the A377

Only long-term restorations and stored airframes are listed at this heavily Auster-flavoured venue. J/1 Autocrat G-AIZY moved briefly to Devon, in September 2012 before settling upon a new home in Kent. The frame of Auster AOP.9 XP286 moved to South Molton, Devon, on 10th September 2012.

◆ **Access:** *Active aerodrome, prior permission* **only | www.eggesfordairfield.co.uk**

❑ G-AFZA	Piper J4A Cub Coupe		39	ex N26198, NC26198. Crashed 21-4-02, CoA 2-12-02. Off-site	12-09
❑ G-AMUI	Auster J/5F		52	ex Liverpool, Stretton, CoA 15-2-66. Frame	12-13
❑ G-AXCZ	Stampe SV-4C		46	ex ZS-VFW, G-AXCZ, F-BCFG. Nord-built. CoA 10-7-83, de-reg 12-2-09	1-10
❑ G-AYDW	Beagle Terrier 2		46	ex King's Lynn, Little Gransden, King's Lynn, Camberley, Cranfield, Bushey, G-ARLM, Auster AOP.6 TW568, LAS, AOPS, 227 OCU, 43 OTU. CoA 1-7-73, de-reg 1-7-85. Frame	12-13
❑ G-BGKZ	Auster J/5K Aiglet Tnr		53	ex Liverpool, Stretton, F-BGKZ. Crashed 30-1-93. Frame	12-13
❑ WT867*	Slingsby Cadet TX.3		51	ex Eaglescott, Syerston, 626 VGS, 635 GS, 618 GS, 616 GS, 617 GS, 623 GS, 123 GS. SOC 14-8-85. In rafters. F/n 6-13	6-13
❑ WZ706	Auster AOP.9	G-BURR	55	ex Middle Wallop, Shrivenham, 7851M (16-6-64), 14 Flt, 656, 1907 Flt, 656	12-13
❑ XA289*	Slingsby Cadet TX.3		52	ex Eaglescott, Syerston, 636 VGS, 621 GS, 634 GS, 617 GS, 622 GS, 89 GS, 92 GS. SOC 14-8-85. In rafters, F/n 6-13	6-13
❑ XP241	Auster AOP.9	G-CEHR	60	ex Middle Wallop, Andrewsfield, Rabley Heath, St Athan, 653, Aden. SOC 13-5-68. Frame	12-13
❑ XX561*	SAL Bulldog T.1		74	ex CFS, 3 FTS, St A UAS, Queens UAS, S'ton UAS, CFS. CoA 25-5-05	12-13

Locally: Not noted since May 2002, Republic Seabee N6191K has been deleted.

❑ G-ASBH	Beagle Airedale	62	CoA 19-2-99	5-02
❑ G-BKSX	Stampe SV-4C	46	ex F-BBAF, Fr mil. Nord-built. CoA 15-6-89	7-10

EXETER

Arden Family Trust: The late Bertram Arden's airframes are held in careful store in the *general* area.

❑ G-AALP	Surrey AL.1	r29	CoA 17-5-40, de-reg 1-12-46	12-97
❑ G-AFGC	BA Swallow II	38	ex BK893, GTS, CLE, RAE, G-AFGC. CoA 20-3-51, de-reg 15-3-10	6-06
❑ G-AFHC	BA Swallow II	38	CoA 20-3-51, de-reg 18-2-59	12-97
❑ G-AJHJ	Auster V	44	ex NJ676, 83 GCS, 440. CoA 27-6-49, de-reg 18-2-59	12-97

Martin Phillips: Spitfire IX RR232 (G-BRSF) moved to Filton and made its first flight there on 18th December 2012, moving on the same day to its new base at Colerne. At a ***private*** workshop in the *general* area, Martin has two other Spitfire projects in their earliest stages: 1940 Mk.IIa P7819 (G-TCHZ) shot down off Dungeness 16th April 1941 and 1943 Mk.IX EN179 (G-TCHO) which failed to return 19th August 1943. The latter was offered for disposal, in the form of recovered remains and the identity, during the summer of 2013.

EXETER AIRPORT EGTE

Is used to store HS.146s, RJs and 'Dash 8s', but these are best considered as just 'passing through'. Pitts S-2A G-BADZ moved to Cotswold, Glos, by May 2012. Last noted with the fire crews in February 2006, Cessna F.172 G-BSHR has been deleted.

❑ G-BAUR	Fokker F.27-200	63	ex JEA, PH-FEP, 9V-BAP, 9M-AMI, VR-RCZ ntu, PH-FEP. CoA 5-4-96, de-reg 25-1-96. Fuselage. Fire crews	5-12

❑ G-BRUA		Cessna 152 II	78	ex Compton Abbas, N49267. CoA 21-11-05, de-reg 5-11-05		1-12
❑ G-JEAT		HS 146-100	87	ex JEA, N171TR, J8-VBB, G-BVUY, B-2706, G-5-071. CoA 23-10-05, de-reg 4-8-04. Dump		1-14

ILFRACOMBE on the A361 north of Barnstaple

A Hunter is stored on an industrial estate.

❑ WT744	'868'	Hawker Hunter GA.11	55	ex Eaglescott, Yeovilton, FRADU, 738, F.4, 247, AFDS. Last flight 16-3-94		9-13

NEWTON ABBOT on the A380 south of Exeter

Andrew Hawkins: The Firefly project is a challenging restoration. He also holds the rear fuselage of AS.5 VT409.

◆ **Access:** *Private location, visits possible* **only** *by prior arrangement* | **griffon74@btinternet.com**

❑ WB440		Fairey Firefly AS.6	50	ex Newton-le-W, Manchester, Heaton Chapel, Newton, Salford, Failsworth, Anthorn, 737, 826, AS.5. SOC 8-3-57. Fuselage		12-13
❑ WD889		Fairey Firefly AS.5	51	ex Haverigg, Sunderland, Failsworth, Anthorn, 771, 814. SOC 2-3-57. Cockpit		12-13
❑ WF145		Hawker Sea Hawk F.1	52	ex Ingatestone, Welshpool, South Molton, Salisbury, Torbay, Brawdy, Abbotsinch, RAE, A&AEE. SOC 21-7-59. Cockpit		12-13

Trago Mills: Or the 'The Big Shop' | **www.trago.co.uk**

❑ G-BDDX		Whittaker Excalibur	76	ex Helston. De-reg 23-6-83		1-14

■ **[1]** Single seat, twin-boom ducted fan pusher design, only made one flight, 1-7-76, built at Bodmin.

UCZ Paintball Park: Close to Trago Mills **Access:** *private location, by prior arrangement* **only** | **www.ucz.info**

❑ G-OPNI		Bell JetRanger II	67	ex G-BXAA, F-GKYR, HB-XOR, G-BHMV, VH-SJJ, VH-FVR. Ditched 5-4-99, de-reg 20-1-00		1-14

PLYMOUTH Scout AH.1 XW281 (G-BYNZ) was sold in late 2012, reportedly to County Tyrone, Northern Ireland.

SOUTH MOLTON south of the A361, south-east of Barnstaple

Dave Taylor - Cockpitmania: *W&R23* (p44) omitted the migration of Chipmunk cockpit WB560 during October 2010, bound for Wigan, but it moved on again. perhaps twice, finally settling upon Norfolk. 'Flea' 'G-ADRZ' was recorded in *W&R23* (p44) as having been sold in 'Yorkshire'. Geographically this was good, more specifically it moved initially to Felixkirk, N Yorks.

Departures: Hunter T.7 cockpit XL564 left in 5-12 settling upon Aylesbury, Bucks; Hunter T.7 cockpit XL609 to Spark Bridge, Cumbria, in 4-12. As noted in *W&R23*, the cockpit of Canberra PR.9 XH174 did indeed arrive - on 26-6-12 - before it moved on again to Leicester, Leics, 7-10-12.

◆ **Access:** *Visits possible* **only** *by prior arrangement* | **cockpitmania@aol.com**

❑ –		Bell JetRanger	~	ex Bolton, Iver Heath. 'Alaskoil' titles		12-13
❑ XK421		Auster AOP.9	57	ex Eggesford, Doncaster, Firbeck, Thurcroft, Firbeck, Hedge End, Fownhope, Long Marston, Innsworth, Bristol, Caldicote, Bristol, 8365M (7-11-63), A&AEE, 1 Wing, Middle Wallop, LAS. Frame		12-13
❑ XP286*		Auster AOP.9	61	ex Eggesford, -?-, Middle Wallop, Hull, Leconfield, Middle Wallop 8044M (9-9-68), West Raynham SF, Middle Wallop. Frame, for spares use. Arrived 10-9-12		12-13
❑ XW927	'02'	HS Harrier T.4	72	ex Ipswich, Hermeskeil, Brüggen, Gütersloh SF, 4, Gütersloh SF, 3, 233 OCU, 4, Wittering SF, 233 OCU, T.2, 233 OCU. Crashed 7-2-92. Cockpit		12-13
❑ –*		DHC Chipmunk T.10	51	ex -?-, Firbeck, Salisbury, Stamford, Blackburn. Forward cockpit. Arrived 11-13	[1]	12-13
❑ –		HS Harrier GR.1	~	ex Welshpool, Market Drayton, Stafford, Abingdon, Hamble. Cockpit	[2]	12-13
❑ 162074		BAe AV-8B Harrier II	~	ex Blackburn, Stamford, Filton, USMC. Painted as 'ZD437', *Michelle*. Cockpit		12-13

■ **[1]** The *likely* bloodline of this Chipmunk that it was written out of *W&R8* (p92) at Radley, Oxfordshire, as 'long gone'. That would make it WG319 SOC 18-7-61 at Valley. As an anonymous front cockpit, devoid of identifying marks, it re-entered in *W&R9* at Blackburn, Lancs; and was acquired from the ATC there in 1992; its travels then as given above. **[2]** The GR.1 cockpit is a 'spare', marked '4 Spare Ser 41H-769733', which falls within the 'XW' range.

TAVISTOCK AERODROME or Brent Tor, or Burnford Common, north of the town

Dartmoor Gliding Society: The following, all last noted in October 2007, have been deleted: Ka.8 BFP, EoN.460-1 BWK, Ka.6 BZQ and Ka.7s FGZ and FTU. | **www.dartmoorgliding.co.uk**

❑ FHU		Schleicher Ka.7	~	BGA.3281, ex RAFGSA R15, RAFGGA, D-5722. CoA 4-3-05. Cockpit, simulator	7-11
❑ XA244*		Slingsby Grasshopper TX.1	53	ex Keevil, Lasham, Cosford, Walsall. Stored	7-13

TOPSHAM between the M5 and the A376 south of Exeter

Home to a *private* collection of fast-jets, visits possible *only* by prior arrangement.

❑ XV359	'035'	HS Buccaneer S.2B	69	ex Culdrose, A2693 [2] (20-3-94), Predannack, Lossiemouth, 208, 237 OCU, 12, 208, 12. Arrived 23-4-05. 809 Sqn colours	3-12
❑ XZ378	'EP'	SEPECAT Jaguar GR.1A	77	ex Shawbury, 6, 41, 17, 31, 20. Arr 14-11-05. 6 Sqn colours	3-12
❑ ZD612	'731'	HS Sea Harrier FA.2	85	ex Yeovilton, St Athan, 899, 800, 899, 800, 801, 899. Arrived 2006. 899 Sqn colours	3-12

TOTNES Last recorded in July 2009, Apace 160 fuselage G-ATOA has been deleted.

DORSET

Includes the unitary authorities of Bournemouth and Poole

BOURNEMOUTH

Streetwise Safety Centre: Among the 'attractions' at the awareness training centre in Bournemouth is the shell of a Twin Squirrel about to 'land' on a Police helicopter pad.

◆ **Access:** *Tours by prior arrangement* **only. Contact:** *1 Roundways, Elliott Road, Bournemouth, BH11 8JJ* | **01202 591330** | **www.streetwise.org.uk**

❑ 'S-WISE'	Aérospatiale Squirrel	~	ex PAS Staverton, N354E, F-GIRL		3-12

BOURNEMOUTH AIRPORT or Hurn EGHH

Bournemouth Aviation Museum (BAM): On the southern perimeter of the airport, co-located with the Adventure Wonderland Theme Park. An excellent wheel-bound exhibit that is working its keep is a former Yellow Buses double-decker that is used to provide views of the activity at the airport.

◆ **Access:** *Follow signs for the airport and then Adventure Wonderland, just off the B3073 Parley Lane.* **Open:** *Daily 10:00 to 16:00, closed Xmas and New Year.* **Contact:** *Merritown Lane, Hurn, Christchurch, BH23 6BA* | **01202 473141** | **aviation.museum@btconnect.com** | **www.aviation-museum.co.uk**

❑ G-BKRL	CMC Leopard	r83	ex airport, Old Sarum, Cranfield. CoA 14-12-91, de-reg 25-1-99. Arrived 18-2-05		1-14
❑ G-CEAH*	Boeing 737-229	75	ex airport, Palmair, OO-SDG. CoA 14-11-07, de-reg 6-11-13. *The Spirit of Peter Bath*. Forward fuselage. Arrived 8-12-13		1-14
❑ G-OPAS	Vickers Viscount 806	58	ex airport, Duxford, Southend, Parcelforce/BWA, BAF, BA, BEA G-AOYN. CoA 26-3-97, de-reg 28-7-97. Arrived 5-12-06. Cockpit	[1]	1-14
❑ 'GO-CSE'*	American AA-5B Tiger G-BFZR	79	ex airport, Fordingbridge, Oxford, EI-BJS, G-BFZR. CoA 24-5-07, de-reg 3-11-05. Travelling exhibit. Arr 9-13		1-14
❑ G-TLET*	Piper Cadet 161	89	ex Shoreham, G-GFCF, G-RHBH, N9193Z. CoA 18-10-12, de-reg 10-6-13. Fuselage. Accident 2011. Arrived 5-6-13	[2]	1-14
❑ –	Vickers Vanguard SIM	~	ex airport , Wycombe Air Park, 'Essex', Hunting, East Midlands. BEA colours		1-14

❑	KF388		NAA Harvard T.2b	45	ex 'KF488' airport, Bournemouth, Wimborne, Sandhurst, 6 FTS, 3 FTS, 1 FTS, 7 FTS. Noorduyn-built. SOC 11-2-57. Arrived 2000. *Billie*	[3]	1-14
❑	WS776	'K'	Gloster Meteor NF.14	54	ex airport, Armthorpe, Sandtoft, North Coates, North Luffenham, Lyneham 7716M 3-5-61), 228 OCU, 85, 25. AWA-built. Arrived 5-2-05		1-14
❑	WT532		EE Canberra PR.7	55	ex airport, Lovaux, Cosford, 8890M / 8728M, RAE Bedford, 13, Wyton SF, 58, 31, 13, 80. Short-built. Arrived 5-7-99. Cockpit		1-14
❑	'WW421'	'P-B'	Percival Provost T.1 WW450 G-BZRE	53	ex airport, Wycombe AP, Armthorpe, Sandtoft, Binbrook, Norwich, Lowestoft, East Kirkby, Tattershall, Lytham, WW450, St Athan '7688M', 7689M (2-11-60), TCCF, 8 FTS, 2 FTS. De-reg 22-2-05. Arrived 10-10-05	[4]	1-14
❑	XE856		DH Vampire T.11 G-DUSK	54	ex airport, Henlow, Catfoss, Long Marston, Lasham, Welwyn GC, Woodford, Chester, St Athan, 219, North Weald SF, 226 OCU. SOC 30-10-67, de-reg 19-3-09. Arrived 6-9-05	[5]	1-14
❑	XG160	'U'	Hawker Hunter F.6A G-BWAF	56	ex airport, Scampton 8831M (2-9-84), 1 TWU, 229 OCU, 111, 43. De-reg 9-12-10. 111 Sqn colours, black		1-14
❑	XH537		Avro Vulcan B.2MRR	59	ex airport, Bruntingthorpe, Ottershaw, Camberley, Abingdon, 8749M (25-3-82), 27, 230 OCU, MoA. Arr 29-10-91. Cockpit		1-14
❑	XL164*		HP Victor K.2	61	ex Brize Norton 9215M (11-11-93), 55, 57, 55, 57, MoA. Cockpit, on loan. Arrived 24-5-13		1-14
❑	XR346		Northrop Shelduck D.1	~	Composite, stored	[6]	1-14
❑	XS463*		Westland Wasp HAS.1	62	ex Charlwood, Crawley, Ipswich, Predannack, Fleetlands, Lee-on-Solent A2647, Wroughton, RAE Thurleigh, A&AEE, *Nubian* Flt, A&AEE, G-17-1. SOC 20-7-75. Boom of XT431. Arrived 21-12-2013	[7]	1-14
❑	XT257		Westland Wessex HAS.3	67	ex airport, East Grinstead, Cosford, Halton 8719M (9-10-81), A&AEE. Arrived 20-1-05. RAF SAR colours		1-14
❑	XX763	'24'	SEPECAT Jaguar GR.1	75	ex Blackstone, St Athan 9009M, Shawbury, 54, 226 OCU. Arrived 26-9-09. 226 OCU colours	[8]	1-14
❑	ZF582		EE Lightning F.53	68	ex Reading. Llantrisant, Luton, Desborough, Portsmouth, Stretton, Warton, R Saudi AF 207, 53-676, G-27-46. Last flown 22-1-86. Arrived 21-9-04. Cockpit		1-14

■ **[1]** Viscount cockpit on loan from the Duxford Aviation Society. See under Gloucestershire Airport, Glos, for *another* 'G-OPAS'. **[2]** Test-bed for the Thielert TME 125 diesel. **[3]** Harvard is a composite and carries the serial KF388, which contributed to the amalgam. That being so, it was SOC 11-2-57 and served with 7, 1, 3 and 6 FTSs respectively. **[4]** Provost T.1 'WW421' has the fuselage of WW450 and the wings of WW421. This exchange occurred during its days at St Athan, when it was even painted up as 7688M (WW421's maintenance serial). **[5]** Owned by Dick Horsfield and Rod Robinson. **[6]** Shelduck drone is a composite, including parts of XV383 and XW578. **[7]** There has been some 'debate' about the identity of this machine, but the 'smart-thinking' is based on an eyeball of the main fuselage plate: F8-565. Others noted have been XS527 - F8-568, and XS529 - F8-570, while XT427 is F8-8288 and XT434 is F8-2895. The plate puts this Wasp nicely in the frame for XS463, while fitted with the boom from XT431. **[8]** Jaguar is on loan from Aviation Trading Ltd - see Woodmancote, W Sussex.

DS Aviation: Sea Vampire T.22 N6-766 (G-VYPO) was offered for sale in late 2011 and was cancelled as sold in South Africa in April 2013. EKW C-3605 C-552 (G-DORN) departed by road on 23rd May 2013 bound for Cowes, Isle of Wight.

◆ **Access:** *Aircraft viewable* **only** *with prior application*

❑	XP924	'134'	DH Sea Vixen D.3 ✈ G-CVIX	63	ex Swansea, Llanbedr, RAE, FAW.2, FRL, RAE, Sydenham, 899, RAFHS. 899 Sqn colours	1-14
❑	XR537	'T'	Folland Gnat T.1 ✈ G-NATY	63	ex Cosford 8642M (10-10-83), 'Red Arrows', 4 FTS	1-14
❑	XW293	'Z'	BAC J Provost T.5A G-BWCS	71	ex 6 FTS, CFS. CoA 3-2-09	1-14
❑	XW419	'125'	BAC Jet Provost T.5A	71	ex Basingstoke, Wycombe AP, Wickenby, Cosford, Halton 9120M (16-9-91), 7 FTS, 1 FTS, RAFC. Fuselage	1-14

Others: In August 2013 all four RR Tynes ran on CL-44-O N447FT, which had taken on an all-silver colour scheme by this time. Despite authorities on both sides of the Atlantic apparently saying it would never fly again, it looks as though this might not be the case. The owner is reported to have said: "Never say never again". Stay tuned...

As ever, there is a frequent throughput of 'legacy' airlines here, but only long-termers are listed.

W&R20 (p50) recorded the departure of the fuselage of Cessna F.172M EI-BAS in August 2005. It was to be found in a recycling yard near Heath End, Hampshire, in October 2012. AA-5B 'GO-CSE' moved over to the museum - above - by 9-13.

All five **Aviation Computer and Consultancy** Venom FB.50s were sold during January 2013, moving to a yard in Portarlington, Ireland: 'VV612' (G-VENI); 'WR360' (G-DHSS), 'WR410' (G-DHUU), 'WR421' (G-DHTT) and J-1573 (G-VICI).

Other departures: Cessna 310Q G-AYND departed 5-13; Sea Prince G-BRFC to St Athan, Wales, arriving 4-5-12; Boeing 737 G-FIGP scrapped 7-12; Baron G-WWIZ was sold in 8-12, becoming G-GAMA; Boeing 737 N419CT was sold in 5-12, becoming HZ-HAA; HS 146 N9070L was scrapped in 4-11; Buccaneer S.2B XX897 departed by road 17-8-12 destined for Shannon, Ireland, arriving there on the 26th.

❑ G-ATPD	HS.125-1B/522	66	ex 5N-AGU, G-ATPD. CoA 14-10-98, de-reg 2-12-03. Dump		1-14
❑ G-AZKS	American AA-1A Trainer	70	ex N6134L. CoA 1-6-10. Spares		1-14
❑ G-BGON	American GA-7 Cougar	79	ex N9527Z. CoA 30-8-08		1-14
❑ G-BPAX*	Cessna 150M	75	ex Wareham. CoA 24-9-10, de-reg 30-7-10, damaged 7-10. Spares. Arrived 4-5-12		1-14
❑ G-FRBA	Dassault Falcon 20C	70	ex FRA, OH-FFA, F-WPXF. CoA 23-9-11, de-reg 6-12-11		1-14
❑ G-GPFI	Boeing 737-229	74	ex European, VH-OZQ, G-GPFI, VH-OZQ, G-GPFI, F-GVAC, OO-SDA, LX-LGN, OO-SDA. CoA 2-4-09, de-reg 19-6-11. Cabin trainer		1-14
❑ D-EFUC*	Cessna 172S	~	stored. Arrived 10-12		1-14
❑ EI-DMR*	Boeing 737-436	92	ex G-DOCR. Arrived 23-3-12		1-14
❑ HZ-BBK*	Boeing 737-3M8 N516WA	91	ex ZK-FDM, HB-IIC, OO-LTG, OO-XTG. Arrived 11-9-10		1-14
❑ LX-ARS	American AA-1B Trainer	~	ex D-EHLD. Spares		1-14
❑ N294AG*	Boeing 737-376	88	ex ZK-JNC, VH-TJB. Arrived 20-12-10		1-14
❑ N470AC	Boeing 737-3L9	90	ex HZ-AMC, B-2653, N2332Q, G-OABD, 9V-TRC, OY-MME		1-14
❑ P4-MMG	Boeing 727-30	65	ex Southend, VP-CMM, VR-CMM, N841MM, N728JE, N72700, N93234Z, D-ABIM. Fuselage		1-14
❑ RP-C-8023	Canadair CL-44-O	61	ex 9G-LCA, 4K-GUP, N447T, EI-BND, N447T, CL-44D4. Allocated N447FT 5-13 - see notes above		1-14
❑ VP-CKA	Boeing 727-82	71	ex Southend, N727FH, N727KS, N46793, CS-TBP. Fuselage		1-14
❑ VR-BEB	BAC 111-527FK	70	ex airliner store, RP-C1181, PI-C1181. Fire dump		1-14
❑ WB556* 'R-UOC'	DHC Chipmunk T.10	50	ex New Milton, Frome, Northolt, Halton, Bicester, Oxf UAS. SOC 12-9-73. Oxf UAS colours. Arrived 14-9-12		1-14
❑ WJ992	EE Canberra T.4	53	ex DRA Bedford, RAE, 76. Avro-built. Fire dump		1-14
❑ –	Hawker Hunter T.7	57	ex Biggin Hill, 'G-ERIC', Bournemouth, Leavesden, Elstree, Hatfield. Stored	[1]	1-14

■ **[1]** The Hunter composite has the cockpit of XJ690.

BOVINGTON off the A352 near Wool, west of Wareham

Tank Museum: Home to the world's finest international collection of armoured fighting vehicles.

◆ **Open:** *Open daily (except Xmas) 10:00 to 17:00.* **Contact:** *Bovington, Dorset, BH20 6JG* | **01929 405096** | **info@tankmuseum.org** | **www.tankmuseum.org**

❑ TK718	GAL Hamilcar I	44	ex Beverley, Christian Malford. Birmingham Railway Carriage-built	[1]	1-14
❑ XM564	Saro Skeeter AOP.12	59	ex Celle, 652, CFS, 12 Flt, 652. 2 RTR colours	[2]	1-14

■ **[1]** Parts of TK718 were used in the creation of the example at Middle Wallop, Hants. **[2]** The last Skeeter flown in BAOR; XM564 was presented to the museum by 2 RTR in 3-69.

CHALMINGTON Moth Minor moved to the realms of Hertfordshire by 2008.

COMPTON ABBAS AERODROME south-east of Shaftesbury EGHA

❑ G-AZRV	Piper Arrow 200	71	ex N2309T. Crashed 30-12-00, CoA 28-5-02. Fuselage, dump	7-12

CORSCOMBE north of the A356, south of Yeovil

A *private* collector keeps a Vampire T.11 in the general area.

❑ WZ450	DH Vampire T.11	52	ex Lashenden, North Weald, Birmingham, Sealand, Wrexham, Woodford, Chester, Shawbury, RAFC, 233 OCU, 202 AFS. SOC 7-1-69	7-13

POOLE on the A35 west of Bournemouth

November-Golf is *thought* to be still in use as a shed (how appropriate!) at a *private* location in the area. The hulk of Tomahawk 112 F-GCTU, last noted in a local holiday park in January 2008, has been deleted.

❑ G-BGNG		Short 330-200	79	ex Bournemouth, Gill, N330FL, G-BGNG. CoA 14-4-97, de-reg 16-8-96. Fuselage	7-10

PORTLAND on the A354 south of Weymouth

Displayed within a marine complex is a Lynx.

❑ XZ250*	'426'	Westland Lynx HAS.3S	78	ex Middle Wallop, 702, 815, 702, 815, 702, Fleetlands, 702, 829, HAS.2, 702, 815, 702. SOC 13-10-10. First noted 5-11	7-13

STINSFORD on the A35 east of Dorchester

Dorset Plant Hire: Has an unusual 'gate guard' - a Cri-Cri in a tree!

❑ N120JN		Colomban Cri-Cri G-BOUT	83	-	1-14

DURHAM and CLEVELAND

The unitary authorities of Hartlepool, Middlesbrough, Redcar and Cleveland, Stockton-on-Tees and Darlington form the region

DURHAM TEES VALLEY AIRPORT or Middleton St George, formerly Tees-side Airport EGNV

International Fire Training Centre: As well as real airframes, the Serco-operated school, has 'synthetic' training rigs.
Access: Strictly *by prior application* **only | www.iftc.org.uk**

❑ G-AWZS		HS Trident 3B-101	71	ex BA, BEA. CoA 9-9-86, de-reg 18-3-86. Whole	12-13
❑ G-AZLS		Vickers Viscount 813	58	ex BMA, SAA ZS-CDV. CoA 9-6-83, de-reg 19-12-86. Fuselage	12-13
❑ 'G-JON'		Short 330-100 G-BKIE	76	ex Newcastle, G-SLUG, G-METP, G-METO, G-BKIE, C-GTAS, G-14-3005. CoA 22-8-93, de-reg 16-9-97	12-13
❑ XP330		W'land Whirlwind HAR.10	61	ex Stansted, 21, 32, 230, 110, 225. SOC 26-1-76	12-13

Others: G-AZNC and the Tomahawk are used by the airport fire services for non-destructive training. **Sycamore Aviation** has a parting-out operation on the airport, types handled during 2013 including Boeing 767 SP-LPE, a variety of A320s and a pair of Ukrainian ATR 42s. Turnover is swift.

❑ G-AZNC		Vickers Viscount 813	59	ex BMA, G-AZLW ntu, SAA, ZS-SBZ, ZS-CDZ. de-reg 27-10-88. Cockpit	12-13
❑ G-BNGR		Piper Tomahawk 112	79	ex N2492F. CoA 1-8-03, de-reg 18-2-05. Trolley-mounted	12-13

FISHBURN AERODROME on the B1278, north of Sedgefield

❑ G-AYYX		MS Rallye Club	71	CoA 9-11-09, de-reg 3-6-11. Fuselage, dumped	12-12
❑ G-RECS		Piper Tomahawk 112	81	ex N5824H, D-EFFX, N23138. CoA 2-5-05, de-reg 9-12-10. Fuselage	1-12
❑ XX711	'X'	SAL Bulldog T.1 G-CBBU	73	ex Newcastle, Lpl UAS, Oxf UAS, QUAS, 13 AEF, Gla UAS, CFS, 13 AEF, QUAS, RNEFTS. De-reg 16-12-10. Dismantled	6-12

HARTLEPOOL

Hartlepool College of Further Education: **Access:** *Busy campus; visits by prior application* **only | www.hartlepoolfe.ac.uk**

❑ XW309	'ME'	BAC Jet Provost T.5	70	ex Cosford 9179M (11-3-93), Shawbury, 6 FTS, 1 FTS	1-14
❑ XW404	'77'	BAC Jet Provost T.5A	71	ex Exeter, St Athan 9049M (16-8-90), 1 FTS. Arrived 15-5-11	1-14
❑ XW405		BAC Jet Provost T.5A	71	ex Exeter, Cosford 9187M (5-5-93), Shawbury, 6 FTS, 1 FTS, 7 FTS, 6 FTS, 1 FTS, RAFC. Plinth-mounted from 11-1-14	1-14
❑ –	TAD.002	Sud Gazelle CIM	~	ex Colsterworth, Arborfield, M' Wallop. Westland-built [1]	1-14

■ [1] Inspection of the CIM reveals it to be a transmission, controls and fuel system rig which is labelled '341 Training Aid Unit 1' with part numbers 89-00-03-27750 - make of that what you will!

SHOTTON COLLIERY west of Peterlee and the A19

Former Army Air Corps engineer Duncan Moyse is in the early stages of establishing a helicopter museum at Shotton Aerodrome, base of the Peterlee Parachute Centre.

❑ XW851	Sud Gazelle AH.1	73	ex Croft (?), Cosford, 847, 3 CBAS, D&TS, IFTU. Westland-built		12-12

THORNABY ON TEES west of the A19 and Middlesbrough

Thornaby Aerodrome Memorial Committee: On a roundabout on the A1045, the Spitfire pays salutes the former airfield.

❑ see below	Supermarine Spitfire V FSM	07	BAPC.301, pole-mounted	[1]	1-14

■ **[1]** Carries colours of Mk.V 'BM481' 'YO-T' of 401 Sqn RCAF, 1943 and F.22 'PK651' 'RAO-B' of 608 (North Riding) Sqn 1948-1950. It was built by GB Replicas.

YEARBY on the B1269 south of Redcar

❑ G-APYB	Tipsy Nipper III	59	CoA 12-6-96		10-13
❑ G-ASFR	Bölkow Bö 208A-1 Junior	63	ex D-EGMO. CoA 31-12-88		10-13
❑ G-BAMG	Lobet Ganagobie	r73	unfinished project. De-reg 5-8-91		10-13
❑ G-BHUO	Evans VP-2	82	CoA 21-12-94, de-reg 23-8-00		10-13
❑ G-BTMW	Zenair CH.701	91	CoA 9-4-96		10-13
❑ G-OOSE	Rutan VariEze	78	unflown project. Damaged		10-13
❑ D-EFNO	Bölkow Bö 208 Junior	~	damaged 1986, spares	[1]	10-13
❑ -	Bölkow Bö 208 Junior	~	spares	[1]	10-13
❑ -	Tipsy Nipper III	~	ex Inverness, Stokesley, Yearby. Unfinished fuselage frame		10-13

■ **[1]** The two Juniors were acquired to assist in the rebuild of G-ASFR; but this project is now stored.

ESSEX

Includes the unitary authorities of Southend and Thurrock

ABRIDGE on the A113, south of the M11/M25 junction

Mayhem Paintball Games: *W&R23* (p49) reported the arrival of the cockpit section of F.27 3C-QSB; well, nearly. On site here is its centre section, arranged close to the nose of the Viscount. The cockpit of 3C-QSB never left Stock, Essex.

◆ **Access: Private** *site, members* **only | www.mayhem-paintball.co.uk**

❑ G-AOHL	Vickers Viscount 802	57	ex Stock, Southend, BAF, BA, BEA. CoA 11-4-80, de-reg 27-3-81. Cockpit		1-12
❑ G-AREE	Piper Aztec 250	60-	ex Stapleford. De-reg 16-12-91. Fuselage		1-12
❑ G-BOIP	Cessna 152 II	79	ex Stapleford, Tattershall Thorpe, Staverton, N49264. Damaged 11-1-90, de-reg 13-1-06. Also tail of C.152 G-BOTB		1-12
❑ G-OBHD*	Short 360-100	87	ex Hinstock, Blackpool, G-BNDK, G-OBHD, G-BNDK, G-14-3714. CoA 5-3-06, de-reg 27-1-11. Arrived 1-8-12		8-12
❑ G-OBPL	EMBRAER Bandeirante 'G-OBWB'	78	ex Stock, Southend, PH-FVB, G-OEAB, G-BKWB, G-CHEV, PT-GLR ntu. CoA 12-12-01, de-reg 27-2-04. Fuselage		1-12
❑ XP854	Westland Scout AH.1	63	ex Ipswich, Bedford, Ipswich, Wattisham, Middle Wallop TAD.043 / 7898M. Crashed 15-5-65		10-13
❑ XX744 'DJ'	SEPECAT Jaguar GR.1	74	ex Ipswich, Coltishall 9251M, Cosford, Shawbury, Warton, 31, 17, 31, 6, 14, 17, A&AEE. Minus fin/rudder. 31 Sqn c/s		2-13
❑ ZD276	Westland Lynx AH.7	83	ex Yeovilton, 655, 671, 656, 661, 652. Crashed 18-3-07. Cabin, fitted with Gazelle fenestron tail		2-13
❑ -	Sud Gazelle	-	with a Scout boom	[1]	1-12

■ **[1]** The Gazelle is *very probably* G-TURP.

ANDREWSFIELD AERODROME or Great Saling, north of the A120, west of Braintree — EGSL

❑ G-BAOB	Cessna F.172M	73	Reims-built. CoA 12-5-07, de-reg 17-12-10		9-10
❑ G-BWEV	Cessna 152 II	79	ex EI-BVU, N47184. Crashed 13-4-08, de-reg 26-10-10		12-09
❑ 319 '8-ND'	Dassault Mystère IVA	c59	ex Sculthorpe, French AF. Last flew 17-10-79, arrived 6-80		2-12

AUDLEY END off the B1383, west of Saffron Walden

Vintage Fabricss : Clive Denney and team work wonders transforming aircraft of all eras. Airframes listed are 'long-termers'.

◆ **Access:** ***Private*** *workshop, visits by prior permission* **only** | **www.vintagefabrics.co.uk**

❑ G-AXUA	Beagle Pup 100		69	ex G-35-150. CoA 5-6-08		7-13
❑ F-BGCJ	DH Tiger Moth	G-BTOG	44	ex France, French AF, Mk.II NM192 n/s. Morris-built		10-13
❑ W2718	Supermarine Walrus I	G-RNLI	34	ex 'Sussex', Southampton, Great Yarmouth, Winchester, Southampton, 276, 751, 764. Saro-built	[1]	10-13

■ **[1]** *Lima-India* is registered to Walrus Aviation, with a Virgin Isles address. Saunders-Roe built W2718 was retired to 15 MU at Wroughton 14-2-46 and acquired by Somerton Airways of Cowes, Isle of Wight. Beyond that it was acquired by the enterprising Norman Grogan who widened the fuselage and turned it into a caravan. Bless, him, he did not throw *any* of it away, leaving it as a time capsule. It was presented to the then Hall of Aviation at Southampton, Hants, in the mid-1980s and in 10-89 was acquired by Spitfire restoration maestro Dick Melton who achieved the vast majority of the process of returning it into a biplane amphibian at Winchester, Hampshire, and then Great Yarmouth, Norfolk.

BOXTED between the A134 and the A12, north of Colchester

Boxted Airfield Historical Group Museum: Punching way above its weight, this small museum tells the story of the 386th BG and Gabreski's 56th FG and much more. The group have the rear fuselage of B-26C-25-MO 41-35253 *Mr Shorty* on loan from the trustees of the Marks Hall Estate at Earls Colne. This artefact does not qualify for a formal inclusion, but, as the largest piece of Marauder extant in the UK, it is well worth a mention.

◆ **Access:** *Off Langham Lane, Langham, near Colchester, CO4 5NW.* **Open:** *Last Sun of month, Mar to end of Oct, 10:00 to 16:00 - check the web-site.* **Contact:** *11 Dunthorne Road, Colchester, CO4 0HZ* | **077747 082085** (museum open hours only) | **richard.boxted.turner@gmail.com** | **www.boxted-airfield.com**

Also: Within the *general* area, a KR-2 is kept. On museum open days it is displayed in 56th FG colours.

❑ G-BUDF	Rand KR-2	94	CoA 3-12-03, de-reg 16-7-12	12-13

BRAINTREE on the A120 east of Colchester

❑ G-AVPV	Piper Cherokee 180C	65	ex 9J-RBP, N11C. CoA 8-3-03	1-12

CHELMSFORD

De Havilland Hornet Project: David Collins continues to work on his exceptional DH Hornet F.1 recreation. The quality of work is exceptional, hence the use of the phrase 'recreation'. David has the long term aim of making as much of a Hornet as possible and it will be finished in the colours of 64 Squadron. During 2011, he took delivery of a large section of Sea Hornet F.20 *wing* that had been in a scrap yard near Lossiemouth. In 2013 the cockpit was displayed at the Hornet pilots' reunion - the first time since the late 1950s that many of the attendees had the opportunity to view their previous 'office'.

◆ **Access:** *Visits* **not** *possible, but appearances at events are publicised in advance.* | **dh103hornet@hotmail.co.uk** | **www.dhhornet50.net**

❑ -	DH Hornet F.1	06	cockpit project	12-13

CLACTON AERODROME EGSQ

Classic Wings: The pleasure flying operation has its maintenance base here and its main site of operation at Duxford, Cambs. Rebuild of Tiger Moth G-ANZZ was completed by August 2012 and it was flying.

❑ G-AGPK	DH Tiger Moth	45	ex N657DH, F-BGDN, French AF, Mk.II PG657, n/s. Morris-built. CoA 23-4-08	2-13
❑ G-ANPE*	DH Tiger Moth	40	ex Duxford, G-IESH, G-ANPE, F-BHAT, G-ANPE, T7397, 19 RFS, 18 EFTS. Morris-built. CoA 9-8-12	2-13

CLACTON ON SEA

East Essex Aviation Museum (EEAM) **and Museum of the 1940s**: Located within a Martello tower.

◆ **Access:** *Within Orchards Holiday Camp at Point Clear, St Osyth.* **Open:** *Apr to Oct Sun 10:00 to 14:00, Mon 19:00 to 21:00, Jun to Sep Wed 10:00 to 14:00.* **Contact:** *Martello Tower, Orchards Holiday Camp, Point Clear, Clacton, CO16 8LJ* | **admin@eastessexaviationsociety.org** | **www.eastessexaviationsociety.org**

❑ 44-14574	NAA P-51D-10-NA Mustang	44	ex 479th FG, 436th FS *Little Zippie*. Crashed off-shore 13-1-45 Recovered 16-8-87	1-14

Locally: The Auster is believed to be extant in the area. At another location, a collector in the *general* area took delivery of a pair of Dragon microlights during October 2012.

❑ G-APAH	Auster 5	57	CoA 5-4-04	8-09
❑ G-MJUZ*	Dragon 150	83	ex Hooton Park, North Coates, Cleethorpes, North Coates. CoA 28-2-87, de-reg 15-11-02. Arrived 16-10-12	10-12
❑ G-MMAI*	Dragon 150	83	ex Hooton Park, North Coates, Cleethorpes, North Coates. CoA 13-7-97, de-reg 30-6-10. Fuselage. Arrived 16-10-12	10-12

COLCHESTER

Charleston Aviation Services: Private *workshop,* **strictly** *viewable by prior application* **only**

❑ LA546	Supermarine Seafire F.46 G-CFZJ	46	ex Newport Pagnell, Newark, Charnock Richard, Carlisle, Anthorn, Lossiemouth Stn Flight. SOC 29-6-51	[1] 12-10
❑ 854	Messerschmitt Bf 109E-7	c40	ex -?-	12-10
❑ 1983	Messerschmitt Bf 109E-7	c40	ex -?-, 5/JG5	12-10

■ **[1]** See also Old Sarum, Wilts.

Merville Barracks: Has a Dakota as a 'guardian' for the HQ of **16 Air Assault Brigade**.

❑ 'KG374' 'YS-DM'	Douglas Dakota IV KP208	45	ex North Weald, Aldershot, Kemble, AFNE, New Delhi, AFNE, HCCF, 24, MEAF, USAAF 44-77087. SOC 18-5-70	11-12

EARLS COLNE AERODROME on the B1024 south of Earls Colne, east of Halstead — EGSR

❑ G-BRBC	NAA T-6G Texan	52	ex It AF MM54099, USAF 51-14470	12-11
❑ SE-HXF	Rotorway Scorpion	~	at local house, off-site	9-13

EAST TILBURY on a minor road east of Tilbury

Thameside Aviation Museum (TAM): Located within the Coalhouse Fort 1860s Victorian Casemate Fortress, TAM's displays include much on the Battle of Britain over Essex. The cockpit of Chipmunk T.10 WG471 departed during April 2013.

◆ **Access:** *At Coalhouse Fort, East Tilbury, RM18 8PB - 'brown signed' from A13.* **Open:** *Last Sun of the month and Bank Hols, Mar to Oct 11:00 to 16:30. Other times by arrangement.* **Contact:** Roger Pickett **07956 801469** | **info@aviationmuseum.co.uk** | **www.aviationmuseum.co.uk** | **www.coalhousefort.co.uk**

❑ 0446	MiG-21UM *Mongol*	~	ex Salisbury, Farnborough, Egyptian AF. Cockpit, stored	12-13

FOULNESS ISLAND on a minor road north-east of Great Wakering

Defence Science and Technology Laboratory, Shoeburyness: The range functions in a small enclave, in the north-east of the 'island', beyond Courtsend. The Sea King is located at the associated Shoeburyness site, south of Great Wakering.

❑ 771	Westland Sea King Mk.47	76	ex Egypt AF. Stripped fuselage	4-12

GREAT DUNMOW on the A120 west of Braintree

Paul and **Andy Wood**:

❑ WP185	Hawker Hunter F.5	55	ex Abingdon, Hendon, Henlow 7583M (30-10-58), 34, 1. AWA-built	3-06

GREAT OAKLEY AERODROME off the B1414 south of Harwich

Percival Aircraft: Mike Biddulph, John Tregilgas, and friends are the centre of excellence for all things Proctor.

❑ G-AHTE	Percival Proctor V	46	ex Nayland, Clacton, Llanelli, Cardiff, Swansea, Llanelli, Hereford, Walsall. CoA 10-8-61	11-13
❑ G-AKEX	Percival Proctor III	43	ex Sweden, SE-BTR, G-AKEX, LZ791, ATA, CFE. Hills-built. Crashed 11-1-51	11-13
❑ G-ANPP	Percival Proctor III	42	ex Thruxton, HM354, BCCF, 21 EFTS, BCCF, Digby SF, 34 Wg CF. Hills-built. De-reg 3-4-89	11-13
❑ G-ANVY '4-47'	Percival Proctor IV	44	ex Sweden, SE-CEA, RM169, 4 RS. Hills-built	11-13

Also:

❑ G-BEDA	Bücker Jungmann	57	ex Spanish AF E3B-504. CASA-built 1.131E. CoA 2-4-00, de-reg 13-8-12	5-13

INGATESTONE on the A12 south-west of Chelmsford

Stuart Gowans: Stuart's ambitious and lovely Spitfire IX reproduction features a Rolls-Royce Merlin, engine bearers and as many other original parts as possible.

❑ N2700*	Fairchild C-119F-FA Flying Boxcar	51	ex Balcombe, Redhill, North Weald, Manston, 3C-ABA, Belg AF CP-9, 51-2700. Cockpit. First noted 10-13	10-13
❑ –	Supermarine Spitfire IX rep	-	see above	10-13

LAINDON north of the A127, near Basildon

❑ G-ARXP	Luton Minor	65	CoA 17-10-95. Fuselage	12-13
❑ G-AWVE	Jodel DR.1050/M1	65	ex Southend, F-BMPQ. CoA 18-5-00. CEA-built. Dismantled	12-13
❑ G-BAGF	Jodel D.92 Bebe	r72	ex F-PHFC. Dismantled	12-13

LAYER MARNEY south of the B1022, east of Tiptree

A new paintball operation, based in Layer Wood, is due to open in the summer of 2014.

❑ XS488* 'XK'	Westland Wessex HU.5	64	ex Market Drayton, Gosport A2712 [3], Wattisham, Halton 9056M (22-1-91), Wroughton, 771, 847, 707, 772, 845, 707, 848. Arrived 11-13	[1]	1-14

■ **[1]** XS488 is fitted with the rear end of XR497.

LONDON SOUTHEND AIRPORT once Southend Airport, or even Rochford EGMC

Following the inevitable increase in the number of 'London' airports, this is the correct title for erm... Rochford. Recent years have seen incredible expansion of the terminal facilities and the infra-structure around it.

Vulcan Restoration Trust (VRT): The 'Return to Power' restoration programme roared into life on 16th November 2013 when all four Olympus engines were run. The Vulcan was last taxied during 2006 and it is hoped that it will move under its own power again in 2014 or 2015. VRT members now receive the excellent and 'reborn' *Vulcan News.*

◆ **Access:** *Regular 'Visit the Vulcan' open days. Other times by appointment.* **Contact:** *PO Box 10486, South Woodham Ferrers, Essex, CM3 9AG* | **vulcan@avrovulcan.com** | **www.avrovulcan.com**

❑ XL426	Avro Vulcan B.2	62 G-VJET	ex Scampton, Waddington, VDF, VHF, Wadd SF, 50, 617, 27, 617, 230 OCU, 617, 230 OCU, 617, 230 OCU, 617, 230 OCU, Scampton, 83. 617 Sqn colours to port, 50 Sqn to stb	[1]	1-14

■ **[1]** XL426 factoids: Replaced with the Vulcan Display Flight with XH558, it made its last flight 19-12-86, clocking up 6,230 flying hours.

Airport: There has been much activity with the storing of HS.146s and RJs and other types, including Airbus A320s, but these have been mostly transient, either swiftly being 'parted out' or put back into service. Only 'long-termers' are listed. On 27th March 2013 the airport took delivery of an 'A319' burning rig previously at Bristol Airport.

Departures: HS 146 RJ100 G-BXAS flew out 25-7-12, bound for Australia as VH-NJH; HS.146 RJ100 G-CGNT flew out 14-8-12; HS.146 RJ100 G-CGNU flew out 22-8-12; HS 146-200 G-FLTA departed to the USA as N147FF 26-8-12 for new life as a fire-bomber; HS 146-200 G-FLTF flew out 15-11-12, becoming N140CA and eventually FAB-105 of the Bolivian Air Force; Baron G-FLTZ became N703JK by 3-12 and was soon flying again; HS 146-200 G-OZRH became N880PA and was ferried to Kent Airport, Kent, on 20-2-13; Boeing 727-95 C5-GAF flew out 30-4-13; BAe ATP CS-TFJ flew out 23-8-13 as SE-MEX; Boeing 737-210C TF-ELL was scrapped by mid-2012, the cockpit moving to Lasham, Hants, by 2-13; Boeing 727-30 9Q-CDC flew out on 23-1-14. Citation II G-JETC was stored following CoA expiry 4-10, it lingered until it was scrapped by 2-13.

❑ G-AKUL	Luscombe Silvaire 8A	46	ex N1462K, NC1462K. CoA 21-5-90	2-14
❑ G-ATRP	Piper Cherokee 140	66	damaged 16-10-81. De-reg 10-11-86	2-14
❑ G-ATXM	Piper Cherokee 180C	65	ex Stapleford, N8809J. CoA 12-10-02, de-reg 25-6-08	2-12
❑ G-AVWM*	Piper Cherokee 140	67	CoA 6-8-10	2-14
❑ G-AYIM	HS 748 Srs 2A/270	70 N687AP	ex Blackpool, G-11-687, CS-TAG, G-AYIM, G-11-5. CoA 21-12-09, de-reg 17-5-11	2-14
❑ G-BPEL	Piper Warrior 151	74	ex C-FEYM. CoA 8-2-92. De-reg 28-2-02	2-14
❑ G-BSZO*	Cessna 152 II	77	ex N24334. CoA 18-1-12, accident 26-6-11	2-14
❑ G-CEBN	HS 146 RJ100	93	ex TC-THE, G-6-238. Parting-out 1-14	2-14
❑ G-CGYV*	HS 146 RJ85	95	ex Brussels Airlines OO-DJO. Arrived 25-1-12	2-14
❑ G-CGZO*	HS 146 RJ85	95	ex Lufthansa D-AVRG, G-6-266. Arrived 7-12-11	2-14
❑ G-CHDT*	HS 146 RJ85	96	ex Brussels Airlines OO-DJS. Arrived 24-1-12	2-14
❑ G-CHFR*	HS 146 RJ85	96	ex Brussels Airlines OO-DJR. Arrived 20-3-12	2-14

❑ G-CHKP*	HS 146 RJ85		97	ex Brussels Airlines OO-DJY. Arrived 11-9-12	2-14
❑ G-CHRF*	HS 146 RJ85		96	ex Brussels Airlines OO-DJX. Arrived 5-12-12	2-14
❑ G-DWJM*	Cessna 550 Citation		81	ex G-BJIR, N6888C. CoA 18-10-10. Fuselage, arrived 4-10	2-14
❑ 'G-FIRE'	BAC 111-401AK	5N-HHH	66	ex HZ-NB2, N5024. Fire crews	2-14
❑ G-FLTC	HS 146-300		91	G-JEBH, G-BTVO, G-NJID, B-1777, G-BTVO, G-6-205. CoA 17-10-09	2-14
❑ G-FLTY	EMBRAER Bandeirante		79	ex G-ZUSS, G-REGA, N711NH, PT-GMH. CoA 5-8-06, de-reg 11-4-06	2-14
❑ G-OCLH*	HS 146 RJ85		95	ex Lufthansa D-AVRH. CoA 22-7-12. Arrived 20-4-12	2-14
❑ G-OFMC	HS 146 RJ100		95	ex Flightline / Ford, G-CDUI, TC-THM, G-6-264. CoA 7-12-09	2-14
❑ G-OSOE	HS 748-2A/275		71	ex Blackpool, Emerald, ZK-MCF, C-GRCU, ZK-MCF, G-AYYG, ZK-MCF, G-AYYG, G-11-9. CoA 11-12-09	2-14
❑ G-TABS*	EMBRAER Bandeirante		79	ex Skydrift, G-PBAC, F-GCLA, F-OGME, F-GCLE, PT-GME. Arrived 29-3-12	2-14
❑ CS-TGX	BAe ATP		90	ex SATA, G-BRLY, TC-THP, G-BRLY	2-14
❑ CS-TGY	BAe ATP		92	ex SATA, G-BTZJ, PK-MTY, G-BTZJ	2-14
❑ F-PYOY	Zenair Zenith 100		~	stored	2-14
❑ I-CLBA*	HS 146 RJ85		96	ex Italia Tour, EI-CNJ, G-6-300. Arrived 20-1-12	2-14
❑ N150JC	Beech Bonanza A35		~	ex Andover, Wick, N8674A. Damaged 18-6-83	2-14
❑ N748D	HS 748-2A/242		71	ex Blackpool, G-SOEI, Emerald, ZK-DES. Mount Cook colours	2-14
❑ 5N-MJB	Boeing 737-322		89	ex Arik Air, N354UA	2-14

■ [1] *Xray-Mike* is/was used Prospects College.

Skylark Airport Hotel: In Aviation Way, on the north-west side of the airport, opposite what was the Historic Aircraft Museum. The three machines are stored in a compound. **www.skylarkhotel.co.uk**

❑ N60256	Beech Bonanza C35	~	ex airport, damaged 28-1-05	2-14
❑ VH-AHL	HS 748-2/228	69	ex airport, RAAF A10-606	2-14
❑ VH-AMQ	HS 748-2/228	68	ex airport, RAAF A10-603	2-14

LONDON STANSTED AIRPORT

EGSS

❑ G-IOIT	Lockheed TriStar 100	76	ex Classic Airways, G-CEAP, SE-DPM, G-BEAL. De-reg 1-10-98. Towing training	10-13
❑ SU-MWC	Boeing 737-683	99	ex Kemble, G-CDKT, SE-DNT. Fuselage, Ryanair inst	4-11

NAVESTOCK west of the A128, south-west of Doddinghurst

❑ G-AFOJ	DH Moth Minor	39	ex London Colney, Navestock, E-1, E-0236, G-AFOJ. *Bugs 2*	11-10
❑ G-MMKT	MBA Tiger Cub 440	r83	de-reg 7-9-94	8-09

NORTH WEALD AERODROME off the A414, junction 7, M11 east of Harlow

EGSX

North Weald Airfield Museum: Based at 'Ad Astra' House, located at the former main gate of the station, with a very impressive memorial dedicated to all those who served at 'Weald and another to the Norwegians. The museum spearheaded the Hurricane gate guardian at the aerodrome entrance - see below.

◆ **Access:** *Off Hurricane Way, from North Weald village – ie the B181 –* **not** *via the aerodrome.* **Open:** *Apr to Nov: Sat, Sun and Bank Hols, 12:00 to 17:00, last entry 16:00. Other times by arrangement. Tours of the airfield can be arranged.* **Contact:** *'Ad Astra House', 6 Hurricane Way, North Weald Aerodrome, Epping, CM16 6AA* | **01992 523010** | **enquiries@northwealdairfieldmuseum.com** | **www.northwealdairfieldmuseum.com**

Note: *The North Weald site is large and aircraft are listed below under their nominal 'keepers'. Airworthy modern general aviation types based are not listed* | **Thinx: 'The Squadron'**, *operated by North Weald Flying Services, is a member-only facility offering great food, a bar and brilliant views of the activity at this superb aerodrome. A series of fly-ins and events are staged during the year - the web-site provides details* | **www.nwflying.co.uk**

❑ 'V7313'	'US-F'	Hawker Hurricane FSM	08	'gate guardian', 56 Sqn colours. *Spirit of North Weald*	1-14

Hangar 11 Collection: Spitfire IX PT879 moved to Sandown, Isle of Wight, in May 2013.

◆ **Access:** *Visits strictly by prior appointment* **only** | **www.hangar11.co.uk**

❑ 'BE505'	'XP-L'	Hawker Hurricane XII ✈	G-HHII	40	ex Sudbury, G-HRLO, RCAF 5403. *Pegs*, 174 Sqn colours	1-14

❑ PL965	'R'	Supermarine Spitfire PR.XI ✈ G-MKXI	44	ex Breighton, N965RF, USA, Rochester, Overloon, Brüggen, Overloon, Deelen, Twenthe, 16, 1 PP		1-14
❑ '2104590'	'44'	Curtiss P-40M-10-CU Warhawk ✈ G-KITT	43	ex '210855', *Red Tails*, TFC Duxford, 'P8196', F-AZPJ, TFC Duxford, N1009N, 'FR870', N1233N, RCAF 840, 43-5802. *Lulu Belle*, Lt Philip R Adair, 80th FG colours		1-14
❑ 472035		NAA P-51D-20-NA Mustang ✈ G-SIJJ	44	ex F-AZMU, N5306M, HK-2812P, HK-2812X, N5411V, 44-72035. *Jumpin Jacques*		1-14

■ **[1]** Spitfire PT879 crashed over the Kola Peninsula while operating with the 767 IAP in Murmansk.

Heritage Aircraft Trust | Gnat Display Team: Hangar 4A. Gnats XR538 (G-RORI) and 'XS111' (G-TIMM - XP504) are airworthy. As with other elements of the site, only long-termers are listed. See also under Bruntingthorpe, Leics.

◆ **Access:** *Visits strictly by prior appointment* **only | www.gnatdisplayteam.org.uk**

❑ G-FRCE		Folland Gnat T.1	63	ex Halton 8604M, XS104, 4 FTS, CFS, 4 FTS. CoA 28-8-08 'Red Arrows' colours	[1]	1-14
❑ XP540	'62'	Folland Gnat T.1	63	ex Cambridge, Bruntingthorpe, Halton 8608M (12-10-78), 4 FTS		1-14
❑ XR538*		Folland Gnat T.1 ✈ G-RORI	63	ex Kemble, Halton 8621M (11-3-79), 4 FTS		1-14
❑ 'XR99<u>2</u>'		Folland Gnat T.1 ✈ G-MOUR / XS102	64	ex 'XR991', Kemble, North Weald, Leavesden, Halton 8624M, 4 FTS, 'Yellowjacks' colours. First flown 10-12-13	[2]	1-14
❑ 'XS111'*		Folland Gnat T.1 ✈ G-TIMM	62	ex 'XM693', Cranfield, Leavesden, Halton 8618M (4-3-79) XP504, 4 FTS, CFS, 4 FTS		1-14
❑ –*	'PF179'	Folland Gnat T.1 XR541	63	ex Bruntingthorpe, USA (?), Humberside, Binbrook, Ipswich, Worksop, St Athan 8602M (17-12-78), CFS, 4 FTS. First noted 3-13	[3]	1-14
❑ '560'		Bell UH-1H ✈ G-HUEY	73	ex Bournemouth, Cranfield, Arg Army AE-413, 73-22077	[4]	1-14

■ **[1]** G-FRCE is registered to Red Gnat Ltd. **[2]** When re-flown as 'XR992' the Gnat took on the black tail adopted by 'Yellowjacks' OC, Sqn Ldr Lee Jones, as a formation aid for the1964 season. **[3]** Turn to *W&R21* (p136) and, under Humberside Airport, you will notice the export to the USA of Gnat XR541 in 2007. Its arrival here does tempt the question; did it ever cross the 'Pond'? 'PF179' relates to the Gnat's time with the **P**ainting and **F**inishing School at St Athan. **[4]** The 'Huey' is registered to the G-HUEY Partnership.

Kennet Aviation: Wasp HAS.1 XT787 (G-KAXT) was disposed off in late 2012 and moved to a new base at Middle Wallop. Scout AH.1 XV118 moved to a paintball arena in the Peterborough, Cambs, area in November 2013.

◆ **Access** *Visits* strictly *by prior appointment* **only**

❑ G-YAKP		Yakovlev Yak-9	47	ex Hungary, SovAF. Stored	[1]	1-14
❑ LA564		Supermarine Seafire F.46	46	ex Newport Pagnell, Redbourn, Newark, Southend, Charnock Richard, Carlisle, Anthorn, 738, 767, A&AEE. SOC 29-6-51		1-14
❑ PK664*		Supermarine Spitfire F.22	45	ex Stafford, South Kensington, Stafford, Cosford, Wyton, Cardington, St Athan, Binbrook, Waterbeach 7759M, 615. SOC 4-2-54. Arrived 9-13		1-14
❑ SX300		Supermarine Seafire F.17 G-RIPH	46	ex G-CDTM, Twyford, Warwick, Leamington Spa, Warrington, Bramcote A2054/ A646, 728. Westland-built	[2]	1-14
❑ SX336	'105'	Supermarine Seafire F.17 G-KASX	46	ex Nottingham, G-BRMG, Cranfield, Twyford, Newark, Warrington, Stretton A2055, Bramcote, 728. Westland-built. 766 Sqn colours. Force-landing, Bondues, France, 1-7-11		1-14
❑ 'XD693'	'Z-Q'	Hunting Jet Provost T.1 G-AOBU	55	ex Cranfield, Winchester, Thatcham, Old Warden, Loughborough, Luton, XM129, G-42-1. CoA 13-3-07. 2 FTS colours		1-14
❑ XT624*		Westland Scout AH.1 G-NOTY	66	ex Plymouth. CoA 28-10-10, de-reg 23-3-11. Arrived 18-8-13		1-14
❑ XW283*		Westland Scout AH.1	69	ex Plymouth, Yeovilton. Arrived 18-8-13		1-14
❑ XW612*		Westland Scout AH.1 G-KAXW	69	ex Lee-on-Solent, Thruxton, G-BXRR. CoA 6-6-12. Arrived 30-1-13	[3]	1-14
❑ NZ3909		Westland Wasp HAS.1 G-KANZ	66	ex Cranfield, RNZN, XT782, Wroughton, 829. Stored		1-14
❑ '8084'		NAA AT-6D Texan ✈ G-KAMY	42	ex LN-AMY, Duxford, LN-LCS ntu, LN-LCN ntu, N10595, 42-85068	[3]	1-14
❑ 126922	'H-503'	Douglas AD-4NA Skyraider ✈ G-RADR	48	ex G-RAID, F-AZED, La Ferté Alais, Gabon AF, FAF No.42, USN 126922. VA-155, dark blue colours	[3]	1-14

■ **[1]** The Yak-9 is registered to Mark Rijkse and Nicholas Richards. **[2]** SX300 is registered to Seafire Displays Ltd. **[3]** Scout XW612, the Texan and 'Spad' are registered to Orion Enterprises of Grand Cayman.

Weald Aviation: A series of jet warbirds and others operate out of the 'Weald' ramp (Hangars 4, 6 and 7) but as they are not part of a collection or 'fleet' as such are not individually listed. 'Long-termers' only are given here. Catalina 'JV928' (N423RS) flew out on 5th March 2013, settling on Biggin Hill, Gtr Lon, at least initially.

◆ **Access:** *Visits strictly by prior appointment* **only** | **www.wealdaviation.com**

❑ G-BWGS		BAC Jet Provost T.5		71	ex XW310, 3 FTS, RAFC, 1 FTS. CoA 2-9-08		1-14
❑ G-BYKJ*		Westland Scout AH.1		67	ex Lee-on-Solent, Thruxton, XV121. CoA 4-1-10. Arrived 30-10-13		1-14
❑ WV322*	'Y'	Hawker Hunter T.8M	G-BZSE	55	ex Exeter, Kemble, Cranwell 9096M, WV322, Kemble, 237 OCU, 764, 736, 809, 764, F.4 92. CoA 19-11-11. Arrived 14-11-12		1-14
❑ WZ507	'74'	DH Vampire T.11 ✈	G-VTII	54	ex Bournemouth, Swansea, Bruntingthorpe, Cranfield, Carlisle, CATCS, 3/4 CAACU, 5 FTS, 8 FTS, 229 OCU. 219 Sqn colours	[1]	1-14
❑ XN459		Hunting Jet Provost T.3	G-BWOT	61	ex CFS, 1 FTS, A&AEE, 1 FTS. CoA 27-3-09, de-reg 24-10-12		1-14
❑ XW311	'MF'	BAC Jet Provost T.5		70	ex Popham, Exeter, Cosford 9180M (11-3-93), Shawbury, 6 FTS		1-14
❑ 1211		MiG-17 *Fresco*	G-MIGG	58	ex Bournemouth, G-BWUF Duxford, Polish AF. SBLim-5 built by PZL-Mielec. North Korean c/s. Engine runs 10-13		1-14
❑ 56498		Douglas C-54D-1	N44914	45	ex BuNo 56498, 42-72525	[2]	1-14
❑ '44-42914'		Douglas DC-4-1009	N31356	46	ex C-FTAW, EL-ADR, N6404	[2]	1-14

■ **[1]** Operated by the **Vampire Preservation Group** | **www.vampirepreservation.org.uk** **[2]** Stored on behalf of Aces High - see Dunsfold, Surrey.

Also: See under Coventry, Warwickshire, for a potential new operator here: Dakotair, the **RAF Transport Command Memorial**. Long-term inmate Beech D.18S N96240 departed by air to France on 29th July 2012. Not noted since February 2006, PZL Gawron SP-CHD has been deleted.

❑ G-AHUN	Globe GC-1B Swift		46	ex Thurrock, EC-AJK, OO-KAY, NC77764. CoA 4-8-95	6-12
❑ G-AKUP	Luscombe Silvaire 8E		48	ex N2774K, NC2774K	9-12
❑ G-APTU	Auster Alpha 5		59	ex Leicester, Sywell, Leicester. CoA 8-6-98	12-09
❑ G-BDXX	Nord NC.854		54	ex airfield, F-BEZQ. CoA 3-7-96. Off-site	4-11
❑ G-FLSH*	Yakovlev Yak-52		87	ex RA-44550. CoA 29-10-10, de-reg 26-3-10. F/n 6-12	1-14
❑ G-LUND	Cessna 340 II		73	ex G-LAST, G-UNDY, G-BBNR, N69452. CoA 17-9-06, de-reg 12-4-11	1-14
❑ 'G-PRAT'	American AA-5	G-BIVV	79	ex Elstree, N26979. CoA 18-7-05, de-reg3-10-08. Fire crews	1-14
❑ G-SEMI	Piper Seminole		78	ex G-DENW, N21439. *Lady Gabriella II*. CoA 23-3-08	7-11
❑ G-TINY*	Zlin Z.526F		72	ex OK-CMD. CoA 1-4-<u>09</u>. First noted 6-12	10-13
❑ G-VDIR	Cessna 310R II		75	ex N5091J. Crashed 4-9-05, de-reg 3-6-06	1-14
❑ N41098*	Cessna 421B		~	first noted 9-12	1-14

PURFLEET on A1090 west of the Dartford Bridge

Purfleet Heritage and Military Centre: Incorporating the **Hornchurch Wing** and housed in the incredible Royal Gunpowder Magazine 18th century arsenal, the centre holds an incredible wealth of aviation artefacts.

◆ **Access:** *Just off the A1090, in Centurion Way, off Tank Hill Road - 'brown signed'.* **Open:** *Thu, Sun and Bank Hols Apr to Oct 10:00 to 16:30; Nov to March 10:00 to 15:00. Closed Dec 25/26 and New Year.* **Contact:** *Alan Gosling, 8 Rapier Close, Purfleet-on-Thames, RM19 1QQ* | **01708 890874** | **purfleet-heritage@blueyonder.co.uk** | **www.purfleet-heritage.com**

RAYLEIGH on the A1095 north-west of Southend-on-Sea

The Cockpit Collection: Nigel Towler's collection is located at a series of sites within the region.

◆ **Access:** The *collection is scattered in various locations and, accordingly, visits are* **not** *possible*

❑ WZ608	DH Vampire T.11		53	ex Market Harbororough, Lutterworth, Bitteswell, Woodford, St Athan, 3 CAACU, 5 FTS, 266, Fassberg SF, 11, 5, Wunstorf SF, 266. SOC 17-11-67. Cockpit	[1]	4-00
❑ 'WZ826'	Vickers Valiant BK.1	XD826	57	ex Cardiff-Wales, Abingdon, Stratford, Cosford, Feltwell 7872M (5-3-65), 543, 232 OCU, 138, 90, 7. Cockpit		4-00
❑ XH560	Avro Vulcan <u>K</u>.2		60	ex Marham, Waddington, 50, Wadd W, 27, Akrotiri Wing, Cott W, Wadd W, Cott W, 230 OCU, 12, MoA, 230 OCU. SOC 5-1-84. Cockpit		4-00

❑ XH669	HP Victor K.2	59	ex Waddington 9092M, 55, 57, Witt Wing, A&AEE. Written off 21-6-90. Cockpit	4-00
❑ XH670	HP Victor B.2	59	ex East Kirkby, Tattershall, Woodford, Radlett, MoA. SOC 31-10-75. Cockpit	4-00
❑ XN795	EE Lightning F.2A	63	ex Foulness, RAE Bedford, A&AEE, BAC. SOC 10-3-77. Cockpit	4-00
❑ XS421	EE Lightning T.5	65	ex Foulness, RAE, 23, 111, 226 OCU. SOC 22-10-75. Cockpit	4-00

■ **[1]** The wings of Vampire WZ608 can be found on WZ518 at Sunderland, N&T.

Also: By January 2011 Lightning F.1A cockpit XG325 had moved from **1476 Squadron Air Cadets** to Thetford, Norfolk.

❑ G-BPUD*	Ryan PT-22 Recruit	41	ex Old Warden, N53189, USAAF 41-15236. CoA 17-2-93. crashed 8-11-92, de-reg 3-3-99	12-13
❑ -	Bücker Jungmann	~	ex Postland, SpanAF. CASA-built 1-131E	12-13

RIDGEWELL on the A1017 south-east of Haverhill

Ridgewell Airfield Commemorative Museum / 381st Bomb Group Memorial Museum: Established in USAAF Station No.167's former hospital. Displays - including the Tony Ince Collection – are dedicated to the 381st and RAF units.

◆ **Access:** *Behind the war memorial off the A1017 between Ridgewell and Great Yeldham.* **Open:** *Second Sun of each month, Apr to Sept, 11:00 to 17:00.* **Contact: 07543 658006 | jim@381st.com | www.381st.com**

SOUTHEND AIRPORT Has gone over to the 'dark side' and is now known as London Southend Airport - which see.

SOUTHEND-ON-SEA

Adventure Island: On Marine Parade, Lost City Adventure Golf has a novel putting hazard. The R22 adorns the pay-booth!

❑ G-AZRX	Gardan Horizon 160	63	ex Great Yarmouth, Tattershall Thorpe (?), F-BLIJ. Crashed 14-8-91, de-reg 21-10-91. Wreck	2-14
❑ G-BOEX	Robinson R22	88	ex Rochester. Crashed 13-8-02, de-reg 11-10-02	2-14

STAPLEFORD AERODROME or Stapleford Tawney, on the A113 south of the M11/M25 junction EGSG

During 2012 a large influx of former AAC Gazelles arrived here, mostly from Colsterworth, Lincs, for re-work or onward sale. At the time of writing, this process was thought to be short-term and accordingly, they are not listed here. Should the cache become longer-term, that will change in *W&R25*. For now, refer to the Colsterworth entry for more details.

❑ G-AZZO	Piper Cherokee 140	67	ex N4471J. CoA 6-8-03, de-reg 8-8-12	1-10
❑ G-BEXO	Piper Apache 160	55	ex OO-APH, N1176P. CoA 10-10-07, de-reg 4-2-09	6-10
❑ G-BHGP	SOCATA TB-10 Tobago	80	CoA 29-5-05, de-reg 4-2-07	1-10
❑ G-BXWC	Cessna 152	83	ex N4794B. Crashed 24-5-07, CoA 12-7-07, de-reg 9-9-10	6-10
❑ G-HERB	Piper Arrow III	78	ex ZS-LAJ, N3504M. Damaged 9-6-09, CoA 2-11-09	1-10
❑ G-JENI	Cessna R.182	78	ex N3284C. CoA 9-7-09	6-10
❑ G-OPJC	Cessna F.152 II	79	ex N68354. Reims-built. CoA 17-10-07, de-reg 25-4-08. Fuselage, dump	6-10

STOCK on the B1007 south of Chelmsford

Hanningfield Metals / H&M Sales: See under Abridge, Essex, for notes on F.27 3C-QSB. Aerial surveillance (of the non-Reaper kind!) in November 2013 revealed the F.27 and a light grey Andover, *likely* XS643. To hulks, last noted in 2009, have been deleted: Short 330 G-DACS and MiG-23MF '50' blue.

◆ **Access:** *Busy and* **private** *yard - visitors by prior arrangement* **only**

❑ 3C-QSB	Fokker F.27-200MAR	81	ex Southend, M-1 RNethAF, PH-EXC. Cockpit	11-13
❑ XS643	HS Andover E.3A	67	ex Manston 9278M, Boscombe Down, 32, A&AEE, 115, 84. Cockpit. See above	10-08
❑ XS791	HS Andover CC.2	64	ex Ely, Bruntingthorpe, Northolt, 32, 60, FEAF VIP Flt, 48, FECS, MECS, Abingdon SF. Fuselage. See above	12-05

STOW MARIES AERODROME north of the B1012 east of South Woodham Ferrers

Stow Maries Great War Aerodrome: Operational from around September 1916, it closed down in 1919 but an incredible number of original buildings remain. A tasteful and thorough restoration has been carried out, including the re-introduction of a flying field. The site serves as a memorial to aircrew lost from 37 Squadron at Stow Maries, Rochford and Goldhanger.

A £1.5 million grant from the National Heritage Memorial Fund, plus help from Essex County Council, Maldon District Council and English Heritage secured the aerodrome in October 2013 and ownership will be transferred to a charitable trust. With the Great Centenary, the team at Stow Maries is planning a range of special events. Fokker E.III replica '422/15' (G-FOKR) moved on to a new home in the North-East in September 2012.

◆ **Access:** *Open Thu, Fri, Sun 10:00 to 16:00 - other times by prior arrangement.* **Contact:** *Stow Maries Great War Aerodrome, Hackmans Lane, Purleigh, Essex, CM3 6RN* | **curator@stowmaries.com** | **www.stowmaries.com**

❑ G-ARUI*	Beagle Terrier 1 ✈	47	ex Southend, Auster AOP.6 VF571, 651, 662. Flew in 19-10-13	[1]	1-14
❑ 'A643'	Sopwith Pup replica	77	BAPC.179, ex 'A7317', Northampton, Coventry, Waltham Abbey, North Weald, *Wings*. 37 Sqn colours	[2]	1-14
❑ 'F235'* 'B'	Rep' Plans SE.5A ✈ G-BMDB	88	ex Boscombe Down. Flew in 28-12-13		1-14

■ **[1]** The Terrier is owned by *W&R* contributor Terry Dann. **[2]** The Pup replica is on loan from Matthew Boddington.

WEST HORNDON west of Basildon, south of the A127

Ricky Kelley | **Access**, *by prior arrangement* ***only*** | **07733 310622** | **ricky.kelley@atos.net**

❑ XW550	HS Buccaneer S.2B	73	ex Stock, St Athan, 16, 15. SOC 18-8-80. Cockpit	3-12

WETHERSFIELD on the B1053 west of Halstead

A Jet Provost arrived at a *private* location in the *general* area during late 2102.

❑ XM473*	Hunting Jet Provost T.3A	60	ex Ipswich, Bedford, Norwich Airport 'G-TINY', Halton 8974M (9-6-88), 7 FTS, 1 FTS, 7 FTS, 1 FTS, CFS, 3 FTS, 1 FTS. First noted 11-12	1-13

WICKFORD north of the A127, west of the A130 and north of Basildon

Paintball Action Park: Part of the Delta Force 'franchise', offering outdoor meetings with machismo and high-speed paint!

◆ **Access:** *By prior arrangement* **only** | **www.paintballgames.co.uk/essex**

❑ XL586	Hawker Hunter T.7	58	ex Melksham, Kemble, Ipswich, Colsterworth, Shawbury, BAe Warton, 1 TWU, 2 TWU, 1 TWU, 229 OCU	[1]	12-13

■ **[1]** T.7 XL586 is fitted with the rear-end of XL578, *but* carries XL586 to port and XL578 to starboard! See under Binbrook, Lincs, for details of the majority of XL578.

GLOUCESTERSHIRE

Includes the unitary authorities of Bristol and South Gloucestershire

ASTON DOWN AIRFIELD south of the A419 west of Cirencester

Cotswold Gliding Club: By December 2013 K.8B ESX was reduced to a fuselage and gone by the following month.

❑ EJF*	Schleicher K.8B	74	BGA.2717. CoA 15-11-09	2-12
❑ EOZ	Schleicher K.8B G-DEJF	64	BGA.2879, ex D-8763	1-14
❑ EQP	Glaser-Dirks DG-202/17	83	BGA.2869, crashed 12-7-92. Cockpit used as a simulator	1-14
❑ FQE	Schleicher K.8B	r89	BGA.3435, ex D-6329. CoA 9-4-01	1-14
❑ –	Slingsby Tutor	c46	BGA.427, ex Stoke, Firbeck, Bickmarsh, RAFGSA.258	1-14
❑ WZ796	Slingsby Grasshopper TX.1	52	ex Nympsfield	1-14
❑ XP493	Slingsby Grasshopper TX.1	61	ex Syerston. Last flight 9-8-84	1-14

BRISTOL

Bristol's City Museum and Art Gallery: In Queen's Road, the Bristol Boxkite 'flies' within the museum.

◆ **Open:** *Mon to Fri 10:00 to 17:00, Sat, Sun, Bank Hols, 10:00 to 18:00.* **Contact:** *Queen's Road, Clifton, Bristol, BS8 1RL* | **0117 9223571** | **general.museum@bristol.gov.uk** | **www.bristol-city.gov.uk/museums**

❑ –	Bristol Boxkite replica	64	BAPC.40, ex Old Warden, Ford, *Those Magnificent Men...*	1-14

M Shed: Sub-titled, 'Your Museum, Your Story'. The cranes on the jetty work, there are buses, boats, locos and lorries that go 'on steam' and an observation gallery provides panoramic views of the incredible so-called 'Floating Harbour'. Perhaps in deference to the long hoped-for exposition at Filton, other than the 'Flea' there is precious little aviation content - hardly a whisper of Concorde. With that in mind, the forward fuselage mock-up has 'moved on'.

◆ **Access:** *'Brown signed' within the city centre and signs for SS* Great Britain *are a good way-point.* **NB** *there is* no *on-site parking.* **Open:** *Tue to Fri 10:00 to 17:00, Sat and Sun 10:00 to 18:00. Note: flash photography not permitted.* **Contact:** *Wapping Road, Bristol BS1 4RN* | **0117 3526600** | **info@mshed.org** | **www.mshed.org**

❑ G-AEHM	Mignet HM.14 'Flea'	36	ex Wroughton, Hayes, Whitchurch, Bristol. *Blue Finch.* De-reg 4-3-39	[1]	1-14

■ **[1]** On loan from the Science Museum; acquired 9-38.

City of Bristol College: Correcting *W&R23* (p57), the college keeps its airframes at the campus on Bradley Stoke Way, close to the junction of the M5 and A38. *W&R23* 'wrote out' several airframes that had apparently out-lived their 'sell-by' date. As is typical, one of these, Queen Air *Delta-Romeo*, last noted in June 1991, is *still* giving good service. By February 2013 Beagle 206 G-ASWJ had moved to Coventry, Warks.

◆ **Access:** *Busy facilities, by prior application* **only** | **www.cityofbristolac.uk**

❑ G-AVDR	Beech Queen Air B80	67	ex Bournemouth, Shobdon, Exeter, A40-CR, G-AVDR. CoA 30-6-86, de-reg 18-5-90. See above		7-12
❑ G-BKGD	Westland WG.30-100	82	ex Weston-super-Mare, Yeovil, Penzance, G-BKBJ ntu. CoA 6-7-93, de-reg 15-4-93	[2]	7-12

■ **[1]** On loan from Helicopter Museum, Weston-super-Mare, Somerset.

University of Bristol, Faculty of Engineering: In the Queen's Building, University Walk, near Tyndalls Park.

◆ **Access:** *Busy campus, by prior application* **only** | **www.bris.ac.uk/engineering/**

❑ XZ649	Westland Lynx AH.7	80	ex Farnborough, Boscombe Down, 657	[1]	10-13

■ **[1]** Lynx XZ649 is fitted with the boom of XZ646.

Others: Projects at a workshop in the area are well long-in-the-tooth, but are thought to be current.

❑ G-ADNL	Miles Sparrowhawk	35	reconstruction	9-03
❑ G-AETG	Aeronca 100	37	ex Hanwell, Booker. Crashed 7-4-69	9-01
❑ G-AEWV	Aeronca 100	37	ex Hanwell. De-reg 7-3-67. Spares	9-01
❑ EI-ALU	Avro Club Cadet	33	ex New Castle, Dublin, G-ACIH	9-01

BRISTOL (FILTON) AIRFIELD closed on 21st December 2013 and is now 'filed' under Filton

BROCKWORTH on the A417 east of Gloucester and the M5

Jet Age Museum / Gloucestershire Aviation Collection: Gamecock replica 'J7904' left the workshop here for Gloucestershire Airport, Glos, in time for the 'pre-season' official opening, in August 2013.

◆ **Access:** No longer available for public inspection - refer to Gloucestershire, Glos, for contact details.

❑ -	Hawker Typhoon Ia or 'b	c42	ex Staverton, Twyford, Chippenham. Forward fuselage	[1]	1-14

■ **[1]** Salvaged from a yard in Chippenham in 1998, the Typhoon's restoration is dedicated to the memory of Michele Clarke.

CHELTENHAM

In the *general* area, **Nick Parker** has a Scimitar cockpit.

❑ XD215	Supermarine Scimitar F.1	57	ex Ottershaw, Foulness, Culdrose A2573 (9-10-67), 764B, 800, 803, A&AEE. Cockpit	6-13

CHIPPING CAMPDEN on the B4081 north of Stow on the Wold

Mike Pyment: At a *private* location, a Comet cockpit has been extensively re-worked with the flight deck in 'live' mode in a challenging link up with flight simulator software.

◆ **Access:** *By prior permission* **only** | **whbandb@yahoo.co.uk** | **www.thecomet4.com**

❑ XV814	DH Comet 4	G-APDF	58	ex Boscombe Down, RAE, MSA, Air Ceylon, BOAC G-APDF. Last flown 28-1-93, acquired 13-8-97. Cockpit	2-12

COTSWOLD AIRPORT or Kemble, on the A429 south-west of Cirencester EGBP

Note: *The site is large and aircraft are given under nominal 'keepers'. Airworthy general aviation types are* not *listed.*

Bristol Aero Collection: The display hangar closed its doors on 28th May 2012 and the job of decanting everything, mostly to Filton, Glos, began. There hopefully the airframes will become a part of the proposed museum/visitor centre.

Departures to Filton, Glos: Bristol Babe replica 'G-EASQ' by 12-12; Britannia cockpit G-ALRX by 12-12; Beagle 206 cockpit G-ATDD by 12-12; Bristol 173 XF785 8-1-13; Sycamore HR.14 XJ917 by 6-13; Concorde EMU forward fuselage by 12-12; Jindivik A92-708 by 12-12; Bolingbroke IV 9048, was noted as 'off-site' in *W&R23* - its cockpit was *already* under restoration at Filton, Glos, at that point and has since been joined by the rest of it. Breaking the trend was Harrier GR.1 XV798, going to Weston-super-Mare, Somerset, 31-10-12.

Bristol Britannia XM496 Preservation Society: Looks after *Regulus*, via a comprehensive restoration policy.

◆ **Open:** *1st and 3rd Sunday of the month, 12:30 to 16:00, during airfield special events, or by prior arrangement.*
Contact: enquiries@XM496.com | www.XM496.com

❑	XM496	Bristol Britannia C.1 G-BDUP	60	ex Lanseria, EL-WXA, 9Q-CJH, CU-T120, Afrek, G-BDUP, Kemble, XM496 99/511. Short-built. *Regulus,* RAF colours [1]	2-14

■ [1] *Regulus* factoids: First flown at Sydenham, 24-8-60, delivered to Lyneham 17-9-60; made last-ever flight by a Britannia when she flew into Kemble, 14-10-97.

Lufthansa Resource Technical Training: See also Doncaster Sheffield, S Yorks.

◆ **Access:** *Visits by prior arrangement* **only**. | **www.lrtt.co.uk**

❑	G-BIBG*	Sikorsky S-76A II+	80	ex Aberdeen, Norwich, 5N-BCE, G-BIBG. CoA 18-8-09, canx 8-12-09. Arrived 13-8-13.	8-13
❑	D-ASDB	VFW-614	77	ex St Athan, Copenhagen, Muk Air OY-RRW, D-ASDB, Luftwaffe 17+03, D-BABS	7-12
❑	N309LJ	Learjet 25	69	ex Staverton, N309AJ, N19FN, N17AR, N3UC, N6GC, N242WT, N954FA, N954GA	1-11
❑	80+55	Bőlkow Bő 105M	~	ex St Athan, HEER	7-12
❑	80+77	Bőlkow Bő 105M	~	ex Hoofddorp, HEER	7-12

Midair Squadron / C2 Aviation: Mike Davis and his team put Canberra PR.9 XH134 into the air as a civilian during 2013. It made its first taxi runs on 12th January and took to the skies on 7th July 2013. C2 Aviation (which takes its name from the hangar it occupies) has been established to look after the 'squadron' that has been formed around the PR.9, and for third-party work. The Hunter T.7s will fly in the same scheme as the Canberra; all are registered to Canberra 134 Ltd.

◆ **Access:** *Visits by prior arrangement* **only**. | **www.midair-squadron.com | www.c2aviation.com**

❑	G-RAXA*	Hawker Hunter T.7 ✈	58	ex G-VETA, St Athan, Kemble, Exeter, G-BVWN ntu, XL600, North Weald, Southall, Fleetlands A2729 (17-10-84), Scampton, 12, 4 FTS, Wattisham SF, 65	1-14
❑	XH134	EE Canberra PR.9 ✈ G-OMHD	59	ex Marham, 39, 1 PRU, 39, 58, MoA. Short-built. First flown 7-7-13. 'Silver' scheme	1-14
❑	XL577*	Hawker Hunter T.7 ✈ G-XMHD	58	ex G-BXKF, Exeter, Navenby, Cranwell 8676M (16-3-81), 2 TWU, 237 OCU, 1 TWU, TWU, 229 OCU. Silver c/s by 11-13	1-14

Also: Canberra PR.9 XH134 first flew as a civilian on 7th July 2013 and is now listed above under Midair Squadron - above. Much storage and parting out of airliners is carried out at Kemble; most of this done by **Air Salvage International**. Most of this activity is too transitory for *W&R*; only long-term items are listed here. The scrapping (sorry, wrong jargon: parting-out) process produces shed-loads of cockpit and flight deck sections, the majority of which must go *somewhere*! During 2011 **Delta Jets** ceased trading, and the relevant airframes listed under that heading in *W&R23* have been incorporated here.

As *W&R* closed for press, former 216 Squadron Tristar KC.1 ZD952 touched down on 3rd January 2014 for decommissioning and scrapping. The others were expected to follow in short order. Processing was expected to be swift; if not, *W&R25* will pick up the pieces!

Departures: Agusta A.109A G-JRSL hulk had gone by 5-13; the fuselage of HS 146 G-JEBV left by road 14-8-12; Boeing 727-31F OO-DHN cockpit moved to North Hykeham, Lincs by 10-12. Delta Jets-based Hunter GA.11 XE689 (G-BWGK) was offered for sale 1-12, it was broken up the following month and the cockpit is *believed* to have been saved;

❑	G-APPA*	DHC Chipmunk 22	52	ex Wellesbourne Mountford area, Carlisle, Glasgow, N5703E, G-APPA, WP917, Glas UAS, 11 RFS, 8 RFS. CoA 14-7-85. Arrived 16-5-12	3-13
❑	G-ARMD*	DHC Chipmunk 22A	50	ex Redditch area, WD297, 666, 1 BFTS. CoA 5-6-76 Arrived 16-5-12	3-13
❑	G-BADZ*	Pitts S-2A	72	ex Exeter. CoA 5-6-00. First noted 5-12	2-13

❑ G-BHSL		Bücker Jungmann		57	ex SpanAF E3B-286. Crashed 6-7-96. CASA-built I-131E. CoA 19-7-96, de-reg 23-8-00		2-13
❑ G-BOVS		Cessna 150M		76	ex N704KC. Cr 6-8-05, de-reg 1-9-05. Scrap area by 11-12		5-13
❑ 'G-ESKY'		Piper Aztec 250D	G-BADI	69	ex Iver Heath (?), North Weald, N6885Y. CoA 29-10-92 Fire crews		5-13
❑ 'G-FIRE'		EMBRAER Bandeirante	SX-BNL	79	ex Trans European, N614KC, PT-GMQ. Fire crews		9-10
❑ G-MKCA		Boeing 747-2B5B		80	ex MK Airlines, 9G-MKR, N778BA, HL7452		2-14
❑ G-MKGA		Boeing 747-2R7F		79	ex MK Airlines, 9G-MKL, N926FT, N639FE, N809FT, EI-BTQ, LX-DCV		2-14
❑ G-ODUB*		EMBRAER Bandeirante		79	ex Kingston-upon-Thames, -?-, Alton, Yeadon, PH-FVC, G-BNIX, N8536J, XC-DAB, PT-GMJ. CoA 6-2-01, de-reg 9-10-02. Fuselage. Arrived 8-7-13		7-13
❑ EI-DYG*		Boeing 737-8AS		08	ex Rome, Ryanair. Damaged 17-3-08. Fuselage. Arrived 9-10. Cabin trainer		1-13
❑ N19CQ*	'A'	HS Dominie T.1		65	Cranwell, XS712, 55, 3 FTS, 6 FTS, 1 ANS, HS. Arrived 14-6-11		8-13
❑ N19CU*	'E'	HS Dominie T.1		65	Cranwell, XS728, 55, 6 FTS, RAFC, 6 FTS, 1 ANS. Arr 13-6-11		8-13
❑ N19EK*	'K'	HS Dominie T.1		66	Cranwell, XS737, 55, 6 FTS, 1 ANS, HS. Arrived 14-6-11		8-13
❑ N19UG*	'H'	HS Dominie T.1		65	Cranwell, XS730, 55, 3 FTS, 6 FTS, 1 ANS. Arrived 14-6-11		8-13
❑ N19UK*	'F'	HS Dominie T.1		66	Cranwell, XS739, 55, 3 FTS, 6 FTS, 1 ANS. Arrived 14-6-11		8-13
❑ N19XY*	'J'	HS Dominie T.1		66	Cranwell, XS731, 55, 3 FTS, 6 FTS, 1 ANS. Arrived 14-6-11		8-13
❑ N25AG		Lockheed JetStar II		76	ex Alton, Kemble, 3C-QRK, P4-CBG, VP-CBH, EC-FQX, EC-232, N20GB, N333KN, N717X, N717, N5528L. Last flown 26-9-06. Fuselage		2-14
❑ N347DK		Douglas Dakota IV ✈		44	ex Weston, Coventry, G-AMSV, F-BSGV ntu, G-AMSV, KN397, 44-76488. Indian AF colours	[1]	8-13
❑ N389DF		Boeing 737-3M8		91	ex KD Avia, EI-DTY, G-IGOV, N250GE, LZ-BOF, N250GE, 9V-TRD, N760BE, N35030. Fire dump		2-14
❑ LZ844*	'UP-X'	Supermarine Spitfire V		43	ex Australia, Brisbane, 'R6915', Point Cook, NZ, Auckland, New Guinea, crashed 12-12-43, RAAF A58-213, LZ844 n/s. Arrived 11-7-11. Stored		8-13
❑ 'WZ868'*	'H'	DHC Chipmunk T.10	G-ARMF	51	ex Redditch area, Wellesbourne, Twyford, WG322, 63 GCF, Leeds UAS, 22 RFS. Damaged 19-6-96, CoA 12-10-98 Arrived 16-5-12		3-13
❑ XE665	'876'	Hawker Hunter T.8C	G-BWGM	55	ex Exeter, Shawbury, Yeovilton, FRADU, 764, Jever SF, 118. CoA 24-6-98, de-reg 16-3-11. Stored		8-13
❑ XH135		EE Canberra PR.9		59	ex Marham, 39, 1 PRU, 39, 13, 58, MoA, Handling Sqn. Arrived 31-7-06		7-13
❑ 'XR540'		Folland Gnat T.1	XP502	62	ex Ipswich, St Athan 8576M, 4 FTS. 'Red Arrows' colours. Displayed		2-14

■ **[1]** The Dakota is thought to still be destined for the Indian Air Force Historic Flight.

DURSLEY on the A4135 south-west of Stroud

Retro Track and Air Ltd: Specialist engine overhaul and airframe company equally at home with historic Grand Prix cars.

◆ **Access:** *Visits* **strictly** *by prior arrangement only* | **www.retrotrackandair.com**

❑ N5719		Glos' Gladiator II	G-CBHO	38	ex Narvik, 263. Abandoned 22-5-40	[1]	1-14
❑ P8208*		Supermarine Spitfire IIb	G-RRFF	41	ex Oxford, Severn estuary, 52 OTU, 1 CACU, 1 CACF, 303. Crashed 26-1-43	[1]	4-13
❑ TE566*		Supermarine Spitfire IX	VH-IXT	45	ex Australia, VH-IXT, South Africa ZU-SPT, crashed 25-4-02, Duxford, G-BLCK, Audley End, Ludham, St Leonards on Sea, Duxford, Israel, IDF/AF 20-32 4X-FOB, Czech AF, 312, TE566. Arrived 11-7-11. Stored		3-13
❑ GA-43		Glos' Gamecock II	G-CGYF	28	ex Finland, Fin AF	[1]	1-14

■ **[1]** All registered to Retro Track and Air.

Chris Wiltshire: Has a Vampire pod in the *general* area.

❑ XD452	'66'	DH Vampire T.11		54	ex Chester, Whixhall, Whitchurch, London Colney, Shawbury, 7990M, 3 FTS, 7 FTS, 1 FTS, 8 FTS, 5 FTS. Pod	8-12

FILTON previously entered as Bristol (Filton) Airport, south of the M5 at Patchway, north of Bristol

Bristol Aerospace Centre: By late 2012 the plans for an element of heritage at Filton had gelled into the Bristol Aerospace Centre, under the guidance of the proven **Bristol Aero Collection Trust**, which has pioneered the commemoration and preservation of the hallowed 'Bristol' name since 1988. The £13.5 million project has backing from Rolls-Royce and BAE Systems, the latter pledging £2m plus 9 acres of land on the northern boundary. The proposed heritage museum and learning centre will incorporate two World War One era hangars, between which a new 'hall' to take Concorde *Alpha-Fox* will be built. In May 2013 persistence was rewarded when the Heritage Lottery Fund allocated a 'first round pass' of £4.4m along with £243,600 to aid progress towards a full go-ahead. Target date for opening is spring 2017.

With the closure of the Bristol Aero Collection museum at Cotswold, Glos, most of the airframes gravitated to the Brabazon hangar for storage; awaiting the new centre. On 23rd December 2013 the Britannia Aircraft Preservation Trust (see under Liverpool, Merseyside) officially handed over the cockpit of Britannia 101 G-ALRX to BAC. It now rests in the hangar in which it was assembled prior to flight test.

◆ **Access:** *Visits* **strictly** *by prior arrangement only.* **Contact**: *PO Box 77, Filton, BS99 7AR* | **0117 9365350** | **enquiries@bristolaero.com** | **www.retrotrackandair.com**

❑ 'G-EASQ'*		Bristol Babe III replica	72	BAPC.87, ex Kemble, Banwell, Stoke, Hemswell, Cleethorpes, Selby. Arrived by 12-12, stored		12-12
❑ G-ALRX*		Bristol Britannia 101	53	ex Kemble, Banwell, Boscombe Down, WB473 / VX447 ntu, Crashed 4-2-54, de-reg 5-4-54. Cockpit. Arrived by 12-12		12-13
❑ G-ATDD*		Beagle 206-1	65	ex Kemble, Filton, Wroughton, South Kensington, Leeds. Damaged 6-73, de-reg 9-4-74. Cockpit. Arrived by 12-12	[1]	12-12
❑ G-BOAF		BAC/Sud Concorde 102	79	ex BA, G-N94AF, G-BFKX. CoA 11-6-04. De-reg 11-6-04. Flew in 26-11-03. External store	[2]	12-13
❑ G-MBTH*		Whittaker MW-4	82	de-reg 11-1-14. First noted 9-13	[3]	9-13
❑ G-ROEI*		Roe I Biplane replica	08	ex Brooklands. Arrived 1-14, stored	[4]	1-14
❑ -*		BAC/Sud Concorde EMU	~	ex Kemble, Brooklands. Test shell, nose. Plus cabin mock-up		12-12
❑ –*		HS 146 RJX 100	c10	ex Swinton, Manchester Airport, Woodford. Unfinished sections. Arrived 6-12-13	[5]	1-14
❑ 'A7288'		Bristol F.2b replica	10	stored	[6]	3-12
❑ XF785*		Bristol 173 Srs 1 G-ALBN	52	ex Kemble, Cosford, Henlow 7648M (10-7-60), G-ALBN. De-reg 21-7-60. Arrived 8-1-13, stored	[7]	6-13
❑ XJ917*	'S-H'	Bristol Sycamore HR.14	57	ex Kemble, Banwell, Helston, Wroughton, CFS, 275. SOC 12-12-72. First noted 6-13, stored		6-13
❑ 9048*	'YO-T'	Bristol Bolingbroke IV	41	ex Kemble, Los Angeles, Chino, RCAF, 8(BR). SOC 21-8-46. Fairchild Canada-built. Dismantled		6-13
❑ A92-708*		GAF Jindivik 3	~	ex Kemble. Llanbedr. Arrived by 12-12, stored	[8]	12-12

■ **[1]** Beagle 206 started life as the Bristol 220 design study, hence the type's place in this collection. **[2]** *Alpha-Fox* factoids: Last UK Concorde built, first flown at Filton 20-4-74 and made the type's last-ever flight, back to its birthplace, on 26-11-03. Withdrawn from BA service 24-10-03, total hours 18,257, landings 6,045. It is on long-term loan from British Airways. **[3]** *Tango-Hotel* was the last aircraft designed, built and *flown* at Filton, by former BAe engineer Mike Whittaker. **[4]** The Roe Biplane is stored on behalf of the Brooklands Museum. **[5]** The RJX composite comprises the cockpit, rear fuselage and wings from still-born Set 396 (c/n E3396) destined for British European (sorry, flybe.com) plus other sections from the closure of the Woodford line. Much of the 146/RJX was built at Filton for assembly at Woodford. **[6]** F.2b replica built by GKN-Aerospace and Rolls-Royce apprentices for the BAC 100 celebrations, 2010. **[7]** Bristol 173 is on loan from the RAF Museum. **[8]** Jindivik represents the first application for the BSE (*née* Armstrong Siddeley) Viper - another Filton product.

Rolls-Royce Heritage Trust - Bristol Branch (RRHT): The Sir Roy Fedden Heritage Centre contains an exceptional array of engines, backed by a vast amount of supportive material, large and small. As well as Bristol and Bristol Siddeley and Rolls-Royce (from 1966), de Havilland and Blackburn powerplants are also represented.

◆ **Access:** *By prior arrangement* **only. Contact: 01332 248181| email via website| www.rolls-royce.com/about/heritage**

Former Airfield: Closed for flying on 21st December 2012, bringing to an end an era that started with Boxkites in 1910. Placards around the huge site offering it redevelopment call the area 'Bristol Brabazon' which at least shows some reference to the past, if not Filton's finest hour. Hundreds of houses plus drive-in take-aways, retail parks and logistics monoliths are destined to render the whole vista unrecognisable before very long. Boeing 747s G-MKKA, and sister G-MKDA, were still laid up in May 2012, and were scrapped. Two other references need 'tidying up'. Mustang 472216 (G-BIXL) departed for an airstrip in Berkshire and was flying again by May 2013. Last noted in February 2000, the AV-8B Harrier (*possibly* 162071) held by Rolls-Royce, has been deleted. The MK Airlines 'hack' Gulfstream I N748AA had been inert within the Brabazon hangar since 11th June 2008. It was moved outside during the summer of 2013 and scrapped on 11th November.

Bombay Nights Takeaway: In Charlton Road just south of the airfield site and close to the golf course.

❑	G-MKSS		HS.125-700B	82	ex *Da Vinci Code,* Biggin Hill, VP-BEK, VP-CEK, C9-TAC, N770TJ. Cockpit		11-13

■ **[1]** *Sierra-Sierra* was cancelled as sold in Russia 15-10-07, becoming RA-02804, but apparently not migrating eastwards.

GLOUCESTER

Gloster Aviation Club: The collection of cockpits has expanded.

◆ **Access:** Not *open to the public, but happy to be contacted by interested parties* | **glosteraviationclub@fsmail.net**

❑	XE339	'149'	Hawker Sea Hawk FGA.6	55	ex Dunsfold, Lee-on-Solent, Culdrose A2635, Halton 8156M (19-1-71), FRU, 801, 803, 800. AWA-built. Cockpit	[1]	2-14
❑	XF383		Hawker Hunter F.6	56	ex Kidlington, North Scarle, Wittering 8706M (19-1-82), Kemble, 12, 216, 237 OCU, 4 FTS, 229 OCU, 65, 111, 263. AWA-built. 65 Sqn colours. Cockpit		2-14
❑	XG331		EE Lightning F.1	59	ex Quedgeley, Staverton, Hucclecote, Barton, Chelford, Long Marston, Innsworth, Staverton, Foulness, Warton, A&AEE. Last flight 28-9-66. Cockpit		2-14
❑	ZF590*		EE Lightning F.53	68	ex Upwood, Binbrook, Lewes, *Wing Commander*, Portsmouth, Warrington, Warton, R Saudi AF 220, 53-679, G-27-49. Last flown 22-1-86. Cockpit. Arrived 9-11-13	[1]	2-14

■ **[1]** Sea Hawk and Lightning F.53 owned by Clive Davies - see also under Bruntingthorpe, Leics.

Also: A scrapyard has the hulk of a Scout. The yard was used as the 'set' for the TV programme *Scrapheap Challenge*.

❑	XP856		Westland Scout AH.1	63	ex Bramley, Middle Wallop, AETW		1-12

GLOUCESTERSHIRE AIRPORT or Staverton

EGBJ

Jet Age Museum operated by the **Gloucestershire Aviation Collection**: From 24th August 2013 the long-awaited museum staged what was called 'Opening Lite', with a handful of airframes and the ability to view work-in-progress which, by May 2014 will see the first phase complete. (Airframes on show during the 'Lite' phase are marked #.) Tenacity and perseverance as scheme after scheme fell over for one reason or another was rewarded during August 2012 when the first ground was cut on the new building. During the summer of 2013 Tewkesbury Borough Council added £9,000 to a previous hand-out of £27,000 towards the scheme. Long-term fund-raising by GAC and grants from other sources also made the £330,000-plus project possible.

Paul Webb is busy building a replica Airspeed Horsa forward fuselage, but this is in early stages and is not formally listed. The workshop at Brockworth, Glos, is working on a Typhoon projects.

◆ **Access:** *Follow signs to the airport.* **Open**: *Every weekend and Bank Hols, 10:00 to 16:00 - and keep an eye on the website for developments. Weekday and group visits by appointment.* **Contact:** *Meteor Business Park, Cheltenham Road East, Gloucester, GL2 9QL* | **01452 260078** | **jetagemuseum@hotmail.co.uk** | **www.jetagemuseum.org**

❑	G-AWZU*		HS Trident 3B-101	71	ex Basingstoke, Stansted, Heathrow, BA, BEA. CoA 3-7-85, de-reg 18-3-86. *Tina.* Cockpit. Arrived 28-11-13	[1]	1-14
❑	–		McBroom Arion hang-glider	~	ex Hucclecote. Stored		1-14
❑	'J7904'*		Gloster Gamecock rep	97	BAPC.259, ex Staverton, Dursley, Staverton. Project unveiled 9-8-98, arrived 10-13. 43 Sqn colours	# [2]	1-14
❑	N5914		Gloster Gladiator II	40	ex Dursley, Norway, 263. Shot down 2-6-40. Recovered 12-98, arrived on-site 20-11-13	[3]	1-14
❑	'V6799'	'SD-X'	Hawker Hurricane FSM	68	BAPC.72, ex 'V7767', Bournemouth, Sopley, Bournemouth Brooklands, North Weald, Coventry, *Battle of Britain.* Acquired 2-7-97. Moved on site 5-4-12. 501 Sqn c/s	# [4]	1-14
❑	'W4041/G'		Gloster E28/39 FSM	05	-	# [5]	1-14
❑	EE425		Gloster Meteor F.3	45	ex Yatesbury, Earls Colne, Andrewsfield, PEE Foulness (16-2-56), 206 AFS, 210 AFS, 206 AFS, 63, 266, 1, 222. Cockpit. Acquired 1-00. Moved back on site 5-4-12		1-14
❑	VW453*	'Z'	Gloster Meteor T.7	49	ex Innsworth 8703M, Salisbury Plain, Hullavington, Ta Qali, 604, 226 OCU, 203 AFS. SOC 12-6-57. Arrived 22-4-13	# [6]	1-14
❑	WF784		Gloster Meteor T.7	51	ex Bentham, Staverton, Quedgeley, Kemble 7895M (30-11-65), 5 CAACU, CAW, FTU, 130, 26. Arrived 1997	#	1-14
❑	WH364		Gloster Meteor F.8	52	ex Kemble 8169M (23-8-71), 601, Safi SF, Takali SF, Idris SF, Takali SF, Safi SF, 85. Arrived 10-9-03. 601 Sqn colours	#	1-14

❑ WK126	'843'	EE Canberra TT.18	54	ex Bentham, Staverton, Hucclecote, N2138J ntu, St Athan, FRADU, B.2, 100, 9. SOC 26-10-90. Acquired 1995. Stored on site	[7]	1-14
❑ WL349	'Z'	Gloster Meteor T.7	52	ex Kemble, 1 ANS, 2 ANS, CFE, 229 OCU. SOC 22-6-76. Stored on site	[8]	1-14
❑ WS807	'N'	Gloster Meteor NF(T).14	54	ex Kemble, Staverton, Bentham, Staverton, Yatesbury, Watton 7973M (6-7-67), Kemble, 1 ANS, 2 ANS. AWA-built. Arrived 7-97. 46 Sqn colours. Stored on site		1-14
❑ XD506		DH Vampire T.11	54	ex Bentham, Staverton, Thrupp, Staverton, Swinderby, Finningley 7983M (7-9-67), CATCS, CNCS, 5 FTS, 206 AFS. Arrived 28-2-98. Stored on site		1-14
❑ XD616		DH Vampire T.11	55	ex Bentham, Staverton, London Colney, Hoddesdon, Old Warden, Woodford, Chester, St Athan, 8 FTS, 1 FTS, 8 FTS, 65. SOC 6-11-67. Arrived 14-5-97. Pod, for spares		1-14
❑ XE664		Hawker Hunter F.4	55	ex Marlborough, ?, HSA, 26. SOC 14-4-59. Cockpit. Acquired 21-2-99. Moved on site 5-4-12	[9]	1-14
❑ XH903	'G'	Gloster Javelin FAW.9	58	ex Bentham, Staverton, Hucclecote, Innsworth 7938M (10-8-67), Shawbury, 5, 33, 29, 33, FAW.7, 23. Acquired 1993. 33 Sqn colours, displayed	# [10]	1-14
❑ XM569		Avro Vulcan B.2	63	ex Bentham, Staverton, Enstone, Cardiff, 44, Wadd Wing, 27, Cott Wing, 27. SOC 21-1-83. Arrived 6-2-97. Back to museum from the Flying Shack by 8-13. Cockpit	# [11]	-1-14
❑ XW264		HS Harrier T.2	69	ex Hucclecote, Innsworth, Dowty, Boscombe Down, HSA. Damaged 11-7-70. Acquired 28-6-94. Cockpit, moved back on site 5-4-12	[12]	1-14

■ **[1]** Donated by Gary Spoors (see also Bruntingthorpe, Laics, and East Midlands, Leics. **[2]** The Gamecock is fitted with a Jupiter IV, on loan from the RAF Museum. **[3]** On 2-6-40, flown by P/O J L Willkie, N5914 was shot down by a 1/ZG 76 Bf 110 flown by Lt Helmut Lent; Willkie was killed. **[4]** Hurricane wears the colours of W/C Ken Mackenzie DECK ARC. **[5]** E28/39 FSM used the mouldings for the Farnborough, Hants, and Lutterworth, Laics, examples. **[6]** VW453 acquired for JAM in 2013 by Tony Mackinnon and Martin Clarke. **[7]** WK126 is on loan from Chris Schaardenberg. **[8]** WL349 is owned by the airport authorities, but stored with JAM. **[9]** Hunter F.4 XE664, on loan from Bob Kneale, was refurbished in 1959 as a T.8 for the FAA with a new cockpit. In 1969 it was rebuilt for the Singapore ADC as T.75 514 (G-9-293 allocated) and is preserved in New Zealand. **[10]** Javelin on loan from the RAF Museum. **[11]** Vulcan cockpit is on loan from Gary Spoors and David Price, via JAM. (For Gary, see also Bruntingthorpe and East Midlands, Leics.) **[12]** The wings of XW264 are on XV798 at Weston-super-Mare, Somerset.

Also: Air experience flight specialists **Tiger Airways** - **www.tigerairways.co.uk** - has a veritable production line of Stampes on the go. **City of Bristol College** staged a clear-out of airframes: Learjet 25 N309LJ moved to Cotswold, Glos, by January 2011; Aztec 250 G-BAUI and Agusta 109 'G-OPAS' joined the fire crews, on the northern and south-west perimeter, respectively. Cessna 337C G-BCBZ was scrapped in late 2012. The cockpit of Vulcan B.2 XM569 moved back to the Jet Age Museum (above) by August 2013.

❑ G-BAUI		Piper Aztec 250D	69	ex City of Bristol College, Bristol, LN-RTS. CoA 15-12-88, de-reg 26-1-89. Fire crews		1-14
❑ G-BEPF*		Stampe SV-4C	46	ex F-BCVD. Nord-built. CoA 12-8-11		1-14
❑ G-BGBA*		Robin R2100A Club	78	ex F-OCBA. CoA 23-10-12. Fuselage		1-14
❑ G-BHFG*		Stampe SV-4C	46	ex F-BJDN, French mil. Nord-built. CoA 17-4-08		1-14
❑ G-BIAX*		Taylor Monoplane	98	CoA 11-5-04		1-14
❑ G-BLWH*		Fournier RF-6B-100	76	ex F-GADF. CoA 5-9-03		1-14
❑ G-BSGK*		Piper Seneca 200T	78	ex N36450. CoA 18-11-09, de-reg 12-10-12		1-14
❑ G-ESTA*		Cessna Citation II	80	ex G-GAUL, N550TJ, N29TC, N2631N. CoA 7-5-10		1-14
❑ G-FORC*		Stampe SV-4C	48	ex G-BLTJ, F-BDNJ. Nord-built. CoA 5-3-12		1-14
❑ G-HIVA*	'6'	Cessna 337A	66	ex G-BAES, SE-CWW, N5329S. CoA 30-8-09		1-14
❑ G-IASL		Beech A60 Duke	68	ex N3ND. CoA 8-3-09, de-reg 5-5-10. Fire crews		1-14
❑ G-NIFE*		Stampe SV-4A	46	ex F-BBBL, French AF, F-BFCE, French AF. Nord-built. CoA 18-8-11		1-14
❑ 'G-OPAS'		Agusta 109	~	ex City of Bristol College, D-HCKV. Fire crews	[1]	1-14
❑ G-PUSH*		Rutan LongEz	00	de-reg 16-3-10		1-14

■ **[1]** See under Bournemouth Airport, Dorset, for a the real G-OPAS.

INNSWORTH west of the B4063, near Parton, north-east of Gloucester

Imjin Barracks: Meteor T.7 VW453 left in style - under a RAF Chinook - on 22nd April 2013 for Gloucestershire, Glos.

LITTLE RISSINGTON AIRFIELD west of the A424, north-west of Burford

Civil operations on the site came to an end by April 2012. The following were removed to a yard at Cricklade, Wilts, by late 2012: Doves G-ARJB and G-DDCD, Devons VP955 (G-DVON) and XA880 (G-BVXR). Dove 8 G-HBBC is reported to have moved to 'Norfolk' by road by January 2012. Last noted in June 2011, Dove 5 G-APSO, Dove 8 G-ARBE and Robin DR.400 G-BAGS are unaccounted for. Norman Freelance G-NACA was flying by 2011 and settled on Henstridge as a base. The five unfinished fuselages, last reported in February 2008, eventually followed *Alpha-Charlie* to Henstridge, Somerset.

At the **RAF enclave** is a Wessex:

❑ XR528		Westland Wessex HC.2	64	ex Lyneham, Gosport, Culdrose, Predannack, St Mawgan, 60, 28, 240 OCU. SOC 5-12-08	7-12

MARSHFIELD on the A420 east of Bristol

At a *private* location in the *general* area, a Jodel is stored.

❑ G-BMEH		Jodel D.150 Mascaret	87	CoA 21-5-08. SAN-built	1-14

MORETON-IN-MARSH on the A44 north-east of Cheltenham

Wellington Aviation Museum: Correcting *W&R23* (p63), the museum/gallery did not close, but transferred sections of Wellington I L7775 to the Stratford Armouries at Pathlow, Warks. Founder of the collection, **Gerry Tyack**, died on 4th January 2014, aged 90. As W&R closed for press, it was hoped that the venture would continue.

◆ **Access:** *Follow signs from the A44/A429.* **Open**: *Tue to Sun 10:00 to 12:30 and 14:00 to 17:00.* **Contact: 01608 650323 | www.wellingtonaviation.org**

The Fire Service College: Increasingly uses purpose-built rigs at the site, including a helicopter (referred to as a 'Merlin') and a jetliner (called a '737'). **Access** *By prior arrangement* **only | www.fireservicecollege.ac.uk**

❑ G-AZDZ		Cessna 172K	69	ex Firbeck, Fownhope, Warmingham, Southend, 5N-AIH, N1647C, N84508. Crashed 19-9-81, de-reg 5-12-83		2-07
❑ G-BAPF		Vickers Viscount 814	58	ex Southend, SE-FOY, G-BAPF, D-ANUN. Hot Air colours. CoA 13-6-90, de-reg 17-6-92		4-13
❑ G-BKRD		Cessna 320	67	ex Sandtoft, D-IACB, HB-LDN, N2201Q. Crashed 5-11-90, de-reg 14-4-92		4-05
❑ G-BNJJ		Cessna 152 II	87	ex Stamford area, Spanhoe, Nayland, Cranfield. Damaged 18-5-88, de-reg 3-2-95. Hulk		6-01
❑ G-BPAD		Piper Seneca 200T	78	ex N21208. Crashed 15-7-92, de-reg 20-2-97. Fuselage		6-01
❑ G-BPJT		Piper Cadet 161	88	ex Oxford, N9156X. Crashed 12-7-92, de-reg 31-10-94		4-03
❑ G-SULL		Piper Saratoga SP	81	ex Stamford, Spanhoe, N82818. Crashed 1-2-95, de-reg 17-5-95		8-98
❑ WT804	'831'	Hawker Hunter GA.11	55	ex Culdrose A2646, A2732 (22-10-85), Shawbury, FRADU, Lossiemouth, 247. Pole mounted, nose in ground		4-13
❑ XM404		Hunting Jet Provost T.3	59	ex Halton, Newton 8055BM (21-11-69), Shawbury, 3 FTS, 2 FTS	[1]	1-12
❑ XP150	'18'	Westland Wessex HAS.3	62	ex Lee-on-Solent A2764, A2719 (8-8-84), Wroughton, 772, 737, 814, HAS.1, 706		4-13
❑ XP680		Hunting Jet Provost T.4	62	ex St Athan 8460M (21-12-75), CAW, 6 FTS. 'Crash' scene		4-13

■ **[1]** Wings marked XM404 can also be found at East Wretham, Norfolk.

OLD SODBURY west of the A46, east of Chipping Sodbury

Lightning F.1A XM173 arrived from Preston, Lancs, on 11th August 2012 for storage. It moved to Malmesbury, Wilts, on 11th February 2013.

TIDENHAM on the A48 north-east of Chepstow

National Diving and Activity Centre Variety in the depths: HS 146-100 G-JEAU (sunk 17-12-07); a 'Cherokee' quoted as having come from "the local police and had been used as a training aid". It is illustrated on the web-site and labelled as a 'Jetstream 2000'!; the forward fuselage of Boeing 747-2B2B 5R-MFT (last noted Feb 2008); the fuselage of Sea Devon C.20 XK896 (G-RNAS - also Feb 2008); Wessex HAS.3 XS122 (Dec 2013) and Wessex HC.2 XT607 (Jan 2012). | **www.ndac.co.uk**

HAMPSHIRE

Includes the unitary authorities of Portsmouth and Southampton

ALTON on the A339 south-west of Farnham

Hillside Nurseries and **Departure Lounge Cafe**: The cafe-cum-airliner flourishes - readers declare that the grub is good.

◆ **Access:** *Beech View, Basingstoke Road, Alton, GU34 4BH.* **Open:** *Cafe -* **not** *necessarily the One-Eleven - open Mon to Fri 09:00 to 17:30, Sat and Sun 10:00 to 17:30* **Contact: 01420 80111** | **pastyfarley@hotmail.com**

❑ G-AWYV	BAC 111-501EX	69	ex Bournemouth, European, 5N-OSA ntu, European, BA, BCAL, Caledonian, BUA. CoA 24-6-04, de-reg 17-12-04. Forward fuselage	1-13

Travelling back to *W&R21* (p64) and the former Air Salvage International site here, the fuselage of Bandeirante G-ODUB was noted leaving by road on 7th September 2006, bound ultimately for Kingston-upon-Thames, Gtr London.

ANDOVER

Pup G-AVDF (last noted Apr 2002) has been deleted. Turnover at the helicopter workshop is swift and the Gazelles previously listed have been deleted: AH.1 G-CDNO (formerly XX432) flying by 2012; AH.1s XX418 (Feb 2010); XZ315 pod (Apr 2010); XZ321 (G-CDNS - Aug 2012); HT.3s XW902 (G-CGJY - Feb 2010, then G-RBIL Dec 2013); XZ933 (G-CGJZ - Mar 2010).

❑ G-AWKM	Beagle Pup 100	68	ex Swansea. CoA 29-6-84, de-reg 28-5-02	10-13
❑ G-BPHW*	Cessna 140	46	ex N76595. CoA 18-6-08, de-reg 14-12-10	10-13

The **Durney Collection** Rapide is *thought* to still be stored in the general area.

❑ G-ALAX	DH Dragon Rapide	45	ex Old Warden, Luton, RL948, ERS, 27 GCF. Brush-built CoA 8-3-67, de-reg 7-12-67. Stored	2-99

AWBRIDGE on the B3084 north of Romsey

The Pembroke cockpit *should* still be at a private location in the area.

❑ WV705	Percival Pembroke C.1	53	ex Wimborne, Bournemouth, BAC, 60, Wildenrath CS, 2 TAF CS, 152, 78, Khormaksar SF, 1417F, Levant CF, Eastleigh SF, MECS. SOC 24-11-70. Cockpit	10-03

Romsey Reclamation Ltd: By early 2012 a Robinson had appeared at the year here. It was written out of *W&R21* (p13) at Barkham, Berks, as 'gone' by January 2008.

❑ G-KENN*	Robinson R22B	87	ex -?-, Barkham, Stamford, Sandtoft. Damaged 31-10-94, de-reg 31-1-95	3-12

BASINGSTOKE on the M3 north-east of Winchester

GJD AeroTech Ltd: The company is involved in the parting out of airliners and most of this work is carried out at Bruntingthorpe, Leics - which see. While there is an administrative base in this area, airframes may well be located in a variety of locations. GJD's Sea Harrier ZA195 is on loan at Tangmere, W Sussex.

◆ **Access:** Private *location,* strictly *viewable by prior application* only | **www.gjdservices.co.uk**

❑ XR810	' Vickers VC-10 C.1K	66	ex St Athan, 10. *David Lord VC*. Last flight 4-11-05. Cockpit	6-10
❑ ZD230	Vickers VC-10 K.4	64	ex St Athan, 101, BA, BOAC G-ASGA. Last flight 16-12-05. Flightdeck	6-10
❑ ZD240	Vickers VC-10 K.4	67	ex St Athan, 101, BA, BOAC G-ASGL. Last flight 4-8-05. Flightdeck	6-10

Also: At Hampshire Fire and Rescue Service, the hulk of Tomahawk 112 G-BGZJ, last noted in January 2012, had gone by March 2012. Trident 3B cockpit G-AWZU moved via Booker, Bucks, to Gloucestershire, Glos, arriving 28th November 2013.

BLACKBUSHE AERODROME on the A30 west of Yateley — EGLK

Well-known landmark, pylon-mounted Robinson R22 G-XIIX, was taken off its lofty perch and roaded away on 17th August 2012. It is thought destined for a new life as a simulator.

❑ G-ARYI	Cessna 172C	62	ex N1560Y. CoA 10-8-03, de-reg 19-11-10	8-13
❑ G-RVSH	Vans RV-6A	04	CoA 11-8-06	8-12

BRAMLEY south-east of Tadley, east of the A340

Army Training Estate Home Counties:

❑ XK970		Westland Whirlwind HAR.10	56	ex Odiham 8789M, Akrotiri, 84, 230, CFS, Khormaksar SAR Flt, 228 JEHU. Poor state		1-14
❑ XZ219*		Westland Lynx AH.7	79	ex Middle Wallop, Fleetlands, 9 Rgt, 1 Rgt, 9 Rgt, 847, 9 Rgt, 3/4 Regt, 656, SFOR, 3 Rgt, 4 Rgt, 1 Rgt, 654, 669, 654, 669, 662, 3 Rgt, 653, 2 Rgt, 662. First noted 3-12	[1]	1-14
❑ XZ300*	'L'	Sud Gazelle AH.1	76	ex Fleetlands, Middle Wallop, 670, 664, 662. Crashed 14-2-97. Westland-built	[2]	1-14
❑ XZ661*	'V'	Westland Lynx AH.7	81	ex Middle Wallop, 671, 653, 1 Rgt, 655, 671, 652, 651. First noted 3-12	[3]	1-14
❑ -	TAD.900	Sud Gazelle AH.1 XW900	74	ex Aborfield, Middle Wallop SEAE, 660. Crashed 25-5-76		1-14

■ **[1]** Lynx XZ219 carries the boom of XZ654. **[2]** Gazelle XZ300 was first noted on site as far back as 7-00, but seems to have dropped off the radar by 4-04. **[3]** Lynx XZ661 carries the boom of another, so far anonymous, Lynx.

CALSHOT at the end of the B3053, south-east of Fawley

Calshot Castle and Heritage Area: The former RFC and RAF seaplane base hosted the last Schneider Trophy races, in 1929 and 1931. The final Sunderlands flew away in October 1953 and from the late 1950s and the slipways were the last resting place of the Saro Princess flying-boats. Calshot closed as an RAF station in May 1961. There are plenty of displays on Calshot's aviation days within the castle and great views of the Solent.

◆ **Access:** *At the end of the B3053 beyond Fawley and signed. Calshot Spit, Fawley, SO45 1BR.* **Open:** *1st Apr to 30th Oct daily, 10:00 to 16:30 - last admission 15:30pm.* **Contact: 023 8089 2077 | calshot.ac@hants.gov.uk | www.calshot.com/castle.html Thinx:** *The massive 'H' shed, now known as the Sunderland Hangar, is 600ft long and is now the incredible Calshot Activities Centre. There is public access to the area beyond museum opening times.*

CHILBOLTON AERODROME or Stonefield Park, east of the A3057, south of Andover

Last noted in May 2001, Luscombe Silvaire N1134K, in use for spares, has been deleted. Piper L-18C G-NICK, last recorded in May 2007, it is thought to have moved to East Anglia.

❑ G-PRIM	Piper Tomahawk 112	78	ex N2398A. CoA 25-12-01. Fuselage	8-11
❑ G-REPM	Piper Tomahawk 112	79	ex N2528D. CoA 9-10-95, de-reg 16-3-01. Cockpit	3-10

FAREHAM on the A27 west of Portsmouth

Fareham College: **Access** by *prior arrangement* **only | www.fareham.ac.uk**

❑ XT780	'636'	Westland Wasp HAS.1	66	ex Fleetlands, A2638 [2], ex A2716 (17-8-83), Fleetlands, 703, 706, 829	1-12

No.**1350 Squadron Air Cadets**: Farm Road

❑ XX745	'GV'	SEPECAT Jaguar GR.1A	74	ex Boscombe Down, Shawbury St Athan 9340M, 54, 16, 6, 16, 6, 226 OCU, 54, 6, 20, 226 OCU. Dam 31-5-00. Cockpit	10-09

FARNBOROUGH

Whittle Memorial: Dramatically displayed on the roundabout to the north of the airfield, close to the Southwood Golf Course, the Gloster E28/39 is a tribute to Sir Frank Whittle. This and the similar monument at Lutterworth, Leics (qv), were financed and built by the Sir Frank Whittle Commemorative Trust.

❑ –	Gloster E28/39 FSM	03	BAPC.285, unveiled 28-8-03	9-13

Prince's Mead Shopping Centre: The SE.5a still provides 'top cover' for the shoppers.

❑ 'D276'	'A'	RAF SE.5a replica	90	BAPC.208, built by AJD Engineering	8-13

FARNBOROUGH AIRFIELD east of the A325, north of Aldershot — EGLF

Farnborough Air Sciences Trust (FAST): The way this site has grown and been refined is a joy to behold. The mass of material held is incredible and only the tip of the iceberg can be displayed at any time. Exhibits are regularly changed, special events staged, and it is hoped to increase the space available within The Old Balloon School, renamed as Trenchard House in honour of one of its earliest 'bosses'. Supporting all aspects of FAST's activities is FASTA - the **Farnborough Air Sciences Trust Association** - which welcomes members, contact details below.

One hundred years after the death of the great aviation pioneer Samuel Franklin Cody, on 7th August 2013, a splendid statue and tribute to the man was unveiled at FAST. Fund-raising for this is still going on, with a pavement of 'named' bricks being laid down. More details on **www.codystatue.org.uk**

Andrew Lee and his dedicated Trident Ground Crew team have restored *Zulu-India* as a 'live' exhibit. Autoland developments with the Trident were a major occupation of RAE, hence its highly appropriate placing at FAST. The cockpit is opened up and 'powered up' most Sundays. See also Feltham, Gtr Lon. | email: **lasaviation@virginmedia.com**

◆ **Access:** *On the A325 - eastern boundary of the airfield - and 'brown signed'.* **Open:** *Sat, Sun and Bank Hols 10:00 to 16:00, other times by arrangement.* **Contact:** *Trenchard House, 85 Farnborough Road, Farnborough GU14 6TF* **01252 375050** | **manager@farnboroughairsciences.org.uk** | FASTA: **membership@farnboroughairsciences.org.uk** **www.airsciences.org.uk**

❑	G-ARRM		Beagle 206-1X	61	ex Shoreham, Kemble, Banwell, Brooklands, Shoreham, Duxford, Shoreham. CoA 28-12-64, de-reg 24-1-68	[1]	1-14
❑	G-AWZI		HS Trident 3B-101	71	ex Lasham, Alton, Reigate, Heathrow, BA, BEA. CoA 5-8-85, de-reg 9-7-87, arr 15-12-04. Cockpit	[2]	1-14
❑	-		Cody biplane replica	07	see notes	[3]	1-14
❑	WT309		EE Canberra B(I).6	55	ex Wycombe Air Park, Boscombe Down, Farnborough, Boscombe Down, A&AEE, HS. Arrived 2-98. Cockpit		1-14
❑	WV383		Hawker Hunter T.7	55	ex Boscombe Down, DERA, RAE, 28, Jever SF, Gütersloh SF, F.4, RAFFC. SOC 21-7-71, arr 13-4-00. *Hecate–Lady of the Night*	[4]	1-14
❑	XP516	'16'	Folland Gnat T.1	63	ex DS&TL, RAE, 8580M (8-2-78), 4 FTS. Arrived 8-6-04	[4]	1-14
❑	XS420		EE Lightning T.5	65	ex Walpole St Andrew, West Walton Highway, Narborough, Binbrook, LTF, 5, LTF, 226 OCU. SOC 16-6-88, arrived 3-9-03	[5]	1-14
❑	XV631		Westland Wasp HAS.1	69	ex RAE site, Wroughton, 829, *Cleopatra* Flt, *Eskimo* Flt, SOC 19-3-84, arrived 11-2-10. Cabin, stored	[4]	1-14
❑	XW241		Sud SA.330E Puma	68	ex DS&TL, RAE Bedford, F-ZJUX. SOC 10-11-88, arrived 29-8-07	[4]	1-14
❑	XW566		SEPECAT Jaguar B.08	71	ex DS&TL, RAE, A&AEE. Last flown 17-6-85, arr 8-6-04	[4]	1-14
❑	XW863*		Sud Gazelle HT.2	73	ex Fairoaks, Cranfield, Arborfield, Middle Wallop TAD.022 (14-11-95), Wroughton, 705. On loan. Arrived 11-6-13		1-14
❑	XW934	'Y'	HS Harrier T.4	73	ex DS&TL, 20, 233 OCU, 1. Arr 28-8-07. 20 Sqn colours		1-14
❑	XZ166		Westland Lynx HAS.2	75	ex QinetiQ, RAE site, A&AEE, Rolls-Royce G-1-2, A&AEE. SOC 18-12-80, arrived 10-09. Cabin, stored		1-14
❑	ZG631		Northrop Chukar D.2 drone	~	stored		1-14
❑	ZJ496		GAF Jindivik 104A drone	~	ex Boscombe Down, Llanbedr, A92-901. Arrived 10-5-05	[4]	1-14
❑	-		EE Lightning	~	procedure trainer	[6]	1-14
❑	-	'35'	X-RAE.1 drone	~	'raspberry ripple' colours		1-14
❑	-		Short MATS-B drone	~	(SBAS-029)		1-14

■ **[1]** The prototype Beagle 206 is owned by the Brooklands Museum (see Brooklands, Surrey). **[2]** The Trident cockpit is on loan from Andrew Lee - see narrative above. **[3]** The incredible Cody is displayed within its own hangar. It is a replica of the British Army Aeroplane No.1A which made the first sustained flight by a British-built aircraft on 16-10-08, just a stone's throw from FAST's site. **[4]** Airframes on loan from DS&TL / QinetiQ. The Jindivik carries 12 mission markers. **[5]** Lightning T.5 on loan from Richard Hall who acquired it from Lakes Lightnings in July 2012 - take a look at **www.xs420.com** **[6]** The procedures trainer is fitted with an ejector seat marked XM171.

Royal Aircraft Establishment Heritage Quarter: Within the Farnborough Business park which occupies much of the former RAE site can be found several listed buildings that reflect the significance of the airfield. The skeletal 1911 balloon hangar has been erected close to its original location and serves as a unique symbol of the Balloon Factory and Royal Aircraft Factory days. The Grade I-listed Building Q121 is the famous wind tunnel building and a local landmark. The former Weapons Testing Building, Q134, is now called **The Hub** and includes a display entitled 'The Secret Factory' and the Aviators Cafe. Also within The Hub is the **National Aerospace Library**, which is open to the general public. More details via **01252 701038** | **hublibrary@aerosociety.com** | **www.aerosociety.com**

Defence Science and Technology Laboratory / QinetiQ: Lynx XZ649, last noted in March 2003, moved to Bristol, Glos. Not reported since February 2002, the anonymous Mi-24 and MiG-23 or -27, have been deleted.

❑	XV344	HS Buccaneer S.2C	67	ex Boscombe Down, RAE, 809, 800, 809. Withdrawn 9-94. *Night bird*. 'Gate'	6-13
❑	162958	HS AV-8B Harrier II	~	ex Basingstoke, St Athan, USMC, VMA-214. Cockpit, sim	12-09

FLEET on the A323 north-west of Aldershot

The flight deck of a Bristol 170 *should* be in the area. Large chunks can also still be found at Enstone.

❑ C-FDFC		Bristol 170 Mk.31	54	ex Enstone, G-BISU Instone, ZK-EPH, NZ5912, ZK-BVI, G-18-194. Crashed 18-7-96. Cockpit	12-05

FLEETLANDS on the B3334 south of Fareham

Vector Aerospace Helicopter Services UK: Rotary wing repair and maintenance is run by the multi-national contractor. From the *W&R* point of view, it is the **Training Centre** that is of interest. Sea King HAS.1 XV669 departed by road on 19th February 2010, with no 'forwarding address'.

❑ XS539	'435'	Westland Wasp HAS.1	64	A2640 [2], ex A2718 [2] (7-1-92), Lee-on-Solent, Portland, 829, 703, 829, 848, 829	[1] 11-12
❑ XW844	'GAZ.4'	Sud Gazelle AH.1	72	ex Wroughton. 659. Westland-built	11-12
❑ XZ213	TAD.213	Westland Lynx AH.1	79	ex Wroughton, Middle Wallop, Wroughton, 659	11-12
❑ ZA133	'831'	Westland Sea King HU.6	81	ex Gosport, 771, 820, 810, 819, 820, 826, 810, 829, 826. SOC 3-4-06	11-12
❑ ZD281*	'K'	Westland Lynx AH.1	83	ex Middle Wallop. First noted 10-12	11-12
❑ QP-31		Westland Lynx HC.28	77	ex Almondbank, Wroughton, Qatar Police	11-12

■ **[1]** Wasp XS539 attacked the Argentine submarine *Santa Fe* with missiles off South Georgia 25-4-82.

GOSPORT on the B3333 south of Fareham

HMS *Sultan*: Defence School of Marine Engineering (DSMarE) On 1st October 2012 what had been Gosport branch of the **Defence College of Aeronautical Engineering** had changed its name to DSMarE. Ultimately, this facility is to re-locate to the tri-service technical training 'campus' at Lyneham, Wilts - which see. Also based here, seemingly with no change to the stationery, is the **Air Engineering and Survival School**. A wholly fictitious unit, **760 Training Squadron**, 'operates' the airframes here and has been given some codes in the '2xx' series. Wessex HU.5 XT771 makes a re-appearance in this edition. It was written out of *W&R22* (p67) as not having been noted since April 2006, but remained steadfastly here!

Departures: **Harrier** GR.3 XV741 offered for tender 8-12, left by road 13-9-12 for Selby, N Yorks; GR.3 XV808 offered for tender 8-12, to Bridgnorth, Shrop, 13-9-12; GR.9A ZD465 arrived from Wittering, Cambs, by 3-12, but moved to Cosford, Shropshire, 7-11-13; **Lynx** AH.7 XZ174 moved to Portsmouth, Hampshire, by 12-11; HAS.3S ZD254 departed to Yeovilton 18-9-13, then moved to a Lincolnshire-based disposal organisation; **Sea Harrier** FA.2 ZD607 to Bicester, Oxfordshire, 23-8-12; **Sea King** HAS.6 XZ921 departed for Colsterworth, Lincs, 5-11-13; HAS.6 ZA128 to Cosford, Shropshire, by 5-12; HC.4 ZD477 arrived by 8-12, then to Bruntingthorpe, Leics, 4-12-13; HC.4 ZD478 to Hixon, Staffs, 2-4-12 and auctioned; HC.4 ZD627 arrived 12-10-12, then to Bruntingthorpe, Leics, 26-11-13; HAS.6 ZD633 departed for Colsterworth, Lincs, 5-11-13; HC.4 ZG822 arrived by 4-12, then to Bruntingthorpe, Leics, 4-12-13; Mk.47 774 and 775 to Hixon, Staffs, 2-4-12. First noted in 12-11, the hulk of **Merlin** HC.3 ZJ138 moved to Boscombe Down, Wilts, by 3-13. **Wessex** HU.5 XS488 departed 11-13, bound ultimately for Layer Marney, Essex; HU.5 XS496 removed by 8-12, likely scrapped; HU.5 XT455 was dumped outside by 11-12 and moved to Hixon, Staffs, 8-13; HU.5 XT761 was written out of this location in *W&R22* (p67); it survived, but by 6-13 moved to Culdrose, Cornwall.

❑ XP110	'55'	Westland Wessex HAS.3	62	ex A2636 [2], A2714 [2], A2728 (25-4-85), Lee-on-Solent, Fleetlands, 737, 706, HAS.1, 737, 706, 737	8-13
❑ XR498*	'X'	Westland Wessex HC.2	63	ex Cosford 9342M, Shawbury, 72, 60, 72, A&AEE. Arrived 11-9-12	8-13
❑ XR518	'O'	Westland Wessex HC.2	64	ex Shawbury, 60, 72, 22, 18, 72, 18	8-13
❑ XS514	'YL'	Westland Wessex HU.5	64	ex A2653 [2], Lee-on-Solent A2740 (7-7-86), 845, 847, 845, A&AEE, 845, 781, 845	8-13
❑ XS568	'441'	Westland Wasp HAS.1	64	ex A2637 [2], Fleetlands A2715 (18-5-83), 829, 771	8-13
❑ XT453	'B'	Westland Wessex HU.5	65	ex Culdrose, Gosport A2666[2], Lee-on-Solent A2756 (22-7-86), Yeovilton, 845, 707, 845, 707	8-13
❑ XT484	'H'	Westland Wessex HU.5	66	ex A2655 [2], Lee-on-Solent A2742 (3-7-86), 845, 846	4-13
❑ XT485	'621'	Westland Wessex HU.5	66	ex A2680 [2], Lee-on-Solent A2769 (30-3-88), 772, Lee SAR Flt, 772, 771, 846, 848, 847	8-13
❑ XT771*	'620'	Westland Wessex HU.5	67	ex A2673 [2], Lee-on-Solent A2761 (11-4-88), 772, 845, 848, 707. See note above	8-13
❑ XV370	'260'	Sikorsky SH-3D Sea King	66	ex A2682 [2], Lee-on-Solent A2771 (8-1-90), ETPS, A&AEE, Yeovil, G-ATYU de-reg 25-10-66	8-13
❑ XV625	'471'	Westland Wasp HAS.1	68	ex A2649 [2], Lee-on-Solent, Culdrose, Manadon A2735 (5-10-71), 829	8-13

❑ XV642	'259'	Westland Sea King HAS.2A	69	ex A2614 [3], Lee-on-Solent A2613 (20-3-91), Yeovil, A&AEE, Yeovil, A&AEE, Yeovil	8-13
❑ XV655	'270'	Westland Sea King HAS.6	69	ex A2805 (10-12-01), 814, 819, 826, 814, 824, 826, 814, 826, 819, 737, 824	8-13
❑ XV660	'269'	Westland Sea King HAS.6	70	ex A2810 (10-12-01), Culdrose, 819, 814, 810, 706, 810, 819, 810, 824, 706	8-13
❑ XV665	'507'	Westland Sea King HAS.6	70	ex A2812 (10-12-01), 810, 820, 810, 824, 706, 819, 826	8-13
❑ XV675	'701'	Westland Sea King HAS.6	70	ex A2622 [3] (1-5-02), 819, 706, 824, A&AEE, 814, 819, 814, 819, 737, 819, A&AEE, 819	8-13
❑ XV676	'ZE'	Westland Sea King HAS.6CR	70	ex 845, 846, Fleetlands, 771, 810, 819, A&AEE, 819, 824, 814, 706, 826, 706, 819, A&AEE, 819. Arrived 18-3-10. Stored	8-13
❑ XV696	'267'	Westland Sea King HAS.6	71	ex A2813 (1-5-02), Culdrose, 814, 819, 826, 810, 825, 814, 820	8-13
❑ XV700	'ZC'	Westland Sea King HAS.6CR	71	824, 814, 819, 814, 706, 814, 819, 814, 825, 706, 820, 810, 849, 846, 845. Arrived 2-4-09	8-13
❑ XV703	'ZD'	Westland Sea King HAS.6CR	71	ex Fleetlands, 845, 846, 771, 819, 820, 819, 826, 706, 814, 826, 706, 820, 824	8-13
❑ XV708	'501'	Westland Sea King HAS.6	71	ex A2643 [3], A2635 [4] (1-5-02), 810, 819, 706, 819, 706, 820, 826, 737	8-13
❑ XV711	'515'	Westland Sea King HAS.6	72	ex A2808 (25-3-02), 810, 819, 814, 824, 814, 706, 820, 706, 824, 706, 814, 819, 814, 819	8-13
❑ XV713	'018'	Westland Sea King HAS.6	72	ex A2804 (19-5-00), Fleetlands, 820, 810, 706, 826, 824, 826, 810, 814, 820	8-13
❑ XV724	'DD41'	Westland Wessex HC.2	68	ex Shawbury, Fleetlands, 22, SARTS, 18. Arrived 15-1-02	8-13
❑ XX443	'Y'	Sud Gazelle AH.1	76	ex Middle Wallop, 658, 662, 663, 3 Regt, 669, 659. Crashed 28-9-97, arrived 18-3-09. Stored	8-13
❑ XZ305	TAD.020	Sud Gazelle AH.1	76	ex Middle Wallop, Arborfield, 3 Regt, 665, 662, 654, GCF. Arrived 26-11-08	8-13
❑ XZ576		Westland Sea King HAS.6	76	ex A2806 (1-5-02), A&AEE, A&AEE, 824, A&AEE, 820	8-13
❑ XZ579	'707'	Westland Sea King HAS.6	77	ex A2843 (25-7-07), Brize Norton, Gosport, 819, 820, 814, 820, 819, 826, 824, 706, 814	8-13
❑ XZ580	'ZB'	Westland Sea King HAS.6CR	77	ex Fleetlands, 846, 845, 846, Boscombe Down, Gosport, 819, 814, 810, 706, 737, 706, 825, 814. Arrived 8-12	8-13
❑ XZ581	'269'	Westland Sea King HAS.6	77	ex A2638 [3], A2627 [3] (1-5-02), Fleetlands, 814, 810, 826, 819, 824, A&AEE, 826, 706, 814	8-13
❑ XZ922	'ZA'	Westland Sea King HAS.6CR	79	846, 845, 846, Boscombe Down, Gosport, 819, 810, 826, 810, 826, 814, 706. Arrived 31-3-10	8-13
❑ XZ930	'Q'	Sud Gazelle HT.3	78	ex A2713 [3] (17-11-00), Shawbury, 2 FTS, CFS. Westland-built	8-13
❑ ZA127	'509'	Westland Sea King HAS.6	80	ex A2846, 706, 810, 826, 810, A&AEE, 820. Arrived 19-7-01	1-13
❑ ZA168	'830'	Westland Sea King HU.6	82	ex A2844 (12-3-09), 771, 820, 849, 820, 810, 819, 826, 814	8-13
❑ ZA170		Westland Sea King HAS.5	82	ex A2830, A2645 [3] (2-4-04), Fleetlands, 706, 810. Black c/s	8-13
❑ ZD625*	'P'	Westland Sea King HC.4	84	ex 848, 846, 848, 846, 845, 846, 707. Arrived by 11-12	8-13
❑ ZD630	'012'	Westland Sea King HAS.6	84	ex Culdrose, 820, 814, 820. Arrived 19-1-04	8-13
❑ ZD634	'503'	Westland Sea King HAS.6	85	ex A2845 (12-3-09), 771, 810, 819, A&AEE, 819	8-13
❑ ZD637	'700'	Westland Sea King HAS.6	85	ex A2811 (15-11-02), 819. 771, 819, 814, 810, 819, A&AEE, 819. Stored	8-13
❑ ZF123*	'WW'	Westland Sea King HC.4	87	ex 848, 846, 848, 772, 846, 772. Arrived 18-5-12	8-13
❑ ZF649		EHI EH-101 PP5	89	ex A2714 [3] (9-4-01), Weston-super-Mare, Yeovil	8-13
❑ ZG816	'014'	Westland Sea King HAS.6	89	ex 820, 819, 820. Arrived 23-7-03	8-13
❑ ZG817	'702'	Westland Sea King HAS.6	90	ex A2814 (19-6-02), 819, 810	8-13
❑ ZG818	'707'	Westland Sea King HAS.6	90	ex Fleetlands, 814, 819, 814. Arrived 6-3-00	8-13
❑ ZG819	'265'	Westland Sea King HAS.6	90	ex A2654 [4], A2641 [4] (19-6-02), 814, 820	8-13
❑ ZG875	'013'	Westland Sea King HAS.6	90	ex A2816 (30-10-00), Yeovilton, 820, 814. Crashed 12-6-99. Wreck	8-13
❑ 776		Westland Sea King Mk.47	75	ex Egyptian Navy. Dumped out by 11-12	1-13

Plus: The following Sea Kings have arrived, but as yet do not come into the long-term storage category. Arrival/first noted dates in brackets: HU.5 XV699 '823' (8-13); HC.4 ZA291 'N' (4-4-13); HC.4 ZA313 'M' (1-13); HC.4 ZD479 'WQ' (27-3-13); HC.4 ZD525 'P' (8-12); HC.4 ZE425 'WR' (7-8-13); HC.4 ZE426 'WX' (1-13); HC.4 ZF119 'WY' (3-4-13); HC.4 ZF121 'T' (1-13); HC.4 ZK507 'F' (8-13).

GREATHAM Wessex HC.2 XR506 departed Longmoor Camp for Selby, N Yorks, on 19th November 2012.

HAMBLE south-east of Southampton

GE Aviation: Hamble Aerostructures became part of GE during the summer of 2013. On the B3397, opposite 'The Harrier' public house, is a Gnat, guarding the former Folland plant. Another example is in store.

❑ XM693		Folland Gnat T.1	60	ex Abingdon, Bicester 7891M (10-8-65), A&AEE	7-13
❑ XP542*	'42'	Folland Gnat T.1	63	ex Southampton, Shrivenham, St Athan 8575M (5-1-78), 4 FTS. Stored. First noted 8-12	8-12

HEATH END on the B3051 north-west of Tadley

J Brant Reclamations: An architectural recycling specialist close to Brimpton Common has a much-battered Cessna. This machine was last noted leaving Bournemouth Airport, Dorset, in August 2005 - see *W&R20*, p50 | **www.jbrant.co.uk**

❑ EI-BAS*		Cessna F.172M	75	ex Bournemouth. Reims-built. Fuselage and wings	10-12

KINGSCLERE on the A339 north-west of Basingstoke

❑ G-AOEX		Thruxton Jackaroo	44	ex Southampton, Tiger Moth II NM175 (Morris-built), 63 GCF, 11 RFS. CoA 3-2-68	8-12
❑ G-BADV		Brochet MB.50	53	ex Ludlow, Dunkeswell, F-PBRJ. CoA 9-5-79	9-05

LASHAM AERODROME west of Golden Pot, north-west of Alton EGHL

Gliding Heritage Centre: Thanks to a bequest by the late Chris Wills, a pioneer of vintage gliders, the first phase of this visitor centre - the Chris Wills Memorial Hangar - was opened on 4th August 2013. The gliders given below represent the 'core' collection, but there is a bewildering list of other types that have been 'volunteered' for occasional loan; the web-site provides details of these. As befitting the world of silent flight, the emphasis is on informality and the 'best time' to visit is quoted as Sunday afternoons. On the first Sunday of each month, the team will try to fly various inmates.

◆ **Access:** *West of Golden Pot, follow signs for the Gliding Centre.* **Open:** *See the narrative above - Sunday afternoons, otherwise by prior application.* **Contact:** *Lasham Airfield, Alton, Hants, GU34 5SS* | **visits@glidingheritage.org.uk** | **www.glidingheritage.org.uk**

❑ G-AEKV*	DZQ	Kronfeld Drone	37	BGA.2510, ex Brooklands, CoA 6-10-60, de-reg 14-1-99. Arrived 1-9-13	[1]	9-13
❑ G-ALJW*		Jacobs Schweyer Weihe	43	BGA.448, ex G-ALJW, BGA.448, Luftwaffe LO+WQ		8-13
❑ ACF*		Abbott-Baynes Scud III ✈	36	BGA.283, ex Dunstable, G-ALJR, BGA.283. Arr 18-7-13	[2]	8-13
❑ ATH*		Slingsby Gull III	39	BGA.643, ex Brooklands, TJ711. CoA 20-6-04. Arr 18-7-13	[1]	8-13
❑ BZM*		Slingsby T.45 Swallow	67	BGA.1365. CoA 4-6-05		8-13
❑ DPG*		München Mü 13D III ✈	57	BGA.2267, ex D-1327	[3]	8-13
❑ DPZ*		Slingsby T.34A Sky	~	BGA.2284, ex Pershore, Ontur, HB-561. Arrived 7-13		7-13
❑ ERZ*		Oberlerchner Mg 19a ✈	55	BGA.2903, ex OE-0324	[4]	8-13
❑ HFZ*		Abbott-Baynes Scud I rep	95	BGA.3922, Brooklands. Arrived 18-7-13	[1]	8-13
❑ -*		Colditz Cock replica	11	ex *Escape from Colditz*	[5]	8-13
❑ –*		Manuel Willow Wren	32	BGA.162, ex Brooklands, Bishop's Stortford. On loan *The Willow Wren*	[1]	8-13
❑ –*		Manuel Hawk	72	BGA.1778, ex Fairoaks. Arrived 26-8-13	[6]	8-13

■ **[1]** On loan from Brooklands Museum, Surrey. **[2]** Scud donated by Laurie Woodage. **[3]** Mü 13 donated by Geoff Moore. **[4]** Mg 19 donated by Alpine Sportflieger Club. **[5]** On loan from its builder, South East Aircraft Services. **[6]** Hawk donated by Tom Coldwell.

Airfield: By August 2013, the fuselage of Boeing 737 G-PJPJ had been painted in US Airways colours and mounted within a huge floodable 'bath'. It was playing the part of Airbus A320 N106US, which ditched in the River Hudson following multiple birdstrikes on 15th January 2009, for a film probably to be called *The Miracle of the Hudson*. In use for cockpit filming was 737 TF-ELL. There is a healthy in-and-out of airliners here, only long-termers are listed.

❑ G-BLGB	Short 360-100	84	ex BRA / Loganair, G-14-3641. Damaged 9-2-98, CoA 31-3-98, de-reg 19-11-98	3-06
❑ EI-DOO	Boeing 737-400	87	ex KD Avia, D-AGEB, N222DZ. 'Fire Trainer'	8-12
❑ OO-DHR	Boeing 727-31	67	ex DHL, N932FT, N1958. Fuselage	11-09
❑ TF-ELL*	Boeing 737-210C	69	ex Southend, N41026, F-GGFI, N4906. Cockpit. See above	8-13
❑ VP-BAA	Boeing 727-51	66	ex Mexican AF TP-05, XC-UJA, Mexican AF TP-01, N477US	3-13
❑ VP-CMO	Boeing 727-212/RE	80	ex N31TR, VR-COJ, N310AS, 9V-SGJ	8-12

❑ 5N-BLH		Boeing 737-522		91	ex VP-BTG, N916UA. Stored	8-12
❑ -*		Boeing 737-500	G-PJPJ	94	ex G-GFFJ, VT-JAZ, 9M-MFH. First noted 3-13 Fuselage, US Airways colours - see above.	8-13

LEE-ON-SOLENT AIRFIELD, or Daedalus Airfield, east of the B3385, south of Fareham — EGHF

B-N Group: A couple of airframes have made the trek from Bembridge.

❑ G-BVHY*	BN-2T-4R Turbo-Islander	00	ex Bembridge. Unflown. De-reg 6-4-04.	2-12
❑ G-BWPM*	BN-2T-4R Turbo-Islander	97	ex Bembridge. Unbuilt kit. De-reg 19-10-00	2-12

Others:

❑ G-AALY	DH Moth	29	ex F-AJKM, G-AALY. CoA 15-5-05. Stored	12-12
❑ G-ACLL*	DH Leopard Moth	34	ex Jurby, AW165, AFEE, 7 AACU, 6 AACU, Ringway SF. CoA 6-12-95. First noted 10-12	12-12

LYMINGTON on the A337 east of Christchurch

Briefly on show at Bournemouth, a Sea Harrier arrived in late 2013 at a *private* location locally.

❑ ZD614*	'122'	HS Sea Harrier FA.2	86	ex Bournemouth, Ipswich, St Athan, Yeovilton, 800, 801, 800, 801, 800, 801, 800, 801, 800. Crashed 8-10-01. Arrived 24-11-13	1-14

MIDDLE WALLOP AIRFIELD on the A343 south-west of Andover — EGVP

Museum of Army Flying (MoAF): This museum is TARDIS-like, there is so much to see. Don 't forget to visit the 'Apache Cafe' which offers views of the activity on the airfield.

Aircraft on loan: Duxford, Cambs: Auster XP281; Southampton, Hants: Skeeter XL770; Sunderland, N&T, Pucará A-528; Winthorpe, Notts: Gazelle XW276.

◆ **Access:** *Off the A343, 'brown signed' from the A303. Middle Wallop, Stockbridge, SO20 8DY.* **Open:** *Daily 10:00 to 16:30 - last entry 16:00.* **Contact: 01264 784421 | info@flying-museum.org.uk| www.armyflying.com**

❑ G-AXKS		Bell 47G-4A		69	ex Bristow, ARWF, G-17-8. Westland-built. CoA 21-9-82, de-reg 9-9-82. Acquired 22-4-82		1-14
❑ 'G285'	'E'	Slingsby Kirby Kite	ACH	36	ex G-ALNH, BGA.285. Acquired 1989		1-14
❑ 'B-415'		AFEE 10/42 replica		82	BAPC.163, ex Wimborne. Acquired 7-82	[1]	1-14
❑ P-5		Hafner Rotachute III		43	8381M, ex Henlow. Acquired 1983	[2]	1-14
❑ N5195		Sopwith Pup	G-ABOX	16	ex Redhill. Acquired, on loan, 1985. CoA 22-4-93	[3]	1-14
❑ 'T9707'		Miles Magister I	T9708	40	ex Cardington, Manchester, Hendon 8378M, Gaydon, Henlow, G-AKKR, 'T9967', T9708, 51 MU, 16 EFTS, 239. CoA 10-4-65, de-reg 16-7-69. Acquired 6-99	[2]	1-14
❑ 'KJ351'		Airspeed Horsa II		45	BAPC.80. Acquired 1968. Fuselage	[4]	1-14
❑ –		Airspeed Horsa II		~	fuselage	[5]	1-14
❑ –		Airspeed Horsa II		~	cockpit	[5]	1-14
❑ 'HH268'		GAL Hotspur II replica		95	BAPC.261. Acquired 13-12-01	[6]	1-14
❑ TJ569		Auster 5	G-AKOW	45	ex PH-NAD, PH-NEG, TJ569, 652, 660, 659. CoA 26-6-82, de-reg 5-8-87. Acquired 10-81		1-14
❑ TK777		GAL Hamilcar I		44	ex Christian Malford. Birmingham Railway Carriage and Wagon Co-built. Forward fuselage	[7]	1-14
❑ WG432	'L'	DHC Chipmunk T.10		51	ex AFWF, LAS, Bri UAS, 19 RFS, Cam UAS, 4 BFTS. Acquired 1997		1-14
❑ WJ358		Auster AOP.6	G-ARYD	52	ex Perth, WJ358, 651, 657, 1913 Flt. De-reg 5-8-87. Acquired 7-80		1-14
❑ WZ721		Auster AOP.9		55	ex Life Guards Air Sqn, 4 RTR, 16 Flt, 14 Flt, 7 Flt, 11 Flt, 6 Flt, 652. SOC 1-9-66. Acquired 1969. *Dragon*, 4 RTR colours		1-14
❑ XG502		Bristol Sycamore HR.14		55	ex gate, Wroughton, Bristol, JEHU. Acquired 1982		1-14
❑ XK776		ML Utility Mk 1		57	ex Cardington, Middle Wallop, A&AEE. Acquired 7-82	[8]	1-14
❑ XL813		Saro Skeeter AOP.12		59	ex ARWF, 4 Regt, 9 Flt. SOC 25-3-68		1-14
❑ 'XM819'		EP Prospector		59	ex Durrington, Middle Wallop, Blackbushe, Lympne. Acquired 14-5-81	[9]	1-14

❑	XP821	'MCO'	DHC Beaver AL.1	61	ex Shawbury, Kemble, St Athan, Defence Attaché, Laos, 130 Flt, 30 Flt RASC, 656. Acquired 2-10-85. White/grey colours	1-14
❑	XP822		DHC Beaver AL.1	61	ex Duxford, Middle Wallop, Shawbury, Kemble, 132 Flt, 667, 18 Flt. Acquired 15-5-93. Displayed outside	1-14
❑	XP847		Westland Scout AH.1	61	ex AETW, Wroughton, Yeovil. Acquired 1984	1-14
❑	XP910	'D'	Westland Scout AH.1	63	ex SEAE. Crashed 13-9-89, acquired 2002. Displayed outside	1-14
❑	XR232		Sud Alouette AH.2	60	ex Historic Flight, Wroughton, A&AEE, Middle Wallop, EW&AU, 656, A&AEE, 16 Flt, 6 Flt, F-WEIP. Acquired 5-92	1-14
❑	XT108	'U'	Bell Sioux AH.1	64	ex Duxford, Yeovilton, Middle Wallop, D&T Flt, Middle Wallop. Agusta-built. Acquired 6-84	1-14
❑	XV127		Westland Scout AH.1	67	ex Fleetlands, Chelsea, Wroughton, 655. Acquired 1995	1-14
❑	XX153		Westland Lynx AH.1	72	ex Yeovil, Wattisham 9320M, Foulness, Westland. Acquired 28-10-03	1-14
❑	XZ675	'H'	Westland Lynx AH.7	81	ex Yeovilton, GDSH Middle Wallop, 671, 4 Rgt, 671, 652. Acquired 7-8-11	1-14
❑	XZ795		Northrop Shelduck D.1 drone	~	'Fleet Target Group, Royal Navy' titles	1-14
❑	ZA209		Short MATS-B drone	~	-	1-14
❑	ZA737		Sud Gazelle AH.1	80	ex 1 Rgt, 847, Fleetlands 'hack', 670, ARWS. Westland-built. Acquired 12-99	1-14
❑	-*		FRL ASAT RPV	~	*Spirit of Kyle*. (ASAT = Advanced Subsonic Aerial Target)	1-14
❑	-*		Tasuma MMT-100 RPV	~	-	1-14
❑	AE-409	'656'	Bell UH-1H Iroquois	72	ex Duxford, Middle Wallop, 656, Stanley, Argentine Army, 72-21506. Acquired 7-82	1-14
❑	111989		Cessna L-19A Bird Dog	51	N33600, ex Fort Rucker, Alabama. Acquired 1982	1-14
❑	'243809'		Waco CG-4A Hadrian	44	BAPC.185, ex Burtonwood, Shrewsbury. Acquired 1985. Fuselage	1-14
❑	70-15990		Bell AH-1F Cobra	70	ex US Army. Acquired 2003	1-14

■ **[1]** The AFEE 10/42 is centred on an original Willys Jeep and on loan from the Wessex Aviation Society. **[2]** Rotachute III and Magister are on loan from the RAF Museum. **[3]** N5195, with an 80hp Le Rhone, was the second Pup restoration by Lt Cdr K C D St Cyrien - G-ABOX being registered 9-84. See under Hendon, Gtr Lon, for his first, N5182 (G-APUP). **[4]** Largest Horsa airframe on show is 'KJ351' (a Thunderbolt II serial) which is an amalgam of TL659, LH208 and 8569M. TL659 was used until salvaged in 1969 as a sports changing room in Abingdon jail. **[5]** Another nose and other large Horsa sections can be found within Hayward Hall. Several other sections are in store. **[6]** GAL Hotspur re-creation has adopted the identity and colours of an example that flew with the Shobdon-based 5 Glider Training School. **[7]** Hamilcar (made up of parts from NX836 and TK718 - see also Bovington, Dorset) is a 'walk-through' exhibit, under restoration. **[8]** ML Utility inflatable had three wing options, 'Clouy', 'Delta' and 'Gadfly'; all are in store. **[9]** Prospector is largely G-APXW, which crashed 9-73, but also has rear fuselage of G-ARDG (see Blackburn, Lancs) and bits of G-APWZ.

Army Air Corps Historic Aircraft Flight / Army Air Corps Reserve Collection Trust: The flight's badge carries a Latin motto which translates as 'Let Their Glory Not Fade'. For some years, the Flight has not been able to act as a display team, with very occasional appearances of single items at events. The website describes the current status as "suspended animation". The spate of civilian registrations paves the way for the aircraft to move to the aegis of CAA Permit to Fly certification. This process is expected to take some time...

◆ **Access**: **Not** *available without prior permission* | **www.army.mod.uk/aviation**

❑	N6985		DH Tiger Moth	G-AHMN	39	ex Mk.II, 2 EFTS, 22 EFTS, Andover SF. Crashed 29-5-00, CoA 27-5-02, de-reg 14-9-00		3-10
❑	WD325	'N'	DHC Chipmunk T.10 ✈		51	ex BFWF, LAS, 12 GCF, 17 RFS	[1]	11-13
❑	XL812		Saro Skeeter AOP.12	G-SARO	59	ex Wattisham, Saxmundham, Middle Wallop. SOC 28-5-69. CoA 30-10-06, de-reg 14-4-10	[1]	4-13
❑	XL814		Saro Skeeter AOP.12		59	ex 1 Wing, 2 Wing, 651		4-10
❑	XP242		Auster AOP.9	G-BUCI	61	ex AFWF, Shrivenham, 653. CoA 19-5-00, de-reg 5-3-01		2-14
❑	XP820		DHC Beaver AL.1 ✈	G-CICP	61	ex 7 Regt, 667, 132 Flt RCT, 130 Flt RCT, 30 Flt RASC, 11 Flt, 656	[1]	2-14
❑	XP884		Westland Scout AH.1		63	ex Arborfield, Middle Wallop. Spares		3-11
❑	XR244		Auster AOP.9 ✈	G-CICR	62	ex AFWF. With AAC HAF from 11-9-81	[1]	2-14
❑	XR379		Sud Alouette AH.2	G-CICS	61	ex Almondbank, 667, 16F, 6(A) Flt, F-WEIN	[1]	2-14
❑	XT131	'B'	Bell Sioux AH.1	G-CICN	64	ex D&T Flight. Agusta-built	[1] [2]	2-14
❑	XT151		Bell Sioux AH.1		65	ex ARWF. Westland-built. Spares		3-11
❑	XT626	'Q'	W'land Scout AH.1	G-CIBW	66	ex 666, Wroughton, 656, BATUS, 656, 663	[1] [2]	2-14

■ **[1]** Listed as on strength with AACHAF, the Skeeter static only. **[2]** Registered to the MoD 10-13 and 11-13

No.**2 (Training) Aircrew Technical Training Detachment / No.70 Aircraft Workshops / Multi-Platform Support Unit** (MPSU): early in 2013, the **Gazelle Depth Support Hub** was renamed as the MPSU, perhaps for the sake of it. Several airframes serve in this role, within Stockwell Hall. The AAC Exhibition Unit has a Gazelle cockpit, used as a travelling recruitment airframe.

MPSU is responsible for supporting the wind-down of AAC Gazelles, and now Lynx (hence multi-platform...). Redundant airframes are stripped of usable items (in a similar manner to the Tornado RTP programme at Leeming, N Yorks) and *quickly* processed therefore not requiring a formal listing within *W&R*. Gazelles are due to remain in Army service until 2018. Last noted on the dump in August 2011, the pod of Lynx AH.7 XZ181 is believed to have expired.

❑ WZ724		Auster AOP.9		55	ex 'WZ670', 7432M (22-5-57), LAS. Tan/brown c/s. Gate		11-13
❑ 'XT123'	'D'	Bell Sioux AH.1	XT827	67	ex Wroughton, Yeovilton, Coypool, 3 CBAS. Westland-built. Gate	[1]	11-13
❑ XT638	'N'	Westland Scout AH.1		66	ex Fleetlands, 666. 666 Sqn badge. Gate		11-13
❑ XX392		Sud Gazelle AH.1		75	ex Shawbury, 3 Flt, 670, ARWS, 3 CBAS. Westland-built. Gate	[2]	11-13
❑ XZ298*		Sud Gazelle AH.1		77	Westland-built. Pod, instructional		1-13
❑ XZ327		Sud Gazelle AH.1		77	ex Fleetlands. Westland-built. Travelling recruiting aid		8-13
❑ XZ613		Westland Lynx AH.7		80	ex Arborfield, 655, 665, A&AEE, Yeovil, 657, 654. Inst	[3]	3-11
❑ XZ672*		Westland Lynx AH.7		81	ex 671, 9 Rgt, 653, 3 Rgt, 655, 656, 1 Rgt, 4 Rgt, 662, 659, 669, 659. Dump. First noted 1-13		11-13

■ **[1]** The Sioux on the gate has its complex side. The plate in the cockpit gives it as WA-S-179, which makes it XT827, latterly with the Historic Flight. **[2]** Gazelle XX392 is displayed at the entrance to the Directorate of Army Aviation, across the road from the airfield gate guards. **[3]** Lynx XZ613 is fitted with the boom of ZD278.

NEW MILTON on the A337 east of Christchurch

Chipmunk T.10 WB556 moved to Bournemouth, Dorset, on 14th September 2012. Another is being restored in the area.

❑ WK638	DHC Chipmunk T.10	G-BWJZ	52	ex Swindon, Long Eaton, Eccleshall. Stamford, Manston, 9 AEF, RAFC, 9 AEF, York UAS, 1 FTS, 1 AEF, Ox UAS, 1 RFS. Crashed 22-8-99, CoA 17-1-02, de-reg 4-4-00 . Cockpit	3-12

ODIHAM AIRFIELD on the A32 south of Odiham EGVO

RAF Odiham:

❑ XA225*		Slingsby Grasshopper TX.1	53	ex Keevil, Upavon, Keevil, Petersfield	7-13
❑ XR453	'A'	W'land Whirlwind HAR.10	62	8873M, ex Foulness, 2 FTS, CFS, 230, 1563 Flt, CFS. Gate	12-13
❑ ZA678	'EZ'	BV Chinook HC.1	81	9229M, ex Fleetlands, 7, N37023. Crashed 24-7-89. Dump	11-13
❑ 82-23762		BV CH-47D Chinook	82	ex US Army. Forward fuselage, procedures trainer	5-12
❑ 86-1677		BV CH-47D Chinook	86	ex US Army. Instructional airframe	5-12
❑ 89-0159		BV CH-47D Chinook	89	ex US Army	11-11
❑ 03-8003	'DT'	BV CH-47F Chinook	02	ex US Army. Unveiled on gate 9-5-12	11-13

Locally: The SIPA is believed to still be stored in the general area.

❑ G-AWLG	SIPA 903	51	ex F-BGHG. CoA 22-8-79	12-97

POPHAM AERODROME on the A303 west of North Waltham EGHP

Cherokee G-BSLM was flying again by 2013. VP-1 G-BFHX (last noted July 2009) and Rans S-10 G-RANZ (July 2007) have been deleted.

❑ G-AVNC	Cessna F.150G	67	Reims-built. CoA 24-5-04	7-11
❑ G-BSTV	Piper Cherokee Six	67	ex N4069R. De-reg 10-5-10	7-12

PORTSMOUTH

Defence College of Policing and Guarding: Southwick Park, the former HMS *Dryad* (which closed in 2004).

❑ XZ174*	Westland Lynx AH.7	77	ex Gosport, Brize Norton, 3 Regt, 655, 662, 655, 652, 651. Cabin. First noted 12-11	7-12

Defence Diving School Since 1997 Wessex HU.5 XT760 has been in a lake off Horsea Island – and it's full of eels!

ROMSEY or Farley, on the A27 north-west of Southampton

A strip in the *general* area holds a number of *W&R* inmates. The following long-in-the-tooth entries have been deleted: Comanche G-ARBO (last noted Feb 2004); Twin Comanche G-ASMA (Jun 2008); Pup G-AXCX (May 2000); Super 2 G-BNHE (Feb 2001); Bölkow Junior F-BRHN; Comanche 180 N5052P and Twin Comanche N8911Y (all three Aug 2005).

❑ G-AOHZ	Auster J/5P Autocar 145		56	CoA 25-9-03		1-12
❑ G-ARUO	Piper Comanche 180		61	ex Bruntingthorpe, N7251P. Cr 19-3-00, de-reg 18-7-00		1-12
❑ G-AVKR	Bölkow Bö 208 Junior		67	ex D-EGRA. CoA 3-9-09		2-11
❑ G-AVPS	Piper Twin Comanche B		67	ex N8393Y. Crashed 30-11-04, de-reg 6-7-05		1-12
❑ G-AZOB	Bölkow Monsun 150FF		72	ex D-EAAZ		3-09
❑ G-BETO	MS Super Rallye		62	ex F-BKED. CoA 11-12-04, de-reg 27-10-06		3-09
❑ EC-AOZ	Piper Pacer	G-BXBB	52	ex N1133C. De-reg 22-4-03		1-12

SOUTHAMPTON

Solent Sky: The proposed 'Aeronautica' development, see *W&R23* p71, was shelved in January 2012. Meanwhile, Solent Sky continues to vibrantly chart the incredible aviation heritage of the entire Solent area. The interior of the Sandringham, including the flight deck, is available for inspection and occasionally cockpits of other exhibits are opened up.

A storage site - *not* available for public inspection - is located well away from the museum. Aircraft held here, or elsewhere in store, are given their own heading from this edition. The museum has an excellent relationship with **424 Squadron, Air Cadets** - see below. The cockpit of Sea Vixen FAW.1 XJ476 is on loan to BDAC at Boscombe Down, Wilts.

◆ **Access:** *Albert Road South, Southampton, SO1 1FR - head for Ocean Village.* **Open:** *Open Tue to Sat and Bank Hols 10:00 to 17:00; Sun 12:00 to 17:00. Also open on Mondays during school holidays 10:00 to 17:00.* **Contact: 02380 635830 | aviation@spitfireonline.co.uk | www.solentskymuseum.org**

❑ 'G-ADZW'		Mignet HM.14 'Flea'		94	BAPC.253, ex Sandown, Lake, Isle of Wight. Arrived 5-00		1-14
❑ G-ALZE		Britten Norman BN-1F		51	ex Cosford, Kemble, Bembridge. De-reg 12-6-89. Arrived 1985		1-14
❑ G-APOI		Saro Skeeter Mk.8		57	ex Middle Wallop, Wattisham, Saxmundham, Middle Wallop. CoA 2-8-00, de-reg 14-4-10. Acquired 3-8-08		1-14
❑ –		SUMPAC man powered		61	BAPC.7, ex Old Warden, Southampton. Arrived 1984	[1]	1-14
❑ –		Airwave hang-glider		80	BAPC.215, prototype. Arrived 1987		1-14
❑ VH-BRC		Short Sandringham 4		43	ex Lee-on-Solent, VP-LVE *Southern Cross*, N158C, VH-BRC, ZK-AMH, JM715. Last flown 2-2-81, arrived 2-3-83. *Beachcomber*	[2]	1-14
❑ 'C4451'		Avro 504J replica		91	BAPC.210, partially sectioned. Unveiled 14-11-91	[3]	1-14
❑ N248		Supermarine S.6A		29	ex Cowes, Southampton, Henlow, Southampton Pier, 'S1596', Eastleigh, Calshot, RAFHSF. Acquired 7-2-76		1-14
❑ 'N546'		Wight Quadruplane rep		87	BAPC.164, ex Wimborne. Arrived 1988		1-14
❑ BB807		DH Tiger Moth	G-ADWO	35	ex Wimborne, Valley SF, 6 FTS, 22 EFTS, 4 FIS, Cam UAS, 510, 24, 20 EFTS, 12 EFTS, G-ADWO. De-reg 15-9-58	[4]	1-14
❑ PK683		Supermarine Spitfire F.24		46	ex Kingsbridge Lane, Kemble, Colerne, Changi 7150M, Singapore Aux AF. Accident 29-9-52. Acquired 7-2-76	[5]	1-14
❑ TG263		Saro SR.A/1		46	ex Duxford, Staverton, Cranfield, G-12-1, TG263. Arrived 1993	[6]	1-14
❑ WK570		DHC Chipmunk T.10 PAX		52	ex Bournemouth, Hamble, Southampton 8211M (4-8-72), 663, Hull UAS, 663, RAFC	[7]	1-14
❑ WZ753		Slingsby Grasshopper TX.1		52	ex Halton, Emanuel School, London		1-14
❑ XJ571	'242'	DH Sea Vixen FAW.2		60	ex Brooklands, Dunsfold, Southampton, Cosford 8140M (30-5-71), Halton, Sydenham, 892, FAW.1, 899, 893. Arrived 5-2-03	[8]	1-14
❑ XK740		Folland Gnat F.1		57	ex Hamble, Cosford 8396M (2-8-61), Bicester, Church Fenton, MoS, Filton. SOC 13-2-61	[4]	1-14
❑ XL770		Saro Skeeter AOP.12		58	ex Middle Wallop, Shrivenham 8046M, Wroughton, 15/19 Hussars, 652, 654. SOC 23-5-68. Arrived 1987	[9]	1-14
❑ XN246		Slingsby Cadet TX.3		59	ex Syerston, 617 GS, 616 GS, 622 GS. SOC 21-8-62. Arrived 1988		1-14
❑ XV760		HS Harrier GR.3		69	ex Dunsfold, Yeovilton A2605 [2] A2614 (30-5-91), Culdrose, St Athan, 3, 4, GR.1, 233 OCU. Cockpit	[8] [10]	1-14
❑ –		Supermarine Swift FR.5 CIM		-			1-14

❑ 'U-1215'		DH Vampire T.11 XE998	55	ex Farnborough, Wisbech, Huntingdon, Horley, Charlwood, Biggin Hill, Warmingham, Wigan, Woodford, Chester, St Athan, 8 FTS, 4 FTS, 8 FTS. SOC 11-12-67	[8]	1-14

■ **[1]** SUMPAC - Southampton University Man-Powered Aircraft. **[2]** Sandringham is on loan from the Science Museum, South Kensington, Gtr Lon. **[3]** Avro 504 built by AJD Engineering, Sudbury, Suffolk. **[4]** Tiger Moth is a composite, with parts from G-AOAC and G-AOJJ. **[5]** Spitfire F.24 and Gnat F.1 are on loan from the RAF Museum, Hendon, Gtr Lon. **[6]** SR.A.1 is on loan from the Imperial War Museum, Duxford, Cambs. **[7]** On loan from 424 Sqn ATC - see below. **[8]** Sea Vixen, Harrier and Vampire are on loan from the Hallett Collection/MCA Aviation USA. **[9]** Skeeter on loan from the Museum of Army Flying, Middle Wallop. **[10]** Much of XV760 was consumed in the Sea Harrier FRS.1 composite XZ493, see Yeovilton, Somerset.

Deep Store: See notes above. By 2012, Spitfire prototype replica 'K5054' (G-BRDV) had moved to Hawkinge, Kent.

❑ G-ASER		Piper Aztec 250B	63	ex Bournemouth, St Leonards, Lydd, Smeeth, Biggin Hill. Crashed 14-9-72, de-reg 24-11-72. Arrived 2009	9-09
❑ –		Mignet HM.14 'Flea'	~	ex Rayleigh. Arrived 9-99	3-04
❑ –		Mignet HM.293	~	unfinished project, fuselage	3-06
❑ WM571		DH Sea Venom FAW.22	54	ex Wimborne, Staverton, ADS, 831, RAE, FAW.21, 891, A&AEE, HS. Last flown 30-4-69. Arrived 24-12-88	4-10
❑ XD332	'194'	Supermarine Scimitar F.1	66	ex Helston, Culdrose SAH-19, Lee-on-Solent A2574 (6-10-67), 764, 736, 807, 804. Arrived 10-3-99	3-13
❑ XF114		Supermarine Swift F.7 G-SWIF	57	ex Bicester, Scampton, Bournemouth, Connah's Quay, Aston Down, CS(A), Cranfield. Arrived 2005. De-reg 19-7-04	4-12

No.**424 Squadron, Air Cadets** has its headquarters within the museum complex - see above - although not open to the public. Within their HQ are several impressive procedure trainers, including a three-axis 'JP' cockpit which *may* be wholly 'synthetic' but *may* also owe its origins to a Mk.3 or Mk.4, although it is emblazoned 'T Mk 5-A' (sic). Chipmunk T.10 PAX WK570 is on show in Solent Sky - above. By August 2012, Gnat T.1 XP542 had returned to its birthplace: Hamble, Hants.

❑ XD596	DH Vampire T.11	54	ex Calmore, St Athan 7939M (14-2-67), CATCS, CNCS, 5 FTS, 4 FTS	4-08
❑ –	Hunting Jet Provost CIM	~	marked 'CRAN 22/2'	3-02

Aero Antiques and AeroTech Ltd: Tiger Moth G-ANFP, last noted in July 2003, moved to Henstridge, Somerset, as far back as April 2010. Completion of 1986 'new-build' Tiger Moth G-DHTM was not proceeded with.

◆ **Access:** *Visits possible* **strictly** *by prior application* **only**

❑ G-ABNX	Robinson Redwing 2	32	ex Redhill, Old Sarum, Shoreham. CoA 12-5-03		7-11
❑ G-ACET	DH Dragon	34	ex Bishop's Stortford, 2779M, AW171, Ringway SF, 6 AACU, G-ACET	[1]	12-09
❑ G-AFJA	Watkinson Dingbat	38	ex Berkswell, Headcorn. Crashed 19-5-75. CoA 18-6-75		10-07
❑ G-AFSW	Chilton DW.2	r39	ex Chilton Manor. Unflown. Stored		1-00
❑ G-ALJL	DH Tiger Moth	40	ex T6311, Fairford SF, 38 GCF, Tarrant Rushton SF, 11 OTU, 25 EFTS. Morris-built. CoA 28-9-50, de-reg 8-12-60		7-03
❑ G-ARTH	Piper Super Cruiser	47	ex EI-ADO. CoA 21-4-95. Stored		7-11
❑ G-EUKS	Westland Widgeon III	28	ex Australia, VH-UKS		7-11

■ **[1]** The Dragon is based on original wings, all else is new-build.

Frank Lund: Keeps his beautifully restored and functioning Canberra cockpit in the area.

❑ WT536	EE Canberra PR.7	55	ex Bruntingthorpe, Cosford 8063M (19-11-69), 80, 31, 13, 17. Short-built. Cockpit	7-10

Hampshire and Isle of Wight Air Ambulance: Has a Bölkow pod in use as a travelling fund-raiser. The operation used to fly Bö 105DBS G-TVAM but currently uses EC 135 G-BZRS. Base is Thruxton, but the headquarters is within Southampton. Until told otherwise, it is 'based' under this heading! **www.hiow-airambulance.org.uk**

❑ G-ESAM	'AM'	Bölkow Bö 105DB	92	ex G-BUIB, G-BDYZ, D-HDEF. De-reg 26-6-03	[1]	4-11

■ **[1]** Original pod from 'DBS-4 upgrade in the early 1990s. G-ESAM, now registered as G-WAAS, flies on.

Also: A collector in the general area has two Vampires and a Gannet.

❑ WN411		Fairey Gannet AS.1	55	ex Abbotsinch, 820. SOC 27-2-62. Cockpit	7-13
❑ 'XD614'	'65'	DH Vampire T.11 WZ572	53	ex Southampton museum, Leeming, 8 FTS, 7 FTS, 202 AFS. SOC 24-4-61. Pod	7-13
❑ XH318	'64'	DH Vampire T.11	56	ex Calmore, Southampton, Ferndown, 7761M (23-10-62), Shawbury, RAFC	7-13

SOUTHAMPTON AIRPORT or Eastleigh

EGHI

Mounted on a roundabout at the approaches to the airport is a substantial model of the prototype Spitfire, K5054. It is large and eye-catching, but is best described as a piece of sculpture.

❑ N6NE	Lockheed JetStar 731	61	ex VR-CCC ntu, N222Y, N731JS, N227K, N12R, N280R. Damaged 27-11-92. Fire crews, poor state		8-11

SWANWICK north-west of Junction 9 of the M27, north of Locks Heath

National Air Traffic Services: Swanwick Centre, in Sopwith Way, gained a Harrier within its grounds in 2012.

❑ XW917*	HS Harrier GR.3	71	ex Boscombe Down, Cottesmore 8975M, Laarbruch, 3, 4, 3. SOC 3-4-88. Arrived 7-8-12		5-13

THRUXTON AERODROME north of the A303 west of Andover

EGHO

Phoenix Aero Services:

◆ **Access:** *Private workshop,* **strictly** *viewable by prior application* **only**

❑ G-BKXP	Auster AOP.6	46	ex Little Gransden, Royston, Oakington, Belgian AF A-14, VT987 n/s		2-12
❑ G-RLEF	Hawker Hurricane XII	42	ex Coventry, RCAF 5385. CCF-built. SOC 30-6-47. Off-site		2-12
❑ NL985	DH Tiger Moth G-BWIK	44	ex -?-, Sywell, Cranfield, Leighton Buzzard, Bushey, Leamington Spa, Hendon, Finningley, Colerne, Cwmfelinfach 7015M, 9 AFTS, 2 GS, Lon UAS, Queens UAS, 11 RFS, 5 RFS, Birm UAS, 16 EFTS, 14 EFTS. Morris-built. Damage 23-5-73	[1]	2-12
❑ Z5207	Hawker Hurricane IIB G-BYDL	41	ex Dursley, Sudbury, Audley End, Russia, 151 Wing, 81	[2]	3-13
❑ 'AG244'	Hawker Hurricane XII G-CBOE	42	ex RCAF 5487. CCF-built. Crashed 22-11-42, SOC 22-3-43	[3]	12-13

■ **[1]** The Tiger Moth restoration project is now identified. It was badly damaged by fire at Hendon 23-5-73 and was replaced by T6296 from Fleet Air Arm stocks (now on show at Hendon, Gtr Lon). It was last noted in *W&R20*, p170, as leaving Sywell for 'Wiltshire'. *India-Kilo* is registered to the proprietor of Phoenix, Phil Lawton. **[2]** *Delta-Lima* is being restored for Phil Lawton, and will wear Finnish Air Force colours as 'HC-465'. **[3]** *Oscar-Echo* is painted in overall 'silver' hue, with a red tail band.

Hampshire and Isle of Wight Air Ambulance: Currently operating an EC135 from the aerodrome, a Bölkow Bö 105 pod is used as a travelling exhibit. It is often kept here; but shares time at the administrative HQ in Southampton, Hampshire.

Access *Does 'the rounds' of shows, otherwise viewable by prior application* **only** | **www.hiow-airambulance.org.uk**

❑ G-BGKP 'AM'	Bölkow Bö 105D	75	ex Bond, North Scottish, D-HDGC. Accident 16-2-81, de-reg 10-7-86. Pod		7-11

Others: During October 2012 four helicopters moved to Lee-on-Solent, Hampshire: Scouts G-BYKJ (XV121, departed 30-10-12); XV130 (G-BWJW - 30-10-12); XV138 (G-SASM - 29-10-12) and Wasp XT793 (G-BZPP - 29-10-12) - the latter first noted here in poor shape during November 2011. By late January 2013, all but had moved on again, this time to <u>Babcary</u>, Somerset. Scout AH.1 XW799 (G-BXSL) moved to the fire dump - see below.

❑ XW799	Westland Scout AH.1 G-BXSL	72	ex Chiseldon, Middle Wallop, GAAS, 657, 656, 658, CoA 19-8-02, crashed 19-11-01, de-reg 7-5-02. Dump by 3-13		3-13

WINCHESTER east of the M3, north of Southampton

Army Training Regiment, Sir John Moore Barracks:

❑ ZB672	Sud Gazelle AH.1	84	ex Shawbury, Fleetlands, 651, 663, 654, 672, 662, 657, 664, 3 Flt, Garrison Air Sqn. Westland-built. Opposite guardroom		4-11

Others: A strip to the north-west holds several 'long-termers'. Jackaroo G-APAJ, last noted in March 2011, had moved on by February 2013. Not recorded since January 2009, Cessna F.150H G-AWUH has been deleted. Stinson 108 G-BHMR and Piper J-5C-65 G-KURK were both flying again by 2013.

❑ G-ARBV	Piper Tri-Pacer 160	57	ex N8633D. CoA 3-7-06. Frame	[1]	1-11
❑ G-AWEI	Druine Condor	68	CoA 10-11-98. Rollason-built		1-11
❑ G-BVRH	Taylorcraft BL-65	40	ex N23929, G-BVRH, N24322, NC24322. CoA 23-9-06		1-11
❑ G-BXSV	Stampe SV-4C	47	ex N21PM, F-BDDB. Nord-built		1-11
❑ G-NGRM	Spezio DAL-1 Tuholer	76	ex N6RM. Cr 24-7-99, CoA 7-2-00, de-reg 26-3-10. Fuselage		1-11

❑ G-OINK	Piper J-3C-65		43	ex G-BJTO, F-BEGK, OO-AAL, 43-30236. CoA 16-7-09, de-reg 11-9-12	1-11
❑ 44-80594	Piper L-4J Cub	G-BEDJ	42	ex F-BDTC, 44-80594. CoA 8-10-96	1-07

■ **[1]** Original fuselage frame, airworthy Tri-Pacer G-ARBV incorporates the fuselage of G-ARDP.

YATELEY The forward cockpit of Chipmunk T.10 WZ876 (G-BBWN) was offered for sale during 2011 and moved on.

HEREFORDSHIRE

BICTON west of the B4361, north-west of Leominster

Oaker Wood Leisure | **Access**, *visits possible* **only** *by prior arrangement* | **www.owlactivities.co.uk**

❑ XP360	'V'	Westland Whirlwind HAR.10	62	ex Upper Hill, Sunderland, Warmingham, Lasham, Fawkham Green, CFS, 225. SOC 31-3-76	3-13

EWYAS HAROLD on the A465 south-west of Hereford

Pontrilas Army Training Area: Last mentioned in *W&R22* (p74) and well-known as the preserve of the 'Herefordshire Gun Club', a Boeing 737 fuselage is in use for special forces training.

❑ 9M-MMI*	Boeing 737-4H6	92	ex Kemble, Malaysia Airlines. Fuselage. Arrived 24-2-13	2-13

HEREFORD Last noted in October 2009, Hunter FGA.9 XG252 moved to France, circa 2010.

KINGTON west of Leominster, on the A44

Martin Aubery - Classic Ultralight Heritage Collection: **Private** *location, visits possible* **only** *by prior arrangement*

❑ G-ADPJ	BAC Drone II	35	ex Selby, Breighton, Wigan, Bristol, Benson, Thetford. Damaged 3-4-55. Also parts from G-AEKU		12-05
❑ G-ARIF	Ord-Hume OH-7 Coupe	61	ex Breighton, Wigan	[1]	11-03
❑ G-ASDF	Edwards Gyrocopter	r62	ex Innsworth, Woking, Coulsdon. De-reg 3-10-63	[2]	3-02
❑ G-BXIY	Blake Bluetit	30	ex North Weald, Old Warden, BAPC.37, Winchester		1-11
❑ G-MBWI	Microlite Lafayette 1	r82	ex Selby, Leeds, Leigh. De-reg 13-6-90		11-03
❑ –	Primary glider	~	ex Innsworth, 'Glos'	[3]	3-02

■ **[1]** The OH-7 is a version of the Luton Minor. **[2]** The Edwards is owned by Computair Consultants. **[3]** The glider was designed in Gloucestershire and is similar to the SG.38, Dagling etc but with a metal frame.

SHOBDON AERODROME north of the A44 west of Leominster EGBS

BA Swallow II G-AFGD took to the air again on 6th June 2013.

❑ G-AGYK	Auster J/1 Autocrat	46	CoA 17-8-07, de-reg 11-2-13. Dismantled	9-10
❑ G-ARVV	Piper Cherokee 160	62	CoA 17-3-09	7-13
❑ G-BVUT*	Evans VP-1	98	CoA 29-9-99	7-13
❑ G-TGRD*	Robinson R22 Beta	97	ex G-OPTS. CoA 24-8-11	7-13
❑ G-TGRS*	Robinson R22 Beta	89	ex G-DELL, N80466. CoA 24-8-11	7-13
❑ N4979B*	Cessna 150	~	dismantled. First noted 9-10	7-13

HERTFORDSHIRE

BENINGTON Last noted in January 2004, Pup 150 G-AXDU has been deleted.

BERKHAMSTED on the A4251 west of Hemel Hempstead

❑ G-AVPD	Jodel D.9 Bebe	69	ex Langley. CoA 6-6-75	11-13

CLOTHALL COMMON on the A507 south-east of Baldock

This entry in *W&R15*, p96, noted: "After many years in store here Auster J/4 Arrow G-AIJS has moved on - destination unknown". That was circa 1996 and it is known to have moved to at least one other location in the UK. By 2008 it was off again, this time heading for France where it is being restored to flying condition by Roger Lane. More details on **www.austerj4.co.uk** The *W&R* wheels may move slowly, but every so often they bring up the occasional nugget!

❑ G-APYU	Champion Tri-Traveler	60	ex Moreton-in-Marsh. Crashed 23-4-72, de-reg 3-4-98	10-99

ELSTREE AERODROME north of Junction 4, M1 EGTR

Pup 100 G-AZDA departed for France during September 2012. *W&R23* (p75) noted Aztec 250E N54211 leaving on a lorry as far back as 6th August 2007. It may well have still been here in December 2008. Either way, by 18th March 2012 it was taking a deep breath ready for submerging at Cliffe, Kent. Twin Comanche N320MR was flying again by September 2012. Some references, all last noted in 2004, have been deleted: AA-5B G-BGPK, Warrior G-BOVH, Cessna 172M G-BSCR, Cessna 150M G-GCNZ, AA-5A G-ODAE, and Navajo 310 ST-AHZ (once G-AXMR) on the dump.

❑ G-AWOE*	Aero Commander 680E	59	ex N3844C. CoA 22-6-10. First noted 3-12	10-13
❑ G-AWTJ	Cessna F.150J	68	Reims-built. CoA 18-12-04, de-reg 18-5-10	10-13
❑ G-AZDE*	Piper Arrow 200B	71	CoA 20-4-08	10-13
❑ G-BAGT	Helio Super Courier	68	ex CR-LGJ. CoA 30-12-09	9-11
❑ G-BARV	Cessna 310Q	73	CoA 18-8-09, de-reg 3-3-11	10-13
❑ G-BGGN	Piper Tomahawk 112	78	CoA 16-9-10, de-reg 29-11-10. Fuselage	6-11
❑ G-BORH	Piper Seneca 200T	80	ex N8261V. CoA 21-3-08, de-reg 21-2-11	10-13
❑ G-DONI*	American AA-5B Tiger	99	ex G-BLLT, OO-RTG. CoA 26-2-10	10-13
❑ G-GLED*	Cessna 150M	75	ex C-GLED. CoA 22-4-11	10-13
❑ G-OARC*	Piper Arrow IV	79	ex EC-HXO, G-OARC, EC-JAF, EC-HXO, G-OARC, G-BMVE, N3071K. CoA 24-3-11	10-13
❑ G-PING*	American AA-5A Cheetah	79	ex G-OCWC, G-WULL, N27153. CoA 25-6-11	10-13
❑ G-WARS*	Piper Warrior 161	97	ex N9281X. CoA 11-11-11	10-13
❑ C-FQIP	Lake LA-4-200	~	ex N1068L. Stored	10-13

HEMEL HEMPSTEAD on the A414 west of St Albans

The Vampire Collection: Alan Allen's former SAAF Vampire T.55 221 was exported to South Africa 13th June 2012.

◆ **Access:** Visits by prior arrangement ***only*** | **alanwz581@gmail.com**

❑ WZ581	'77'	DH Vampire T.11	53	ex Ruislip, Bushey, Keevil, Exeter, 3/4 CAACU, 229 OCU, 233 OCU, 25. SOC 16-12-71. Pod	2-14
❑ XT439	'605'	Westland Wasp HAS.1	65	ex King's Lynn, Bruntingthorpe, Cranfield, Wroughton,829, 703, 829, 845. Crashed 25-3-86. Arrived 10-5-02	2-14

HITCHIN on the A505 north-east of Luton

Philip and **Tony Leaver**:

❑ G-KAYT		Robinson R22 Beta	88	ex G-EIST, N9081H. Crashed 31-8-94, de-reg 18-1-95. Sim	3-12
❑ –		HS Harrier GR.1	~	ex Llantrisant, Welshpool, Stafford, Abingdon, Hamble [1]	3-12
❑ XV759	'O'	HS Harrier GR.3	69	ex Bruntingthorpe, South Molton, Welshpool, Llantrisant, Pendine, St Athan, 233 OCU, 1417 Flt, 233 OCU, 1, 233 OCU, 1, GR.1, 233 OCU. SOC 10-7-89. Cockpit, simulator	3-12

■ [1] The GR.1 cockpit is *thought* to be the original fitted to XV779 - see Wittering Cambs. It carries FL/R 41H 725624.

Also: The Martin is believed to still be underway in the area. At a separate location, an Auster is under long term rebuild.

❑ G-AEYY	Martin Monoplane	37	ex Bishop's Stortford, Meir. De-reg 3-6-98	4-05
❑ G-AOZL	Auster J/5Q Alpine	57	ex Earls Colne, Southend. CoA 28-5-88	12-13

LEAVESDEN south of Abbots Langley, north of the A41

Studios: Eon Productions. During March 2013 a pair of Lynx AH.7 cabins, reportedly XZ205 and XZ217, were offered for sale from here. Both had been used for static shots masquerading as UH-60 Blackhawks. (See also Barby, Northants.) The references here are long-in-the-tooth and three, last noted in February 2005, have been deleted: Tiger 'F-ZWWW' plus the hulks of a Cessna 172 and a Pilatus PC-6.

◆ **Access: Strictly** *by prior permission*

❑ –	Bede BD-5J	~	ex *Octopussy*		9-08

LONDON COLNEY south of the A414, south-east of St Albans

De Havilland Aircraft Museum: Early in 2014 the 'Heritage Centre' suffix was dropped in favour of DHAM and references to the Mosquito Aircraft Museum dropped, to better reflect the purpose. Billed on the website as "The oldest aircraft museum in the UK", this pioneering museum traces its roots to Walter Goldsmith who opened up Salisbury Hall to the public from 1955 and in September 1958 brought the prototype Mosquito on to the site as an added attraction. Regular public open days started in the very early 1960s; hard on its heels came the Shuttleworth Collection in 1963. (Both the Science Museum and the Imperial War Museum pre-date this, but both are not *dedicated* aircraft museums.)

To celebrate this longevity, DHAM announced planning approval and the launch of a £1m new display hangar on 13th January 2014. Fund raising is under way - take a look at the DHAM website for how *you* can help.

Elements of the cockpit of HS.125-1 G-ARYA were insufficient for a formal listing and have been deleted. Otter VP-FAK was kept on behalf of its owners and moved on during late 2012. Chipmunk T.10 WP869 also departed during late 2012.

◆ **Access:** *South of Junction 22 of the M25 to the south-east of London Colney, access from the B556.* **Open:** *First Sun of Mar to last Sun of Oct, Tue, Thu, Sat 12:00 to 17:30, Sun and Bank Hols 10:30 to 17:30.* **Contact:** *Salisbury Hall, London Colney, St Albans, AL2 1BU* | **01727 826400** | **museum@dehavillandmuseum.co.uk** | **www.dehavillandmuseum.co.uk**

❑ G-ABLM	Cierva C.24		31	ex Hatfield. CoA 16-1-35, de-reg 12-39. Arrived 7-80	[1]	1-14
❑ G-ADOT	DH Hornet Moth		35	ex Hatfield, Old Warden, Stoke Ferry, Stapleford, Houghton-on-the-Hill, X9326, 5 GCF, 23 OTU, 24 GCF, 6 AONS, Halton SF, 2 CPF, G-ADOT. CoA 5-10-59, de-reg 18-9-63		1-14
❑ G-AKDW	DH Dragon Rapide		45	ex Aviodome, Amsterdam store, F-BCDB, G-AKDW, YI-ABD, NR833. Arrived 1994. *City of Winchester*		1-14
❑ G-ANRX	DH Tiger Moth		39	ex Belchamp Walter, Mk.II N6550, SLAW, 25 EFTS, 18 EFTS, 241, 14 EFTS, 56 ERFTS. CoA 20-6-61, de-reg 8-6-67. Arrived 1976. Crop duster. *Border City*		1-14
❑ G-AOTI	DH Heron 2D		56	ex Biggin Hill, Exeter, G-5-19. CoA 24-6-87, de-reg 17-10-95. Arrived 19-8-95		1-14
❑ G-AREA	DH Dove 8		61	ex Hatfield. CoA 8-9-87, de-reg 19-9-00. Arr 2000. BAe c/s		1-14
❑ G-ARYC	HS.125 Srs 1		63	ex Hatfield, Filton, R-R. CoA 1-8-73, de-reg 31-3-76. Arrived 1979. R-R (stb), Bristol Siddeley Engines (pt) colours		1-14
❑ G-AVFH	HS Trident 2		71	ex Heathrow, BA, BEA. Forward fuselage. De-reg 12-5-82. Arrived 7-82. BEA colours		1-14
❑ G-JEAO	HS 146-100		83	ex Filton, Air France Express/JEA, G-UKPC, C-GNVX, N802RW, G-5-512, PT-LEP, G-BKXZ, PT-LEP. CoA 4-6-05, de-reg 2-11-09. Arrived 27-7-09. Fuselage	[2]	1-14
❑ –	DH.88 Comet FSM		90	BAPC.216, ex 'G-ACSS', St Albans, Kings Langley, Wroughton, Australia. Arrived 2001	[3]	1-14
❑ –	Airspeed Horsa I / II		c44	BAPC.232, composite fuselage, rear of Mk.II TL615		1-14
❑ –	DH Comet 2 SIM		~	ex Wroughton, Crawley. Arrived 1996	[4]	1-14
❑ D-IFSB	DH Dove 6	G-AMXR	52	ex Hatfield, BFS, D-CFSB, Panshanger, Srs 2A G-AMXR, N4280V. Last flew 24-10-78, arrived 3-79		1-14
❑ F-BGNX	DH Comet 1XB	G-AOJT	53	ex Farnborough, G-AOJT, Air France F-BGNX. Last flight 27-6-56. Arrived 20-3-85. Fuselage, Air France colours		1-14
❑ J-7326	DH Humming Bird	G-EBQP	24	ex Hatch, Audley End, Bishop's Stortford. Arr 25-3-03	[5]	1-14
❑ W4050 *and* E-0234	DH Mosquito prototype		40	ex Hatfield, Chester, Hatfield, Panshanger, Hatfield, RR, DH, A&AEE, E-0234. Last flown 12-43, arrived 9-58	[6]	1-14
❑ LF789 'R2-K'	DH Queen Bee		43	BAPC.186, ex 'K3584', Hadfield, Droylesden, Redhill, St Athan, Pilot-less Aircraft Unit, Manorbier, St Athan. Scottish Aviation-built. SOC 23-11-46. Arrived 13-4-86		1-14
❑ TA122 'UP-G'	DH Mosquito FB.6		45	ex Soesterberg, Delft, 4, 2 GCS, 48, 4, 605, 417 ARF. SOC 30-6-50. Arrived 26-2-78. 605 Sqn and/or 4 Sqn c/s	[7]	1-14

❑ TA634	'8K-K'	DH Mosquito TT.35	G-AWJV	45	ex Speke, *Mosquito Squadron*, Speke G-AWJV, Aldergrove, 3 CAACU, APS Schleswigland, APS Ahlorn, APS Sylt, 4 CAACU. Last flown 16-7-68. De-reg 19-10-70. Arrived 10-70. 571 Sqn colours	1-14
❑ TJ118		DH Mosquito TT.35		45	ex Elstree, *Mosquito Squadron*, *633 Squadron*, Exeter, 3/4 CAACU, 3 CAACU. SOC 18-9-61. Cockpit/fuselage sections	1-14
❑ VV217		DH Vampire FB.5		48	ex Sunderland, Barnham, Bury St Edmunds, 'VV271', 7323M (23-3-56), Oakington, DH. Arrived 12-8-09. Stored, off-site	1-14
❑ WM729		DH Vampire NF.10		52	ex Gloucestershire, London Colney, Ruislip, Bingley, Bradford, Church Fenton, CNCS, 2 ANS, 25, 151. SOC 30-11-59. Arrived 22-6-94. Cockpit, stored, off-site	1-14
❑ WP790	'T'	DHC Chipmunk T.10	G-BBNC	52	ex Rush Green, WP790, Bir UAS, Wales UAS, PFTS, AOTS, 1 ITS, RAFC, Man UAS, G&S UAS, Stn UAS, 24 GCF, 5 RFS, 17 RFS. SOC 5-11-73. De-reg 23-9-74. B'ham UAS c/s	1-14
❑ WR539		DH Venom FB.4		56	ex Staverton, L' Colney, Fownhope, Cardiff, 'Midlands', Cosford, 8399M, Kai Tak, 28, 60. SOC 4-7-62. Stored	1-14
❑ WX853		DH Venom NF.3		55	ex Debden 7443M (10-7-57), Shawbury, 23. Stored, off-site	1-14
❑ XG730	'499'	DH Sea Venom FAW.22		57	ex Southwick, Portsmouth, Lee-on-Solent, ADS, Sydenham, 893, 894, 891. SOC 13-7-70. Arr 28-10-78. 894 Sqn c/s	1-14
❑ XJ565	'127'	DH Sea Vixen FAW.2		60	ex RAE, 899, 893, 766B. SOC 29-7-76. Arrived 31-10-76. 899 Sqn colours	1-14
❑ XJ772	'H'	DH Vampire T.11		55	ex Brooklands, Wisley, Shawbury, CATCS, 1 FTS, 8 FTS, RAFC, RNorAF 15018 'PX-G'. SOC 3-2-71. Arrived 29-3-94	1-14
❑ XK695		DH Comet C.2(R)	G-AMXH	56	ex Stock, Newton 9164M (10-11-92), Duxford, Wyton, 51, 216, Srs 2 G-AMXH. De-reg 2-3-55, last flown 10-1-75. Arrived 17-12-95. Cockpit	1-14
❑ J-1008		DH Vampire FB.6		c55	ex Hatfield, Swiss AF. Arrived 11-5-75	1-14
❑ J-1790		DH Venom FB.54	G-BLKA	57	ex 'WR410', 'Norfolk', Bournemouth, Bruntingthorpe, Cranfield, G-BLKA, G-VENM ntu, Swiss AF J-1790. CoA 14-7-95, de-reg 13-10-00. Arrived 23-10-03	1-14

■ **[1]** The de Havilland-built Cierva C.24 is on loan from the Science Museum, acquired 9-35. **[2]** The 146 first flew at Hatfield 8-11-83 and made its last flight, into Filton, on 7-1-03. **[3]** The stored DH.88 Comet FSM was built in Australia for use in the film *The Great Air Race*. Owned by Ralph Steiner, it will re-appear in the colours of G-ACSP *Black Magic*, in taxiable condition. **[4]** The Comet SIM was built at the same time as the cockpits for the first two prototypes and was used for structural tests. It then went to the DH Servicing School and was later converted into a simulator. It is now fitted with Mk.4 instrumentation. **[5]** The Humming Bird uses the wings of the Martin Monoplane G-AEYY, which itself used a set of DH.53 wings, very likely from J7325. The project is on loan from Terry Pankhurst and Peter Kirk and is under restoration to fly, with a Bristol Cherub, at which point it will leave the collection. The original G-EBQP crashed 21-7-34. **[6]** 'Mossie' prototype W4050 was built at Salisbury Hall and first flown from a field alongside the house on 25-12-40 by Geoffrey de Havilland JR, landing at Hatfield. It wears its serial to port and its manufacturer's test identity to starboard. **[7]** Mosquito FB.6 TA122 is being rebuilt using the wing of TR.33 TW233 acquired in Israel. The codes 'UP-G' relate to TA122's days with 605 Squadron in May 1945 and with its use with 4 Sqn in Germany 1949-1950. (And *possibly* during its time in between with 2 Group's comms unit at Evere!)

PANSHANGER AERODROME east of Welwyn Garden City, south of the B1000 EGLG

While the wings of Tomahawk G-BSKC were still here in November 2012, the rest of it was not, and its has been deleted.

❑ G-BEEU	Piper Cherokee 140F	73	ex PH-NSE, N11C. Cr 27-1-09, CoA 4-3-10, de-reg 18-9-12	11-12
❑ G-DTOO	Piper Tomahawk 112	78	ex Seething. Crashed 9-7-94, de-reg 31-1-95	11-12
❑ N93938	Erco Ercoupe 415C	~	fuselage, stored	7-12

RUSH GREEN on the B656, west of Stevenage

An Auster AOP.9 has gravitated to a *private* airstrip. This machine was written out of *W&R22* (p52) and leaving North Weald, Essex, by March 2008 for 'Scotland'. It seems never to have gone north o' the border.

❑ XN437*	Auster AOP.9	G-AXWA	59	ex North Weald, ?, Lashenden, Welling, Biggin Hill, Luton, Odiham, Maghull, Hoylake, St Athan, 653, 8 Ind Recce Flt. SOC 28-11-67	3-12

ST ALBANS Not noted since 2010, the Cessna cache has been deleted: FRA.150L G-AZZX, 150H N7263S, 172M N13253 and the anonymous 150K.

ISLE OF MAN

The Island is a self-governing British Crown Dependency - it is part of the British Isles, but not part of the United Kingdom, or the European Union for that matter

ANDREAS AERODROME

❑ G-BZXL		Whittaker MW-5 Sorcerer	01	CoA 2-7-04, de-reg 21-4-10		8-08
❑ G-BMFI		SZD-45A Ogar	76	CoA 30-5-08		7-11
❑ G-DCVA	CVA	LET L13 Blanik	73	BGA.1830, *Boggles the Blanik*. CoA 29-9-09, de-reg 17-6-11		7-11
❑ G-MMTD		Hiway Demon 175	83	CoA 10-9-03		8-08
❑ G-MSTC		American AA-5A Cheetah	79	ex G-BIJT, N26950. Cr 17-6-06, CoA 27-4-08, de-reg 31-8-10		3-11

ISLE OF MAN AIRPORT or Ronaldsway EGNS

Manx Aviation and Military Museum: Run by the Manx Aviation Preservation Society, the museum charts the island's varied aviation history and occupies wartime buildings on the airport site.

◆ **Open:** *10:00 to 16:30 Sat, Sun and Bank Hols. Also daily throughout the TT motorcycle races practice week to the end of Sep; or by appointment.* **Contact:** *c/o 47 Fuchsia Grove, Ballasalla, Isle of Man, IM9 2DT* | **01624 829294** | **airmuseum@manx.net** | **www.maps.org.im**

❑ G-BGYT		EMBRAER Bandeirante P1	79	ex Keenair, N104VA, G-BGYT, PT-SAA. CoA 12-1-06, de-reg 26-9-06. Manx Airlines colours		12-13
❑ 9041		Bristol Bolingbroke IVT	41	ex Nanton, Canada, RCAF. Fairchild Canada-built. SOC 1-10-46. Arrived 21-6-04. Cockpit, off-site		12-13

Airport:

❑ –		Eider Duck	c66	BAPC.282, displayed within the terminal	[1]	8-13
❑ EI-WYO		Piper Navajo 310	~	stored		8-13
❑ SE-LGV*		BAe ATP	91	ex West Air Cargo, N857AW, G-11-034. Stored, first noted 7-11		8-13

■ **[1]** Single-seat pusher-configured homebuild, unflown.

JURBY west of Andreas

Leopard Moth G-ACLL, last noted in September 2010, was noted 'road-running' in the Manchester area during September 2012. It eventually settled upon Lee-on-Solent, Hampshire. By July 2011 the site was clear with Bergfalke CEV and Spitfire FSM BAPC.283 unaccounted for.

ISLE OF WIGHT

BEMBRIDGE (ISLE OF WIGHT) AERODROME south-west of Bembridge EGHJ

B-N Group: The factory remains at Bembridge, but the flying side is centred on Lee-on-Solent, Hants. BN-2Ts G-BVHY and G-BWPM moved to Lee-on-Solent, Hampshire, by 2012. Islander AL.1 ZG994 appears not to have been here for static tests. Not noted since January 2004, the fuselages of Trislander G-BEVR and BN-2T G-BVHX have been deleted.

◆ **Access:** *Visits* **strictly** *by prior permission*

❑ G-AXZK	BN-2A-26 Islander		70	ex V2-LAD, VP-LAD, G-AXZK, G-51-153. CoA 16-4-06, de-reg 25-2-11. Engine rig	12-13
❑ G-BVYE	BN-2B-20 Islander		95	CoA 21-2-95, de-reg 27-11-98. Fuselage, dumped	12-13
❑ 'G-OUCH'	Beech Musketeer	G-ASJO	63	CoA 12-2-01, de-reg 20-10-05. Fire dump - poor state	12-13
❑ G-RAPA	BN-2T-4R prototype		81	CoA 31-7-91, de-reg 3-5-02. Stripped out on dump	12-13

Also: Freeland G-NACI was flying again by late 2012 and moved over to Sandown.

❑ G-AMVP	Tipsy Junior	52	ex Sandown, OO-ULA. CoA 12-10-11	12-13

Britten Norman Aircraft Preservation Society: With assistance from the **Bembridge Heritage Society** the aim is to restore *Charlie-November* ready for its 50th birthday.

◆ **Access:** *Visits* **strictly** *by prior permission* | **Contact enquiries@bnhistorians.co.uk** | **www.bnhistorians.co.uk**

❑ G-AVCN	BN-2A Islander	66	ex airfield, Puerto Rico, N290VL, F-OGHG, G-AVCN	12-13

COWES on the A3020, north of the island

Cliftongrade Ltd: The scrap dealers use the Phantom cockpit to advertise their business.

❑ XT863	'AS'	McD Phantom FG.1	68	ex Abingdon, 43, 111, 892, 767. SOC 24-2-89. Cockpit	12-13

Also: At a workshop on an industrial estate a 'Schlepp' is being restored.

❑ C-552*	EKW C-3605 ✈ G-DORN	48	ex Bournemouth, HB-RBJ, SwissAF C-552. CoA 28-4-10. Arrived 23-5-13	12-13

◆ **Thinx:** *At The Prospect in the delightful High Street can be found a real gem - the* ***Sir Max Aitken Museum****. Set inside an 18th century sail-maker's loft, this was the home of Sir Max Aitken* BT DSO DFC *from 1947 until his death in 1985. The vast bulk of the exhibits are maritime, but there are memorabilia of his night-fighting days and 601 (County of London) Squadron* - **01983 293800 | www.sirmaxaitkenmuseum.org**

EAST COWES on the A3021, north of the island and, well, east of Cowes!

A *private* collector in the *general* area has taken on a Tornado cockpit, while Sea Harrier FA.2 ZH807 moved to Selby, N Yorks, by December 2012.

❑ ZE168*	Panavia Tornado F.3	86	ex Leeming RTP, 25. Cockpit, first noted 2-13	12-13

◆ **Thinx:** *Inside the iconic Columbine Hangar - where Saunders-Roe built many flying-boats, ending up with the enormous Princess, two of which never flew - is the* ***Classic Boat Museum Gallery****. This is essentially boating memorabilia and small artefacts and the aviation 'flavour' is limited, but it is well worth the visit.* | **01983 244101** | **www.classicboatmuseum.org**

ISLE OF WIGHT (SANDOWN) AERODROME north of the A3056, west of Sandown EGHN

Airframe Assemblies: During late 2013/early 2014 the company re-located lock-stock-and-barrel to a new hangar on the north perimeter. The craftsmen continue an impressive throughput of restorations.

Departures: Spitfire V EP122 was worked on from early 2012, departing to Biggin Hill, Gtr Lon, 5-13. Mk.IX LZ842 to Biggin Hill, Gtr London, 13-11-12. The fuselage of Mk.XVIII SM845 (SE-BIN) arrived from Duxford 10-12, returning to Duxford, Cambs, 5-13.

◆ **Access: Private** *premises - visits* **strictly** *by prior permission*

❑ BH238	Hawker Hurricane IIb		42	ex Front Line Sandown, Russia, Soviet AF. Wreck		12-13
❑ BS410	Sup' Spitfire Tr.9	G-TCHI	42	ex 315. Crashed 13-5-43	[1]	12-13
❑ EE602*	Supermarine Spitfire V		42	ex Aldershot, 453, 129, 66. Westland-built. Crashed 17-7-43. Arrived mid-2013		12-13
❑ PT879*	Supermarine Spitfire IX	G-BYDE	45	ex North Weald, Romford, Sandown, Romford, Murmansk, 767 IAP, Sov AF, PT879 no RAF service. Crashed 18-5-45 Arrived 5-13.		12-13
❑ RM927	Supermarine Spitfire XIV	G-JNMA	44	ex High Wycombe, USA, Southend, Charnock Richard, Ostend, Belg AF SG-25, RAF, 29 MU, 403. Stored	[2]	12-13
❑ TP298	Supermarine Spitfire FR.XVIII	N41702	44	ex USA N41702, Duxford, India inst, IAF HS662, RAF TP298 n/s. Crashed 19-5-94. Stored		12-13
❑ -	Supermarine Spitfire IX		~	static fuselage project from original parts		12-13

■ **[1]** BS410 is being rebuilt for Martin Phillips - see also Exeter, Devon. **[2]** RM927 was registered to Paul Andrews in March 2009 - see also Wycombe Air Park, Bucks, and Kemble, Glos, for the rest of his fleet.

Also: During October 2013, Aztec 250 G-ESKY departed by road, thought bound for scrapping. Cherokee 235 G-BAMM was broken up and carted away for scrap during December 2013.

❑ G-BRDN	MS Rallye Club	68	ex OY-DTV. CoA 27-4-02, de-reg 11-2-10. Stored, off site	12-13
❑ G-OMOG	American AA-5A Cheetah	78	ex L' Upham, G-BHWR, N26892. CoA 15-4-02, de-reg 23-7-01	12-13

NEWPORT on the A3054, middle of the island

Kept in *separate* and *private* locations are two homebuilds.

❑ G-AZJE	Gardan GY-20 Minicab	74	ex Sandown. CoA 7-7-82	12-13
❑ G-BCMF	Levi Go-Plane	r74	flown only one, 16-11-74, de-reg 5-12-83	12-13

RYDE on the A3054, east of Newport

❑ G-ELIZ*	Denney Kitfox II	92	damaged 1993, CoA 5-11-93	12-13

SHANKLIN on the A3055 east of Newport

Jungle Jim's Adventure Play: Within the Summer Arcade on the Esplanade is a zebra-striped Rallye.

❑ G-BIRB	MS Rallye 100T	74	ex Manston, Firbeck, Carlisle, Hooton Park, Moston, Carlisle, F-BVAQ. CoA 16-6-90, de-reg 13-7-92	12-13

WHIPPINGHAM on the A3021 south of East Cowes

Lashed to a tree in a woodland 'encampment' near here is a microlight.

❑ G-MNCZ	Solar Pegasus XL-T	r85	de-reg 6-5-87	12-13

YARMOUTH on the A3054 west of Newport

A *private* owner here has a damaged Bulldog. One side has been painted as the prototype, G-AXEH.

❑ G-CCOA	SAL Bulldog 122	75	ex Ghana AF G-111, G-BCUU. Dam 22-8-01, re-reg 16-6-02	12-13

KENT

Includes the unitary authority of Medway

ASHFORD on the M20 west of Folkestone

The Jackaroo and Airedale are *believed* held at a private strip, the Varsity is with a private owner.

❑ G-ANFY	Thruxton Jackaroo	43	ex Tiger Moth I NL906 (Morris-built), 9 RFS, 23 EFTS, 9 FTS. CoA 25-5-68, de-reg 22-2-73	1-96
❑ G-ASBY	Beagle Airedale	62	ex St Ives, 'Overseen', Royston. CoA 22-3-80, de-reg 20-4-10	6-00
❑ WF408	Vickers Varsity T.1	52	ex Bruntingthorpe, East Grinstead, Northolt, 2 SoTT Cosford 8395M (12-11-73) 2 SoTT, 6 SS, 2 ANS, 1 RS, 11 FTS, 201 AFS. Cockpit	8-09

Also: A pair of cockpits arrived in the area by late 2011. Both *may* have moved on again...

❑ XH136*	'W'	EE Canberra PR.9	59	ex Spanhoe, Bruntingthorpe, Cosford 8782M (8-2-83), 1 PRU, A&AEE, 39, 13, 58, Moa. Short-built. Cockpit	1-12
❑ XV165*		HS Buccaneer S.2B	66	ex Spanhoe, Bruntingthorpe, Farnborough, Staverton, Bentham, Staverton, Hucclecote, Heathrow, Stock, Shawbury, 12. Cockpit. 12 Sqn colours	11-11

BELTRING on the A228 north of Paddock Wood

Hop Farm Family Park: In what must be the ultimate in farm diversification this site seems to offer everything from garden centre to 'gig' venue to an annual event they claim as "the world's largest military spectacular" (that was World War Two, surely?). In the equestrian zone, a Seneca fuselage serves as a jump.

◆ **Access:** *'Brown signed' at the junction of the A228 and B2160 north of Paddock Wood.* **Open:** *Daily 10:00 to17:00 daily.* **Contact: 01622 872068 | www.thehopfarm.co.uk**

❑ G-BAGZ	Piper Seneca 200	72	ex EI-AWS, G-BAGZ, N15067. De-reg 22-9-81	[1]	2-10

■ **[1]** *Golf-Zulu* was cancelled as sold in the USA as N474EW.

BRENCHLEY east of the B2160, east of Royal Tunbridge Wells

❑ G-ATKH	Luton LA.4A Minor	67	ex Rochester. CoA 4-8-06	9-06
❑ G-AYXO	Luton LA.5 Major	r71	ex Beeston Rylands. De-reg 2-9-91	9-06

BRENZETT on the A2070 north-west of New Romney

Romney Marsh Wartime Collection incorporating **Brenzett Aeronautical Museum Trust**: To emphasize the wider nature of the exhibits; the organisation was renamed during 2013. Canberra WH657 has been reduced to a cockpit section.

◆ **Access:** *'Brown signed' at the junction of the A259 and A2070 - east of the village.* **Open:** *Weekends Easter to end of Oct, also Bank Hols, 11:00 to 17:30.* **Contact:** *Ivychurch Road, Brenzett, Romney Marsh, TN29 0EE* | **01797 344747** | **www.brenzettaero.co.uk**

❑ G-AMSM	Douglas Dakota 4	43	ex Booker, Brenzett, Duxford, Brenzett, Lydd, Skyways, Eagle, Starways, KN274, TCDU, 77, St Eval SF, Azores SF, 43-49948. Damaged 17-8-78, de-reg 11-9-78. Cockpit. Air Freight colours		1-14
❑ V7350	Hawker Hurricane I	40	ex Robertsbridge, 85. Crashed 29-8-40. Cockpit	[1]	1-14
❑ WH657	EE Canberra B.2	52	ex Godalming, Cranfield, RAE, 231 OCU. SOC 29-11-77. Cockpit		1-14
❑ XK625	DH Vampire T.11	56	ex Firbeck, North Weald, Southend, Woodford, St Athan, 4 FTS, 1 FTS, 7 FTS. SOC 4-12-68		1-14

■ **[1]** Sgt Frank Walker-Smith was shot down by Bf 109s and he successfully baled out of V7350 and it crashed at Etchington, Kent.

CANTERBURY Woodhams Sprite BAPC.17 is thought to have moved on, with no 'forwarding address'.

CAPEL LE FERNE on the B2011 north-east of Folkestone

National Battle of Britain Memorial: Dubbed - wisely - 'a modern day place of pilgrimage', the deeply-moving statue of a pilot sitting, contemplating the English Channel, set against a huge three-bladed propeller akin to the ancient chalk figures found on the South Downs. The Christopher Foxley-Norris Memorial Wall carries the names of all who took part in the Battle. Planning permission for 'The Wing' visitor centre was granted in March 2012 with the aim of having it officially opened in July 2015 - the 75th anniversary of the Battle of Britain. Estimated to cost £2.8m, fund-raising for this incredible project had reached the half-way mark as *W&R* went to press - take a look at the website to see how you can help the appeal which has 'Staying True to the Few' as its campaign 'banner'.

◆ **Open:** *Car park / visitor centre Mar to Oct daily 10:00 to 17:00; winter car park and memorial weekends 10:00 to 16:00.* **Contact:** *PO Box 337, West Malling, ME6 9AA* **01732 870809** | **battleofbritain@btinternet.com** | **www.battleofbritainmemorial.org**

❑ 'P2970'	'US-X'	Hawker Hurricane I FSM	03	BAPC.291, 56 Squadron colours. *Little Willie*	[1]	1-14
❑ 'R6775'	'YT-J'	Supermarine Spitfire I FSM	04	BAPC.299, 65 Sqn colours	[2]	1-14

■ Both FSMs were built by GB Replicas. **[1]** Hurricane was donated by the Tory Family Association; it is in the colours of Plt Off Geoffrey Page when he was shot down and badly burnt on 12-8-40. **[2]** Spitfire is in the colours of Supermarine test pilot Fg Off Jeffrey Quill.

CHATHAM east of Rochester

The Historic Dockyard Chatham:

◆ **Access:** *North of the A231, well signed.* **Open:** *Mid-Feb to late Oct daily 10:00 to 18:00. Weekends only Nov. Closed Dec and Jan.* **Contact:** *Historic Dockyard, Chatham ME4 4TZ* | **email via website** | **01634 823800** | **www.thedockyard.co.uk**

❑ WG751	'710'	Westland Dragonfly HR.5	52	ex Gosport, Condover, Ramsgreave, Ancoats, *The Last Caravan*, Wisbech, Blackbushe, Fleetlands, RAF HS, Lossiemouth SF, HR.3, Yeovilton SF, 705. SOC 16-9-65. 705 Sqn colours	1-14

Royal Engineers Museum and Library: Among the exhibits are the medals etc of James McCudden VC DSO* MC* MM.

◆ **Access:** *On the B2004 north of Chatham.* **Open:** *Tue to Fri* (**not** *Mon) 09:00 to 17:00, weekends and Bank hols 11:30 to 17:00.* **Contact:** *Prince Arthur Road, Gillingham, ME4 4UG* | **01634 822839** | **mail@re-museum.co.uk** | **www.re-museum.co.uk**

❑ –		Military balloon	~	basket only. RAFM loan	3-12
❑ XZ964	'D'	HS Harrier GR.3	80	ex St Athan, 1417 Flt, 233 OCU, 3, 233 OCU, 1. *Ninja One*	3-12

CHATTENDEN on the A228 north of Rochester

Defence Explosive Ordnance Disposal, Munitions and Search School: The 'JP' is indoors in the Lodge Hill Camp site. The 'Doodlebug' is reported to be moving on.

❑ –		Fieseler Fi 103 (V-1)	c44	BAPC.158, inside the camp	5-00
❑ XM410		Hunting Jet Provost T.3	60	ex North Luffenham, Halton 8054AM (23-10-69), Shawbury, RAFC, 7 FTS, 2 FTS	4-11
❑ XT907	'W'	McD Phantom FGR.2	68	ex 9151M (10-1-93), 74, 56, 228 OCU, 54, 6, 228 OCU	12-13

CHISLET north of the A28 south-east of Herne Bay

❑ G-ANWX	Auster J/5L Aiglet Trainer	54	crashed 1-8-93, de-reg 24-9-93	8-05
❑ G-ASAX	Beagle Terrier 2	46	ex AOP.6 TW533, 652, LAS, AOPS, 663. CoA 1-9-96	8-05

CLIFFE at the end of the B2000, north of Rochester

Buckland Lake Reserve - Polaris Scuba: Has two airframes in the depths: Aztec 250E N54211 (submerged circa Mar 2012, last noted Aug 2013) and the fuselage of Falcon 20 9M-BCR (last reported Aug 2013). **www.bucklandlake.eu**

DOVER

Dover Museum: As well as the V-1 replica, other items of interest include a piece of Blériot's cross-Channel Type XI.

◆ **Open:** *Mon to Sat, daily 10:00 to 17:30, Sun 10:00 to 15:00. Closed Sun, Sep to Mar.* **Contact:** *Market Square, Dover, CT16 1PB* | **01304 201066** | **museumenquiries@dover.gov.uk** | **www.dovermuseum.co.uk**

❑ –	Fieseler Fi 103 (V-1) FSM	c00	BAPC.290		6-13

FOLKESTONE

A *private* strip in the general area holds several airframes.

❑ G-BECU	Bücker Jungmann	51	ex Spanish AF E3B-384. CASA-built. De-reg 1-12-77		4-10
❑ G-BECW	Bücker Jungmann	53	ex Spanish AF E3B-423. CASA-built. CoA 4-11-06	[1]	7-13
❑ G-RIXA	Piper J-3C-65 Cub	48	ex 7Q-YDF, 5Y-KEV, VP-KEV, VP-NAE, ZS-AZT		4-10
❑ -	Bücker Jungmann	~	frame		8-09

■ **[1]** *Reportedly* a composite, with parts from G-BECY, the former E3B-459.

At another, *private*, location in the general area, a Yak-3 is being restored.

❑ '21'	Yakovlev Yak-3 G-CDBJ	03	ex RA-44553. CoA 12-5-09		3-12

GRAVESEND on the A226 east of Dartford

A Buccaneer S.1 cockpit is with a local collector at a *private* location.

❑ XN928	Blackburn Buccaneer S.1	62	ex Manston, Bruntingthorpe, Cardiff, St Athan 8179M (10-9-74), 736, 809, 801. Desert pink, *Glenfiddich*, *Jaws* and *Liz*. Cockpit		12-11

Gravesend Police College: Specialist Training Centre

❑ G-AVMK	BAC 111-510ED	68	ex Bournemouth, European, BA, BEA. CoA 8-8-00, de-reg 1-3-02. Fuselage		5-07

HAWKINGE on the A260 north of Folkestone

Kent Battle of Britain Museum: Founder and leading light of the museum, **Mike Llewellyn** MBE, died on 16th October 2013. The depth and intensity of the displays is exceptional and serve as fine tribute to his determination and vision. The museum occupies buildings used during the Battle of Britain by the famous RAF station. The full-size models are occasionally repainted with new identities and it is not easy to keep track of them!

◆ **Access:** *Signed off the A260 to the west of the town.* **Open:** *Apr, May and Oct, 10:00 to 16:00 daily; Jun to Sep 10:00 to 17:00 daily; last admission one hour before.* ***NB*** *not open on Mondays other than Bank Hols.* **Note:** *Photography, notebooks and bags are* **not** *permitted within the museum.* **Contact:** *Aerodrome Road, Hawkinge Airfield, Folkestone, CT18 7AG* | **01303 893140** | **kentbattleofbritainmuseum@btinternet.com** | **www.kbobm.org**

❑ 'G-AAAH'	DH Moth replica	81	BAPC.168, ex Croydon, Gatwick. *Jason*. Stored		6-11
❑ –	Fieseler Fi 103 (V-1) FSM	64	BAPC.36, ex Old Warden, Duxford, Old Warden, *Operation Crossbow*		6-11
❑ –	M'schmitt 'Bf 109' FSM	68	BAPC.66, ex '1480', Chilham Castle, *Battle of Britain*		6-11
❑	M'schmitt 'Bf 109' FSM	68	BAPC.74, ex '6357', '6', Higher Blagdon, *Battle of Britain*		6-11
❑ 'D-3-340'	DFS Grunau Baby	~	ex Ramsgate		6-11
❑ 'K5054'	Supermarine Spitfire rep	c88	BAPC.297, ex Luton, Lowestoft, Luton	[1]	6-11
❑ 'K5054'*	Supermarine Spitfire proto rep G-BRDV	84	ex Southampton, Sandown, Keevil. CoA 18-2-95, de-reg 19-5-00	[2]	12-12
❑ 'N2532' 'GZ-H'	Hawker Hurricane FSM	99	BAPC.272, 32 Sqn colours		6-11
❑ 'N3289' 'DW-K'	Supermarine Spitfire FSM	68	BAPC.65, ex Chilham Castle, *Battle of Britain*. 610 Sqn colours		6-11
❑ 'N3313' 'KL-B'	Supermarine Spitfire FSM	68	BAPC.69, ex Higher Blagdon, Stoneleigh, *Battle of Britain*. 54 Sqn colours		6-11
❑ 'N7033'	NAA Harvard IIb FX442	44	Bournemouth, Fordingbridge, Bournemouth, Sandhurst, Hullavington, 501, 226 OCU, 203 AFS, 61 OTU. SOC 14-12-56		8-12

❑	'N9181'		DH Tiger Moth	~	ex Bedford area	8-12
❑	'P2921'	'GZ-L'	Hawker Hurricane FSM	99	BAPC.272, 32 Sqn colours	6-11
❑	'P3059'	'SD-N'	Hawker Hurricane FSM	99	BAPC.273, ex Chilham Castle, *Battle of Britain*, 501 Sqn c/s	6-11
❑	'P3208'	'SD-T'	Hawker Hurricane FSM	68	BAPC.63, ex 'L1592', Higher Blagdon, *Battle of Britain*. 501 Sqn colours	6-11
❑	'P3679'	'GZ-K'	Hawker Hurricane FSM	99	BAPC.278, 32 Sqn colours	6-11
❑	'MK356'	'2I-V'	Sup' Spitfire IX FSM	~	– [3	6-11
❑	–		Hawker Hurricane FSM	~	ex Lowestoft. 'RF-U' 303 Squadron colours	6-11
❑	'425/17'		Fokker Dr.I FSM	78	BAPC.133, ex Winthorpe, Higher Blagdon	6-11
❑	-*		Fokker Dr.I replica	c04	ex Manston, Halton, *Flyboys*	12-12
❑	-*		Gotha G.IV replica	c04	ex Manston, Halton, *Flyboys*. Forward fuselage	12-12
❑	'14'		Messerschmitt 'Bf 109' FSM	68	BAPC.67, ex Coventry, North Weald, Newark, *Battle of Britain*. JG52 colours	6-11

■ **[1]** *This* 'K5054' is an unfinished project started as an all-metal faithful reproduction by Barry Gennard in Luton. **[2]** This one is full-scale, but with wooden airframe and powered by a converted Jaguar V-12; built 1984 by Viking Wood Products. **[3]** The Spitfire IX FSM has a real counterpart, at Coningsby, Lincs, and there is yet *another* MK356 at Cosford, Shropshire!

Peter Smith: The collection is *thought* unchanged. Peter has a Chipmunk PAX on loan at Brooklands, Surrey - which see.

◆ **Access**: *Airframes stored in a variety of places, visits are* **not** *possible*

❑	G-AAXK	Klemm L 25	30	ex Sevenoaks, CoA 29-11-60, de-reg 18-3-91. Fuselage	3-02
❑	–	RAF BE.2c FSM	76	BAPC.117, ex Manston, Sevenoaks, Brooklands, North Weald, *Wings*	3-02
❑	–	Supermarine Spitfire FSM	c90	BAPC.190, ex Barton, Chelford, 'K5054', Sevenoaks	3-02
❑	EJ922	Hawker Typhoon Ib	43	ex Manston, Brooklands, Sevenoaks, Biggin Hill, Southend, Brooklands, Brownhills, 3. Gloster-built. SOC 13-3-47. Cockpit	3-04
❑	–	RAF 'SE.5a' FSM	~	ex Sevenoaks, Coventry. Poor state	3-02
❑	–	Hawker Typhoon I	~	ex Manston, Brooklands, Sevenoaks, Innsworth, Leeds, Cheltenham, Kemble. Cockpit	3-02

KENT AIRPORT, or Kent International Airport even, more reasonably Manston EGMH

Spitfire and Hurricane Memorial Museum: The superb Hurricane and Spitfire are both examples of the workmanship of Medway APS, Rochester. There is a wealth of other material to see and the superb 'Merlin Cafeteria' to sample.

◆ **Access:** *Signed off the A253 Ramsgate road.* **Open:** *Mar to Oct 10:00 to 17:00, Nov to Feb 10:00 to 16:00, daily. Closures at Xmas and New Year* **Contact:** *The Airfield, Manston Road, Ramsgate, CT12 5DF* **01843 821940** | **spitfire752@btconnect.com** | **www.spitfiremuseum.org.uk**

❑	'BN230'	'FT-A'	Hawker Hurricane IIc LF751	44	ex Rochester, Bentley Priory, Waterbeach 5466M (21-7-45), 24 OTU, 1681 BDTF. 43 Sqn colours [1]	1-14
❑	TB752	'KH-Z'	Supermarine Spitfire XVI	45	8086M, ex Rochester, Manston 7256M / 7279M, SOC 28-9-55. Lyneham, 5 CAACU, 103 FRS, 102 FRS, 403, 66. *Val* (port). 403 Sqn colours [2]	1-14

■ **[1]** Hurricane 'BN230' is a composite, with parts from Mk.II Z3687 and Mk.IIc PG593 and is on loan from the RAF Museum. See Bentley Priory, Gtr Lon, for *another* 'BN230'. **[2]** The Spitfire is on loan from the RAF Museum.

RAF Manston History Museum: Located in the old MT building, the museum is run by the RAF Manston History Society and concentrates on the 90-year history of Manston, both military and civil. Extensive support displays are very absorbing; the wartime street recreation is exceptional.

W&R23 (p84) recorded the former Flyboys Fokker Dr.I as being disposed of during 2010; it was bound eventually for Hawkinge, Kent, as was the Gotha replica during 2012.

◆ **Open:** *Daily Mar to Oct 10:00 to 16:00. Nov to Feb Sat and Sun 10:00 to 16:00.* **Contact:** *Manston Road, Manston, Ramsgate, CT12 5DF* | **01843 825224** | **www.rafmanston.co.uk**

❑	G-BXVZ*	PZL Iskra TS-11	77	ex airfield, Shoreham, SP-DOF. De-reg 24-4-09. Arr 8-13	1-14
❑	G-SSWP	Short 330-100	79	ex Southend, CS-DBY, 5N-OJU ntu, G-BGNB, N330VM, G-BGNB, G-14-3030. CoA 28-8-03, de-reg 8-10-04. Arrived 8-04. Cockpit	1-14
❑	–	Huntair Pathfinder	~	ex Indonesia. Arrived 2003	1-14
❑	'B_619'	Sopwith 1½ Strutter rep	c04	ex Halton, *Flyboys*. Arrived 2005	1-14
❑	'VM791'	Slingsby Cadet TX.3 XA312	53	ex Kenley 8876M, 636 GS, 634 GS, 2 GC, GIS. SOC 22-4-68. Arrived 1999	1-14

❑ 'WD615'		Gloster Meteor TT.20 WD646	52	ex North Weald, Elmdon, Cosford 8189M (10-12-71), 5 CAACU, 3/4 CAACU, AWA, CSE. AWA-built. Arrived 1997 85 Sqn, NF.11 colours	1-14
❑ WP772	'4'	DHC Chipmunk T.10	52	ex Lyneham, Colerne, Abingdon, St Athan, Middle Wallop, BFWF, QUAS, Hull UAS, 17 RFS. Arrived 1999	1-14
❑ WT205		EE Canberra B.15	55	ex Eastwood, Foulness, MoA, 9. SOC 31-8-72. Short-built. Arrived 14-10-00. 9 Sqn colours. Cockpit	1-14
❑ XA231		Slingsby Grasshopper TX.1	53	ex Stockport, 'Sealand', Cosford 8888M, Warwick, Kimbolton, Petersfield. Arrived 1999	1-14
❑ XG226		Hawker Hunter F.6A	56	ex Faversham, Manston, Faygate, Catterick 8800M (15-2-83), 1 TWU, TWU, 229 OCU, 92, 66, 92. Cockpit. 92 Sqn colours	1-14
❑ XL190		HP Victor K.2	61	ex St Mawgan 9216M (27-9-93), 55, 232 OCU, Witt Wing, 139. Arrived 6-2-99. Cockpit	1-14
❑ XN380	'67'	Westland Whirlwind HAS.7	60	ex Lashenden, Wroughton, 705, 771, 829, 824, 825. SOC 9-3-77. Arrived 13-10-01. *Doris*. USAF H-19 colours	1-14
❑ XS482	'A-D'	Westland Wessex HU.5	63	ex DSFCTE, Farnborough, A&AEE, 848. SOC 20-2-86. SAR colours	1-14
❑ XV352		HS Buccaneer S.2B	67	ex Gravesend, Manston, Stock, St Athan, Lossiemouth, 237 OCU, 208. Cockpit	1-14
❑ XZ106	'FD'	SEPECAT Jaguar GR.3A	76	ex Ipswich, St Athan, 2, 41, SAOEU, GR.1, 41, 16, 54. SOC 3-5-05	1-14
❑ ZA325	'TAX'	Panavia Tornado GR.1	80	ex St Athan 9338M, Cosford, St Athan, 15, TTTE. SOC 13-8-03. Cockpit	1-14
❑ -	'A-I'	Nieuport 17 rep	c04	ex Halton, *Flyboys*. Arr 2005. Travelling airframe, stored	1-14
❑ -		Nieuport 17 rep	c04	ex Halton, *Flyboys*. Arrived 2005. Fuselage	1-14
❑ -		Fieseler Fi 103 (V-1) rep	c04	pole-mounted 'gate guardian'	1-14
❑ '117415'	'TR-415'	Lockheed T-33A/N Silver Star	56	N36TH, ex North Weald, G-BYOY, N333DV, N134AT, N10018, N134AT, RCAF 21231. Canadair-built. De-reg 8-6-05. Arrived 3-2-10. 512th FIS colours	1-14

Defence Fire Training and Development Centre (DFTDC): Note the name change.

❑ WK124	'CR'	EE Canberra TT.18	54	ex 9093M, Wyton, 100, 7, B.2, 213, 59, 103. Avro-built. Flew in 26-3-91	6-11
❑ XR503		Westland Wessex HC.2	63	ex Boscombe Down, Gosport A2705[2], RAE, A&AEE, MoA	6-11
❑ XS714	'P'	HS Dominie T.1	66	ex 9246M, Finningley, 6 FTS, RAFC, CAW. Arrived 11-95	6-11
❑ XV229		HS Nimrod MR.2	69	ex Kinloss, Kin Wg, StM Wg, K Wg, 42, A&AEE, MR.1, Kin Wg. Flew in 26-5-10, last-ever MR.2 flight	6-11
❑ XV411	'L'	McD Phantom FGR.2	69	ex 9103M (11-7-91), 19, 56, 29, 92, 19, 92, 2, 41, 14. Poor state	6-11
❑ XV725	'C'	Westland Wessex HC.2	68	ex Cosford, Gosport A2707 [2], Shawbury, 72, 18. Arrived 11-08	6-11
❑ XV864		HS Buccaneer S.2B	68	ex 9234M (28-3-94), 12, 237 OCU, 16. Poor state	6-11
❑ XW768	'N'	HS Harrier GR.3	71	ex Gosport, Cosford, Halton 9072M (10-8-90), 4, 1, 4, 20	6-11
❑ XW870	'F'	Sud Gazelle HT.3	73	ex 9299M, Shawbury, 2 FTS, CFS. Crashed 8-8-95	6-11
❑ XX116		SEPECAT Jaguar GR.3A	73	ex St Athan, 16, 226 OCU, 6, Indian AF JI-008, G-27-316, GR.1, 226 OCU, JOCU. Arrived 26-9-05	6-11
❑ XZ215*		Westland Lynx AH.7	79	ex Middle Wallop, 9 Regt. Arrived 10-12	10-12
❑ XZ966	'G'	HS Harrier GR.3	73	ex Cottesmore 9221M (13-10-93), St Athan, 1417 Flt, 4, 1417 Flt, 233 OCU, 1, 1417, 1. Poor state	6-11
❑ ZE165*	'GE'	Panavia Tornado F.3	86	ex Shawbury, 43. Arrived 20-3-13	3-13
❑ ZE204*	'FC'	Panavia Tornado F.3	86	ex Shawbury, Leuchars, 25. Arrived 20-3-13	3-13
❑ ZE360	'O'	McD F-4J(UK) Phantom	c67	ex 9059M, 74, USN 155574. Last flown 22-2-91	6-11
❑ ZH553*	'RT'	Panavia Tornado F.3	93	ex Shawbury, Leuchars, 56, 11, 56, 11, 56, 29. Arrived 20-3-13	3-13

■ **[1]** Wessex XR503 is fitted with the tail of XT463 - the rest of the latter can be found at Hixon, Staffs.

Airport: Manston continues to act as a storage centre for 'mature' jetliners; as usual only longer-term inmates are listed. Predictably, the hyped-up reports of TS-11 G-BXVZ being bought for an enormous fee by the proprietors of a Sussex eatery (as quoted in *W&R23*, p85) did not materialise. *Victor-Zulu* moved instead into the care of the RAF Manston History Museum - see above - in August 2013. The fuselage of Boeing 707 N707QJ had gone by June 2013. DC-10-30 5X-JOE was broken up and removed during June 2012. DC-8-55F 9G-MKA was scrapped and removed during December 2013.

❑ LV-AZF	Boeing 747-267B	83	ex Southern Winds, N230AL, LV-AZF, N230AL, G-VRUM, TF-ATV, G-VRUM, B-HIF, VR-HIF, N6066U		8-13
❑ N309TD	Boeing 747-269M	82	ex 9K-ADD		8-13
❑ N880PA*	HS 146-200	85	ex Southend, G-OZRH, EI-DDF ntu, N188US, N364PS. Arrived 20-2-13. Engine test-bed		2-13
❑ TF-AMC	Boeing 747-2B3F	79	ex Air Atlanta, F-GBOX. Scrapped 6-13, cockpit extant		6-13
❑ TF-ARU	Boeing 747-344	83	ex Air Atlanta, ZS-SAF		8-13

LASHENDEN AERODROME or Headcorn, on the A247 south of Headcorn — EGKH

Lashenden Air Warfare Museum (LAWM): During April 2012 the museum acquired a 40ft x 55ft building to form a new display hall. Planning permission was granted in August 2013 and construction started the following month. Restoration of the Fi 103R-IV 'Reichenberg' was completed by Auktionhaus fur Historische Technik at Geisenhausen, Germany, to a very high standard. The £33,000 project returned during March 2013 and is stored awaiting the new display building.

The loan agreement regarding the F-100F and Mystère expired at the end of 2007. The airframes have been patiently awaiting removal or scrapping ever since. In fairness to LAWM, they have been moved to the 'Aerodrome' section below as the airframes have long since ceased to be the museum's responsibility.

◆ **Open:** *Sat, Sun and Bank Hols 10:30 to 18:00, May to Sep; Sun and Bank Hols 10:30 to 15:30, Mar to May and Oct to Dec.* ***Closed*** *Jan and Feb. Other times by prior arrangement* **Note** *Photos, note taking, sketching within the buildings possible* ***only*** *by prior, written, permission* **Contact:** *c/o Lashenden Aerodrome, Ashford, TN27 9HX* **01622 631799 | lashendenairwar@aol.com | www.lashendenairwarfaremuseum.co.uk**

❑ ZF587	EE Lightning F.53	68	ex Reading, Portsmouth, *Wing Commander,* Portsmouth, Stretton, Warton, R Saudi AF 215, 53-691, G-27-61. Last flown 29-8-68. Cockpit	[1]	2-14
❑ 100549	Focke-Achgelis Fa 330A-1 Bachstelze	c44	ex Manchester, Liverpool, Blackpool, Lavenham, Hullavington, Biggin Hill, Farnborough		2-14
❑ –*	Fieseler Fi 103R-IV	44	BAPC.91, ex Germany, Lashenden, Rochester, Horsham, Farnborough, Dannenburg. Arrived 4-3-13	[2]	2-14

■ **[1]** The Lightning cockpit was split vertically for use in the sci-fi film *Wing Commander*. It is on loan from Mike Coleman. **[2]** Almost certain to have originated at Dannenberg and captured 23-4-45; piloted V-1 'Reichenberg', w/nr quoted as 6/2080.

Aerodrome: Damaged Turbulent G-APNZ moved to Derby, Derbyshire, by February 2013.

❑ G-AHAV	Auster J/1 Autocrat	46	ex HB-EOM ntu. CoA 21-6-75, de-reg 28-3-06. Stored, off-site		4-08
❑ G-ARHL	Piper Aztec 250	61	CoA 23-11-79, de-reg 15-3-01. Fire dump		4-08
❑ G-ASKP	DH Tiger Moth	35	ex Mk.II N6588, 9 EFTS, 9 ERFTS. CoA 14-3-09		5-12
❑ G-AWGA	Beagle Airedale	62	ex Biggin Hill, Sevenoaks, Biggin, Bicester, EI-ATA, G-AWGA, D-ENRU. CoA 3-7-86, de-reg 30-9-86		4-08
❑ G-AZVJ	Piper Seneca 200	72	ex N4529T. CoA 21-8-03, de-reg6-2-09. Dumped		6-13
❑ G-BAKD	Piper Seneca 200	72	ex N1378T. CoA 30-12-07, de-reg 17-11-11. Dumped		6-13
❑ G-BFMR	Piper Pacer 125	50	ex N7025K. CoA 6-3-06		4-08
❑ G-BLYP	Robin R3000/120	85	CoA 5-5-01		3-12
❑ G-BPZD	Nord NC.858S	50	ex F-BEZD. Crashed 1-7-06. CoA 26-6-07		3-12
❑ G-BSZG	Stolp Starduster	56	ex N70P. CoA 4-7-00		3-13
❑ N5240H	Piper Clipper	~	dismantled		3-12
❑ -	Airbus A300B4	~	ex HeavyLift. Cockpit, simulator		3-12
❑ 84 '8-NF'	Dassault Mystère IVA	c57	ex Sculthorpe, French AF. Last flown 17-10-79	[1]	12-13
❑ 56-3938 '11-MU'	NAA F-100F-16-NA Super Sabre	56	ex Sculthorpe, French AF. Last flown 24-5-77 Arrived 2-4-79. Stored	[1]	12-13

■ **[1]** See notes under LAWM, above.

LYDD AIRPORT — EGMD

Two hulks, both last noted in August 2005, have been deleted: Trislander G-AZLJ and Cessna 336 G-PIXS. At least the cabin of the latter had moved to Elvira, Portugal, by April 2009.

LYMINGE east of the B2068, north of Hythe

A *private* strip here has become a haven for T.67s.

❑ G-BLTW	Slingsby T.67B Firefly	85	CoA 15-9-06	5-10
❑ G-BLUX	Slingsby T.67M-200 Firefly	85	ex G-7-145, G-BLUX, G-7-113. CoA 27-4-07	5-10

❑ G-BOCL		Slingsby T.67C Firefly	86	CoA 26-2-07		5-10
❑ G-BONU		Slingsby T.67B Firefly	86	ex Hinton-in-the-Hedges. CoA 29-6-00		5-10

RICHBOROUGH Last noted in October 2007, Whirlwind HAR.10 XJ727 has been deleted.

ROCHESTER AERODROME on the A229 south of Rochester EGTO

Medway Aircraft Preservation Society Ltd: Notching up another incredible restoration, the Rochester team bade farewell to Defiant N1671 when it returned to Hendon, Gtr London, on 6th December 2012. Not content with this, the team turned their skills on a Phoenix UAV and took delivery of the former Rochester-built Short Scion in June 2013. Next RAF Museum project is Lysander III R9125 which was due from Hendon as *W&R* went to press.

◆ **Access:** *Workshop is open to the public on Sun, Mon and Wed 09:00 to 13:00. Airport rules must be observed – the threshold of Runway 34 needs negotiating via traffic lights.* **Contact:** *c/o AFIS Unit, Rochester Airport, Maidstone Road, Chatham, ME5 9SD* | **01634 204492** | **info@mapsl.co.uk** | **www.mapsl.co.uk**

❑ G-AEZF*		Short Scion II	37	ex Redhill, East Tilbury, Southend, M5. CoA 5-5-54, de-reg 22-1-70. Arrived 12-6-13	[1]	1-14
❑ 'XT005'*		Northrop Shelduck D.1	~	ex Gillingham	[2]	1-14
❑ ZJ303*		GEC Phoenix UAV	~	engineless, first noted 7-12		1-14

■ **[1]** Pobjoy Airmotors and Aircraft-built at Rochester, first flying 9-12-37 as a floatplane. Test flown with 'B Condition' (or 'trade-plate') markings as M5 1941. **[2]** Acquired from Gillingham ATC during 1992. Identity unknown, but it is known that it was the fifth in a batch, so the serial reflects this.

BAE Systems: *W&R23* recorded the departure of gate guard Lightning F.53 ZF581 to Bentwaters in May 2011. This was replaced at the facility close to the threshold of Runway 20 by a more recent product, a Phoenix UAV.

❑ -*		GEC Phoenix UAV	~	Army markings, on gate, first noted 7-12		1-13

Also:

❑ G-BXVC		Piper Turbo Arrow IV	79	ex Redhill, D-ELIV, N2152V. Cr 22-8-98, de-reg 22-1-03. Dump		6-13
❑ WZ589	'19'	DH Vampire T.11	53	ex Lashenden, Woodford, Chester, St Athan, 56. SOC 30-10-67		9-02
❑ XE956		DH Vampire T.11 G-OBLN	55	ex Pen-Coed, Bridgend, St Albans, Hatfield, CATCS, 1 FTS, 8 FTS, 3 CAACU, APS, 67. SOC 2-2-71. De-reg 14-2-05		5-04

ROYAL TUNBRIDGE WELLS

A collector in the general area specialising in Ducati motorcycles has expanded his collection to include aircraft.

◆ **Access: Private** *collection, visits by prior arrangement* **only**

❑ XX841		SEPECAT Jaguar T.4	75	ex Ipswich, Shawbury, 6, 16, T.2, 6, ETPS, 41, 226 OCU. SOC 15-8-05. 6 Sqn colours		6-10
❑ XZ364	'FS'	SEPECAT Jaguar GR.3A	76	ex Ipswich, Shawbury, 41, 54, GR.1, Gulf Det, 54, 2. SOC 28-11-05. Cockpit		6-10
❑ ZE350*	'T'	McD F-4J(UK)	c67	ex Welshpool, Stock, Pendine, Laarbruch 9080M (10-10-91), 74, USN 153768, NATC. Cockpit		6-11
❑ ZH799		HS Sea Harrier FA.2	96	ex Ipswich, St Athan, Yeovilton, 899, 801, 800, 801		6-10

SEVENOAKS

In the *general* area is a helicopter cache.

❑ XR502	'Z'	Westland Wessex HC.2 N486KA	63	ex G-CCUP (de-reg 7-1-13), Colsterworth, Fleetlands, 60, 72, WTF, 18, 1 FTU. SOC 16-3-00		12-13
❑ XV722	'WH'	Westland Wessex HC.2	68	ex Hixon, Shawbury, 2 FTS, CATCS, 18, 72, 18		12-13
❑ XV731	'Y'	Westland Wessex HC.2	68	ex Redhill area, Fleetlands, 72, WTF, 240 OCU, 18, 78		12-13
❑ XX414		Sud Gazelle AH.1	75	ex Hurstbourne Tarrant, Gosport, 671, Fleetlands, 651, 661, 662, 663, 660. Westland-built		4-13

Also:

❑ G-APJZ		Auster J/1N Alpha	57	ex St Albans, 5N-ACY, VR-NDR ntu, G-APJZ. Cr 10-11-75		12-97

SHOREHAM west of the A225 north of Sevenoaks EGKA

Shoreham Aircraft Museum: SAM is a superb museum based upon an extensive number of 'digs', all beautifully researched and presented. Included in the incredible selection of artefacts is the rear fuselage skin from Bf 109 *Black 6*. The museum is carrying out an incredible project to erect stone memorials to honour the RAF Battle of Britain pilots that were killed in combat in crashes within a ten-mile radius. The tea room is exceptional!

◆ **Open:** *Sat, Sun and Bank Hols 10:00 to 17:00, or by prior arrangement. Special events staged regularly.* **Contact:** *High Street, Shoreham Village, Sevenoaks, TN14 7TB* | **01959 524416** | **mail@shoreham-aircraft-museum.co.uk** | **www.shoreham-aircraft-museum.co.uk**

❑	TB885	Supermarine Spitfire XVI	44	ex Kenley, *Reach for the Sky* as 'R1247', Cosford	[1]	4-08
❑	-	Junkers Ju 88A-1	c42	ex Norway. Cockpit		12-13

■ [1] The remains of Spitfire XVI are in deep store and ***not*** available for inspection. It saw no operational service.

TONBRIDGE Spitfire I X4276 is now listed under Biggin Hill, Gtr London.

WHITFIELD Swallow CAX and Schleicher Ka 7 EVB, both last noted in December 2005, have been deleted.

LANCASHIRE

Includes the unitary authorities of Blackburn with Darwen, and Blackpool

BLACKBURN

A *private* collector has two projects in the general area.

❑	G-ARDG	EP Prospector	61	ex Haverhill, Redhill, Washington, Durrington, Middle Wallop, Shoreham, Lympne. 'Pod', poor state	[1]	9-10
❑	WD377	DHC Chipmunk T.10	51	ex Haverhill, Dumfries, 12 AEF, Glas UAS, HCEU, 11 RFS, 2 BFTS. Crashed 29-7-66. Cockpit	[2]	9-10

■ **[1]** At least the rear end of EP.9 G-ARDG is incorporated within the composite on show at Middle Wallop, Hampshire. **[2]** The rear fuselage of WD377 can be found under Upper Ballinderry, N Ireland.

BLACKPOOL AIRPORT on the B6430, south of Garstang, west of the M6 EGNH

Airport: Pitts S-1 G-BTEF was flying by 2010. Two entries have been deleted: Cherokee G-AVWE (last noted Aug 2000) and AA-5 G-BCEO (Jan 2004). The hulk of Short 330 G-SSWA on the dump was unrecognisable by March 2011 and has been deleted. Several other entries are well long-in-the-tooth, but are *believed* to be extant.

❑	G-AWKP	Robin DR.253 Regent	68	Damaged 8-6-98, de-reg 13-10-98. Fuselage	10-03
❑	G-AWUA	Cessna P.206D	68	ex Thruxton, N8750Z. Damaged 16-10-87, de-reg 11-8-98	10-03
❑	G-BJZX	Grob G-109	82	ex D-KGRO ntu. Crashed 15-5-98, de-reg 18-3-02	10-03
❑	G-BLWD	Piper Seneca II	80	ex ZS-KKV, ZS-XAT, N8253E. Crashed 8-9-02	10-03
❑	G-BMJG	Piper Arrow 200	69	ex ZS-TNS, ZS-FYC, N9345N. Crashed 11-10-98, de-reg 15-4-99. Fuselage	10-03
❑	G-BSPF	Cessna T.303 Crusader	82	ex OY-SVH, N3116C. De-reg 28-8-98	10-03
❑	G-KBPI	Piper Warrior 161	78	ex Goodwood, G-BFSZ, N9556N	11-11
❑	G-LYDD	Piper Navajo 300	70	ex Lydd, G-BBDU, N6796L. Damaged 17-7-91, de-reg 30-3-93. Dump	10-03
❑	–	BAe ATP	~	ex Chadderton. Fuselage, dump	7-10

BURNLEY on the M65, north-east of Blackburn

Pennine Aviation: David Stansfield and friends work on a series of projects, the Albemarle and the Hadrian being the largest. A fascinating remnant is a substantial proportion of Bell P.400 Airacobra BX195, including all of the tail unit, many cockpit items, the Alison engine and propeller blade.

◆ **Access:** Not *available for public inspection.* **Contact**: *54 Hillcrest Avenue, Cliviger, Burnley, BB10 4JA*

❑	–	AW Albemarle	~	ex Bacup, Carlisle, Westnewton. Cockpit section etc	5-08
❑	–	Waco Hadrian	~	ex Bacup. Cockpit	5-08

CAPERNWRAY on the A6 north of Carnforth

Capernwray Diving Centre: Has several submerged hulks: Cessna F.150L G-BFWL (last noted Apr 2010); HS 748-2A G-BVOV (sunk 29th March 2010); Dragonfly HR.3 WP503 (Apr 2010); Wessex HU.5 XS491 (Apr 2010). **www.dive-site.co.uk**

CHORLEY on the A6 south of Preston

International Fire Training and Development Centre: Washington Hall; the facility is spread over 28 acres.

◆ **Access:** *by prior arrangement* **only | www.washingtonhall.co.uk**

❑ –		BAe ATP	~	ex Chadderton, c/n 2070, fuselage	1-13

Also: Auster 5C G-AKSZ was flying by mid-2012.

COCKERHAM on the A588 between Lancaster and Fleetwood

Last noted in November 2008 Minimax G-MWWE has been deleted.

❑ G-BKPC		Cessna A.185F Skywagon	79	ex N4599E. CoA 11-11-07	12-09

ECCLESTON on the B5250 south of Leyland

Bygone Times Antique Warehouse: This huge emporium occasionally offers airframes among the Poole pottery.

◆ **Access:** *At Grove Mill, The Green, off the B5250 - 'Brown signed' - check for opening times.* **Contact: 01257 451889 | www.bygonetimes.co.uk**

❑ 'A4850'		RAF SE.5a scale rep	c68	BAPC.176, ex Chorley, Barton, Firbeck, Pontefract	10-11

Delph Scuba Diving Centre: Has two submerged airframes: the forward fuselage of a Short 360, and Jet Provost T.4 XP688; both last noted June 2012. **www.thedelph.com**

KIRKHAM on the A583 between Blackpool and Preston

A Wasp is kept at a *private* address in the *general* area.

❑ XS570*	'445'	Westland Wasp HAS.1	64	ex Birkenhead, Glasgow, Plymouth, Lee-on-Solent, A2699, 829. SOC 4-12-91	3-12

LYTHAM ST ANNE'S south of Blackpool

Representing the presentation aircraft *Lytham St Anne's*, a Spitfire V FSM was unveiled at Fairhaven Lake on the Inner Promenade on 21st June 2012. As part of the fund-raising for the memorial, the **Spitfire Display Team** came into being. A Spitfire cockpit using a large number of original fittings was used as a travelling exhibit, mounted within a trailer. This moved to Shannon, Ireland, in March 2013. The team have a Mk.IX FSM in 611 Squadron colours which is used as a travelling display and is available for hire.

◆ **Contact: info@w3644.com | www.w3644.com | www.spitfiredisplayteam.co.uk**

❑ 'W3644'	'QV-J'	Sup' Spitfire Vb FSM	12	unveiled 21-6-13. *Lytham St Anne's*, 19 Sqn colours	[1]	12-13
❑ 'BS435'	'FY-F'	Sup' Spitfire IX FSM	~	ex Delabole, 'RB159', Hooton Park. *Lucy*. 611 Sqn colours. Travelling display	[2]	12-13

■ **[1]** 'W3644' was flown by Sgt Alan Lever Ridings of 19 Sqn on an escort for RAF Bostons on 23-6-42; he was shot down and killed. **[2]** 'BS435' wears the colours of 611 (West Lancashire) Sqn, it was shot down 5-2-43 and Sqn Ldr H T Armstrong killed.

Blue Bird Project: A workshop in the area is rebuilding the BSE Orpheus-powered boat *Bluebird K7* in which Donald Campbell met his fate on Windermere on 4th January 1967. The engine donor airframe is stored. The team are also well into the restoration of the Fleet Air Arm Museum's Barracuda's tail surfaces; with more of the project due in course.

◆ **Access:** *By prior application* **only | www.bluebirdproject.com**

❑ XM708		Folland Gnat T.1	61	ex Bruntingthorpe, Kings Langley, Locking, Halton 8573M (2-12-77), 4 FTS, CFS, HS	3-13

PRESTON

BAE Systems Engineering Training Centre: Marsh Lane. **Private** *location, visits possible* **only** *by prior arrangement*

❑ ZA328		Panavia Tornado GR.1	81	ex BAE	[1]	2-10

■ **[1]** Factoids: first flown on 13th July 1981, last flight (its 781st) on 12th December 2002; total time 1,093 hours.

Phil Elsden: Took delivery of a 'JP' cockpit and is making good progress with its restoration.

◆ **Access: Private** *location, visits possible* **only** *by prior arrangement* | **XW315JP5a@gmail.com**

❑ XW315*		BAC Jet Provost T.5A	70	ex Wolverhampton, Long Marston, 'Lincs', CFS, 3 FTS, CFS. Damaged 5-7-84. Cockpit. Arrived 27-6-12	2-14

Others: Lightning F.1A XM173 was put up for sale in June 2012; it moved to Old Sodbury, Glos, on 11th August 2012. Wessex HU.5 XT469 moved by November 2012 to Bowgreave, Lancs, but by January 2014 had settled upon Weeton, Lancs.

❑ XT469*		Westland Wessex HU.5	65	ex Kirkham, Stafford, 8920M, Wroughton, 771, 847, 772, 846, 848, 847, 848. SOC 27-9-07	11-12

SAMLESBURY on the A59 east of Preston

BAE Systems / Spirit AeroSystems: Lightning F.53 ZF580 came down off display during February 2013. It was trucked to Newquay, Cornwall, on 11th March 2013. There, Gateguards UK is using it to create a mould and the 'gate' here is due to be guard by an full-scale model built from this exercise. It is reported that an F-35 FSM (I *refuse* to call it a Lightning II!) will also appear here and doubted that the 'real' Lightning will return.

WARTON AIRFIELD on the A584 west of Preston EGNO

BAE Systems: *W&R23* (p89) wrote Harrier GR.5 ZD353 out of this location as gone by 2011; it was destined for Ipswich, Suffolk. Former Overseas Training Unit Tornado GR.1 ZA359 left by road 24th January 2014 for Selby, N Yorks.

❑ XS928	'AD'	EE Lightning F.6	67	ex Binbrook, 5-11, 56, 11, 56, 74, 5, 11. SOC 13-6-88. 5 Sqn c/s	1-14
❑ ZA101		HS Hawk Mk.50 G-HAWK	76	ex G-HAWK, ZA101, XX155 ntu. De-reg 13-3-90. Apprentices	11-11
❑ ZA327		Panavia Tornado GR.1	80	ex Leeming. Cockpit	4-08
❑ ZA411	'TT'	Panavia Tornado GR.1	83	ex St Athan, 617, 15, 617, 2, 20, 16. Static trials	12-11
❑ ZK531*		HS Hawk T.53	c80	ex Brough, Warton, Indonesian AF LL-5306, G-9-471. Arrived by 1-13	8-13
❑ ZK532*		HS Hawk T.53	c80	ex Brough, Warton, Indonesian AF LL-5315. Arrived by 1-13	8-13

No.**967 Squadron Air Cadets**: On the Bank Lane site.

❑ WT520		EE Canberra PR.7	55	ex Lytham St Annes, Eaglescott, Burntwood, Swinderby 8184M (8-10-71), 8094M ntu, CAW, 31, 17, 1, 17, 31, 80. Short-built. Cockpit	10-11

WEETON on the B5260 west of Blackpool, north of the M55 EGNH

A Wessex is kept at a *private* address in what is now called Weeton Camp, once home to 8 School of Technical Training.

❑ XT469*		Westland Wessex HU.5	65	ex Bowgreave, Kirkham, Stafford, 8920M, Wroughton, 771, 847, 772, 846, 848, 847, 848. SOC 27-9-07	1-14

LEICESTERSHIRE

Within the administrative county boundaries of Leicestershire are the unitary authorities of Leicester - and far from a county - the People's Republic of Rutland!

BRUNTINGTHORPE AERODROME between the M1 and the A50 south of Leicester

Cold War Jets Collection / Bruntingthorpe Aviation / C Walton (Aviation Division) Ltd: Run the airfield complex and custodians of a superb - and largely 'live' - collection of aircraft. It seems like only yesterday, but during November 2013 celebrated *three decades* of operation with the runway 'gathering' that I couldn't resist using on page 130 and it appears on the rear cover. It was in August 1983 that David Walton and his family-run organisation acquired what was then Chrysler UK's proving ground. Since then the site has blossomed into a variety of uses and is a major employer in the area.

◆ **Access:** *Off the B5414 near Shearsby, follow signs for the Proving Ground.* **Open:** *Every Sun 10:00 to 16:00. Other times by prior arrangement.* ***Please note****: admission need not necessarily provide access to all areas. There are no catering facilities on the airfield. Special events staged when several aircraft are fired up and taxied, in association with other airfield operators - details published in the aviation press* **Contact:** *Bruntingthorpe Airfield, Lutterworth, LE17 5QS* | **0116 2799300** | **www.bruntingthorpeaviation.com**

❑ 'G-ASDA'		Boeing 747-212B	SX-OAD	79	ex Olympic, 9V-SQH. *Olympic Flame*. Flew in 12-6-02		1-14
❑ F-BTGV	'1'	Aerospacelines Super Guppy 201		70	ex Airbus Skylink, N211AS Flew in 1-7-96	[1]	1-14
❑ XM715		HP Victor K.2		63	ex 55, 232 OCU, 543, 232 OCU, 100, 139. Flew in 25-11-93. *Teasin' Tina*. Taxiable		1-14
❑ XS235		DH Comet 4C	G-CPDA	63	ex XS235, Boscombe Down, DTEO, A&AEE, BLEU. *Canopus*. Flew in 30-10-97. De-reg 27-3-08. Taxiable		1-14
❑ XV226		HS Nimrod MR.2		68	ex Kinloss, MR.1, Kinloss/St Mawgan Wing. Last flew 27-4-10. Taxiable		1-14
❑ XX145*		SEPECAT Jaguar T.2A		74	ex Woodhouse, Cranwell, Boscombe Down, ETPS, 226 OCU, JOCU. Arrived 12-4-12	[2]	1-14
❑ XX900		HS Buccaneer S.2B		76	ex St Athan, 208, 12, 208, 216, 12, 208. Arrived 27-10-94. Taxiable		1-14
❑ XZ382		SEPECAT Jaguar GR.1		77	ex Coltishall, Halton 8908M (29-10-86), Shawbury, 14, 17. Arrived 22-2-99. British racing green and Jaguar (as in cars) logo	[3]	1-14
❑ ZA326*		Panavia Tornado GR.1		83	ex Boscombe Down, DERA, RAE Bedford. Arrived 1-10-13	[4]	1-14
❑ -		Gloster Meteor TT.20	WM234	52	ex Enstone, Lasham, Aborfield, TT.20 FRL, NF.11 68, 264. AWA-built. Arrived 3-2-11. Suez stripes, on gate by 11-13	[5]	1-14
❑ 85	'8-MV'	Dassault Mystère IVA		c59	ex East Midlands, Sculthorpe, French AF. Last flown 15-5-79. 'Desert' colours, on gate	[6]	1-14
❑ 1018		PZL Iskra 100	G-ISKA	78	ex Polish AF. Flew in 5-7-96. De-reg 24-5-10. Taxiable		1-14

■ **[1]** *Golf-Victor* was the first 337SGT conversion, first flying 24-8-70. It is based on a Boeing C-97 airframe(s). More details on **www.superguppy.co.uk** **[2]** XX145 is on long-term loan to David Walton. **[3]** XZ382 is on loan from a US owner. It *may* eventually travel to Florida. **[4]** ZA326 factoids: first flown 31-3-83 and last flown 13-12-05 by which time it was the last flying GR.1. Donated by Elliott Atkins, who is leading the restoration team - keep an eye on **www.za326.com**. **[5]** Meteor is a complex composite, with the centre section, wings and tailplane from ex Israeli DF/AF 1953-built NF.13 4X-FNA / 5616, ex RAF WM366, A&AEE and RRE; the cockpit from TT.20 WM234 (service history quoted above); and rear fuselage of F.8 VZ462 from Biggin Hill. It is due to leave Bruntingthorpe during 2014. **[6]** Mystère held on behalf of the National Museum of the USAF, USA.

Airliners: Scrapping, sorry, parting-out, has continued at the site. There are now two organisations carrying out such work: **GJD AeroTech Ltd** (see also below) and **Aircraft Recovery, Recycling, Care and Maintenance Ltd** (ARRCAM). Examples have been: KLM Boeing 737-400s in late in 2011; Spanair Airbus A321 in April 2012, a pair of former Transero 737-300s in late 2012 which have lingered, Qatar Freight Airbus A300Fs in November 2013 and a Cathay Pacific 747-400 in January 2014. Processing is carried out at a brisk pace and only 'long-termers' are listed.

❑ VP-BGX*	Boeing 747-346	88	ex Transaero, N6046P, JA8189, N741UN. Flew in 3-12-12	1-14
❑ VP-BGY*	Boeing 747-346	87	ex Transaero, N6009F, JA8179, N743UN. Flew in 29-10-12	1-14

Beech Restorations and **Tomcat T6 Restorations**: Adrian Marshall, Philip Turland, Ben Brown and friends are restoring *Naval Encounter* and G-TOMC and other projects for third parties. Broussard 3303 (G-CBGL) first flew on 10th May 2013. As well as the projects given below, the team has recently been busy repainting the Meteor and Mystère on display at the gate and on Tim Darrah's airworthy Beech 18 G-BKGL.

◆ **Access:** *Exhibited at open days, otherwise by prior arrangement* ***only***. **Contact**: **philipstudfast@btconnect.com** | **www.beechrestorations.com**

Bruntingthorpe continues after the photo-spread, on page 129

BEDFORDSHIRE

English Electric Lightning T.5 XS458
Cranfield, September 2013
Richard Hall

Hawker Hunter F.1 WT612
Henlow, July 2013
Ian Humphreys

Percival Mew Gull G-AEXF
Shuttleworth, July 2013
(at Breighton prior to departure, with 'Mini-me')
Andy Wood

BEDFORDSHIRE

Sopwith Camel replica G-BZSC
Shuttleworth, September 2013
Roger Richards

Avro 504K 'E3273'
Shuttleworth, July 2013
Ken Ellis

Grumman F4F 86690
Shuttleworth, August 2012
Tim R Badham

BERKSHIRE

Westland Lynx AH.9 XZ170
Arborfield, March 2012
Roger Richards

Agusta A.109A ZE412
Arborfield, March 2012
Roger Richards

Fairey Gannet AS.4 XA459
White Waltham, May 2013
Ian Haskell

BERKSHIRE

Miles Student 2 G-MIOO
Woodley, June 2013
Tim R Badham

Miles Martinet TT.1 TF-SHC
Woodley, June 2013
Tim R Badham

CAMBRIDGESHIRE

Fairchild A-10A Thunderbolt II 80-0219
Alconbury, April 2012
Richard Flagg

CAMBRIDGESHIRE

Avro Shackleton MR.3/3 XF708
Duxford, October 2013
Col Pope

Westland Lynx AH.7 XZ194
Duxford, July 2013
Ken Ellis

Junkers Ju 52 '4V+GH'
Duxford, September 2012
Col Pope

C

V

G
9

CAMBRIDGESHIRE

Heinkel He 162A-1 120235
Duxford, July 2013
Ken Ellis

Bristol Bolingbroke IVT G-BPIV
Duxford, roll-out 12th August 2013
(starboard in *very* temporary Finnish colours)
Both Col Pope

In fond memory of Graham Warner
1929-2014

CAMBRIDGESHIRE

Aircraft Restoration Co Spitfire line-up: Mk.Ia N3200, PR.XI PL983, PR.XIX PS853, Mk.Vb AB910
Duxford, February 2013
Col Pope

Supermarine Spitfire Ia P9374
Duxford, January 2013
Col Pope

Hawker Sea Fury T.20S WG655
Duxford, July 2013
Ken Ellis

CAMBRIDGESHIRE

Bristol Beaufighter XI 'A19-144'
Duxford, July 2013
Ken Ellis

Gloster Meteor T.7 WF877
Duxford, November 2012
Steve Buckby

British Aerospace Harrier GR.7A ZD469
Wittering, September 2013
Terry Dann

CHESHIRE

The Aeroplane Collection line-up: foreground: Tutor, behind: Gannet T.2, Vampire T.11 XD624
Hooton Park, November 2013
Dave Arkle

Panavia Tornado GR.1 ZA399
Knutsford, August 2013
Dave Harding

Hawker Siddeley Sea Harrier FA.2 ZA691
Winsford, April 2012
Dave Harding

CORNWALL

Hawker Sea Hawk F.1 WF225
Culdrose, June 2013
Terry Dann

Fairey Gannet ECM.6 XG831
Davidstow Moor, April 2013
Roger Richards

Gloster Meteor TT.20 WM167
Newquay, June 2013
Tim R Badham

CORNWALL

British Aircraft Corp 111-539 ZH763
Newquay, August 2013
Richard Hall

DEVON

Hawker Siddeley 146-100 G-JEAT
Exeter, May 2012
Ian Haskell

DORSET

CMC Leopard G-BKRL
Bournemouth, July 2012
Mike Cain

DORSET

Boeing 737-229 G-CEAH
Bournemouth, December 2013
Mike Phipp

Vickers Viscount 806 G-OPAS and
EE Lightning F.53 ZF582
Bournemouth, May 2013
Mike Cain

American AA-5B Tiger 'GO-CSE'
Bournemouth, September 2013
Ian Haskell

ESSEX

Dassault Mystère IVA 319
Andrewsfield, February 2012
Ken Ellis

Supermarine Walrus I W2718
Audley End, July 2013
Jon Wickenden

Lockheed TriStar 100 G-IOIT
London Stansted, October 2013
Jon Wickenden

8-ND

Dalby

L-1011

ESSEX

Avro Vulcan B.2 XL426
Southend, November 2013
Phil Whalley

Cessna Citation G-DWJM
Southend, June 2013
Mike Cain

Sopwith Pup replica 'A643'
Stow Maries, May 2012
Phil Whalley

GLOUCESTERSHIRE

Westland Lynx AH.7 XZ649
Bristol, November 2012
Phil Adkin

Bristol Britannia C.1 XM496
Cotswold, June 2013
Ken Ellis

Folland Gnat T.1 'XR540'
Cotswold, July 2013
Mike Phipp

GLOUCESTERSHIRE

English Electric Canberra PR.9 XH134
Cotswold, September 2013
(Performing at Goodwood)
Phil Whalley

Agusta A.109A G-JRSL and
EMBRAER Bandeirante G-ODUB
Cotswold, August 2013
Alf Jenks

Gloster Gamecock replica 'J7904'
Gloucestershire Airport, November 201
Les Woodward

GLOUCESTERSHIRE

Gloster Javelin FAW.9 XH903
Gloucestershire Airport,
February 2012
Ian Haskell

HAMPSHIRE

Royal Aircraft Factory SE.5A replica
'D276'
Farnborough, August 2013
Roger Richards

Hawker Siddeley Buccaneer S.2C
XV344
Farnborough, February 2013
Les Woodward

THE Willow Wren

US AIRWAYS

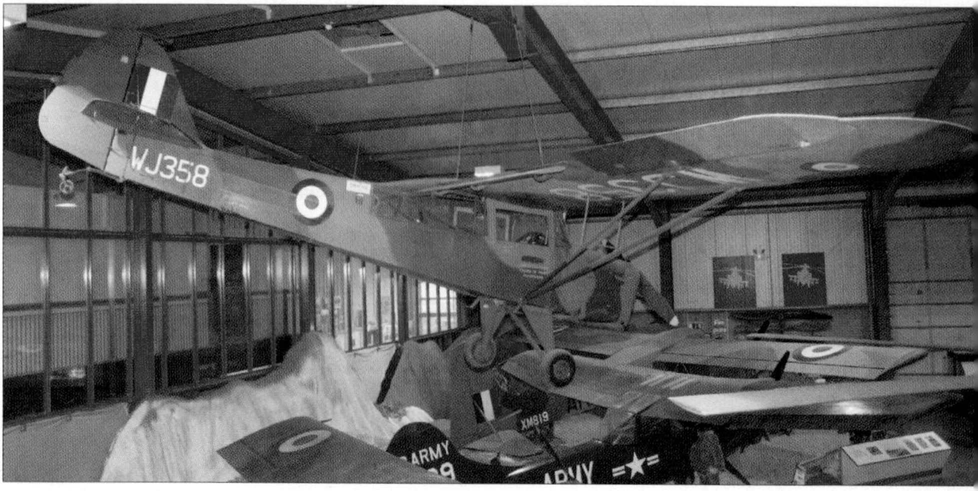
WJ358
XM819
ARMY
ARMY

HAMPSHIRE

Manuel Willow Wren BGA.162
Lasham, August 2013
Tim R Badham

Boeing 737-5H6 G-PJPJ
Lasham, September 2013
Tom Singfield

Auster AOP.6 WJ358
Middle Wallop, October 2012
Mike Cain

HAMPSHIRE

Boeing CH-47F Chinook 03-8003
Odiham, May 2013
Jon Wickenden

HEREFORDSHIRE

Westland Whirlwind HAR.10 XP360
Bicton, March 2013
Phil Adkin

HERTFORDSHIRE

Westland Wasp HAS.1 XT439
Hemel Hempstead, October 2013
Ben Brown

HERTFORDSHIRE

Hawker Siddeley 125 Srs 1 G-ARYC
London Colney, July 2013
Roger Richards

De Havilland Dove 6 D-IFSB
London Colney, July 2013
Roger Richards

KENT

Boeing 747-344 TF-ARU, Boeing 747-269M N309TD and Douglas DC-8-55F 9G-MKA
Kent Airport, June 2013
Phil Whalley

KENT

Fieseler Fi 103R-IV, with visiting Nord 1002 G-ETME
Lashenden, August 2013
Richard Foord-LAWM

LEICESTERSHIRE

Gloster Meteor TT.20 WM234
Bruntingthorpe, February 2013
Alf Jenks

English Electric Lightning F.6s XR728 and XS904 in QRA shed
Bruntingthorpe, July 2012
Richard Hall

F
ROYAL AIR FORCE

LEICESTERSHIRE

Vickers VC-10s
Bruntingthorpe, December 2012
Nigel Bailey-Underwood

Vickers VC-10 K.3 ZA147 - making the type's final touch down
Bruntingthorpe, 25th September 2013
Ian Haskell

Vickers VC-10s: K.4 ZD241, K.3 ZA149, C.1K XR808, K.3 ZA147
Bruntingthorpe, September 2013
Francis Wallace

LEICESTERSHIRE

Douglas Boston IIIA
Hinckley, July 2012
Ken Ellis

Cessna FA.152 Aerobat G-LEIC and Elster G-BMWV
Leicester, August 2013
Alf Jenks

LINCOLNSHIRE

Hawker Siddeley Sea Harrier FA.2 ZE697
Binbrook, September 2012
Tony McCarthy

LINCOLNSHIRE

Avro Lancaster I PA474
Coningsby, May 2013
(saluting Derwent Dam)
Phil Whalley

English Electric Lightning F.6 XR753
Coningsby, June 2012
Richard Hall

McDonnell Phantom FGR.2 XT891
Coningsby, June 2012
Richard Hall

LINCOLNSHIRE

Panavia Tornado F.3 ZE760
Coningsby, June 2012
Richard Hall

Hawker Siddeley Dominie T.1 XS727
Cranwell, December 2013
Howard Heeley

Douglas C-47A Skytrain 2100882
East Kirkby, May 2013
Andy Wood

G-JXLI
JETSTREAM
41
BRITISH AEROSPACE

Ifor Williams
Trailers

AA
XR770

LINCOLNSHIRE

British Aerospace Jetstream 41 'G-JXLI'
Humberside, January 2013
Brian Downs

Hawker Siddeley Harrier GR.3 XV810
and Lightning F.6 XS932
Metheringham, June 2013
(attending *CockpitFest*)
Ken Ellis

English Electric Lightning F.6 XR770
Waddington, May 2012
Alf Jenks

GREATER LONDON

Supermarine Spitfire IX MK912
Biggin Hill, November 2012
Steve Buckby

Supermarine Spitfire XVI RW382
and Mk.IX TD314
Biggin Hill, November 2012
Steve Buckby

Hawker Hunter F.1 WT555
Greenford, July 2013
Rowland Benbrook

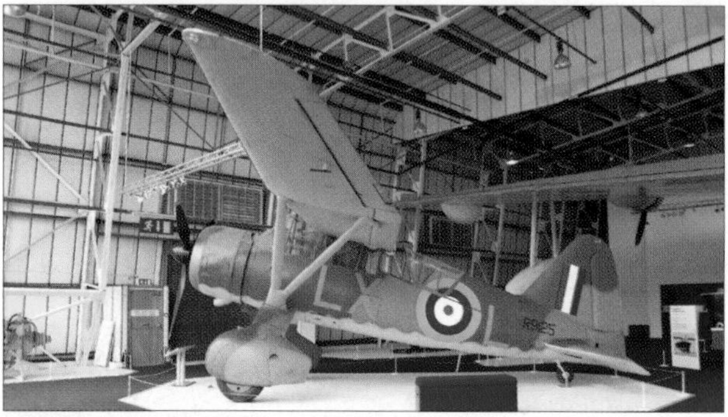

GREATER LONDON

Boulton Paul Defiant I N1671
Hendon, August 2013
Ken Ellis

Westland Lysander III R9125
Hendon, September 2012
Ken Ellis

Short Sunderland MR.5 ML824
Hendon, September 2012
Ken Ellis

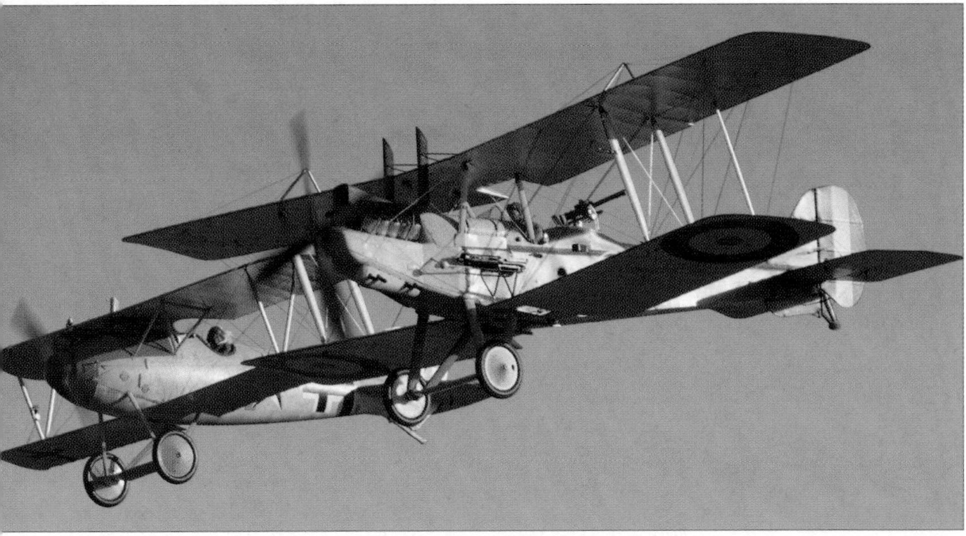

GREATER LONDON

Royal Aircraft Factory RE.8 'A3930' and Albatros D.Va 'D.7343'
Hendon (performing at Shuttleworth, August 2012)
Steve Buckby

Sopwith Dolphin 'C3988'
Hendon, September 2012
Ken Ellis

Hanriot HD.1 HD-75
Hendon, September 2012
Ken Ellis

GREATER LONDON

Sopwith Snipe E6655
Hendon, August 2013
Ken Ellis

Cody Military Biplane 304
South Kensington, November 2012
Ken Ellis

Royal Aircraft Factory SE.5A G-EBIB
South Kensington, November 2012
Ken Ellis

GREATER LONDON

Avro 504K D7560
South Kensington, November 2012
Ken Ellis

GREATER MANCHESTER

Mignet 'Flying Flea' 'G-ADYO'
Manchester, November 2013
Brian Downs

MERSEYSIDE

Hawker Siddeley 748-1/105 G-BEJD
Liverpool, May 2012
Ken Ellis

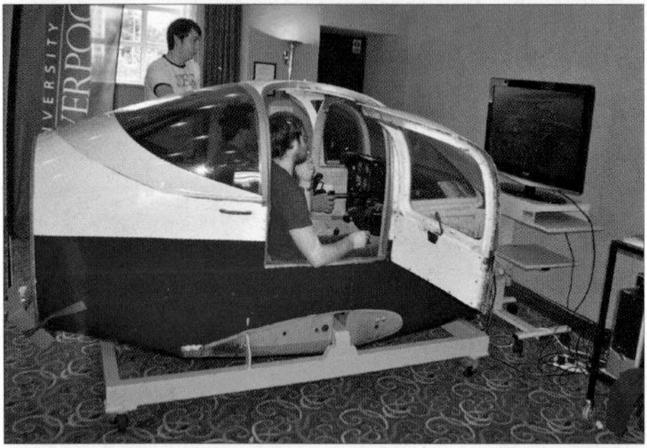

MERSEYSIDE

Hawker Siddeley 747-2A/334 G-ORAL and Jetstream 41 G-JMAC
Liverpool, May 2012
Ken Ellis

Piper Tomahawk 112 G-LFSD
Liverpool, June 2013
David S Johnstone

WEST MIDLANDS

Supermarine Spitfire IX ML427 and Hurricane IV 'P3395'
Birmingham, November 2013
Jon Wickenden

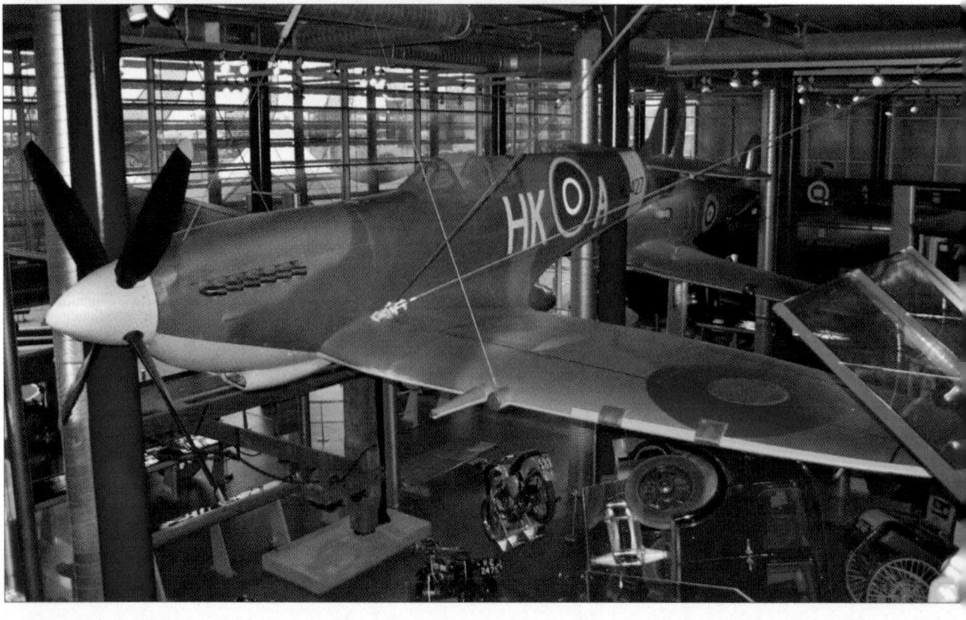

❑ G-AJJS	Cessna 120		47	ex Sywell, 8R-GBO, VP-GBO, VP-TBO, N1106M, YV-T-CTA, NC2786N. Crashed 9-5-10, CoA 15-11-11	[1]	1-14
❑ G-BKRN	Beech D.18S		52	ex Cranfield, Perth, Prestwick, CF-DTN, RCAF inst A675, RCAF 1500. CoA 26-6-83. US Navy colours, *Naval Encounter*		1-14
❑ G-HRVD	NA Harvard IV		53	ex Felthorpe, Swanton Morley, Wellesbourne Mountford, Thruxton, G-BSBC, Mozambique, Port AF 1741, WGAF BF+055, AA+055, 53-4629. CCF-built. Stored	[3]	1-14
❑ -	Fairey Battle I		~	ex Canada, RCAF. Substantial remains		1-14
❑ –	NA Harvard IIb		~	ex Kenilworth, Henlow. Forward cockpit section	[4]	1-14
❑ 3019	NA Harvard II	G-CPPM	41	ex Canada, Trenton, Uxbridge (Ontario), RCAF 3019, 1 FTS, 1 SFTS, 8 SFTS. RCAF colours	[5]	1-14
❑ 51-14700	NA T-6G-NT Texan	G-TOMC	42	ex Stoke-on-Trent, Eccleshall, North Weald, Coventry, *Empire of the Sun*, La Ferté Alais, FAF, USAF, USAAF 42-44514. *Texan Tomcat*	[6]	1-14

■ **[1]** Cessna 120 is registered to the Juliet Sierra Group. **[2]** Harvard G-HRVD was registered to Phil Earthey 2-13 - see Norwich, Norfolk.. **[4]** Harvard cockpit is being restored for the Midland Aircraft Recovery Group - see Kenilworth, Warks. It has the constructor's number 14-2441 with a build date of 11th January 1944. That would make it *possibly* former 3 FTS Mk.IIb KF741. It was acquired, circa 1986, from the RAF Museum store at Henlow. Comments? **[5]** The former RCAF Harvard II is owned by Steve Wilch. **[6]** In Algeria, the French knew armed Texans as 'Tomcats' because of their growl – hence the identity. *Mike-Charlie* is registered to Texan Restoration.

The Buccaneer Aviation Group: (Known, lovingly, as T-BAG!) XW544 was fully repainted by March 2012 and now boasts a full complement of wing pylons. Work is complete on the front cockpit of XX889 and work has begun on the rear 'office'. T-BAG was responsible for moving S.2B XV168 from Brough, E Yorks, to Elvington - turn to Brough for more details.

◆ **Access:** *By prior arrangement* **only** *plus at open days and special events*. **Contact: thebuccavgroup@btinternet.com | www.thebuccaneeraviationgroup.com**

❑ XW544	'Y'	HS Buccaneer S.2B	72	ex Shawbury, Cosford 8857M (21-5-85), Shawbury, 16, 15. Arrived 3-10-04. 16 Sqn colours. Taxiable	1-14
❑ XX889	'T'	HS Buccaneer S.2B	75	ex Kemble, Staverton, Bentham, Staverton, Enstone, St Athan, 12, 208, 12, 16. Arrived 8-5-11. 208 Sqn colours	1-14
❑ XX894	'020'	HS Buccaneer S.2B	75	ex Farnborough, Kemble, Bruntingthorpe, St Athan, 208, 16, 12, 208, 12. Arrived 28-9-03. 809 Sqn colours. Taxiable	1-14

GJD AeroTech Ltd: (Headquartered as Basingstoke, Hants - which see.) The company is also very active in airliner parting-out - see page 96. A leading light in GJD is Gary Spoors, who also has an impressive collection in his own right - see below.

VC-10 C.1K XR808 arrived on 29th July 2013. It is destined for the RAF Museum, it transpired that a landing at Cosford, Shropshire, would not be possible and it was ferried to Bruntingthorpe for dismantling. Arrangements to move XR808 were still to be finalised as *W&R24* went to press.

On 25th September 2013 VC-10 K.3 ZA147 touched down at Bruntingthorpe and its Conway 301s fell silent. It had clocked 14,800 hours of flying with the RAF, bringing its grand total to around 50,000 - it started life as a civvie with East African Airways. Captained by Brize Norton's OC, G/C Steve Lushington, ZA147 had made the last-ever flight by one of the most attractive jet transports ever. A quick factoid: in April 1987 ZA147 achieved a world record for a non-stop (it was 'tanked' twice) flight from London to Perth, Australia, taking 15 hours 53 minutes. Parts reclamation began quickly; it is thought that the cockpit will be saved and may go to Scotland.

Departures: **Hercules** C.3s XV221 and XV301 moved to Hixon, Staffs, by 4-13 and 18-2-13, respectively. **VC-10** C.1Ks XV101, XV102, XV105 and XV107, all of which flew in during late 2011, had been processed by 5-12. C.1K XV108 flew in 7-12-12 and was processed by 9-13, the forward fuselage of XV108 going to East Midlands, Leics, 16-11-13.

◆ **Access:** Private *location*, strictly *viewable by prior application* only | **www.gjdservices.co.uk**

❑ XR808*	'R'	Vickers VC-10 C.1K	66	ex 101, 10. *Kenneth Campbell VC*. Flew in 29-7-13. See notes above	1-14
❑ XV104*	'U'	Vickers VC-10 C.1K	67	ex 101, 10. *James McCudden VC*. Flew in 4-11-12. Broken up by 1-13. Cockpit	1-14
❑ XV106*	'W'	Vickers VC-10 C.1K	67	ex 101, 10. *Arthur Scarf VC*. Flew in 7-12-12. Broken up by 9-13. Cockpit	1-14
❑ XV109	'Z'	Vickers VC-10 C.1K	68	ex 101, 10. *Thomas Mottershead VC*. Flew in 31-3-10. Cockpit	1-14
❑ ZA147*	'F'	Vickers VC-10 K.3	66	ex 101, 10, East African 5H-MMT. Flew in 25-9-13. See notes above. Engineless by 1-46	1-14
❑ ZA149*	'H'	Vickers VC-10 K.3	69	ex 101, 10, East African 5X-UVJ. Flew in 25-9-13. Broken up by 12-13. Forward fuselage	1-14

A celebration of three decades of aviation preservation at Bruntingthorpe, staged in November 2013. *Steve Buckby*

GJD AeroTech Ltd continued:

❑ ZD477*	'E'	Westland Sea King HC.4		84	ex Gosport, 845, 846, 845, 846, 845, 846, 845, 846, 845, 846. Arrived 4-12-13		1-14
❑ ZD627*	'WO'	Westland Sea King HC.4		84	ex Gosport, 848, 846, 707. Arrived 26-11-13		1-14
❑ ZG822*	'WS'	Westland Sea King HC.4		90	ex Gosport, Yeovilton, 848, 846, 845, 846, 845, 846, 848, 846, 848, 846. Arrived 27-11-13		1-14

Lightning Preservation Group:

◆ **Access:** *Regular open days, otherwise by prior appointment only.* **Contact: email via website | www.lightnings.org.uk**

❑ XP703		EE Lightning F.3		63	ex Norwich, Coltishall, Bruntingthorpe, Warton, MoD, 29, 56, 74. Last flown 23-5-75. Arrived 7-10. Cockpit		1-14
❑ XR728	'JS'	EE Lightning F.6		65	ex Binbrook, 11, LTF, 5, 56, 23, 11, 23. Last flown 24-6-88		1-14
❑ XS904	'BQ'	EE Lightning F.6		66	ex BAe Warton, Binbrook, 5-11 pool. Last flown 21-1-93		1-14

Phoenix Aviation | Phoenix Aviation Museum: The famed Baron 'car' G-AYKA was acquired by Dave Thomas - see below. Cessna F.150L G-BAXX departed for 'Peterborough' on 12th November 2013.

◆ **Access**: *Viewing by prior arrangement* **only.**

❑ XH592	'L'	HP Victor B.1A		58	ex Cosford 8429M (17-10-74), St Athan, 232 OCU, TTF, 232 OCU, Honington Wing, 15. Cockpit		1-14
❑ XN582	'95'	Hunting Jet Provost T.3A		61	ex Teversham, Cambridge, Teversham, Cosford 8957M (11-3-88), 7 FTS, 1 FTS, 3 FTS, RAFC. Arr 21-7-05. Taxiable		1-14
❑ XP883		Westland Scout AH.1		63	ex Oaksey Park, Boscombe Down, 658, 655, 652. Arrived 1-4-04	[1]	1-14
❑ 'XR993'		Folland Gnat T.1	XP534	63	ex North Weald, Cranfield, G-BVPP, XP534, Halton 8620M, 4 FTS, CFS, 4 FTS,CFS, 4 FTS. Dam 17-9-04, CoA 14-1-05, de-reg 22-5-09. Arrived 17-9-04. 'Red Arrows' colours	[3]	1-14
❑ XT630	'X'	W'land Scout AH.1	G-BXRL	66	ex Burbage. Crashed 16-10-99, de-reg 20-3-00. Arr 10-02		1-14
❑ XV328	'BZ'	EE Lightning T.5		66	ex Cranfield, Binbrook, LTF, 5, LTF, 5, 29. SOC 29-6-88. Cockpit		1-14

■ **[1]** The boom of XP883 is to be found on another Scout - see Plymouth, Devon. **[2]** Being restored to taxiable condition for the Heritage Aircraft Trust, North Weald, Essex.

Gary Spoors: During March 2013 took delivery of some decidedly heavy metal. Previously listed under 'Also', it is time Gary's aircraft were listed separately. After a respray by Beech Restorations - see above - Meteor WM234 was put on display at the gate and so moves to the Cold War Jets listing above. See also The Buccaneer Aviation Group, above, Gloucestershire, Glos, and East Midlands, Leics.

◆ **Access**: *Viewing by prior arrangement* **only**

❑ XP672	'03'	Hunting Jet Provost T.4	62 G-RAFI	ex Retford, Ipswich, North Weald, Bournemouth, Jurby, Halton 8458M, SoRF, CAW, CATCS, CAW, 2 FTS. CoA 11-3-00, de-reg 22-11-10. Arrived 28-7-11. Taxiable		1-14
❑ XX494	'B'	HP Jetstream T.1	75	ex Retford, Ipswich, Shawbury, Cranwell, 45, 3 FTS, 45, 6 FTS, METS. Last flown 22-3-04. Arrived 11-8-11		1-14
❑ ZD241*	'N'	Vickers VC-10 K.4	68	ex 101, G-ASGM, BOAC. Arrived 21-3-13, acquired 5-13. Taxiable		1-14
❑ ZD610*	'006'	HS Sea Harrier FA.2	85	ex Dunsfold, Yeovilton, 800, 899, 801, 800, 899, 801, 899. Arrived 2-5-12		1-14
❑ 37+86*		McD F-4F Phantom	~	ex Spanhoe, Bruntingthorpe, WGAF. Cockpit. Arrived 26-3-12		1-14

Dave Thomas: Previously listed under 'Also', the collection is now given its own sub-heading. Strikemaster G-UPPI was stripped for spares by January 2013 and the hulk removed. Given under the GJD heading in W&R23, the hulk of Koliber 160 G-BZAJ was broken down for produce by January 2012.

◆ **Access**: *Viewing by prior arrangement* **only**

❑ G-AYKA*	'AY'	Beech Baron 55A	64	ex Phoenix, Shoreham, Elstree, HB-GEW, G-AYKA, D-IKUN, N8683M. Cr 18-6-89, de-reg 28-2-90. 2 Sqn marks!	[1]	1-14
❑ WT806		Hawker Hunter GA.11	55	ex Shoreham, Ipswich, Shawbury, Abingdon, Chivenor, FRADU, CFS, 14. SOC 26-11-94. Arrived 22-12-10		1-14
❑ XJ494	'121'	DH Sea Vixen FAW.2	59	ex Kings Langley, Farnborough, FRL, A&AEE, HSA, Sydenham, 899, Sydenham, 892. SOC 4-12-83. Arrived 22-6-99. Restoration to taxi		1-14
❑ XM365		Hunting Jet Provost T.3A	60 G-BXBH	ex North Weald, Norwich, Binbrook, Shawbury, 1 FTS, 3 FTS, 2 FTS. CoA 31-8-01, de-reg 10-10-02. Arr 25-5-10		1-14
❑ XN494*	'43'	Hunting Jet Provost T.3A	60	ex Charlwood, Crawley, Bruntingthorpe, Middle Wallop, Halton 9012M (10-3-90), 1 FTS, RAFC. Arrived 19-8-13		1-14
❑ XW290*	'MA'	BAC Jet Provost T.5A	69	ex Cosford, 9199M (6-7-93), Shawbury, 3 FTS, RAFC, CFS. Arrived 11-12-13		1-14
❑ XX467		Hawker Hunter T.7	58 G-TVII	ex Exeter, Kemble, Perth, 1 TWU, Jordan AF 836, Saudi AF 70-617, G-9-214, XL605, 66, 92. SOC 13-10-83. Arrived 28-6-11		1-14

■ **[1]** Baron *Kilo-Alpha* was turned into a car as part of a training exercise at Shoreham!

Also: The 'fleets' of Gary Spoors and Dave Thomas, previously listed under this heading, have been 'promoted' and are given above. Gnat T.1 'PF179' (XR541) moved to North Weald, Essex, by March 2013.

◆ **Access**: *Viewing by prior arrangement* **only**

❑ G-TORE	'42'	Hunting Jet Provost T.3A	59	ex London, Ipswich, Cranfield, XM405, 1 FTS, RAFC, 1 FTS, 2 FTS. CoA 5-5-95, de-reg 2-2-04. Arrived 2-4-10		1-14
❑ - -		Auster	~	unfinished frame, basis of restoration	[1]	1-14
❑ WT333		EE Canberra B(I).8	56 G-BVXC	ex Farnborough, Bedford, RAE, C(A). Flew in 28-1-95. De-reg 22-4-03. Taxiable	[2]	1-14
❑ XL565	'Y'	Hawker Hunter T.7	58	ex Kemble, Ipswich, Colsterworth, Shawbury, Lossiemouth, FRADU, 237 OCU, 4 FTS, 208, 8, West Raynham SF, 8, 1417 Flt, 8, Hawker. SOC 10-10-93. Arr 21-3-02. Taxiable	[3]	1-14
❑ XN584	'E' *and* '88'	Hunting Jet Provost T.3A	61	ex Halton 9014M (10-9-90), 1 FTS, CFS, RAFC, CFS, RAFC, TWU, RAFC. Arrived 27-3-95. Taxiable	[4]	1-14
❑ 22+35		Lockheed F-104G Starfighter	62	ex Lasham, Manching, JbG34, KE+413, DD+105 Messerschmitt-built. Arrived 28-5-10	[5]	1-14
❑ '53'		Aero L29 Delfin	c66 395189	ex Rosehill Market Drayton, Boboc, Romanian AF. Arrived 11-2-10. Engine running 6-12	[6]	1-14

■ **[1]** The anonymous Auster frame is owned by John and Mark Wood. **[2]** Roger Wintle, Steve Reglar, Clive Davies and Andy Bromley own WT333 which was built as a B(I).8 but was later fitted with the cockpit from B.2 WK135. **[3]** XL565 is owned by Geoffrey Pool - see also Delfin '53'. **[4]** 'JP' XN584 is owned by Clive Davies - see also Gloucester, Glos. The wings of XN584 are fitted to T.4 XP627 at Sunderland, N&T. **[5]** F-104 is owned by Tony Ions and Alan Quatermaine - long term aim is to acquire a J79 and get it taxying! **[6]** The Delfin is owned by Mark Boffin, Geoffrey Pool (see also XL565) and Graham Smith.

Off-site: At a nearby business park is a workshop specialising in Comanche and 'Twin Com' spares.

❑ G-ASCJ	Piper Comanche 250	60	ex 5N-AEB, N7197P. Crashed 10-9-86, de-reg 8-1-87		1-14
❑ G-ATFK	Piper Twin Com' 160	65	ex Romsey, N7642Y. Crashed 12-6-89, de-reg 21-10-92		1-14
❑ G-ATWR	Piper Twin Com' 160B	66	ex N8025Y. Crashed 14-9-93, de-reg 18-4-95		1-14
❑ G-AVCY	Piper Twin Com' 160B	66	ex N8241Y. Crashed 9-3-91, de-reg 17-7-91		1-14
❑ G-AVVI	Piper Twin Comanche 160B	67	ex Shipdham, EI-AVD, G-AVVI, N8241Y. Crashed 6-4-91, de-reg 29-9-97		1-14
❑ G-BAWN	Piper Twin Com' 160C	69	ex N8790Y. Crashed 31-3-98, de-reg 23-6-98		1-14

COALVILLE on the A511 north-west of Leicester

Snibston Discovery Museum: Set on a former colliery, the centre has much to offer on the region's industrial heritage.

◆ **Access:** *East of the A511 and A447 junction and 'brown signed'.* **Open:** *Nov to Mar weekdays 10:00 to 15:00, weekends and Bank Hols, 10:00 to 17:00; Apr to Oct daily 10:00 to 17:00.* **Contacts:** *Ashby Road, Coalville, LE67 3LN* | **01530 278444** | **snibston@leics.gov.uk** | **www.snibston.com**

❑ G-AGOH	Auster J/1 Autocrat	45	ex Winthorpe, Leicester. CoA 24-8-95, de-reg 7-8-08		1-14
❑ XP280	Auster AOP.9	61	ex Leicester, St Athan, 6 Flt, 651. SOC 6-11-74		1-14

Deep store: Not available for inspection without prior arrangement.

❑ G-AFTN	Taylorcraft Plus C2	39	ex Heavitree, HL535, 43 OTU, 652, 651, G-AFTN. CoA 1-11-57, de-reg 31-1-99.	[1]	8-13
❑ G-AIJK	Auster J/4 Archer	46	ex Leicester, Stratford. CoA 24-8-68, de-reg 8-8-68. Frame		8-13
❑ VZ728	R&S Desford Trainer G-AGOS	45	ex Perth, Strathallan, Thruxton, RAE, Desford. CoA 28-11-80, de-reg 9-11-81		2-10

■ **[1]** *Tango-November* is the oldest surviving Auster type.

COTTESMORE north of the B668, north-east of Oakham

RAF Cottesmore: After the ensign was lowered, the station morphed into **Kendrew Barracks** as of 2nd April 2012. From the point of view of *W&R*, it seems to be game over.

DISEWORTH on the B5401 south of East Midlands Airport

Two Bulldogs are stored in the general area.

❑ XX633	'X'	SAL Bulldog T.1	74	ex Shawbury, Northum UAS, 2 FTS. SOC 10-5-01	9-12
❑ XX671	'D'	SAL Bulldog T.1	75	ex Wellesbourne M, Shawbury, Birm UAS, 2 FTS. SOC 10-8-01	9-12

EAST MIDLANDS AIRPORT, or Castle Donington EGNX

Aeropark: Supporting the Aeropark is the **East Midlands Airport Volunteers Association**. The team continues to make great progress. During 2014 a second Romney hut is due to be erected; the intention is that the first one will house several airframes and the engine collection, while the new one will become a restoration workshop.

Wessex HAS.1 XS876 moved to a location in Norfolk, on 4th April 2012 before setting off for Greece that December.

◆ **Access:** *Airport west of Junction 23A of the M1 and well signed. Airport main entrance is off the A453 and Aeropark signed from there - on northern perimeter, site postcode DE74 2PR.* **Open:** *May to Sep Thu 10:30 to 16:00, Sat 12:00 to 17:00, Sun 10:30 to 17:00; Oct to Apr Sun 10:30 to 17:00 or dusk if earlier. Also Bank Hols other than Xmas and New Year.* **Contact:** *29 Sandringham Avenue, Stapenhill, Burton-on-Trent, DE15 9BJ* | **01332 850463** *during Aeropark opening hours* | **grahamv@eastmidlandsaeropark.org** | **www.eastmidlandsaeropark.org**

❑ G-ANUW	DH Dove 6	55	ex Long Marston, Welshpool, North Weald, Stansted, CAFU. CoA 22-7-81, de-reg 5-6-96. Arrived 31-10-09		1-14
❑ G-APES	Vickers Merchantman	61	ex Hunting, ABC, BEA. *Swiftsure*. CoA 2-10-95, de-reg 28-2-97. BEA colours Cockpit		1-14
❑ G-ASDL	Beagle Terrier 2	50	ex Long Eaton, Eccleshall, G-ARLN, Auster AOP.6 WE558, LAS. CoA 18-5-07; de-reg 17-8-04. Arrived 1-12	[1]	1-14
❑ G-BBED	MS Rallye 220	73	ex King's Croughton. CoA 13-9-87. Arrived 11-9-10		1-14
❑ G-BEOZ	AW Argosy 101	60	ex ABC, N895U, N6502R, G-1-7. CoA 28-5-86, de-reg 19-11-87. Arrived 6-87. Elan colours, *Fat Albert*		1-14
❑ G-CSZB	Vickers Viscount 807	57	ex Coleorton, Southend, N141RA ntu, G-CSZB, VQ-GAB, ZK-NAI, SP-LVC, G-AOXU. *Viscount Scotland*. CoA 24-1-97, de-reg 19-8-98. Arrived 4-03. Cockpit	[2]	1-14

❑ G-FRJB		Britten SA-1 Sheriff	r81	ex Sandown. De-reg 6-2-87. Arrived 1-7-86. Unflown		1-14
❑ -		Schleicher K-8	~	-		1-14
❑ -		EoN Primary	~	ex Doncaster. Stored		1-14
❑ WH740		EE Canberra T.17	53	ex Cosford 8762M, 360, B.2, RNZAF, Upwood SF, 40, 18. SOC 1-12-82. Arrived 8-12-91		1-14
❑ WL626	'P'	Vickers Varsity T.1 G-BHDD	53	ex Coventry G-BHDD, 6 FTS, 1 ANS, 2 ANS, 201 AFS. SOC 12-4-76. Last flown 8-11-79. De-reg 21-11-09	[3]	1-14
❑ WM224	'X'	Gloster Meteor TT.20	52	ex North Weald 'WM311', East Dereham, Swanton Morley 8177M (15-10-71), 5 CAACU, 3 CAACU, 3/4 CAACU, NF.11, 29, 228 OCU. AWA-built. Arrived 12-1-03		1-14
❑ WM367		Gloster Meteor NF.13	53	ex Long Marston, Firbeck, North Weald, Powick, Boscombe Down, A&AEE. SOC 17-8-72. AWA-built. Arrived 11-10-08. Cockpit	[3]	1-14
❑ WP784	'RCY-E' *and* 'M'	DHC Chipmunk T.10	52	ex Long Marston, Hemel Hempstead, Booker, Boston, Holbeach, Wellingborough, Reading, Benson, Abingdon, 6 AEF, Leeds UAS, Aber UAS, 8 FTS, Man UAS, QUAS, Air Attaché Paris, 5 RFS, 17 RFS. SOC 21-6-72. 5 RFS colours. Arrived 11-10-08	[4]	1-14
❑ WS760		Gloster Meteor NF(T).14	54	ex Yatesbury, Loughborough, Cranfield, Bushey, Duxford, Brampton, Upwood 7964M (23-8-67), 1 ANS, 64, 237 OCU. AWA-built. Arrived 11-11-06. Off-site		1-14
❑ WV382		Hawker Hunter GA.11	55	ex Long Marston, Smethwick, A2724, Lee-on-Solent A2730 (5-2-85), Shawbury, Kemble, FRADU, FRU, 738, F.4, 67. Arrived 24-1-09		1-14
❑ WW442*	'N'	Percival Provost T.1	54	ex Charlwood, Kings Langley, Leverstock Green, Cranfield, Booker, St Merryn, Houghton-on-the-Hill, Kidlington, Halton 7618M (10-10-59), CNCS, 3 FTS. First noted 9-13	[1]	1-14
❑ XD447	'50'	DH Vampire T.11	54	ex Long Marston, East Kirkby, Tattershall, Woodford, Chester, St Athan, 8 FTS, RAFC, 5 FTS. SOC 1-12-67. Arrived 3-10-09		1-14
❑ XD459	'63'	DH Vampire T.11	54	ex Doncaster, East Mids, Bruntingthorpe, Long Marston, Bennington, Cranfield, Bushey, Keevil, 3/4 CAACU, 229 OCU,233 OCU, 151, 253, 56. SOC 6-1-72. Off-site	[5]	1-14
❑ XD534	'41'	DH Vampire T.11	54	ex Welshpool, Barton, Chelford, Hadfield, Wythenshawe, Cheadle, Woodford, Chester, Shawbury, 7 FTS, CFS, 9 FTS, 10 FTS. SOC 30-10-67. Arrived 2004	[6]	1-14
❑ XG588		Westland Whirlwind Srs 3 G-BAMH	55	ex Cuckfield, Bristow VR-BEP, G-BAMH, Redhill, HAR.3 XG588, 705, 701, *Warrior* Flt, *Albion* Flt. SOC 10-10-69. Arrived 5-86		1-14
❑ XG737		DH Sea Venom FAW.22	58	ex Long Marston, Rhoose, Yeovilton, FRU, 894, 893, RAE, 891. SOC 27-3-69. Arrived 31-10-09		1-14
❑ 'XJ714'		Hawker Hunter 'FR.10'	56	ex Long Marston. Arrived 23-5-09	[7]	1-14
❑ XL569		Hawker Hunter T.7	58	ex Abingdon, Cosford 8833M (2-9-84), 2 TWU, 1 TWU, 12, 216, 237 OCU, Laarbruch SF, 15, 237 OCU, 12, 2 TWU, 1 TWU, TWU, 229 OCU. Arrived 20-2-93		1-14
❑ XM575		Avro Vulcan B.2	63	G-BLMC ntu, ex 44, Wadd Wing, Scampton Wing, 617. SOC 25-1-83, last flight 21-8-83		1-14
❑ XP568		Hunting Jet Provost T.4	62	ex Long Marston, Faygate, Hatfield, Shawbury, RAFC. SOC 1-10-71. Arrived 25-10-08		1-14
❑ XT604		Westland Wessex HC.2	66	ex Hixon, Colsterworth, Fleetlands, 22, 103, 78, Muharraq SAR Flt, 78. SOC 16-3-00. Arrived 11-7-02	[8]	1-14
❑ XV108*	'Y'	Vickers VC-10 C.1K	68	ex Bruntingthorpe, 10. *William Rhodes-Moorhouse VC.* Last flight 7-11-12. Forward fuselage. Arrived 16-11-13	[9]	1-14
❑ XV350		HS Buccaneer S.2B	67	ex Shawbury, Warton, RAE. Arrived 11-12-93		1-14
❑ XW664		HS Nimrod R.1	71	ex 51, A&AEE, 51. Last flown 12-7-11, on site 19-11-11		1-14
❑ XX457	'Z'	Sud Gazelle AH.1	76	ex Long Marston, Arborfield TAD.001, 2 Flt, 662, 656, ARWF, GCF. Arrived 11-10-08		1-14
❑ ZF588	'L'	EE Lightning F.53	68	ex Warton, R Saudi AF 53-693, G-27-63. Last flown 14-1-86. Arrived 8-1-89. 74 Sqn colours		1-14

■ **[1]** Terrier and Provost are on loan from Dave Warren. **[2]** Viscount cockpit is owned by Colin Jacobs. **[3]** Varsity and Meteor NF.13 are owned by Graham Vale. **[4]** WP784 is a complex composite. **[5]** XD459, owned by D Hardy, has the wings and booms from XE872. **[6]** XD534 is owned by Chris Fairhall; and is fitted with the wings and tail of XD382. **[7]** Single-seat Hunter is a complex beast; with an unused F.6 cockpit from Stafford, the centre section of F.6 XG226, the rear end of a Danish T.7 and the wings from PH-NLH. **[8]** XT604's rear fuselage is fitted to XT760 - see Portsmouth, Hants. **[9]** VC-10 on loan from Gary Spoors - see also Bruntingthorpe, Leics, and Gloucestershire, Glos.

Airport: Boeing 767-222 G-CECU touched down on 15th May 2008 for storage. It was scrapped in early April 2011.

❑ TC-ALM		Boeing 727-230	71	ex Air Alfa, TC-IKO, TC-JUH, TC-ALB, N878UM, D-ABDI. Fire crews		8-13

HINCKLEY south-west of Leicester

Exceptional work by craftsman Steve Milnthorpe has taken the project started by the Douglas Boston-Havoc UK Preservation Trust and turned it into a museum piece to drool over. It has been fitted out to Boston IIIA configuration and will be presented in 88 Squadron colours. Other items held include port inner mainplane, landing gear, Boston-fit Wright Cyclone, some rear fuselage and tailplane parts.

◆ **Access:** *Please note that visits are* **only** *possible by prior arrangement*

❑ -		Douglas Boston IIIA	43	forward fuselage - see notes	[1]	2-14

■ **[1]** Based upon the forward fuselage of A-20G-30-DO 43-9628 *Lady Constance* of the 388th BS, 312th BG, which crashed in New Guinea 16-4-44. The restoration includes elements of Boston IIA Z2186 ex 418 Sqn RCAF which crashed in Snowdonia 17-10-42.

HUSBANDS BOSWORTH AERODROME south of the A427, south of the village

Last noted in September 2009, spares-ship Wilga 35 HA-SEU has been deleted. | **www.thesoaringcentre.co.uk**

❑ XK790		Slingsby Grasshopper TX.1	55	ex Halton. Stored		8-13

LEICESTER

Leicester Aircraft Restoration Group: Max La Rue-Blood and his father, Ritch, make excellent progress with their Chipmunk. The anonymous Auster AOP.6 fuselage frame had moved on by 2013. **Access:** *By prior arrangement* **only**

❑ WZ869	'6'	DHC Chipmunk T.10 PAX	53	ex Bruntingthorpe, South Molton, ?, Handforth 8019M, 1 FTS, RAFC, Dishforth SF, Benson SF, Oxf UAS, Dur UAS, 64 GCF, Colerne SF. Crashed 20-5-68. Cockpit. RAFC colours		6-13

Also: An Aeronca, K8 glider and Canberra cockpit are at *separate* locations in the *general* area.

❑ G-BRFI		Aeronca 7DC Champion	46	ex Londonderry area, Ballymoney, N1058E, NC1058E. Damaged 1990. CoA 19-2-91		6-04
❑ FQD		Schleicher K8b	r89	BGA.3434		1-12
❑ XH174*		EE Canberra PR.9	60	ex South Molton, Welshpool, Staffordshire, Basingstoke, Shawbury, St Athan,1 PRU, 39, 13, 39, MoS, 39, 58. Cockpit. Arrived 7-10-12		10-12

LEICESTER AERODROME or Leicester East or Stoughton, south-east of Leicester EGBG

The cabin of Cessna 152 G-IBRO was removed in 2009 to become a rescue trainer at Shuttleworth, Beds.

❑ G-AEXZ		Piper J2 Cub	38	CoA 2-11-78. Off site		8-92
❑ G-AMTD		Auster J/5F Aiglet Trainer	52	ex EI-AVL, G-AMTD. Crashed 7-8-93, de-reg 15-1-99. Off-site		10-07
❑ G-ARDJ		Auster D.6/180	60	crashed 30-5-86. CoA 7-7-88. Off site		10-07
❑ G-BMWV*		Putzer Elster B	61	ex Nayland, D-EEKB, Luftwaffe 97+14, D-EBGI. CoA 27-10-06. Arrived 13-7-13		12-13
❑ G-CGYM*		NAA Harvard IIb	43	ex Chalgrove, Indian AF HT291, FS787, 20, 43-12628. Noorduyn-built. Arrived by 8-12	[1]	12-13
❑ G-LEIC*		Cessna FA.152 Aerobat	85	Reims-built. CoA 1-7-98, de-reg 29-11-11. Cr 19-5-11	[2]	12-13
❑ G-MWPS		Renegade Spirit	90	CoA 1-7-98. Fuselage frame		6-11
❑ 'PL256'	'TM-L'	Supermarine Spitfire IX FSM	c87	ex Delabole, Castle Donington, Leicester, Donington, Holland, 'H-25' *Baby Bee*, 'MK735'. 504 Sqn colours	[3]	12-13
❑ –*		Westland Wallace replica	c89	ex Old Warden, Hatch. Fuselage frame. Arrived 1-13	[1]	12-13
❑ -		Fieseler Fi 103 V-1 FSM	c91	ex Delabole, Castle Donington, Leicester	[3]	12-13

■ **[1]** Harvard and Wallace frame are destined for the Indian Air Force Historic Flight. **[2]** G-LEIC is used as an instructional airframe for school parties. **[3]** Spitfire is believed to be TDL Replicas-built; both it and the V-1 are displayed courtesy of the Wheatcroft Collection.

LOUGHBOROUGH on the A6 north of Leicester

Charnwood Museum: The 1956 King's Cup-winning Auster J/1N commemorates the wonders worked at nearby Rearsby.

◆ **Access:** *Granby Street, Loughborough, LE11 3DU.* **Open:** *Apr to Sep, Tue to Sat 10:00 to 16:30, Sun 14:00 to 17:00; Oct to Mar, Tue to Sat 10:00 to 15:00, Sun 12:00 to 15:00 -* **NB** *closed Mondays.* **Contacts: 01509 233754 | museum@charnwood.gov.uk | www.leics.gov.uk/museums**

❑ G-AJRH	'7'	Auster J/1N Alpha	47	ex Leicester, Harrogate, Wigan. CoA 5-6-69, de-reg 18-1-99	12-13

University; **Department of Aeronautical & Automotive Engineering**: EAP ZF534 moved to Cosford, Shropshire, on 27th March 2012. BAE Systems provided a replacement.

❑ ZH200*		HS Hawk 200	87	ex Brough, Warton. Arrived 5-12	11-12

LUTTERWORTH

Lutterworth Museum: Includes much Sir Frank Whittle and Power Jets material and an incredible archive.

◆ **Access:** *At Wycliffe House, Gilmorton Road, Lutterworth, Leics, LE17 4DY - off the A426 (Market Street).* **Open:** *Tue, Thu and Fri 10:00 to 16:00, Sat 10:00 to 13:00. Check website for winter openings. Other times by appointment.* **Contact: 01455 555585 | www.lutterworthmuseum.com**

Whittle Memorial: Dramatically displayed to the south of the town on the A426 roundabout is a superb tribute to the Gloster E28/39 as a tribute to Sir Frank Whittle. This and the similar monument at Farnborough, Hants (qv) were financed and built by the Sir Frank Whittle Commemorative Trust.

❑ –		Gloster E28/39 FSM	02	BAPC.284	11-13

Phil Cartwright: Keeps his *CockpitFest* champion Phantom cockpit at a private location in the general area.

❑ 37+86*		McD F-4F Phantom II	72	ex Market Drayton, Bruntingthorpe, Poland, GAF, WGAF, 72-1196. Cockpit	6-12

MELTON MOWBRAY

Tutor BGA.473 moved to Hooton Park, Cheshire, on 10th June 2012. Cadet BGA.1255 travelled to Lasham, Hampshire, to act as a wing donor for a Motor Cadet project.

NORTH LUFFENHAM north of the A6121 south-west of Stamford

St George's Barracks: On the eastern side of the former airfield was an **RAF Explosive Ordnance Disposal** enclave; airframe-wise at least, this wound down during 2013. Harrier GR.3 XV804 departed the enclave for Ipswich, Suffolk, 6th March 2013, followed on 16th May 2013 by Phantom FGR.2 XT905, also bound for Ipswich, Suffolk. Whirlwind HAR.10 XP344, last noted in November 2012, is believed to have been removed.

SALTBY AERODROME Last noted in September 2005, FRED G-BMOO has been deleted.

SHAWELL south of Lutterworth, east of the A5

Skirmish Paintball Games Leicester: **Access:** *busy site, by prior permission* **only | www.skirmishpaintballleicester.co.uk**

❑ XT770	'P'	Westland Wessex HU.5	67	ex Bruntingthorpe, St Athan, Halton 9055M (23-1-91), Wroughton, 845, 707, 781	7-08

STANFORD north-east of Rugby, near Swinford

Stanford Hall and **Percy Pilcher Museum**: Within the stables block is a display devoted to Percy Pilcher RN. Pilcher crashed at Stanford Hall on 30th September 1899 and died of his injuries two days later. There also is a memorial to the pioneer in the grounds. (The original craft he was piloting is in reclusive store - see under East Fortune, Scotland.)

◆ **Access:** *At the M6, M1, A14 junction (No.19) take the minor road off the A14 roundabout for Swinford, well signed to the north of the village of Stanford on Avon. Stanford Hall, Lutterworth, LE17 6DH.* **Open:** *Sun and Bank Hols, Easter to end of Sep 13:30 to 17:30 (last admission 17:00).* **Note:** *the Pilcher exhibit is available via a 'grounds' ticket and does not need entry to the house.* **Contact: 01788 860250 | enquiries@stanfordhall.co.uk | www.stanfordhall.co.uk**

❑ -		Pilcher Hawk replica	58	BAPC.45, ex Coventry, Bitteswell	1-14

STONEY STANTON on the B581 east of Hinckley

Stoney Cove - The National Diving Centre: Within the waters Wessex HU.5 XT768 (down at 70ft); the forward fuselage of Viscount 814 G-AWXI (23ft) and Partenavia P.68 G-LOUP (60ft). All last reported June 2011. **www.stoneycove.com**

WIGSTON south-east of Leicester

Graham Smith: Harrier GR.3 XV810 moved to Metheringham, Lincs, by early 2013.

◆ **Access: Private** *location, visits by prior arrangement* **only**

❑ XW763	HS Harrier GR.3	71	ex Bruntingthorpe, Wigston, Bruntingthorpe, Duxford, St Athan 9041M, 9002M ntu, 4, GR.1, 1453 Flt, 1, A&AEE, 1, 233 OCU. SOC 22-3-89. Cockpit	6-10

WOODHOUSE north of Woodhouse Eaves, east of the village, south of Loughborough

Welbeck Defence Sixth Form College: Jaguar T.2A XX145 moved on to Bruntingthorpe, Leics, on 10th April 2012.

◆ **Access:** *Busy campus, visitors* **strictly** *by prior arrangement* | **www.welbeck.mod.uk**

❑ XX381	Sud Gazelle AH.1	74	ex Middle Wallop, Shawbury, 847, 9 Regt, 3 Regt, 662, 664, 658, 2 Flt, 658, 6 Flt, RCS, 3 CBAS. Westland-built	2-12

LINCOLNSHIRE

Includes the unitary authorities of North Lincolnshire and North-East Lincolnshire

BARKSTON HEATH AIRFIELD on the B6403 north of Grantham EGYE

Hunter F.6A XE606 moved to Waddington, Lincs, on 10th April 2013.

❑ WT339	EE Canberra B(I).8	56	ex Cranwell 8198M (22-5-72), 16, 3, 14, 88. Short-built. Dump, poor state	9-13

BINBROOK on the B1203 north-east of Market Rasen

Charles Ross: Chairman of the Lightning Association (see below), Charles has an example in his garden and a small museum dedicated to the subject. Charles also owns F.1A XM192 at Woodhall Spa, Lincs.

◆ **Access:** *Admission by prior arrangement* **only**

❑ XR725	'BA'	EE Lightning F.6	65	ex Rossington, Binbrook, 11, F.3, 11, 5, LTF, 5, 56, 74, 5, 23. SOC 24-6-88	6-12
❑ XS899	'E'	EE Lightning F.6	66	ex Norwich, Coltishall, Bruntingthorpe, Cranfield, Binbrook, 11, 5-11 pool, 23, 5. SOC 24-6-88. Cockpit. 23 Sqn colours	6-13

BINBROOK AIRFIELD north of the B1203, north of the village

RAF Binbrook Heritage Centre: During 2011 a 2-acre site was acquired within the former RAF station in association of Roy Whitleley's Lincair. An incredible amount of work has been carried out in clearing the site, but there is much to be done before public access is possible. Previously listed under the LA (below), the T.5 cockpit now 'moves' to this entry. **Access:** *Visits by prior permission* **only**. **Contact: lincair@binbrook.demon.co.uk | www.binbrook.demon.co.uk**

❑ XS457	EE Lightning T.5	65	ex Grainthorpe, North Coates, New Waltham, Laceby, Binbrook, 5, 11, 5, LTF, 11, 226 OCU. SOC 21-9-87. Cockpit	6-12

Lightning Association: Via the LA's *incredible* website, which has to be 'grazed' to appreciate just how much is there, Lightning fans are united. **Access:** *Visits by prior permission* **only**. **Contact: email via website | www.lightning.org.uk**

❑ XR724	EE Lightning F.6	65	ex G-BTSY (de-reg 26-5-92), Shawbury, BAe Warton, 11, F.3, 11, 5, 11, 5, LTF, 11. Arrived 23-7-92	6-12

Also:

❑ XL578*	'77'	Hawker Hunter T.7	58	ex Woodhall Spa, Gainsborough, Kemble, Norwich, Bruntingthorpe, Cranfield, St Athan, 1 TWU, TWU, 229 OCU. SOC 26-7-84. Arrived 8-3-13	[1]	4-13

❑ XS177*	'N'	Hunting Jet Provost T.4	63	ex Metheringham, Ipswich, Cosford, Valley 9044M (24-4-90), Shawbury, CATCS, 3 FTS, 2 FTS. Arrived by 10-12		10-13
❑ ZE697	'006'	HS Sea Harrier FA.2	88	ex Charlwood, St Athan, 801. 899. 800. 899. 800. 801, 899, FRS.1, 801, 800		6-12

■ **[1]** The Hunter is a composite, with the rear end of XG290. The cockpit of XG290 can be found under Boscombe Down, Wilts. For the tail of XL578, see under Wickford, Essex.

BOSTON

Tony Smith: Is *believed* to still keep two airframes at a *private* location in the general area.

❑ G-MJBN		Aerolights Eagle Rainbow	r82	ex Glatton. De-reg 6-9-94. Stored	12-06
❑ –		Stewart Ornithopter	c65	BAPC.61, ex North Coates, Louth, Tumby Woodside, East Kirkby, Tattershall, Wigan, Irlam, S Reston. *Bellbird II*	12-06

Also: A *private* workshop in this general area holds some 'long-termers'. One of these, Super Cub G-PULL, had moved to East Winch, Norfolk, by November 2012. Super Cub G-AXGA had moved on by October 2013.

❑ G-AYVT		Brochet MB.84	r71	ex Tattershall Thorpe, Sunderland, F-BGLI. Damaged 28-6-77, de-reg 3-9-81	10-13
❑ F-BBGH		Brochet MB.100	~	ex F-WBGH	10-13
❑ F-PFUG		Adam RA-14	~	-	10-13

Others: Travel back to *W&R22*, p129. Here the moving on of Lightning F.3 cockpit XP757 was noted, with no forwarding address. It is now to be found at Stamford, Lincs.

COLSTERWORTH on the A1 north of Stamford

Witham Specialist Vehicles Ltd: A wholesale exodus of Gazelle AH.1s to Stapleford Tawney, Essex, where turnover or further disposal is thought to be swift, hence no 'forwarding reference': XW848 (by 5-12), XW909 (5-12), XW913 (17-7-12), XX371 (5-12 - becoming G-CHLU), XX383 (5-12), XX386 (7-12), XX394 (7-12), XX398 (10-12), XX409 (10-12 - to G-CHYV), XX416 (7-12), XX437 (10-12), XX438 (5-12), XX439 (7-12 - to G-CHLW), XX445 (7-12), XX455 (5-12), XX456 (6-12), XX462 (7-12), XZ291 (10-12), XZ296 (9-12), XZ304 (5-12), XZ314 (10-12), XZ324 (5-12), XZ338 (10-12 - to G-CHZF), XZ344 (5-12), ZA726 (5-12), ZA728 (7-12), ZB673 (7-12), ZB688 (9-12 - to G-CHMF, gaining a permit in 2013 for a Cypriot owner).

◆ **Access:** *Visits possible* **only** *by prior arrangement* | **www.mod-sales.com**

❑ XZ292		Sud Gazelle AH.1	76	ex Shawbury, 645, 3 Regt, 656, 664, 656, 663, 656, 654, 669, 662. Westland-built	5-10
❑ XZ921*	'269'	Westland Sea King HAS.6	79	ex Gosport, Fleetlands, 820, 814, 810, 706, 706, 820. Arrived 6-11-13	11-13
❑ ZA776		Sud Gazelle AH.1	80	ex Shawbury, Yeovilton, 847, 3 CBAS. Westland-built	5-10
❑ ZD633*	'014'	Westland Sea King HAS.6	84	ex Gosport, 820, 810, 814, 810, 820, 706. Arrived 6-11-13	8-13

CONINGSBY AIRFIELD south of the A153, south-east of Woodhall Spa EGXC

Battle of Britain Memorial Flight (BBMF) and **Visitor Centre**: Spitfire XVI TE311 was air tested on 19th October 2012 and joined the fleet in the 2013 season. Spitfire F.21 LA255 moved to Leuchars, Scotland, on 20th August 2012, to join the 'new' 1 Squadron. The guided tour 'experience' is an *essential* part of the visit - don't miss out!

The **RAF Memorial Flight Club** has been established which offers free entry to the Visitor Centre and other goodies. Funds raised go directly to the upkeep of BBMF: **www.memorialflightclub.com**

◆ **Access:** *'Brown signed' from the A153; located in Dogdyke Road, on the western perimeter of the base.* **Open:** *Mon to Fri except Bank Hols 10:00 to 17:00. Guided tours from 10:30 to 15:30 (15:00 Nov to Feb) Normally closed at weekends, Bank Holidays and two weeks at Christmas - check on the website.* **Note:** *Access to the BBMF hangar is via guided tour* **only**. *Please note that it is advisable to check in advance relating to the movements of the Flight, as it may be that some, or all, of the aircraft may be away visiting an event. Occasionally, due to RAF commitments and stand down, access to the hangar cannot be guaranteed.* **Contact:** *Battle of Britain Memorial Flight Visits, RAF Coningsby, Lincoln LN4 4SY* | **01522 782040** | **bbmf@lincolnshire.gov.uk** | **www.raf.mod.uk/bbmf**

❑ P7350	'EB-G	Supermarine Spitfire IIa ✈	40	ex *Battle of Britain* G-AWIJ, Colerne, 57 OTU, CGS, 64, 616, 603, 266. Joined BBMF 1968. 41 Sqn colours	[1]	2-14
❑ AB910	'MD-E'	Supermarine Spitfire Vb ✈	41	ex *Battle of Britain*, BBMF, G-AISU, 29 MU, RWE, 527, 53 OTU, 402, 242, 133, 130, 222. BBMF from 1965. 133 Sqn colours from 5-12	[2]	2-14

❑	'EN398'	'JE-J'	Sup' Spitfire IX FSM	~	ex Duxford, built by GB Replicas. On loan		2-14
❑	LF363	'YB-W'	Hawker Hurricane IIc ✈	44	ex Audley End, Coningsby, Biggin Hill SF, 41, 41 GCF, Waterbeach SF, Odiham SF, Thorney Island SF, FCCS, M' Wallop SF, 61 OTU, 41 OTU, 62 OTU, 26, 63, 309, 63. Joined Biggin Hill Stn Flt 1951. 17 Sqn colours	[3]	2-14
❑	MK356	'5J-K'	Supermarine Spitfire IX ✈	44	ex St Athan, Abingdon, 5690M St Athan, Henlow, Bicester, Hawkinge, Halton, 84 GSU, 443. 126 Sqn c/s, *Kay*	[4]	2-14
❑	PA474	'KC-A'	Avro Lancaster I ✈	45	ex 44, Wroughton, Cranfield College, RAE, FRL, 82. Joined BBMF 20-11-73. *Thumper Mk.III*. 617 Sqn c/s from 9-12	[5]	2-14
❑	PM631	'S'	Supermarine Spitfire ...PR.XIX ✈	45	ex THUM Flt, Buckeburg SF, 206 OCU, 203 AFS. Joined Biggin Hill Stn Flt 13-6-57. 541 Sqn colours		2-14
❑	PS915		Supermarine Spitfire PR.XIX ✈	45	ex Samlesbury, Preston, Brawdy, St Athan, Coningsby, Brawdy, Leuchars 7548M/7711M, West Malling, Biggin Hill, THUM Flt, 2, PRDU, 541. *The Last!*, 81 Sqn c/s	[6]	2-14
❑	PZ865	'EG-S'	Hawker Hurricane II ✈	44	ex 'P2619' 'US-B' *Angels One-Five*, Hawker G-AMAU. Joined BBMF 29-3-72. 34 Sqn, SEAC, colours	[7]	2-14
❑	TE311	'4D-V'	Supermarine Spitfire XVI ✈	45	ex EP&TU, 7241M, 'MK178' 'X4474', France, Abingdon, Henlow, Wattisham, CAACU, 103 FRS, 102 FRS, 83 GSU. First flew 19-10-12. 74 Sqn colours	[8]	2-14
❑	WG486	'G'	DHC Chipmunk T.10 ✈	51	ex Newton, Gatow SF, ARWF, 3 AEF, Bri UAS, 3 AEF, Bri UAS, Liv UAS, PFS, 1 FTS, ITS, AOTS, ITS, RAFC, MECS, 114, 651, 657, 2 FTS, 63 GCF, 9 RFS, 5 BFTS	[9]	2-14
❑	WK518	'C'	DHC Chipmunk T.10 ✈	52	ex Newton, 1 AEF, Lon UAS, Hull UAS, Leeds UAS, Hull UAS, Coltishall SF, FWS, Cam UAS, Hull UAS, Cam UAS, Mcr UAS, Liv UAS, 63 GCF, RAFC. Hull UAS c/s	[9]	2-14
❑	ZA947	'UK'	Douglas Dakota III ✈	42	ex DRA, RAE, Farnborough, West Freugh, 'KG661', RCAF 661, 42-24338. *Kwicherbichen*, 233 Sqn colours	[10]	2-14

■ **[1]** P7350 represents Mk.IIa N3162 as flown by Flt Lt Eric Lock DSO DFC*, 1940. **[2]** AB910 was due back from major maintenance at Duxford, Cambs, in May 2014 in 64 Sqn colours, as flown by Flt Lt Tony Cooper. Very much a 'warbird', on 19-8-42 AB910 took part in the ill-fated Dieppe raid; Flt Sgt 'Dixie' Alexander was credited with the destruction of a Do 217 in it that day. **[3]** LF363 should appear in 2014 in 1 Sqn colours, as flown by Arthur Clowes. **[4]** MK356 was repainted in late 2013 into the colours of ML214 of 126 Sqn, as flown by S/L John A Plagis DSO DFC. See under Cosford, Shropshire, and Hawkinge, Kent, for 'other' MK356s! **[5]** PA474 represents Mk.I DV385 based at Woodhall Spa which took part in the raids on the *Tirpitz* in Tromso fjord 28-10-44 and 12-11-44. It carried out 50 'ops' and dropped 15 x 12,000lb Tallboy bombs. **[6]** PS915 represents PS888 of 81 Sqn which flew the last ever RAF operational Spitfire sortie, on 1-4-54. **[7]** PZ865 returned from restoration by Arco at Duxford on 10-4-13 and carries the colours of HW840 with 34 Sqn, flown by F/L Jimmy Whelen DFC. **[8]** TE311's restoration consumed fellow TB382 as a source of spares. It wears the colours of 74 CO S/L Tony Reeves DFC, 1945. **[9]** WG486 taken on charge 31-12-51 and WK518 28-1-52 and still going strong, the last of their breed in UK military service. **[10]** Rolled out at Manchester on 5-4-11 having been resprayed by Air Livery. It represents FZ692 of 233 Sqn.

RAF Coningsby:

❑	'XP765'	'A'	EE Lightning F.6	XS897	66	ex Doncaster, Firbeck, Rossington, Binbrook, 5, 11, 5, 11, 56, 74. SOC 5-2-88. 29 Squadron, displayed	[1]	12-13
❑	XR753	'XI'	EE Lightning F.6		65	ex Leeming 8969M (25-5-88), Binbrook, 11, 5-11 pool, 23, FCTU, F.3. 11 Sqn colours, displayed	[2]	1-12
❑	XT891	'Z'	McD Phantom FGR.2		68	9136M (10-6-92), ex 74, 228 OCU, 56, 228 OCU, 29, 228 OCU, 29, 228 OCU, 29, 228 OCU, 56, 228 OCU, 6, 54, 228 OCU, 54. Gate, 228 OCU colours		1-12
❑	XW924		HS Harrier GR.3		71	ex Cottesmore 9073M, Laarbruch, Halton, 3, 4, 1, 233 OCU, GR.1, 4, 20, 4. 3 Squadron, displayed		1-12
❑	ZE760	'AP'	Panavia Tornado F.3		88	ex St Athan, ItAF MM7206, RAF, 5. 229 OCU colours. Gate		1-12
❑	ZJ943	'DK'	Eurofighter Typhoon FGR.4		07	ex 11, Landing accident at China Lake 23-4-08. Fuselage	[3]	12-11

■ **[1]** XS897 is owned by Lakes Lightnings - see Spark Bridge, Cumbria - and is on a ten-year loan to 29 Squadron. Only F.3s were flown by 23 Squadron, so it has been given a small ventral tank, but retains the conical camber wings of the F.6. **[2]** XR753 is displayed outside XI Squadron's Typhoon headquarters on the southern perimeter - see under Tangmere, W Sussex, for its doppelgänger. **[3]** ZJ943 was delivered to Coningsby 10-1-08 and was written off 74 days later.

CRANWELL AIRFIELD on the A17/B1429 north-west of Sleaford EGYD

Cranwell Aviation Heritage Centre: Located close to the airfield, the centre charts the history of Cranwell and gives notes on the other airfields on the North Kesteven Airfield Trail. Also boasting a souvenir shop, flight simulator and archive film show, it is an excellent stop-off when visiting Cranwell and/or the trail.

◆ **Access:** *'Brown signed' off the A17 on minor road to North and South Rauceby.* **Open:** *Daily, Apr to Oct, 10:00 to 16:30 daily; Nov to Mar, 10:00 to 16:00 Sats and Suns only.* **Contact:** *Heath Farm, North Rauceby, Sleaford, NG34 8QR* | **01529 488490** *or* **01529 308102** | **cranwellaviation@n-kesteven.gov.uk** | **www.cranwellaviation.co.uk**

❑ XE946		DH Vampire T.11	55	ex Cardington, Henlow, Bicester 7473M (25-9-57), Habbaniya SF, Nicosia SF. Cockpit	12-13
❑ XP556	'3'	Hunting Jet Provost T.4	61	ex Bruntingthorpe, Halton 9027M (15-2-90), Shawbury, CATCS, SoRF, 6 FTS, RAFC	12-13

RAF Cranwell: The Spitfire 'guards' the Selection Centre, the Dominie and 'JP' are along the B1429 through the camp.

❑ 'P8448'	'DO-R'	Supermarine Spitfire FSM	90	BAPC.225, ex Swanton Morley	12-13
❑ XS710	'O'	HS Dominie T.1	65	ex Cosford 9259M (7-10-96), Cranwell, 3 FTS, 6 FTS, CAW. Fire pits	10-13
❑ XS727	'D'	HS Dominie T.1	65	ex 55, 3 FTS, 6 FTS, 1 ANS. 'Gate' by 9-13	10-13
❑ XW353	'3'	BAC Jet Provost T.5A	71	ex 9090M (18-7-91), 3 FTS, RAFC, CFS, 3 FTS, RAFC. 'Gate'	10-13
❑ XZ138		HS Harrier GR.3	76	ex 9040M (25-3-76), SIF, St Athan, 1, 233 OCU, 1453 Flt, 1, 3, 4, 3. Cockpit	5-11
❑ ZA717	'C'	BV Chinook HC.1	82	ex 9238M, St Athan, Fleetlands, 78, 7 1310F, 18, N37056. Crashed 25-7-89. Fuselage	10-11

Training Consolidation Flight: The flight was wound down, with all of the airframes put up for tender, or other use, by late 2012. Jaguar departures to Cosford, Shropshire: T.2A XX141 23-4-13; GR.1 XX821 4-4-12; T.2 XX837 7-8-12; GR.1A XX965 17-10-12; GR.1A XZ358 by 8-13; T.2 ZB615 by 8-13. Harrier GR.3 XZ132 moved to Selby, N Yorks, 14-11-13.

❑ XX396	'N'	Sud Gazelle HT.3	75	ex 8718M, EPTT, St Athan, Abingdon, Henlow, 2 FTS. Westland-built. Crashed 30-6-81. See above	5-11
❑ XX747	'08'	SEPECAT Jaguar GR.1	74	ex Halton 8903M (23-5-86), Shawbury, Gibraltar Det, 6, 20, 31, 226 OCU. Gulf pink colours, *Sadman.* See above	5-11

Cranwell North: The gliding club has at least one long term inmate.

❑ EHB*	'K3'	Schleicher Ka 3	~	BGA.2689, ex RAFGGA 559. CoA 28-5-05	11-13

RAF Exhibition, Production and Transportation Unit (EP&TU): The airframes are based on a former airfield close by and run by a contractor. EP&TU is 'parented' by the Cranwell-based Directorate of Recruitment and Selection and, for that reason, the 'fleet' is listed under this heading. Access to the 'detached' site is *not* possible and indeed many of the airframes spend their time in 'transit camps' elsewhere to minimise vehicle usage. EP&TU also has two Eurofighter Typhoon cockpit mock-ups, both of which include interactive segments. These, 'Chinook' 'IR808' and a 'Hercules' - the latter owing more to Crane Fruehauf than to Lockheed Georgia - are *not* considered as deserving of a 'formal' listing. The cockpit mock-up of Jaguar GR.1 'XZ363' and Harrier GR.7 FSM 'ZH139' were offered for disposal in 2011 and are thought to have moved on.

❑ 'XX226'	'74'	HS Hawk T.1 FSM	78	BAPC.152, ex St Athan, 'XX262', Abingdon, 'XX162'. 74 Sqn colours	7-00
❑ 'XX227'		HS Hawk T.1 FSM	81	BAPC.171, ex 'XX253', St Athan, 'XX297', Abingdon, 'XX262'. 'Red Arrows' colours	9-11
❑ 'ZA556'	'Z'	Panavia Tornado GR.1 FSM	80	BAPC.155, ex St Athan, 'ZA368' 'ZA446' Abingdon, 'ZA600', 'ZA322'. Grey colours, 13 Sqn colours	7-04
❑ 'IR206'	'IR'	Eurofighter Typhoon FGR.4 FSM	c02	Trailer-mounted, 17 Squadron colours	8-13

CROWLAND AERODROME on the A1073 south of Spalding

❑ G-BBRX*	SIAI-Marchetti S.205-18	66	ex LN-VYH, OO-HAQ. CoA 15-6-10, de-reg 25-8-10. F/n 4-12	7-13

Also: A private collector in the *general* area has a Noralpha project.

❑ 'F-OTAN-6'	Nord Noralpha	G-BAYV	48	ex Barton, Chelford, Sevenoaks, Booker, Hawkinge, Maidstone, Ford, F-BLTN, French AF. Crashed 23-2-74, de-reg 28-4-83. Fuselage	12-11

DIGBY east of the B1188 north of Sleaford

Within the historic station the **RAF Digby World War Two Sector Operations Room** has been lovingly restored.

◆ **Open:** *Suns, May to Oct, at 11:00, guided tours* ***only****. Groups by prior arrangement.* **Contact: 01526 327272** *- weekdays 08:00 and 17:00* | **www.raf.mod.uk/rafdigby**

Joint Services Signals Organisation Digby:

❑ 'MJ832'	'DN-Y'	Supermarine Spitfire FSM	89	BAPC.229, ex 'L1096', Church Fenton. *City of Oshawa*, 416 Sqn colours. Displayed	12-13

EAST KIRKBY AERODROME on the A155 west of Spilsby

Lincolnshire Aviation Heritage Centre (LAHC): Run by the Panton family as a memorial to brother Christopher, who was killed on the horrific Nürnberg raid of 30-31st March 1944, and as a tribute to Bomber Command as a whole. On 9th June 2013, **Fred Panton** died aged 82. The writer would be hard-pressed to beat the LAHC's own tribute to a determined and genial man: "a gentleman, a loving and caring family man and an inspiration to us all. He will remain in the thoughts and spirit of the centre forevermore." There is not an inch of LAHC that is not steeped in the vision and drive of Fred.

With this in mind, *Just Jane* was due to be rolled out on 29th March 2014 to commemorate the 70th anniversary of the Nürnberg raid. The codes on either side of the fuselage have been slightly amended, to pay tribute to Fred and his brother, Harold, who rescued NX611 and brought it to life at East Kirkby.

Displays include the famous watch tower, the incredible escape exhibition, a blast shelter, 'Blitz' display and much more. There are regular 'in steam' days with the Lancaster and especially moving are the night-time runs and a now annual airshow - all well recommended. Lancaster G-ASXX is the subject of a long-term project to put it back into the air. C-47A *Drag 'Em Oot* is based and available occasionally for taxi rides (a la *Just Jane*) when not flying elsewhere.

Acting in support of the taxiable Lancaster is the **East Kirkby Lancaster Association** - subscribing helps in its upkeep and brings benefits, including an annual newsletter. Two other groups are based within LAHC: **Lincolnshire Aircraft Recovery Group**: 'Prize' exhibit is the very substantial Spitfire BL655. **Lincolnshire Aviation Preservation Society**: Main project is the painstaking restoration of AE436, the Brian Nicholls Hampden Project and Proctor IV NP294.

◆ **Open:** *Easter to Oct Mon to Sat 10:00 to 17:00, last admission 16:00; Nov to Easter Mon to Sat 10:00 to 16:00, last admission 15:00.* **Note:** *Not open on Sundays.* **Contact:** *East Kirkby, near Spilsby, PE23 4DE* | **01790 763207** | **enquiries@lincsaviation.co.uk** | **www.lincsaviation.co.uk**

❑ -*		Druine Turbulent	~	fuselage in workshop rafters. First noted 8-12		1-14
❑ AE436	'PL-J'	HP Hampden I	41	ex Coningsby, Henlow, Sweden, 144. Crashed 4-9-42. EE-built. Forward fuselage, etc	[1]	1-14
❑ BL655		Supermarine Spitfire Vb	41	ex Dorrington Fen, 416, 129, 341, 164, 602, 416. Crashed 1-7-43. Substantial fuselage section	[2]	1-14
❑ NP294		Percival Proctor IV	44	ex Tattershall, Friskney, Poynton, Andover, Cosford, 4 RS, 2 RS. Hills-built. SOC 22-3-55	[1]	1-14
❑ NX611	'DX-F' *and* 'LE-H'	Avro Lancaster VII G-ASXX	45	ex Scampton, 8375M, Blackpool, Hullavington, Lavenham, Biggin Hill, Aéronavale, WU-15, St Athan, Llandow. Austin Motors-built. *Just Jane*, 57 Sqn colours to stb, 630 Sqn to port. *City of Sheffield*. Taxiable - see above	[3]	1-14
❑ WH957		EE Canberra E.15	55	ex Bruntingthorpe, Cosford 8869M, 100, 98, B.6, 98, Akrotiri Wing, 32, Hemswell SF, Upwood SF, 21, 542, 617. Short-built. Cockpit		1-14
❑ -		Heinkel He 111 mock-up	~	ex New Zealand, East Kirkby, others, *Battle of Britain*. Cockpit, in blitz display building		1-14
❑ 2100882	'3X-P'	Douglas C-47A Skytrain ✈ N473DC	42	ex N5831B, C-FKAZ, CF-KAZ, RCAF, TS422, 435, 1 HGSU, 42-100882. *Drag 'Em Oot*		1-14

■ **[1]** Hampden and Proctor with LAPS. **[2]** Spitfire Vb with LARG. **[3]** Codes altered in early 2014 - 'F' for Fred Panton, 'H' for Harold.

ELSHAM west of the A15, north-east of Brigg

RAF Elsham Wolds Association Memorial Garden and Memorial Room: A poignant commemoration housed in the premises of the Anglian Water Treatment Plant at the end of one of the old runways.

◆ **Access:** *From J5 of the M180 on the minor roads to Elsham village.* **Open:** *By prior appointment* **only** | **01652 653247** | **www.walter9.info/RAFEW/**

FENLAND AERODROME west of the B1168 and Holbeach St Johns — EGCL

SOCATA Diplomate G-HOLY was removed during May 2012 for reduction to spares to help a flyer in Ireland. Last noted in June 2007, Cherokee Six G-BRNZ has been deleted.

❑ G-AHAP	Auster J/1 Autocrat	46	ex March. CoA 20-2-91. Off-site	12-09
❑ G-AMRF	Auster J/5F Aiglet Trainer	52	ex VT-DHA, G-AMRF. *Grey Dove*. CoA 31-3-07. Off-site	6-13
❑ G-AWBA*	Piper Cherokee Arrow 180	68	CoA 29-3-12, de-reg 2-3-12. Fuselage. First noted 4-12	7-13

❑ G-AZLO	Cessna F.337F	71	ex Bourn, Land's End. Reims-built. CoA 22-4-82, de-reg 4-12-86	6-13
❑ G-BLVS	Cessna 150M	75	ex EI-BLS, N45356. CoA 14-12-07	6-13
❑ G-BORY	Cessna 150L	71	ex N6792G. CoA 21-7-09, de-reg 19-10-00	6-13
❑ G-BSUW*	Piper Seneca 200T	77	ex N2360M. CoA 7-9-10	6-13
❑ G-BSXI*	Mooney M.20E	70	ex N6766V. CoA 9-6-11	6-13

FLEET HARGATE on the A17, east of Holbeach

Harold Payne: The Hunter is within the grounds of the 'Anglia Motel' and looked after by **2430 Squadron, Air Cadets**.

❑ WT680 'J'	Hawker Hunter F.1	54	ex Aberporth, Weeton 7533M (22-1-57), DFLS, West Raynham SF	11-13

GLENTHAM on A631 west of Market Rasen

❑ XD595	DH Vampire T.11	54	ex Altrincham, Woodford, Chester, St Athan, 1 FTS, Oakington SF, 7 FTS, 4 FTS. SOC 6-11-67. Cockpit	1-12

HAXEY off the A161, north-west of Gainsborough

Andrew Exton:

❑ XR759	EE Lightning F.6	65	ex Rossington 'TVI759', Binbrook, 5-11 pool, 56, 74, 5. SOC 24-6-88. Cockpit. 56 Sqn colours	6-12

HIBALDSTOW AERODROME on the B1206 south of Brigg

Two long-termers have been deleted: Rallye G-AWXY (last noted July 2001) and IS.28M G-BKAB (February 2008).

❑ G-ANHR	Auster 5	44	ex MT192, 662. CoA 20-7-86. Frame		12-13
❑ G-ASDK*	Beagle Terrier 2	48	ex G-ARLM, Auster AOP.6 VF631, 654, 652, 656. CoA 4-11-10		12-13
❑ G-BWCO	Dornier Do 28D-2	79	ex EI-CJU, N5TK, 5N-AOH, D-ILIF. CoA 19-5-99, de-reg 30-1-0	9	8-13
❑ G-BZHL*	NAA Harvard IIB	44	ex Wickenby, Egypt, FT118 n/s. SOC 11-7-46. Arrived 6-13		8-13
❑ HA-NAH*	Technoavia SMG-92 Finist	~	ex Spain, RA44484. Arrived 9-10-12. Crashed 1-7-12		8-13
❑ 115	Dornier Do 28D-2	~	ex Kenyan Air Force. Stored		8-13
❑ 117	Dornier Do 28D-2	~	ex Kenyan Air Force. Stored		8-13

HUMBERSIDE AIRPORT or Kirmington EGNJ

Global Aviation: 'JP' T.3A XM376 (G-BWDR) was exported to a museum in Turkey, perhaps as early as April 2009.

◆ **Access:** *By prior arrangement* **only**

❑ G-BWSH	Hunting Jet Provost T.3A	60	ex XN498, 1 FTS, 3 FTS, RAFC. CoA 8-7-03	1-13
❑ 1115	BAC Strikemaster 80A	73	ex RSaudi AF, G-27-226. Stored	3-11
❑ 1129	BAC Strikemaster 80A	76	ex RSaudi AF, G-27-295. Stored	3-11

Spitfire Ltd: Richard Lake's Buchón and Spitfire are due to be joined by Spitfire XVIII SM845 (G-BUOS) - see Duxford, Cambs. The latter - then registered SE-BIN - arrived here on 12th July 2012, before moving, via Duxford, to Sandown, Isle of Wight, on 21st September 2012.

◆ **Access:** *By prior arrangement* **only**

❑ TD248 'CR-S'	Supermarine Spitfire XVI ✈ G-OXVI	45	ex Duxford, Audley End, Braintree, Earls Colne, Sealand, Hooton Park 7246M, 610, 2 CAACU, 695. 74 Sqn colours	[1]	8-13
❑ – 'I->>'	Hispano Buchón ✈ G-AWHE	48	ex Duxford, USA N109ME, *Battle of Britain* G-AWHE, Span AF C4K-31.JG53 colours	[1]	8-13

■ **[1]** TD248 carries codes that co-incide with initials of Spitfire Ltd's chief pilot, AM Cliff Spink. See also under Flixton, Suffolk for 'another' TD248. **[2]** G-AWHE flies in the colours of Major Erich Gerlitz's Bf 109F of JG53.

Also: The fuselage of Jetstream 41 G-GCJL was broken up during July 2013 and removed.

❑ G-AVMP	BAC 111-510ED	68	ex Iver Heath, Bournemouth, European, BA, BEA. Forward fuselage. CoA 6-4-01, de-reg 12-11-02. Fire crews	11-10
❑ G-CDYI	BAe Jetstream 41	93	ex N305UE, G-4-019	2-11
❑ 'G-JXLI'	BAe Jetstream 41	97	ex Prestwick. c/n 41105. Unflown fuselage, fire crews	1-13

INGHAM west of the B1398, north-west of Scampton

RAF Ingham Heritage Group: The volunteers secured a 25-year lease on the former Airmen's Mess building during 2012 and since have been working feverishly to refurbish the building and to provide support infrastructure.

◆ **Access: Not yet open** - *keep an eye on the website* | **enquiries@rafingham.co.uk** | **www.rafingham.co.uk**

KIRTON-IN-LINDSEY on the B1398 north-east of Gainsborough

❑ WZ757 Slingsby Grasshopper TX.1 52 ex Rufforth, Locking, Chichester. Stored [1] 6-12

■ **[1]** The frame of WZ757, 'tail feathers' of WZ768 and wings of XK820 ('fuselage' at Bridge of Weir, Scotland).

LINCOLN

Mark Rumble: Has the former Balderton Lightning F.2A and is embarking on an ambitious restoration.

◆ **Access: Private** *location, access by prior arrangement* **only** | **markrumble@btopenworld.com**

❑ XN728 'V' EE Lightning F.2A 61 ex Balderton, Coningsby, Wildenrath 8546M (1-4-77), 92. Cockpit 2-14

LOUTH Not noted since 1998, Stewart Ornithopter BAPC.161 has been deleted.

MESSINGHAM on the A159 south of Scunthorpe

❑ XK417 Auster AOP.9 G-AVXY 56 ex Melton Mowbray, Tattershall Thorpe, Wisbech, Henstridge, Thruxton, 652, LAS. SOC 7-11-67. CoA 9-7-00 4-12

METHERINGHAM on the B1191 west of Woodhall Spa

Metheringham Airfield Visitor Centre: Based in what was part of the bomber base's communal site is an excellent display showing life at Metheringham and 106 Squadron. There is a very active **Friends of Metheringham Airfield**.

Hunter FGA.9 XE624 moved to Wickenby, Lincs, by June 2012. Jet Provost T.4 XS177 was put up for disposal in early 2012 and moved to Binbrook, Lincs, by October 2012.

◆ **Access:** *Westmoor Farm, Martin Moor, on the B1189 south-east of Metheringham and signed close to the site.* **Open:** *Easter to Oct, Wed 11:00 to 16:00, Sat, Sun and Bank Hols 11:00 to 17:00. Other times by prior arrangement.* **Contact:** *Westmoor Farm, Martin Moor, Metheringham, Lincoln, LN4 3BQ* | **www.metheringhamairfield.com**

❑ XS186 '10' Hunting Jet Provost T.4 64 ex Ipswich, North Luffenham, Halton 8408M (7-10-74), St Athan, Kemble, Shawbury, CAW [1] 4-13

■ **[1]** The 'JP' is on loan from Paul Flynn.

Richard Scarborough: Keeps his award-winning Lightning in the general area

❑ XS932 EE Lightning F.6 67 ex Market Drayton, Farnborough, Shoreham, Bruntingthorpe, Rossington, Binbrook, 5, 11, 56, 11. SOC 24-6-88. Cockpit 6-13

❑ XV810* 'K' HS Harrier GR.3 71 ex Wigston/Bruntingthorpe, St Athan, Abingdon, 9038M, St Athan, 233 OCU, 4, 20. SOC 16-1-89. Cockpit. 4 Sqn colours 6-13

NEW YORK on the B1192 south of Coningsby

❑ XS416 'DU' EE Lightning T.5 64 ex Grainthorpe, New Waltham, Rossington, Binbrook, 5, LTF, 11, 74, 226 OCU. SOC 24-6-88 10-13

❑ ZA361 'TD' Panavia Tornado GR.1 81 ex St Athan, Marham, 15, TTTE. Fuselage 10-13

NORTH COATES AERODROME north of the A1031, south of Humberston

North Coates Heritage Collection: A small display of artefacts, images and models relating to the history of the airfield 1914 to 1992 has been put together in an area of 200 sq ft within the North Coates Flying Club premises.

Open: *Weekends and Bank Hols 10:00 to 17:00 summer and 10:00 to 15:00 Nov to Mar.* **Contact: 01472 388850** | **brianstafford169@btinternet.com** | **www.northcoatesflyingclub.co.uk**

❑ G-ASME* Bensen B.8M 66 CoA 10-8-12. Spares for B.8MR G-BIHX. First noted 8-12 1-14

❑ CEK Slingsby T.21B(T) 59 BGA.1482, ex RAFGSA.369, XN147. CoA 7-5-05. Stored [1] 1-14

❑ N259SA Cessna F.172G 66 ex Skegness, EI-BAO, G-ATNH. Reims-built 1-14

■ **[1]** Motor-glider conversion.

NORTH HYKEHAM east of the A1434, south of Lincoln

The cockpit section of a Boeing 727 had appeared in the Lindum Business Park by late 2012.

❑ OO-DHN*	Boeing 727-31F	69	ex Kemble, Alton, Lasham, 'N9748C', DHL, N260NE, N97891. De-reg 13-11-03. Cockpit. First noted 10-12	5-13

NORTH MOOR AERODROME near Messingham, south of Scunthorpe

❑ G-BMHC	Cessna U.206F	76	ex Grindale, N10TB, G-BMHC, N8571Q. Crashed 20-10-05	4-13

NORTH SCARLE east of the A1133, north of Swinderby

Ground Equipment Supplies Ltd: The cockpit of Lightning F.1A XM191 moved to Selby, N Yorks, by October 2013.

◆ **Access:** *Private location, visits possible* ***only*** *by prior arrangement* | **www.groundequipmentsupplies.co.uk**

❑ 'WT720' 'B'	Hawker Hunter F.51	56 E-408	ex Sealand, Cranwell 'XF979', Brawdy 8565M, Dunsfold, G-9-436 (10-4-76), Esk.724, Dan AF E-408. 74 Sqn colours	1-14

SANDTOFT AERODROME south of the M180, between Sandtoft and Westgate EGCF

❑ G-BBLM	MS Rallye 100S	73	CoA 8-5-08, de-reg 30-11-10. 'Gate guardian'/rescue trainer	1-14
❑ G-BEYT*	Piper Cherokee 140	64	ex D-EBWP, N6280W. CoA 29-6-11. First noted 7-13	1-14
❑ G-BIFB*	Piper Cherokee 150	65	ex 4X-AEC. CoA 29-5-09. First noted 3-12	1-14
❑ G-BNSY*	Piper Warrior II	80	ex N4512M. CoA 6-11-09. First noted 7-13	1-14
❑ G-BOFY*	Piper Cherokee 140	74	ex N43521. CoA 29-7-09. First noted 3-12	1-14
❑ G-BSJZ	Cessna 150J	69	ex N60661. CoA 20-11-99	1-14
❑ G-DLTR*	Piper Cherokee 180	70	ex G-AYAV. CoA 6-11-09. First noted 3-12	1-14
❑ G-OZOO*	Cessna 172N Skyhawk II	76	ex G-BWEI, N73767. CoA 17-8-09. First noted 7-13	1-14

Delta Salvage: The extensive yard close to the aerodrome, on the Delta Business Park, is home to the amazing all-pink combo of Grumman AA-1 and Suzuki 4x4 - registration D164 MBH - that was illustrated in *W&R22* (p238) when it made an appearance at Glastonbury. **Access:** *By prior arrangement* **only** | **www.deltasalvage.com**

❑ -	American AA-1 hybrid	~	fuselage and tail mounted on a Suzuki 4x4 - see above First noted 5-12	1-14

SCAMPTON AIRFIELD on the A15 north of Lincoln EGXP

RAF Scampton Museum: Located within one of the World War Two hangars, the collection extends to over 400 items, including a Blue Steel stand-off missile and substantial components from HP Hampden I P1206 previously of 49 Squadron which was shot down on a raid on 8th November 1941 and salvaged in the Netherlands. The entire history of the airfield, from the 'Expansion Period' to the 'Red Arrows' and of course centring on 617 Squadron the 'Dam Busters' is covered. Visits include a tour of famous sites on the base.

[In another hangar is the **Museum of RAF Fire-Fighting** which is available by prior application only: 07912 658402 | museumofraffirefighting@hotmail.co.uk | **www.museumofraffirefighting.com**]

◆ **Access:** *Open all year round,* occasionally *on public holidays,* not *open during the Christmas season. Visits by prior arrangement* ***only*** *and valid photo identification (eg driving licence or passport)* ***essential***. **Contact: 07748 630832** or **01522 500738** | **museum1993@hotmail.co.uk** | **www.raf.mod.uk/rafscampton**

❑ XR757	EE Lightning F.6	65	ex Grainthorpe, New Waltham, Rossington, Binbrook, 5-11 pool, 23, 5. SOC 24-6-88. Cockpit	[1]	10-13
❑ XX320	HS Hawk T.1A	80	ex Cranwell, Shawbury, 208, 100, 19, 2 TWU, 1 TWU. Crashed 20-8-08. 208 Sqn colours. Cockpit	[2]	11-11

■ **[1]** XR757 is on loan from Trevor Garrod. **[2]** XX320 is owned by Dave Wright.

RAF Scampton: The 'Red Arrows' HQ is guarded by a Gnat within the base and a Hawk is being prepared for similar duties.

❑ XR571	Folland Gnat T.1	63	ex Cranwell, Scampton, Cosford, Kemble, Brampton 8493M (7-5-76), Kemble, 4 FTS		10-13
❑ XX253	HS Hawk T.1A	78	ex 'Red Arrows'. Displayed	[1]	10-13
❑ XX349*	HS Hawk T.1W	81	ex Valley, 100, 208, 19, 74, 4 FTS, 100, TWU, 4 FTS. Cockpit, fire section. First noted 6-13		7-13

■ **[1]** XX253 collided with XX233 over Kastelli, Crete.

Hawker Hunter Aviation: HHA is a major contractor for the military and aerospace industry and much of its fleet is beyond the terms of reference for *W&R*. Airframes under major restoration or long term store only are mentioned here.

◆ **Access:** *Visits* **only** *possible by prior appointment* | **www.hunterteam.com**

❑ XE685*	'861'	Hawker Hunter GA.11 G-GAII	55	ex St Athan, Exeter, Yeovilton, Hurn, FRADU, FRU, 764, Yeovilton SF, 764, 738, F.4 98, 93. Flew in 22-5-12. Spares use. CoA 15-8-12	10-13
❑ XF994	'873'	Hawker Hunter T.8C G-CGHU	56	ex Boscombe Down, Shawbury, Yeovilton, FRADU, 759, F.4, 229 OCU, AFDS, 66. SOC 17-3-98	2-11
❑ XL587	'Z'	Hawker Hunter T.7 G-HPUX	58	ex Duxford, Scampton, 8807M (2-3-84), 208, 237 OCU, 1 TWU, 229 OCU	4-09
❑ XV235*		HS Nimrod MR.2	69	ex Kinloss, Kin Wing, Kin & St M Wing, 42, Kinloss, St M, 236 OCU. Forward fuselage, stored	3-12
❑ XX885		HS Buccaneer S.2B G-HHAA	74	ex Lossiemouth 9225M (25-11-93), 12, 208, 12, 208, 216, 16	8-13
❑ 98+14		Sukhoi Su-22M *Fitter*	~	ex WTD-61 Manching, Luftwaffe, East German AF	8-13

Also: The report of Canberra cockpit WK118 being here, since *W&R22*, is in error. It remained in Worcester, Worcs.

❑ XP282		Auster AOP.9 G-BGTC	61	ex Melton Mowbray, Norfolk, 1 Air Dispatch Rgt, 14 ADR, 2 Flt, 651. SOC 12-10-79. Damaged 2-10-96	6-11

SKEGNESS (WATER LEISURE PARK) or Ingoldmells, on the A52 north of Skegness

Some tidying up; the following, last noted in August 2008, have been deleted: Rallye G-AZEE, Cessna F.172G EI-AOK and Geronimo PH-NLK.

❑ G-ARCW		Piper Apache 160	60	ex N2187P. *Mockingbird IV*. CoA 24-8-07	11-12
❑ G-ASWW		Piper Twin Comanche 160	64	ex N7531Y. Damaged, CoA 23-1-10, de-reg 12-8-09	9-10
❑ G-AVPI		Cessna F.172H	67	Reims-built. CoA 30-5-03, stored	9-10
❑ G-MJPV		Eipper Quicksilver MX	83	CoA 17-8-04. Stored in rafters	7-13
❑ XS456	'DX'	EE Lightning T.5	65	ex Wainfleet, Binbrook, LTF, 11, 56. SOC 13-7-88	8-13

SLEAFORD on the A15 and A17 south of Lincoln

David Ballicki: Keeps his 'JP' cockpit in the *general* area.

❑ G-BYED		BAC Jet Provost T.5 XW302	70	ex Market Drayton, Chester, Londonderry, N166A, XW302, 6 FTS, 3 FTS, RAFC, 1 FTS. Crashed 12-2-01, de-reg 30-12-04. Black/yellow scheme. Cockpit	6-13

SPALDING west of the A16, north of Peterborough

Skycraft Ltd: The famed 'Chop Shop' continues to process a large number of light aircraft types for spares. Turn-around is swift and the team has a good web-site where you can virtually browse for the wotsit you've long needed.

◆ **Access:** *Visits by prior arrangement* **only** | **www.sky-craft.co.uk**

Also:

❑ G-AFVN		Tipsy Trainer 1	39	ex Fenland. CoA 2-1-03, de-reg 20-11-06	7-12

SPILSBY on the B1195 west of Skegness

A **private** strip in the *general* area has served as a long-term store for Auster types.

❑ G-AHAR		Auster J/1 Autocrat	46	ex North Weald, F-BGRZ. Frame	7-13
❑ G-AHSO		Auster J/1N Alpha	46	CoA 6-4-95, de-reg 6-4-09	7-13
❑ G-AIGP		Auster J/1 Autocrat	46	CoA 30-10-73, de-reg 31-10-73	7-13
❑ G-AIPV		Auster J/1 Autocrat	46	CoA 7-2-05	7-13
❑ G-AJDW		Auster J/1 Autocrat	47	ex Luton area. CoA 17-1-77, de-reg 20-11-96. Frame [1]	7-13
❑ G-AVOD		Beagle D5/180 Husky	67	crashed 31-7-92, de-reg 8-9-92	7-13

■ **[1]** The wings of G-AJDW can be found at Flitwick, Beds.

Also: On 25th May 2012 an auction of the Spilsby Soaring Trust was held. As well as the structure of a steel 'blister' hangar, going under the hammer were: Slingsby Swallow BGA.2210 (which moved to Spanhoe, Northants); SZD Bocians BGA.1274, SP-2445 plus another; and a Slingsby Falke. Bocian SP-2445 plus probably the anonymous example are thought to have been used in the 'Grasshopper' 'sculpture' displayed at the Glastonbury Festival 2013.

STAMFORD

The Lightning cockpit is being restored by **Martyn** and **Aiden Steele** and was an award winner at *CockpitFest* 2012.

◆ **Access:** *Visits by prior arrangement* **only**

❑ XP757*	EE Lightning F.3	64	ex Boston, Woodhall Spa, Keighley, Siddal, Binbrook, 29, 23. SOC 13-11-75. Cockpit		6-13

Also: SZD Pirat G-DDFW arrived late in 2013 for spares recovery. In February 2014 its cockpit moved to a location in Gloucestershire for use in a high-flying simulator project.

❑ WG303		DHC Chipmunk T.10 PAX	51	ex Bicester 8208M (4-8-72), Shawbury, Kemble, Ox UAS, Gatow SF, Wittering SF, Marham SF, Bir UAS, 5 RFS, 2 BFTS	[1]	1-14
❑ WT914*	FED	Slingsby Cadet TX.3	52	BGA.3194, ex Tibenham, Kenley. CoA 7-2-87		1-14
❑ MM52-2420*		Piper L-18C Super Cub	52	ex Spanhoe, Lakenheath area, Embry-Riddle, It AF, USAF. Arrived 1-14	[1]	1-14

■ **[1]** The rear fuselage of WG303 can be found at Carlisle, Cumbria. **[2]** The L-18 restoration project is *likely* N917CS.

STURGATE AERODROME south-east of Gainsborough, near Heapham EGCS

❑ G-BDDG	Jodel D.112	58	ex F-BILM. CoA 28-7-04	1-14

STURTON on the B1207 north of Hibaldstow, south-west of Brigg

Revenge Paintball: Within the war zones is a camouflaged Cherokee with subtle markings. **www.revengepaintball.com**

❑ 'NA+ZI'	Piper Cherokee	~	camouflaged hulk	6-09

SUTTON BRIDGE on the A17 west of King's Lynn

A Nord 1002 is *thought* still stored at a *private* location in the general area.

❑ G-ASUA	Nord 1002 Pinguoin	45	ex Elstree, F-BFDY. Crashed 30-7-64, de-reg 5-1-65	12-05

TATTERSHALL on the A153 south-west of Coningsby

A storage yard on a minor road to the north-west holds a trio of Whirlwinds, long since thought to have moved on. In *W&R15* (p129) XJ407 was reported as leaving circa 1994. XP329 was written out of *W&R18* (p145) as unaccounted for; XP328 was in print until *W&R20* (also p145) when it was declared that the yard had been cleared by September 2005.

◆ **Access: Strictly** *by prior arrangement* **only**

❑ XJ407*		Westland Whirlwind HAR.10	N7013H	54	ex G-BKHB (de-reg 15-6-88), XJ407, Northolt, 32, 103, 110, HAR.4, 22, 155. SOC 15-6-88. Trailer-mounted	11-13
❑ XP328*		Westland Whirlwind HAR.10	G-BKHC	61	ex Northolt, 32, 21, 28, 110, 225, 110, 225. Crashed 22-8-88, de-reg 4-6-90. Cabin	11-13
❑ XP329*	'V'	Westland Whirlwind HAR.10		61	ex Shawbury, Lee-on-Solent, Akrotiri 8791M (10-7-82), 84, 230, 110, 225. SOC 10-7-82. Cabin	9-13

TATTERSHALL THORPE on the B1192 south-east of Woodhall Spa

Thorpe Camp Visitor Centre: The former No.1 Communal Site (or 'Thorpe Camp') of RAF Woodhall Spa is a superb visitor centre. Themes include life in Lincolnshire during World War Two, the history of Woodhall Spa, including its resident units: 97, 617, 619 and 627 Squadrons. There is a small workshop area, which is viewable from within one of the buildings.

It is probably unfair to zoom in on one exhibit, but one stands out for many reasons, the amazing, massive arrester gear salvaged from the end of one of Woodhall's runways. This was intended to stop a Lancaster, fitted with a special hook, from over-runs and Woodhall prototyped the operational version. Moving this huge contraption up out of its pit and across to Thorpe Camp must have been an epic task.

Omitted from *W&R23*, for no reason other than operator senility, was the centre's incredible Fairchild Argus replica!

◆ **Access:** *On the B1192 south of the former RAF Woodhall Spa.* **Open:** *Sun and Bank Hols 13:00 to 17:00, Easter to Oct plus Wed in Jul and Aug, 13:00 to 17:00. Other times by appointment.* **Contact:** *Lancaster Farm, Tumby Woodside, Mareham-le-Fen, Boston, PE22 7SP* | **01526 342249** | **mjhodgson@lancfile.demon.co.uk** | **www.thorpecamp.org**

Thinx: *A short distance from the Visitor Centre is the 'Blue Bell' - strongly recommended. Take the B1192 to Woodhall and visit the Dambuster memorial - more details under Woodhall Spa.*

❑ 'G-AEXF'		Percival Mew Gull replica	11	-	[1]	1-14
❑ –		DH Tiger Moth replica	11	-		1-14
❑ 'EV771'		Fairchild Argus replica	c97	BAPC.294, ex Southampton		1-14
❑ XM192	'K'	EE Lightning F.1A	61	ex Hemswell, Binbrook, Wattisham 8413M (28-5-74), Wattisham TFF, Binbrook TFF, 226 OCU, 111. 111 Sqn c/s	[1]	1-14

■ **[1]** Mew Gull made by a team led by John Lord. See Shuttleworth, Beds, and Hendon, Gtr Lon, for *other* G-AEXFs! **[2]** The Lightning is on loan from Charles Ross (see Binbrook, Lincs).

WADDINGTON AIRFIELD on the A607 south of Lincoln EGXW

RAF Waddington Heritage Centre: Volunteers have created a superb Heritage Centre in a building that in World War Two housed the catering squadron headquarters. Among the many exhibits are remains of 463 Squadron Lancaster I PD259 which crashed in Scotland on a training detail on 31st August 1944, with the loss of all seven crew.

◆ **Access:** *Main gate on the A607.* **Open:** *By prior arrangement* **only. NB** *Valid photo ID needed.* **Contact: 01522 727367 | WAD-Heritagecentre@mod.uk | www.raf.mod.uk/rafwaddington**

RAF Waddington: Phantom FGR.2 XV497 moved by road to Ipswich, Suffolk, on 24th November 2012. By the author's reckoning, this was the first 'legit' disposal in the civilian world, other than to museums. Does this mean that the treaty obligations on the wonder from St Louis no longer apply?

❑ 'XE620'*	'B'	Hawker Hunter F.6A XE606	56	ex Barkston Heath, 'XE673', Cottesmore, Laarbruch 8841M (29-11-84), 8737M ntu, 1 TWU, TWU, 229 OCU, 92, 74, 65, 54, CFE. Arrived 10-4-13. 8 Sqn colours, displayed.	[1]	7-13
❑ XM607		Avro Vulcan B.2	63	8779M (19-1-83), ex 44, 101, 35. Displayed		1-14
❑ XR770	'AA'	EE Lightning F.6	65	ex Grainthorpe, New Waltham, Laceby, Binbrook, 11, 5-11 pool, 56, 23, 74. SOC 10-6-88	[2]	1-14
❑ ZH105		Boeing Sentry AEW.1	91	ex 8. *Sneezy*. Spares recovery - fuselage by 6-13		6-13

■ **[1]** Hunter serves as the 8 Sqn 'mascot'. **[2]** Lightning is loaned by Lesley and Dave Blissett and is the 5 Squadron 'mascot'.

WAINFLEET south-west of Skegness

Aerial Application Collection: Dispersed store, visits are ***only*** possible by prior arrangement.

❑ G-AOGI	DH Tiger Moth	42	ex OO-SOA, G-AOGI, Mk.II DF186, 608, Valley SF, 21 EFTS. Morris-built. CoA 23-8-91	1-12
❑ G-AWLX	Auster J/2 Arrow	46	ex Gloucester, F-BGJQ, OO-ABZ. CoA 23-4-70	1-12
❑ G-BFBP	Piper Pawnee 235D	77	ex Rush Green. Crashed 11-5-78, de-reg 21-6-78. Cockpit	1-12
❑ G-BFEY	Piper Pawnee 235D	77	ex Old Buckenham. CoA 19-1-87, de-reg 17-7-90. Frame	1-12
❑ G-NRDC	NDN Fieldmaster	81	ex Sandown, Old Sarum. CoA 17-10-87, de-reg 3-2-95. Fuse.	1-12
❑ –	NDN Fieldmaster EMU	c81	ex Sandown, Old Sarum. Fuselage	1-12

WALCOTT on the B1189 south of Woodhall Spa

Andy Rawden: Was restoring the cockpit of HS.125 5N-AAN to Dominie status; then acquired a Dominie! (This location is a good illustration of the pitfalls of British geography; there are *two* Walcots (one 't') also in the county, east of Grantham and north of Scunthorpe.) *Access*: Private location, by prior arrangement *only*.

❑ 5N-AAN*		HS.125-3B/RA	67	ex Newark, Sunderland, Woolsington, Biggin Hill, F-GFMP, G-AVAI, LN-NPA, G-AVAI. Cockpit, trailer mounted. Arrived 23-12-13	12-13
❑ XS735*	'R'	HS Dominie T.1	66	ex Penwyllt, St Athan, CTTS, Sealand, Cranwell 9246M (28-10-96), 55, 6 FTS, RAFC, CAW. Arrived 15-8-13	8-13

WALTHAM on the B1203 south of Grimsby

Waltham Windmill Trust and Preservation Society: Part of the extensive site surrounding the windmill is the **RAF Grimsby Exhibition**, situated in a Nissen hut. This is dedicated to the personnel and Lancasters of 100 Squadron and other units that flew from Waltham (or Grimsby) airfield, located to the east of the windmill. (The A16 cuts through the former airfield's eastern perimeter.)

◆ **Access:** *Signed off the B1203, near Norman Corner.* **Open:** *The site is open all year. Times for access to the windmill vary - check the website. The RAF Grimsby Exhibition is open Easter to October, Sat, Sun and Bank Hols 14:00 to 17:00.* **Contact:** *Waltham Windmill, Brigsley Road, Waltham, DN37 0JZ* | **01472 822236** | **www.walthamwindmill.org.uk**

WICKENBY (LINCOLN) **AERODROME** north of the B1399, north-east of Lincoln EGNW

The former wartime tower acts as both a **Visitor Centre** and the **RAF Wickenby Memorial Museum**. The **Wickenby Register** - 12 and 626 Squadron Association - has it archives here. The 'Icarus Memorial' at the aerodrome entrance is dedicated to the 1,080 personnel of the two squadrons who gave their lives while the units were resident, 1942 to 1945. The cafe in the tower specialises in a warm welcome and great grub!

◆ **Open:** *Daily except Xmas - times vary, check before setting out. Anyone wishing to refer to the extensive archive should make prior arrangement.* **Contact:** *The Control Tower, Wickenby Aerodrome, Langworth, Lincoln, LN3 5AX.* **01673 885000 | rafwmm@hotmail.com | www.wickenbymuseum.co.uk**

Vintage Skunk Works: The name and logo, pay homage to Lockheed's famed research and development centre at Palmdale, California. The former Millom 'Pou Maquis' is painted in RAF post-war trainer colours, complete with yellow 'T-bands'. This is to link in with similarly-marked resident Terrier 2 VX927 (G-ASYG) which is used by the local charity **Flights for Life** which is devoted to giving children with serious illnesses a flight in an historic aircraft. The 'Flea' is used as a travelling attraction and 'sit-in' experience for the charity. For more details take a look at: **www/flightsforlife.co.uk**

Auster 5 G-AIKE was airworthy by late 2013. Harvard IIB G-BZHL had moved to Hibaldstow, Lincs, by July 2013.By May 2012 a Tempest firewall/windscreen/cockpit section acquired during the restoration of Tempest MW763 moved to Wycombe Air Park, Bucks.

◆ **Access:** *Visits are* **not possible**. *Occasional appearances at special events and airshows*

❑ G-ACDJ		DH Tiger Moth		33	ex BB729, Dyce SF, 28 EFTS, 1 EFTS. Crashed 18-8-05, CoA 18-8-07		9-13
❑ G-AKPI		Auster 5		44	ex Breighton, Skegness, Humberside, NJ703, 652, 660. CoA 15-6-01	[1]	8-13
❑ G-ANNN		DH Tiger Moth		45	ex Tattershall Thorpe, Eccleshall, Hatch, Mk.II T5968, Wattisham SF, 61 GCF, 3 RFS, 28 EFTS, 57 OTU. Morris-built. De-reg 6-11-00		15-11
❑ G-AOBV		Auster J/5P Autocar		55	ex Cheshunt, Laindon, Stapleford Tawney, Benington. CoA 7-4-71, de-reg 14-11-91		2-07
❑ G-BYYU		DHC Chipmunk T.20	N1360A	59	ex Little Staughton, Bedford, Spanhoe, CS-DAP ntu, PortAF 1360. De-reg 9-5-01		1-12
❑ G-BZVW		Ilyushin Il-2M3		42	ex Lancing, Russia	[2]	6-12
❑ G-BZVX		Ilyushin Il-2M3		42	ex Lancing, Russia		6-08
❑ G-CFXT		NAF N3N-3		42	ex N45299		10-13
❑ G-OOSY		DH Tiger Moth		43	ex Hawarden, Burslem, Stoke-on-Trent, Eccleshall, F-BGFI, FAF, Mk.II DE971 n/s. Morris-built		9-13
❑ G-SHOW		MS Alcyon		56	ex Spanhoe, -?-, Bruntingthorpe, Cranfield, Booker, F-BMQJ, FAF 125. CoA 24-5-83		6-12
❑ -		Lakes Waterbird replica		11	under construction	[3]	1-12
❑ N9606H		Fairchild PT-26 Cornell	G-CEVL	42	ex Martham, Earls Colne, Andrewsfield, Southend, USA, FJ662, 42-15491. Stored	[4]	6-12
❑ T7793*		DH Tiger Moth	G-ANKV	40	ex Booker, Croydon, Redhill	[5]	6-12
❑ MW763	'HF-A'	Hawker Tempest II	G-TEMT	45	ex Sandtoft, Brooklands, Chichester, India, IAF HA586, RAF MW763	[6]	1-12
❑ XE624*	'G'	Hawker Hunter FGA.9		56	ex Metheringham, Leicester area, Bruntingthorpe, Brawdy 8875M (4-10-85), 1 TWU, 2 TWU, TWU, 229 OCU, West Raynham SF, 1. Arrived by 5-12		11-13
❑ –	'F-4L'	Mignet HM.280		97	BAPC.260, ex Millom. *Flying Flea*	[7]	1-12
❑ 963		SZD Bocian		~	ex Egyptian AF. Stored		7-12
❑ 354		MS 315E D2	G-BZNK	32	ex France, F-BCNK, French AF		10-13
❑ -	'856'	Nord Norvigie	G-CDWE	50	ex France, F-WFKF, F-BFKF. French military colours		10-13
❑ HA604		Hawker Tempest II	G-PEST	45	ex Sandtoft, Brooklands, Chichester, India, IAF, RAF MW401. Stored	[6]	3-10
❑ C-558		EKW C-3605	G-CCYZ	48	ex Spanhoe, N31624, Norwich, Little Gransden, Wycombe AP, Lodrino, Swiss AF. Stored		6-12

■ **[1]** It is intended to finish *Papa-India* as a floatplane in the colours of Auster AOP.V TJ207 which was tested at MAEE 1945-1946. **[2]** Under restoration for the RAF Museum and will be displayed within the 'Milestones of Flight' hall; in exchange for a Spitfire restoration project. **[3]** Faithful replica of a two-seat biplane floatplane built by Avro for E W Wakefield of the Lakes Flying Co, Windermere, 1911. Parts of the original are held by the RAF Museum at Stafford, Staffs. **[4]** Cornell had previously been thought to be ex FH678, 42-14361. Current thinking is quoted above, but there is a *possibility* that the airframe is a composite. It is under restoration for a Lincolnshire-based group. **[5]** The identity is debatable; G-ANKV was not converted (at Croydon?) and cancelled from the register in 9-56. **[6]** G-TEMT and G-PEST are registered to Tempest Two Ltd. **[7]** See narrative, above, for more details.

Others:

❑ G-BGWN	Piper Tomahawk 112	79	ex N9693N. CoA 17-7-08	1-12
❑ G-LUFT	Putzer Elster C	60	ex Rufforth, Humberside, North Coates, G-BOPY, D-EDEZ. De-reg 12-7-07	1-12
❑ G-MWWP	Rans S-4 Coyote	92	CoA 1-8-00, de-reg 4-6-10	6-11
❑ N91384	Aero Commander 690A	73	ex SE-FLN	6-13

WOODHALL SPA on the B1191 and B1192 south-west of Horncastle

Hunter T.7 XL578 moved on 8th March 2013 to Binbrook, Lincs.

◆ **Thinx:** *At the junction of the B1191 and B1192 in Woodhall Spa is the impressive 'Dambuster' memorial and the newly-inaugurated 617 Squadron commemoration. Another 'must' is the 'Petwood Hotel' which was the Officers' mess for, in turn, 97, 619 and 617 Squadrons. The 'Squadron Bar' has loads of memorabilia.* **www.petwood.co.uk**

GREATER LONDON

Greater London constitutes the following boroughs: Barking and Dagenham, Barnet, Bexley, Brent, Bromley (including Biggin Hill!), Camden, City of Westminster, Croydon, Ealing, Enfield, Greenwich, Hackney, Hammersmith and Fulham, Haringey, Harrow, Havering, Hillingdon, Hounslow, Islington, Kensington and Chelsea, Kingston upon Thames, Lambeth, Lewisham, Livingston, Merton, Newham, Redbridge, Richmond upon Thames, Southwark, Sutton, Tower Hamlets, Waltham Forest, Wandsworth

...which leads us, of course, to Mornington Crescent

BENTLEY PRIORY between the A409 and A4140 north of Harrow

The Bentley Priory Museum: Administered by the Bentley Priory Battle of Britain Trust was officially opened on 12th September 2013 and tells the story of the magnificent country house's role as the HQ of Fighter Command.

◆ **Access:** *Within the new housing development, which is gated - do not let that put you off, security guards will show you where to park* | **Open** *Mon, Wed and the third Sat of the month* | **Contact** *Mansion House Drive, Stanmore, HA7 3FB* | **020 89505526 | enquiries@bentleypriory.org | www.bentleypriory.org**

❑ 'R6595'*'DW-O'	Supermarine Spitfire FSM	11	610 Sqn colours, pole-mounted		1-14
❑ 'BN230'* 'FT-A'	Hawker Hurricane FSM	89	BAPC.218, ex St Mawgan, Bentley Priory, 'P3386'. 43 Sqn colours. Returned by 9-12, pole-mounted	[1]	1-14

■ **[1]** See also Manston, Kent, for *another* 'BN230'.

BIGGIN HILL AIRPORT EGKB

Biggin Hill Heritage Hangar Ltd / The Spitfire Company (Biggin Hill) Ltd: Peter Monk's impressive facility was officially opened on 12th June 2012. As well as Peter's expanding collection, other warbirds are looked after and under restoration. Clive Denney was at the helm of Mk.XVI RW382 (G-PBIX) for its post-restoration first flight on 18th September 2013.

◆ **Access:** *Strictly by prior permission* **only.** *Open days and special events are staged, more details on the website.* **Contact** *Biggin Hill Airport, Biggin Hill, TN16 3BN* | **01959 576767 | www.bigginhillheritagehangar.co.uk**

❑ 'P3886'* 'UF-K'	Hawker Hurricane X ✈	G-CHTK	41	ex Chino, USA, N33TF, Sudbury G-TWTD, Lancing, See Hurricane I AE977, 760, 759. CCF-built. Arrived 7-12, first flown 5-9-12. 601 Sqn colours	[1]	1-14
❑ X4276*	Supermarine Spitfire I	G-CDGU	40	ex Breighton, 54. Crashed 28-12-40. Stored, off-site	[1]	1-14
❑ X4650 'KL-A'	Supermarine Spitfire I ✈	G-CGUK	40	ex Duxford, Audley End, Bentwaters, 'Kent', 'Yorkshire', 54. Collision 28-12-40. 54 Sqn colours	[2]	1-14
❑ EP122*	Supermarine Spitfire V		42	ex Sandown, Malta, 1435 Flt, 185, 249. Crashed 27-3-43. Arrived 5-13		1-14
❑ 'FE788'*	NAA Harvard II ✈	G-CTKL	41	ex G-BKWZ ntu, It AF MM54137, RCAF 3064. Noorduyn-built. RAF colours	[3]	1-14
❑ LZ842* 'EF-F'	Supermarine Spitfire IX	G-CGZU	43	ex Sandown, Australia, UK, South Africa, SAAF, RAF 232. Accident 27-4-50. Arrived 13-11-12	[4]	1-14
❑ MK912 'SH-L'	Supermarine Spitfire IX ✈	G-BRRA	44	ex Canada CF-FLC, Duxford, Audley End, Paddock Wood, G-BRRA, Brussels, Belg AF SM-29, RNethAF H-59, H-119, MK912, 341, 312. 64 Sqn colours, *Borough of Bromley*	[5]	1-14

❑ RW382 '3W-P'	Supermarine Spitfire XVI ✈	45 G-PBIX	ex Sandown, USA N382RW, Audley End, Braintree, Uxbridge 8075M, Leconfield, Church Fenton 7245M, C&RS, 3 CAACU, 604. First flown 18-9-13. 322 Sqn c/s	[6]	1-14
❑ TA805 'FX-M'	Supermarine Spitfire IX ✈	44 G-PMNF	ex Duxford, Sandown, Oxford, SAAF Museum, SAAF, TA805, 234, 183. *Spirit of Kent*, 234 Sqn colours	[1]	1-14
❑ TD314 'FX-P'	Supermarine Spitfire IX ✈	44 G-CGYJ	ex Sandown, Tonbridge, Bentwaters, Canada, South Africa, SAAF, 234, 183. 234 Sqn colours. First flown 7-12-13	[7]	1-14
❑ TE184* 'EJ-C'	Supermarine Spitfire XVI ✈	45 G-MXVI	ex Germany, Booker, Duxford, Halton, North Weald, St Merryn, Holywood, Aldergrove, Finningley, Cranwell, Henlow, Bicester, Royton 6850M, Long Benton, CGS, 607, 226 OCU, 203 AFS. CoA 30-5-02. Arrived 10-3-12	[8]	3-12
❑ TE517*	Supermarine Spitfire IX	45 G-JGCA	ex Booker, G-CCIX, Winchester, Nailsworth, G-BIXP, Duxford, Israel DF/AF 2046, Czech AF, RAF TE517, 313. Arrived 10-12-12	[5]	1-14
❑ 42-29854* '44-R'	Piper L-4H Cub ✈	43 G-BMKC	ex F-BFBA, USAAF 43-29854. *Little Rock-ette* First noted 2-12	[9]	1-14

■ **[1]** Registered to Peter Monk. **[2]** [X4650 registered to Comanche Warbirds. **[3]** *Kilo-Lima* registered to Simpson Marine Ltd. **[4]** LZ842 registered to M A Bennett. **[5]** Registered to High Wycombe-based P M Andrews - see also Wycombe, Bucks, and Sandown, Isle of Wight. **[6]** RW382 is registered to the wonderfully-named Pemberton-Billing LLP - P-B was the flamboyant founder of Supermarine. **[7]** Registered to Kent-based K M Perkins. **[8]** TE184 registered to Leicestershire-based S R Stead. **[9]** Cub registered to Joe Hirst.

Also: Kraguj G-RADA and UTVA-66 YU-DLG moved to Linton-on-Ouse, N Yorks, by December 2012. Some tidying up, with last noted dates in brackets, the following have been deleted: Cessna 150 G-APZR (Jun 2005), Cessna A.152 G-BHJA (Feb 2009), Archer 181 G-BOBZ (Feb 2009) and Hughes 269C G-ZBHH (Jun 2006).

❑ G-AOGE	Percival Proctor III	42	ex BV651, Halton SF, 2 GCS, FAA 755, 756. CoA 21-5-84, de-reg 19-1-99	2-12
❑ G-AOKH	Percival Prentice 1	48	ex VS251, 3 FTS, CFS, 2 FTS. Blackburn-built. CoA 2-8-73, de-reg 17-6-92	4-01
❑ G-YUGO	HS.125-1B/522	66	ex Dunsfold, G-ATWH, HZ-BO1, G-ATWH. CoA 19-4-91. De-reg 29-3-93. Dump	6-05
❑ -	Civilian Coupe	~	unfinished airframe, No.7	10-95
❑ N666AW	Piper Navajo 325	~	stored, minus wings by 2-11	6-11

St George's Chapel of Remembrance: Famed for its 17 stained glass windows and a vast amount of memorabilia, the chapel was built in 1951. It was formulated in the style of the original RAF Biggin Hill Station Chapel which was opened in 1943, but was burned to the ground in 1946.

◆ **Access:** *Signed off the A233 Biggin Hill road.* **Open:** *All week, 11:00 to 16:00. Services on Sat and Sun* | **01959 570353**

❑ 'K9998' 'QJ-K'	Supermarine Spitfire FSM	10	gate guardian. 92 Sqn colours	[1]	10-13
❑ 'P2991' 'GZ-L'	Hawker Hurricane FSM	10	gate guardian. *Blue Peter*, 32 Sqn colours	[2]	10-13

■ **[1]** The Spitfire represents that flown by Plt Off Geoffrey Wellum. **[2]** The Hurricane is in the colours of Flt Lt Peter Brothers.

Biggin Hill Battle of Britain Supporters' Club and **Trust**: Fund-raising for the planned **Battle of Biggin Hill Battle of Britain Centre** continues. The club stages events and links its members via its journal, *The Bump*. **www.bhbobsc.org.uk**

No.**2427 Squadron Air Cadets:**

❑ WZ846	DHC Chipmunk T.10	53 G-BCSC	ex Chatham, G-BCSC, Bicester 8439M (10-3-75), Manston, Wales UAS, AOTS, 202, 228, CFE, W Raynham SF, G&S UAS, Bri UAS, 1 AEF, St Athan, Nott UAS, 63 GCF, Edn UAS, S'ton UAS. De-reg 21-1-75	8-12

CATFORD south of Greenwich, on the South Circular, A205

Catford Independent Air Force: Alan Partington's collection. **Access**: *Visits by prior arrangement* **only**

❑ –	Mignet HM.14 'Flea'	~	unfinished	[1]	6-13
❑ XH783	Gloster Javelin FAW.7	58	ex Wycombe, Sibson, Aylesbury, Halton 7798M (31-7-63), 64, 25, GWTS, A&AEE. Cockpit		6-13
❑ –	Supermarine Spitfire V FSM	~	built by Feggans Brown for *Piece of Cake*. Cockpit		6-13
❑ –	HS Harrier	~	cockpit	[2]	6-13

■ **[1]** The 'Flea' has a plaque saying 'Made at Capel'. **[2]** The Harrier is thought to be an unused GR.1 cockpit section and may have come from Richmond Air Cadets. It is 41H/729048 which puts it between GR.1s XV810 and XW630.

CHESSINGTON on the A243 north of J9 of the M25

World of Adventures: The website states it is Britain's wildest adventure, so it must be true. Within, the giant aquarium called 'Azteca' contains sharks, rays and parrot fish... and, of course, a Cessna.

◆ **Open:** *See the web-site for details* | **0871 6634477** | **www.chessington.com**

❑ -		Cessna 150 / 152		~	*Azteca*, fuselage and wings	7-11

CROYDON on the A23 in south London

Croydon Airport Visitor Centre: The visitor centre within the former terminal building (Airport House) is run in association with the **Croydon Airport Society**.

◆ **Access:** *On the A235, at Airport House, Purley Way. Croydon, CR0 0XZ.* **Open:** *1st Sun of each month, 11:00 to 16:00 - or by prior arrangement.* **Contact: 07932 081600** | **cas.cavc@hotmail.co.uk** | **www.croydonairport.org.uk**

❑ 'G-AOXL'		DH Heron 2D	G-ANUO	54	ex Biggin Hill, Exeter. CoA 12-9-86, de-reg 9-8-96. Pole-mounted at entrance [1]	1-14

■ **[1]** G-ANUO is painted as 'G-AOXL' of Morton Air Services. The *real* G-AOXL made the last passenger flight from Croydon, on 3-9-59.

No.**2157 Squadron Air Cadets**: Not noted since January 2000, Cessna F.172G G-ATFX has been deleted.

DULWICH on the A205 South Circular, south of Peckham

Dulwich College: *Private school, access* **only** *by prior permission* | **www.dulwich.org.uk**

❑ WB627		DHC Chipmunk T.10		50	ex 9248M (27-3-96), Cambridge, 5 AEF, 1 AEF, Lon UAS, Cam UAS, 2 SoTT, 22 GCF, Debden SF, Jurby SF, 8 RFS, 18 RFS	12-10

FELTHAM on the A312 south-east of Heathrow

Heathrow Trident Collection: Kevin Bowen's collection of Trident memorabilia includes uniforms, manuals, instruments, part of a flight deck and cabin, a reference library and much more. Andrew Lee (who has the cockpit of Trident 3B G-AWZI at Farnborough, Hants - which see) has also contributed material for this extensive tribute.

◆ **Access:** *By prior arrangement* **only** | **g-awzk@msn.com**

GREENFORD on the A40 west of the city

Vanguard Holdings: The Hunter is back on show; the Vampire and Lightning are **not** available for inspection.

❑ WT555		Hawker Hunter F.1	55	ex Cosford, Locking 7499M (22-11-57), A&AEE, Dunsfold	1-14
❑ XK632	'67'	DH Vampire T.11	56	ex Denham, Leavesden, Hemel Hempstead, Bushey, Keevil, Exeter, 3/4 CAACU, CFS. SOC 6-1-72. Pod	1-14
❑ XP745	'H'	EE Lightning F.3	64	ex Boulmer 8453M (25-9-75), Leconfield, 29, 56	1-14

GREENWICH east of the A102 Blackwall Tunnel Approach, just south of the 'Dome'

Emirates Aviation Experience: Opened on 5th June 2013, this high-tech, 300 square metre visitor centre includes such gems as a Rolls-Royce Trent 800 built entirely of Lego and a film presentation entitled *Be the Baggage*. An impressive full-scale mock-up of an Airbus A380 allows access to the flight deck; this is more a part of the building than an 'airframe' and is not listed formally. Please note that although the opening times are expansive, to allow for a 'flow' of visitors, each day is split into a series of 'sessions' and it is best to use the enquiry form within the website to help plan a visit.

◆ **Access:** *In East Parkside, east of the A102. Nearest tube is North Greenwich.* **Open:** *Daily 08:00 to 19:00* **but see** *the website regarding pre-buying tickets.* **Contact**: **enquiries via the website** | **www.aviation-experience.com**

HAYES west of the A312, north of Junction 3 of the M4

London Motor Museum: With a huge variety of cars of all eras and capabilities, during January 2014 the museum acquired another 'gate guardian', an AB 204. The helicopter is displayed next to a yellow Reliant van belonging to Trotters Independent Trading, with the registration plate DEL BOY... no idea what that is about. It would be nice to think that the 'chopper' is a nod to a former Hayes industry, originally Fairey then Westland, which was just a stone's throw away, in North Hyde Road. The last machines coming out of the factory were Pumas in the late 1970s.

◆ **Access:** *In Nestles Avenue, close to the Hayes and Harlington railway station.* **Open:** *Daily, other than Xmas, 10:00 to 18:00.* **Contact:** *3 Nestles Avenue, Hayes, UB3 4SB* | **0800 1950777** | **info@londonmotormuseum.co.uk** | **www.londonmotormuseum.co.uk**

❑ 'MM80270'		Bell 204B		~	MM8027<u>9</u>, ex Cormano, It AF. Agusta-built. Arrived 1-14	1-14

HENDON north-west London, near the end of the M1

Royal Air Force Museum, London: On 15th November 2012 Hendon clocked up its 40th birthday, having grown from 40 aircraft in four hangars to over 100 in six and in that time over 10 million visitors. Plans, including Heritage Lottery funding, to re-develop the exhibitions in the Grahame-White Factory building, in readiness for the centenary of World War One were announced on 5th February 2013. The Camel and Fokker D.VII presently in 'Milestones' were due to move across to the 'Factory' and it *might* be that some airframes will be suspended within the building. Three aircraft, at the time of writing, the Pup, 'Strutter' and Bristol M.1C were due to move to Cosford, Shropshire, to take part in the centenary exhibition there. Other airframes are destined for Stafford. A special exhibition on the Royal Air Force of Oman - and remember Hendon's Omani 'gate guard' - is scheduled for later in 2014. This will include the Provost T.1 and Pioneer CC.1 from Cosford.

See under Cosford and Bruntingthorpe, Leics, for details of the VC-10 acquisition and Lyneham, Wilts, for the background to the Comet C.2. As predicted in the *Preface* of *W&R23*, early in December 2013 it was announced that the museum would not be preserving a Tristar.

Precision Aerospace Productions at Wangaratta, Victoria, Australia, is near to completing Douglas A-20G Havoc 43-9436 *Big Nig* for the museum. Two Spitfires from the museum's 'working stock' at Stafford, Staffs, will go to Precision when the project is complete. During 2012 a remarkably intact Curtiss Kittyhawk Ia was discovered in the Egyptian desert. With RAF Museum input this was salvaged and moved to secure storage. Government-to-government discussions were in hand in early 2014 about the museum taking this significant airframe on. It may well be that Spitfire F.22 PK664 was/is involved in this - see Stafford, Staffs.

There is a very active **Society of Friends of the RAF Museum** with a variety of activities which also publishes a journal – *The Flying M* – details of membership from the address below. Of course, there is the RAF Museum 'North' and the Michael Beetham Conservation Centre at **Cosford, Shropshire**, and the storage site at **Stafford, Staffs**.

The RAF Museum has long had a vigorous loan policy with the following to be found elsewhere: **Brooklands**, Surrey: Valiant cockpit; **Coventry**, Warks: Meteor WS838; **Duxford**, Cambs, Canberra WH725, Fi 103 (V-1); **Filton**, Glos, Bristol 173 G-ALBN; **Gloucestershire Airport**, Glos, Javelin XH903; **Manchester**, Gtr Man, several airframes; **Manston**, Kent, Hurricane and Spitfire: **Middle Wallop**, Hants, Magister T9708 and Rotachute III; **South Kensington**, Gtr Lon, P.1127; **Southampton**, Hants, Gnat F.1 XK740, Spitfire F.24; **Tangmere**, W Sussex: Hunter, Meteor, Phantom, Swift; **Woodley**, Berks, Jet Gyrodyne; **Yeovilton**, Somerset, P.1052, Dragonfly VX595, Supermarine 510. Overseas: **Munich, Germany**: a Fi 103 (V-1) and **Soesterberg, Netherlands**: Dornier Do 24T-3 HD5-1.

◆ **Access:** *On Grahame Park Way, signposted from the end of the M1 and A41.* **Open:** *Daily 10:00 to 18:00 all week, except Christmas and New Year. Last admission 17:30.* ***Note***: *The Grahame White Factory is closed 12:00 to 13:30.* **Contact:** *Hendon, London, NW9 5LL* | **020 8205 2266** | **london@rafmuseum.org** | **www.rafmuseum.org**

'Gate guardians':

❑	'Z3427'	'AV-R'	Hawker Hurricane FSM	90	BAPC.205, ex 'BE421'. 121 'Eagle' Sqn colours		1-14
❑	'MH486'	'FT-E'	Supermarine Spitfire FSM	90	BAPC.206, 43 Sqn colours		1-14
❑	853		Hawker Hunter FR.10	57	ex Oman, Thumrait, SOAF, RJorAF 853, XF426, 229 OCU, 2, 208. Acquired 6-9-03. Pole-mounted	[1]	1-14

■ **[1]** The Hunter FR.10 was a gift from the Sultan of Oman.

'Historic Hangars' and **Bomber Command Hall**: By March 2013 BE.2b '687' had transferred to the Grahame-White Factory - see below. Moth G-AAMX departed to Stafford, Staffs, on 15th May 2012. On 7th November 2013 Typhoon Ib MN235 moved to Cosford, Shropshire.

❑	G-FAAG		AW R.33 airship	17	Vickers-built. Dismantled 5-28. Control gondola		1-14
❑	'G-RAFM'		Robinson R22 G-OTHL	87	ex Redhill. CoA 2-3-00, de-reg 8-2-00. 'Hands-on'	[1]	1-14
❑	-		American AA-5B Tiger	77	ex 'G-ROWL', Cabair, Elstree. Cockpit	[1]	1-14
❑	-*		Lockheed TriStar SIM	~	BA colours		1-14
❑	N9050T		Douglas Dakota III	44	ex Rochester, Cosford, Fleet, Thruxton, Hal Safi, 5N-ATA, PH-MAG, G-AGYX, KG437, 42-92656. Forward fuselage		1-14
❑	'A6526'		RAF FE.2b	17	ex Cosford, Stafford, Wyton, Cardington, Leiston. Acquired 4-76	[2]	1-14
❑	'E2466'	'I'	Bristol F.2b	18	BAPC.165, ex Cardington, Weston-on-the-Green. Acquired 1965. Semi-skeletal		1-14
❑	F1010		Airco DH.9A	18	ex Cardington, Krakow, Berlin, 110. Force-landed 5-10-18 and captured. Westland-built. Acquired 15-6-77.	[3]	1-14
❑	'K2227'		Bristol Bulldog IIA	30	ex Hatch, Cardington, Old Warden, Henlow, Filton, G-ABBB, Science Museum, R-11. Crashed 13-9-64, de-reg 22-9-61. Acquired 31-3-99. 56 Sqn colours		1-14
❑	K4232		Avro Rota I (C.30A)	34	ex Spain, Cardington, SE-AZB, K4232, SAC. Acquired14-6-78		1-14
❑	K4972		Hawker Hart Trainer	35	ex Cosford, Cardington, Hendon, St Athan, 1546 ATC, Carlisle, Wigton 1764M, 2 FTS. AWA-built. Acquired 16-10-63		1-14

❑ K6035		Westland Wallace II	35	ex Hatch, Henlow, Newark, Cranwell, 2361M, EWS, 502. Acquired 4-77. Fuselage, partially covered	[4]	1-14
❑ L5343		Fairey Battle I	39	ex Cosford, Rochester, Hendon, St Athan, Henlow, Leeming, Iceland, 98, 266. Crashed 13-9-40. Acquired 21-11-72. 98 Sqn colours	[5]	1-14
❑ N5628		Gloster Gladiator II	39	ex 263. Lost in Norway 4-40. Acquired 8-68. Forward fuselage		1-14
❑ N9899		Supermarine Southampton I	25	ex Cardington, Henlow, Felixstowe (as houseboat), wrecked at moorings, Calshot, 23-11-28, 480 Flt, MAEE, 480 Flt. Acquired 9-67. Fuselage		1-14
❑ R5868	'PO-S'	Avro Lancaster I	42	ex Scampton 7325M, 467, 83. Metropolitan-Vickers-built. Acquired 3-72. 467 Sqn colours		1-14
❑ W1048	'TL-S'	HP Halifax II	42	ex 8465M, Henlow, Lake Hoklingen, Norway, 35, 102. EE-built. Force-landed 27-4-42. Acquired 25-8-73. 35 Sqn c/s		1-14
❑ W2068	'68'	Avro Anson I	39	ex Duxford, 9261M, Australia, VH-ASM, W2068, 4 SFTS, 3 SFTS. Acquired 19-4-96. Fuselage on 'Queen Mary' trailer		1-14
❑ BL614	'ZD-F'	Supermarine Spitfire Vb	42	ex Rochester, Manchester, St Athan, 'AB871', Colerne, Wattisham, Credenhill 4354M (6-12-43), 118, 64, 222, 242, 611. Acquired 10-72. 222 Sqn colours		1-14
❑ 'DD931'	'L'	Bristol Beaufort VIII	44	ex 9131M, Cardington, Chino, New Guinea, RAAF. DAP-built. Acquired 1991. 42 Sqn colours	[6]	1-14
❑ FE905		NAA Harvard IIB	43	ex Cardington, Winthorpe, Cardington, Royston, London Bridge, Southend, LN-BNM, Danish AF 31-329, RCAF, 41 SFTS, FE905, 42-12392. Noorduyn-built. Acquired 3-85		1-14
❑ 'FX760'	'GA-?'	Curtiss Kittyhawk IV	43	ex Cosford 9150M, Wyton, Cardington, Hendon, USA. Acquired 29-5-92. 112 Sqn colours		1-14
❑ 'KL216'	'RS-L'	Republic P-47D-40-RA Thunderbolt	45	ex Cosford 9212M, Duxford, Cardington, Bitteswell, Yugoslav AF 13064, USAAF 45-49295. Acquired 7-86. 30 Sqn colours		1-14
❑ KN751	'F'	Consolidated Liberator VI	44	ex Cosford, Colerne, Ind AF 6 Sqn HE807, RAF KN751, 99. Ford-built. Acquired 1-7-74. 99 Sqn, Cocos Islands, c/s	[7]	1-14
❑ LB264		Auster I	42	ex Cosford, G-AIXA, Spanhoe, 22 EFTS, 1 EFTS, A&AEE. CoA 21-2-07, de-reg 13-12-02, acquired 23-10-02		1-14
❑ MP425	'G'	Airspeed Oxford I	43	ex Cardington, Winthorpe, Cardington, G-AITB, Shawbury, Perth, MP425, 7 FTS, 18 (P)AFU, 1536 (BAT) Flt. Standard Motors-built. CoA 24-5-61, de-reg 31-10-61, acquired 3-69. 1536 Flt colours		1-14
❑ MT847*	'AX-H'	Supermarine Spitfire FR.XIV	45	ex Manchester, Cosford, Weeton, Middleton St George, Freckleton, Warton, 6960M (28-5-52), 226 OCU, A&AEE. Arrived 9-2-14	[8]	2-14
❑ PK724		Supermarine Spitfire F.24	46	ex Finningley 7288M (4-11-55), Gaydon, Norton, Lyneham, n/s. Acquired 20-2-70		1-14
❑ 'PR536'	'OQ-H'	Hawker Tempest II	46	ex Duxford, Cardington, Chichester, Indian AF HA457, RAF. Acquired 13-11-91. 5 Sqn colours		1-14
❑ RD253		Bristol Beaufighter TF.10	44	ex St Athan 7931M, Portuguese AF BF-13, RD253. Acquired 1965		1-14
❑ VS618		Percival Prentice T.1	49	ex G-AOLK, Southend, Southend, VS618, 9 MU, 22 FTS. CoA 17-9-10, de-reg 9-2-10. Acquired 9-10-09		1-14
❑ VT812	'N'	DH Vampire F.3	47	ex Cosford, Wyton, Hendon, Cosford, Shawbury, Colerne 7200M, Cardington, 602, 601, 614, 32. Acquired 9-6-64		1-14
❑ WE139		EE Canberra PR.3	53	ex 8369M, Henlow, 231 OCU, 39, 69, 540. Acquired 23-4-69		1-14
❑ WH301		Gloster Meteor F.8	51	ex Henlow 7930M, Kemble, 85, CAW, 609, DFLS. Acquired 17-2-67		1-14
❑ WP962	'C'	DHC Chipmunk T.10	53	ex 9287M, Newton, 3 AEF, Bri UAS, AAC, Lon UAS, 61 GCF, 662. Acquired 5-5-00		1-14
❑ WV783		Bristol Sycamore HR.12	50	ex Rochester, Wyton, Cardington, Fleetlands, Henlow 7841M, HDU Old Sarum, CFS, ASWDU, G-ALSP de-reg 26-3-52. Acquired 1995. CFS colours		1-14
❑ WZ791		Slingsby Grasshopper TX.1	52	ex 8944M, Syerston, Halton, High Wycombe, Hove. Acquired 8-8-91		1-14

❑	XA302	HAK	Slingsby Cadet TX.3	52	ex Syerston, BGA.3786, 622 GS, 661 GS, CGS, 2 GC, 671 GS,615 GS, 613 GS, 126 GS, 123 GS, 22 GS. CoA 24-5-96, acquired 5-5-05	[9]	1-14
❑	XG154		Hawker Hunter FGA.9	56	ex 8863M, St Athan, 1 TWU, 229 OCU, 54, 43, 54. AWA-built. Acquired 30-5-85. 8 *and* 43 Sqn colours		1-14
❑	XG474	'O'	Bristol Belvedere HC.1	62	ex 8367M, Henlow, 66, 26, 66. Acquired 7-8-69. 66 Sqn c/s		1-14
❑	XL318		Avro Vulcan B.2	61	ex 8733M, Scampton, 617, 230 OCU, Wadd Wing, 617, 230 OCU, Scamp Wing, 617. Acquired 1-1-82		1-14
❑	XM463	'38'	Hunting Jet Provost T.3A	60	ex 1 FTS, RAFC. Acquired 6-3-91. Fuselage, 'hands-on'		1-14
❑	XM717		HP Victor K.2	63	ex Cardington, Marham, 55, 57, 55, 543, Witt W, 100. Acquired 2-3-94. *Lucky Lou*. Cockpit		1-14
❑	XP299		Westland Whirlwind HAR.10	61	ex Cosford 8726M, 22, 230, 1563F, Queen's Flt, 230, CFS. Acquired 30-11-81. 22 Sqn colours		1-14
❑	XS925	'BA'	EE Lightning F.6	67	ex 8961M, Binbrook, 11, 5-11 pool. Acquired 26-4-88. 11 Sqn colours		1-14
❑	XV424	'I'	McD Phantom FGR.2	69	ex 9152M, St Athan, Wattisham, 56, 228 OCU, 29, 92, 228 OCU, 29, 228 OCU, 111, 29. Acquired 12-11-92		1-14
❑	XV732		Westland Wessex HCC.4	69	ex Shawbury, 32, Queen's Flight. Acquired 26-3-02		1-14
❑	XW323	'86'	BAC Jet Provost T.5A	70	ex 9166M (23-10-92), Shawbury, 1 FTS, RAFC. 1 FTS colours		1-14
❑	XW547	'R'	HS Buccaneer S.2B	72	ex Cosford 9169M, Shawbury, 9095M, Gulf Det, 12, 237 OCU, 208, 12, 216, 12, 237 OCU, 12. Acquired 20-1-93 *Guinness Girl / Pauline / The Macallan*. Pink colours		1-14
❑	XW855		Sud Gazelle HCC.4	73	ex Shawbury, Fleetlands, 32. Westland-built. Acquired 1-4-03		1-14
❑	ZA457	'AJ-J'	Panavia Tornado GR.1	83	ex St Athan, 2, 617, RAF Gulf Det, 17, 15, 9, 617, 9, TOEU. Acquired 28-7-03		1-14
❑	ZE686		Grob Viking TX.1	85	ex Syerston, Kirkbymoorside, BGA.3099. Cockpit	[10]	1-14
❑	ZE887	'GF'	Panavia Tornado F.3	88	ex Leuchars, 111, 43, 25, 11, 5, 11, 43, 229 OCU. Acquired 18-10-10. 43 Sqn colours	[11]	1-14
❑	ZJ116	'IOI'	EHI EH.101 PP8	90	ex Brize Norton, Yeovil, G-OIOI, G-17-01. CoA 5-5-94, de-reg 1-4-96, acquired 20-11-02		1-14
❑	–		Bristol Beaufighter	c42	ex East Fortune, Hendon, Duxford, Hendon, Cranfield. Cockpit	[12]	1-14
❑	A16-199	'SF-R'	Lockheed Hudson IIIA	42	ex Strathallan, G-BEOX, VH-AGJ, VH-SMM, 3 Comms Unit, 2 Sqn, 13 Sqn, RAAF A16-199, FH174 n/s, 41-36975. De-reg 12-12-81. Acquired 14-7-81. RAAF 13 Sqn colours		1-14
❑	920	'QN'	Supermarine Stranraer	40	ex Queen Charlotte Airlines CF-BXO, RCAF 920. Canadian Vickers-built. Acquired 7-70		1-14
❑	10639	'6'	Messerschmitt Bf 109G-2	40	ex Duxford G-USTV, Benson, Northolt, Lyneham 8478M, Henlow, Wattisham, Stanmore Park, Sealand, CFE-EAF, 1426 Flt, RN228, Lydda, 3 Sqn Gambut, III/JG77. Erla-built. Crashed 12-10-97, de-reg 24-9-98. Acquired 10-3-02		1-14
❑	120227	'2'	Heinkel He 162A-2	44	ex St Athan 8472M, Colerne, Leconfield, VN679, AM.65, Farnborough, Leck, JG1. Acquired 1961. JG1 colours		1-14
❑	584219	'38'	Focke-Wulf Fw 190F-8/U1	44	ex St Athan 8470M, Gaydon, Henlow, Fulbeck, Wroughton, Stanmore, Wroughton, Brize Norton, AM.29, Farnborough, Karup. JG54 colours. Acquired 9-70		1-14
❑	'34037'		NAA TB-25N-20-NC Mitchell	44	ex 8838M, Blackbushe, N9115Z, *Hanover Street*, *Catch-22*, USAAF 44-29366. Acquired 25-10-82		1-14
❑	44-83868	'N'	Boeing B-17G-95-DL Flying Fortress	45	ex Stansted, N5237V, Andrews AFB, TBM Inc, Aero Union, USN PB-1W 77233. Douglas, Long Beach-built. Acquired 13-10-83. 94th BG, 332nd BS colours		1-14
❑	83-24104	'BN'	BV CH-47D Chinook	84	ex Boeing, US Army. Fuselage 'walk-in' exhibit. 18 Sqn, RAF colours		1-14

■ **[1]** The Robinson and AA-5 were gifted from Cabair and are in the kids' 'Aeronauts' area. **[2]** FE.2 is based on an unfinished nacelle built by sub-contractor Richard Garrett and Sons of Leiston and stored at their factory for close on 60 years. Much of the work creating the rest of the airframe was carried out by John McKenzie of Aircraft and Weapon Reproductions of Southampton 1987 to 2007, with completion by Guy Black's Retrotec. **[3]** 'Nin-Ack' was the 13th of 18 donated to 110 Sqn and a panel reads: 'Presented by His Highness the Nizam of Hyderabad No.12A' - the potentate was clearly superstitious! The fuselage was acquired from Krakow, wings and much else created/acquired in-house. **[4]** Other Wallace fuselage and wing parts are held at Stafford, Staffs.

[5] Original restoration of Battle L5343 included substantial elements of the centre fuselage of a former RCAF Battle I, believed to be L5340, and other parts from P2183. **[6]** Beaufort is a composite: forward fuselage from A9-557, rear from A9-559, centre section from A9-591, all salvaged from Tadji, Papua New Guinea and all Department of Aircraft Production built. **[7]** Liberator carries 'SNAKE' alongside its serial number, denoting an aircraft destined for Air Command South East Asia and not to be diverted to other taskings or theatres. **[8]** The FR.XIV Spitfire arrived for a temporary exhibition 'Britain from Above', but, as *W&R* closed for press, was not expected to return to Manchester. **[9]** Cadet donated by Bill Walker OBE. **[10]** Viking cockpit *may* be from ZE655. Whichever, it was tested to destruction in mid-1986 in a fatigue rig at Syerston. **[11]** Tornado F.3 factoids: During its first stint with 43 Sqn, it was deployed to Dhahran for Operation GRANBY, 8-90 to 1-91. ZE887's last flight was 4-3-10, having clocked 4,966 hours total time. **[12]** Beaufighter cockpit is thought to be from a 1941-1942-built Merlin XX Mk.IIf.

Battle of Britain Experience:

❑ K8042		Gloster Gladiator II	37	ex 8372M, Biggin Hill 'K8442', 61 OTU, 5 (P)AFU, A&AEE. Acquired 11-65. 87 Sqn colours		1-14
❑ 'L8756'	'XD-E'	Bristol Bolingbroke IVT	42	ex Boscombe Down, RCAF 10001. Fairchild Canada-built. Acquired 25-4-66. 139 Sqn colours as Blenheim IV		1-14
❑ N1671*	'EW-D'	Boulton Paul Defiant I	38	ex Rochester, Hendon 8370M, Finningley, 285, 307. Acquired 23-7-68, arrived 6-12-12		1-14
❑ P2617	'AF-F'	Hawker Hurricane I	40	ex 8373M, 71 MU, 9 FTS, 9 SFTS, 1, 607, 615. Acquired 5-72. 607 Sqn colours		1-14
❑ P3175		Hawker Hurricane I	40	ex 257. Shot down 31-8-40. Acquired 1978. Wreck		1-14
❑ R9125	'LX-L'	Westland Lysander III	40	ex 8377M, 161, 225. Acquired 3-61. 225 Sqn colours		1-14
❑ T6296		DH Tiger Moth II	41	ex 8387M, Yeovilton SF, BRNC, RNEC, Stretton, 7 EFTS, 1 EFTS. Morris-built. Acquired 15-3-72		1-14
❑ X4590	'PR-F'	Supermarine Spitfire I	40	ex Cosford 8384M, Finningley, 53 OTU, 303, 57 OTU, 66, 609. Acquired 1-72. 609 Sqn colours		1-14
❑ ML824	'NS-Z'	Short Sunderland MR.5	44	ex Pembroke Dock, Aéronavale, 330, 201. Acquired 11-1-71. 201 Sqn colours		1-14
❑ A2-4		Supermarine Seagull V	35	ex Cardington, Wyton, VH-ALB, RAAF A2-4. Acquired 5-72		1-14
❑ 4101	'12'	Messerschmitt Bf 109E-4	40	ex St Athan 8477M, Henlow, Biggin, Fulbeck, Wroughton, Stanmore, Pengam Moors, Stafford, DG200, 1426 Flt, A&AEE, DH Hatfield, Hucknall, RAE, JG51, JG52, JG51. Erla-built. Force-landed 27-11-40. Acquired 9-69		1-14
❑ 360043	'D5+EV'	Junkers Ju 88R-1	43	ex St Athan 8475M, Henlow, St Athan, Biggin Hill, Fulbeck, Wroughton, Stanmore, PJ876, 47 MU, CFE, 1426 (EA) Flt, RAE. Defected 9-5-43. Acquired 9-69		1-14
❑ 494083	'RI+JK'	Junkers Ju 87G-2 'Stuka'	c44	ex St Athan 8474M, Henlow, St Athan, Biggin Hill, Fulbeck, Wroughton, Stanmore, Eggebek. Acquired 9-69		1-14
❑ 701152	'NT+SL'	Heinkel He 111H-20/R1	44	ex St Athan 8471M, Henlow, Biggin Hill, Fulbeck, Stanmore Park, RAE, 56th FG USAAF, Luftwaffe. Acquired 9-69		1-14
❑ 730301	'D5+RL'	Messerschmitt Bf 110G-4/R6	44	ex St Athan 8479M, Biggin Hill, Stanmore Park, 76 MU, RAE, AM.34, Karup, I/NJG3. Acquired 8-73		1-14
❑ –		Fieseler Fi 103 (V-1)	45	BAPC.92, ex Cardington, St Athan		1-14
❑ MM5701	'13-95'	Fiat CR-42 Falco	40	ex St Athan 8468M, Biggin Hill, Fulbeck, Wroughton, Stanmore Park, AFDU, RAE, BT474, 95 SCT. Force-landed Orfordness 11-11-40. Acquired 1968		1-14
❑ E3B.521		Bücker Bü 131 Jungmann	56	ex Spain, Spanish AF. '781-3'. CASA-built. Acquired 23-1-97		1-14

Grahame-White Factory: Refer to the beginning of this section for details of the World War Once centenary plans. **The 'Factory' is closed to the public from 3rd March 2014** to allow for preparations for the centenary exhibition and is due to re-open in November 2014. Three aircraft, believed to be the Pup, the 'Strutter' and the M.1C will move to Cosford, Shropshire, for its Great Centenary exhibition. The Tabloid and Vimy are destined for storage at Stafford, Staffs.

Part of the Albatros-RE.8-Snipe replicas exchange, Hanriot HD.1 HD-75 was exported to New Zealand in December 2012, arriving in February 2013. Never an RFC/RAF airframe, it was always anomalous; the plan is to put it back in the air.

❑ No.433	Blériot XXVII		1911	BAPC.107, ex Stafford, Cosford, Wyton, Hendon 9202M, Cardington, Heathrow, RAeS, Hendon, Nash, Brooklands Acquired 5-63		1-14
❑ '168'	Sopwith Tabloid replica	G-BFDE	80	ex Cardington, Hendon, Cardington, G-BFDE. CoA 4-6-83, de-reg 8-12-86. Acquired 23-3-83. See notes above		1-14
❑ '687'*	RAF BE.2b replica		88	BAPC.181, ex Cardington. Acquired 6-92		1-14
❑ '2345'	Vickers FB.5 Gunbus replica	G-ATVP	66	ex Cardington, Hendon, Brooklands, G-ATVP. CoA 6-5-69, de-reg 27-2-69. Acquired 10-6-68	[1]	1-14

❑	'3066'		Caudron G.3 G-AETA	16	ex 9203M, Henlow, Stradishall, Heathrow, RAeS, Hendon, Nash, Brooklands, G-AETA ntu, OO-ELA, O-BELA. Acquired 1964		1-14
❑	'A3930'*	'B'	RAF RE.8 replica	12	ex New Zealand, ZK-TVC. Acquired 28-8-12. 9 Sqn colours	[2]	1-14
❑	'A8226'		Sopwith 1½ Strutter replica G-BIDW	80	ex Cardington, Land's End, '9382', G-BIDW. CoA 29-12-80, de-reg 4-2-87. Acquired 1-81. See notes above		1-14
❑	'C3988'		Sopwith 5F1 Dolphin	18	ex Cosford, 'D5239', Wyton, Cardington. Acquired 6-67	[3]	1-14
❑	'C4994'		Bristol M.1C replica G-BLWM	87	ex Cardington, 'C4912', Hucknall, G-BLWM. CoA 12-8-87, de-reg 12-5-88, acquired 8-87. See notes above		1-14
❑	'E449'		Avro 504K	18	ex 9205M, Henlow, Abingdon, Heathrow, RAeS, Nash collection, Brooklands. Acquired 3-63	[4]	1-14
❑	F938		RAF SE.5a G-EBIC	18	ex Henlow 9208M, Biggin Hill, Heathrow, Brooklands, Wroughton, Brooklands, 'B4563', Colerne, RAeS, Brooklands, Hendon, Nash collection, Savage Skywriting, G-EBIC, F938, 84 Sqn. CoA 3-9-30, de-reg 31-12-38. Acquired 12-64		1-14
❑	'F8614'		Vickers Vimy replica G-AWAU	69	ex 'H651', Wisley, Brooklands, G-AWAU. Damaged 14-6-69, CoA 4-8-69, de-reg 19-7-73, acquired 12-70 *Triple First*. See notes above	[1] [5]	1-14
❑	'N5182'		Sopwith Pup G-APUP	16	ex 9213M (31-8-93), Blackbushe, Old Warden, G-APUP, Musée de l'Air, Chalais Meudon, Dover Defence Flight, Walmer DF, 9 Sqn RNAS, 3 Sqn RNAS, 8 Sqn RNAS, 1 Wing, A8736 ntu. CoA 28-6-78, de-reg 4-10-84. Acquired 6-82 See notes above	[6]	1-14
❑	N5912		Sopwith Triplane	17	ex 8385M, Henlow, 49 MU, 5 MU, Cardington, Sch of Air Fighting, Redcar, Sch of Air Fighting, Marske. Oakley-built. Acquired 1964		1-14
❑	'D.7343/17'		Albatros D.Va replica	12	ex New Zealand, ZK-TVD. Acquired 28-8-12, f/n 3-13	[7]	1-14

■ **[1]** Gunbus and the Vimy built by the Brooklands-based Vintage Aircraft and Flying Association, first flying 14-6-66 and 3-6-69, respectively. **[2]** RE.8 built by The Vintage Aviator Ltd, fitted with a 'reverse-engineered' RAF 4a; unveiled at Old Warden 28-8-12; exchange for Farman F-HMFI (see Cosford, Shrop) and Hanriot HD-75 (see above). Original rudder, wing and fuselage parts found in a garage in Coventry by the Northern Aircraft Preservation Society. **[3]** The Dolphin uses many original parts. The rear fuselage comes from C3988 and this has been adopted as its identity. **[4]** Avro 504K 'E449' is a composite of G-EBJE (fuselage) and Type 548A G-EBKN (wings), both of which used to ply their joy riding trade from Shoreham, and was originally with the Nash Collection. **[5]** The Vimy was badly damaged in a fire while on the ground at Manchester Airport 14-6-69; it was substantially rebuilt to static status and handed over to the RAFM in June 1972. The name *Triple First* denotes the first Atlantic, Australia and South Africa flights undertaken by Vimys. **[6]** The story goes that Lt Cdr K C D St Cyrien MBE was allowed to bring this machine out of museum storage for return to flight and that he did it piece by piece over a series of years! In 2-59 he registered G-APUP as a Pup *replica*, but changed this in 1973 to an *original*. Lt Cdr St Cyrien was also responsible for G-ABOX, currently at the Museum of Army Flying, Middle Wallop, Hants. **[7]** D.Va built by The Vintage Aviator Ltd, fitted with original Mercedes D.III ex RAFM stocks; unveiled at Old Warden 28-8-12; exchange for Farman F-HMFI (see Cosford, Shrop) and Hanriot HD-75 (see above).

'Milestones of Flight': Within this hall can be found the **'TrailBlazers'** exhibition. Kicking this off was the story of Alex Henshaw with the AJD Engineering-built Mew Gull replica. The Camel and Fokker are destined to move to the Grahame-White building for the World War One centenary exhibition.

See under Gainsborough, Lincs, for the Ilyushin Il-2 that is destined for display here. Bf 109G-2 10639 moved to the Historic Hangars by March 2013. Early in 2012 Mohawk G-AEKW moved to Stafford, Staffs.

❑	'G-AEXF'		Percival Mew Gull replica	08	ex Sudbury. Acquired 17-4-08	[1]	1-14
❑	–		Clarke Chanute glider	1910	BAPC.100, ex Wyton, Hendon, Cardington, Hayes, South Kensington. Acquired 1983	[2]	1-14
❑	–		*Nulli Secundus I* replica	~	BAPC.296, Army Balloon Factory airship gondola, 1907		1-14
❑	No.164		Blériot XI	c1910	BAPC.106, ex Cosford 9209M, Cardington, Hendon, Colerne, Hendon, Heathrow, RAeS, Hendon, Nash collection, Brooklands. Acquired 1964		1-14
❑	E6655*	'B'	Sopwith Snipe	11	ex New Zealand. Acquired 28-8-12	[3]	1-14
❑	F6314	'B'	Sopwith F1 Camel	18	ex Cosford 9206M, Wyton, Hendon, Heathrow, Colerne, Hendon, RAeS, Hendon, Nash Collection, Brooklands, 'H508', Tring, Waddon. Acquired 9-1-64	[4]	1-14
❑	'J9941'		Hawker Hart	35	ex HSA, 'J9933', G-ABMR. CoA 11-6-57, de-reg 2-2-59. Acquired 1972. 57 Sqn colours		1-14
❑	–		Supermarine Spitfire FSM	03	BAPC.293, built by Concepts & Innovations. Lobby		1-14

❑	DG202/G		Gloster F9/40 Meteor	42	ex Cosford, Colerne, Yatesbury, Locking 5758M, Moreton Valance. Acquired 1965		1-14
❑	'KK995'	'E'	Sikorsky Hoverfly I KL110	44	ex Bicester, Henlow, Cranfield, 705, King's Flt, TCDU, 43 OTU, USAAF 43-46596. Acquired 14-1-66	[5]	1-14
❑	NV778		Hawker Tempest TT.5	44	ex Cosford, Wyton, Cardington, Hendon, 8386M, Leeming, Middleton St George, North Weald, Foulness, 233 OCU, Napier. Acquired 8-65. 233 OCU colours		1-14
❑	TJ138	'VO-L'	DH Mosquito TT.35	45	ex St Athan 7607M, Swinderby, Finningley, Colerne, Bicester, Shawbury, 5 CAACU, 98. Acquired 6-67. 98 Sqn c/s		1-14
❑	XZ997	'V'	HS Harrier GR.3	82	ex 9122M, 233 OCU, 1453 Flt, 4, 1, 4. Acquired 4-12-91. 4 Sqn colours		1-14
❑	ZH588		Eurofighter Typhoon DA2	94	ex Brize Norton, Coningsby, Warton, BAE Systems. Acquired 22-1-08	[6]	1-14
❑	8417/18		Fokker D.VII	18	ex Cardington, Hendon 9207M, Cardington, Hendon, Cardington, Heathrow, RAeS, Hendon, Nash collection, Brooklands, Versailles, OO- ?, Belgian AF (?), Jasta 71 Ostdeutsche Albatros Werke-built. Acquired 3-66	[4]	1-14
❑	112372	'4'	Messerschmitt Me 262A-2a	45	ex Cosford 8482M, St Athan, Cosford, Finningley, Gaydon, '110880', Cranwell, Farnborough, VK893. Twenthe. Acquired 1972	[7]	1-14
❑	'413317'	'VF-B'	NAA P-51D-30-NA Mustang	44	ex N51RT, N555BM, YV-508CP, N555BM, N4409, N6319T, 44-74409. Acquired 18-11-03. 4th FG, 336th FS colours, *The Duck*	[8]	1-14
❑	–		Lockheed-Martin F-35 FSM	10	installed 9-11		1-14

■ **[1]** See under Shuttleworth, Beds, for the flying G-AEXF and Tattershall Thorpe, Lincs, for another replica. **[2]** The Clarke Chanute biplane glider is on loan from the Royal Aero Club through the Science Museum; acquired 1914. **[3]** Snipe built by The Vintage Aviator Ltd, with original wings, fuselage, tailplane and Bentley; unveiled at Old Warden 28-8-12; exchange for Farman F-HMFI (see Cosford, Shrop) and Hanriot HD-75 (see above). **[4]** The Camel and Fokker are *expected* to move to the Grahame-White building for the World War Once centenary exhibition. **[5]** The majority of the Hoverfly is KL110 despite it wearing 'KK995'; the latter was delivered to Cranfield 5-51 and there was probably some exchange of parts. **[6]** DA2 factoids: First flown at Warton, Lancs, 14th August 1993; adopted the all-black colour scheme in the summer of 2000; last-ever flight into Coningsby, Lincs, 29th January 2007 for spares recovery; moved by road to Brize Norton, Oxfordshire, October 2007 for McDD Globemaster loading trials. **[7]** History track revised to reflect recent thinking on the Me 262; it is very *likely* 112372. **[8]** P-51 'The Duck' was donated by Bob Tullius of Group 44 Inc, who based it at Sebring, Florida.

Locally: Martin and Sam Churchill are turning the Canberra nose into a flight simulator.

❑	WJ731	EE Canberra B.2T	53	ex Dunstable, Willington, Wyton, Wyton SF, 231 OCU, 7, 231 OCU, 50, 90. Cockpit, trailer-mounted	8-09

KINGSTON-UPON-THAMES

Kingston College Aviation Village: The new campus was initiated on 3rd October 2012 by which time two airliners were at the Penrhyn Road site. The fuselage of Bandeirante G-ODUB had arrived by this time, but see notes under Alton, Hampshire, for a 'time-lag' with this machine. It was not here for long, moving to Cotswold, Glos, on 8th July 2013.

◆ **Access:** *Very busy access* **only** *by prior permission* | **www.kingston-college.ac.uk**

❑	-*	HS 146	~	cockpit	10-12

Also:

❑	XG209	'66'	Hawker Hunter F.6	56	ex Chelmsford, Stock, Halton, Cranwell, Halton 8709M (17-11-81), 12 DFLS, 111, 14. Cockpit	1-14

LONDON

Bomber Command Memorial: The incredible memorial and its seven aircrew statues was official unveiled on 28th June 2012 in Green Park. It is a moving and long-overdue national tribute to the 55,573 aircrew that perished during World War Two. **www.bombercommand.com**

Andrew Martin International: Interior designers of Walton Street, SW3. A brightly-polished Gnat cockpit - complete with 'foreplanes' - is displayed. | **www.andrewmartine.co.uk**

❑	XS100	Folland Gnat T.1	64	ex Fyfield, Bournemouth, Ipswich, Halton 8561M (14-11-77), 4 FTS. Forward fuselage	[1]	1-14

■ **[1]** The remainder of XS100 was at North Weald, Essex, by 3-13.

Mutoid Waste Company / MuTATE Britain: This 'travelling art co-operative' stages regular exhibitions within London and an annual extravaganza at the Glastonbury festival. **www.mutatebritain.com**

❑ XK911	'519'	Westland Whirlwind HAS.7	57	ex Melksham, Chipping Sodbury, Adlington, Derby, Colton, Ipswich, Wroughton, Lee-o-Solent, Arbroath A2603,771, 829, *Ark Royal* Flt, 824, 820, 845. SOC 6-2-70		11-12
❑ XX375		Sud Gazelle AH.1	74	ex Shawbury, 8 Flt, 663, 670, 658, 2 Flt. Westland-built		7-10

Queen Mary and Westfield College: Part of the University of London, the Mile End Campus, Engineering Department, is in Bancroft Road, off the Mile End Road. **Access**, *busy campus, access by prior arrangement* **only | www.qmul.ac.uk**

❑ G-BVYE		BN-2B-20 Islander	95	ex Bembridge. Over-stressed 28-8-96, de-reg 27-11-98		11-03

Slimelight Night Club: Last noted in May 2011, Jaguar GR.3 XZ118 and Harrier FA.2 ZE695 were scrapped.

LONDON HEATHROW AIRPORT EGLL

British Airways Heritage Collection - Speedbird Centre: Now within the corporate headquarters at Harmondsworth.

◆ **Open:** *Visits welcome by prior arrangement* **only**. **Contact**: *Waterside (HDGA), PO Box 365, Harmondsworth, UB7 0GB* | **020 8562 5777** or **5737 | www.britishairways.com/travel/museum-collection**

BA Engineering Base: A purpose-built fire rescue rig, a sort of collision of a DC-10 and 747 is in a pen in this area.

❑ G-BOAB		BAC/Sud Concorde 102	76	ex BA, G-N94AB. CoA 19-9-01, de-reg 4-5-04	[1]	2-14

■ **[1]** *Alpha-Bravo* factoids: Withdrawn from BA service 15th August 2000, total hours 22,297, landings 7,810.

DHL / Gate Gourmet: Close to the Colnbrook bypass.

❑ -		Boeing 737	~	forward fuselage, DHL colours		9-11

NORTHOLT AIRFIELD on the A4180 north-west of Northolt EGWU

RAF Northolt: The Spitfire is located alongside the 32 Squadron hangar complex, on the southern edge, close to the A40. The Hurricane is situated close to the former SHQ building.

❑ 'L1684'		Hawker Hurricane FSM	89	BAPC.219, ex 'L1710', Biggin Hill	[1]	8-13
❑ 'MH314'	'SZ-G'	Supermarine Spitfire FSM	89	BAPC.221, ex 'EN526', 'MH777' 'RF-N'. 316 Sqn colours	[2]	8-13

■ **[1]** The Hurricane is in the colours of G/C Stanley Vincent, station CO during the Battle of Britain. **[2]** The Spitfire is in the colours of W/C Aleksander Gabszewicz, who flew EN526 from Northolt gaining three 'kills' in it.

◆ **Thinx** : *Spare some time to visit the Polish Air Force Memorial located at the junction of the A40 and the A4180 at the south-eastern tip of the airfield. There is a pull-in off the A4180 to allow inspection of this imposing monument.*

ROEHAMPTON on the A306 north of Kingston

Kingston University: School of Engineering, Roehampton Vale campus, Friars Avenue.

◆ **Access:** *Busy campus, by prior arrangement* **only | www.kingston.ac.uk**

❑ N121EL		Learjet 25	~	ex N121GL ntu, N82UH ntu, N10BF ntu, N102PS, N671WM, N846HC, N846GA		9-03

SIDCUP on the A271, south-east London

Lost Island Encounter | World of Golf: A very 'different' golfing range, pitch-and-putt, crazy golf - call it what you will - has among the attractions on 'Manuwago Island' a Cherokee in a 'crashed' pose.

◆ **Access:** *Off the A20 to the south of the town* | **www.worldofgolf.co.uk**

❑ G-BOSU		Piper Cherokee 140	73	ex N55635. Crashed 6-06, de-reg 12-7-07. Zebra stripes		1-11

SOUTH KENSINGTON on the A4 west of Westminster

Science Museum (ScM): The **Flight Gallery** holds some of the UK's most iconic airframes. The museum picked up the Cody biplane from 4 Squadron at Farnborough on 26th November 1913 and it has been with the museum ever since. It follows that in November 2013 the first whole airframe to be owned by a UK museum clocked up a centenary with its hosts. The engine 'stacks' are a work of art, allowing close inspection of an incredible array of powerplants, including the original Whittle unit that was fitted to W4041/G when 'Gerry' Sayer first flew it at Cranwell on 15th May 1941.

The 'large object' store is at **Wroughton**, Wilts. Other ScM airframes can be found at: **Bristol**, Glos ('Flea' G-AEHM), **Hendon**, Gtr Lon (Clarke Chanute); **London Colney**, Herts (C.24 G-ABLM), **Southampton**, Hants (Sandringham VH-BRC) **Yeovilton**, Somerset (Concorde G-BSST, Ohka, Vampire LZ551). From early 2012, the **Museum of Science and Industry, Manchester**, became part of the National Museum of Science and Industry group.

◆ **Access:** *In Exhibition Road, off the Cromwell Road. Nearest tube is South Kensington.* **Open:** *Daily 10:00 to 18:00, except Xmas.* **Contact**: *Exhibition Road, South Kensington, London SW7 2DD* | **0870 8704868** | **www.sciencemuseum.org.uk**

Flight Gallery:

❑	G-EBIB		RAF SE.5a	18	ex 'F939', Hendon, Savage Skywriting G-EBIB, F937, 84 Sqn. Wolseley-built. CoA 6-6-35, de-reg 1-12-46. Acquired 24-7-39		2-14
❑	G-AAAH		DH Moth	28	CoA 23-12-30, de-reg 12-31. *Jason*. Acquired 21-1-31 Amy Johnson's Australian flight machine, 5-30		2-14
❑	G-ASSM		HS.125-1/522	65	ex Wroughton, Chester, Southampton, 5N-AMK, G-ASSM. Acquired 16-3-89	[1]	2-14
❑	G-AZPH		Pitts S-1S	70	ex Meppershall, Chessington, N11CB. *Neil Williams*. Damaged 10-5-91, de-reg 8-1-97. Acquired 10-91		2-14
❑	DFY		Schempp-Hirth Cirrus	c75	BGA.2097, ex Army GA. Acquired 1992		2-14
❑	–*		Frost Ornithopter	1902	wings, flapping mechanism etc. Acquired 1925	[2]	2-14
❑	–		Roe Triplane	1909	BAPC.50, ex Newton Heath. Last flown 10-09. Acquired 1925	[3]	2-14
❑	–		Blériot XI	c1909	cockpit. Acquired 1920	[4]	2-14
❑	–		JAP-Harding Mono	1910	BAPC.54, Blériot-based, presented by JAP Ltd in 1930		2-14
❑	–		Antoinette Monoplane	1910	BAPC.55, ex Robert Blackburn, Colwyn Bay. Acquired 1926. Minus starboard wing, port wing uncovered		2-14
❑	–		Vickers Vimy IV	18	BAPC.51, Alcock and Brown's transatlantic machine, 1919. Acquired 15-12-19. Starboard fuselage undercovered		2-14
❑	–		Wright Flyer replica	48	BAPC.53, Hatfield-built. Acquired 1948		2-14
❑	–		Lilienthal replica	76	BAPC.124, built for the museum	[5]	2-14
❑	304		Cody Military Biplane	1912	BAPC.62, ex Farnborough, 4 Squadron, wrecked 31-3-13. Handed over to the museum 26-11-1913		2-14
❑	J8067		Hill Pterodactyl I	25	ex Yeovil, Farnborough, RAE, Westland, RAE. Acquired 1951. Starboard wing uncovered		2-14
❑	L1592	'KW-Z'	Hawker Hurricane I	38	ex 9 PAFU, 5 PAFU, 9 AOS, SDF, 615, 43, 17, 43, 17, 56. Acquired 16-12-54. 615 Sqn colours		2-14
❑	P9444	'RN-D'	Supermarine Spitfire Ia	40	ex Sydenham (London), 53 OTU, 61 OTU, 58 OTU, 72. SOC 10-8-44. Acquired 16-12-54. 72 colours		2-14
❑	S1595	'1'	Supermarine S.6B	31	ex RAFHSF. Acquired 18-4-32. Schneider winner 1931	[6]	2-14
❑	W4041/G		Gloster E28/39	41	ex RAE, Gloster. Acquired 28-4-46	[7]	2-14
❑	AP507	'KX-P'	Cierva C.30A G-ACWP	34	ex Halton, Sydenham (London), 76 MU, 5 MU, 529, 1448 Flt, Duxford Calibration Flt, RAE, G-ACWP. Avro-built. Acquired 24-5-46. 529 Sqn colours		2-14
❑	XN344		Saro Skeeter AOP.12	60	ex Middle Wallop 8018M, 654, 652. SOC 27-5-68		2-14
❑	XP831		Hawker P.1127	60	ex Hendon 8406M, RAE Bedford, Dunsfold. Arrived 31-5-92	[8]	2-14
❑	1364	'BTT-3'	TTL Banshee 300 UAV	~	donated 1996		2-14
❑	–		Short Bros Gas balloon	1910	basket. Acquired c1912		2-14
❑	–		Balloon Factory Airship	1910	No.17, *Beta II*, gondola. Acquired c1917		2-14
❑	–	'448'	Douglas Dakota IV	44	ex Ottawa, RCAF, KN448, 436, 10, 44-76586. Acquired 1976. Cockpit		2-14
❑	210/16		Fokker E.III	16	BAPC.56, captured 1-4-16 and allocated XG4. Acquired 27-2-18. Stripped airframe	[9]	2-14
❑	191316	'6'	Me 163B-1a Komet	43	ex Halton, 3 MU, 47 MU, 6 MU, Farnborough, Husum, II/JG.400. Acquired 1958		2-14
❑	442795		Fieseler Fi 103A-1 (V-1)	44	BAPC.199, sectioned		2-14

■ **[1]** HS.125 wears UK markings, these were cancelled when it was exported to Nigeria, 28-5-80. Upon return to the UK, it was not restored to the UK civil register. **[2]** Every time the author looks at the Frost in its glass case, he's debated a 'formal' listing, but there is a lot of it, including its 'cockpit'. Second machine built by E P Frost, 3hp engine, wings covered with artificial feathers; there is evidence of 'flight'. First example was presented to Richard Shuttleworth in 1925 - assumed broken up. **[3]** Alliott Verdun Roe made the first sustained flight by a British national in a British designed and built aeroplane 23-7-09 at Lea Marshes. **[4]** Lilienthal original held at Wroughton, Wilts. **[5]** This Blériot was the first aircraft to fly the Irish Sea 22-4-12 - Denys Corbett Wilson piloting.

[6] S1595, piloted by Flt Lt J Boothman at Calshot, 13-9-31 secured the Schneider Trophy for the UK at 340.05mph. **[7]** First British jet, first flew at Cranwell 15-5-41, pilot P E G 'Gerry' Sayer. **[8]** P.1127 prototype - first tethered hover 21-10-60 - on loan from the RAF Museum. **[9]** The 'Eindecker' was being ferried from Valenciennes to Wasquehal to start its operational career when it force-landed behind the lines. It was evaluated at Upavon and retrospectively given the captured aircraft serial XG4, but probably never wore it.

Making of the Modern World: Any visit to the SCM should include *at least* this hall as well; among the treasures here is Stephenson's Rocket locomotive. The 504 and the Lockheed 'fly' prominently, but the SC.1 and the 'Flying Bedstead' seem to evade some visitors. The SC.1 is mounted, without its undercarriage, against a wall, behind the V-2 rocket. The 'Bedstead' is in 'flying' pose close to the Apollo command module.

❑ NC5171N	Lockheed 10A Electra G-LIOA	35	ex Wroughton, G-LIOA, Orlando, N5171N, NC243 Boston-Maine AW, NC14959 Eastern. Acquired 21-6-82. De-reg 26-4-02		2-14
❑ D7560	Avro 504K	18	ex Middle Wallop, South Kensington, Hull, Waddon, 3 TDS. Acquired 22-1-20		2-14
❑ XG900	Short SC.1	57	ex Wroughton, Yeovilton, Wroughton, Hayes, South Kensington, RAE Bedford. Acquired 22-6-71		2-14
❑ XJ314	R-R Thrust Measuring Rig 'Flying Bedstead'	53	ex Wroughton, Yeovilton, East Fortune, Strathallan, Hayes, South Kensington, crashed 16-9-57, RAE Bedford, RAE Farnborough, R-R. Acquired 9-1-61	[1]	2-14

■ **[1]** The official name is the Rolls-Royce Thrust Measuring Rig, but it is universally known as the 'Flying Bedstead'.

SOUTH LAMBETH on the A3203 east of Lambeth Palace

Imperial War Museum London: As these words hit the screen, the IWM was deep in the throes of its £35 million re-vamp and closed to the public. It will open again in July 2014 to start the task of commemorating the centenary of World War One. From late 2012 to January 2013, all of the airframe exhibits headed north for Duxford, Cambs. Just *which* exhibits will return was unconfirmed, leaving a quandary about how to present this entry. Accordingly, the reader is to **refer to the section 'South Lambeth airframes' under Duxford** with the promise that all will have settled down by *W&R25*! Aircraft listed below are known to have arrived.

IWM, of course, runs a series of sites. From a *W&R* point of view the other dominant one is Duxford, Cambs, but there is also IWM North at Manchester, Gtr Man. For completeness, there are two other London-based sites: HMS *Belfast* and the Churchill War Rooms - both brilliant venues.(Details via the website below.)

Departures: Fw 190A-8 733682, on loan from the RAF Museum, was returned it to its care, going to Cosford, Shropshire, 20-12-12. Plus the following, all to Duxford, Cambs: BE.2c 2699 (by 10-12), Camel N6812 (by 10-12), Spitfire I R6915 (13-12-12 - but see below), Lancaster I cockpit DV372 (9-12), Halifax A.VII cockpit PN323 (9-12), He 162A-1 120235 (1-13), Mustang '472218' (9246) (21-12-12, the A6M *Zeke* cockpit (10-12), Fi 103F-1 477663 (10-12).

◆ **Access: RE-OPENS JULY 2014.** *Lambeth Road, London SE1 6HZ. Nearest tube, Elephant and Castle*. **Open:** *10:00 to 18:00 daily. Closed 24-26th Dec*. **Contact: 020 7416 5000 | mail@iwm.org.uk | www.iwm.org.uk | www.1914.org**

❑ R6915*	Supermarine Spitfire I	40	ex Duxford, South Lambeth, Cardiff, RNDU, 57 OTU, 61 OTU, 609. SOC 21-6-47. Arrived 15-1-14	2-14
❑ ZD461*	BAe Harrier GR.9A	89	ex Duxford, Cottesmore, 4, 20, GR.7, 1. Damaged 26-1-10, SOC 14-12-10. Acquired 14-3-12, arrived 2-12-13	2-14

TOLWORTH north of the A3, south of Kingston

No.**1034 Squadron Air Cadets**: Queen Mary Close.

❑ XZ130	'A'	HS Harrier GR.3	76	ex Cosford 9079M, 4, 3, 233 OCU, 3, 1453 Flt, 1, 4, 20. 4 Sqn colours	10-08

UPMINSTER south-east of Romford, west of J29 of the M25

Delta Force Paintball: Within the 'Flight DF777 Jet Hijack' arena, a four-engined airliner - aka what looks like a Jetstream - awaits saviours in camouflage, spitting Post Office Red from potent weaponry!

❑ -	HP Jetstream	~	fuselage - see above	10-11

UXBRIDGE on the A4020 south of the town

RAF Uxbridge Battle of Britain Bunker: Guided tours of 11 Group's command bunker, 60ft below ground level and in use from 1939 to 1958 are available by prior booking. There is an exceptional collection of artefacts.

◆ **Open:** *Guided tours every weekday, at 10:00 and 14:00 - other times by prior arrangement. All* **must** *be booked in advance.* **Contact: 01895 238154 | 11gpenquiries@btconnect.com | www.raf.mod.uk/battleofbritainbunker**

❑ 'P9301'	'RF-E'	Hawker Hurricane FSM	10	gate guardian. 303 Sqn colours	8-13
❑ 'BS239'		Supermarine Spitfire FSM	10	gate guardian	8-13

WOOLWICH near the A205 South Circular, south-east London

Firepower - The Royal Artillery Museum: The home of the Royal Regiment of Artillery's international collection of 800 artillery pieces – from bronze guns to missile systems. Within the 'Field of Fire' theme can be found experiences of 20th century warfare with the Auster AOP.9 dramatically suspended above.

◆ **Access:** *Close to Woolwich ferry and Woolwich Arsenal station.* **Open:** *Tue to Sat 10:30 to 18:00 - last admission 16:30 - so,* **closed** *Sun and Mon.* **Note:** *The 'Field of Fire' exhibition is* **only** *open twice a day – check for times.* **Contact:** *Royal Arsenal, Woolwich, London SE18 6ST* | **020 8855 7755 | info@firepower.org.uk | www.firepower.org.uk**

❑ XR271	Auster AOP.9	62	ex Larkhill, St Athan, Middle Wallop. NEA 8-11-68	12-12
❑ XT583	Northrop Shelduck D.1	~	-	3-12

GREATER MANCHESTER

Includes the unitary authorities of Bolton, Bury, Manchester, Oldham, Rochdale, Stockport, Tameside, Trafford, Warrington and Wigan

ASHTON-UNDER-LYNE - See under Stalybridge, Gtr Man

LEVENSHULME on the A6 south-east of Manchester

No.**1940 Squadron Air Cadets**: St Oswald's Road. 'JP T.3' XM474 cockpit moved to South Reddish, Gtr Man, by late 2013.

❑ WG418	DHC Chipmunk T.10	51	ex 8209M (4-8-72), Woodvale, Hamble, Jever SF, Lon UAS, G-ATDY (de-reg 19-1-68), 61 GCF, QUB UAS, Lon UAS, 3 BFTS, 16 RFS	[1]	1-06

■ **[1]** The rear end of WG418 is at London Colney, Herts.

MANCHESTER

Imperial War Museum North: The building is designed to represent a shattered globe, and three 'shards' of this 'Air', 'Earth' and 'Water' plus the Main Exhibition Space are the main elements. IWM, of course, runs a series of sites. From a *W&R* point of view the two dominant ones are Duxford, Cambs, and South Lambeth, Gtr Lon.

◆ **Access:** *'Brown signed' from the end of the M602. Nearest Metrolink is MediaCityUK.* **Open:** *Daily (except Xmas) 10:00 to 17:00 - last admission 16:30.* **Contact:** *The Quays, Trafford Wharf Road, Trafford Park, Manchester M17 1TZ* | **0161 836 4000 | iwmnorth@iwm.org.uk | www.iwm.org.uk/north**

❑ 159233	'CG'	HS AV-8A Harrier	74	ex Yeovilton, VMA-231, USMC	3-12

Spitfire FR.XIV MT847 leaving the Air and Space Gallery of the Museum of Science and Industry, Manchester, 9th February 2104. *Courtesy and copyright Trustees of the Royal Air Force Museum*

Museum of Science and Industry (MOSI): From early 2012, the National Museum of Science and Industry combine, headed by the Science Museum welcomed MOSI into to the group. (See under South Kensington, Gtr London.) The **Air and Space Gallery** occupies what was the Lower Campfield Market Hall. The **Revolution Manchester Gallery**, in the Great Western Warehouse site, includes a replica of the world's first aircraft to fly with a fully enclosed cockpit - the Avro Type F.

Most of the airframes here are on loan, from the **RAF Museum** - see Hendon, Gtr Lon, and Cosford, Shropshire, among others - and from **The Aeroplane Collection** - see under Hooton Park, Cheshire, for TAC's main entry. As well as on-site storage for smaller items, MOSI has a site at Swinton, Gtr Man - which see.

The cockpit of Vulcan B.2 XM602 is on loan at Woodford, Gtr Man. Spitfire FR.XIV MT847 moved to Hendon, Gtr London, on 9th February 2014. Stored Jet Provost T.4 XS179 moved to Nantwich, Cheshire, on 15th January 2013.

◆ **Open:** *Daily from 10:00 to 17:00, including Bank Hols but excluding Dec 23-25 and New Year.* **Contact:** *Liverpool Road, Castlefield, Manchester M3 4FP* | **0161 832 2244** | **email via impenetrable website** | **www.mosi.org.uk**

Air and Space Gallery:

❑ G-EBZM	Avro Avian IIIA	28	ex Higher Blagdon, Peel Green, Lymm, Liverpool, Huyton, Manchester, Hesketh Park. CoA 20-1-38, de-reg 1-12-46	[1]	1-14
❑ G-ABAA	Avro 504K	c18	ex 'H2311', 9244M, Henlow, Heathrow, RAeS, Hendon, Nash collection, Brooklands. CoA 11-4-39, de-reg 1-1-39	[2]	1-14
❑ G-ADAH	Dragon Rapide	35	ex East Fortune, Peel Green, Booker. CoA 9-6-47, de-reg 18-2-59. Allied Airways colours, *Pioneer*	[1]	1-14
❑ 'G-ADYO' 'BHP.1'	Mignet HM.14 'Flea'	36	BAPC.12, ex East Fortune, Chester-le-Street, Newcastle, Wigan, Stockport, Rishworth. Dismantled	[1] [3]	1-14
❑ G-APUD	Wallis-Bensen B.7MC	59	ex Firbeck, Nostell Priory, Wigan, Biggin Hill. CoA 27-9-60, de-reg 27-2-70	[1]	1-14
❑ G-AWZP	HS Trident 3B-101	71	ex Heathrow, BA, BEA. CoA 14-3-86, de-reg 27-6-86. Cockpit		1-14
❑ G-AYTA	MS Rallye Club	71	ex Moston, Wickenby. CoA 7-11-88, de-reg 12-5-93. 'Hands on' exhibit		1-14
❑ G-BLKU	Colt 56 SS hot-air balloon	84	ex Newbury. CoA 29-4-91, de-reg 1-5-92	[4]	1-14
❑ G-BYMT	Pegasus Quantum 15-912	99	ex Strathaven. De-reg 10-8-10		1-14
❑ G-CFTF	Roe Triplane I replica	09	flight trials 10-09. Kept off-site	[5]	1-14
❑ G-MJXE	Mainair Tri-Flyer	82	ex Droylesden, Blackpool. CoA 21-3-95, de-reg 19-10-00	[1]	1-14
❑ BQT	EoN 460 Srs 1	64	BGA.1156, ex Seighford, Staffs GC, EGC / BGA.2666, BGA.1156. CoA 18-4-97. Dismantled		3-12
❑ '14'	Roe Triplane replica	c53	BAPC.6, ex London, Southend, Irlam, Peel Green, Old Warden, Woodford. *Bullseye Avroplane*	[1] [6]	1-14
❑ –	Volmer VJ-23 Swingwing	77	BAPC.175, ex Old Warden	[7]	1-14
❑ –	Wood Ornithopter	c68	BAPC.182, ex Hale. Stored, dismantled		3-12
❑ –	Hiway Spectrum	c80	BAPC.251, ex Lytham. Built c 1980. Stored		3-12
❑ –	Flexiform hang-glider	c82	BAPC.252, ex Lancaster. Built Macclesfield c 1982. Stored		3-12
❑ –	Mignet HM.14 'Flea'	c86	stored, unfinished		3-04
❑ –	Skyhook Safari	c79	stored	[8]	3-12
❑ WG763	EE P.1A	55	ex Henlow 7816M, RAE. Last flight 7-12-59. Arr 17-8-82	[2]	1-14
❑ WR960	Avro Shackleton AEW.2	54	ex Cosford, 8772M (28-11-82), 8, 205, A&AEE, 210, 42, 228	[2]	1-14
❑ WZ736	Avro 707A	53	ex Waddington, Cosford, Finningley, Colerne 7868M, RAE Bedford, A&AEE, Avro	[2]	1-14
❑ XG454	Bristol Belvedere HC.1	60	ex Henlow, 8366M, Abingdon, A&AEE, Bristol, Old Sarum, Belvedere Trials Unit. Accident 30-8-61	[2]	1-14
❑ 997	Yokosuka Ohka 11	c44	BAPC.98, ex 8485M, Henlow, Cottesmore, Cranwell	[2]	1-14

Revolution Manchester Gallery:

❑ -	Avro Type F replica	10	in the 'Revolution' gallery in main museum	1-14

■ **[1]** Airframes on loan from The Aeroplane Collection. **[2]** Airframes on loan from the RAF Museum. **[3]** Painted in the colours of a 'Flea' built by Brian Henry Park in Wigan; the link being that the Scott A.2S engine from the original G-ADYO is fitted to BAPC.12. **[4]** Colt on loan from the British Balloon Museum and Library. **[5]** Triplane built by the Roe Heritage Group, is registered to Eric Alliott Verdon-Roe, grandson of 'AV', and powered by a 9hp JAP. **[6]** Triplane acquired by NAPS (later TAC) from Shuttleworth 24-10-69. **[7]** Flown by David Cook across the Channel 9-5-78 - first hang-glider to do so. Last flown 8-5-81 and presented to Shuttleworth; to Manchester 29-9-93. **[8]** Skyhook flown by Len Gabriel London to Paris 27-8-79 and presented to the museum by Len.

No.**184 Squadron Air Cadets**: Mauldeth Road West.

❑ XN466	Hunting Jet Provost T.3A	60	ex Radcliffe, 1 FTS, 7 FTS, 1 FTS. Crashed 29-1-63. Cockpit	11-07

MANCHESTER AIRPORT or Ringway EGCC

Runway Visitor Park: A series of viewing platforms allow great photographic possibilities of the airliners taxying by and 'Ringways' has huge windows allowing all-weather noshing and ogling!

- **Access:** *Off the A538 Wilmslow Road, between M56 Junction 6 and the airport tunnels. 'Brown signed' from access roads; on Sunbank Lane and Wilmslow Old Road - WA15 8XQ.* **Open:** *Daily from 8.30am to dusk - times may change in winter.* **Contact: 0161 4893932 | runwayvisitorpark.enquiries@manairport.co.uk | www.manchesterairport.co.uk/manweb.nsf/content/ concordeviewingpark**
- **Thinx:** *On the northern boundary of the airport, close to the threshold of Runway 24 Right, is the HQ of* W&R's *publishers,* **Crécy Publishing**, *and its sister company Airplan Flight Equipment. The well-stocked shop is always well worth a visit! Located beyond the end of the airport spur of the M56, off West Ringway Road, turn north into Shadowmoss Road and then turn right into the Ringway Trading Estate - M22 5LH* | **0161 4990023** | **www.crecy.co.uk**

❑ G-AWZK	HS Trident 3B-101	71	ex Heathrow, BA, BEA. CoA 14-10-86, de-reg 29-5-90 Arrived 11-9-05. BEA colours		1-14
❑ G-BOAC	BAC/Sud Concorde 102	75	ex BA, G-N81AC. CoA 16-5-05, de-reg 4-5-04. Arrived 31-10-03	[1]	1-14
❑ G-DMCA	Douglas DC-10-30	80	ex Monarch, N3016Z. CoA 11-3-03, de-reg 3-11-03. Arrived 19-12-03. Cockpit		1-14
❑ G-IRJX	HS 146 RJX 100 T2	01	ex Woodford, G-6-378. de-reg 20-2-03. Arrived 6-2-03	[2]	1-14
❑ XV231	HS Nimrod MR.2	71	ex Kinloss, Kin Wing, Kin & St M Wing, 42, 203, 236 OCU. Arrived 27-4-06		1-14

■ **[1]** *Alpha-Charlie* factoids: Withdrawn from BA service 30-8-03, total hours 22,260, landings 7,730. This 'hot-rod' is looked after by Heritage Concorde - more of them on **www.heritageconcorde.com** - and is on long-term loan from British Airways. **[2]** The RJX is run in co-operation with Salford University's Department of Aeronautical Engineering, as an instructional airframe *and* exhibit. *Juliet-Xray* first flew 23-9-01 and last flew 6-2-03 when it arrived at its new home with a total of 198:23 hours and 135 landings.

Airport: Last noted in February 2007, the forward fuselage of Islander 'G-FOXY' (G-BLDX) was scrapped circa 2011 by a Northwich scrap dealer. On 18th May 2013 Trident 2E 'G-SMOKE' (G-AVFG) was scrapped and removed.

❑ –	BAe ATP	~	ex Chadderton. Unfinished fuselage. Fire crews	9-04

MANCHESTER (BARTON) AERODROME EGCB

or even City of Manchester Airport - on the A57 south of the M62/M63 junction at Eccles

Last noted here in December 2003, Scheibe SF-25A G-BECF was up for grabs via a pixelated auction in mid-2012, with a Morpeth, Northumberland, address. Another that slipped the net was Stinson HW-75 G-BMSA which was re-registered in May 2009 as G-MIRM and flying from a strip in the Warrington area by 2012. Bulldog T.1 XX522 (G-DAWG) moved by road to Blackpool, Lancs, 16th June 2012 and was quickly back in the skies. Two long-in-the-tooth references have been deleted: Cessna 210 G-ASXR (last noted Nov 2004) and Tiger Cub G-MMEP (Jun 2001).

❑ G-APUY	Druine Turbulent	63	CoA 10-6-86	1-14
❑ G-AREV	Piper Tri-Pacer 160	58	ex N9628D. CoA 29-1-08	1-14
❑ G-AZGF	Beagle Pup 150	69	ex PH-KUF, G-35-076. CoA 2-5-98	1-14

MANCHESTER WOODFORD AIRFIELD - listed under 'Woodford', see below

OLDHAM

Oldham College: Rochdale Road. **Access**: *by prior arrangement* **only** | **www.oldham.ac.uk**

❑ EI-CKR	Boeing 737-2K2	95	ex Prestwick, Ryanair, PH-TVR, C-FICP, PH-TVR, D-AJAA ntu, PH-TVR. Fuselage	2-06

ROYTON on the A671 north of Oldham

No.**1855 Squadron Air Cadets**: Park Lane.

❑ WS726	'H'	Gloster Meteor NF(T).14	53	ex 7960M (19-6-67), Kemble, 1 ANS, 2 ANS, 25. AWA-built. 25 Sqn colours	8-11

SALFORD south-west of Manchester

University of Salford, Faculty of Science, Engineering and Environment: Airframes are *believed* unchanged.

◆ **Access:** *By prior arrangement* **only** | **www.salford.ac.uk**

❑ OO-WIO		Cessna FRA.150L	~	ex Blackpool, F-BUMG. Reims-built. Simulator	7-05
❑ –		Volmer VJ-23 hang-glider	~	donated by Peter Barlow	7-99
❑ –		Rotec Rally 2B	~	ex North Coates, Binbrook	10-03

SOUTH REDDISH astoundingly *south* of *Reddish*, east of the A6, north of Junction 1 on the M60

No.**1804 Squadron Air Cadets**: Took on a Jet Provost cockpit by October 2013.

❑ XM474		Hunting Jet Provost T.3	60	ex Levenshulme, 8121M (15-12-70), Firbeck, Heaton Chapel, Warrington, Shrewsbury, Shawbury, 6 FTS, CFS. Cockpit	10-13

STALYBRIDGE on the A6018 east of Ashton-under-Lyne

Top Gun Flight Simulator Centre: The flight simulator operation previously at Ashton-under-Lyne has relocated the short distance to Stalybridge. The Delfin was 'written out' of *W&R23*, but serves on as a simulator. Off-site a Queen Air is stored.

◆ **Access:** *Private location, visits by prior permission only* | **www.topgunflightsimulator.co.uk**

❑ G-KEAB*		Beech Queen Air B80	67	ex Ashton-under-Lyne, Accrington, Bruntingthorpe, Shoreham, Manston, G-BSSL, G-BFEP, F-BRNR, OO-VDE. De-reg 24-5-91. Fuselage, stored off-site	10-12
❑ XK637*	'56'	DH Vampire T.11	56	ex Millom, Royton, Woodford, Chester, St Athan, 4 FTS, 7 FTS. SOC 30-11-67. Stored	10-12
❑ '47'*	692147	Aero L29 Delfin	~	ex Ashton-under-Lyne, Market Drayton, Romanian AF. Cockpit, simulator	10-12

STOCKPORT on the A6 south-east of Manchester

Roger Light: Campbell-Bensen B.8 G-ASNY is on loan to the Newark Air Museum at Newark Showground, Notts.

Access **Private** *collection, visits possible by prior arrangement* **only**

❑ G-ATLH		Fewsdale Tiger Mk.1	r65	ex Thornaby-on-Tees. De-reg 10-2-82	4-09
❑ G-AXIY		Bird Gyroplane	r69	de-reg 9-8-91	4-09

Peter and **Mike Rolfe**: **Private** *location, visits by prior permission* **only** | **http://WN957.webs.com**

❑ WN957		Hawker Hunter F.5	54	ex 'Devon', Welshpool, Llanbedr, Stafford, N Weald, Chivenor, Leconfield, St Athan 7407M (21-2-57), RAE. AWA-built. Cockpit	6-12
❑ XG692	'668'	DH Sea Venom FAW.22	57	ex Baxterley, Hatton, Alcester, Wellesbourne Mountford, Sydenham, Castlereagh, Sydenham, 750. SOC 20-8-70. Pod	6-12

SWINTON on the A580, M60 J14, in north-west Manchester

Museum of Science and Industry: Storage facility. See under Manchester, Gtr Man, for the museum itself. The cockpit of Vulcan B.2 XM602 returned to its birthplace, Woodford, Gtr Man, on 20th April 2013. The unfinished RJX (c/n E3396) moved to Filton, Glos, 6th December 2013.

◆ **Access: Strictly** *by prior arrangement only*

❑ ZE966		Panavia Tornado F.3	89	ex St Athan, 111, 56, 11, 25, 11, 43	3-12

WESTHOUGHTON on the A58 south-west of Bolton

A Draken is stored in a yard in the area.

❑ A-011		SAAB A.35XD Draken	c62	ex Grainthorpe, New Waltham, Danish AF Esk.729	1-13

WIGAN north-west of Manchester

Ponsford Collection: See Breighton, E Yorks, and Selby, N Yorks, for the bulk of Nigel's 'fleet'.

◆ **Access:** *By prior arrangement* **only**.

❑ CHQ		Slingsby Tandem Tutor	59	BGA.1559, ex Bury St Edmunds, Leeds, RAFGSA.316, XN247, 622 GS. CoA 1-7-82	1-14
❑ –		Addyman STG	c35	BAPC.15, ex Warmingham, Wigan, Harrogate	1-14
❑ RA848		Slingsby Cadet TX.1	c44	ex Harrogate, Wigan, Handforth. Cockpit	1-14

WOODFORD between the A5102 and A523 south-west of Poynton

Avro Heritage Centre: In mid-2013 the centre re-located to the Old Fire Station and began consolidating at its new home. Prior to this, Vulcan XM603 trundled across on 17th February 2013 and the cockpit of XM602 arrived from storage at Swinton. Previously given under this location, restoration of Avro 504L G-EASD is now listed under Scarborough, N Yorks.

◆ **Access:** *By prior arrangement* only. **Contact**: *Avro Heritage Centre, Chester Road, Woodford, Stockport, SK7 1QR* | **0161 4400487 | avroheritage@gmail.com | www.avroheritage.com**

❑ XM602*	Avro Vulcan B.2	63	ex Swinton, Bruntingthorpe, Woodford, St Athan 8771M (16-3-83), 101, Wadd Wing, 35, 230 OCU, Wadd W, Cott W, 12. Cockpit. Arrived 20-4-13	[1]	1-14
❑ XM603	Avro Vulcan B.2	63	ex 44, 101, Wadd Wing, Scampton Wing, 9. Flew in 12-3-82		1-14

■ **[1]** XM602 is on loan from MOSI - see Manchester, above.

Former BAE Systems site: A few things to clear up from *W&R23* (p154) and *W&R22* (p149) thanks to Mike Higginbottom and Ken Haynes. First off, the price paid by Avro Heritage (the former JCB Real Estate organisation and *not* to be confused with the above) was given as a real bargain, even in these days of austerity: I typed £100, it should have read a credit card-trembling £100m! The far from unflown RJX prototype G-ORJX departed by road to Prestwick, Scotland, on 7th June 2011 - see under that entry for more. The first production RJX was G-6-391, destined for British European. This first flew on 9th January 2002 and last took to the air seven days later, clocking just 8:55 hours and five landings. The fin and wings were cut off on 17th October 2002 and the fuselage moved outside on 24th January 2004. Chevron Aerospace started dismantling it in May 2004 and it was finally cut up in early July. Unflown RJX85 c/n E2395 was used in two evacuation/rescue trials in October 2003 and July 2005. It was scrapped by Sandbach Car and Commercial Dismantlers on 17th September 2009. As *W&R* went to press, the bulldozers were poised...

MERSEYSIDE

Includes the unitary authorities of Knowsley, Liverpool, St Helens, Sefton and Wirral

BIRKDALE on the A565 south-west of Southport

No.**281 Squadron Air Cadets**: In Upper Aughton Road, keep a 'Chippax'.

❑ WG477	DHC Chipmunk T.10 PAX	51	8362M (22-8-73), ex CoAT Hamble G-ATDP (de-reg 15-1-68), G-ATDI, Marham SF, MECS,114, Bri UAS, Abn UAS, 11 RFS, 2 BFTS, 25 RFS, Liv UAS, 25 RFS. Off-site	10-10

BIRKENHEAD DOCKS Wasp HAS.1 XS570 moved to Kirkham, Lancs, on 21st March 2012.

LIVERPOOL

Crowne Plaza Hotel: With the blessing of the hotel management, the **Speke Aerodrome Heritage Group** nurtures its collection. Located on the 'old' airport site, Speke, the superb hotel is a development of the 1930s terminal building. The 'new' airport (opened in 1986) is called Liverpool (John Lennon) - see below. Until 20th February 2014, the hotel had been 'guarded' by a replica Rapide; this has been dismantled and stored awaiting a decision on its future.

◆ **Access:** *On the A561 Widnes to Liverpool Road.* **Open:** *Sat 11:00 to 16:00 - other times by prior arrangement.* **Contact:** *Rob Taylor, 69 Knaresborough Road, Wallasey, CH44 2BQ* | **info@spekeaero.org | www.spekeaero.org**

❑ 'G-AJCL'	DH Dragon Rapide FSM	01	BAPC.280, ex 'G-ANZP', 'G-AEAJ'. Stored, off-site	[1]	2-14
❑ G-AMLZ	Percival Prince 6E	52	ex Haverigg, Caernarfon, Coventry, VR-TBN ntu, G-AMLZ. CoA 18-6-71, de-reg 9-10-84. Shell Aviation colours	[2]	2-14
❑ G-BEJD	HS 748-1/105	61	ex Squires Gate, Emerald, LV-HHE, LV-PUF. CoA 29-3-06, de-reg 8-4-10	[3]	2-14
❑ G-JMAC	BAe Jetstream 4100	92	ex Woodford, Prestwick, G-JAMD, G-JXLI. CoA 6-10-97, de-reg 21-5-03. *Spirit of Speke*	[4]	2-14
❑ G-ORAL	HS 748-2A/334	77	ex Hooton Park, Blackpool, Reed, Emerald, Janes, G-BPDA, G-GLAS, 9Y-TFS, G-11-8. CoA 12-11-07, de-reg 15-6-09. *The Paper Plane*. Cockpit	[5]	2-14

❑ G-SEXY		American AA-1 Yankee	70	ex G-AYLM. Damaged 11-2-94, de-reg 15-11-00. Stored	2-14
❑ WH291		Gloster Meteor F.8	51	ex Wycombe Air Park, Lasham, Kemble, 229 OCU, 85, CAW, 257. SOC 10-2-76. 79 Sqn colours. Dismantled	2-14

■ **[1]**.The *real* G-AJCL served with Cambrian Airways as *Flint* 1949-1959 and frequented the apron on the opposite side of the hotel. **[2]** *Lima-Zulu* factoids: last flown 13-11-73, total time 2,858 hours. **[3]** This puts many of the 'biggie' museums to shame: it is the only Srs 1 (15 built) surviving; so it's the oldest 748 extant; and the only complete civilian 748 preserved in the UK. **[4]** See Humberside, Lincs, for *another* 'G-JXLI'. **[5]** *The Paper Plane* and the Meteor are on loan from Mike Davey - see below and Newark Showground, Notts.

Britannia Aircraft Preservation Trust: Sharing the apron at Speke is BAPT which continues to make progress with the challenging restoration of *Charlie-Fox*. See Filton, Glos, for notes on Britannia 101 cockpit G-ALRX..

◆ **Access:** *By prior arrangement* **only**. **Contact:** *12 Northway, Lewes, BN7 1DS* | **01273 476283** | **britboss1@aol.com** | **www.bristol-britannia.com**

❑ G-ANCF		Bristol Britannia 308F	59	ex Kemble, Banwell, Brooklands, Manston, 5Y-AZP, G-ANCF, LV-GJB, LV-PPJ, G-ANCF ntu, G-14-1, G-18-4, N6597C ntu, G-ANCF. CoA 12-1-81, de-reg 21-2-84. British Eagle colours, Short-built. *New Frontier*	2-14

Jordan and **Robbie Burgess**: Make great progress with the restoration of their AV-8B cockpit.

◆ **Access:** *By prior arrangement* **only** | **www.av-8blucy.blogspot.com**

❑ 162730		HS AV-8B Harrier II	86	ex Peterborough, Charlwood, St Athan, Wyton, St Athan, USMC. *Lucy*. Forward fuselage, trailer-mounted	3-13

Mike Davey - F-4 Phantom Preservation Society: As well as his airframes on site at the Crown Plaza - see above - Mike has others in store off-site and here serves as a good place under which to list them. See also Newark Showground, Notts, for Mike's other Phantom. With so much phabulous Phantom hardware to hand, it may well be that Mike has the largest collection of F-4-bilia in private hands in the world!

◆ **Access:** *At dispersed locations, not available for inspection*

❑ G-AGPG*		Avro XIX Srs 2	45	ex Market Drayton, Hooton Park, Chadderton, Brenzett, Southend, Pye, Ekco, Avro. CoA 13-12-71; de-reg 5-11-75. Cockpit. Arrived by 4-13	12-13
❑ WL405*		Gloster Meteor T.7	52	ex Hooton Park, Bruntingthorpe, Yatesbury, Chalgrove, Farnborough, BCCS, 1 GCF, 231 OCU, Wittering SF, JCU, Hemswell CF. SOC 1-4-69. Arrived 7-12	12-13
❑ ZE352	'G'	McD F-4J(UK) Phantom	67	ex Hooton Park, Haverigg, Preston, Hooton Park area, Stock, Foulness, Pendine, Laarbruch 9086M (30-8-84), 74, Wattisham, 74, USN 153783, VX-4, VMFA-333. Cockpit. Arrived 7-12	12-13
❑ -		McD Phantom SIM	~	ex Leuchars. Redifon-built	12-13

Liverpool University: Within the vast campus a former John Lennon Tomahawk has been converted into a simulator.

❑ G-LFSD		Piper Tomahawk 112	82	ex Liverpool Airport, G-BNPT, G-LFSD, N91522. Cr 9-9-06, CoA 13-7-08, de-reg 26-10-10. Fuselage, simulator	6-13

LIVERPOOL (JOHN LENNON) **AIRPORT** or Speke — EGGP

❑ EI-CIJ		Cessna 340	73	ex G-BBVE, N69451. Forward fuselage by 6-12	6-12

NEW BRIGHTON on the A554 north of Birkenhead

Fort Perch Rock: The fort has a great strapline: 'Defending Merseyside's Heritage since 1829'. Home of the **Warplane Wreck Investigation Group** since 1977; this coastal defence fort is amazing enough, but WWIG's extensive recovery items, including the 'Luftwaffe over Merseyside' exhibition, are incredible.

◆ **Access:** *Off the A554. Fort Perch Rock, Marine Promenade, New Brighton, CH45 2JU.* **Open:** *Tue to Sun (ie* **not** *Mon) 10:00 to 17:00. Also all Bank Hols and all week during school holidays.* **Contact**: **0797 6282120** | **www.fortperchrock.org**

WOODVALE AIRFIELD on the A565 north of Formby

RAF Woodvale: What must be regarded as one of the most tenacious RAF stations of recent decades gained a 'gate guardian' in June 2013. Its last incumbent was Phantom FGR.2 XV468 which was scrapped in July 2001 - see *W&R18*, p159

❑ XW420*	'MU'	BAC Jet Provost T.5A	71	ex Cosford 9194M (7-6-93), ex 1 FTS, RAFC. Arrived 25-6-13. Gate	9-13

WEST MIDLANDS

Within the administrative regional county boundaries can be found the unitary authorities of Birmingham, Coventry, Dudley, Sandwell, Solihull, Walsall and Wolverhampton

BIRMINGHAM

Thinktank – Millennium Discovery Centre, the former **Birmingham Science Museum**:

◆ **Access:** *South of the A38/A4540 junction, near New Street Station.* **Open:** *Daily 10:00 to 17:00, last entry 16:00 - not open during the Xmas hostilities.* **Contact:** *Millennium Point, Curzon Street, Birmingham, B4 7XG* | **0121 202 2222** | **findout@thinktank.ac** | **www.thinktank.ac**

❑ 'P3395'	'JX-B'	Hawker Hurricane IV KX829	43	ex Loughborough, 631, 1606 Flt, 137. SOC 8-3-46 1 Sqn colours	[1]	1-14
❑ ML427	'HK-A'	Supermarine Spitfire IX	44	ex Castle Bromwich, St Athan, South Marston, Millfield, Hucknall, 6457M (15-10-47), FLS, 3501 SU. FLS colours		1-14

■ **[1]** In the colours of Flt Lt Arthur 'Darky' Clowes DFM.

John Fawke: *W&R* last mentioned John in the 18th edition, under Solihull, W Midlands. A move of house dropped him off the radar, as occasionally happens. John is working on the oldest Spitfire components extant and makes great progress, although the project does not (yet) merit a formal listing. Jeffrey Quill lifted Mk.I K9851, the 64th production example, into the air for the first time at Eastleigh on 23rd January 1939. Four days later it joined 19 Squadron at Duxford. It became 2467M at Kirkham, Lancs, in March 1941. It was cut up and buried but rediscovered and John intends his long-term static reconstruction to incorporate as many original parts as possible.

◆ **Access:** *Private location, viewing by prior arrangement* **only** | **j.fawke1@btinternet.com**

COVENTRY

Coventry University: The Faculty of Engineering and Computing moved its Aerospace Workshop from Alma Street, Hillfields to Gulson Road. The Harrier T.4 made the move on 10th September 2012. On the same day, Scout AH.1 XR635 moved to Coventry Airport, Warks, on loan to the Midland Air Museum.

◆ **Access:** *Busy campus, visits by prior arrangement* **only** | **wwwm.coventry.ac.uk**

❑ XW270	HS Harrier T.4	70	ex Ipswich, Bruntingthorpe, Cranfield, Wittering, 4, 1, 233 OCU, 1, 233 OCU. SOC 10-2-92	[1]	6-13

■ **[1]** Fitted with the wings of XV748 - which is to be found whole at Elvington, N Yorks. The cockpit is fitted out as a flight sim.

Also: Previously given under this location, Chilton DW.1A G-AFSV is now listed under Warwick, Warks. P-51D Mustang restoration project 413954 (G-UAKE), last noted in February 2006, has moved on to another Midlands workshop.

HOCKLEY HEATH east of junction 4, M42, south of Solihull

Delta Force Paintball Solihull: (Also known as Delta Force Paintball Birmingham). Within this large site is an Aztec at Pablo Escobar's Jungle Airstrip - your chance to wipe out a Colombian drug baron! The Aztec was previously erroneously listed under Ollerton, Cheshire, and was 'written out' of this location in *W&R20* (p159) but appears never to have moved.

◆ **Access:** *Busy site, access by prior arrangement* **only** | **www.paintballgames.co.uk**

❑ G-SHIP*	Piper Aztec 250F	76	ex Hockley Heath, Coventry, Birmingham, N62490. Crashed 4-12-83, de-reg 13-2-89	5-12

SANDWELL east of the M5 and the junction of the A4182 and A4252, north of Smethwick

West Midlands Fire Service Academy: Dartmouth Road **Access:** *Visits by prior arrangement* **only** | **www.wmfs.net**

❑ G-WMCC	BAe Jetstream 3102	81	ex Birmingham Airport, G-31-601, G-TALL, G-31-601. CoA 1-11-99, de-reg 26-11-97	10-11

WILLENHALL on the A454 west of J10 of the M6

Triple-R Solutions Ltd: Rose Hill. The Lansen was broken up by October 2013; the cockpit survives.

❑ G-BMSG	SAAB Lansen	56	ex Cranfield, Swedish AF, Malmslatt, Fv32028. Cockpit	10-13

WOLVERHAMPTON

Boulton Paul Aircraft Heritage Project: Two years short of the centenary of the founding of Boulton Paul Aircraft, the curtain was brought down on the exceptional heritage project and the site in Wobaston Road was vacated in April 2013. As related in *W&R23*, Moog Aviation Group relocated to a brand-new factory site nearby, and the former BP plant is to be redeveloped. A helping hand was extended by RAF Museum Cosford and the extensive archive has moved to the storage site at Stafford. Large artefacts and the project airframes moved to storage at Cosford, Shropshire - which see. Making the move were the following: P-6 replica 'X-25' and the Overstrand forward fuselage replica on 23rd April 2013; Defiant replica 'L7005', Balliol T.2 WN149, Hunter T.53 cockpit 'XE531' (ET-272) all in April 2013.

Other departures: The unfinished fuselage of ANEC Missel Thrush G-FBPI moved out prior to the closure; destination unknown. Slingsby Tutor CFZ moved to Keevil, Wilts, by February 2013. StART airframes Canberra T.`7 cockpit WJ576, Balliol T.2 WN534, Grasshopper TX.1 XP494 and Jet Provost T.4 XR662 all moved, at least initially, to Baxterley, Warks.

Mick Boulanger and **Mark Ray**: 'JP' T.5 XW315 cockpit moved to a new home in Preston, Lancs, on 27th June 2012.

No.**1046 Squadron Air Cadets**: Bee Lane, Fordhouses.

❑ WK576*	DHC Chipmunk T.10 PAX		52	ex Lichfield, 8357M (10-8-73), AOTS, 3/4 CAACU, Cam UAS, Oxf UAS, Lon UAS, Cam UAS, Lon UAS, Cam UAS, Hull UAS, Cam UAS, Bir UAS, Cam UAS, 22 RFS. First noted 6-12	9-13

NORFOLK

ATTLEBOROUGH on the A11 south-west of Norwich

Last noted in April 2006, Evans VP-1 G-PFAG, Robinson R22 G-SUMT plus an anonymous one, Slingsby T.59 CSA and Schleicher K8B FCQ have been deleted.

BIRCHAM NEWTON between the B1153 and B1155 north-east of Docking

RAF Bircham Newton Memorial Project: There are times when you think you've got your finger on the pulse, then circumstances remind you that this was *never* the case... Opened on 28th July 2005, the volunteers of this project have erected memorials and established a treasure trove of a museum dedicated to the famous RAF station (1918-1962) and its satellite field at Docking. The airfield is home of a major campus for the Construction Industry Training Board.

◆ **Open:** *Regular open days - see the website for details. Other times by appointment.* **Contact: email via website | www.rafbnmp.org.uk**

BODNEY CAMP on the B1108 west of Watton

Army Training Estate (ATE) **East**: South of the camp is an extensive training area, centred upon Stanford Water and referred to as STANTA, for Stanford Training Area. See also East Wretham, below.

❑ XS872	Westland Wessex HAS.1	65	ex Wroughton, Farnborough, A2666, Leatherhead, Wroughton, *Eagle* SAR Flt, 706, 820. SOC 18-5-78	12-13

CANTLEY on the B1140 south of Acle

Great British Aircraft Spares: Bruce Gordon's Vampires multiply! He keeps them and the DHAHC Venom pod in the area. The latter is a long term restoration project. **Access:** *Airframes within a **private** store* | **www.gbairspares.co.uk**

❑ WZ584	'K'	DH Vampire T.11	G-BZRC	53	ex Armthorpe, Sandtoft, North Coates, St Albans, Hatfield, CATCS, 1 FTS, 2 CAACU, 32. SOC 11-12-70, de-reg 22-2-05		9-13
❑ XD547*	'Z'	DH Vampire T.11		54	ex Elgin, Felixkirk, Dumfries, Aberfoyle, Strathallan, Milngavie, Glasgow, CATCS, 8 FTS, 1 RS, 263. SOC 22-3-71	[1]	9-13
❑ XE979*	'54'	DH Vampire T.11		55	ex Birlingham, Standish, Woodford, Chester, St Athan, 1 FTS, 8 FTS, RAFC. SOC 12-12-68. Cockpit		9-13
❑ XH328		DH Vampire T.11		56	ex London Colney, Duxford, Bournemouth, Cranfield, Hemel Hempstead, Croxley Green, Bushey, Keevil, Exeter, 3 CAACU, 60. SOC 22-6-71. Pod		9-13
❑ J-1632		DH Venom FB.50	G-VNOM	56	ex London Colney, Cranfield, Bridgend, Bruntingthorpe, Cranfield, Swiss AF. FAF-built. Pod. De-reg 27-6-11		9-13

■ [1] XD547 has the wings of XD425 – see Seaton Burn, N&T.

COLTISHALL east of the B1150, north of Coltishall

During January 2013 Norfolk County Council bought a substantial (600-plus acres) chunk of the site for development, alongside the existing HMP Bure, which occupies much of the domestic site. Plans are at an early stage, but an early project was the clearing of undergrowth from a World War Two fighter pan; there will be a heritage element within the grand plan. As *W&R* closed for press, this was a long way from fruition.

EAST WINCH AERODROME north of the A47, east of the village and south of Gayton

❑ G-PULL*	Piper Super Cub 150	57	ex Boston, Tattershall Thorpe, PH-MBB, ALAT 18-5356. Crashed 13-6-86, de-reg 25-11-87. Frame	11-12
❑ SE-EAN	Cessna 150B	~	fuselage	10-11

EAST WRETHAM east of the A1075 north of Thetford

Thorpe Camp: See also the 'northern' end of this area, listed under Bodney Camp, Norfolk.

❑ XM386	'08'	Hunting Jet Provost T.3	59	ex St Athan, Halton 8076M (2-2-70), Shawbury, 2 FTS, CFS [1]	6-12
❑ XT643		Westland Scout AH.1	66	ex Waterbeach, Wroughton, 660, 661	6-12

■ **[1]** The wings alongside the fuselage of XM386 are from XM404 - see Moreton-in-Marsh, Glos.

FAKENHAM south of the A148, between King's Lynn and Holt

A Terrier is under restoration locally.

❑ G-ARLP*	Beagle Terrier	48	ex T.10 / AOP.6 VX123, 663, 661.	12-13

FRETTENHAM east of the A140, south west of Coltishall

New Farm Aviation Heritage Group: Material held includes the remains of 458th BG, 754th BS B-24H 42-50404 *Belle of Boston* which crashed on take-off from Horsham St Faith (Norwich Airport) on 8th May 1944.

◆ **Open:** *Occasional special events, otherwise by appointment* **only. Contact:** *nfahg@yahoo.com* | **http://sites.google.com/site/nfaviationheritagecroup/**

GREAT YARMOUTH

Sea-Front Crazee Golf, has the hulk of a Centurion as part of the course.

❑ G-MANT	Cessna 210L II	75	ex Oxford, G-MAXY, N550SV. Cr 16-2-92, de-reg 3-4-92	6-06

Vauxhall Holiday Park, in 'Louie the Lion's Adventure Golf', is an Aerobat.

❑ G-BPRO	Cessna A.150K	70	ex N221AR. CoA 24-3-99, de-reg 23-11-00	6-06

HARDWICK or Shelton Common, east of the A140, west of Bungay

93rd Bomb Group Museum: An incredible museum set in three Nissen huts, with another under renovation and the all-important Mess (sorry, that would be Chow) Hall on the former Station 104's Communal Site A. Displays are exceptional and the welcome is warm!

◆ **Open:** *Third Sun of each month, May to Oct. 10:00 to 17:00 plus special events - see the website. Other times by appointment.* **Contact:** *Paul Thrower, 12 St David's Close, Long Stratton, NR15 2PP* | **01508 531405** | **email via website** | **www.93rd-bg-museum.org.uk**

❑ XK418	Auster AOP.9	56	ex South Molton, Lasham, Basingstoke, Thruxton, Netheravon, Middle Wallop 7976M (24-7-57), 19 MU, 12 Flt, Middle Wallop, LAS. Frame	12-11

HETHEL north of the B1135, east of Wymondham

389th Bomb Group Memorial Exhibition and **Home for the 466th BG Attlebridge**: Volunteers have restored Station 114's wartime chapel and the buildings around it; a unique element of Eighth Air Force history.

◆ **Access:** *Within the grounds of Potash Farm, Hethel. Turn off the B1135 into Potash Lane, close to the Lotus Engineering facility, and carry on past the Lotus plant, then follow the signs.* **Open:** *Second Sun of the months of Apr to Oct, 10:00 to 16:00 - other times by appointment.* **Contact:** *The Old Chapel, Potash Farm, Potash Lane, Hethel, Norwich, NR14 8EY* | **01953 607147** | **hethel389@hotmail.co.uk** | **www.hethel389th.wordpress.com**

Note: *The control tower is within the secure Lotus site and available for inspection* **only** *by prior arrangement.*

LITTLE SNORING AERODROME
Last noted in October 2005, PL-4A G-FISK has been deleted.

MARHAM AIRFIELD south of the A47 west of Swaffham EGYM

RAF Marham: With the **Tornado Training School** (TTS) Tornado GR.4 ZA594 returned to service by 2013 with another taking its place. The **Tornado Maintenance Flight** (TMF) has a purpose-built cockpit as a training aid. Another cockpit training aid was delivered in late 2013.

❑ XH169		EE Canberra PR.9	60	ex 39, 1 PRU, 39, 58. Short-built. *End of an Era*. Unveiled 20-11-07. 'Gate'		7-13
❑ XH673		HP Victor K.2	60	ex 8911M (2-7-86), 57, B.2, Witt Wing, 139. Outside SHQ. 55 and 57 Sqn colours		12-13
❑ ZA267		Panavia Tornado F.2	80	ex 9284M, Boscombe Down. Instructional		8-12
❑ 'ZA305'		Panavia Tornado IDS	~	cockpit, TMF - see above		8-12
❑ ZA356		Panavia Tornado GR.1	80	ex St Athan, 15. Cockpit, TTS		8-12
❑ ZA407		Panavia Tornado GR.1	83	ex 9336M, 617, TWCU. Plinth-mounted, in the camp	[1]	11-13
❑ ZA549	'060'	Panavia Tornado GR.4	81	ex 15, 13. TTS. First noted 12-11		12-13
❑ -*	'GS400'	Panavia Tornado IDS	~	cockpit, ex Selby. Arrived 10-13		10-13

■ **[1]** ZA407 last flew 22-11-01 and was unveiled 2-11-04.

NARBOROUGH south of the A47, north-west of Swaffham

Wellesley Aviation: *Private* location, by prior arrangement **only**.

❑ WH850	EE Canberra T.4	54	ex Winthorpe, Barton, Chelford, Samlesbury, St Athan, Laarbruch SF, Wildenrath SF, 14, 88, Marham SF. SOC 26-11-81. Cockpit	11-13

NEATISHEAD east of the A1151, north of Hoveton, near Horning

RAF Air Defence Radar Museum: On 9th August 2012 ownership of the museum site was transferred from the MoD to the Board of Trustees of the museum, thus ensuring its long-term prospects. Dedicated to every aspect of radar, air defence and battle management and housed in the original 1942 Operations Building, exhibits include a Battle of Britain 'Ops' Filter Room, a 'Cold War' era 'Ops' Room and a ROC Field Post. The Jaguar is within the RAF Coltishall Heritage Memorial Room.

◆ **Access:** *'Brown signed' off the A1062, Hoveton road.* **Open:** *Second Sat of each month all year, Bank Hols and every Tue and Thu, early Apr to end of Oct. Times: 10:00 to 17:00. Group visits by prior arrangement.* **Contact:** *Neatishead, Norwich, NR12 8YB* | **01692 631485** | **curator@radarmuseum.co.uk** | **www.radarmuseum.co.uk**

❑ XX979	SEPECAT Jaguar GR.1A	75	ex Coltishall 9306M, St Athan, DTEO, A&AEE. Cockpit	2-14

NORWICH

County Hall: In Martineau Lane, off the A1054 between Lakenham and Old Lakenham south of the city centre.

❑ XW563	SEPECAT Jaguar S.07	70	ex Coltishall, 8563M (26-1-78), 'XX822', Brüggen. *Spirit of Coltishall*. Displayed, plinth-mounted	[1]	4-12

■ **[1]** Composite, based upon the cockpit and forward fuselage of S.07 XW563 which first flew 12-6-70.

◆ **Thinx:** *Well worth a visit is the* ***2nd Air Division Memorial Library*** *inside The Forum on Millennium Plain in the middle of Norwich. Huge resources devoted to the illustrious history of the crews of the B-24-equipped 2nd AD stationed at bases all around the city. Plenty of memorabilia on show, along with the amazing 'Friendly Invasion' mural. Open Monday to Saturday* | **01603 774747** | **www.2ndair.org.uk**

Classic Aero Services: Phil Earthey and team have a workshop in the *general* area. (Phil owns Harvard G-HRVD - see Bruntingthorpe, Leics.) Fiat G.46 MM53211 moved to Shipdham, Norfolk, by August 2012. A fascinating re-registration in June 2012 was G-ARKD to the Classic Flying Machine Collection. CAC-built Mustang Mk.22 A68-5, became VH-BVM in 1953 and then *Kilo-Delta* in February 1961 in the name of Edinburgh-based Ronald Flockhart. It was intended for an Australia to UK speed attempt, but was abandoned at Athens, Greece, after a fire in the cockpit on 7th September 1961. It was reported to have been scrapped in the 1970s. For now, we'll give it a mention, but not a formal listing.

◆ **Access: Private** *workshop,* **strictly** *viewable by prior application* only

❑ G-WGHB	Lockheed T-33A/N Silver Star Mk.3	58	ex Booker, Gainsborough, Sandtoft, Portsmouth, S'ton, Coventry, Duxford, Southend, CF-EHB, CAF 21640, 133640. Canadair-built. CoA 13-6-77, de-reg 24-2-12	7-09

❑	G-CCOY		NAA Harvard II	42	ex Bruntingthorpe, Norwich, Swansea, 'Exeter', 'FT323', Cranfield, Bushey, East Ham, Port AF 1513, SAAF 7426, EX884 n/s, 41-33857. CCF-built	[1]	5-13
❑	44-72181		NAA P-51D-20-NA Mustang G-CEBW	44	ex 336th FS, 4th FG *Sunny VIII*. Crashed 29-5-45 Restoration project	[2]	11-08

■ **[1]** *Oscar-Yankee* is registered to Classic Flying Machine Collection. **[2]** P-51D project is registered to Dental Insurance Solutions Ltd.

Also: Last noted in June 2009; the hulk of Cessna 150E G-ATAT has been deleted. A Skeeter is kept in the general area.

❑	XN351*		Saro Skeeter AOP.12 G-BKSC	59	ex Saxmundham, Lossiemouth, Inverness, Shobdon, Cardiff, Higher Blagdon, Old Warden, Wroughton, 3 RTR, 652, 651. CoA 8-11-84, de-reg 11-10-00		1-14

NORWICH AIRPORT or Horsham St Faith EGSH

City of Norwich Aviation Museum (CNAM): RAF **100 Group Association** bases its exceptional collection within CNAM. (email **raf100groupassociation@gmail.com**). Other displays show the history of RAF Horsham St Faith, Bomber Command, the 8th Air Force, the role of women in aviation and local aviation pioneers. Grasshopper TX.1 XP458, long since noted as stored, was returned to its owner "many moons ago".

◆ **Access:** *From the A140, follow 'brown signs', ensuring you turn* right *at the church in Horsham St Faith.* **Open:** *Apr to Oct: Tue to Sat, 10:00 to 17:00; Sun and Bank Hols 12:00 to 17:00.* Note ***not*** *'normal' Mondays. Nov to Mar: Wed, Fri and Sat 10:00 to 16:00, Sun 11:00 to 15:00. Closed Christmas and New Year.* **Contact:** *Old Norwich Road, Horsham St Faith, Norwich, NR10 3JF* | **01603 893080** | **admin@cnam.co.uk** | **www.cnam.co.uk**

❑	G-ASAT*		MS Rallye Club	62	ex Defford. CoA 2-8-02, de-reg 18-1-11, arrived 12-6-12	[1]	1-14
❑	G-ASKK		HP Herald 211	63	ex Air UK, PP-ASU, G-ASKK, PI-C910, CF-MCK. CoA 19-5-85, de-reg 29-4-85. Arrived on site 1985		1-14
❑	G-BHMY		Fokker Friendship 200	62	ex KLM uk, Air UK, F-GBDK, F-GBRV ntu, PK-PFS, JA8606, PH-FDL. CoA 22-5-99, de-reg 27-2-03		1-14
❑	G-BTAZ		Evans VP-2	90	ex airport, unflown project. De-reg 12-3-09. Arrived 2006		1-14
❑	G-OVNE		Cessna 401A	69	ex airport, N401XX, N171SF ntu, N71SF, N6236Q. CoA 8-10-92, de-reg 8-2-94. Arrived 2006		1-14
❑	–		Westland Whirlwind I	06	forward fuselage. *Crikey!*	[2]	1-14
❑	WH984		EE Canberra B.15	55	ex Mold, Bruntingthorpe, Hinckley, Bruntingthorpe, Cosford 8101M (6-8-70), HS, B.6, 9, Binbrook SF, 9. Short-built. Arrived 30-11-05. 32 Sqn colours. Cockpit	[3]	1-14
❑	WJ633	'EF'	EE Canberra T.17	54	ex Wyton, St Athan, Wyton, 360, B.2, 231 OCU, 100. HP-built. Arrived 2007. Cockpit	[4]	1-14
❑	WK654	'B'	Gloster Meteor F.8	52	ex 'WL135' Neatishead 8092M, Kemble, 85, CFE, Odiham SF, AWFCS, 247. SOC 9-4-70. Arrived 25-11-95. 245 Sqn colours		1-14
❑	WM267		Gloster Meteor NF.11	53	ex ?, Walpole, Firbeck, Hemswell, Misson, 151, 256, 11. AWA-built. SOC 30-10-67. Arrived 11-9-06. Cockpit		1-14
❑	–		Supermarine Scimitar CIM	~	–		1-14
❑	'XE683'	'G'	Hawker Hunter F.51	56	ex 'XF383' Cardiff-Wales, 'WV309', 'XF383', Dunsfold, G-9-437 (9-12-75), DanAF Esk.724 E-409. Arrived 7-10-95. 74 Sqn colours		1-14
❑	'XG168'	'10'	Hawker Hunter F.6A XG172	56	ex North Weald, Ipswich, Scampton 8832M (2-9-84), 1 TWU, 229 OCU, 263, 19. Arrived 2-2-01. 79 Sqn colours	[3]	1-14
❑	XM612		Avro Vulcan B.2	64	ex 44, Wadd Wing, Scampton Wing, 9. SOC 19-1-83. Arrived 30-1-83		1-14
❑	XN967	'233'	HS Buccaneer S.1	63	ex Coltishall, Weybourne, Fleckney, Helston, Culdrose A2627, SAH-20, Lossiemouth, 736, 809. SOC 23-1-70. Arrived 2006. Cockpit		1-14
❑	XP355		Westland Whirlwind HAR.10	62	ex G-BEBC (de-reg 5-12-83), Faygate, 8463M (6-2-76), 38 GCF, 21, CFS. Arrived 15-6-80. 22 Sqn colours		1-14
❑	XV255		HS Nimrod MR.2	70	ex Kinloss, Kin Wing, A&AEE, 42, Kin Wing, 42, StM Wing. Arrived 24-5-10		1-14
❑	XV426	'P'	McD Phantom FGR.2	69	ex Coltishall, Coningsby, 56, 19, 56, 23, 29, 228 OCU, 56, 111, 31, 31. Arrived 2007. 56 Sqn colours. Cockpit		1-14
❑	XW268	'720'	HS Harrier T.4N	70	ex Faygate, Yeovilton, 899, 233 OCU, T.2, 233 OCU. Accident 27-6-94. Arrived 8-5-08	[5]	1-14

❑ XX109	'GH'	SEPECAT Jaguar GR.1	72	ex Coltishall 8918M (21-10-86), Warton, A&AEE. Arrived 1-9-04. 54 Sqn colours		1-14
❑ XX830		SEPECAT Jaguar T.2	74	ex Coltishall 9293M, Warton, Shawbury, St Athan, ETPS, A&AEE, 226 OCU. Last flown 29-9-99. Arr 2006. Cockpit	[6]	1-14
❑ XZ375		SEPECAT Jaguar GR.1	76	ex Coltishall, St Athan 9255M (20-9-96), Warden Det, 54, Gulf Det, 54, 14, 20. *The Avid Guardian Reader*. Arrived 2006. Cockpit	[6]	1-14
❑ 3088	'BTT-3'	TTL Banshee 300 drone	~	–		1-14
❑ 121	'8-MY'	Dassault Mystère IVA	c57	ex Sculthorpe, FAF. Last flown 27-7-81, arrived 31-1-82		1-14
❑ 53-686 *and* G-AWON		EE Lightning F.53 ZF592	68	ex Portsmouth, Luxembourg, *Wing Commander*, Stretton, Warton, R Saudi AF 223, 53-686, 1305, G-AWON, G-27-56. Last flown 22-1-86, arrived 6-2-02	[3] [7]	1-14
❑ 16718	'TR-999'	Lockheed T-33A-5-LO	51	ex Sculthorpe, Turkish AF ntu, FAF. Arrived 31-5-86. USAF colours, 47th BW		1-14

■ **[1]** The Rallye has come 'home' having bashed the circuit with the Norfolk and Norwich Aero Club 8-63 to 11-69. **[2]** Built by the late Ray Wood of Thetford as a reminder of an extinct type - W E W Petter's incredible Whirlwind twin-Peregrine fighter. **[3]** Canberra cockpit WH984, Hunter F.6A 'XG168' and Lightning ZF592 / 53-686 are on loan from John Sheldrake. **[4]** Canberra cockpit WJ633 is on loan from Richy Doel - see Wyton, Cambs. **[5]** Harrier is on loan from Dan Lander - see also Aylesbury, Bucks. **[6]** Jaguar cockpits are on loan from The Coltishall Cockpit Collection. **[7]** As illustrated in the colour section, ZF592 carries Saudi markings to port and G-AWON to starboard; it appeared as *Oscar-November* at Farnborough 1968.

Airport: Heralds G-ATIG and G-AVEZ, last noted early in 2006, were scrapped during mid-2008. The airport is used for storage of jetliners awaiting re-use and from late 2013 KLM UK Engineering commenced parting out, with a pair of RJ85s being the first for processing. Fokker 100s, F-GIOG, F-GNLG and F-GNLH had all departed by August 2013.

❑ G-BCDN	Fokker Friendship 200	63	ex Air UK, PH-OGA, JA8615, LV-PMR ntu, PH-FDP. CoA 19-7-96, de-reg 28-1-98. Training airframe	6-12
❑ G-BCDO	Fokker Friendship 200	63	ex Air UK, PH-OGB, JA8621, PH-FEZ. *Lord Butler*. Damaged 19-7-90, de-reg 27-1-95. Fuselage. Tech college, inst	6-12
❑ EI-RJW*	HS 146 RJ85		ex Air France, N535XJ, G-6-371. Parting out	8-13
❑ EI-WXB	HS 146 RJ85		ex Northwest, N504XJ, G-6-311. Parting out	8-13

Offshore Fire and Survival Training Centre: An extensive facility on the northern perimeter of the airport.

◆ **Access: Strictly** *by prior appointment* **only | www.petans.co.uk**

❑ N5880T	Westland WG.30-100	83	ex Weston-super-Mare, Yeovil, Air Spur, G-17-31	8-13

OLD BUCKENHAM AERODROME south of the A11, east of the B1077 near Attleborough EGSV

Taylorcraft G-AHSD was flying by mid-2012 and it was joined the following year by Tiger Moth G-BYLB.

❑ G-BKVA	MS Rallye 180	79	ex SE-GFS, F-GBXA. CoA 20-7-11	9-11

REYMERSTON near East Dereham

Wallis Autogyros: Wg Cdr Kenneth Horatio Wallis MBE, pioneer of autgyros, wartime Wellington pilot, designer and builder of sports cars, motorcycles, speed boats and many more talents and skills, died, aged 97 on 1st September 2013. President of the Norfolk and Suffolk Aviation Museum since 1976, his loss was also felt across the preservation movement. For a superb account of an incredible man read *The Lives of Ken Wallis - Engineer and Aviator Extraordinaire* by Ian Hancock and published by N&SAM - see under Flixton, Suffolk.

On 24th September 2013, the flight shed at Reymerston was emptied and the 'gyros were taken to a location in Bedfordshire, to await a decision on their future. As *W&R* was closing for press, this situation remained and it is felt better to await *W&R25* to chart the outcome. Believed moved to Bedfordshire were: **WA-116**s G-ARRT; G-ASDY; G-ATHM; G-AVDG, G-AXAS, G-BGGU, G-BMJX; G-SCAN; **WA-117**s G-AVJV; G-VIEW; G-VTEN; **WA-118** G-AVJW; **WA-120** G-AYVO; **WA-121** G-BAHH; **WA-122**s G-BGGW; G-BLIK; **WA-201** G-BNDG. WA-116 XR944 (G-ATTB) is reported to have moved to a site in Norfolk by November 2013. G-ARZB *Little Nellie*, was on loan to the National Motor Museum, Beaulieu.

See also Filxton, Norfolk, for the Wallbro Monoplane replica and *Little Nellie II* and Manchester, Gtr Man, for the Wallis-Bensen B.7 G-APUD, first flown 23rd May 1959 to start an exceptional dynasty.

SEETHING AERODROME east of the B1332, north of Bungay EGSJ

Station 146 Control Tower Museum: Run by the **Station 146 Seething Tower Association**. The control tower has been restored and contains a museum dedicated as a living memorial to the Liberator-equipped 448th BG. The brochure and website sums it all up well: "One building: a whole airfield of memories".

◆ **Access:** *From the Thwaite St Mary road to the south.* **Open:** *First Sun May to Oct, 10:00 to 17:00. Other times by appointment.* **Contact**: *Toad Lane, Seething, Norfolk, NR15 1AL* | **email via website** | **www.seethingtower.org**

Aerodrome: Rex Ford continues to make persistent, patient progress with the magnificent Q.6.

❑ G-AFFD	Percival Q.6	38	ex Isle of Man, Sutton Coldfield, Duxford, Redhill, G-AIEY ntu, X9407, MCS, 510, Old Sarum SF, Halton SF, Heston SF, Northolt SF, 6 AACU, G-AFFD. CoA 31-8-56	1-14

SHIPDHAM AERODROME off the A1075 south-west of East Dereham EGSA

A clear up of references at this lovely aerodrome. Last noted in February 2008, Blaniks BXR and DEY have been deleted. The latter, at least, was reported to have been broken up. (Blaniks were grounded for wing spar inspections in 2010 and many owners seemed to decide to draw a line on operating the type.) During early 2010 Blanik D-5826 (FDV - BGA.3186) was noted in poor state and sectioned and is also thought to have moved on or been scrapped. One that missed the 'net' completely was an anonymous EoN Primary which had been stored, dismantled, at Shipdham since at least 2006. The pioneers at the Norfolk and Suffolk Aviation Museum tracked it down and on 29th October 2013 the 'fuselage' and tail feathers made the journey to Flixton, Suffolk, with the wings following in due course.

❑ G-AYUM	Slingsby T.61A	71	ex Watton, Swanton Morley. CoA 10-6-02		4-10
❑ G-BGRC	Piper Cherokee 140B	69	ex Swanton Morley, SE-FHF. CoA 26-10-97, de-reg 13-12-11		9-11
❑ N556MA	Beagle Pup 100	68	ex G-AWEB. Crashed 14-7-05		4-10
❑ WZ797	Slingsby G'hopper TX.1	52	ex Upwood, Shenington, Locking, Wimborne. Off-site		10-13
❑ MM53211* 'ZI-4'	Fiat G.46-IV	~	BAPC.79, ex Norwich, France, Duxford, Lydd, Southend, Shoreham, It AF. First noted 8-12	[1]	4-13

■ **[1]** The Fiat has long been the subject of just-what-is-its-identity syndrome; another option for an Italian serial number is MM52799.

SWANTON MORLEY east of the B1110, north of East Dereham

Two Nords are kept *separately* in the general area.

❑ No.37	Nord 3400	G-ZARA	60	ex Boston, Stixwould, Breighton, Coventry, La Ferté Alais, ALAT F-MMAB. De-reg 30-6-97	6-09
❑ No.124	Nord 3400	G-BOSJ	60	ex La Ferté Alais, ALAT F-MMAB. Damaged 12-6-94	6-09

TERRINGTON ST CLEMENT north of the A17, east of King's Lynn

Terrington Aviation Collection: The 'JP' is stored in the area. See also under West Walton Highway, Norfolk.

❑ XM468	Hunting Jet Provost T.3	60	ex King's Lynn, Stock, St Athan, Halton 8081M (6-5-70), Shawbury, 6 FTS, RAFC. Stored	7-10

THETFORD

A *private* collection of cockpits is located in the *general* area.

❑ WW664		Hawker Hunter F.4	55	ex Spanhoe, Cottesmore, Newark, Winthorpe, Newark, Harrogate, HSA, 26. Cockpit	[1]	3-13
❑ XG325*		EE Lightning F.1	59	ex Rayleigh, Southend, Wattisham, Foulness, DH Hatfield, A&AEE. SOC 23-6-65. Cockpit		3-13
❑ XN650*	'456'	DH Sea Vixen FAW.2	61	ex Spanhoe, Bruntingthorpe, Newton Abbot, Welshpool, Bruntingthorpe, Cardiff, Culdrose A2639, A2620, A2612 (3-3-72), RAE, 892. Cockpit. Arrived 9-10		3-13
❑ 764*		MiG-21SPS *Fishbed*	~	ex Northampton, Wycombe Air Park, East GermAF. Cockpit		3-13

■ **[1]** The rest of WW664 became the prototype T.8B in 1958 for the Fleet Air Arm and later went to Singapore as a T.75.

THORPE ABBOTTS off the A140 at Dickleburgh, north of Scole

100th Bomb Group Memorial Museum: Contents of the tower museum are exceptional (as is the website), offering poignant insights into the life and times of the men and machines of the 'Bloody Hundredth'.

◆ **Access:** *'Brown signed' from the A140 and the A143.* **Open:** *Mar to Oct, weekends and Bank Hols, 10:100 to 17:00; Weds May to Sep, 10:00 to 17:00. Last admission 16:00. Closed Nov to Feb. Other times by appointment.* **Contact:** *Common Rd, Dickleburgh, Diss, IP21 4PH* | **01379 740708** | **100bgmm@tiscali.co.uk** | **www.100bgmus.org.uk**

TIBENHAM north of the B1134, north of Diss

Black Barn Aviation: Specialise in 'Stearmen' and other US classics at a ***private*** workshop. Already a staunch supporter of the Norfolk and Suffolk Aviation Museum, BBA kindly donated a composite Stearman, based on PT-27 42-15662, and it moved to Flixton, Suffolk, on 26th June 2012. Last noted in August 2008, N2S-3 Kaydet G-BRHB has moved on.

❑ G-FANC		Fairchild 24R-46	46	ex Felthorpe, N77647, NC77647. Burnt out 18-2-03, CoA 26-5-03, de-reg 30-7-03		1-12
❑ N1325M		Boeing N2S-5 Kaydet	~	ex USA, BuNo 43390		3-12
❑ N1328		Fairchild 24KS	~	ex USA, NC1328		3-12
❑ N57783		Stinson L-5 Sentinel	~	ex USA. Frame		3-12
❑ N68427		Boeing N2S-4 Kaydet	~	ex USA, BuNo 55771		8-13

Others: Chris Jefferson keeps the Kensinger in the locality. A Tiger Moth restoration is also in the area.

❑ G-ASSV		Kensinger KF	53	ex Deopham Green, Brenchley, Deopham Green, Tonbridge, Bobbington, N23S. Crashed 2-7-69		5-09
❑ N6965	'FL-J'	DH Tiger Moth	G-AJTW 38	ex Mk.II N6965, 13 OTU, 16 EFTS, 13 OTU, 418, Northolt SF, 24, 81, 613. Crashed 7-6-99, CoA 9-9-00. 81 Sqn colours		5-11

WATTON on the A1075, south of East Dereham

No.**611 Volunteer Gliding School**:

❑ XP490	JJN	Slingsby Grasshopper TX.1	61	BGA.4552, ex Swanton Morley, Ipswich, Syerston, Grantham. CoA 21-7-99. Stored		4-12

Also: Evans VP-1 G-BBXZ moved on, within the county. Last noted in February 2006, Mong Sport G-BTOA has been deleted.

WEST WALTON HIGHWAY on the A47 north-east of Wisbech

Fenland and West Norfolk Aviation Museum: Run by the Fenland and West Norfolk Aircraft Preservation Society. The museum has a close association with the **Terrington Aviation Collection** - see also Terrington St Clement, Norfolk.

◆ **Access:** *At Bamber's Garden Centre, Old Lynn Road – signed off the A47/B198 junction.* **Open:** *Weekends, Bank Hols, Mar and Oct 10:00 to 17:00, also Wed 13:00 to 16:00. Other times by appointment.* **Contact:** *Old Lynn Road, West Walton, Wisbech, PE14 7DA* | **email via website** | **http://fawnaps.webs.com**

❑ G-ARNH		Piper Colt 108	61	ex Chatteris, Elstree. Dam 1-9-72, de-reg 24-5-73. Off-site		4-08
❑ WR971	'Q'	Avro Shackleton MR.3/3	56	ex Narborough, Cosford 8119M (14-12-70), 120, Kinloss Wing, 201, 120, Kinloss Wing, CA. Arrived 2002. Fuselage		1-14
❑ XD434	'25'	DH Vampire T.11	54	ex Marham, Barton, Woodford, Chester, St Athan, 5 FTS, 7 FTS. SOC 1-12-67. Arrived 3-89		1-14
❑ XM402	'18'	Hunting Jet Provost T.3	59	ex Narborough, West Raynham, Halton, Newton 8055AM (21-11-69), Shawbury, 6 FTS, 2 FTS. Arrived 10-9-95		1-14
❑ XN983		HS Buccaneer S.2B	65	ex Terrington St Clement, 12, 208, 15, 12, 809, A&AEE, RR. SOC 10-4-94. Arrived 2002. Cockpit	[1]	1-14
❑ XS459	'AW'	EE Lightning T.5	65	ex Narborough, Binbrook, 5, LTF, 56, 29, 226 OCU. SOC 21-6-88. Arrived 4-94		1-14
❑ –		Hunting Jet Provost CIM	~	procedure trainer, on loan from March Air Cadets. Arr 2000		1-14
❑ 526	25887	MiG-29 *Fulcrum*	~	ex Fairford. Crashed 21-7-93. Arrived 2000. Cockpit	[1]	1-14

■ [1] On loan from the Terrington Aviation Collection.

WEYBOURNE on the A149 west of Cromer

Muckleburgh Collection: Bannered as Britain's largest working military collection, there is much to fascinate here, including 'live' tank demonstrations during school holidays - check in advance for details.

◆ **Access:** *Mar to Oct 10:00 to 17:00 daily; last admission 16:00.* **Contact:** *Military Camp, Weybourne, NR25 7EG* | **01263 588210** | **info@muckleburgh.co.uk** | **www.muckleburgh.co.uk**

❑ WD686	'S'	Gloster Meteor NF.11	52	ex Duxford, RAE Bedford, Wroughton, TRE Defford. AWA-built. SOC 2-11-67. Arrived 1991. 141 Sqn colours		1-14
❑ XZ968	'3G'	HS Harrier GR.3	80	ex Marham 9222M (13-10-93), St Athan, 233 OCU, 1417 Flt, 1, 4		1-14
❑ ZJ385		GEC Phoenix UAV	~	-		4-13
❑ –		Fieseler Fi 103 V-1 replica	~	on ramp		1-14

WYMONDHAM on the A11 south-west of Norwich

No.**1986 Squadron Air Cadets**: The Hunter has been transformed into a superb flight simulator.

❑ –		Hawker Hunter F.6	c57	ex Duxford. Cockpit. 74 Sqn colours	[1]	5-11

■ **[1]** A *possible* identity for the Hunter cockpit is XE612.

NORTHAMPTONSHIRE

AYNHO on the B4031 south west of Brackley

A Sea Harrier is kept at **private** premises in the general area.

❑ ZD582	'123'	HS Sea Harrier FA.2	85	ex Henley-on-Thames, Shawbury, Colsterworth, Shawbury, 800, 899, 800, 899, FRS.1, 801, 800	8-09

BARBY south of the M45, north of Daventry

WarFighters: Olney Fields Farm, Onley Lane. By December 2010 Lynx AH.7 XZ218 had left, probably ultimately destined for Leavesden, Herts. It was 'dressed' as a UH-60 Blackhawk for a film. Lynx AH.7 XZ175 departed by road 26th November 2013. **Also**: Stored not far from the above, is *another* Lynx.

❑ XZ664	Westland Lynx AH.7	81	ex Ipswich, Staverton, Middle Wallop, 663, 3 Rgt, 1 Rgt, Fleetlands, 653, 657, 655, LCF, 651. Crashed 23-2-01	2-13

BRACKLEY on the A43 east of Banbury

❑ G-BLLV	Slingsby T.67C	84	ex Turweston, Wellesbourne. CoA 10-11-00, de-reg 27-2-03	3-11
❑ G-BLRG	Slingsby T.67B	85	ex Turweston. CoA 17-7-00, de-reg 5-2-09	3-11

CORBY

Frank and **Lee Millar**: See under Newark, Notts, for their Canberra PR.9 cockpit.

❑ XE849	'V3'	DH Vampire T.11	54	ex Barton, Shobdon, Mildenhall, Long Marston, Yatesbury, Monkton Farleigh, Conington, Ware, St Athan 7928M (13-10-66), 3 CAACU (?),CATCS, CNCS, 5 FTS, 7 FTS, 1 FTS, 4 FTS. Stored, dismantled	6-12

CROUGHTON on the B4031 south-west of Brackley

USAF Croughton, 422nd ABG: Two airframes guard the gate.

❑ '63000'	'000'	NAA F-100D-11-NA Super Sabre	54-2212	54	ex Upper Heyford, Sculthorpe, French AF. Last flown 6-1-76	6-13
❑ '63428'	'WW'	Republic F-105G-RE Thunderchief	62-4428	62	ex Upper Heyford, Davis-Monthan 'FK095', 128 TFS, Georgia ANG. 561 TFS, Korat, colours	6-13

Also: A small lake north of the B4031, close to the main gate of the base, was drained in December 2013 revealing an Apache that had been 'planted' there in 1994 for use by a diving club.

❑ G-BFSK*	Piper Apache 160	56	ex Turweston, Kidlington, OO-NVC, OO-HVL, OO-PIP. De-reg 5-12-83. See notes above	1-14

HARRINGTON south-east of Market Harborough

'Carpetbagger' Aviation Museum: Centred upon the hardened group operations building of what was once USAAF Station 179 and home of the clandestine 492nd and 801st BGs. Restored to its wartime state, it houses exhibitions describing the covert operations carried out by the US from Harrington and by the RAF from Tempsford, Beds. Working in support of the museum is the **Harrington Aviation Museum Society**. In the former Paymaster's building is the **Northants Aviation Museum** run by the Northamptonshire Aviation Society.

◆ **Access:** *Take the minor road south out of Harrington village, towards Lamport, and turn right after the A14 – follow signs. (This will take you westerly on a track paralleling the A14.) Also signed from the A43 near Broughton.* **Open:** *From Easter to Oct weekends and Bank Hols, 10:00 to 17:00. Other times by prior arrangement.*

***Please note**: Photography is not possible within the museum without prior consent.* **Contact:** *Sunny Vale Farm Nursery, off Lamport Road, Harrington, NN6 9PF* | **01604 686608** | **enquiries@harringtonmuseum.org.uk** | **www.harringtonmuseum.org.uk**

❑	G-APWK	Westland Widgeon	59	ex Corby (?), Sywell, *Eye of the Needle*, Yeovil. De-reg 10-7-73. Forward fuselage	3-12

◆ **Thinx:** *On the Harrington to Lamport road is a memorial to the 492nd and 801st. At this point, good views of the former airfield and the Grade 2 listed Thor IRBM pads can be had.* ***Please note**: the majority of the airfield site is* privately owned *and not available for inspection without prior arrangement.*

HINTON-IN-THE-HEDGES AERODROME just west of Brackley

❑	G-ASOX	Cessna 205A	64	ex Bournemouth, Newcastle, N4856U. CoA 1-8-92	5-13
❑	ENY*	Schleicher ASK.13	~	ex RAFGSA R17. CoA 2-6-04. Fuselage	6-13

IRTHLINGBOROUGH on the A6 north-west of Higham Ferrers and Rushden

Allens Metals: The yard on the banks of the River Nene has a Navajo fuselage as a signboard/attraction.

◆ **Access:** *Busy yard, by prior arrangement* **only** | **www.scrapmetal-northampton.co.uk**

❑	G-ISFC*	Piper Navajo B	73	ex Little Staughton, G-BNEF, N7574L. CoA 25-5-08, de-reg 23-5-13. Fuselage, first noted 4-13	9-13

KETTERING

Chariots: Inside the futuristic building in Kettering Venture Park (Pytchley Road, the A509 near the A 14 junction) a Baby Great Lakes 'flies' over the fleets of limos and high-powered skate boards for sale. | **www.chariotsspecialistcars.com**

❑	G-BGEI*	Oldfield Baby Great Lakes	80	ex Temple Bruer. CoA 21-6-12. First noted 5-12	9-13

■ **[1]** *Echo-India* factoids: Tested at Samlesbury, Lancs, for PFA permit clearance 26-8-80 by Wg Cdr Roland Beamont CBE DSO* DFC*.

Tresham College: In the campus (main entrance on Windmill Avenue, near Wickstead Park) is a BAC 1-11 used by the Travel and Tourism and Uniformed Public Service courses. **Access:** *Visitors* **strictly** *by prior arrangement* | **www.tresham.ac.uk**

❑	G-AVMJ	BAC 111-510ED	68	ex Watford, Horton, Bournemouth, Farnborough, Bournemouth, Filton, BA, BEA. CoA 17-11-94, de-reg 11-5-01. Fuselage	9-13

■ **[1]** *Mike-Juliet* factoids: First flew 15-7-68, last flew with BA 13-1-92, ferry to Hurn. Final flight Hurn-Filton 25-5-93.

KING'S CLIFFE south of the A47, west of Peterborough

John Tempest: Keeps his project at a *private* location in the general area.

❑	G-ARUL	Le Vier Cosmic Wind	c59	ex Halfpenny Green, N22C. Crashed 29-8-66 [1]	12-05

■ **[1]** About 90% of the parts from the *original* Cosmic Wind G-ARUL are held plus other components. (G-ARUL, as *Ballerina II* and a build date of 1973, is airworthy and based at Duxford, Cambs.)

NORTHAMPTON

W&R23 (p166) wrote out the cockpit of MiG-21 764. It had moved to Thetford, Norfolk, by January 2011.

NORTHAMPTON AERODROME or Sywell, north-east of Northampton, off the A43 EGBK

Sywell Aviation Museum: The museum gained an impressive 'gate guardian' in the form of the only whole Hunter F.2 surviving; thanks to the IWM for gifting it. *Echo-Sierra* came courtesy of well-known Tiger aficionado Ken Broomfield. It replaced G-BHLT which was returned to its owners in August 2013.

◆ **Access:** *Car parking for the museum (no charge) doubles as a viewing area for the aerodrome.* **Open:** *Weekends and Bank Hols 10:00 to 16:30, Easter to end of Sep. Other times by appointment.* **Contact:** *Sywell Aerodrome, NN6 0BN* | **sywellaviationmuseum@gmail.com** | **www.sywellaerodrome.co.uk/museum.php**

❑	G-AOES*	DH Tiger Moth	41	ex Baxterley, Redhill, Biggin Hill, Cosford, Mk.II T6056, Waddington SF, Benson SF, 18 EFTS. Morris-built. Crashed 26-9-99, CoA 15-6-02. Fuselage. Arrived 3-13	2-14
❑	WG419	DHC Chipmunk T.10 PAX	51	ex Armthorpe, Finningley 8206M (2-8-72), Laarbruch SF, Gütersloh SF, Ahlhorn SF, Oldenburg SF, CFS, Abn UAS, Bir UAS, 15 RFS, 4 BFTS, 6 RFS. Arrived 2008	2-14

❑ WN904*		Hawker Hunter F.2	54	ex Waterbeach, Duxford, Newton, Melksham, Halton 7544M (31-3-58), 257. 1 Sqn colours to stb, 56 Sqn to port. Arrived 2-8-12	[1]	2-14
❑ WZ820		Slingsby Grasshopper TX.1	52	ex Shoreham, Lancing College. Arrived 2001		2-14
❑ XD599	'A'	DH Vampire T.11	54	ex Ingatestone, Welshpool, Shobdon, Caernarfon, Bournemouth, Blackbushe, Staverton, Stroud, CATCS, RAFC, 1. SOC 15-12-70. Arrived 10-10-04. Cockpit		2-14

■ **[1]** WN904 will be returned to 257 Sqn colours, coded 'Q', from its days at Horsham St Faith in 1954. She is unofficially called 'Heidi' after a former girlfriend of a SAM member. Both share certain attributes: "Great looker, fast mover, but *very* high maintenance!"

Aerodrome: As well as the Aeronca, Matthew Boddington has acquired a venerable Tiger Moth, once flown by his late father, Charles, with the Barnstormers, for restoration. Across at **Virtual Aerospace**, the cockpit of Jet Provost T.3 'XN493' (XN137) did not stay long, moving on to pastures new in early 2012. The company has a fixed-based Boeing 737NG simulator available for professional and enthusiast 'flights' - **www.virtual-aerospace.com**

❑ 'G-ACSS'	DH.88 Comet FSM	97	BAPC.257, ex London Colney, Hatfield. *Grosvenor House*. Stored	[1]	12-13
❑ G-AEXD	Aeronca 100	37	ex Hanwell. CoA 20-4-70	[2]	12-13
❑ G-AKIN	Miles Messenger 2A ✈	47	-	[3]	12-13
❑ G-APVT*	DH Tiger Moth	35	ex K4254, Colerne SF, 81 GCF, 60 GCF, 18 RFS, Lon UAS, 6 EFTS, 1 GTS, 101 OTU, 17 EFTS, 7 EFTS, 14 EFTS, 20 ERFTS, 24. Crashed 29-7-73		12-13
❑ G-ARAM	Piper Super Cub 150	60	ex N10F. Crashed 4-7-01, CoA 22-6-02		12-13
❑ G-FILL	Piper Navajo C	79	ex OO-EJM, N3521. CoA 13-10-11. Fuselage, spares		12-13
❑ -*	Robinson R22	~	pod, travelling demo with Sloane Helicopters. F/n 3-11		12-13

■ **[1]** The DH.88 is perhaps best described as *nearly* a full-scale replica! It is actually seven-eighths scale. It is planned to install this inside the Hangar One entertainment complex alongside the 'Aviator Hotel'. **[2]** G-AEXD includes parts from G-AESP. To further complicate matters, the airworthy G-AEVS at Breighton, E Yorks (which see) contains parts from G-AEXD! **[3]** The Sywell Messenger Trust looks after G-AKIN. Owned by the Spiller family since August 1949 and based at Sywell since May 1952, *India-November* clocked up 60 years residency in 2012. This loyalty to base is probably only surpassed by the Shuttleworth Moth G-EBWD.

SPANHOE AERODROME south-east of Harringworth

Windmill Aviation: See under Newark-on-Trent for an exceptional restoration; temporarily resident. 'Super Tiger' G-AOAA moved to Lavenham, Suffolk, for completion in October 2013. Cessna F.172M G-BAOS, Cessna 120 G-BRJC and J/1 'MT182' (G-AJDY) were flying again by 2012. Rikki McClain's (see below) Nord Norvigie 54 (G-CGWR) arrived on 14th March 2011 for restoration; Windmill's Carl Tyers was at the helm for its first flight on 20th October 2012. Piper L-18C MM52-2420 arrived by October 2013, but moved on to Stamford, Lincs, in later January 2014.

◆ **Access**, *by prior arrangement* **only**

❑ G-APKM	Auster J/1N Alpha	58	ex Newark. CoA 9-1-89		1-12
❑ G-APVG	Auster J/5l Aiglet Tnr	59	ex Bedford, ZK-BQW. CoA 20-3-00		1-12
❑ G-ARNN	Globe GC-1B Swift	46	ex Tatenhill, Leicester, VP-YMJ, VP-RDA, ZS-BMX, NC3279K. Crashed 1-9-73, de-reg 26-1-11. Off-site		10-08
❑ G-ARYZ	Beagle Airedale	62	CoA 26-2-01. Stored		6-10
❑ G-ASWF	Beagle Airedale	64	ex Newark-on-Trent, Leicester. CoA 27-4-83, de-reg 3-2-89		8-10
❑ G-BCPK*	Cessna F.172M Skyhawk	74	ex Little Staughton, D-ELOB. CoA 12-1-01. Spares		12-13
❑ G-BPHX	Cessna 140	47	ex Enniskillen, N2252N, NC2252N. Crashed 23-5-92		8-10
❑ G-BSOE	Luscombe Silvaire 8A	46	ex Sturgate, N1604K, NC1604K. Off-site		6-11
❑ G-BTBV*	Cessna 140	47	ex Little Staughton, N2474N, NC2474N. CoA 6-8-03		12-12
❑ G-BTYX*	Cessna 140	76	ex Uckfield. Rochester, N76568. CoA 23-2-98, de-reg 10-4-01 First noted 12-12		12-12
❑ -*	Cessna 140	~	ex Uckfield. Fuselage, spares		12-12
❑ -*	Cessna 140	~	ex Little Staughton. Fuselage, spares		12-12
❑ G-CFGE	Stinson 108-1	46	ex Gainsborough, Hibalstow, Little Gransden, ZS-BHW, NC97127. Off-site		6-10
❑ EI-AYL	Beagle Airedale	63	ex Abbeyshrule, G-ARRO, EI-AVP ntu, G-ARRO. CoA 1-2-86		6-10
❑ EI-BAL	Beagle Airedale	62	ex Abbeyshrule, G-ARZS. De-reg 29-6-79		6-10
❑ EI-BBK	Beagle Airedale	62	ex Abbeyshrule, G-ARXB, EI-ATE ntu, G-ARXB. CoA 11-11-83		6-10
❑ J-95	EKW D-3801	~	ex Switzerland, Swiss AF. Frame, off-site	[1]	5-05
❑ J-146	EKW D-3801	~	ex Switzerland, Swiss AF. Frame, off-site	[1]	5-05
❑ –	EKW D-3801	~	ex Switzerland, Swiss AF. Frame, off-site	[1]	5-05

■ **[1]** The EKW D-3801 was a Swiss development of the MS.406 single-seat fighter.

Others: Rikki McClain's cockpits moved on as follows: Canberra PR.9 XH136 and Buccaneer S.2B XV165 to Ashford, Kent by November 2011 and Sea Vixen FAW.2 XN650 to Thetford, Norfolk, by January 2012. See above for the restoration of Rikki's Norvigie 54. Two gliders are stored locally:

❑ BVS*	SZD Bocian 1D	~	BGA.1274, ex Spilsby. Arrived 9-12	12-13
❑ -*	Slingsby Swallow	~	BGA.2210, ex Spilsby, RAFGGA.539. Arrived 9-12	12-13

WELDON at the junction of the A43 and A605 east of Corby

Warwickshire and Northamptonshire Air Ambulance: The forward fuselage of an A.109 is kept here and used as a travelling fund-raiser for G-WNAA which operates from Northampton Aerodrome. **www.wnaa.co.uk**

❑ G-HIMJ	Agusta A.109E	03	crashed 14-3-04, CoA 15-4-06, de-reg 14-7-04. Forward fuselage	12-09

NORTHUMBERLAND and TYNESIDE

The five unitary authorities of Gateshead, Newcastle-upon-Tyne, Sunderland, North Tyneside and South Tyneside comprise the 'counties'

BAMBURGH on the B4130 east of Belford and north-west of Seahouses

Bamburgh Castle Aviation Artefacts Museum: In the West Ward, within the former laundry is the superb **Armstrong Aviation Museum**. Two rooms cover local aviation history, including wreckage from local 'digs'.

◆ **Open:** *Feb to Oct daily 10:00 to 16:45, last entry 16:00; Nov to Feb, weekends only 11:00 to 16:30, last admission 16:00.*
Contact: *Bamburgh, NE69 7DF* | **01668 214515** | **administrator@bamburghcastle.com** | **www.bamburghcastle.com**

BOULMER AIRFIELD east of Alnwick

RAF Boulmer: Flying will cease at the base between 2015 and 2017 with 202 Squadron giving up the Sea Kings, to be replaced by more modern, privately-operated, hardware at Humberside Airport. There are no plans to close the RAF Station, which has a major surveillance and control training role.

❑ XV415	'E'	McD Phantom FGR.2	68	ex 9163M, 56, 74, 228 OCU, 23, 56, 92, 29, 228 OCU, 56, 228 OCU, 31, 228 OCU, 41, 228 OCU, 41, 54, A&AEE. Gate	1-14

ESHOTT AERODROME east of the A1 south of Fenton

❑ G-ASYK*		Piper Twin Comanche 160	64	ex Bruntingthorpe, N7543Y. Crashed 11-5-96, de-reg 30-10-96. Fuselage	7-13
❑ G-BWVR*	'52'	Yakovlev Yak-52	87	ex LY-AKQ, Sov AF 134. IAV Bacau-built. CoA 7-12-06	7-13
❑ G-MWKX*		Microflight Spectrum	90	CoA 14-5-04. F/n 9-12	7-13
❑ G-MYAY*		Microflight Spectrum	92	CoA 21-12-00, de-reg 27-10-10. F/n 9-12	7-13

MORPETH

A *private* workshop and airstrip, in the *general* area.

❑ G-BPMN*	Taylor Coot A	r78	de-reg 9-5-94	8-13
❑ G-MNKG*	Solar Pegaus Photon	87	CoA 11-6-95	6-13
❑ G-MNWY*	CFM Shadow C	88	CoA 19-8-03	6-13
❑ G-MVJJ*	Aerial Arts Chaser	88	CoA 5-8-08	6-13
❑ YU-DLG*	UTVA 66	~	ex Linton-on-Ouse, Biggin Hill, Yugoslav AF 51109. Arrived 9-2-13	6-13

BlackStone Aviation:

❑ G-APOL		Druine Turbulent		63	ex Charterhall. Damaged 24-7-93, de-reg 13-9-00	8-13
❑ 'K5673'*		Isaacs Fury II	G-BZAS	00	CoA 4-7-04	6-13
❑ 42-58687	'IY'	Taylorcraft DF-65	G-BRIY	43	ex N59687, NC59687, TG-6 42-58678. CoA 10-7-98	8-13

NEWCASTLE AIRPORT or Woolsington EGNT

Newcastle Aviation Academy: Note that the Rye Hill Campus is also used - see below.

◆ **Access:** *Visits possible* **only** *by prior arrangement* | **www.ncl-coll.ac.uk**

❑ G-AZMF		BAC 111-530FX	72	ex Bournemouth, European, 7Q-YKJ, G-AZMF, PT-TYY, G-AZMF. CoA 22-1-04, de-reg 10-3-06. Forward fuselage	1-14
❑ G-BBYM		HP Jetstream 200	69	ex Cosford, Cranfield, BAe, G-AYWR, G-8-13. CoA 20-9-98, de-reg 7-6-00	1-14
❑ C-GWJO		Boeing 737-2A3	69	ex Westjet, HR-SHO, CX-BHM, N1797B, N1787B	1-14
❑ N37LW		Piper Aztec 250 G-EEVA	60	ex Fishburn, Kirknewton, G-EEVA, G-ASND, N4800P	1-14
❑ XM355	'D'	Hunting Jet Provost T.3	59	ex Bruntingthorpe, Shobdon, Cambridge, Bruntingthorpe, Halton 8229M (17-10-73), Shawbury, 1 FTS, 7 FTS, CFS. Blue/white colours	1-14
❑ XM419	'102'	Hunting Jet Provost T.3A	60	ex St Athan 8990M (15-3-89), 7 FTS, 3 FTS, CFS, RAFC, CFS, 3 FTS, RAFC, 6 FTS, RAFC, 2 FTS	1-14

Also: Twin Comanche G-ASYK is best listed under Eshott, N&T. Cherokee G-AWBH had moved on by November 2013. **Offshore Training Newcastle** opened up for operations on 30th May 2013 with a mock-up oil rig heli-deck plus a helicopter rig for fire-rescue exercises.

NEWCASTLE UPON TYNE

Auster 5 G-ANFU moved to Sunderland, N&T by mid-2012. As predicted in *W&R23*, Phil Moore's Chipmunk T.10 PAX WB670 moved to Carlisle, Cumbria, on 13th December 2012. The Whirlwind is with a *private* individual in the *general* area and not as given in *W&R23*.

❑ XJ723	Westland Whirlwind HAR.10	55	ex Montrose, Wroughton, 202, 228, HAR.4, 155. SOC 29-3-79. Off-site	3-13

SEATON BURN east of the A1, north of Newcastle upon Tyne

Spit4Hire: Neil and Amanda McCarthy unveiled their GB Replicas-built Spitfire FSM 'P7895' at Linton-on-Ouse on 3rd May 2013. Bedecked in 72 Squadron colours, this was very appropriate venue as Linton is the current base of 72 (flying Tucanos.). The Spitfire was available for hire until it was acquired by the Ulster Aviation Society and moved to Long Kesh, N Ireland, on 21st December 2013. A Spitfire cockpit section/simulator is available for hire.

◆ **Access:** *Visits possible* **only** *by prior arrangement* | **07904 034301** | **spit4hire@gmail.com** | **www.spit4hire.com**

❑ -*		Supermarine Spitfire FSM	13	cockpit/sim, travelling demo		7-13
❑ XD425	'M'	DH Vampire T.11	54	ex Millom, Dumfries, West Freugh, Stranraer, Woodford, Chester, St Athan, 8 FTS, 5 FTS, 7 FTS, 202 AFS. SOC 30-11-67. Pod. 6 Sqn colours	[1]	7-13

■ **[1]** The wings of XD425 are on XD547 at Cantley, Norfolk.

SOUTH SHIELDS on the A1018 north of Sunderland

Karl and **Sam Edmondson**: Auster AOP.5 'TJ398' took to the air on 30th September 2013 - inside the hold of a RCAF CC-130J from Brize Norton bound for the National Artillery Museum at Shilo, Manitoba, Canada.

SUNDERLAND site of the former Usworth aerodrome, west of Sunderland

North East Land, Sea and Air Museums (NELSAM): A lot of planning, forward vision and determination came to fruition in 2012 when like-minded teams across the region came together to turn the **North East Aircraft Museum** into NELSAM, a wide-reaching museum complex encompassing all forms of motive power. Using a building donated by the Port of Sunderland, the **Military Vehicle Museum** rolled-in the first of its extensive exhibits in January 2012. Since then, the **North East Electrical Traction Trust** has also joined in and, as *W&R* went to press, the tracks were laid and its tram shed was due to be commissioned. Aspirations of all involved are limitless - as the new name indicates - NELSAM looks set to create something much greater than the constituent parts!

Acquired as a source of spares, the hulk of Bell 47D-1 G-ASOL was reduced to produce by mid-2012. The cockpit of Viscount 813 G-AZLP moved to Brooklands, Surrey, by late 2013.

◆ **Access:** *On Old Washington Road, east of Washington between the A1290 and A1231. 'Brown signed' off the A1290 and A19 .* **Open:** *Apr to Oct daily, 10:00 to 17:00; Nov to Mar 10:00 to dusk - last admission one hour before closing.* **Contact:** *Old Washington Road, Sunderland, SR5 3HZ* | **0191 5190662** | **info@nelsam.org.uk** | **www.nelsam.org.uk**

❑ 'G-ADVU'		Mignet HM.14 'Flea'		93	BAPC.211, ex Stoke-on-Trent. Arrived 1994	[1]	12-13
❑ 'G-AFUG'		Luton Minor		54	BAPC.97, ex Stoke-on-Trent, Sunderland, Sibson, Sywell, Sunderland, Stanley. Arrived 10-98. Stored, in container		12-13
❑ G-ANFU*		Auster 5 Alpha		45	ex Newcastle, Sunderland, Bristol, TW385, 663, 227 OCU, 13 OTU. CoA 25-8-76. Stored	[2]	10-12
❑ G-APTW		Westland Widgeon		59	ex Helston, Southend, Westland. CoA 26-9-75, de-reg 24-8-72. Arrived 1993		12-13
❑ G-ARAD		Luton Major		60	ex local, Borgue. De-reg 16-10-02. Arrived 4-6-01. Stored	[3]	12-13
❑ G-ARHX		DH Dove 8		61	ex Doncaster, Sunderland, Booker, Southgate, Leavesden. CoA 8-9-78, de-reg 6-12-78. Arrived 1992		12-13
❑ G-ARPO		HS Trident 1C		65	ex Middleton St George, BA, BEA. CoA 12-1-86, de-reg 18-1-84. Arrived 31-7-11	[4]	12-13
❑ G-AWRS		Avro Anson C.19		46	ex Strathallan, Kemps, Junex, Hewitts, TX213, WCS, 22 GCF, OCTU, 18 GCF, 2 TAF CS, 527, CSE, RCCF. SOC 6-9-68. CoA 10-8-73, de-reg 30-5-84. Arrived 6-8-81		12-13
❑ G-BEEX		DH Comet 4C		61	ex East Kirkby, Tattershall, Woodford, Lasham, Dan-Air, Egypt Air/UAA SU-ALM. Last flight 15-10-76, de-reg 19-5-83. Arrived 1989. Cockpit		12-13
❑ G-MBDL		AES Lone Ranger		81	de-reg 13-6-90. Arrived 1989. Stored		12-13
❑ G-OGIL		Short 330-100		81	ex Gill, G-BITV, G-14-3068. Dam 1-7-92, de-reg 12-11-92 Arrived 4-93		12-13
❑ DUC		Carmam M.100S		r78	BGA.2383, ex Carlton Moor, F-CCSA. CoA 6-5-88. Arr 2009		12-13
❑ –		Brown Helicopter		62	BAPC.96, ex Stanley		12-13
❑ –		Bensen B.7		c67	BAPC.119, ex Stanley		12-13
❑ –		Olympus hang-glider		c85	BAPC.228. Arrived 1989. Stored, in its bag!		3-12
❑ WA577		Bristol Sycamore 3		r49	ex King's Heath, Shirley, St Athan 7718M (12-4-61), A&AEE, G-ALST (de-reg 17-10-50).		12-13
❑ WB685		DHC Chipmunk T.10		50	ex Leeds, Irlam, Edn UAS, Lyneham SF, 8 RFS, 1 RFS. SOC 19-7-72. Arrived 1986	[5]	12-13
❑ WD790		Gloster Meteor NF.11		52	ex Darlington, Leeming, 8743M (30-10-81), RAE Llanbedr, RRE, Ferranti, TRE. Arrived 30-10-85. Cockpit		12-13
❑ WG724	'932'	Westland Dragonfly HR.5		52	ex Chester-le-Street, Leyburn, Darlington, Blackbushe, Fleetlands, Lossiemouth SF, FRU, Ford SF, Eglinton SF SOC 16-9-65. Acquired 3-75		12-13
❑ WJ639		EE Canberra TT.18		54	ex Samlesbury, 7, B.2, 57. HP-built. SOC 9-12-81. Arr 8-88		12-13
❑ WL181	'X'	Gloster Meteor F.8		54	ex Chester-le-Street, Acklington, Kemble, CAW, Tangmere SF 34. SOC 3-11-71. Acquired 18-3-75. 92 Sqn colours		12-13
❑ WZ518	'B'	DH Vampire T.11		53	ex Chester-le-Street, Handforth, Pomona Dock, 5 FTS, Oldenburg SF, 2 TAF CF, 14. SOC 30-10-67. Acq 11-10-75	[6]	12-13
❑ WZ767		Slingsby Grasshopper TX.1		52	ex Halton. Arrived 4-85. On loan. Stored		12-13
❑ XG680	'438'	DH Sea Venom FAW.22		56	ex Sydenham, ADS, 891, Merryfield SF. SOC 20-1-70. Arr 7-81		12-13
❑ XL319		Avro Vulcan B.2		61	ex 44, Wadd W, 35, 230 OCU, 617, 230 OCU, Scamp W, 617. Flew in 21-1-83		12-13
❑ XM833		Westland Wessex HAS.3		60	ex Lasham, Wroughton, 737, 820, 814, HAS.1, 819, 700H SOC 24-11-81		12-13
❑ XN258	'589'	Westland Whirlwind HAR.9		59	ex Helston, Culdrose SF, *Hermes* SAR Flt, HAS.7, Lossiemouth SF / SAR Flt, 705, A&AEE. SOC 27-6-74. Arrived 1993		12-13
❑ XN696	'751'	DH Sea Vixen FAW.2		61	ex Flixton, Wisbech area, Walpole, Farnborough, RAE, Tarrant Rushton, FRU, 899, 893, FAW.1, 899, A&AEE, 899. SOC 10-11-81. Arrived 2-3-11. Cockpit	[7]	12-13
❑ XP627		Hunting Jet Provost T.4		62	ex London Colney, Hatfield, Shawbury, 6 FTS, 3 FTS, 1 FTS. SOC 1-10-71. Arrived 25-11-80. Fuselage	[8]	12-13
❑ 'XS933'	'BE'	EE Lightning F.53	ZF594	68	ex Warton, ZF594, R Saudi AF 53-696, G-27-66. Last flown 14-1-86. Arrived 4-89	[9]	12-13
❑ XT148		Bell Sioux AH.1		65	ex Weston-super-Mare, Halton, Panshanger, Wroughton, ARWF. Agusta-built. Arrived 20-11-93. Stored		12-13
❑ XZ335		Sud Gazelle AH.1		77	ex Shawbury, 6 Flt. Westland-built. Stored, in container		11-12
❑ 'XZ177'	'T'	Sud Gazelle 1	G-SFTA	73	ex Carlisle, 'XZ345', G-SFTA, HB-XIL, G-BAGJ, XW858 ntu. Westland-built. Crashed 7-3-84, de-reg 21-5-86. Arrived 11-86. 'ARMY' black/green camo		12-13

❑ A-522		FMA Pucará	c80	ex Yeovilton, St Athan 8768M (27-9-82), Stanley, Argentine AF. Arrived 24-7-94	[10]	12-13
❑ E-419		Hawker Hunter F.51	56	ex Dunsfold, G-9-441, Dan AF Esk.724. Last flown 10-4-76. Acquired 12-7-77		12-13
❑ 146	'8-MC'	Dassault Mystère IVA	c59	ex Sculthorpe, French AF. Last flown 3-5-78, arrived 30-4-82	[11]	12-13
❑ 42157	'11-ML'	NAA F-100D-16-NA	54	ex Sculthorpe, French AF, USAF 54-2147. Last flown 24-5-77, arrived 4-78	[11]	12-13
❑ 55-4439	'WI'	Lockheed T-33A-1-LO	55	ex Sculthorpe, French AF, USAF 55-4439. Last flown 25-1-78, arrived 5-6-79	[11]	12-13
❑ -		Fieseler Fi 103 (V-1) FSM	~	ex Pickering. Arrived 2011		3-12
❑ 16171		NAA F-86D-35-NA Sabre	52	ex Hellenikon, Greek AF, USAF 51-6171. Arrived 7-87. *Sabre Knights*, 325th FIS USAF colours		12-13
❑ 26541		Republic F-84F-40-RE Thunderstreak	53	ex Hellenikon, Greek AF, USAF 52-6541 Arrived 9-10-85		12-13
❑ –		HP C-10A Jetstream EMU	c68	ex Doncaster, Sunderland, Wycombe Air Park, Bushey, West Ruislip, Stanmore, St Albans, Radlett. RAF colours. Cockpit		12-13

■ **[1]** Flea 'G-ADVU' incorporates parts from an original, built in Congleton, Cheshire. **[1]** The Auster is a composite, with G-ANFU's forward fuselage, a 'spare' rear AOP.6 frame, stb wing of G-AKPH and port from an AOP.6. **[3]** G-ARAD is an unflown project; construction started 1959. **[4]** Take a look at **www.savethetrident.org** for details of the restoration of *Papa-Oscar* and how you can help. **[5]** Chipmunk WB685 is a composite, including the rear of WP969 (G-ATHC) and wings of WP833. **[6]** WZ518 is fitted with the wings of WZ608, the 'pod' of which can be found at Rayleigh, Essex. **[7]** The Sea Vixen cockpit is owned by Hugh Newell. **[8]** 'JP4' XP627 has the wings of Mk.3 XN584, see Bruntingthorpe, Leics, for the fuselage. **[9]** See under Farnham, Surrey, for the *real* XS933. **[10]** The Pucará is on loan from the Fleet Air Arm Museum. **[11]** Airframes from the National Museum of the USAF's Loan Program.

No.**2214 Squadron Air Cadets**: Phantom FGR.2 cockpit XV460 moved to Ipswich, Suffolk, in March 2013.

❑ XD622	DH Vampire T.11	55	ex Leeming, Barkston Ash 8160M (2-7-71), Shawbury, 118, RAFC	6-13

NOTTINGHAMSHIRE

Includes the unitary authority of Nottingham

COLWICK south-east of Nottingham, south of the A612 ring road

St John the Baptist Primary School: Has an innovative classroom. **Access:** *By prior arrangement* **only**

❑ G-SSWO	Short 360-100	83	ex Millom, Blackpool, Emerald, SE-KLO, N343MV, G-BKMY ntu, G-14-3609. CoA 4-12-04, de-reg 6-6-07	2-12

FARNSFIELD south of the A617, east of Mansfield

Wonderland Pleasure Park: **Access**, *on the A614 and 'brown signed'* | **www.wonderlandpleasurepark.com**

❑ 'V7467'	'LE-D'	Hawker Hurricane FSM	01	BAPC.288, 242 Sqn colours	[1]	3-10

■ **[1]** The Hurricane up the pole here is not to be confused with the one in similar stance at High Wycombe, Bucks!

HUCKNALL AERODROME south of the town EGNA

Drone 2 G-AEDB moved on to Wiltshire-based owners in mid-2012. Two long-in-the-tooth references have been deleted: Nipper 2 G-ARXN (last noted Jun 2007) and Jodel DR.220 G-BKOV (Feb 2006).

MANSFIELD on the A60 north of Nottingham

No.**384 Squadron Air Cadets**: Botany Avenue

❑ WT507	EE Canberra PR.7	54	ex Halton 8548M (11-3-71) 8131M ntu, St Athan, 31, 17, 58, A&AEE, 58, 527, 58. Cockpit	1-12

NEWARK-ON-TRENT

Cliff and **David Baker**: Long since mourning the absence of Harriers overhead the writer's gaff, the 'circuit' at Spanhoe, Northamptonshire, to the south across the Welland valley has become all-important in keeping spirits up. So what has this to do with Cliff and David's devotion to all things Auster? In early August 2013 a large-ish single-engined type drew the eye. A pause to watch what was thought to be Fokker Instructor G-BEPV, owned by another set of aviating brothers, Malcolm and Stephen Isbister. No, this was bigger and 'stockier'; then it dawned what it was - Auster Agricola G-CBOA. Carl Tyers of the resident Windmill Aviation was at the helm for the first flight, out of the Baker's strip on 10th August 2013 and ferried this ground-breaking and exceptional restoration to Spanhoe for flight test and sign-off. Sixteen days later it attended a fly-in at its birthplace of 1966, Rearsby. With *Oscar-Alpha* taking to the air, it departs the confines of *W&R*. This incredible achievement has so far been very under-spoken, perhaps 2014 will bring it rightfully to the forefront as it gladdens the hearts of many more people.

Agricola G-CBOA visiting Rearsby, August 2013. *Nigel Bailey-Underwood*

◆ **Access:** *The workshop/store is* **not** *open to the public and visits are* **strictly** *by prior permission*

❑ G-AHHK	Auster J/1 Autocrat	46	ex Shobdon, Cranfield. Dam 3-86, CoA 22-3-70, de-reg 3-4-89. Frame	[1]	1-08
❑ G-AIJI	Auster J/1N Alpha	47	ex East Midlands, Elsham Hall, Goxhill, Kirmington. Damaged 12-1-75, de-reg 12-3-75. Frame, spares		1-08
❑ G-AKWT	Auster 5	44	ex East Midlands, Elsham Hall, Goxhill, Stroxton Lodge, Tollerton, MT360, 26, 175, 121 Wing, 181, 80, 486, 56, 19. Crashed 7-8-48, de-reg 3-9-48. Frame		1-08
❑ G-ALNV	Auster 5	44	ex Nottingham, Leicester, RT578, 341, 329. CoA 4-7-50, de-reg 1-5-59		3-09
❑ 'G-AMKL'	Auster 'B.4'	~	nearing completion	[2]	3-09
❑ G-ANHW	Auster 5D	45	ex Shipdham, TJ320, 664. CoA 9-3-70, de-reg 15-12-71		3-09
❑ G-ANHX	Auster 5D	45	ex Leicester, TW519, 661, A&AEE. Crashed 28-3-70		3-09
❑ G-AOCP	Auster 5	45	ex TW462, 666. Damaged 4-70, de-reg 24-6-71	[3]	1-08
❑ G-ARGB	Auster 6A	46	ex Waddington, VF635, 662, 1901 Flt. CoA 21-6-74, de-reg 30-5-84		3-09
❑ G-AROJ	Beagle Airedale	62	ex Leicester, Thorney, HB-EUC, G-AROJ. CoA 8-1-76, de-reg 21-1-80		1-08
❑ G-ARTM	Beagle Terrier 1	50	ex Chirk, Auster T.7 WE536, 651, 657, Schwechat SF. Crashed 28-5-70, de-reg 12-9-73		1-08
❑ G-ARXC	Beagle Airedale	62	ex Kirton-in-Lindsey, EI-ATD, G-ARXC. CoA 27-6-76, de-reg 12-4-89		3-09
❑ EI-AMF	Taylorcraft Plus D	42	ex Abbeyshrule, G-ARRK, G-AHUM, LB286, Coltishall SF, 309, 70 GCF, 84 GCF, 22 EFTS, 43 OTU, 653		2-07

❑ F-BBSO		Auster 5		45	ex Taunton, G-AMJM, TW452, 62 GCF. Frame	3-09
❑ –	c/n 3705	Auster D.6-180		~	ex White Waltham, Rearsby. Frame	1-08
❑ –		Beagle Terrier 3		~	ex White Waltham, Rearsby. Frame	1-08
❑ WZ729		Auster AOP.9	G-BXON	55	ex Singapore, 7 Flt, 656, 652. SOC 13-9-74	3-09

■ **[1]** This J/1N frame, originally thought to be the second fuselage used by G-AIGR, is now *believed* to be from J/1 G-AHHK. **[2]** A reproduction of the Auster rear-loading ambulance one-off, the B.4, is under way. This will wear the original's identity of G-AMKL, which was scrapped at Rearsby in 1956. It is based on an as yet unidentified 'donor' airframe. **[3]** Auster 5 G-AOCP is a composite, it includes parts from G-AKOT.

NEWARK SHOWGROUND, or Winthorpe, on the A46 north-east of Newark-on-Trent

Newark Air Museum (NAM): Founder-member and stalwart supporter **David Westacott** died on 17th May 2013, aged 76. With a fascination with all things motive transport - he was also heavily into locomotives - David's National Service was with the RAF and he then joined the Royal Observer Corps. Always hands-on at Newark, David was a powerhouse in helping to make this museum the incredible place it is today. In more recent times he worked hard to establish NAM's vibrant cafe and more behind-the-scenes. People of the calibre of David *made* the UK preservation movement. He inspired countless people - including the writer - in his time and his endeavours and vision will shine on at Newark.

NAM's dynamic growth and maturity continues to delight; as does its comprehensive collecting policy. It has a scope that rivals the 'nationals'. Top among its many special events, NAM is host to the annual *CockpitFest* - see the Appendix.

The anonymous Swift CIM, on loan from Higgins Aviation, was acquired to act as back-up for the Swift restoration project at Selby, N Yorks, and moved northwards by June 2013. The cockpit of HS.125-3B 5N-AAN moved to Walcot, Lincs, on 23rd December 2013.

◆ **Access:** *Signed from the A1, A46 and A17, on Newark Showground, off Drove Lane, Winthorpe, NG24 2NY.* **Open:** *Daily Mar to Oct 10:00 to 17:00, Nov to Feb daily 10:00 to 16:00 - last entry an hour before closing. Closed Dec 24, 25, 26 and Jan 1.* **Contact:** **01636 707170 | enquire@newarkairmuseum.org | www.newarkairmuseum.org**

❑ G-AHRI	DH Dove 1	46	ex Long Marston, East Kirkby, Tattershall, Little Staughton, 4X-ARI, G-AHRI. De-reg 18-5-72. Arrived 13-5-89. Iraq Petroleum Trans Co colours		2-14
❑ G-ANXB	DH Heron 1	54	ex Biggin Hill, Fairflight, BEA, G-5-14. CoA 25-3-79, de-reg 2-11-81. Arrived 27-10-81. BEA c/s, *Sir James Young Simpson*		2-14
❑ G-APNJ	Cessna 310	56	ex Shoreham, EI-AJY, N3635D. CoA 28-11-74, de-reg 5-12-83. Arrived 4-3-04		2-14
❑ G-APRT*	Taylor Monoplane	59	CoA 31-7-12, de-reg 16-4-12. Arrived 10-4-12	[1]	2-14
❑ G-APVV	Mooney M.20A	59	ex Skelmersdale, Barton, N8164E. Crashed 11-1-81, de-reg 3-4-89. Arrived 13-12-95		2-14
❑ G-ASNY	Bensen B.8	c64	ex Eccles. De-reg 17-12-91. Arrived 20-4-09	[2]	2-14
❑ G-AXMB	Slingsby Motor Cadet	71	ex Ringmer, BGA.805, VM590 (Cadet TX.1 1946). CoA 9-7-82, de-reg 9-1-92. Arrived 18-8-02		2-14
❑ G-BFTZ	MS Rallye Club	68	ex Firbeck, Hooton Park, Warmingham, Fownhope, Rhoose, F-BPAX. CoA 19-9-81, de-reg 14-11-91. Arrived 27-1-96. *Kathy-S*		2-14
❑ G-BJAD	Clutton FRED Srs 2	r81	ex Retford. Uncompleted project, de-reg 13-3-09. Arr 9-1-02		2-14
❑ G-BKPG	Luscombe Rattler Strike	r83	ex Egginton, Tatenhill. De-reg 31-7-91. Arrived 16-12-00		2-14
❑ G-CCLT	Powerchute Kestrel	93	ex Nantwich. De-reg 9-12-03. Arrived 27-10-03		2-14
❑ 'G-MAZY'	DH Tiger Moth	c41	ex Innsworth, Staverton, Newark, Thruxton. Arrived 25-6-95. Partially covered	[3]	2-14
❑ G-MBBZ	Volmer VJ-24W	r81	ex Old Sarum. CoA 3-9-93, de-reg 29-11-95. Arr 16-10-98		2-14
❑ G-MBUE	MBA Tiger Cub 440	r82	ex Retford, Worksop. De-reg 6-9-94. Arrived 16-7-94. *The Dormouse Zeitgeist*		2-14
❑ G-MBVE	Hiway Skytrike	r82	de-reg 13-6-90, arrived 21-6-95		2-14
❑ G-MJCF	Maxair Hummer	r82	de-reg 24-1-95, arrived 17-1-06		2-14
❑ G-MJDW	Eipper Quicksilver MX	82	ex Horncastle. CoA 5-5-07. Arrived 15-12-07		2-14
❑ G-MNRT	Aviasud Sirocco 377GB	86	ex Mansfield area. CoA 18-8-01. Arrived 28-6-05	[4]	2-14
❑ CDX*	SZD Pirat	r68	BGA.1470, ex Darlton. CoA 6-1-07. Stored		2-14
❑ –	Lee-Richards Annular rep	64	BAPC.20, ex Shoreham, Winthorpe, *Those Magnificent Men...*		2-14
❑ –	Mignet HM.14 'Flea'	36	BAPC.43, ex East Kirkby, Tattershall, Wellingore. Arr 9-3-94		2-14
❑ –	Mignet HM.14 'Flea'	36	BAPC.101, ex Tumby Woodside, East Kirkby, Tattershall, Sleaford. Arrived 9-3-94. Battered fuselage		2-14
❑ –	Zurowski ZP.1 helicopter	c77	BAPC.183, ex Burton-on-Trent. Arrived 26-4-85. Unflown		2-14
❑ –	Ward Gnome	~	unflown. Fitted with a Citroen 2CV		2-14

❑ –		Slingsby Firefly CIM	~	ex Barkston Heath. Arrived 1-11. Cockpit procedure trainer.		2-14
❑ –*		Tasuma CSV 30 UAV	~	on launcher. First noted 6-13	[5]	2-14
❑ –*		Tasuma CSV 30 UAV	~	'Navigator'. First noted 6-13	[5]	2-14
❑ –*		Tasuma Observer UAV	~	RAF roundels. First noted 6-13	[5]	2-14
❑ VH-UTH		GAL Monospar ST-12	35	ex Innsworth, Winthorpe, Booker, Croydon, Panshanger, Biggin Hill, Australia, New England Airways. Arrived 18-3-68		2-14
❑ KF532		NAA Harvard IIB	44	ex Lossiemouth, 781, 799, 727, 799, 733, 758. SOC 9-4-54. Noorduyn-built. Arrived 24-8-10. Cockpit		2-14
❑ RA897		Slingsby Cadet TX.1	c44	stored		2-14
❑ TG517		HP Hastings T.5	48	ex 230 OCU, SCBS, BCBS, 202, 53, 47. Flew in 22-6-77		2-14
❑ VL348		Avro Anson C.19	46	ex Southend, G-AVVO (re-reg 16-9-72), Shawbury, 22 GCF, 24 GCF, Colerne SF, 62 GCF, HCMSU, RCCF. SOC 15-11-67. Arrived 11-72		2-14
❑ VR249	'FA-EL'	Percival Prentice T.1	48	ex G-APIY, 1 ASS, RAFC. SOC 17-8-57. CoA 18-3-67, de-reg 19-4-73. Flew in 8-7-67. RAFC colours		2-14
❑ VZ608		Gloster Meteor FR.9	51	ex Hucknall, Shoreham, MoS, RR. Arr 2-70. RB.108 test-bed		2-14
❑ VZ634		Gloster Meteor T.7	48	ex Wattisham 8657M, 5 MU, Leeming SF, Stradishall SF, 41, 141, 609, 247. SOC 15-11-71. Arrived 16-12-85		2-14
❑ WB491		Avro Ashton 2	51	ex Woodford, Rhoose, Dunsfold, Farnborough, Rolls-Royce, RAE, Tudor 2 G-AJJW, TS897. SOC 13-2-62. Arrived 26-2-03. Forward fuselage	[6]	2-14
❑ WB624		DHC Chipmunk T.10	50	ex Hooton Park, Firbeck, Long Marston, Warmingham, East Midlands, Wigan, Dur UAS, Abn UAS, Henlow, St Athan, 22 GCF, Debden, Jurby SF, 8 FTS, 18 RFS. SOC 14-7-72. Arrived 14-9-95		2-14
❑ WF369	'F'	Vickers Varsity T.1	51	ex 6 FTS, AE&AEOS, AES, 2 ANS, 201 AFS. SOC 1-4-76, flew in same day. 6 FTS colours.		2-14
❑ WH779		EE Canberra PR.7	54	ex East Midlands, Boscombe Down, Farnborough, Marham, RAE, 100, 13, Wildenrath 8129M (10-3-71), Brüggen, 31, 80, 13, 542. Arrived 7-11-10. Cockpit	[7]	2-14
❑ 'WH792'		EE Canberra PR.7 WH791	54	ex Cottesmore 'WH717' 8187M (19-11-71), St Athan, 8176M and 8165M ntu, 81, 58, 82, 542. Arrived 29-11-98. 31 Sqn colours	[8]	2-14
❑ WH863		EE Canberra T.17	53	ex Marham 8693M, 360, A&AEE, B.2, RAE, IAM. Short-built. SOC 29-5-81. Arrived 10-7-90. Cockpit	[9]	2-14
❑ WH904	'04'	EE Canberra T.19	53	ex Cambridge, 7, 85, T.11, W Raynham TFF, 228 OCU, B.2 35, 207. (Short-built) SOC 4-6-80. Arrived 1-10-85	[10]	2-14
❑ WK277	'N'	Supermarine Swift FR.5	55	ex Congresbury, Wisley, Cosford, Leconfield 7719M (9-11-61), 2, F.4, RAE. Arrived 18-8-69. 2 Sqn colours		2-14
❑ WM913	'456'	Hawker Sea Hawk FB.3	54	ex Fleetwood, Sealand 8162M, Culdrose A2510 (14-7-61), Abbotsinch, 736, 700, 895, 897, 806. Arrived 1-7-84		2-14
❑ WR977	'B'	Avro Shackleton MR.3/3	57	ex Finningley 8186M (3-11-71), 203, 42, 206, 203, 42, 201, 206, 201, 220. Arrived 1-5-77. 42 Sqn colours	[11]	2-14
❑ WS692	'C'	Gloster Meteor NF.12	53	ex Cranwell, Henlow 7605M (8-7-59), 72, 46. AWA-built. Arrived 31-10-81		2-14
❑ WS739		Gloster Meteor NF(T).14	54	ex Misson, Church Fenton 7961M (12-10-67), Kemble, 1 ANS, 2 ANS, 25. AWA-built. Arrived 21-1-84. 25 Sqn c/s		2-14
❑ WT651	'C'	Hawker Hunter F.1	54	ex Lawford Heath, Halton, Credenhill, Weeton 7532M (22-11-57), 229 OCU, 233 OCU, 229 OCU, 222. Arrived 17-1-92. 222 Sqn colours		2-14
❑ WT933		Bristol Sycamore 3	51	ex Sutton, Strensall, Halton 7709M (18-11-60), A&AEE, G-ALSW (de-reg 26-3-51). Arrived 17-6-80		2-14
❑ WV606	'P-B'	Percival Provost T.1	54	ex Halton 7622M (20-11-55), 1 FTS. Arrived 2-72		2-14
❑ WV787		EE Canberra B.2/8	52	ex Abingdon 8799M (23-12-83), A&AEE, Ferranti, ASM. Arrived 24-11-85. Hefner 'bunny' logo, A&AEE colours		2-14
❑ WW217	'351'	DH Sea Venom FAW.21	55	ex Cardiff, Ottershaw, Culdrose, Yeovilton, ADS, 891, 890. SOC 20-8-70. Arrived 18-12-83. 890 Sqn colours		2-14
❑ WX905		DH Venom NF.3	53	ex Henlow, Hendon, Yatesbury 7458M (14-10-57), 27 MU, 23. Arrived 16-5-89. 23 Sqn colours		2-14
❑ XA239		Slingsby Grasshopper TX.1	53	ex 'Northampton'		2-14

❑ XB261		Blackburn Beverley C.1	55	ex Duxford, Southend, A&AEE. SOC 6-10-71. Arrived 25-5-04. Cockpit		2-14
❑ XD593	'50'	DH Vampire T.11	54	ex Woodford, Chester, St Athan, 8 FTS, CFS, FWS, 5 FTS, 4 FTS. SOC 12-12-68. Arrived 30-3-73. CFS colours		2-14
❑ XH992	'P'	Gloster Javelin FAW.8	59	ex Cosford 7829M (21-2-64), Shawbury, 85. Arrived 22-8-81. 85 Sqn colours		2-14
❑ XJ560	'243'	DH Sea Vixen FAW.2	59	ex RAE Bedford, Farnborough, Halton 8142M (29-6-71), 893, 899, 892, 890. Arrived 10-8-86. 893 Squadron colours		2-14
❑ XL764	'J'	Saro Skeeter AOP.12	58	ex Nostell Priory, Rotherham, Middle Wallop, Arborfield 7940M (13-3-67), Hayes, A&AEE, MoA, AAC, Saro, AAC. Arrived 16-7-80		2-14
❑ XM383	'90'	Hunting Jet Provost T.3A	60	ex Crowland, Scampton, 7 FTS, 1 FTS, RAFC, 6 FTS, BSE, 2 FTS, A&AEE, 2 FTS. Arrived 12-11-94. 7 FTS colours		2-14
❑ XM594		Avro Vulcan B.2	63	ex 44, Scampton Wing, 617, 27. SOC 19-1-83. Flew in 7-2-83. 44 Sqn colours	[11]	2-14
❑ XM685	'513'	Westland Whirlwind HAS.7	59	ex Panshanger, Elstree, Luton, G-AYZJ (de-reg 29-12-80), Fleetlands, Lee-on-Solent, 771, *Ark* Ship's Flt, 847, 848. SOC 24-3-71. Arrived 17-6-80. 771 Sqn colours		2-14
❑ XN573	'E'	Hunting Jet Provost T.3	61	ex Blackpool Airport, Kemble, 1 FTS, CFS. SOC 28-5-76. Arrived 15-4-89. Cockpit		2-14
❑ XN819		AW Argosy C.1	61	ex Finningley 8205M (10-7-72), 8198M ntu, Shawbury, Benson Wing, 105, MoA. Cockpit section, in small display hall		2-14
❑ XN964	'118'	Blackburn Buccaneer S.1	63	ex Bruntingthorpe, E Midlands, Brough (10-10-76), Pershore, RRE, RAE, 803, 736, 801. Arrived 26-2-88. 801 Sqn colours		2-14
❑ XP226		Fairey Gannet AEW.3	62	ex Lee-on-Solent, Southwick, Lee-on-Solent, A2667 (28-3-79), Lossiemouth, Ilchester, 849. Arrived 7-11-82. 849 'D' Flt colours		2-14
❑ XR534	'65'	Folland Gnat T.1	63	ex Dunholme Bridge, Valley 8578M (2-12-77), 4 FTS, CFS. Arrived 2-12-00. 4 FTS colours		2-14
❑ XS417	'DZ'	EE Lightning T.5	64	ex Binbrook, LTF, 5, 11, 5, 11, LTF, 56, 23, 11, 23, 226 OCU. SOC 29-7-88. Arrived 5-9-88. Lightning Training Flt colours		2-14
❑ XT200	'F'	Bell Sioux AH.1	65	ex Middle Wallop. Westland-built. Arrived 1978		2-14
❑ XV490	'R'	McD Phantom FGR.2	69	ex Nantwich, Bruntingthorpe, Wattisham, 74, 228 OCU, 92, 56, 22, 92, 56, 23. SOC 1-10-92. Cockpit. 74 Sqn c/s	[12]	2-14
❑ XV728	'A'	Westland Wessex HC.2	68	ex Fleetlands, 72, 2 FTS, CFS, 18. Arrived 18-8-98. *Argonaut*		2-14
❑ XW276		Sud Gazelle 03	70	ex Sunderland, Wroughton, Southampton, Middle Wallop, Farnborough, Leatherhead, F-ZWRI	[13]	2-14
❑ XX492	'A'	HP Jetstream T.1	75	ex Culdrose, Cranwell, 45, 3 FTS, 45, 6 FTS, METS. Arrived 9-12-04. 45 Sqn colours		2-14
❑ XX634	'T'	SAL Bulldog T.1	74	ex Wellesbourne Mountford, Shawbury, Liv UAS, Man UAS, EMUAS, CFS, 3 FTS, CFS, Cam UAS, 2 FTS. Arr 9-1-06. CFS c/s		2-14
❑ XX753		SEPECAT Jaguar GR.1	75	ex RAF EP&TU, Bottesford, 9087M, St Athan, Abingdon, Shawbury, 54, 226 OCU, 6. Arr 1-5-10. 16 Sqn c/s. Cockpit		2-14
❑ XX829	'GZ'	SEPECAT Jaguar T.2A	74	ex Ipswich, Shawbury, St Athan, 54, 16, 6, 226 OCU, 6, 54. Arrived 21-3-12. 54 Sqn colours		2-14
❑ ZA176	'126'	HS Sea Harrier FA.2	81	ex Yeovilton, 801, 800, 801, 899, 801, 899, 800, 801, 899, 801, 809, 800, 809, 899. Arrived 21-7-04. 800 Sqn c/s		2-14
❑ –	TA200	Auster AOP.9	56	ex Middle Wallop. SOC 28-3-63. Fuselage frame	[14]	2-14
❑ –		Hunting Jet Provost CIM	~	procedures trainer.		2-14
❑ –		Folland Gnat T.1 CIM	~	ex Melton Mowbray. Procedures trainer		2-14
❑ –	'DB001'	McD Phantom CIM	~	ex Wattisham. Full-axis simulator		2-14
❑ –*		HP Victor SIM	~	ex Ashby de Launde, Elvington, Marham, Warton. Arr 5-10-13		2-14
❑ –		EE Canberra PR.9	~	ex Corby, Stock, Rhoose, Brough, Boscombe Down. Short-built. Arrived 14-11-00. Cockpit	[15]	2-14
❑ –		SAL Bulldog T.1 CIM	~	ex Newark, Newton	[16]	2-14
❑ AR-107		SAAB S.35XD Draken	71	ex Scampton, Esk.729, RDanAF. Arrived 29-6-94		2-14
❑ 83	'8-MS'	Dassault Mystère IVA	~	ex Sculthorpe, French AF. Last flown 3-5-78, arrived 9-78. ET.1/8 colours		2-14
❑ 56321		SAAB Safir	56	ex G-BKPY (for ferry flight, de-reg 8-2-02), Norwegian AF. Flew in 14-7-82		2-14

❑ Fv37918	'57'	SAAB AJSH.37 Viggen	76	ex Cranwell, RSwAF, F21 and F10 Wings. Arrived 25-6-06		2-14
❑ '458'		MiG-23ML *Flogger*	~	ex Chester, Latvia, USSR. (024003607). Arrived 22-5-02. Polish colours	[17]	2-14
❑ '71'		MiG-27K *Flogger*	~	ex Chester, Latvia, USSR. (61912507006). Arrived 22-5-02 Soviet AF colours	[17]	2-14
❑ 42-12417		NAA Harvard IIB	42	ex Earls Colne, Harrington, East Tilbury, Windsor, N Weald, Dutch AF B-163, RCAF FE930, 42-12417. Arrived 24-8-10		2-14
❑ 51-9036		Lockheed T-33A-1-LO	51	ex '5547', Sculthorpe, French AF. Last flown 30-5-78. Arrived 1979. 48th FIS colours	[18]	2-14
❑ 54-2223		NAA F-100D-16-NA Super Sabre	54	ex Sculthorpe, French AF. Last flown 24-5-77, arrived 5-78. USAF colours, 32nd TFW	[18]	2-14

■ **[1]** G-APRT is the prototype Taylor JT.1 Monoplane, designed and built by John Taylor and first flown at White Waltham 4-7-59. **[2]** *November-Yankee* is on loan from Roger Light - see Stockport, Gtr Man. **[3]** Tiger Moth 'G-MAZY' is *very* likely BAPC.21. A composite, it is mostly G-AMBB/T6801, in which case it is: ex Scampton SF, 6 FTS, 18 EFTS. **[4]** Sirocco was built by Midland Ultralights at Bitteswell, Leics. **[5]** The three RPV-thingies were built by Tasuma (UK) of Blandford Forum. **[6]** Laid down at Woodford as Tudor 2 G-AJJW, TS897 ntu, but completed as an Ashton. **[7]** The exceptionally restored PR.7 WH779 is on loan from Darren Green - **www.wh779.webs.com** - it was an award-winner at *CockpitFest* 2013. **[8]** PR.7 'WH792' on loan from 81 Squadron Association. **[9]** T.17 cockpit is on loan from Aaron Braid. **[10]** T.19 WH904 was built by Shorts Brothers and Harland as a B.2 and therefore the forward fuselage *should* have a plate reading SHB-0-2388. Inspection found the cockpit to have the plate EEP71123, which would make it WH651. The logic works out like this... WH651 was issued to English Electric for conversion from a B.2 to a T.4 on 5th July 1956 and in this process it would have been fitted with a new-build T.4 cockpit. It looks as though the old cockpit passed on to Boulton Paul for use in the B.2 to T.11 conversions. WH904 was issued to BP on 17 10-57 for T.11 fit. It received the cockpit of WH651. (And later was further converted to T.19 status.) **[11]** The Shackleton and the Vulcan are owned by Lincolnshire's Lancaster Association. **[12]** Phantom cockpit is on loan from Mike Davey (see also Liverpool, Merseyside). **[13]** Gazelle is on loan from the Museum of Army Flying, Middle Wallop, Hants. **[14]** The Auster AOP.9 is very probably XR268 or *perhaps* XS238. The plate reads 'B5-10-1185 - issue 72 -10-9-62 and a mod plate reads 'AUS/R-10/74' - any help? **[15]** The PR.9 cockpit, owned by Frank and Lee Millar, is believed to be an unflown 'boiler plate' for development and/or installations trials. See also Corby, Northants. **[16]** The Bulldog CIM is on loan from Higgins Aviation, Newark, Notts. **[17]** The *Floggers* are on loan from Hawarden Aviation Services, Hawarden, Wales. **[18]** Airframes from the National Museum of the USAF's Loan Program.

NOTTINGHAM AERODROME or Tollerton, south of the A52, east of the city — EGBN

Last noted in July 2008, Seabee N6210K is confirmed as having returned to the USA.

❑ G-BGGF	Piper Tomahawk	CoA 15-10-94, de-reg 4-12-02. Stored	2-12
❑ G-GRAY	Cessna 172N	ex N4859D. Ditched 2-4-93, de-reg 27-9-00. Fuselage, dumped	2-12
❑ G-OATS	Piper Tomahawk	ex N9659N. Crashed 27-10-05, de-reg 16-1-06. Fuselage, dumped	9-13

RETFORD AERODROME or Gamston, off the B6387 south of East Retford — EGNE

Cessna A152 G-FLAP and GA-7 Cougar G-REAT, both not reported since August 2008, have been deleted.

SYERSTON AIRFIELD off the A46 south-west of Newark-on-Trent — EGXY

RAF Syerston: The Jaguars were for use in Officer Cadet training, under the command of RAF College, Cranwell, Lincs, but were expected to be put up for disposal early in 2014. The airfield is also the base of the **Central Glider Maintenance Flight**; turn-over of Viking gliders is reasonably swift and only long-term items are given here.

❑ XX739	'I'	SEPECAT Jaguar GR.1	74	ex Cosford 8902M (27-5-86), Halton, Shawbury, Gibraltar Det, 6, 226 OCU	12-13
❑ XX751	'10'	SEPECAT Jaguar GR.1	74	ex Cosford 8937M (29-5-87), Abingdon, 226 OCU, 14	12-13
❑ ZE550	'VX'	Grob Viking T.1	84	ex 615, 614, 626, CGS, 622, BGA.3025. Damaged	7-11
❑ ZE556		Grob Viking T.1	84	ex Stapleford, Beeston, Syerston, BGA.3031, CGHF, Arbroath, 662 VGS, 636 VGS, 631 VGS, 661 VGS, 622 VGS. Crashed 12-4-02. Cockpit	10-12

TOTON Harrier T.4 XW267 moved to Ipswich, Suffolk, during January 2014.

WORKSOP on the A57/A60 east of Sheffield

Phil Jarvis keeps a skeletal Harrier cockpit at a *private* location in the *general* area. See also Doncaster, S Yorks.

❑ XV806	HS Harrier GR.3	71	ex South Molton, Boscombe Down, Culdrose A607[3], A2602[2] (18-4-91), Cosford, 4, 3, 4, 20. Cockpit, skeletal	6-13

OXFORDSHIRE

ABINGDON

Lodge Hill Garage: West of the A4183, close to its junction with the A34

❑	'N3310'	'AI-A'	Supermarine Spitfire FSM	~	ex Wellesbourne Mountford, Winthorpe. Displayed	10-12

BANBURY

Last recorded in June 2008, the fuselage of Cessna 150A G-ARRF has been deleted.

BENSON AIRFIELD east of the A4074, east of Wallingford — EGUB

RAF Benson: The Wessex is displayed outside 606 (Chiltern) Squadron RAuxAF's HQ.

❑	'PL904'		Supermarine Spitfire FSM	89	BAPC.226, ex 'EN343', gate [1]	7-13
❑	XS507	'27'	Westland Wessex HU.5	64	ex Gosport, Lee-on-Solent A2674 [2], A2762 (21-3-88), 772, 845, 707, 848, 847, 772, 2 FTS, 772, 707, 846, 845, 707	7-13
❑	XW201		Sud Puma HC.1	71	ex 230, 33, 27, 230 OCU, 230, 240 OCU. Westland-built. Inst	11-13

■ **[1]** The Spitfire represents the PR.XI flown by Flt Lt Duncan McCuaig DFC of 541 Sqn which departed Benson on 28-9-44 bound for a recce of Bremen and failed to return and is dedicated to his memory.

Locally: David Webb's Hunter cockpit travels extensively to events around the country.

❑	WV381	'732'	Hawker Hunter GA.11	55	ex Culham, Kemble, Farnborough, FRADU, FRU, FWS, 222. Crashed 2-11-72. Cockpit	6-13

BICESTER

Defence Storage and Distribution Agency: *Not* the aerodrome, but signed as 'MoD Bicester'.

❑	ZA319	'TAV'	Panavia Tornado GR.1	79	ex 9315M (19-3-02), St Athan, 15, TTTE	10-13
❑	ZD607*		HS Sea Harrier FA.2	85	ex Gosport, St Athan 9328M, Warton, St Athan, 800, FRS.1, 801, 800, 801, 800, 801, 800, 899. Crashed 2-7-00. Arrived 23-8-12	10-13

BICESTER AERODROME on the A421 north-east of Bicester — EGDD

In July 2012 an organisation called Bomber Command Heritage launched a campaign to acquire the airfield. This bid was unsuccessful, the grass airfield and the former technical site going to **Bicester Heritage Ltd** by March 2013. BHL's website declares the intention to be: "the UK's first and only business campus dedicated to historic motoring and aviation". The plan being to attract 'cottage industries' and other specialist concerns. These plans were in their early days as &R went to press - keep an eye on: **www.bicesterheritage.co.uk**

Windrushers Gliding Club Last noted in March 2004, Capstan BPT was flying again by 2012. | **www.windrushers.org.uk**

❑	BBU*		Slingsby Skylark 2B	58	BGA.845, CoA 8-11-09. First noted 4-12	4-12
❑	BJQ*		Slingsby Capstan	61	BGA.1009, CoA 1-6-08. First noted 4-12	4-12
❑	DWF		DFS Grunau Baby IIB	c48	BGA.2433,ex Keevil, AGA.16, RNGSA.1-13, VW743. CoA 9-1-02	1-12

Also: A Chipmunk is under restoration in the general area.

❑	WB763*		DHC Chipmunk T.10	50 G-BBMR	ex St Mawgan, Bodmin, Tollerton, Twyford, Camberley, Feltham, Southall, 2 FTS,4 FTS, AOTS, 1 ITS, 1 AEF, Bri UAS, 3 AEF, AAC, 652, Odiham SF, 24 RFS, 14 RFS. CoA 1-11-05. First noted 10-12	2-13

BRIZE NORTON AIRFIELD on the A4095 south-west of Witney — EGVN

RAF Brize Norton: The **Defence Movements School** and the **Joint Air Delivery Test and Evaluation Unit** keep airframes for teaching techniques and trials. The Dakota is displayed outside the **47 Air Despatch Squadron** hangar. With the demise of the VC-10 the forward fuselage of ZD234, used as a procedures trainer, was disposed of.

❑	-*	'YS-DH'	Douglas Dakota IV	44 G-AMPO	ex Lyneham, Coventry, Air Atlantique, G-AMPO, LN-RTO, G-AMPO, KN566, Oakington SF, 77, 62, Waterbeach SF, 1 1381 CU, 133 CU, 238, 44-76853. CoA 29-3-97. de-reg 18-10-01. 271 Sqn colours. Arrived 16-9-12	9-13

❑ XV304		Lockheed Hercules C.3A	68	ex LTW, C.1, 30-47, USAF 66-13547. Wheels-up landing 6-5-10. Fuselage, instructional	11-13
❑ XZ994	'O'	HS Harrier GR.3	81	ex 9170M, St Athan, 1417 Flt, 233 OCU, 1417F, 233 OCU	11-13
❑ ZB684		Sud Gazelle AH.1	83	ex 9330M, Fleetlands, 667, 665, 655. Westland-built	11-13

CHALGROVE AIRFIELD on the B480 north-west of Watlington — EGLJ

Martin-Baker: Meteor T.7 WL419 *Asterix* and T.7(mod) WA638 act as flying test-beds for MB. Two anonymous cockpits, last recorded in March 2005 have been deleted: MiG-19 and IAI Lavi.

❑ EE416	Gloster Meteor III	46	ex Wroughton, South Kensington, MB. Cockpit	3-12
❑ –	Northrop F-5A F/Fighter	63	ex Greek AF, 63-8418. Cockpit, dump	7-12
❑ 65-10450	Northrop AT-38B Talon	65	cockpit	7-12

■ **[1]** Almost certainly this is/was a Shenyang F-6.

Reflight Airworks: Tiger Moth G-CGYN moved to Leicester and was flight tested there during September 2012. It was air-freighted out to India through Heathrow on 23rd September 2012. By August 2012 Harvard G-CGYM had followed to Leicester, Leics. (A Dakota is also being prepared for the Flight, see Cotswold, Glos.)

ENSTONE AERODROME on the B4030 east of Chipping Norton

❑ G-ARET	Piper Tri-Pacer 160	60	ex North Moreton. CoA 20-5-83	10-10
❑ G-AVGJ	Jodel DR.1050	61	ex F-BJYJ. SAN-built. CoA 22-4-85, de-reg 10-6-93	5-05
❑ G-AWAC	Gardan Horizon 180	67	crashed 22-7-03, CoA 11-6-04	8-11
❑ G-AWSP	Druine Condor	69	CoA 23-1-95. Rollason-built	6-13
❑ G-AXPF	Cessna F.150K	69	Reims-built. CoA 22-4-02	6-13
❑ G-BNCG	QAC Quickie Q-2	91	Crashed 21-8-97, de-reg 12-1-98	10-10
❑ G-MVHI	Thruster TST Mk.1	88	CoA 10-3-06	10-10
❑ G-MVOV*	Thruster TST Mk.1	89	CoA 10-9-10	7-13
❑ G-SION	Piper Tomahawk 112	81	ex N32661. Crashed 2-7-97, CoA 28-12-00, de-reg 9-9-02	8-11
❑ F-WREI	Gardan Horizon 180	~	ex France. Spares for G-AWAC - see above	8-11

GROVE on the A417 north-west of Wantage

Grove Technology Park: Located on the western edge of the former airfield. | **www.grovetechpark.com**

❑ J-1758	DH Venom FB.54	57	ex Lambourn, North Weald, N203DM, Cranfield, G-BLSD, SwAF. Federal A/c Factory-built. De-reg 5-6-96. Displayed	7-13

HENLEY-ON-THAMES on the A4155 north of Reading

No.**447 Squadron Air Cadets**: Friday Street

❑ XS218	Hunting Jet Provost T.4	64	ex Woodley, Halton 8508M (23-2-77), Shawbury, 3 FTS. Cockpit	9-11

Also: In the *general* area: a Vampire is at a **private** address.

❑ J-1169	DH Vampire FB.6	~	ex Samedan gate, Swiss AF	4-13

KIDLINGTON on the B4260 north of Oxford

Malcolm Coe: Keeps a Buccaneer at a *private* location.

❑ XX895	HS Buccaneer S.2B	75	ex Woking, St Athan, Lossiemouth, 208, 12, 237 OCU, 12, 237 OCU, 16, 15, 12. SOC 13-1-95	12-11

OXFORD

The cockpit of Spitfire II P8088 (G-CGRM) moved temporarily to Brooklands, Surrey, on 14th December 2011. Spitfire II restoration project P8208 changed hands during March 2013 and is now listed under Dursley, Glos.

OXFORD AIRPORT, or Kidlington

EGTK

Airplan Flight Equipment: Sister company to the publishers of *Wrecks & Relics*, AFE has an EoN 460 'flying' in the saleroom.

◆ **Access:** *Chancerygate Business Centre, in Langford Lane, about four minutes' walk from the airport's main entrance, on the southern boundary, on a minor road between the A44 and A4260 - look for the Mercedes showroom.* **Open:** *Mon to Fri 09:00 to 17:30 and Sat 09:00 to 17:00.* **Contact: 01865 | tech@afeonline.com | www.afeonline.com**

❑ G-APWL	BRK	EoN 460 Srs 1A	59	BGA.1172, ex Eaglescott, BGA.1172, G-APWL, RAFGSA.268, G-APWL. CoA 26-4-00, de-reg 18-2-10. Displayed	2-14

SHENINGTON AERODROME west of the A422, north-west of Banbury

Shenington Gliding Club: *Busy gliding site, prior permission required* | **www.shenington-gliding.co.uk**

❑ G-BJVC		Evans VP-1	84	fuselage	8-10
❑ GCG	'S81'	Schleicher K.8B	~	BGA.3722, ex D-5227. CoA 24-10-04	5-13
❑ HCM*		Schleicher K.7	~	BGA.3838, ex D-5669. CoA 29-8-02	6-12
❑ D-1155*		Schleicher K.8B	~	first recorded stored in 1999!	6-12
❑ SE-UCF		Slingsby Venture T.2	81	ex ZA664. Stored	6-13

SHRIVENHAM east of Swindon, south of the A420

Defence Academy of the United Kingdom: Harrier GR.3 XV744 moved to Tangmere, W Sussex, on 14th March 2013.

❑ XT621		Westland Scout AH.1	66	ex Wroughton, 655, 656, 666, 664, 666	6-13
❑ XV122	'A'	Westland Scout AH.1	68	ex Almondbank, Wroughton. Displayed	6-13
❑ ZJ369*		GEC Phoenix UAV	~	-	6-13
❑ 69-16445		Bell AH-1F Cobra	69	ex US Army, 1/1CAV, Budingen. 'IFOR' markings	6-13
❑ 70-15154		Bell OH-58CR Kiowa	70	ex Lyneham (transit), US Army	6-13

SOUTHMOOR off the A420/A415 west of Abingdon

❑ XL563		Hawker Hunter T.7	57	ex Hereford 9218M (7-10-93), Kempston, Farnborough, IAM	7-12

STEVENTON on the B4017 south of Abingdon

Robin Phipps: Keeps his Sea Vixen cockpit at a *private* location near here. His Buccaneer cockpit is at Coventry, Warks.

❑ XN647	'707'	DH Sea Vixen FAW.2	61	ex Bruntingthorpe, Helston, Culdrose SAH-10, A2610 (25-2-71), 766, 892, FAW.1, 766, 899. Cockpit	11-13

UPPER HEYFORD or Heyford Park, north of the B4030, north of Oxford

Heyford Park: You will have to turn to *W&R14* (p162) for the last entry on the once superb USAF base, home of the 'Swinger' and in 1994 closing rapidly. It is now an obligatory store for row upon row of cars and an expanding industrial park. A small museum run by Don Todd has been created in what was the base commander's building.

◆ **Access:** *By prior arrangement with North Oxfordshire Consortium* **only | 01869 238200 | www.raf-upper-heyford.org**

WALLINGFORD on the A4130 east of Didcot

A yard here has dealt with surplus airframes from nearby Benson.

❑ XT681	'U'	Westland Wessex HC.2	67	ex Benson 9279M (23-9-97), Shawbury, 72, WTF, 18. Hulk	10-13

SHROPSHIRE

Includes the unitary authority of Telford and Wrekin

ALVELEY By October 2013 the cockpit of Canberra B.2 WF911 had made the trek to Long Kesh, N Ireland.

ASTLEY east of the A49 north of Shrewsbury

❑ G-AWGM		M-P Kittiwake II	68	ex Hanworth, Halton. Damaged 18-1-86, de-reg 4-3-99	9-95

BRIDGNORTH

Millington Engineering: Roy Millington and friends are lovingly restoring a Harrier.

Access: *By prior arrangement* **only | www.millingtonengines.com**

❑ XV808* 'DD08'	HS Harrier GR.3	71	ex Gosport, Culdrose, A2687[2] (11-7-94), 9076M, 233 OCU, 3, GR.1 20, 4. Arrived 13-9-12		12-13

COSFORD AIRFIELD south of Junction 3 of the M54 EGWC

Royal Air Force Museum: See below - and the front cover - for the Goodwin Sands Dornier, which surfaced during June 2013. Plans were being finalised in January 2014 to bring VC-10 C.1K XR808 by road to Cosford - see under Bruntingthorpe, Leics. Cosford will be staging a special World War One centenary exhibition later in 2014 and this will feature three airframes from Hendon, Gtr Lon - see under that heading for details. In return a special 'do' on the Royal Air Force of Oman at Hendon during 2014 will see the Provost T.1 and Pioneer CC.1 move 'down south'.

There is a superb cafe within the visitor centre, with views over the active airfield. The **Aerospace Museum Society** provides a vital link in both the restoration of exhibits and the running of the museum and special events.

◆ **Access:** '*Brown signed' from Junction 3 of the M54.* **Open:** *Mar to Oct 10:00 to 18:00 daily - last entry 17:00; Nov to Feb 10:00 to 17:00 daily - last entry 16:00. Closed Xmas and New Year - check the website for full details. Annual airshow - extra charges apply.* **Contact:** *Cosford, Shifnal, Shropshire, TF11 8UP* | **01902 376200** | **cosford@rafmuseum.org** | **www.rafmuseum.org**

Hangar 1: The cockpit of Vulcan B.1 XA893 had moved to the 'Deep Store' - see below- by March 2012. Jet Provost T.3 XM351 had moved to Hangar 2 by November 2013. Jetstream T.1 XX496 had moved outside by August 2013.

❑ G-EBMB	Hawker Cygnet	25	ex Hendon, Cardington, Henlow, Lympne No.14. De-reg 30-11-61, acquired 1968		1-14
❑ G-ACGL '6'	Comper Swift	33	ex Hatch, Stafford, Timperley, Wigan, Stockport, Kinver. CoA 22-3-40, de-reg 1-12-46, arrived 3-11-11		1-14
❑ G-AEEH	Mignet HM.14 'Flea'	36	ex St Athan, Colerne, Bath, Whitchurch. Acquired 1966		1-14
❑ 'G-AFAP'	Junkers Ju 52/3m	54	ex Spanish AF, Cuatro Vientos, Escuela de Paracaidistas, Ala Mixed 46, Ala de Tansport, CASA 352L T2B-272, T2B-272, Escuela de Paracaidistas, CASA 352A T2-272. CASA-built. Last flew 31-5-78. British Airways colours		1-14
❑ 'G-AJOV'	Westland Dragonfly HR.3 WP495	53	ex Biggin Hill, Banstead, Warnham, Wimbledon, Blackbushe, Culdrose SF, 705, *Victorious* Flt, *Centaur* Flt, *Victorious* Flt, HR.1, Culdrose SF, Ford SF. SOC 1-6-64, arrived 2-80. BEA colours		1-14
❑ G-APAS	DH Comet 1XB	53	ex Shawbury 8351M, XM823, G-APAS, G-5-23, Air France, F-BGNZ. De-reg 22-10-58, last flown 8-4-68, arrived 17-9-78. BOAC colours		1-14
❑ 'FS628'	Fairchild Argus II	43	ex Rochester, G-AIZE, Cosford, Henlow, Hanwell, G-AIZE, N9996F, 43-14601. CoA 6-8-66, de-reg 6-3-73, acquired 2-73. SEAC colours		1-14
❑ 'RG904'* 'Z'	Supermarine Spitfire FSM	12	*Haldane Place*, 441 Sqn colours	[1]	1-14
❑ TX214	Avro Anson C.19	46	ex Henlow 7817M, HCCS, MCS, RCCF, Staff College CF, 1 FU, 16 FU. Acquired 29-8-63		1-14
❑ VP952	DH Devon C.2/2	47	ex St Athan 8820M, 207, 21, WCS, SCS, Upavon SF, TCCF, MCS, BCCS, HCCS, A&AEE, MCCF, AAFCE, Hendon SF, HS. Last flown 5-7-84		1-14
❑ WE600	Auster C4	51	ex St Athan, Swinderby, Finningley 7602M, Trans-Antarctic Expedition, 663. Acquired 1964. Skis	[2]	1-14
❑ WL679	Vickers Varsity T.1	53	ex 9155M, Farnborough, RAE, BLEU, RAE. Last flown 27-7-92	[3]	1-14
❑ WP912	DHC Chipmunk T.10	52	ex Hendon 8467M, Man UAS, RAFC, ITS, Cam UAS, CFS, 2 FTS, Lon UAS, FTCCS, HCCS, 8 FTS. Acquired 14-12-76	[4]	1-14
❑ WV746	Percival Pembroke C.1	55	ex 8938M, 60, 207, 21, WCS, TCCF, FTCCS, BCCS, HS, 2 TAFCF. Acquired 13-4-87. 60 Sqn colours		1-14
❑ XD674	Hunting Jet Provost T.1	54	ex store, St Athan, Swinderby, Finningley, Bicester 7570M, 71 MU, A&AEE, AS Bitteswell, Hunting. Last flown 4-6-57		1-14
❑ XJ918 *and* 8190M	Bristol Sycamore HR.14	56	ex 2 SoTT 8190M, 32, MCS, Kemble, Wroughton, 110, Seletar, A&AEE, 275. Acquired 1983		1-14
❑ XL703 'Z'	SAL Pioneer CC.1	56	ex store, Manchester, Henlow 8034M (1-10-68), 209, 230	[5]	1-14

❑ XP411		AW Argosy C.1	62	ex 2 SoTT 8442M (22-5-75), 6 FTS, Kemble, 70. Acq 4-88		1-14
❑ XR525	'G'	Westland Wessex HC.2	64	ex Shawbury, 72, 60, 72, Benson SF, SAR Wing, Benson SF, 72. Acquired 13-5-04. *Sunshine*, 72 Sqn colours		1-14
❑ XR977	'3'	Folland Gnat T.1	64	ex 2 SoTT 8640M, Red Arrows, 4 FTS. Last flown 5-10-79. 'Reds' colours		1-14
❑ XS639		HS Andover E.3A	67	ex 9241M, Northolt, 32, 115, C.1, 32, 46. Last flown 13-7-94. 32 Sqn colours		1-14
❑ XX654	'3'	SAL Bulldog T.1	74	ex Shawbury Newton, CFS, 3 FTS, CFS, 3 FTS, Bri UAS, 2 FTS. Acquired 1993		1-14
❑ 7606M	'P-C'	Percival Provost T.1 WV562	54	ex Cranwell, Henlow 7606M (30-6-59), 22 FTS. Acquired 9-79	[5]	1-14
❑ 418947		Fieseler Fi 103 (V-1)	c44	BAPC.94, ex 8583M, Westcott		1-14

■ **[1]** The Spitfire, claimed to be the only 1:1 'Airfix' 'kit', was assembled during a James May TV programme called *Toy Story* at Cosford in 2009. It was removed during 2010, going to Gateguards (UK) Ltd at Newquay, Cornwall, for what the museum termed "maintenance and strengthening". It returned in October 2010 and occupies space that could be taken up by a *real* exhibit. **[2]** WE600 is one of two specially-modified Auster T.7s. **[3]** WL679 made the last-ever flight by the type, into Cosford, on 27-7-92. **[4]** The Chipmunk was used by the Duke of Edinburgh during his flying training. **[5]** Pioneer and Provost are due to move to Hendon, Gtr Lon, for a special exhibition during 2014.

Hangar 2 - Test Flight: By March 2012 Meteor T.7 WA634 had gone to the 'Deep Store' - see below. With the arrival of the EAP, Tornado P.02 XX946 was rolled across to the MBCC - see below.

❑ WG760		EE P.1A	54	ex Binbrook, Henlow, Bicester 7755M, St Athan, Warton, A&AEE. Acquired 1-86		1-14
❑ WG768		Short SB.5	52	ex Topcliffe, Finningley 8005M, ETPS, RAE Bedford, RAE Farnborough, A&AEE, RAE Bed', A&AEE. Last flown 7-3-68	[1]	1-14
❑ WG777		Fairey FD.2	56	ex Topcliffe, Finningley 7986M, RAE Bedford. Acq 8-9-67		1-14
❑ WK935		Gloster Meteor F.8(mod)	53	ex St Athan, Colerne 7869M, RAE. AWA-built. Acquired 12-1-65. Prone-pilot		1-14
❑ WZ744		Avro 707C	53	ex Topcliffe, Finningley, Colerne 7932M, RAE, Avro. Last flown 7-6-66, acquired 17-4-67		1-14
❑ XD145		Saro SR.53	56	ex Brize Norton, Henlow, Westcott, A&AEE. Last flown 20-10-59, arrived 2-3-82	[2]	1-14
❑ XE670		Hawker Hunter F.4	55	ex deep store, St Athan 8585M / 7762M, Abingdon, Bicester, 93, 26. Cockpit		1-14
❑ XF926		Bristol 188	63	ex 8368M, Foulness Island, RAE. L/flown 12-1-64. Arr 3-9-72		1-14
❑ XM351	'Y'	Hunting Jet Provost T.3	58	ex 2 SoTT, Halton 8078M (25-2-70), Shawbury, 3 FTS, 7 FTS, 2 FTS. Acquired 6-96. Education area		1-14
❑ XN714		Hunting 126/50	63	ex RAE Bedford, NASA Ames and Moffett, Holme-on-Spalding Moor, RAE. Last flown 9-11-67, arrived 30-4-74		1-14
❑ XR220		BAC TSR-2 XO-2	64	ex Henlow 7933M, Boscombe Down, A&AEE. Never flown. Acquired 20-6-67, arrived 4-5-75		1-14
❑ XS695		HS Kestrel FGA.1	65	ex Wyton, Cardington, Yeovilton, Culdrose 'SAH-6', Manadon A2619 (10-5-73), A&AEE, RAE, CFE, Tri-Partite Eval Sqn, A&AEE, RAE. Crashed 1-3-67. On display from 1-14	[3]	1-14
❑ XX765		SEPECAT Jaguar GR.1 (m)	75	ex Loughborough, Warton, BAe, GR.1, 226 OCU, 17, 14. Last flown as GR.1 4-8-78, last flown as ACT 11-84	[4]	1-14
❑ ZF534*		BAe EAP	85	ex Loughborough, Warton. Last flown 1-5-91, Arrived 27-3-12	[5]	1-14

■ **[1]** The T-tail rear fuselage of the Short SB.5 is displayed alongside WG768. **[2]** SR.53 first flew on 16-5-57 and last flew 20-10-59 with a total time of just under 18 hours in 46 sorties. **[3]** The Kestrel was placed on RAF Museum charge 10-5-74 but moved to Manadon on extended loan, before coming back into the fold. **[4]** XX765 is much-modified Active Control Technology (ACT) test-bed. The machine was the world's first to fly with an all-digital quadruplex 'fly-by-wire' control system, on 21-10-81 with Chris Yeo at the helm. **[5]** EAP factoids: first flown at Warton 8-8-86, total time 191 hours, 21 minutes.

Hangar 3 - 'Warplanes': Spitfire PR.XIX PM651 was taken off display by March 2012 and in November 2013 was air-freighted to Kuwait, for 'indefinite loan' that will include display at several venues, including Bahrain.

❑ K9942	'SD-D'	Supermarine Spitfire I	39	ex Hendon 8383M, Rochester, Hendon, 71 MU Bicester, Fulbeck, Wroughton, Newark, Cardiff, 53 OTU, 57 OTU, 72. Acquired 9-11-71. 72 Sqn colours	1-14
❑ LF738	'UH-A'	Hawker Hurricane II	44	ex Rochester, Biggin Hill, Wellesbourne Mountford, 5405M, 22 OTU, 1682 BDTF. Acquired 8-2-84. 1682 BDTF c/s	1-14

❑ RF398		Avro Lincoln B.2/4A	45	ex 8376M, Henlow, Abingdon, 151, CSE, BCBS. AWA-built. Last flown 30-4-63		1-14
❑ TA639	'AZ-E'	DH Mosquito TT.35	45	ex 7806M, CFS, 'HJ682', 3 CAACU, Aldergrove TT Flt, B.35. Acquired 5-7-67. 627 Sqn, Guy Gibson, colours		1-14
❑ XK724		Folland Gnat F.1	56	ex Cranwell, Bicester, Henlow 7715M. Acquired 14-8-85		1-14
❑ ZG477		BAe Harrier GR.9A	90	ex Cottesmore, 1, 4, 800, QinetiQ, GR.7/A, 3, 1, 3, 4 Arrived 19-12-01. '1969-2010' markings	[1]	1-14
❑ –		Hawker Hind (Afghan)	37	BAPC.82, ex Hendon, Kabul, RAfghan AF, RAF. Acq 20-1-68		1-14
❑ A-515		FMA Pucará	78	ex 9245M, ZD485, A&AEE, Yeovilton, Stanley, Arg AF A-515, Mauritania AF M4 / 5T-MAB ntu. Last flown (as ZD485) 9-9-83. Gr 3 de Ataque colours		1-14
❑ L-866		Consolidated PBY-6A Catalina	45	ex 8466M, Colerne, Danish AF Esk.721, 82-866, BuNo 63993. Acquired 29-5-74		1-14
❑ 191614	'14'	Messerschmitt Me 163B-1a Komet	44	ex 8481M, Biggin Hill, Westcott, Brize Norton, Farnborough, Hussum, II/JG400. Acquired 1975	[2]	1-14
❑ 420430	' '3U+CC'	Messerschmitt Me 410A-1/U2	43	ex St Athan 8483M, Cosford, Fulbeck, Wroughton, Stanmore Park, Brize Norton, Farnborough, AM.72, Vaerlose		1-14
❑ 475081	'GM+AK'	Fieseler Fi 156C-7 Storch	44	ex St Athan, Coltishall, Bircham Newton, Finningley, Fulbeck, Halton 7362M (3-8-56), VP546, RAE, AM.101, Farnborough. Mraz-built. Arrived 6-4-89		1-14
❑ 733682*		Focke-Wulf Fw 190A-8/R6	43	ex South Lambeth, 9211M, ex Duxford, South Lambeth, Biggin Hill, Cranwell, Brize Norton, Farnborough AM.75. Arrived 20-12-12 - see notes under MBCC	[3]	1-14
❑ –		Focke-Achgelis Fa 330A-1	43	ex 8469M, Henlow, Farnborough. Acquired 9-67		1-14
❑ 16336	'24'	Kawasaki Ki-100-1b	c44	BAPC.83, ex MBCC, Hendon, Cosford, St Athan 8476M, Cosford, Henlow, Biggin Hill, Fulbeck, Wroughton, Stanmore, Sealand, Japanese Army		1-14
❑ 5439		Mitsubishi Ki-46-III *Dinah*	44	BAPC.84, ex St Athan 8484M, Biggin Hill, Fulbeck, Wroughton, Stanmore, Sealand, ATAIU-SEA. Arrived UK 8-46, Cosford 3-89. 3 Sqn, 81st HQ Rec Group, colours		1-14
❑ –		Yokosuka Ohka 11	c45	BAPC.99,ex St Athan 8486M, Cosford, Westcott		1-14
❑ J-1704		DH Venom FB.54	56	ex 'Cold War', Greenham Common. Swiss AF. Acq 8-6-79		1-14
❑ '413573'	'B6-V'	NAA P-51D-25-NA Mustang	44	ex Hendon 9133M, Halton, N6526D, RCAF 9289, 44-73415. Acquired 1991. *Isabel III*, 361st FS, 357th FG c/s		1-14

■ **[1]** GR.9 factoids; Operation WARDEN Incerlik, Turkey, 1993-1994; Operation ALLIED FORCE, Gioia del Colle, Italy, 1999; Operation HERRICK, Kandahar, Afghanistan, 2008-2009. Made final departure from HMS *Ark Royal* 24-11-10 and took part in the 'Farewell to Harrier' formation 15-12-10. Completed 4,191 flight hours and 3,969 landings. **[2]** Komet is marked '191461' on the port fin. **[3]** Fw 190A was modified to be the upper component of a Mistel S3B flying-bomb combination and was mounted on a Ju 88H when captured. It joined the collection at Cranwell from 18-9-46 and remained on loan from the RAF Museum during its time at IWM.

Goodwin Sands Dornier: On 10th June 2013 the Goodwin Sands Dornier Do 17Z was successfully raised from its watery grave 50ft down. The engines did not come up with the first lift, but were later recovered. The airframe moved to Cosford and a highly-specialised conservation programme, lasting at least two years, has been initiated. It is displayed within two hydration poly-tunnels alongside Hangar 3, still in the lifting frames. The airframe is sprayed in citric acid and sodium hydroxide for ten minutes, every 20 minutes, around the clock to neutralise the salt and prevent further corrosion. Once stabilised, the Dornier will be prepared for display at Hendon.

❑ 1160*	'5K+AR'	Dornier Do 17Z-2	40	ex Goodwin Sands, 7/KG3. Shot down 26-8-40. Hulk, salvaged from sea. Arrived 6-13	1-14

National 'Cold War' Exhibition:

❑ KN645		Douglas Dakota C.4	44	ex 'KG374', 8355M, Colerne, AFN CF, MinTech, AFN CF, MinTech, AFN HQ, SHAPE CF, Malta CF, BAFO CS, 2nd TAF CS, 44-77003. Acquired 1-5-74. Transport Command colours	1-14
❑ TG511		HP Hastings T.5	48	ex 8554M, 230 OCU, SCBS, BCBS, 202, 47. Acquired 16-8-77	1-14
❑ TS798	G-AGNV	Avro York C.1	45	ex 'MW100', Shawbury, Brize Norton, Staverton, 'LV633', G-AGNV, Skyways, BOAC, TS798. CoA 6-3-65, de-reg 7-5-65. acquired 16-5-72	1-14
❑ WS843	'J'	Gloster Meteor NF(T).14	54	ex Hendon, St Athan, Henlow 7937M, St Athan, Kemble, 1 ANS, MoA, 228 OCU. AWA-built. Acquired 13-3-67. 16 Sqn colours	1-14
❑ XA564		Gloster Javelin FAW.1	54	ex 2 SoTT, Locking 7464M, Filton. Acquired 9-75	1-14

❑ XB812	'U'	NAA Sabre F.4	53	ex Hendon, 9227M, Duxford, Rome, Italian AF MM19666, XB812, 93, 112, RCAF (no service) 19666. Acquired 31-1-94. 93 Sqn colours		1-14
❑ XD818		Vickers Valiant BK.1	56	ex Hendon, Marham 7894M, 49 'A' Flt. Acquired 25-5-65, arrived 8-05. 49 Sqn colours		1-14
❑ XG337		EE Lightning F.1	59	ex 2 SoTT 8056M, Warton, A&AEE, Warton. Acquired 10-83		1-14
❑ XH171	'U'	EE Canberra PR.9	60	ex 2 SoTT 8746M, 39, 13, 39 MoA, 58. Short-built. Last flight 13-7-82. 39 Sqn colours		1-14
❑ XH672		HP Victor K.2	60	ex 9242M (26-3-94), Shawbury, 55, 57, 543, MoA. Last flown 30-11-93. *Maid Marion.* 55 Sqn colours	[1]	1-14
❑ XL568	'X'	Hawker Hunter T.7A	58	ex Cranwell 9224M (19-11-93), Lossiemouth, 12, 74, MoA, 74, HS. Acquired 12-2-02. 74 Sqn colours		1-14
❑ XL993		SAL Twin Pioneer CC.1	58	ex Henlow 8388M (6-2-69), Shawbury, 21, 78		1-14
❑ XM598		Avro Vulcan B.2	63	ex 8778M, 44, Wadd Wing, Cott Wing, 12. Arrived 20-1-83. 44 Sqn colours		1-14
❑ 'XN972'		Blackburn Buccaneer S.1 XN962	63	ex Hendon, Cosford, St Athan, 'XN972', Abingdon 8183M, Foulness, 736, 800, 809. . Acquired 7-95. Cockpit		1-14
❑ XR371		Short Belfast C.1	67	ex Hucknall, Kemble, 53. Arrived 6-10-78. *Enceladus.* 53 Sqn colours		1-14
❑ XV591	'013'	McD Phantom FG.1	69	ex St Athan, 111, 43, 892. 892 Sqn Trans-Atlantic c/s. Cockpit		1-14
❑ 503		MiG-21PF *Fishbed* G-BRAM	c66	ex Farnborough, Bournemouth, G-BRAM, N610DM, North Weald, Hungarian AF. De-reg 16-4-99, acquired 18-10-06. Hungarian AF colours		1-14
❑ 1120 red		MiG-15*bis* (Lim-2)	55	ex Hendon, Cardington, South Lambeth, Hendon, Middlesborough, Polish AF. Acq29-10-86. Polish AF c/s		1-14
❑ 74-0177		GD F-111F Aardvark	64	ex Mildenhall, AMARC, 27th TFW, 48th TFW, 366th TFW, 347th TFW. Last flown 10-95, arrived 3-11-05. 492nd FS USAFE colours		1-14
❑ 68-8284		Sikorsky MH-53M Pave Low	68	ex Brize Norton, Baghdad, *Desert Thunder*, 20th SOS, 67th ARRS, SEA. Acquired 17-12-08		1-14

■ **[1]** Victor XH672 flew during the Falklands conflict, including the BLACK BUCK raids and had the highest sortie score during Operation GRANBY - 52 'ops'. When it landed at Shawbury (for roading to Cosford) on 30-11-93 it made the last flight by a Victor.

Michael Beetham Conservation Centre: Part of the Albatros-RE.8-Snipe exchange, Farman F-HMFI was exported to New Zealand during December 2012, arriving in February. Never an RFC/RAF airframe, its part in the core collection was always anomalous. Ki-100-1B 16336 moved to Hangar 3 by August 2013. Fw 190A-8 733682 arrived from South Lambeth on 20th December 2012 and was readied for display at the MBCC. It moved to Hangar 3 in October 2013. Kestrel FGA.1 XS695 was completed and moved to Hangar 2 in January 2014. Typhoon Ib MN235 is being prepared for a loan to Canada. The fuselage of Brigand TF.1 RH746 and Vampire T.11 XD515 have been 're-filed' under 'Deep Store' - see below.

◆ **Access:** *Viewing on Friday afternoons by prior arrangement* **only** *to groups, max 20 persons. Annual open week in early November - see RAF Museum web-site for details* | **01902 376208**

❑ P1344	'PL-K'	HP Hampden TB.I	42	ex 9175M, Wyton, Cardington, Hatch, Petsamo, USSR, 144, 14 OTU. Forced down 4-9-42	[1]	1-14
❑ MF628		Vickers Wellington T.10	44	ex Hendon 9210M, Abingdon, St Athan, Biggin Hill, Hendon, Heathrow, Wisley, Vickers, *Dam Busters*, 1 ANS		1-14
❑ MN235*		Hawker Typhoon Ib	44	ex Hendon, Shawbury, Smithsonian, USAAF FE-491. Gloster-built. Acq 19-11-68. Arrived 7-11-13. See above		1-14
❑ XX946	'WT'	Panavia Tornado P.02	74	ex Hendon, Honington 8883M (5-2-86), Laarbruch, Honington, Warton. Acquired 16-11-94		1-14
❑ 7198/18		LVG C.VI	18	ex Old Warden, 9239M, G-AANJ (CoA 8-5-04, de-reg 11-12-03), Stanmore, Colerne, Fulbeck. Last flown 20-9-03, arr 12-11-03		1-14

■ **[1]** The Hampden is being restored 'half-and-half' - one side fully restored, the other allowing inspection of the interior. At some stage in its operational career it was fitted with the tailboom of Short-built Hereford I L6012. This was SOC on 20-10-41 while serving with the Jurby-based 5 BGS following a collision with an Anson. The Hereford was a Hampden powered by Napier Daggers

Outside:

❑ XG225		Hawker Hunter F.6A	56	ex 8713M (15-2-82), Weapons School, 2 SoTT, Kemble, 229 OCU, 92, 74, 20. Acquired 1988. 'Gate'. 237 Sqn colours	1-14

❑	'XM497'		Bristol Britannia 312F G-AOVF	57	ex Southend, 9Q-CAZ, G-AOVF, Stansted, Donaldson, British Eagle, BOAC. Last flown 2-5-84, De-reg 21-11-84. RAFASC colours, *Schedar*		1-14
❑	XS709	'M'	HS Dominie T.1	64	ex Cranwell, 55, 3 FTS, 6 FTS, 1 ANS, CAW, 1 ANS, A&AEE, G-37-65 Rolls-Royce. Last flight 11-2-11		1-14
❑	XV202		Lockheed Hercules C.3	67	ex Brize Norton, 47, Lyneham TW, C.1, Lyneham TW, 48, USAF 66-8552. Last flown 12-8-11		1-14
❑	XV249		HS Nimrod R.1	70	ex Kemble, Waddington, 51, MR.2 Kinloss W, St Mawgan W, 42, MR.1, Kinloss, 203, Kinloss. 'Nimrod R.1 1974-2011' titles. Last flown 29-7-11, arrived 3-12. Unveiled 28-9-12	[1]	1-14
❑	XX496	'D'	HP Jetstream T.1	75	ex 'Cold War', Cranwell, 45, 6 FTS, 3 FTS. SAL-built. Arrived 22-3-04. 45 Sqn colours		1-14
❑	204		Lockheed SP-2H Neptune	61	ex Dutch Navy, 320 Sqn, Valkenburg, 5 Sqn, 321 Sqn. Last flight 22-7-82. 320 Sqn colours		1-14

■ **[1]** The Nimrod made the last-ever flight by the breed (into Kemble) on 29-7-11, completing 18,488 flying hours.

Boulton Paul Aircraft Heritage Project: During 2012 the project was informed that use of the former Boulton Paul factory built in Wolverhampton, West Midlands, would come to an end and the hunt was on for new premises. This proved impossible, but the RAF Museum lent a helping hand with an offer of storage while the possibility of accommodation within the Cosford site is examined. Airframes listed below are in deep store and are ***not*** available for inspection.

❑	'X-25'*		BP P.6 replica	01	BAPC.274, ex Wolverhampton. Arrived 23-4-13		4-13
❑	-*	'F'	BP Overstrand replica	11	forward fuselage, completed mid-2012. 101 Sqn colours Arrived 23-4-13		4-13
❑	'L7005'*	'PS-B'	BP Defiant replica	02	BAPC.281, ex Wolverhampton. 264 Sqn colours. Arrived 28-4-13	[1]	4-13
❑	WN149*	'AT'	BP Balliol T.2	54	ex Wolverhampton, Bacup, Salford, Failsworth, RAFC. Arrived 28-4-13	[2]	4-13
❑	'XE531'*		Hawker Hunter T.53	58	ex Wolverhampton, North Weald, Bruntingthorpe, Bournemouth, Bruntingthorpe, Bitteswell, Hatfield G-9-430 (1-12-75), RDanAF Esk.724, ET-272, 35-272. Cockpit. Arrived 4-13	[3]	4-13

■ **[1]** Defiant re-creation uses an original turret and parts from salvaged remains. The rear fuselage of N3378 and others are displayed in a diorama depicting the Bleaklow Moor crash site. **[2]** Balliol is described as 'half restoration, half replica'. [3] The Hunter cockpit is painted as the one-off RAE test-bed T.12 which was written off 17-3-82.

Deep store: *Not* available for inspection. The cockpit of Hunter F.4 XE670 went on display by November 2013.

❑	RH746		Bristol Brigand TF.1	46	ex Kemble, Sunderland, Failsworth, CS(A), ATDU Gosport, Bristol, ATDU, A&AEE, Bristol. Fuselage. Stored		3-12
❑	VX573		Vickers Valetta C.2	50	ex 8389M, Henlow, Wildenrath CF, Buckeburg CF. *Lorelei*		4-10
❑	WA346		DH Vampire FB.5	51	ex Cardington, Cosford, Henlow, Hendon, 3/4 CAACU, 1 FTS, 7 FTS, 130, 98, 102 FRS. EE-built. SOC 10-10-60	[1]	4-10
❑	WA634		Gloster Meteor T.7(mod)	49	ex St Athan, Martin-Baker. Acquired 8-74		3-12
❑	WD931		EE Canberra B.2	51	ex Aldridge, Pershore, RRE, RAE. SOC 13-5-65. Cockpit	[2]	4-10
❑	WE982		Slingsby Prefect TX.1	50	ex 8781M, Cardington, Henlow, Syerston, Manston, ACCGS, CGS, 1 GC, 621 GS, 612 GS, 644 GS, 643 GS, 166 GS, 143 GS		4-10
❑	WL732		BP Sea Balliol T.21	54	ex Henlow, A&AEE, Lossiemouth, Anthorn.		4-10
❑	XA893		Avro Vulcan B.1	56	ex Abingdon, Bicester 8591M (10-6-63), A&AEE. Cockpit		3-12
❑	XD515		DH Vampire T.11	54	ex Rugeley, Winthorpe, Misson, Linton-on-Ouse 7998M, 3 FTS, 7 FTS, 1 FTS, 5 FTS, 206 AFS. Stored		9-08
❑	XT903	'X'	McD Phantom FGR.2	68	ex Wyton, Leuchars, 56, 228 OCU, 92, 228 OCU, 23, 228 OCU, 2, 228 OCU. Cockpit		4-10
❑	-		Hawker P.1121	58	ex Henlow, Cranfield. Fuselage sections		4-10
❑	6130		Lockheed Ventura II	42	ex SAAF Museum, SAAF, RAF AJ469, n/s		4-10
❑	'6771'		Republic F-84F-51-RE	52	ex Rochester, Southend, Belgian AF FU-6, 52-7133		4-10

■ **[1]** The Vampire FB.5 has the booms of VX461. **[2]** The Canberra B.2 cockpit carries the c/n EEP.71038 which *should* make it WD956 (which had no operational life, undertaking RED DEAN missile trials), comments? WD956 was issued from Vickers, Brooklands, 30-4-57 to 15 MU, Wroughton, and sold for scrap 1964. Was the nose grafted to WD931?

Defence School of Aeronautical Engineering (DSAE): From 1st October 2012 the Defence *College* of Aeronautical Engineering was renamed as 'School'. DSAE Cosford 'parents' the schools at Arborfield, Berks, and Gosport, Hampshire. See under Lyneham, Wiltshire, for the current state-of-the-art on tri-service technical training.

What is still called **1 School of Technical Training** is split into a series of squadrons and flights, each teaching specialist elements: **Avionics and Mechanic Training Squadron**; **Aerosystems Training Wing** - comprising the **Avionics Training Flight** and the **Weapons Training Flight**; the **Airfield Squadron** - aka the unofficial 238 Squadron; and a **Battle Damage Repair Flight**. No attempt has been made to delineate which airframes are with which elements in the listing below.

Departures: **Jet Provost** T.5As XW290 to Bruntingthorpe, Leics, 11-12-13; XW299, XW301 and XW410 to Selby, N Yorks, 31-1-13; T.5As XW318, XW358, XW360, XW361, XW425 and XW434 to Selby, N Yorks, 16-1-13; T.5As XW321, XW328, XW330 to Ipswich, Suffolk, 16-10-13; XW367, XW370, XW416, XW432 to Ipswich, Suffolk, 9-10-13; T.5A XW364 to Halton, Bucks, 18-10-12, arriving 22-10-12; T.5A XW420 to Woodvale, Merseyside, 25-6-13; **Tornado** GR.1 ZA399 to Selby, N Yorks, 29-5-13; **Wessex** HC.2 XR498 to Gosport, Hants, 11-9-12. Last recorded in July 1999, synthetic Jaguar training rig 'XX110' (BAPC.169) has been deleted.

❑ XM362		Hunting Jet Provost T.3	59	ex 8230M, Halton, Kemble, Shawbury, 3 FTS, 2 FTS. Arrived 21-3-73. 'Cutaway' and camouflaged	10-13
❑ XV643	'262'	Westland Sea King HAS.6	69	ex 9323M, St Athan, Gosport A2657[4] (24-3-00) Culdrose, 819, 849, 819, 814, 820, 819, 824, 814, A&AEE	10-13
❑ XV653	'63'	Westland Sea King HAS.6	69	ex 9326M, Gosport, 810, 706. Arrived 15-10-02	10-13
❑ XV659	'62'	Westland Sea King HAS.6	70	ex 9324M, Gosport, Fleetlands, 810, 814, 819, 706, 826, 824, 819, 814, FTU, 824. Arrived 7-10-02	10-13
❑ XV701	'64'	Westland Sea King HAS.6	71	ex Gosport, Cosford, Gosport A2809 (10-12-01), 814, 820, 810, 819, A&AEE, 819, 706, 824. *Lulabelle.*	10-13
❑ XW320	'71'	BAC Jet Provost T.5A	70	'9015M', 9016M (19-12-89), ex Halton, 1 FTS, Leeming SF, 3 FTS, RAFC	10-13
❑ XW327	'62'	BAC Jet Provost T.5A	70	ex Halton 9130M (9-12-91), CFS, 7 FTS, 6 FTS, 7 FTS, 1 FTS, CFS, RAFC	10-13
❑ XW375	'52'	BAC Jet Provost T.5A	71	ex 9149M (7-6-93), Halton, CFS, 6 FTS, RAFC	10-13
❑ XW418	'MT'	BAC Jet Provost T.5A	72	ex 9173M (17-12-92), Shawbury, 1 FTS, 7 FTS, CFS, 3 FTS, Leeming SF, 3 FTS	10-12
❑ XW430	'MW'	BAC Jet Provost T.5A	72	ex 9176M (20-1-93), 1 FTS, CFS, 3 FTS, Leeming SF, 3 FTS	4-13
❑ XW436	'68'	BAC Jet Provost T.5A	72	ex Halton 9148M (18-5-92), 1 FTS, CFS, 3 FTS, Leeming SF, 3 FTS, RAFC	10-13
❑ XW852		Sud Gazelle HCC.4	73	ex 9331M, St Athan, Fleetlands, 32. Westland-built	10-13
❑ XW897		Sud Gazelle AH.1	74	ex Shawbury, 3 Regt, 663, 654, 663, 658, 671, 670, 669, 664, 658, 660. Westland-built. Arrived 7-1-09. '238 Sqn' c/s	10-13
❑ XW899	'Z'	Sud Gazelle AH.1	74	ex Shawbury, 6 Flt, 658, 662, 653, 655, 663, 660. Westland-built. Arrived 7-1-09. '238 Sqn' colours	10-13
❑ XX110	'EP'	SEPECAT Jaguar GR.1	74	ex 8955M (3-12-87), Shawbury, 6, A&AEE, BAC. *Baghdad or Bust* (stb)	10-13
❑ XX112	'EA'	SEPECAT Jaguar GR.3A	73	ex Coltishall, 6, GR.1, 6, A&AEE. Arrived 13-6-07	10-13
❑ XX117	'ES'	SEPECAT Jaguar GR.3A	73	ex St Athan, 16, GR.1, 16, 6, SAOEU, 226 OCU, 54, Indian AF JI004, G-27-317, A&AEE, 6, 226 OCU, JOCU. L/flown 1-7-05	10-13
❑ XX119	'AI'	SEPECAT Jaguar GR.3A	73	ex Coningsby, 6, GR.1, 54, 16, 226 OCU, 8898M ntu, 226 OCU, A&AEE, 54, 226 OCU, JOCU. Last flown 29-3-06. 'Tiger' c/s	10-13
❑ XX141*	'T'	SEPECAT Jaguar T.2A	74	ex Cranwell 9297M, 6, 16, 226 OCU, 6, 226 OCU, JOCU. Arrived 23-4-13	10-13
❑ XX412		Sud Gazelle AH.1	75	ex Shawbury, 847, 3 CBAS. Westland-built. Arrived 7-1-09. '238 Sqn' colours	10-13
❑ XX723	'EU'	SEPECAT Jaguar GR.3A	74	ex Shawbury, 6, 41, 54, DERA, GR.1, 54, 6, 54, 226 OCU. Arrived 24-4-07	10-13
❑ XX724	'EC'	SEPECAT Jaguar GR.3A	74	ex Coltishall, 6, T.2, 54, Shawbury, 54, 226 OCU, A&AEE. *Ecoops* (pt), *Egleno* (stb). Last flown 12-6-07	10-13
❑ XX725	'T'	SEPECAT Jaguar GR.3A	74	ex Coningsby, 41, 54, SAOEU, GR.1, 54, SAOEU, 54, 6, Indian JI010, G-27-235, 54, 226 OCU. Last flown 2-7-07. Desert pink colours	10-13
❑ XX726	'EB'	SEPECAT Jaguar GR.1	74	ex Halton 8947M (9-12-87), Shawbury, 6	10-13
❑ XX727	'ER'	SEPECAT Jaguar GR.1	74	ex 8951M, Shawbury, 6, 54, 6, JOCU. Last flown 26-7-84	10-13
❑ XX729	'EL'	SEPECAT Jaguar GR.3A	74	ex Coltishall, 6, GR.1, SAOEU, 6, 54, 226 OCU, 6, 54, Indian JI012, G-27-326, 6, 226 OCU. *Eliam*. Arrived 18-5-07	10-13
❑ XX738	'ED'	SEPECAT Jaguar GR.3A	74	ex Coltishall, 6, GR.1, SAOEU, 54, 6, Shawbury, 54, Indian AF JI016, G-27-329, 6. Arrived 13-5-07	10-13
❑ XX743	'EG'	SEPECAT Jaguar GR.1	74	ex Halton 8949M (3-12-87), Shawbury, 6	10-13

❑ XX746	'S'	SEPECAT Jaguar GR.1A	74	ex Halton 8895M (23-5-86), Shawbury, 226 OCU, 14, 17, 6, 31, 226 OCU		10-13
❑ XX748	'EG'	SEPECAT Jaguar GR.3A	74	ex Coltishall, 6, GR.1, 54, 14, 226 OCU. *Egaz*. Last flown 18-5-07		10-13
❑ XX752	'EK'	SEPECAT Jaguar GR.3A	75	ex Coltishall, 6, 41, 16, GR.1, 6, Shawbury, 54, 226 OCU, 54. Arrived 16-6-07		10-13
❑ XX756	'W'	SEPECAT Jaguar GR.1	75	ex 8899M (23-5-86), 14, 20, 226 OCU, 14		10-13
❑ XX766	'EF'	SEPECAT Jaguar GR.3A	75	ex St Athan, 6, 16, GR.1, 6, 54, 226 OCU, 17. Arr 31-1-06		10-13
❑ XX767	'FK'	SEPECAT Jaguar GR.3A	75	ex Shawbury, 41, 54, GR.1, 54, 17, 31, 14, 226 OCU, 14. Last flown 11-4-06		10-13
❑ XX818	'DE'	SEPECAT Jaguar GR.1	75	ex Halton 8945M (4-11-87), Shawbury, 31, 20, 17		10-13
❑ XX819	'CE'	SEPECAT Jaguar GR.1	75	ex 8923M (19-12-86), Shawbury, 226 OCU, 20, 17		10-13
❑ XX821*	'P'	SEPECAT Jaguar GR.1	75	ex 8896M (23-5-86), Cranwell, Coltishall, 41, 14, 17. Black colours. Arrived 4-4-12		10-13
❑ XX824	'AD'	SEPECAT Jaguar GR.1	75	ex Halton 9019M (10-1-90), Shawbury, 14, 17, 14		10-13
❑ XX825	'BN'	SEPECAT Jaguar GR.1	75	ex 9020M, Halton, Shawbury, 17, 31, 14		10-13
❑ XX833		SEPECAT Jaguar T.2A	75	ex Boscombe Down, QinetiQ, DERA, RAE, 41, 14, 20, 226 OCU. QinetiQ titles	[1]	10-13
❑ XX835	'EX'	SEPECAT Jaguar T.4	75	ex Coningsby, 6, 41, T.2, 41, 6, 54, RAE, 226 OCU. Last flown 1-7-07		10-13
❑ XX837*	'Z'	SEPECAT Jaguar T.2	75	ex Cranwell, Cosford, Halton 8978M (29-9-88), Shawbury, 226 OCU. Black colours. Arrived 7-8-12		10-13
❑ XX840	'EY'	SEPECAT Jaguar T.4	75	ex Coltishall, 6, 16, T.2, St Athan, Shawbury, 41, 2, 226 OCU, 17. Last flown 12-6-07		10-13
❑ XX847	'EZ'	SEPECAT Jaguar T.4	76	ex Coltishall, 6, 16, T.2, St Athan, 41, Shawbury, 226 OCU, 31, 20, 14, 2, 226 OCU. Last flown 18-5-07		10-13
❑ XX958	'BK'	SEPECAT Jaguar GR.1	75	ex 9022M, Shawbury, 17, 14. Last flown 12-3-85		10-13
❑ XX959	'CJ'	SEPECAT Jaguar GR.1	75	ex 8953M, Shawbury, 20, 14. Last flown 4-7-84		10-13
❑ XX965*	'C'	SEPECAT Jaguar GR.1A	75	ex Cranwell 9254M (18-9-96), Coltishall, 16, 226 OCU, 54, 14. 16 Sqn colours. Arrived 17-10-12		10-13
❑ XX967	'AC'	SEPECAT Jaguar GR.1	75	ex 9006M, Shawbury, 14, 31. Arrived 2-11-89		10-13
❑ XX968	'AJ'	SEPECAT Jaguar GR.1	75	ex 9007M, Shawbury, 14, 31. Arrived 1-11-89		10-13
❑ XX969	'01'	SEPECAT Jaguar GR.1	75	ex 8897M (23-5-86), 226 OCU, 31		10-13
❑ XX970	'EH'	SEPECAT Jaguar GR.3A	75	ex Coltishall, 6, GR.1, 6, 226 OCU, 17, 31. Arrived 13-6-07		10-13
❑ XX975	'07'	SEPECAT Jaguar GR.1A	76	ex Halton 8905M (23-9-86), Shawbury, 226 OCU, 17, 31		10-13
❑ XX976	'BD'	SEPECAT Jaguar GR.1	76	ex Halton 8906M (22-10-86), Shawbury, 17, 31		10-13
❑ XZ103	'EF'	SEPECAT Jaguar GR.3A	76	ex Coltishall, 41, SAOEU, GR.1, 41, Shawbury, 2. *Exfoxy 2004-2009*. Arrived 12-6-07		10-13
❑ XZ104	'FM'	SEPECAT Jaguar GR.3A	76	ex St Athan, 41, 6, 2. Arrived 27-10-05		10-13
❑ XZ109	'EN'	SEPECAT Jaguar GR.3A	76	ex Shawbury, 6, SAOEU, GR.1, 6, 54, 2. Arrived 29-8-07		10-13
❑ XZ112	'GW'	SEPECAT Jaguar GR.3A	76	ex Shawbury, 41, 54, GR.1, 54, Shawbury, 2. L/flown 12-4-06		10-13
❑ XZ114	'EO'	SEPECAT Jaguar GR.3A	76	ex Shawbury, 6, 41, GR.1, Shawbury, 41. Last flown 11-4-06		10-13
❑ XZ115	'ER'	SEPECAT Jaguar GR.3A	76	ex Shawbury, 6, 16, GR.1, SAOEU, 41, Shawbury, Gulf Det, 41, 2, 41. Arrived 24-10-06		10-13
❑ XZ117	'ES'	SEPECAT Jaguar GR.3A	76	ex Shawbury, 41, 6, GR.1, Warden Det, 54, 41. Arr 17-11-09		10-13
❑ XZ322	'N'	Sud Gazelle AH.1	77	ex St Athan 9283M, Shawbury, 670, ARWS, 6 Flt		8-12
❑ XZ358*	'L'	SEPECAT Jaguar GR.1A	76	ex Cranwell, 9262M (18-10-96), ex Coltishall, 41, Warden Det, 41, Gulf Det, 41. 41 Sqn colours. First noted 8-13		10-13
❑ XZ367	'EE' *and* 'GP'	SEPECAT Jaguar GR.3	76	ex Ipswich, Coltishall 9321M, Shawbury, Warden Det, GR.1, 54, Gulf Det, 54, 2, 226 OCU, 2	[2]	10-13
❑ XZ368	'E'	SEPECAT Jaguar GR.1	76	ex 8900M (23-5-86), Coltishall, 14, 6, 14		10-13
❑ XZ370	'JB'	SEPECAT Jaguar GR.1	76	ex 9004M, Shawbury, 14, 17. Arrived 18-10-89		10-13
❑ XZ371	'AP'	SEPECAT Jaguar GR.1	76	ex 8907M (23-5-86), Shawbury, 14, 17		10-13
❑ XZ374	'JC'	SEPECAT Jaguar GR.1	76	ex 9005M, Shawbury, 14, 20. Last flown 13-8-85. Stored		8-12
❑ XZ377	'EP'	SEPECAT Jaguar GR.3A	77	ex St Athan, 6, GR.1, 6, 16, 6, 54, 226 OCU, 2, 31, 20. Arrived 6-7-07		10-13
❑ XZ383	'AF'	SEPECAT Jaguar GR.1	77	ex 8901M (23-5-86), Coltishall, 14, 17		10-13
❑ XZ384	'BC'	SEPECAT Jaguar GR.1	77	ex 8954M (3-12-87), Shawbury, 17, 31, 20		10-13
❑ XZ389	'BL'	SEPECAT Jaguar GR.1	77	ex Halton 8946M (13-11-87), Shawbury, 17, 31, 20		10-13
❑ XZ390	'DM'	SEPECAT Jaguar GR.1	77	ex 9003M, Shawbury, 2, 20, 31. Last flown 25-4-85		10-13

❑	XZ391	'ET'	SEPECAT Jaguar GR.3A	77	ex Coltishall, 6, GR.1, 6, 16, 54, 226 OCU, 54, 31. Last flown 12-4-06		10-13
❑	XZ392	'EM'	SEPECAT Jaguar GR.3A	77	ex Coltishall, 16, GR.1, Shawbury, 54, 20, 31. Arrived 12-6-07		10-13
❑	XZ398	'EQ'	SEPECAT Jaguar GR.3A	77	ex Coltishall, 6, 41, GR.1, 41, 54, 41, 6, Indian AF J1007, G-27-323, Warton. Arrived 18-5-07		10-13
❑	XZ399	'EJ'	SEPECAT Jaguar GR.3A	76	ex Coltishall, 6, GR.1, 226 OCU, 6, 226 OCU, 6, 14, 6. *Ejordan 2004-2007 - Sleep Well Mighty Cat!* Arrived 12-6-07		10-13
❑	XZ941	'B'	Sud Gazelle HT.2	78	ex 9301M, St Athan, Shawbury, 2 FTS, Odiham hack, CFS		8-12
❑	XZ991	'3A'	HS Harrier GR.3	81	ex 9162M, St Athan 9162M, 233 OCU, 4, 1417 Flt, 233 OCU, 1, R-R, 1, 3, 1		6-13
❑	ZA128*	'010'	Westland Sea King HAS.6	81	ex Gosport (10-10-02), 820, 706, 820. First noted 5-12		10-13
❑	ZA131	'271'	Westland Sea King HAS.6	81	ex Gosport A2639[3], Cosford, Gosport, A2628[3] (19-6-02), 814, 820, 826, 810, 826. *Fanny*		10-13
❑	ZA169	'515'	Westland Sea King HAS.6	82	ex Gosport A2844 (12-3-09), 820, 771, 810, 814, 820, 819, 820, 706, 820		10-13
❑	ZA320	'TAW'	Panavia Tornado GR.1	79	ex 9314M (8-4-02), St Athan, 15, TTTE		10-13
❑	ZA323	'TAZ'	Panavia Tornado GR.1	83	ex 9339M, St Athan, 15, TTTE. Arrived 18-8-03		10-13
❑	ZA357	'TTV'	Panavia Tornado GR.1	81	ex 9341M, St Athan, 15, TTTE. Arrived 18-8-03		10-13
❑	ZA450	'TH'	Panavia Tornado GR.1	83	ex 9317M, St Athan, 15, 12, 617, 12, 27, 20, 15. Arr 14-5-02		10-13
❑	ZA771		Sud Gazelle AH.1	80	ex Shawbury, 654, 664, 656, 662, 656, 663, 664, 656, 664, 670, ARWS. Arrived 7-1-09. '238 Sqn' colours		10-13
❑	ZB615*		SEPECAT Jaguar T.2	82	ex Cranwell, Boscombe Down, ETPS. Frist noted 8-13		10-13
❑	ZD465*	'55'	BAe Harrier GR.9A		ex Gosport, Wittering, Cottesmore, BAE Warton. wfu 12-10. Arrived 7-11-13		11-13
❑	ZD939		Panavia Tornado F.2	85	ex St Athan, Warton, St Athan, 229 OCU. Cockpit		10-13
❑	ZE340	'GO'	Panavia Tornado F.3	87	ex 9298M, Coningsby, 56. Rear fuselage of ZE758. Arrived 4-9-01. 43 Sqn colours		10-13
❑	ZJ695	001	GenFly Mk.2	c02	Typhoon training rig	[3]	8-13
❑	ZJ696	002	GenFly Mk.2	c02	Typhoon training rig	[3]	8-13
❑	ZJ697	003	GenFly Mk.2	c02	Typhoon training rig	[3]	8-13
❑	ZJ698	004	GenFly Mk.2	c02	Typhoon training rig	[3]	8-13
❑	ZK006		Typhoon training aid	c02	-	[3]	8-13
❑	ZK007		Typhoon training aid	c02	-	[3]	8-12
❑	ZK008		Typhoon training aid	c02	-	[3]	8-13

■ **[1]** Jaguar XX833 factoids: total flying time 5,335 hours - 1,070 of these since arriving at Boscombe in April 1994; it has had five bird strikes, one lightning strike and nine different engines. **[2]** XZ367 was supplied in response to a tender issued in 2009, it seems DCAE mis-calculated how many GR.3s it would need. **[3]** DCAE has four sophisticated Eurofighter Typhoon purpose-built training rigs, called GenFlies. These have the capacity to generate over 100 different faults, to really annoy the trainees. They have been allocated serials not because they are intended to fly, but because they have a full maintenance schedule, just like a live airframe. Other 'sims' in use include a barrage of Emulator Test Rigs, AV001 to AV018.

PT Flight: (Bob Mitchell) Keeps a store on the airfield - this is *not* available for inspection. See also Sleap, Shropshire.

❑	G-AYKZ	SAI KZ-VIII	49	ex Coventry, HB-EPB, OY-ACB. CoA 17-7-81. Stored	5-02
❑	G-BADW	Pitts S-2A	72	ex museum. CoA 6-9-95	5-02

Others: The Spitfire is 'on guard' in the parade ground.

❑	'MK356'	Sup' Spitfire IX FSM	03	BAPC.298, on parade ground	[1]	10-12

■ **[1]** Note that the decidedly *real* MK356 can be found at Coningsby, Lincs, while *another* 'MK356' is at Hawkinge, Kent.

Warped Paintball: In a field near Junction 3 of the M54, adjacent to the RAF station.

◆ **Access:** *By prior arrangement only* | **www.warpedpaintball.co.uk**

❑	G-HERA*	Robinson R22	90	ex Halfpenny Green, Blackpool. CoA 15-6-99, de-reg 21-8-99. Pod. First noted 5-12	5-12
❑	XZ318	Sud Gazelle AH.1	77	ex Shawbury, Fleetlands, Yeovil, Fleetlands, 656, 664, 657, 664, 656, 670, ARWS, A&AEE. Westland-built. Crashed 2-1-97. Pod	5-12

DONNINGTON south of the A518, north-east of Telford

HQ Defence Storage and Disposition Centre: This huge logistics base has a Harrier on show.

❑	XZ971	'U'	HS Harrier GR.3	81	ex Shawbury, Benson 9219M (13-10-93), HOCU, 1417 Flt, 233 OCU. Gate	7-13

LUDLOW on the A49 north of Leominster

Despite the longevity of its 'last noted' date, the Swift is believed to still be stored in the area.

❑ G-ABUS		Comper Swift	32	ex Heathfield. CoA 19-6-79		2-91

MARKET DRAYTON on the A53 north-east of Shrewsbury

Retro Aviation: A specialist company providing airframes for all purposes, restoration services, film work, spare parts and the moving and packing of airframes. In the cold light of day, the state of Avro XIX G-AGPG, universally known as 'Aggie-Paggie', was beyond help but it could help other projects; it was recovered for spares in February 2012. Thanks to Mike Davey and Jonathan Howard, the cockpit was declared a viable proposition and, after some initial restoration work, went on to win a *W&R* award at *CockpitFest* 2013 - see Appendix C. It is listed under Liverpool, Merseyside. Similar logic lay with Anson T.21 VS562; its wings were shipped to Australia to help with a static Mk.I project. The forward fuselage moved to Shannon, Ireland, by July 2013.

Short 360 G-OBHD moved to Abridge, Essex, on 1st August 2012. The cockpit of Jaguar GR.1 XX826 arrived from Welshpool on 30th February 2012, by July 2013 it had moved on to Shannon, Ireland.

◆ **Access:** *Visits by prior arrangement* ***only***. **Contact: 01630 684040 | rp@retroaviation.com | www.retroaviation.com**

❑ G-TEXA		BAe Jetstream 4100	95	ex Inverness, N318UE, G-4-041. De-reg 16-5-11. Cockpit		3-12
❑ -		BAe ATP	~	ex Coventry, Atlantic Airlines. Cockpit		3-12
❑ AX246		Avro Anson I	41	ex Canada, RCAF, 33 SFTS	[1]	3-12
❑ XN597*	'X'	Hunting Jet Provost T.3	61	ex Blackpool, Millom, Firbeck, Levenshulme, Stamford, Firbeck, Sunderland, Stoke-on-Trent, Bournemouth, Faygate, 7984M, 2 FTS. Damaged 28-6-67. Cockpit. Arrived 17-2-12		2-12
❑ -		Panavia Tornado F.3 SIM	~	ex Leuchars		3-12
❑ '42'	792642	Aero L29 Delfin	~	ex Catshill, Market Drayton, Romanian AF. Cockpit	[2]	3-12

■ [1] This machine was supplied to Canada 27-11-41 and transferred to the RCAF 1-12-44 - no further details. [2] The cockpit of the L29 has been converted into a simulator and is used as a fund-raising tool for Help for Heroes.

NEWPORT on A41 north-east of Telford

In the *general* area is Vaughan K Meers' Provost (see also Abbots Bromley, Staffs, Baxterley, Warks, and Penkridge, Staffs).

❑ WW388	'O-F'	Percival Provost T.1	54	ex Sleap, Hemswell, Firbeck, Long Marston, Cardiff-Wales, Llanelli, Chinnor, Chertsey, Cuxwold, Chessington, Halton 7616M (13-10-59), 2 FTS		2-12

PEPLOW or Child's Ercall, south of Market Drayton, west of the A41

At a *private* location on the former airfield, two aircraft are stored.

❑ G-AVKP		Beagle Airedale	63	ex SE-EGA. CoA 26-9-03		8-08
❑ G-BCFW		SAAB Safir	62	ex PH-RLZ. CoA 24-7-06		8-08

REDNALL east of the A5 and Oswestry

Rednall Paintball Arena: Based on the wartime airfield (for which the spelling is Rednal and the signs will show you Rednall Industrial Estate) is an outside leisure complex offering motorcycling, paintballing and laser shooting which includes the control tower. The Wessex takes pride of place in front of the former watch tower.

◆ **Access:** *Busy place, full of flying paint; visits by prior arrangement* only | **www.rednallpaintballarena.com**

❑ XT480	'468'	Westland Wessex HU.5	66	ex Hixon, Fleetlands, A2617[2] (13-12-90), A2603[2], Wroughton, 771, 847, 772, 846, 707		5-12

SHAWBURY AIRFIELD on the B5063 north of Shawbury EGOS

Assault Glider Trust: Within the base, AGT has made exceptional progress with its complete Horsa and CG-4 reproductions, Dakota tug and Tiger Moth. AGT has an informal parts-exchange with the Silent Wings Museum at Lubbock, Texas; the CG-4 having come from them. The Trust's aim is to create a memorial in the Midlands to all Service personnel; assigned to glider-borne operations - the aircrew, ground crews and airborne regiments - and to the civilians involved in the manufacture and assembly of assault gliders.

◆ **Access:** ***Strictly*** *by prior permission - at* least *one month's notice required.* **Contact:** *Assault Glider Trust, RAF Shawbury, SY4 4DZ* | **01939 250009 | assaultglidertrust@gmail.com | www.assaultglidertrust.co.uk**

❑ EM840		DH Tiger Moth	G-ANBY 43	ex -?-, Rochester, Mk.II, 21 EFTS. Morris-built	[1]	2-14

❑ KG651		Douglas Dakota III	42	ex Coventry, SU-AZI, G-AMHJ, ZS-BRW, KG651, 1333 CU, 1383 CU, 24, 109 OTU, 42-108962. CoA 5-12-00, de-reg 23-1-03	2-14
❑ 'LH291'		Airspeed Horsa replica	01	BAPC.279	2-14
❑ '241079'		Waco CG-4 Hadrian replica	03	ex Lubbock, Texas. Fuselage	2-14

■ **[1]** EM840 served with 21 EFTS at Booker, where many Glider Pilot Regiment pilots were taught. As G-ANBY, this machine was last heard of, unconverted, at Rochester in April 1960 when it was said to have been scrapped! Where has it been since?

Aircraft Maintenance and Storage Unit (AM&SU) operated for the Defence Aviation Repair Agency by FBHeliservices.

Departures: **Gazelle** AH.1 XX403 and XX447 to MPSU, Middle Wallop, Hampshire 16-1-14; ZB674 returned to service by 3-12; ZB679 to MPSU, Middle Wallop, Hampshire; **Hawk** T.1W XX310 returned to service 28-6-13; T.1A XX311 returned to service 17-10-12; T.1A XX325 returned to service 17-12-12; **Tornado** the following moved by road to Leeming, N Yorks, for the RTP programme: **F.3** ZE737 - 10-10-12; **GR.4** ZA446 - 1-8-12; ZA470 - 31-7-12; ZA563 - 4-9-12; ZA608 - 10-10-12; ZD708 - 4-9-12; ZD892 - 1-8-12; ZG769 - 31-7-12. The last three **F.3**s, ZE165, ZE204, ZH553, moved to Manston, Kent, 20-3-13.

❑ XX403		Sud Gazelle AH.1	75	ex Gosport, Shawbury, 671, Middle Wallop, 670, 656. Arrived 12-10-10 [1]	10-13
❑ XW200		Sud Puma HC.1	71	ex 33, 240 OCU, HOCF. Westland-built. Crashed 9-4-01. Arrived 2-7-01	1-14
❑ XW202		Sud Puma HC.1	71	ex Benson, 33, 230, 33, 27, 230, 1563 Flt, 33, 1563 Flt, 33, 1563 Flt, 33, 240 OCU, 230, A&AEE, 230, 240 OCU, 230, 240 OCU. Westland-built. Arrived 25-7-05	1-14
❑ XW206*		Sud Puma HC.1	71	ex Boscombe Down, Benson, 72, 230, 33, 230, 33, 1563 Flt, 33, 1563 Flt, 33, 240 OCU, 33. Arrived 26-6-12	1-14
❑ XW207*		Sud Puma HC.1	71	ex Boscombe Down, 33, 230, 33, 1563 Flt, 33, 1563 Flt, 33, 32, 33, 240 OCU, 33. Westland-built. Crashed 19-4-00. Arrived 26-6-12	1-14
❑ XW208*		Sud Puma HC.1	71	ex Boscombe Down, 33, 230, 33, 72, 33, 230, 240 OCU, 33, 240 OCU, 33, 240 OCU, 33. Arrived by 8-12	1-14
❑ XW218		Sud Puma HC.1	71	ex 1563 Flt, 33. 230, 72, 33, 72, 18, 230, 33, 18, 230, 33, 230, 240 OCU, 230. Westland-built. Cr 15-4-07, arr 5-3-08	1-14
❑ XX160		HS Hawk T.1	77	ex 208, 19, 208, DERA, TEE, DERA, RAE. Arrived 18-6-07	1-14
❑ XX161*		HS Hawk T.1W	77	ex Valley, 19, 208, RAFAT, 4 FTS, CFS, 4 FTS, CFS. Arrived 22-8-12	1-14
❑ XX165*		HS Hawk T.1A	77	ex 208, FRADU, 4 FTS, CFS, 74, CFS, 4 FTS, CFS. Arr 16-3-12	1-14
❑ XX167*		HS Hawk T.1W	77	ex 208, 4 FTS, TWU, 4 FTS. Arrived 27-2-12	1-14
❑ XX168		HS Hawk T.1	77	ex Valley, FRADU, 208, 100, 6 FTS, 74, 4 FTS. Arrived 10-6-09	1-14
❑ XX169		HS Hawk T.1	77	ex 19, 92, FRADU, 19, 74, 6 FTS, 234, 4 FTS. Arrived 17-5-11	1-14
❑ XX171		HS Hawk T.1	77	ex 208, 19, 208, 74, CFS, 4 FTS. Arrived 20-5-11	1-14
❑ XX172		HS Hawk T.1	77	ex Yeovilton, FRADU, 19, 4 FTS, 234, 4 FTS. Bird strike 15-12-06. Arrived 14-11-07. Trial installations airframe	1-14
❑ XX173		HS Hawk T.1	77	ex FRADU, 6 FTS, 4 FTS. Arrived 19-7-05	1-14
❑ XX174*		HS Hawk T.1	77	ex 208, 19, 6 FTS, 19, 74, 4 FTS. Arrived 14-1-13	1-14
❑ XX175		HS Hawk T.1	77	ex 208, FRADU, 208, 19 CFS, 4 FTS. Arrived 4-6-10	1-14
❑ XX176*		HS Hawk T.1W	77	ex 208, 100, 92, 19, CFS, 4 FTS. Arrived 14-1-13	10-13
❑ XX178*		HS Hawk T.1W	77	ex 208, 19, 92, 234, 4 FTS. Arrived 27-11-12	10-13
❑ XX181*		HS Hawk T.1W	77	ex 208, 19, 208, 100, TWU, 4 FTS. Arrived 5-9-12	10-13
❑ XX185		HS Hawk T.1	77	ex Marham, 208, 6 FTS, 19, 4 FTS. Arrived 13-9-11	1-14
❑ XX190	'CN'	HS Hawk T.1A	77	ex 100, 208, 74, 4 FTS, 74, 1 TWU, 2 TWU, 1 TWU, TWU. Arrived 30-6-08	10-13
❑ XX191		HS Hawk T.1A	78	ex 19, 4 FTS, 208, 234, 1 TWU, TWU. Arrived 12-7-10	10-13
❑ XX194*	'CP'	HS Hawk T.1A	78	ex 100, 74, TWU. Arrived 8-5-13	1-14
❑ XX195		HS Hawk T.1W	78	ex 208, 4 FTS, 19, 208, 100, 2 TWU, 1 TWU, TWU. Arr 2-2-10	10-13
❑ XX220*		HS Hawk T.1A	78	ex 208, FRADU, St Athan, FRADU, TWU, CFS, TWU. Arr 4-11-11	1-14
❑ XX222*		HS Hawk T.1A	78	ex 100, 208, 74, TWU. Arrived 15-7-11	1-14
❑ XX224*		HS Hawk T.1W	78	ex 208, 19, CFS, 4 FTS, CFS, 4 FTS. Arrived 6-9-12	1-14
❑ XX225		HS Hawk T.1	78	ex 208, FRADU, 208, 19, 4 FTS. Arrived 3-8-07	1-14
❑ XX226		HS Hawk T.1	78	ex Yeovilton, 100, 74, CFS, 74, 4 FTS. Accident 20-4-07. Arrived 13-11-07. Trial installations airframe	1-14
❑ XX228		HS Hawk T.1A	78	ex 208, 100, 2 TWU, 1 TWU. Arrived 8-11-07	1-14
❑ XX231*		HS Hawk T.1W	78	ex 208, 74, 92, 19, 4 FTS, RAE, 4 FTS. Arrived 27-9-11	1-14

❑	XX232		HS Hawk T.1	78	ex 208, 19 , 6 FTS, 74, 4 FTS. Arrived 26-9-07		10-13
❑	XX234*		HS Hawk T.1	78	ex 208, FRADU, 234, 74, 4 FTS. Arrived 21-7-11		1-14
❑	XX235		HS Hawk T.1W	78	ex 208, 19, 208, 19, 74, CFS, 4 FTS. Emergency landing 28-5-09		1-14
❑	XX237*		HS Hawk T.1W	78	ex RAFAT, 4 FTS. Arrived 2-10-11		1-14
❑	XX238		HS Hawk T.1	78	ex 208, 19, 74, 19, 6 FTS, CFS, 4 FTS. Arrived 11-6-08		1-14
❑	XX239		HS Hawk T.1W	78	ex 19, 74, 208, 74, 208, 19, CFS, 4 FTS. Arrived 14-2-06		10-13
❑	XX247		HS Hawk T.1A	78	ex 19, 100, 1 TWU, 2 TWU, 1 TWU. Arrived 7-4-11		1-14
❑	XX244*		HS Hawk T.1A	78	ex RAFAT, 208, FRADU, 4 FTS. Arrived 7-13		1-14
❑	XX248	'CJ'	HS Hawk T.1A	78	ex 100, 1 TWU, 2 TWU, 1 TWU. Arrived 4-10-07		1-14
❑	XX260		HS Hawk T.1A	79	ex RAFAT. Bird strike 7-8-11, arrived 24-8-11		1-14
❑	XX265		HS Hawk T.1A	79	ex 19, 100, 92, 2 TWU, 1 TWU. Arrived 6-10-10		1-14
❑	XX266*		HS Hawk T.1A	79	ex RAFAT. Arrived 11-9-13		1-14
❑	XX278*		HS Hawk T.1	79	ex RAFAT, 208, BAE, 19, 100, 19, 100, 19. Arrived 12-13		1-14
❑	XX283*		HS Hawk T.1W	79	ex 208, 100, TWU. Arrived 7-2-13		10-13
❑	XX284*	'CA'	HS Hawk T.1A	79	ex 100, 208, 100, TWU. Arrived 11-12-08		1-14
❑	XX286*		HS Hawk T.1A	79	ex 208, 234, 19, TWU. Arrived 5-9-12		1-14
❑	XX289*	'CO'	HS Hawk T.1A	79	ex 100, 19, TWU. Arrived 4-7-12		10-13
❑	XX290	'U'	HS Hawk T.1W	79	ex 100, FRADU, 208, 100, 234, 4 FTS, RAFAT, 4 FTS. Arrived 15-4-04		1-14
❑	XX292		HS Hawk T.1W	79	ex RAFAT, 19, 92, 4 FTS. Arrived 12-10-09		1-14
❑	XX294*		HS Hawk T.1	79	ex RAFAT, 4 FTS. Arrived 2-6-11		1-14
❑	XX295		HS Hawk T.1W	79	ex 19, 208, 6 FTS, 4 FTS. Arrived 9-3-06		10-13
❑	XX296		HS Hawk T.1	79	ex 208, 74, 4 FTS. Arrived 21-1-04		1-14
❑	XX299		HS Hawk T.1W	79	ex 208, 100, 19, 208, 74, 92, 4 FTS. Arrived 2-4-08		1-14
❑	XX303*		HS Hawk T.1	80	ex 208, 74, 19, CFS, 74, 1 TWU. Emergenccy landing 8-10-13		1-14
❑	XX306*		HS Hawk T.1A	80	ex RAFAT, 4 FTS. Arrived 22-10-12		1-14
❑	XX307*		HS Hawk T.1	80	ex 208, RAFAT, 4 FTS. Arrived 17-10-12		10-13
❑	XX308*		HS Hawk T.1	80	ex RAFAT, 4 FTS. Arrived 18-4-13		1-14
❑	XX309		HS Hawk T.1	80	ex St Athan 'hack', 208, 19, 6 FTS, 234, 4 FTS. Arrived 15-2-06. Welsh dragon colours		10-13
❑	XX312*		HS Hawk T.1W	80	ex 208, 19, 74, 100, 1 TWU, 4 FTS. Arrived 9-5-12		1-14
❑	XX313*		HS Hawk T.1W	80	ex 208, 74, 19, CFS, 19, 4 FTS. Arrived 16-8-12		1-14
❑	XX314		HS Hawk T.1W	80	ex Valley, 19, 100, 208, 4, 4 FTS, 2 TWU, 4 FTS. Arr 18-10-11		1-14
❑	XX331*		HS Hawk T.1A	80	ex 100, 2 TWU. Arrived 29-6-11		1-14
❑	XX335*		HS Hawk T.1A	80	ex 100, 19, 2 TWU. Arrived 24-6-11		1-14
❑	XX338*		HS Hawk T.1W	81	ex 208, 19, 208, 19, 4 FTS. Arrived 12-9-13		1-14
❑	XX345*	'CE'	HS Hawk T.1A	81	ex 100, 19, 92, TWU. Arrived 3-12-08		1-14
❑	XX350		HS Hawk T.1A	81	ex 19, 4 FTS, 74, 1 TWU. Arrived 30-4-08		10-13
❑	XX351		HS Hawk T.1A	81	ex 4 FTS, 100, 19, 208, 234, 1 TWU. Arrived 29-5-08		1-14
❑	XX378	'Q'	Sud Gazelle AH.1	74	ex Gosport, Shawbury, Middle Wallop, 671, 2 Flt, 671, 667, 670, 655, 2 Flt. Arrived 12-10-10	[1]	1-14
❑	XX379	'Y'	Sud Gazelle AH.1	75	ex 6 Flt, 658, 3/4 Rgt, 8 Flt, 658, 656, 2 Flt. Arrived 3-09	[1]	2-12
❑	XX399	'D'	Sud Gazelle AH.1	75	ex 671. Arrived 7-4-10	[1]	2-12
❑	XX431*	'43'	Sud Gazelle HT.2	75	ex 9300M Airman's Tng Sch, 705, FONA, 705. Arrived 23-1-97; on storage site by 10-13	[1]	1-14
❑	XX442	'E'	Sud Gazelle AH.1	76	ex 666, 658, 664, 659, 669. Arrived 23-2-09	[1]	1-14
❑	XX460		Sud Gazelle AH.1	76	ex 671, 3/4 Rgt, 9 Rgt, 662, 664, 669, 662. Arrived 17-6-09	[1]	10-13
❑	XZ294	'X'	Sud Gazelle AH.1	76	ex 658, 669, 664, 661, GCF. Arrived 9-3-09	[1]	10-13
❑	XZ295		Sud Gazelle AH.1	76	ex 12 Flt, 7 Flt, 662. Arrived 17-3-09	[1]	2-12
❑	XZ303		Sud Gazelle AH.1	76	ex 6 Flt, 3/4 Rgt, 663, 656, 662, 663, GCF. Arrived 3-09	[1]	1-14
❑	XZ311		Sud Gazelle AH.1	76	ex 671, 6 Flt, 664, 7 Flt. Arrived 8-9-09	[1]	1-14
❑	XZ323	'J'	Sud Gazelle AH.1	77	ex 671. Arrived 7-4-10	[1]	2-12
❑	XZ328		Sud Gazelle AH.1	77	ex 671, 6 Flt, 666, 3 Rgt, 662, 654, 651, 665. Arrived 9-7-09	[1]	10-13
❑	XZ331	'D'	Sud Gazelle AH.1	77	ex 666, 654, 3/4 Rgt, 669, 654, 663, 657, 665. Arr 9-3-09	[1]	2-12
❑	XZ337	'Z'	Sud Gazelle AH.1	77	ex 658, 6 Flt, 3/4 Rgt, 664, 667, 656, 657, 658, 659, 669. Arrived 9-3-09	[1]	1-14
❑	XZ343		Sud Gazelle AH.1	78	ex 665, 3/4 Regt, 661, 4 Regt, 1 Regt, 661, 652, 12 Flt, 663, ARWS, 661. Arrived 3-4-06	[1]	10-13
❑	XZ349	'U'	Sud Gazelle AH.1	79	ex 671. Arrived 7-4-10	[1]	2-12
❑	ZA773	'F'	Sud Gazelle AH.1	80	ex 666, 665, 655, 665, 655. Arrived 31-10-05	[1]	1-14

❑ ZA775		Sud Gazelle AH.1	80	ex 665, 656, 658. Arrived 29-9-05	[1] 10-13
❑ ZB665		Sud Gazelle AH.1	80	ex 665, UNFICYP, FONAC, Fleetlands 'hack'. Arr 10-1-06	[1] 10-13
❑ ZB667*		Sud Gazelle AH.1	80	ex Middle Wallop, 665, 16 Flt, UNFICYP Flt. Arr 16-1-14	[1] 1-14
❑ ZB690		Sud Gazelle AH.1	80	ex Yeovil. 665, 16 Flt. Arrived 12-2-06	[1] 10-13
❑ ZE449*		Sud Puma HC.1	c75	ex Boscombe Down, 230, Weston-super-Mare, 9017M, Port Stanley, Argentine Prefectura Naval PA-12. Crashed 9-7-09. Arrived 25-7-12	1-14
❑ ZF160		Short Tucano T.1	88	ex 1 FTS, 3 FTS, RAFC, 7 FTS. Arrived 8-2-02	1-14
❑ ZF161		Short Tucano T.1	88	ex 72, 1 FTS, CFS, 1 FTS, 6 FTS, 7 FTS, A&AEE. *Qucahas Nek*. Arrived 29-3-06	1-14
❑ ZF163		Short Tucano T.1	89	ex 1 FTS, CFS, 1 FTS, 7 FTS. Arrived 19-7-01	1-14
❑ ZF166		Short Tucano T.1	89	ex 1 FTS, CFS, 1 FTS, CFS, 3 FTS, RAFC, 7 FTS, A&AEE, 7 FTS Arrived 14-4-02	1-14
❑ ZF203		Short Tucano T.1	89	ex 72, 1 FTS, CFS. Arrived 5-12-03	1-14
❑ ZF211		Short Tucano T.1	89	ex 1 FTS, CFS, 1 FTS, 7 FTS. Arrived 23-5-01	1-14
❑ ZF212		Short Tucano T.1	89	ex 1 FTS, DERA, 1 FTS, CFS. Arrived 16-3-06	1-14
❑ ZF242		Short Tucano T.1	90	ex 1 FTS, CFS, 1 FTS, 6 FTS, 7 FTS. Arrived 3-11-06	1-14
❑ ZF263		Short Tucano T.1	90	ex 1 FTS, 3 FTS, 7 FTS. Arrived 4-7-02	1-14
❑ ZF268		Short Tucano T.1	90	ex 1 FTS, CFS. Arrived 15-2-06	1-14
❑ ZF286		Short Tucano T.1	91	ex 1 FTS, CFS. Arrived 11-5-06	1-14
❑ ZF288		Short Tucano T.1	91	ex 1 FTS, CFS. Arrived 4-7-02	1-14
❑ ZF315		Short Tucano T.1	91	ex 1 FTS, 3 FTS. Arrived 22-3-06	1-14
❑ ZF318		Short Tucano T.1	91	ex 1 FTS, CFS. Arrived 28-11-01	1-14
❑ ZF345		Short Tucano T.1	91	ex 207, 1 FTS, 207, 1 FTS, CFS. Arrived 23-5-06	1-14
❑ ZF350		Short Tucano T.1	91	ex 1 FTS, RAFC. Arrived 25-5-02	1-14
❑ ZF372		Short Tucano T.1	91	ex 1 FTS, CFS. Arrived 24-8-00	1-14
❑ ZF376		Short Tucano T.1	92	ex 1 FTS. Arrived 2-7-01	1-14
❑ ZF380		Short Tucano T.1	92	ex 1 FTS, CFS. Arrived 23-5-01	1-14
❑ ZF405		Short Tucano T.1	92	ex 1 FTS, 6 FTS. Arrived 21-6-06	1-14
❑ ZF408		Short Tucano T.1	92	ex 1 FTS. Arrived 7-8-01	1-14
❑ ZF410		Short Tucano T.1	92	ex 1 FTS, CFS, 1 FTS. Arrived 8-2-06	1-14
❑ ZF412		Short Tucano T.1	92	ex 1 FTS. Arrived 8-6-00	1-14
❑ ZF414		Short Tucano T.1	92	ex 1 FTS, CFS, 1 FTS, RAFC. Arrived 14-4-00	1-14
❑ ZF416		Short Tucano T.1	92	ex 1 FTS, CFS, 1 FTS. Arrived 22-3-06	1-14
❑ ZF418		Short Tucano T.1	92	ex 1 FTS, 6 FTS. Arrived 6-3-06	1-14
❑ ZF446		Short Tucano T.1	92	ex 1 FTS, 6 FTS. Arrived 15-3-06	1-14
❑ ZF447		Short Tucano T.1	92	ex 72, 1 FTS, CFS, 1 FTS, RAFC. Arrived 8-9-05	1-14
❑ ZF449		Short Tucano T.1	92	ex 1 FTS, CFS, 1 FTS. Arrived 2-7-02	1-14
❑ ZF483		Short Tucano T.1	92	ex 72, CFS, 1 FTS. *Jason*. Arrived 9-11-06	1-14
❑ ZF484		Short Tucano T.1	92	ex 1 FTS, CFS, 1 FTS. Arrived 25-4-03	1-14
❑ ZF486		Short Tucano T.1	92	ex 1 FTS. Arrived 4-9-03	1-14
❑ ZF487		Short Tucano T.1	92	ex 1 FTS. Arrived 27-2-06	1-14
❑ ZF488		Short Tucano T.1	92	ex 1 FTS. Arrived 15-2-00	1-14
❑ ZF490		Short Tucano T.1	92	ex 1 FTS. Arrived 30-9-03	1-14
❑ ZF492		Short Tucano T.1	92	ex 1 FTS. Arrived 24-8-06	1-14
❑ ZF513		Short Tucano T.1	92	ex 72, CFS, 1 FTS. *Basuto*. Arrived 9-3-06	1-14
❑ ZF514		Short Tucano T.1	92	ex 1 FTS. Arrived 27-2-06	1-14
❑ ZF516		Short Tucano T.1	92	ex 1 FTS, 3 FTS. Arrived 1-12-99	1-14
❑ ZG844*		BN Islander AL.1	87	ex 1 Flt, G-BLNE. Arrived 23-7-12	10-13
❑ ZG847		BN Islander AL.1	87	ex 1 Flt, G-BLNV. Arrived 25-8-11	10-13
❑ ZG989*		BN Islander ASTOR	88	ex BN, G-DLRA. Arrived 29-3-12	[2] 10-13
❑ ZG993		BN Islander AL.1	88	ex 1 Flt, G-BOMD. Arrived 1-7-10	10-13
❑ ZH821*		EHI Merlin HM.1	97	ex Yeovil. Arrived 1-10-13	1-14
❑ ZH822*		EHI Merlin HM.1	97	ex Culdrose, Fleetlands, DERA. Arrived 30-6-10	1-14
❑ ZH823*		EHI Merlin HM.1	97	ex Culdrose, DERA. Arrived 26-5-10	1-14
❑ ZH825*	'583'	EHI Merlin HM.1	98	ex Fleetlands, 824, 700. Arrived 25-1-12	1-14
❑ ZJ258		Aérospatiale Squirrel HT.1	97	ex DHFS, G-BXEO. Crashed 14-12-04	2-12
❑ ZJ259		Aérospatiale Squirrel HT.1	97	ex DHFS, G-BXFJ. Collided 10-1-07 with ZJ263	1-14
❑ ZJ263		Aérospatiale Squirrel HT.1	97	ex DHFS, G-BXHK. Collided 10-1-07 with ZJ259	10-13

■ **[1]** The Gazelles, of course, are Westland-built. [2] When ZG989 left for Shawbury, it was the last BN movement out of Bembridge.

Also: Gazelle HT.2 XX431 moved to the storage site by October 2013 - see above.

❑ XR516	'V'	Westland Wessex HC.2	64	ex Gosport, 9319M, A2709 [2], Shawbury, 2 FTS, 18. Gate, 60 Sqn colours	[1]	1-14
❑ XS713	'C'	HS Dominie T.1	65	ex Cranwell, 55, 3 FTS, 6 FTS, 1 ANS, CAW, 1 ANS, CAW, 1 ANS. Arrived 23-2-11. Dump		1-14
❑ XT773		Westland Wessex HU.5	67	ex Cosford, St Athan, Abingdon 9123M (2-10-91), Wroughton, 771, 845, 847, 772, 845, 707. Dump		1-14
❑ XV123		Westland Scout AH.1	67	ex Thruxton, Ipswich, Weston-super-Mare, Fleetlands	[2]	1-14

■ **[1]** Wessex XR516 has been 'adopted' by 60 Squadron, which flies Bell Griffins from the base. **[2]** The Scout is displayed by 660 Squadron, AAC, who fly Squirrels from here. This machine is *believed* to be privately owned.

SHREWSBURY

Roger Marley: Roger's exceptional Typhoon project continues to progress. The aim is to represent a late-series Mk.Ib. It is fitted with the rear fuselage of Sea Fury FB.11 VW589 and Roger has Napier Sabre which will be fitted.

◆ **Access:** *Private collection, access available* **only** *by prior permission* | **roger.marley@btopenworld.com**

❑ JP843	'PR-L'	Hawker Typhoon Ib	ex Sleap, Market Drayton. 609 Sqn colours	[1]	12-13

■ **[1]** The cockpit, firewall, front and rear spar, fishplate joints, flying controls and most cockpit fittings are all original. The rear fuselage is a replica. The portside fuselage panel came from JP843, which first served with 197 Squadron. After that it joined 609 (West Riding) Squadron and was lost on operations 27-7-44. It was hit by flak, and its pilot, Flt Sgt P M Price, was killed. It is believed that the panel was removed in the UK and was found in a farmer's field on the south coast.

SLEAP AERODROME south-west of Wem EGCV

Wartime Aircraft Recovery Group Aviation Museum: As well as the airframes there are plenty of aero engines and artefacts recovered from 'digs' - including WAG's 'founder', 61 OTU Spitfire IIa P7304 involved in a mid-air collision near High Ercall on 22nd August 1943 and recovered in 1977. *W&R23* (p188) recorded Spitfire FSM 'EN398' moving to Taunton, Devon, during 2007, this was not so.

◆ **Open:** *2nd and 4th Sun in summer,* often *open Sat pm. Otherwise by prior arrangement.* **Contact:** *WARG, 2 Fields View, Lodmore Lane, Burleydam, Whitchurch, SY13 4BD* | **wargsleap@gmail.com** | **01630 672969**

❑ 'K7271'		Hawker Fury II replica	79	BAPC.148, ex Market Drayton, Cosford. Stored, dismantled		10-11
❑ 'EN398'	'JE-J'	Supermarine Spitfire IX FSM	~	ex Cannock	[1]	7-12

■ **[1]** Spitfire FSM with *original* instrumentation etc is on loan from Keith Jones.

Former **PT Flight**: Bob Mitchell's collection is stored here. See also Cosford, Shropshire.

Access *Private collection, access available* **only** *by prior permission*

❑ G-AEUJ		Miles Whitney Straight	37	ex Cosford, Sutton Coldfield, Marple, East Midlands, Bournemouth. CoA 4-6-70		2-08
❑ G-AFRZ		Miles Monarch	38	ex Cosford, Sutton Coldfield, Shipdham, G-AIDE, W6463, Kemble, 10 GCF, FTCCF, 13 EFTS, G-AFRZ. CoA 29-6-70		10-11
❑ G-AWIW		Stampe SV-4B	47	ex Cosford, Colerne, F-BDCC. Nord-built. CoA 6-5-73		2-08
❑ G-RIDE		Stephens Akro	76	ex N81AC, N55NM. CoA 13-8-92		2-08
❑ N1344		Ryan PT-22 Recruit	41	ex Cosford, 41-20877	[1]	10-11
❑ N49272	'23'	Fairchild PT-23-HO	42	ex Cosford, USAAF 42-49413	[1]	10-11
❑ N56421	'855'	Ryan PT-22 Recruit	41	ex Cosford, 41-15510	[1]	10-11
❑ N58566		Vultee BT-15 Valiant	42	ex Cosford, USAAF 42-41882	[1]	10-11

■ **[1]** Registered to Flying Heritage Inc of Ventura, California.

Also: By April 2012 Tiger Moths G-ALWS and T8191 (G-BWMK) had moved to Henstridge, Somerset.

❑ G-BLWW	Taylor Mini-Imp	85	CoA 4-6-87, de-reg 13-10-00	3-11

SOMERSET

Includes the unitary authorities of North-West Somerset and Bath and North-East Somerset

BABCARY east of the A37, east of Somerton

A **private** local workshop disposed of five Gazelles by January 2012 to a Hampshire workshop: HT.2 XW887 (G-CBFD - last noted Sep 2008), AH.1 XW892 (G0CGJX - Nov 2010), HT.2 XZ938 (Sep 2008), AH.1 ZA730 (G-FUKM), AH.1 ZA767 (Oct 2008).

❑ XT793*		Westland Wasp HAS.1 G-BZPP	67	ex Lee-on-Solent, Thruxton, Yeovilton, East Dereham, Bruntingthorpe, Fleetlands, HHU, 829, A&AEE, 829, HHU. De-reg 7-9-12. First noted 1-13	1-13
❑ XV130*	'R'	Westland Scout AH.1 G-BWJW	70	ex Lee-on-Solent, Thruxton, 666. CoA 25-1-06, de-reg 13-11-12. First noted 1-13	1-13
❑ XV138*		Westland Scout AH.1 G-SASM	67	ex Lee-on-Solent, Thruxton, East Dereham, Almondbank, Wroughton, 658. First noted 1-13	1-13

BRISTOL AIRPORT or Lulsgate

EGGD

Paintball Adventure West: Located on the edge of the airport; the Wessex is within the 'Mission Impossible' game zone.

◆ **Access:** *Available* **only** *by prior permission* | **www.paintball-adventures.co.uk**

❑ G-AWOX	Westland Wessex 60	68	ex Weston-super-Mare, Bournemouth, W-s-M, G-17-2, G-AWOX, 5N-AJO, G-AWOX, 9Y-TFB, G-AWOX, VH-BHE, G-AWOX, VR-BCV, G-AWOX, G-17-1. CoA 13-1-83, de-reg 23-11-82	2-10

BURNHAM ON SEA south of Weston-super-Mare, on the B3140

A collector in the *general* area has a Britannia cockpit. *Available* **only** *by prior permission* | **www.silverscouters.co.uk**

❑ 5Y-AYR	Bristol Britannia 307F	57	ex Bournemouth, African Cargo, G-ANCD, Gemini, Lloyd, BUA, Air Charter, 4X-AGE El Al, N6595C, G-ANCD, G-18-3. Cockpit	1-14

DRAYCOTT Last recorded in January 2008, Bocian FUD has been deleted.

FELTON west of the A38, north-east of Bristol Airport

❑ XN551	'100'	Hunting Jet Provost T.3A	61	ex St Athan 8984M (6-2-89), 7 FTS, RAFC, 1 FTS, 3 FTS, 6 FTS, RAFC	7-13

HENSTRIDGE AERODROME south of the A30, east of Henstridge Marsh

EGHS

Cassutt IIIM G-BFMF was back in the air by 2012. The fuselage of Warrior 161 had gone by April 2013. Last noted in September 2009, Hiller UH-12 N5025J has been deleted.

❑ G-ALYG	Auster 5D	44	ex Charlton Mackrell, Heathrow, Irby-on-Humber, MS968, 661, 653. CoA 19-1-70. Frame	4-05
❑ G-ALWS*	DH Tiger Moth	39	ex Sleap, Welshpool, Bromsgrove, Rothesay, Strathallan, Perth, Mk.II N9328, Upwood SF, 6 FTS, 15 EFTS, 17 EFTS, 15 EFTS, 19 EFTS, Duxford SF, Farnborough SF. F/n 4-12	4-13
❑ G-ANFP*	DH Tiger Moth	39	ex Southampton, Fownhope, London Colney, Denham, Rush Green, N9503, 2 RFS, 7 RFS, 2 RFS, 4 RFS, 4 EFTS. CoA 1-7-63, de-reg 9-8-66. Frame. First noted 4-10	4-13
❑ G-BDYD	Rockwell Commander 114	76	ex N1914J. CoA 16-12-08, de-reg 24-11-09. Fuselage	2-11
❑ G-BECC	MS Rallye 150ST	76	CoA 15-5-00, de-reg 30-1-06. Stored, in container	2-14
❑ G-BERW	Rockwell Commander 114	77	ex N4884W. CoA 6-5-07, de-reg 27-7-07. Fuselage	2-14
❑ -*	Norman Freelance	c88	ex Little Rissington, Coventry, Sandown. Fuselage	1-14
❑ -*	Norman Freelance	c88	ex Little Rissington, Coventry, Sandown. Fuselage	1-14
❑ -*	Norman Freelance	c88	ex Little Rissington, Coventry, Sandown. Fuselage	1-14
❑ -*	Norman Freelance	c88	ex Little Rissington, Coventry, Sandown. Fuselage	1-14
❑ -*	Norman Freelance	c88	ex Little Rissington, Coventry, Sandown. Fuselage	1-14

❑ T8191*	DH Tiger Moth	G-BWMK 41	ex Sleap, Lee-on-Solent, Mk.II T8191, FAAHF, Yeovilton SF, Culdrose SF, Yeovilton SF, BRNC, Lossiemouth SF, Arbroath SF, Culdrose SF, Bramcote, Gosport, 3 FF, 22 EFTS, 4 FIS, 3 EFTS. Morris-built. First noted 4-12	4-13

Also: Close to the aerodrome, a Lightning has arrived.

❑ XS919*	EE Lightning F.6	66	ex Dinton, Farnsfield, Devonport, Lower Tremar, Binbrook, 11, 5, 11, 5, 56, 11. SOC 10-4-88. First noted 1-14	1-14

KEW STOKE north of Weston-super-Mare

Mark Templeman:

❑ XF940	Hawker Hunter F.4	56	ex Portishead, Boscombe Down, Salisbury, Cove, Farnborough, ETPS, 74, 71. Crashed 13-10-61. Cockpit. Red c/s	1-12

MARKSBURY on the A39 west of Bath

Hamburger Hill: **Access:** *Available* **only** *by prior permission* | **www.hamburgerhill.co.uk**

❑ XE668	'832'	Hawker Hunter GA.11	55	ex Predannack, A2647 [2], Culdrose SAH A2733 (8-2-85), Yeovilton, FRADU, 738, F.4, 26, 4	7-11
❑ XT762		Westland Wessex HU.5	66	ex Predannack, A2661 [2], Culdrose A2751 (28-7-87), Lee-on-Solent, Wroughton, RAE Bedford, A&AEE, 848	12-13
❑ S-887		Sikorsky S-55C	~	ex Weston-super-Mare, Panshanger, Elstree, RDanAF	7-11

POOLE on minor road north of Wellington

Managed Asset Services Ltd: Poole Industrial Estate.

◆ **Access:** *Hunter on external display, interior access available* **only** *by prior permission* | **www.masl-uk.com**

❑ XG164	Hawker Hunter F.6		ex Shawbury, Halton 8681M (2-4-81), Kemble, West Raynham SF, 74, 111. Displayed	[1]	6-13

■ **[1]** Hunter XG164 has the starboard wing of T.7 XL623. The port wing is at Beck Row, Suffolk. The fuselage of XL623 – with *altogether* different wings – is at Woking, Surrey!

PORTISHEAD west of the M5, Junction 19

Skirmish Paintball Games (Bristol) | **Access**, *available* **only** *by prior permission* | **www.skirmishbristol.co.uk**

❑ S-882	Sikorsky S-55C	~	ex Weston-super-Mare, Panshanger, Elstree, Dan AF Esk.722	12-11

SPARKFORD on the A303 north-east of Yeovil

A pair of 'Hueys' are stored at a local industrial estate.

❑ N250DM*	Bell UH-1H Iroquois	66	ex 66-16114. First noted 4-12	1-14
❑ N338CB*	Bell UH-1H Iroquois	66	ex N312RB, 66-16118. First noted 4-12	1-14

TAUNTON

Spitfire Spares: Specialising in trading in World War Two artefacts, spares etc, the organisation has created a taxiable Spitfire IX, powered by a Rolls-Meteor V-12 tank engine and available for hire. The plan is to make the 'Gunbus' also taxi.

◆ **Access:** *Available* **only** *by prior permission* | **www.spitfirespares.com**

❑ 'A1452'		'Vickers Gunbus'	85	BAPC.234, ex Sywell, 'GBH-7', Swindon, Sleap, High Halden, Hawkinge, Manston, Chelford, Coventry, Old Warden, White Waltham, *Sky Bandits, Gunbus. Bombay 3*	[1]	3-12
❑ 'EN398'	'JE-J'	Sup' Spitfire IX FSM	~	see notes above		3-12

■ **[1]** The 'Vickers Gunbus' film mock-up is displayed within the 'Hangar One' entertainment complex alongside the 'Aviator Hotel'. It is much more DH.2 than FB.5, having been based upon G-BFVH which flies from Wickenby, Lincs.

UPPER VOBSTER on minor road west of Frome

Vobster Quay: HS 748-2A G-AVXJ (last noted December 2011) is split into three sections, the cockpit and tail at 39ft down, with the centre section at 85ft. **Access:** *Private site, visits by prior permission* ***only*** | **www.vobsterquay.co.uk**

WEDMORE on the B3139 west of Wells

Castle Farm Camping and Caravanning: Neil Banwell, site owner, keeps a SHAR. It is displayed outside during the summer.

◆ **Access:** *Private site, visits by prior permission* ***only***.

❑ XZ494	'128'	HS Sea Harrier FA.2	80	ex St Athan, 800, FRS.1, 899, 801, 899, 800, 899, 801, 800, 899. 800 Sqn colours		10-13

WELLS Not noted since October 2009, Airtourer G-AZMN has been deleted.

WESTON-SUPER-MARE AERODROME on the A371 east of Weston-super-Mare

The Helicopter Museum (THM): Every so often, the passage of time serves to supply a jolt, normally as a reminder of quickly it goes by. A note from Elfan ap Rees, THM's Chairman of Trustees and the founder of this exceptional endeavour, brought one of those shocks... a pleasant one, mind! THM is celebrating 25 years of being open to the public and there is a hope that a special publication charting the history of this collection will be published to mark this significant milestone.

The THM team is working on a new project that will involve Heritage Lottery Funding to replace the existing entrance area with an imposing two-storey feature which will have record-breaking Lynx G-LYNX as its centre-piece. Additional display space, conference facilities, much improved catering and retail areas also feature in the scheme. The project could also see the 1936 control tower restored and a new hangar devoted to machines built at Weston-super-Mare.

It can't merit a formal listing, even though it is bigger than some of the complete rotorcraft at IHM, but Boeing XCH-62 73-22012 certainly deserves a mention. A prototype heavy-lift helicopter it was cancelled before it could fly. The nose wheels and main landing gear were acquired from Fort Rucker, Alabama, in 2009.

Subject to operational conditions, there are regular helicopter experience flight days; loads of special events, including a new interactive area and film theatre; tours of the restoration hangar; kids play area with a Westland 30 to 'fly' and regular 'Open cockpit' days. The 'HeliWorld' gift shop is excellent, and the great 'Choppers' cafe offers 'Heliburgers'. The **Reserve Collection** is listed separately - below. Cricket G-AXRA has moved from display to the 'Reserve'. To claw back a little space for this entry *only*, W-s-M has been substituted for Weston-super-Mare.

◆ **Open:** *All year Wed to Sun 10:00 to 17:30 (16:30 Nov to Mar), plus Bank Holidays, other than Xmas and New Year.* **Also** *daily during Easter and late Jul to early Sep - check with website.* **Contact:** *The Heliport, Locking Moor Road, Weston-super-Mare, BS24 8PP* | **01934 635227** | **helimuseum@btconnect.com** | **www.helicoptermuseum.co.uk**

❑ G-ALSX	Bristol Sycamore 3	50	ex Duxford, Staverton, G-48/1, G-ALSX, VR-TBS ntu, G-ALSX. CoA 24-9-65, de-reg 31-1-66	[1]	1-14
❑ G-AODA	Westland Whirlwind Srs 3	55	ex Redhill, Bristow, 9Y-TDA, EP-HAC, G-AODA. *Dorado*. CoA 23-8-91, de-reg 23-9-93. Arrived 7-8-93		1-14
❑ G-AOUJ	Fairey Ultra Light Helicopter	56	ex Staverton, Innsworth, W-s-M, Harlow, White Waltham, XJ928. CoA 29-3-59, de-reg 26-2-69. Arrived 2010		1-14
❑ G-AOZE	Westland Widgeon 2	57	ex Cuckfield, Shoreham, 5N-ABW, G-AOZE. Arrived 1986		1-14
❑ G-ASTP	Hiller UH-12C	61	ex Biggin Hill, Thornicombe, 'Wales', Thornicombe, Redhill, N9750C. CoA 3-7-82, de-reg 24-1-90. Arrived 12-10-89		1-14
❑ G-ATFG	Brantly B.2B	65	ex East Fortune, Newport Pagnell. CoA 25-3-85, de-reg 25-9-87. Arrived 21-1-04	[1]	1-14
❑ G-AVNE *and* G-17-3	Westland Wessex 60 Srs 1	67	ex Bournemouth, W-s-M, G-17-3, 5N-AJL, G-AVNE, 9M-ASS, VH-BHC, PK-HBQ, G-AVNE. CoA 7-2-83, de-reg 23-11-82. Arrived 1987		1-14
❑ G-AWRP	Cierva Grasshopper III	69	ex Blackpool, Heysham, Shoreham, Redhill. CoA 12-5-72, de-reg 5-12-83. Arrived 1993		1-14
❑ G-BAPS	Campbell Cougar	73	CoA 20-5-74, de-reg 21-1-87. Acquired 5-76		1-14
❑ G-BGHF	Westland WG.30-100	79	ex Yeovil, Westland. CoA 1-8-86, de-reg 29-3-89. Acquired 22-12-88	[2]	1-14
❑ G-BIGP	Bensen B.8M	81	ex Shrewsbury. CoA 20-10-07, de-reg 27-11-08		1-14
❑ G-BVWL	Air & Space 18A	66	ex East Fortune, Kinnetties, SE-HIE, N90588, N6152S. De-reg 18-10-00. Arrived 22-11-07		1-14
❑ G-EHIL	EHI EH-101 PP3	87	ex Yeovil, ZH647. De-reg 28-4-99. Arrived 26-11-99	[3]	1-14
❑ G-ELEC	Westland WG.30-200	83	ex Westland, W-s-M, Yeovil, G-BKNV. CoA 28-6-85, de-reg 27-2-98. Arrived 7-12-01		1-14
❑ G-HAUL	Westland WG.30 TT300	86	ex G-17-22, Yeovil. CoA 27-10-86, de-reg 22-4-92. Arr 1991		1-14
❑ G-LYNX	Westland Lynx Mk.7(mod) ZB500	79	ex Yeovil, W-s-M, Yeovil, ZB500, ZA500 ntu, G-LYNX, De-reg 27-2-98. Arrived 18-1-95	[4]	1-14
❑ G-OAPR	Brantly B.2B ✈	65	ex G-BPST ntu, N2280U	[1]	1-14

❑ G-ORVB		McCulloch J-2	G-HEKY	71	ex G-ORVB, G-BLGI ntu, G-BKKL ntu, Bahrain Public Security BPS-3, N4329G. De-reg 30-1-09. Arrived 21-12-08		1-14
❑ G-OTED		Robinson R22		81	ex Elstree, G-BMYR, ZS-HLG. CoA 17-2-02, De-reg 26-3-02. Arrived 2-02		1-14
❑ G-WBAT*		Julian CD Wombat		90	ex Breeqhou, St Merryn, G-BSID. De-reg 29-4-09. Arr 9-7-13		1-14
❑ G-BYMP*		Campbell Cricket		99	ex Cheshire, Newtownards. Arrived 16-1-14		1-14
❑ –		Hafner R-II		32	BAPC.10, ex Middle Wallop, Locking, W-s-M, Higher Blagdon, Old Warden, Yeovil, Heston, Vienna		1-14
❑ –		Murray M-1 Helicopter		54	BAPC.60, ex Wigan, Salford. Arrived 10-95		1-14
❑ –		Watkinson CG-4		77	BAPC.128, ex Horley, Bexhill. Arrived 1978.	[5]	1-14
❑ –		Westland WG.33 EMU		78	BAPC.153, ex Yeovil. Arrived 1980	[6]	1-14
❑ –		Bensen B.8M		84	BAPC.264, ex Westbury-on-Trym. Unflown		1-14
❑ –		Bensen B.8M Gyro-Boat		c65	BAPC.289, ex Brooklands, Glasgow. Arrived 11-10-03		1-14
❑ –		Husband Modac Hornet		02	ex Sheffield. 'Hopped' only. Arrived 13-11-04		1-14
❑ –		Agusta A.109A		~	ex Denham, Helicopter Film Services. Arrived 2012. Fuselage		1-14
❑ –*		Yamaha Motors RPH		86	-	[7]	1-14
❑ D-HMQV		Bölkow Bö 102 Helitrainer		60	ex Bückeburg, Germany	[1] [8]	1-14
❑ DDR-SPY		Kamov Ka-26 *Hoodlum*		73	ex D-HOAY, Germany, Interflug DDR-SPY. Arrived 12-6-95		1-14
❑ F-OCMF	'335'	Sud Super Frelon		67	ex Aérospatiale, Olympic, F-BTRP, F-WKQC, F-OCZV, F-RAFR, F-OCMF, F-BMHC, F-WMHC. Arrived 28-4-93. Olympic colours, *Hermes*	[9]	1-14
❑ F-WQAP		Sud SA.365N Dauphin		79	ex Eurocopter, Marignane, F-WZJJ. Acquired 19-3-03	[10]	1-14
❑ N114WG		Westland WG.30-160		84	ex Yeovil, Westland Inc, G-EFIS, G-17-8. Arrived 10-1-97. Forward fuselage		1-14
❑ OO-SHW		Bell 47H-1		56	ex Thruxton, G-AZYB, LN-OQG, SE-HBE, SABENA OO-SHW. Crashed 21-4-84, de-reg 22-4-85	[1]	1-14
❑ SP-SAY		Mil Mi-2 *Hoplite*		85	ex PZL-Swidnik, Hiscso, ZEUS. PZL-built. Arrived 24-11-97		1-14
❑ AP506		Cierva C.30A		34	ex Staverton, Tewkesbury, AP506, 529, 1448 Flt, 74 Wing, 5 RSS, G-ACWM, Autogiro Fg Club, Hanworth. Avro-built. De-reg 17-3-59. Arrived 1986. Frame	[1]	1-14
❑ WG719		Westland Dragonfly HR.5		52	ex G-BRMA 'WG718', Shawbury, W-s-M, Yeovilton, Yeovilton SF, 705. SOC 5-5-70. De-reg 30-3-89. Acq 11-73	[1]	1-14
❑ XD163	'X'	Westland Whirlwind HAR.10		54	ex Wroughton, 8645M, CFS, Akrotiri SAR Flt, MoA, 228, 275, 155, MoA. SOC 20-3-80	[1]	1-14
❑ XE521		Fairey Rotodyne Y		57	ex Cranfield, White Waltham. Sections. Acquired 1981	[1] [11]	1-14
❑ XG452		Bristol Belvedere HC.1		60	ex G-BRMB, Ternhill, Cosford, 2 SoTT 7997M (8-12-67). De-reg 3-7-96. Acquired 5-11-74		1-14
❑ XG462		Bristol Belvedere HC.1		61	ex Henlow, W-s-M, 72, 66. Crashed 5-10-63. Cockpit. Arrived 1989	[1]	1-14
❑ XK940	'911'	Westland Whirlwind HAS.7		57	ex G-AYXT, Tibenham, Redhill, Northampton, Heysham, Carnforth, Panshanger, Elstree, Luton, Blackpool, Fleetlands, 771, Culdrose SF, 705, 825, 824, 845. SOC 24-3-71. CoA 4-2-99, de-reg 8-8-00. Arrived 6-6-00	[1] [12]	1-14
❑ XL811		Saro Skeeter AOP.12		59	ex Stoke-on-Trent, Warmingham, Southend, 9/12 Lancers, 17F, 656, 651. SOC 27-5-68. Arrived 1993	[1]	1-14
❑ XL829		Bristol Sycamore HR.14		57	ex Bristol, 32, MCS, Khormaksar SAR Flight. SOC 18-12-71. Arrived 17-10-07		1-14
❑ XM328	'653'	Westland Wessex HAS.3		60	ex Culdrose, A2644 [2], A2727 (9-5-85), Wroughton, Culdrose SAR Flt, 772, 737, A&AEE, HAS.1, A&AEE. Arrived 3-04. *The Sow*		1-14
❑ XM330		Westland Wessex HAS.1		59	ex Farnborough, RAE, ATDU, ETPS, RAE Farnborough, A&AEE, HS. SOC q6-6-83. Arrived 16-5-94		1-14
❑ XP165		Saro P.531-2		60	ex W-s-M, HAM Southend, ETPS, A&AEE, RAE, A&AEE. Last flown 28-5-1. Acquired 10-5-83		1-14
❑ XR486		Westland Whirlwind HCC.12		64	ex G-RWWW, Redhill, Tattershall Thorpe, St Athan, 32, QF, 32, QF. CoA 25-8-96, de-reg 10-7-00. Arr 8-6-00	[1]	1-14
❑ XT190		Bell Sioux AH.1		65	ex Wattisham, Soest, Middle Wallop, UNFICYP. Westland-built. Arrived 8-6-95		1-14
❑ XT443	'422'	Westland Wasp HAS.1		66	ex Oldmixon, Sherborne, 703. SOC 7-5-87. Arrived 18-1-95. HMS *Aurora* titles		1-14

❑ XV733		Westland Wessex HCC.4	69	ex Shawbury, Queen's Flight. Arrived 15-11-01		1-14
❑ XV798*		HS Harrier GR.1	70	ex Kemble, Banwell, Foulness, PCB rig, Dunsfold, 20, 233 OCU. Crashed 23-4-71. Arrived 31-10-12	[13]	1-14
❑ XW839		Westland Lynx 00-05	74	ex Yeovilton, A2624 [2], A2657 (1-11-88), A2710, Manadon, BS Eng. Arrived 11-1-96. 'HMS Thunderer' titles		1-14
❑ XX910		Westland Lynx HAS.2	74	ex Yeovilton, DERA/RAE Farnborough, Aberporth, A&AEE. Arrived 5-12-00	[14]	1-14
❑ ZB686		Sud Gazelle AH.1	83	ex Middle Wallop, 9322M, ex Fleetlands, 665, 655. Westland-built. Trailer mounted, travelling exhibit		1-14
❑ ZE477		Westland Lynx 3	84	ex G-17-24, Yeovil, Westland. Arrived 1989		1-14
❑ 'ZS782'*		Westland Wideye EMU	82	'stealth' remote-piloted helicopter	[7]	1-14
❑ -*		Westland Mote RPH	75	first noted 7-12	[7]	1-14
❑ -*		Westland Wisp RPH	76	first prototype	[7]	1-14
❑ -*		Westland Wideye RPH	79	pre-production	[7]	1-14
❑ A-41	ACB	Sud Alouette II	67	ex Belgian Army. Arrived 19-2-08		1-14
❑ 622		Piasecki HUP-3 Retriever	54	ex Philadelphia, N6699D, RCN, 51-16622. Arrived 1991		1-14
❑ 09147		Mil Mi-4 *Hound*	c57	ex Prague, Sechov, Tabor, Czech AF. Arrived 1-94		1-14
❑ FR-108	'CDL'	Sud-Ouest Djinn	59	ex France, ALAT F-MCDL. Arrived 1991		1-14
❑ 81+00		Bölkow Bö 105M	84	ex Donauworth, Laupheim, Heer, D-HZYR. Arr 3-5-07	[15]	1-14
❑ 96+26		Mil Mi-24 *Hind-D*	81	ex Basepohl, Luftwaffe, East German 421. Arrived 20-2-95		1-14
❑ MM80927	'CC-49'	Bell 206C JetRanger	74	ex Italy, Carabinieri. Agusta-built. Arrived late 2012		1-14
❑ MM81205		Agusta A.109A Mk.II	86	ex Frosinone, Guardia di Finanza GdiF-128. Arrived 6-10-10		3-12
❑ 1005	'05'	WSK SM-2	~	ex Polish Air Force. Arrived 10-6-91		3-12
❑ 2007	'07'	Mil Mi-1 *Hare*	59	ex Poland. Soviet colours. WSK-built SM-1. Arrived 2-9-93		3-12
❑ 618		Mil Mi-8PS *Hip*	~	ex Poland, Polish AF, 37 PST, 36 SPLT. Arrived 5-2-10	[16]	3-12
❑ 66-16579		Bell UH-1H-BF Iroquois	67	ex US Army, UH-1D. Arrived 29-8-92		3-12
❑ 67-16506		Hughes OH-6A Cayuse	68	ex US Army. Arrived 8-99		3-12

■ **[1]** Airframes on loan from Elfan ap Rees. **[2]** WG.30 prototype, first flown 10-4-79. **[3]** EH-101 factoids: First flown at Yeovil 30-9-88, retired 2-99 with 653 hours in 581 flights. **[4]** G-LYNX established a world air speed record in 8-86 of 249.1mph. **[5]** CG-4 is a man-powered rotorcraft. **[6]** WG.33 - engineering mock-up of a single-seat ultra-light observation helicopter. **[7]** RPH - remote-piloted helicopter; the Yamaha was built for agricultural use; Wideye 'ZS782' had 'stealth' characteristics (!). **[8]** Although bolted firmly down on to a base-plate, the Helitrainer was capable of flight, but intended as a fully-functioning procedure and flight trainer. **[9]** Frelon started life as SA.321 c/n 116. It is in Olympic Airways colours as worn at the 1969 Paris Salon. **[10]** First production SA.365N, modified to fly-by-wire test-bed; retired in 2001. **[11]** The Rotodyne project was cancelled in February 1962 and XE521 stored at White Waltham and eventually broken up. As couple of times in *W&R*, the rules are broken and although there is not cockpit, the fuselage sections and rotor pylon are substantial enough to be formally listed. **[12]** Registration G-AYXT was also allocated to XK907, but not taken up - see Coventry, Warks. **[13]** Harrier is fitted with the wing of T.2 XW264 –see Gloucestershire Airport, Glos, for the rest of it. XV798 was used for Pegasus plenum chamber burning (PCB) ground trials. **[14]** During refurbishing at Yeovilton XX910 was fitted with the boom of Danish MK.80 S-142. **[15]** Bö 105M donated by Eurocopter. **[16]** *Hip* is a VIP version - square, not round, windows, delivered to Poland in the 1970s, serving until retirement in 2005. It flew with 37 Air Assault Regiment (PST), Leznica Wielka, Lodz.

Reserve Collection: Available for inspection only by special arrangement - check with the contacts above. Several hulks used for spares or potential exchange have been scrapped: JetRanger G-BODW and the anonymous example; Bölkow Bö 105Ds G-PASA and G-PASB.

❑ G-ANFH	Westland Whirlwind Srs 1	53	ex Redhill, Great Yarmouth, Bristow, BEAH. CoA 17-7-71, de-reg 2-9-77	[1]	1-14
❑ G-ANJV	Westland Whirlwind Srs 3	54	ex Redhill, Bristow and VR-BET. De-reg 1-8-74		1-14
❑ G-ARVN	Cierva Grasshopper 1	63	ex Shoreham, Redhill. CoA 18-5-63, de-reg 14-3-77		1-14
❑ G-ASCT	Bensen B.8M	r62	ex Hungerford. CoA 11-11-66, de-reg 20-9-73. Arrived 1993. Major components		1-14
❑ G-ATBZ	Westland Wessex 60 Srs 1	65	ex Austria, Bournemouth, G-17-4, W-s-M. CoA 15-12-81, de-reg 23-11-82. Arrived 1988		1-14
❑ G-AVKE	Gadfly HDW-1	67	ex Southend, Thruxton. De-reg 12-10-81. Arrived 1978	[1]	1-14
❑ G-AXFM	Cierva Grasshopper III	r69	ex Blackpool, Heysham, Shoreham, Redhill. De-reg 5-12-83. Arrived 1993	[2]	1-14
❑ G-AXRA	Campbell Cricket	69	de-reg 25-10-90. Arrived 10-13		1-14
❑ G-AZAU	Cierva Grasshopper III	r71	ex Blackpool, Heysham, Shoreham, Redhill. De-reg 5-12-83. Arrived 1993	[2]	1-14
❑ G-TPTR	Bell AB.206B JetRanger II	79	ex Lyneham, G-LOCK, N2951N, N2951W. Crashed 1-3-89. de-reg 9-10-94. Agusta-built. Arrived 13-10-07.		

❑	–		Bensen B.6 gyroglider	c60	BAPC.212. Major components		1-14
❑	–		Cranfield Vertigo	c82	BAPC.213, ex Yeovil, Cardington, Yeovil	[3]	1-14
❑	N5840T		Westland WG.30-100	82	ex Yeovil, Air Spur, G-BKFF. Arrived 10-1-97		1-14
❑	XG596	'66'	Westland Whirlwind HAS.7	57	ex Wroughton A2651 (7-1-76), 705, 829, 771, 705, 737 Arrived 11-7-77	[1]	1-14
❑	XL736		Saro Skeeter AOP.12	58	ex Saxmundham, Stuttgart, Moordrecht, 1 Flt, 655, Middle Wallop. Ground accident 25-9-68. Minus tailboom		1-14
❑	XL767		Saro Skeeter AOP.12	58	ex Saxmundham, Stuttgart, Moordrecht, 19 Regt, 26 Regt, 17 Flt, 652, 9 Flt, 1 Flt, 652, 1 Wing. SOC 21-11-68		1-14
❑	XM557		Saro Skeeter AOP.12	59	ex Saxmundham, Stuttgart, Moordrecht, 5 Flt, 652, 17Flt, 652, 4 Flt, 654, 652, 1 Wing. Minus tailboom		1-14
❑	XN345		Saro Skeeter AOP.12	60	ex Saxmundham, Stuttgart, Moordrecht, 26 Regt, 17 Flt, 652, 17 Flt, 654, 655, 1 Wing. SOC 20-10-69		1-14
❑	XP404		Westland Whirlwind HAR.10	62	ex Finningley, Benson 8682M (10-10-82), 22, SAR Wing, 202, 228. Arrived 1991		1-14
❑	XP886		Westland Scout AH.1	63	ex Yeovil Tech, Arborfield, Wroughton, 652, 660, 651		1-14
❑	XR526		Westland Wessex HC.2	64	ex Yeovil, Sherborne, Farnborough, Odiham 8147M, 72. Damaged 27-5-70. Arrived 26-8-99		1-14
❑	XS149	'61'	Westland Wessex HAS.3	63	ex Manadon, Wroughton, Templecombe, Lee-on-Solent, 737, HAS.1, 819, 845, 706. Arrived 1987	[4]	1-14
❑	XS486	'F' *and* '524'	Westland Wessex HU.5	64	ex Colerne 9272M (31-5-91), Wroughton, Lee-on-Solent, Wroughton, 772, 771, 707, 848, 707, A&AEE, 707, 848, 707, 848. Union Jack-painted nose		1-14
❑	XT472	'XC'	Westland Wessex HU.5	66	ex Hullavington, Netheravon, Middle Wallop, Lyneham, Wroughton, 845, 847, 845. SOC 10-9-82. Arrived 1987		1-14
❑			Westland WG.30-300 EMU	~	ex Yeovil. Transmission rig, using parts from c/n 022		1-14
❑	S-881		Sikorsky S-55C	54	ex Panshanger, Elstree, Dan AF Esk.722. Spares		1-14
❑	S-886		Sikorsky S-55C	54	ex Panshanger, Elstree, Dan AF Esk.722		1-14

■ **[1]** Airframes on loan from Elfan ap Rees. **[2]** G-AXFM second prototype Grasshopper III, ground-running rig. **[3]** G-AZAU, unfinished third prototype: centre section, floor pan, dynamics system. **[3]** Vertigo, a man-powered rotorcraft. **[4]** Wessex HAS.3 XS149 is fitted with the rear fuselage of Srs 60 G-17-6.

WESTON ZOYLAND AERODROME on the A372 east of Bridgwater

❑	WV499	'G'	Percival Provost T.1 G-BZRF	53	ex Exeter, Wycombe Air Park, Armthorpe, Sandtoft, North Weald, St Athan, Weeton 7698M, 6 FTS. De-reg 22-2-05	12-07
❑	WW453		Percival Provost T.1 G-TMKI	55	ex Clevedon, Cranfield, Thatcham, Strathallan, Perth, Hunting, 1 FTS, 2 FTS. De-reg 3-10-11	7-13

YEOVIL AIRFIELD to the west of Yeovil

EGHG

AgustaWestland: The hulk of Lynx AH.1 XX907 departed 5th July 2011 for a scrapyard in Stafford, Staffs. Merlin HM.1 ZH821 moved to Shawbury, Shrop, on 1st October 2013.

❑	G-BKKI		Westland WG.30-100	83	de-reg 8-1-91. External store		12-13
❑	XZ671		Westland Lynx AH.7	81	ex Fleetlands, Yeovil, Wroughton, 652. Cr 24-1-85. Trials	[1]	10-10
❑	–	'961'	EHI EH.101 EMU	~	static test airframe. Stored		3-02

■ **[1]** XZ671 is fitted with the boom of ZE377.

Yeovil Technical College:

❑	ZA129	Westland Sea King HAS.6	80	ex Westland - Yeovil, Gosport, Fleetlands, 810, 820, 826, 706. SOC 24-1-01. Cockpit	10-08

YEOVILTON AIRFIELD on the B5131, south of the A303, north of Yeovil

EGDY

Fleet Air Arm Museum (FAAM): An all-absorbing visit, with 'Carrier' and 'Leading Edge' representing the best of innovation. The 'Falklands 30' exhibition proved very popular and has been extended in duration. There is an observation window that allows visitors to see progress in the restoration/conservation workshop and another that overlooks the ramp giving views of activity on the Fleet Air Arm base. The 'Swordfish' restaurant is excellent. There is a very active **Friends of the FAAM**. Membership enquiries via the museum.

FAAM aircraft can be found at the following: Coventry, Warks, Gannet XA508; Sunderland, Tyneside, Pucará A-522; Woodley, Berks, Gannet XG883. And, a little further away, Scimitar F.1 XD220 now with the Empire State Aerosciences Museum. MB.339AA 0767 has been signed over to the South Yorkshire Aircraft Museum at Doncaster, S Yorks.

The following have moved through to Cobham Hall, see below: Barracuda DP872, Firefly VH127, Lynx XZ699. Martlet AL246 moved to the Restoration Workshop - see below - in 2011, but was back on show in time for the opening of the Battle of the Atlantic exhibition in July 2013.

◆ **Access:** *On the B5131, east of Ilchester and north of Yeovil. 'Brown signed' off the A303 with access through Ilchester from the west, or immediately after West Camel from the east.* **Open:** *Daily (other than Xmas) Apr to Oct 10:00 to 17:30 and Wed to Sun Nov to Mar 10:00 to 16:30.* **Contact:** *RNAS Yeovilton, Box D6, Ilchester, BA22 8HT* | **01935 840565** | **info@fleetairarm.com** | **www.fleetairarm.com**

Main Halls: Dave Morris and his team spent from 2011 to mid-2013 in the Restoration Workshop pealing back the paint on Martlet I AL246, in a similar manner to work carried out on Corsair KD431. The upper surfaces revealed a two-tone green camouflage, believed applied by Grumman at Bethpage prior to delivery. Under wing, AL246 was painted with one black and one cream-coloured wing, in the 'high recognition' style for fighters of 1940. The fuselage carried evidence of the code 'M2-R' from its days with 768 Squadron at Machrihanish in 1941. Work completed, this striking restoration was returned to the main halls by July 2013.

Gulf War veteran Lynx HAS.3 XZ720 was handed over to the museum on 26th April 2012 and was briefly on show in the Falklands exhibition, but had moved to Cobham Hall - see below - by October 2013. Albacore 'N4389' moved to Cobham Hall, see below, by October 2013. The Ohka had moved to the workshop by December 2013. More inter-hall shuffles were due to be made as *W&R* went to press!

❑ –		Short S.27 replica		79	BAPC.149, ex Lee-on-Solent. Acquired 1980		2-14
❑ 8359		Short 184		15	ex Duxford, South Lambeth, Crystal Palace, Buncrana, Rosyth, Dundee, Killingholme. Westland-built. Forward fuselage. Bomb damaged 31-1-41 at S Lambeth. Acquired 28-1-76	[1]	2-14
❑ L2301		Supermarine Walrus I		39	ex Arbroath, Thame, G-AIZG de-reg 5-1-49, EI-ACC, IAC N18, L2301 - no service. Acquired 6-12-66		2-14
❑ L2940		Blackburn Skua II		40	ex Lake Grotli, Norway, 800. Crashed 27-4-40. Arrived 1974		2-14
❑ N1854		Fairey Fulmar II	G-AIBE	40	ex Lossiemouth, Fairey G-AIBE, CoA 6-7-59, de-reg 30-4-59, A&AEE. Acquired 1962		2-14
❑ 'N6452'		Sopwith Pup rep	G-BIAU	83	ex Whitehall, G-BIAU. CoA 13-9-89, de-reg 10-3-97. Acquired 10-6-85		2-14
❑ 'P4139'		Fairey Swordfish II	HS618	43	ex 'V6105', 'W5984', Manadon A2001, Donibristle, 834. SOC on board HMS *Hunter* 5-8-43. Acquired 1962		2-14
❑ Z2033	'275'	Fairey Firefly TT.1		44	ex Duxford, Staverton, G-ASTL de-reg 2-3-82, SE-BRD, Z2033, 731. Acquired 25-7-00. 1771 Sqn c/s, *Evelyn Tentions*		2-14
❑ AL246		Grumman Martlet I		40	ex Loughborough, 768, RAE, 882, 802. Acquired 1963. See notes above		2-14
❑ DP872		Fairey Barracuda II		43	ex Andover area, Yeovilton, Enagh Lough, 769. Crashed 18-1-44. Acquired 1968. Forward fuselage	[2]	2-14
❑ EX976		NAA Harvard IIA		41	ex Portuguese AF 1657, EX976, 41-33959. Acquired 1981		2-14
❑ KD431	'E2-M'	Vought Corsair IV		44	ex Cranfield, 768, 1835, BuNo 14862. Acquired 1964. 768 Sqn colours		2-14
❑ KE209		Grumman Hellcat II		45	ex Lossiemouth SF, Stretton, Anthorn, BuNo 79779. Last flown 7-54. Acquired 1970		2-14
❑ SX137		Supermarine Seafire F.17		45	ex Culdrose, 'W9132', Yeovilton SF, 764, 759, 1831, Culham. Last flown 16-7-60, acquired 1964		2-14
❑ VX595		Westland Dragonfly HR.5		49	ex Portland, Gosport, Fleetlands, Henlow, Fleetlands, ETPS, RAE, ETPS, A&AEE, AFEE, A&AEE, AFEE. Acquired 23-11-98	[1]	2-14
❑ WJ231	'115'	Hawker Sea Fury FB.11		51	ex Wroughton, Yeovilton 'WE726', Yeovilton SF, FRU. Acquired 1965		2-14
❑ WN493		Westland Dragonfly HR.5		53	ex Culdrose, Culdrose SF, 705, 701, A&AEE. Acquired 19-10-66		2-14
❑ XB446		Grumman Avenger ECM.6B		45	ex Culdrose SF, 831, 751, 820, USN 69502, VC-11, VT-87. Acquired 9-4-68. 'Invasion stripes' and 1944 camouflage		2-14
❑ XP142		Westland Wessex HAS.3		62	ex Wroughton, Yeovilton A2720, 737, 706, 814, 706, 845. Acquired 26-7-82. *Humphrey*	[3]	2-14
❑ XZ499	'003'	BAe Sea Harrier FA.2		81	ex St Athan, 801, 800, 801, 899, 800, 801, 800, 809, 801. Arrived 13-11-02	[4]	2-14

❑	XZ574		Westland Sea King HAS.6	76	ex Gosport, 771, 810, 820, 819, 810, 820, 826. Acquired 9-6-08	[5]	2-14
❑	AE-331		Agusta A.109A ZE411	80	ex 7 Rgt, Middle Wallop, Yeovilton, Middle Wallop, 846, Arg Arm CAB.601. Acquired 10-10. Argentine colours		2-14
❑	100545		Focke-Achgelis Fa 330A-1 Bachstelgze	44	ex Wroughton, Yeovilton, Higher Blagdon, Cranfield, Farnborough. Acquired 25-8-93		2-14
❑	01420		MiG-15*bis Fagot*	64	ex North Weald, Gamston, Retford, G-BMZF, Polish AF. Aero-built SBLim-2A. De-reg 23-2-90. Acquired 14-5-87 North Korean colours		2-14

■ **[1]** Aircraft on loan: Short 184 from the Imperial War Museum; Vampire LZ551 - Science Museum; Dragonfly VX595 - RAF Museum. **[2]** The long-term restoration of Barracuda II DP872 will use the substantial wreckage of Mk.II LS931 from its crash site on the Scottish Isle of Jura, plus other parts from MD953 and PM870. More of the airframe of DP872 is stored in Cobham Hall. The 'tail feathers' are being worked on at Lytham St Anne's, Lancs. **[3]** *Humphrey* attacked the Argentine submarine *Santa Fe* with depth charges 25-4-82 off South Georgia. **[4]** Sea Harrier XZ499 is fitted with the tail fin of ZA195. **[5]** Sea King XZ574 factoids: entered service 6-10-76; detached to HMS *Invincible* for Operation CORPORATE 4-82 to 9-82 and flown by - among others - HRH Prince Andrew; total time upon retirement 9,168 hours; handed over to the museum 9-7-08.

'Carrier': Technically, Wessex XT769 is in Hall 2 - but as the method of 'conveyance' to 'Carrier', it really belongs here! By October 2013, Gannet AEW.3 XL503 had moved to Cobham Hall, see below.

❑	LZ551/G		DH Vampire 1	44	ex Waddon (Science Museum), DH, RAE, 778, A&AEE, RAE. SOC 13-8-47. Acquired 1966	[1]	2-14
❑	WA473	'102'	Supermarine Attacker F.1	51	ex Abbotsinch, 736, 702, 800. SOC 16-6-58, acquired 1964		2-14
❑	WV856		Hawker Sea Hawk FGA.6	54	ex RAE, 781, 806.AWA-built. Acquired 7-67		2-14
❑	XA466	'777'	Fairey Gannet COD.4	57	ex Wroughton, Yeovilton, Lee-on-Solent, Lossiemouth, 849. Acquired 12-12-78		2-14
❑	XD317	'112'	Supermarine Scimitar F.1	59	ex FRU, RAE, 800, 736, 807. Acquired 18-9-69		2-14
❑	XN957	'630'	Blackburn Buccaneer S.1	63	ex 736, 809, 801. SOC 10-11-72. Acquired 1974		2-14
❑	XS590	'131'	DH Sea Vixen FAW.2	66	ex 899, 892. Acquired 26-11-70. 899 Sqn colours		2-14
❑	XT482	'ZM'	Westland Wessex HU.5	66	A2656 [2], ex A2745, Lee-on-Solent, Wroughton, 707, 845, 847, 707, 771, 707. Acquired 24-2-94	[2]	2-14
❑	XT596		McD Phantom FG.1	66	ex Scampton, Holme-on-Spalding Moor, RAE Thurleigh, H-o-s-M, Hucknall, Patuxent River, Edwards. Arr 19-1-88		2-14
❑	XT769		Westland Wessex HU.5	67	ex Lee-on-Solent, Wroughton, Culdrose, 771, 772, 771, 846, 848. Acquired 3-11	[2]	2-14
❑	XV333	'234'	HS Buccaneer S.2B	66	ex 208, 12, 15, 16, FAA, 237 OCU, 12. Arrived 23-3-94 801 Sqn colours		2-14

■ **[1]** Sea Vampire on loan from the Science Museum and it is occasionally referred to as a Sea Vampire 10. Piloted by Lt Cdr Eric 'Winkle' Brown, it made the world's first-ever landing by a pure-jet on a carrier - HMS *Ocean* - 3-12-45. **[2]** Visitors to 'Carrier' exhibition travel to the flight deck 'on board' Wessex XT769 and disembark from XT482!

'Leading Edge': The inter-active and quite superb display hangar devoted to aviation technology. Centre piece is Concorde 002 and entrance to the interior of this, the most iconic of the UK-built examples, is free!

❑	G-BSST		BAC/Sud Concorde 002	69	CoA 30-10-74, de-reg 21-1-87. Flew in 4-3-76	[1]	2-14
❑	N5419		Bristol Scout D replica	90	ex Kemble, Banwell, Cardington, USA. Arrived 30-11-98	[2]	2-14
❑	VR137		Westland Wyvern TF.1	49	ex Cranfield, Yeovil. Acquired 2-66	[3]	2-14
❑	WG774		BAC 221	64	ex East Fortune, RAE Bedford, Filton, Fairey Delta 2. Last flight 9-6-73. Arrived 1-80	[4]	2-14
❑	XA127		DH Sea Vampire T.22	54	ex CIFE, 736. SOC 12-8-65. Pod		2-14
❑	XL580	'723'	Hawker Hunter T.8M	66	ex FRADU, FOFT, 764. Acquired 26-11-94. 899 Sqn colours		2-14
❑	XP841		Handley Page HP.115	61	ex Cosford, Colerne, RAE Bedford. Last flown 1-2-74. Acquired 6-6-79		2-14
❑	XP980		Hawker P.1127	63	A2700, ex Culdrose, Tarrant Rushton, RAE Bedford, Cranwell, A&AEE. Acquired 6-3-89		2-14
❑	XZ493	'001'	HS Sea Harrier FRS.1	80	ex Dunsfold, Yeovilton, Lee-on-Solent, 899, 801. Ditched 15-12-94, acquired 1-3-95. 801 Sqn colours	[5]	2-14

■ **[1]** UK prototype Concorde G-BSST is on loan from the Science Museum; it first flew on 9-4-69 and clocked a total of 836 flight hours and made 438 landings. **[2]** Bristol Scout D is on loan from Sir George White; its 'serial' is actually its US civil registration. **[3]** The Wyvern was from a pre-production batch of 20 TF.1s, powered by the 24-cylinder RR Eagle 22, but this one did not fly. **[4]** Build date given is that of its second guise as ogival wing test-bed for Concorde, prior to that is was the first FD.2, first flying 6-10-55 and achieving the world air speed record of 1,132mph on 10-3-56. **[5]** The FRS.1 is a complex composite. Rebuilt for museum purposes by BAe at Dunsfold, the forward fuselage of XZ493 was grafted on to the wings and rear fuselage of Harrier GR.3 XV760. The cockpit of XV760 can be found at Southampton, Hants.

Restoration Workshop: (From this edition, listed separately.) At the end of the 'Carrier' tour can be found the workshop area, which is glass-walled to provide visitors with a great view of what's going on without delaying the technicians. See under the Main Halls listing for details of the incredible detective work carried out on Martlet I AL246.

❑ 'N5579'		Gloster Sea Gladiator II	39	ex Dursley, Cardington, Norway. Acquired 17-7-02. Frame		2-14
❑ 15-1585		Yokosuka Ohka 11	c45	BAPC.58, ex Hayes, South Kensington. Acquired 1977	[1]	2-14

■ **[1]** Ohka on loan from the Science Museum.

Cobham Hall: Home of the FAAM's reserve collection, archive and much more. Wessex XP142 *Humphrey* moved to the main museum site by May 2012. Sea Gladiator 'N5579' is now listed under the Restoration Workshop, see above. Gannet COD.4 XA466 moved to 'Carrier' with the AEW.3 XL503 coming the other way. Fa 330 100545 moved to the Main Halls. Albatros D.Va 'D.5397' was disposed of to a UK owner during 2012, before being exported to the USA as N428UT in late 2012.

◆ **Access:** *Occasional open days, otherwise only by prior appointment. Contact details as given above*

❑ 'G-ABUL'		DH Tiger Moth	XL717	40	ex G-AOXG, Mk.II T7291, 24 EFTS, 19 EFTS. Morris-built. De-reg 31-10-56. Acquired 1972		2-14
❑ G-AZAZ		Bensen B.8M		71	ex Wroughton, Houndstone, Yeovilton, Manadon. De-reg 19-9-75. Acquired2-12-99		2-14
❑ G-BGWZ		Eclipse Super Eagle h-g		79	ex Wroughton, Houndstone, Yeovilton. De-reg 5-12-83		2-14
❑ 'B6401'		Sopwith Camel replica		69	ex 'C1701', N1917H, G-AWYY. CoA 1-9-85, de-reg 25-11-91. Acquired 1985	[1]	2-14
❑ 'N2078'		Sopwith Baby floatplane		16	ex Fleetlands, Heathrow, RAeS, Nash collection, Brooklands. Acquired 5-70. *The Jabberwock*	[2]	2-14
❑ 'N4389'	'4M'	Fairey Albacore	N4172	41	ex FAAM, Land's End, Yeovilton, Wroughton, 828. Crashed 1-4-41. Acquired 1983		2-14
❑ 'N5459'		Sopwith Triplane replica		76	ex 'N5492', Chertsey. *Black Maria*. Acquired 25-3-87 BAPC.111, 10 (Naval) Sqn, 'B' Flight colours		2-14
❑ 'S1287'		Fairey Flycatcher replica		79	ex Andover, Middle Wallop, Duxford, Middle Wallop, Yeovilton, G-BEYB. De-reg 12-7-96. Acquired 5-6-96. 405 Flt colours	[3]	2-14
❑ VH127	'200'	Fairey Firefly TT.4		47	ex Wroughton, Yeovilton, Culdrose, FRU, 700, 737, 812. Acquired 29-11-72		2-14
❑ VV106		Supermarine 517		48	ex Wroughton, Lee-on-Solent, Cosford, St Athan, Colerne, Cardington, Halton 7175M, RAE. Acq 2-90	[4] [5]	2-14
❑ VX272		Hawker P.1052		48	ex Wroughton, Lee-on-Solent, Cosford, St Athan, Colerne, Cardington, Halton 7174M. Acquired 2-90	[4]	2-14
❑ WM292	'841'	Gloster Meteor TT.20		53	ex Bruntingthorpe, Cardiff, Yeovilton, FRU, Kemble, NF.11 527. AWA-built. Acquired 4-6-69		2-14
❑ WP313	'568'	Percival Sea Prince T.1		53	ex Wroughton, Kemble, 750, Sydenham SF, 750, Lossiemouth SF, 750. Acquired 1-87		2-14
❑ WS103	'709'	Gloster Meteor T.7		52	ex Wroughton, Crawley, Wroughton, Lee-on-Solent, FRU, Kemble, Yeovilton Standards Sqn, Anthorn. SOC 19-1-71. Acquired 8-1-71		2-14
❑ WT121	'415'	Douglas Skyraider AEW.1		51	ex Culdrose, 849, USN VC-12, VC-11 124121. SOC 22-9-60. Acquired 1962	[6]	2-14
❑ WV106	'427'	Douglas Skyraider AEW.1		50	ex Culdrose, Helston, Culdrose, 849, Donibristle, Abbotsinch, US Navy VC-12 124086. Acquired 1964. SOC 23-9-60. 849 Sqn colours		2-14
❑ WW138	'227'	DH Sea Venom FAW.22		55	ex AWS, 831, 809. Acquired 9-69. Suez stripes		2-14
❑ XA129		DH Sea Vampire T.22		54	ex Wroughton, Yeovilton, CIFE, 736. Acquired 14-7-70		2-14
❑ XA864		Westland Whirlwind HAR.1		53	ex Wroughton, Yeovilton, RAE, A&AEE, RAE, CA, G-17-1. Acquired 10-3-70		2-14
❑ XB480	'537'	Hiller HT.1		53	ex Wroughton, Yeovilton, Manadon, A2577, 705. Acquired 5-10-71		2-14
❑ XE340	'131'	Hawker Sea Hawk FGA.6		55	ex Montrose, Strathallan, Wroughton, Staverton, Brawdy, 801, 898, 897, 800. Acquired 21-10-70		2-14
❑ XG574	'752'	Westland Whirlwind HAR.3		55	ex Portland, Wroughton, Yeovilton, Wroughton, Lee-on-Solent, A2575, 771, 705, 701. Acquired 12-3-75		2-14
❑ XG594	'517'	Westland Whirlwind HAR.3		57	ex East Fortune, Strathallan, Wroughton, Lee-on-Solent, 771, A&AEE, Fleetlands, 705, 846, 737, 701, RAE Bedford, 700. Acquired 23-5-70		2-14

❑ XJ481		DH Sea Vixen FAW.1	58	ex Fleetlands, Southampton, Ilkeston, Yeovilton, Portland, Yeovilton, Boscombe Down, LRWE. Acquired 7-3-74		2-14
❑ XK488		Blackburn NA.39	58	ex Filton, BSE, DHE, Blackburn, RAE, DHE, Blackburn. Acquired 22-7-67	[7]	2-14
❑ XL503	'070'	Fairey Gannet AEW.3	61	ex RRE, 849, A&AEE, RAE, 849, A&AEE. Acquired 26-4-73. 849 Sqn 'D' Flt colours		2-14
❑ XL853		Westland Whirlwind HAS.7	58	ex Portland, Fleetlands, Southampton, Middle Wallop, Lee-on-Solent, A2630, Wroughton, Yeovilton SF, 824. Acquired 7-12-98		12-13
❑ XN332		Saro P.531 G-APNV	58	ex Portland, Wroughton, Yeovilton, Wroughton, Yeovilton, Manadon A2579 (6-5-63), 771, RAE, 700, RAE, 700, A&AEE, G-APNV. De-reg 1-10-59. Acquired 7-10-71		2-14
❑ XN334		Saro P.531	58	ex Wroughton, Crawley, Weston-super-Mare, Yeovilton, Arbroath A2525 13-9-62), RAE, 771, 700, RAE, 700. Ditched 4-3-62. Acquired 22-7-83		2-14
❑ XN462	'17'	Hunting Jet Provost T.3A	60	ex Wroughton, Sharnford, Shawbury, 1 FTS, 2 FTS, CFS, 3 FTS, 7 FTS, 1 FTS. Acquired 25-3-98	[8]	2-14
❑ XS508		Westland Wessex HU.5	64	ex A2677[2], A2766 (14-4-88), Lee-on-Solent, Wroughton. Acquired 28-6-93		2-14
❑ XS527		Westland Wasp HAS.1	63	ex Wroughton, 829, 703, A&AEE. Acquired 31-7-86	[9]	2-14
❑ XS574		Northrop Shelduck D.1	~	dismantled		2-14
❑ XT176	'U'	Bell Sioux AH.1	65	ex Wroughton, 3 CBAS. Acquired 6-6-94		2-14
❑ XT427	'606'	Westland Wasp HAS.1	65	ex Helston, Yeovilton, Wroughton, Lee-on-Solent, 829, 703, 829. Acquired 28-3-84		2-14
❑ XT765	'J'	Westland Wessex HU.5	66	ex Gosport A2665[2], A2755, Lee-on-Solent, 845, Lee SAR Flt, 772, 846, 845. Acquired 3-11		2-14
❑ XT778	'430'	Westland Wasp HAS.1	66	ex A2642[2], A2722 (23-3-88), ex Portland, West Moors, Lee-on-Solent, 829, Yeovilton, Wroughton, Lee-on-Solent, A&AEE. Acquired 15-2-99. *Achilles* Flt colours		2-14
❑ XW864	'54'	Sud Gazelle HT.2	73	ex Shawbury, 705, Wroughton. Westland-built. Acq 21-10-02		2-14
❑ XW994		Northrop Chukar D.1 drone	~	dismantled		2-14
❑ XZ699*		Westland Lynx HAS.3	80	ex Yeovilton, Fleetlands, 815, 702. Acquired 11-06		2-14
❑ XZ720*	'410'	Westland Lynx HAS.3GMS	80	ex Fleetlands, 815, 829,815. 815 Sqn, 216 Flt colours. HMS *Gloucester* titles. Handed over 26-4-12	[10]	2-14
❑ ZB604*	'722'	HS Harrier T.8N	83	ex Wittering, Shawbury, Yeovilton, 899, T.4, 899. 899 Sqn colours		2-14
❑ ZD433	'45A'	BAe Harrier GR.9A	89	ex Cottesmore, 800. Acquired 20-12-11	[11]	2-14
❑ -		Fairey IIIF	~	fuselage frame		2-14
❑ AE-422		Bell UH-1H Iroquois	74	ex Wroughton, Yeovilton, Stanley, Arg Army, 74-22520. Acquired 6-6-89		2-14
❑ 0729	'411'	Beech T-34C-1 Turbo-Mentor	78	ex Wroughton, Yeovilton, Stanley, Pebble Island, Arg Navy Acquired 7-7-83		2-14
❑ '102/17'		Fokker Dr.I replica	68	BAPC.88. Acquired 1975	[12]	2-14

■ **[1]** Camel replica built by Slingsby. **[2]** Sopwith Baby 'N2078' is a composite, using parts from the sequential 8214 and 8215. Both of these machines, ordered in 1915, were passed on to the Italian government to act as pattern aircraft in July 1916, for production by Macchi. This would go a long way to explaining the Italian tricolour on the rudder of the components acquired by R G J Nash. **[3]** Flycatcher built by Westward Airways (aka Viv and Rod Bellamy). **[4]** The Supermarine 510 and P.1052 are on loan from the RAF Museum. **[5]** On 14-12-52 Supermarine *510* VV106 suffered a wheels-up landing at Farnborough. It was returned to Supermarine on 10-7-53 for repair and to have a hinged rear fuselage fitted. This substantial modification was given the design number 517. **[6]** For reasons best known to someone, Skyraider WT983 was painted correctly as 'WT' but given the 'last-three' of its US Navy serial number and this stuck throughout its career. **[7]** Third prototype Buccaneer - also designated NR/A.39 - with non-folding wings, was first flown 10-31-58. **[8]** The Jet Provost was donated by a former RN pilot who earned his wings on this very aircraft while with 1 FTS – where a large number of Navy pilots received their training. **[9]** XS527 also let rip at the *Santa Fe*, with SS.12 missiles. **[10]** XZ720 served almost from new during the Falklands, but came to fame during the first Gulf War when it attacked - and 'killed' - five Iraqi Navy ships with Sea Skua missiles. **[11]** The GR.9 is kept in its battle-weary condition and as such have nicknamed it *Dirty Harry*! **[12]** Triplane based on a Lawrence Parasol airframe, making it a five-eighths scale replica.

Royal Navy Historic Flight (RNHF) /**Fly Navy Heritage Trust**: Working to support the operation of the Flight is the Swordfish Trust. As *W&R* closed for press it was hoped that Swordfish W5856, last flown in 2003, will re-join the 'circuit'. Last noted in July 2010, Sopwith Pup project B1807 (G-EAVX) is believed to have returned to a workshop in Somerset.

◆ **Access: Not** *available for public inspection, but the aircraft are frequently at airshows.* **Contact:** *RNHF Support Group, RNAS Yeovilton, Ilchester, BA22 8HT* | **01935 456279** | **www.royalnavyhistoricflight.org** | **www.fnht.co.uk**

❑ W5856	'4A'	Fairey Swordfish I G-BMGC	41	ex Brough, Strathallan G-BMGC, de-reg 2-9-91, Alabama, RCN, Wroughton, Manston. Blackburn-built. 820 Sqn colours by 11-13	[1]	2-14
❑ LS326	'5A'	Fairey Swordfish II ✈ G-AJVH	43	ex Westland, White Waltham, G-AJVH, de-reg 30-4-59, Worthy Down, 836. Blackburn-built. 836 Sqn colours. *City of Liverpool*		2-14
❑ NF389		Fairey Swordfish III	44	ex Brough, Yeovilton, Brough, Lee-on-Solent, 781, ATDU, 4 Ferry Flt. Blackburn-built. Stored		2-14
❑ VR930	'110'	Hawker Sea Fury FB.11 ✈	48	ex Brough, Yeovilton, Boscombe Down, Lee-on-Solent, Wroughton, Yeovilton, 8382M, Colerne, Dunsfold, FRU, Lossiemouth, Anthorn, 801, Anthorn, 802. 802 Sqn colours		2-14
❑ VX281	'120'	Hawker Sea Fury T.20S ✈ G-RNHF	49	ex North Weald, USA, N281L, N8476W, G-BCOW, DLB D-CACO, G-9-64, VX281, 738, 736. 799 Sqn colours	[2]	2-14
❑ WB657	'908'	DHC Chipmunk T.10	49	ex BRNC, Leeds UAS, 16 RFS, 25 RFS, Leeds UAS, 25 RFS. Withdrawn, spares use		2-14
❑ WK608	'906'	DHC Chipmunk T.10 ✈	50	ex BRNC, Bri UAS, 7 FTS, 3 FTS, Edn UAS,11 RFS.		2-14
❑ WV908	'188'	Hawker Sea Hawk FGA.6	55	ex Dunsfold, Yeovilton, Dunsfold, Yeovilton, Culdrose SF, Halton 8154M, Sydenham A2660, 738, 806, 898, 807. AW-built. Last flown 2010, 806 Sqn colours		2-14
❑ WV911	'115'	Hawker Sea Hawk FGA.6	55	ex Dunsfold, Lee-on-Solent A2622[2], A2626, Fleetlands, Lee-on-Solent A2526 (31-10-62), 700, 804. AW-built. Spares		2-14

■ **[1]** In the colours of Lt Hugh de Graaf Hunter who was awarded a DSC for his part in the attack on the *Bismarck* launched from the *Ark Royal*, 5-41. **[2]** VX281 is registered to Naval Aviation Ltd.

Others: The **Engineering Training School** (ETS) uses instructional airframes. The **Flight Safety and Accident Investigation Unit** is no longer resident. There is a Lynx **R**eturn **to P**roduce programme here, the majority of the candidates being too fleeting to list. Wessex HU.5 XT765 was replaced on display by XT458 and moved to Cobham Hall, see above, by early 2011.

Departures: **Gazelle** HT.2 XW890 moved to Middle Wallop, Hants, 14-11-13 for return to service; **Harrier** GR.1 XV280 cockpit to Culdrose, Cornwall, by 4-13; T.8N ZB604 was transferred to the FAAM (above) by 8-13.

❑ XS513		Westland Wessex HU.5	64	ex A2681[2], Gosport, A2770 (14-3-87), Lee-on-Solent, 772, 845, 772, 845, 707, 846, 845, 846, 845, 707, 846, 848, 845, 848. Dump		7-13
❑ XT458	'P'	Westland Wessex HU.5	65	ex Gosport, A2679 [2], A2768 (15-3-88), Lee-on-Solent, 772, 845, 772, 845, 846, 845, 707, A&AEE, 781. 845 Sqn c/s. Displayed outside Command HQ from 14-8-12		11-13
❑ XV586*	'AJ'	McD Phantom FG.1	69	ex Leuchars 9067M, 43, 892. Arrived 16-5-12. Stored		11-13
❑ XV755	'M'	HS Harrier GR.3	69	ex A2606[3], A2604 (22-5-91), 233 OCU, 3, 233 OCU, 3, 233 OCU, 1, 233 OCU, 1, 233 OCU. Dump		12-13
❑ XW630		HS Harrier GR.3	71	ex A2671[2], Gosport, A2759 (15-5-91) Lee-on-Solent, 3, 4, 3, 20. FAA colours. Dump		12-13
❑ XW784		M-P Kittiwake I	71	ex G-BBRN, CoA 8-9-05. Stored		11-12
❑ XZ228*		Westland Lynx HAS.3GMS	76	ex 815,HAS.2, 815, 702, 815, A&AEE. Arrived 19-6-12		8-12
❑ XZ236 *and* 'LST1'	'302'	Westland Lynx HMA.8	77	ex Fleetlands A2851 (17-6-09), Boscombe Down, Fleetlands, 702, DERA, DTEO, HAS.3, Westland, HAS.2, A&AEE. ETS		6-12
❑ XZ728	'326'	Westland Lynx HMA.8DSP	80	ex A2852, Fleetlands, 815, HAS.3, 702, 815, HAS.2, 815. Crashed 25-2-97. SOC 20-9-04. 'Gate'		12-13
❑ ZB601		HS Harrier T.4	82	ex Dunsfold, St Athan, ETS Yeovilton, 899, 233 OCU. SOC 5-6-00, spares reclaim		12-13
❑ ZD267 *and* 'LST2'		Westland Lynx HMA.8	83	ex A2853, Fleetlands, DTEO, HAS.3, A&AEE. ETS SOC 25-1-08		3-12
❑ ZD578	'122'	HS Sea Harrier FA.2	85	ex St Athan 9329M, 801, 899, 801, 899, 801, FRS.1, 800, 801, 899, 801, 800, A&AEE, 800, 899. SOC 4-12-02 'Gate'. 800 Sqn colours (port), 801 (stb)		12-13
❑ ZF115*	'WV'	Westland Sea King HC.4	86	ex 848, 845, 848, Gosport A2815, A&AEE. ETS from 27-2-13		12-13
❑ 'ZH800'	'123'	HS S' Harrier FA.2 ZH801	96	ex Cottesmore, Yeovilton, 800, 899, 801, 899. Stored		12-13
❑ 'ZH801'	'001'	HS S' Harrier FA.2 ZH800	96	ex Cottesmore, Greenwich, Yeovilton, 899, 801, 800. Stored		12-13
❑ –		HS Sea Harrier FA.2 EMU	~	cockpit, orientation trainer with ETS	[1]	9-02
❑ -		Westland Lynx CIM	~	-	[2]	6-12

❑ RG-05	Westland Lynx static rig	~	ex Weston-super-Mare, Blackpool, Coventry, Yeovil. Dump		3-08
❑ 773	Westland Sea King Mk.47	75	c/n WA.823, ex Gosport, Egyptian Navy. Dump, on side		12-13

■ **[1]** The Sea Harrier orientation trainer was made by Ogle Design Ltd of Letchworth, Herts. **[2]** Purpose-built maintenance trainer, built at Almondbank, 1977.

STAFFORDSHIRE

Includes the unitary authority of Stoke-on-Trent

ABBOTS BROMLEY on the B5014 south of Uttoxeter

Staffordshire Aircraft Restoration Team: Vampire T.11 XD445 moved to Baxterley, Warks, in May 2013. See also Abbots Bromley, Staffs, Baxterley, Warks, Newport, Shrop, and Penkridge, Staffs.

❑ DBU	Schempp-Hirth Goevier 3	~	BGA.1992, ex D-5233, Wolverhampton. CoA 19-7-87	5-12

Also:

❑ G-ARAS	Champion Tri-Traveler	60	Crashed 4-5-98, CoA 22-6-01. Stored	9-13

ALREWAS on the A513 east of the town, midway between Lichfield and Burton

National Memorial Arboretum: This 150-acre site, containing 160-plus memorials, should long ago have been included as a site readers really should go and see. Planting started in 1997 and the scope of the commemorations and landscaping is breath-taking. Just some of the memorials of an aeronautical nature are: Berlin Airlift, Coastal Command, Operation MARKET-GARDEN, various RAF commemorations , including the RAF Wood; Royal Auxiliary Air Force, Suez, and so on.

◆ **Access:** *Brown-signed from the A513 and the A38.* **Open:** *Daily, other than Xmas - 09:00 to 17:00.* **Contact:** *Croxall Road, Alrewas, DE13 7AR* | **01283 792333** | **info@thenma.org.uk** | **www.thenma.org.uk**

BASSETT'S POLE at the junction of the A38 and A453, north-east of Sutton Coldfield

A paintballing field here has a Whirlwind to shoot at.

❑ XP350	Westland Whirlwind HAR.10	62	ex Bruntingthorpe, Helston, Chivenor, 22, 225. SOC 3-3-82. With boom of XK969	[1]	5-10

BUCKNALL on the A52 east of Stoke-on-Trent

Kingsland Primary School: Eaves Lane | **Access**, *visits possible* **only** *by prior arrangement*

❑ G-SSWE	Short 360-100	86	ex Market Drayton, Coventry, SE-IXE, G-BNBA ntu, G-14-3705. CoA 22-8-05, de-reg 6-6-07. *The King's Wings*	2-11

BURSLEM on the A50 north-west of Stoke-on-Trent

Supermarine Aero Engineering: See also Stoke-on-Trent. *Visits possible* **only** *by prior arrangement* | **www.supermarine.net**

❑ SL611	Supermarine Spitfire XVI	45	ex Scafell, 603, 111 OTU. Crashed 20-11-47	1-05

CANNOCK Harrier GR.1 XV281 moved to Welshpool, Wales, by June 2013.

CHEDDLETON on the A520 south of Leek

❑ G-BFAA	Gardan Horizon 160	65	ex F-BLVY. CoA 18-11-90, de-reg 6-1-12	4-10

HEDNESFORD on the A460 northeast of Cannock

Martyn Jones: *Should* still have his 'JP' cockpit.

❑ XM417	'D'	Hunting Jet Provost T.3	60	ex Fownhope, Halton 8054BM (23-10-69), Shawbury, 6 FTS, 7 FTS, 2 FTS. Cockpit	8-94

HIXON on the A51 east of Stafford

Air & Ground Aviation Ltd: The company has extensive warehousing and storage facilities close to, and on, the former airfield. Airframes brought to the site(s) are normally processed for spares recovery quickly, including a variety of Lynx from Yeovilton, and as such do not merit a 'formal' listing. The company owns Wessex HC.2 XT672 at Stafford, Staffs.

Auctioneers Malcolm Harrison staged a massive sale of stock here on 20th and 21st November 2013. Such was the size of the task that the 20th was devoted to Lot 1 onwards and the following date to Lot 1000 onwards! Included were Hercules C.3s XV221 and XV301 (Lots 1431 and 1430 respectively - high bid £9,500 each, did not reach reserve); Phantom FGR.2 XV499 (Lot 1433 - high bid £17,000, did not reach reserve), several Sea Kings and shedloads of spares-extracted Lynx, plus lots of vehicles, some missiles (!), office equipment, spares and two airworthy helicopters, R22 G-SHRT and Squirrel G-EJOC. The first of upwards of 30 gutted former AAC and FAA Lynxes began to arrive on site in April 2012, but the bulk appeared from the spring of 2013 onwards. As such they were too transitory for *W&R*, although some may make formal appearances in *W&R25*. By the end of November nearly all the Lynx had moved on, along with three Sea Kings. The latter were former Egyptian Mk.47s 774 (Lot 1435) and 775 (Lot 1437) which arrived from Gosport, Hampshire, on 2nd April 2012 and an FAA example - *probably* HC.4 ZD478. This trio had moved to a scrapyard in Rotherham, S Yorks, by January 2014.

◆ **Access: Strictly** *by prior arrangement* **only | www.airandground.com**

❑ XT455*	'U'	Westland Wessex HU.5	65	ex Gosport A2654 [2], Lee-on-Solent A2741 (3-7-86), 845, 707, 845, 846, 845, 707. Arrived 8-13	8-13
❑ XV197		Lockheed Hercules C.3	67	ex Boscombe Down, Lyneham, .LTW, 242 OCU, LTW, 24-36 pool, 36, USAF 66-13542. Dismantled	12-13
❑ XV217		Lockheed Hercules C.3	67	ex Lyneham, LTW, Lyneham Wing, 24-36 pool, 36, USAF 66-8567. Dismantled	12-13
❑ XV220		Lockheed Hercules C.3	67	ex Lyneham, LTW, 242 OCU, Lyneham Wing, 70, Lyneham Wing, 24-36 pool, 36, USAF 66-8570. Dismantled	12-13
❑ XV221*		Lockheed Hercules C.3	67	ex Bruntingthorpe, Lyneham, LTW, C.1, 242 OCU, LTW, 40-47 pool, 47, 66-8571. First noted 4-13, see above	12-13
❑ XV301*		Lockheed Hercules C.3	68	ex Bruntingthorpe, Lyneham, LTW, C.1, 70, Fairford Wing, 30-47 pool, 66-13544. Arrived 18-2-13, see above	12-13
❑ XV305		Lockheed Hercules C.3	68	ex Lyneham, LTW, 70, Fairford Wing, 47, 30, USAF 66-13548. Dismantled	12-13
❑ XV499*	'I'	McD Phantom FGR.2	69	ex Leeming, 74, 19, 228 OCU, 29, 228 OCU, 29, 228 OCU, 23, 19, 92, 41, 228 OCU, 29, 228 OCU, 6, 228 OCU. SOC 5-10-92. Arrived 13-2-13, see above	12-13
❑ XV720		Westland Wessex HC.2	68	ex Gosport A2701 [2], Fleetlands, SARTU, 22, 18	4-13
❑ ZA135	'705'	Westland Sea King HAS.6	81	ex Fleetlands, Gosport, 771, 849, 820, *Gannet* SAR Flt, 819, 820, 819, 810, 706, 820. SOC 7-10-09	11-13

LICHFIELD north-west of Tamworth

Whittington Barracks: The helicopters are displayed within the camp.

❑ XR601		Westland Scout AH.1	64	ex Arborfield, BATUS, 657, 665, 666. Damaged 26-8-79	11-12
❑ XT466	'XV'	Westland Wessex HU.5	65	ex Gosport, A2617 [4], Weeton 8921M (3-2-87), Cosford, Wroughton, 847, 771, 848, 845	11-12
❑ ZE413		Agusta A109A	98	ex 8 Flt	11-12

No.**1206 Squadron Air Cadets**: Last noted in November 2003, Chipmunk T.10 PAX WK576 moved to Wolverhampton, W Mids, by June 2012.

LONGTON on the A50 south of Stoke-on-Trent

Motor Clinic: On the Trentham Road, have a 'JP' on show.

❑ XM425	'88'	Hunting Jet Provost T.3A	60	ex King's Lynn, Bruntingthorpe, Halton 8995M (10-4-89), 7 FTS, 1 FTS, RAFC, 3 FTS, CFS	11-12

PENKRIDGE between the A449 and M6 south of Stafford.

Staffordshire Aircraft Restoration Team: See also Abbots Bromley, Staffs, Baxterley, Warks, and Newport, Shrop.

◆ **Access:** *Visits possible* **only** *by prior arrangement*

❑ G-MJIA*	Flexiform Striker	82	CoA 20-9-96, first noted 6-12		6-12
❑ 'PD685'	Slingsby Cadet TX.1	~	ex Wolverhampton, Stoke-on-Trent, ATC. Fuselage	[1]	3-12

❑ WT877	Slingsby Cadet TX.3	51	ex Wolverhampton, Walsall, Swinderby, St Athan GC, Syerston, 621 GS, 625 GS, 643 GS, 22 GS. SOC 21-8-86	6-12

■ [1] Restored to represent an example that served from Walsall with 43 Gliding School.

RUGELEY on the A51 east of Stafford

❑ WW444 'D'	Percival Provost T.1	54	ex Sibson, Coventry, Bitteswell, Shawbury, CAW, 5 AEF, 6 FTS, 3 FTS, 22 FTS. SOC 4-5-67	6-11

STAFFORD (Beaconside, west of the city)

Royal Air Force Museum Reserve Collection: As well as the airframes and countless smaller artefacts, the following substantial parts deserve a mention, if not a 'formal' listing: Armstrong Whitworth Whitley V N1498; English Electric Ayr flying-boat; Short Stirling III LK488 fuselage and tail sections of an RE.8, Sopwith Snipe and Westland Wallace components.

Spitfire F.22 PK664 moved to North Weald, Essex, during September 2013. Two of the Spitfires held in 'stock' are destined for Australia, in exchange for the A-20G Havoc. For both of these, see under see under Hendon, Gtr Lon.

◆ **Access:** *Viewing is possible* **only** *via prior arrangement*

❑ G-AAMX*	DH.60GM Moth	29	ex Hendon, Cosford, Shoreham, NC926M. Moth Corp-built CoA 7-5-94, de-reg 19-8-96. Arrived 15-5-12	10-13
❑ G-AEKW*	Miles Mohawk	36	ex Hendon, Cosford, Hatch, Cosford, Hatch, Wyton, USA, Tablada, Spain, HM503, MCCS, Turnhouse SF, G-AEKW	10-13
❑ G-AHED	DH Dragon Rapide	46	ex Cosford, Wyton, Cardington, Henlow, Dominie II RL962, Witney. Brush-built. CoA 17-4-68, de-reg 3-3-69	10-13
❑ A301	Morane BB	16	ex Wyton, Cardington, Hendon. Fuselage	10-13
❑ R9371	HP Halifax II	41	ex Innsworth, Glos scrapyard, Lossiemouth, 10. Crashed 9-3-42. Cockpit	8-13
❑ Z7197	Percival Proctor III G-AKZN	40	ex Hendon 8380M, St Athan, Swinderby, Finningley, G-AKZN, AST, 18 EFTS, 1 RS, 2 SS. CoA 29-11-63	10-13
❑ DG590	Miles Hawk Major G-ADMW	35	ex Cosford, Wyton, Cardington, Middle Wallop, Henlow 8379M, Ternhill, G-ADMW, Swanton Morley SF, Wyton SF, G-ADMW. CoA 4-6-83, de-reg 16-9-86	10-13
❑ HS503	Fairey Swordfish IV	43	BAPC.108, ex Cosford, Wyton, Cardington, Cosford, Henlow, Canada, RCAF, 754, 745. SOC RCAF 21-8-46	10-13
❑ LA226	Supermarine Spitfire F.21	45	ex Cosford, Wyton, Cardington, St Athan, Shawbury, Abingdon, Biggin Hill, South Marston, London, South Marston, Little Rissington, 7119M (18-1-54), 3 CAACU, 122	10-13
❑ SL674 'RAS-H'	Supermarine Spitfire XVI	45	ex Cosford, Wyton, Cardington, St Athan, 8392M, Biggin Hill, Little Rissington, 501, 17 OTU. 612 Sqn colours	10-13
❑ 'TB675' '4D-V'	Supermarine Spitfire XVI RW393	45	ex Hendon, Cosford, Stafford, Cosford, St Athan, Turnhouse 7293M (27-3-56), 602, 3, CAACU, 31, FCCS, 203 AFS	10-13
❑ VX275	Slingsby Sedbergh TX.1	48	ex Cosford, Wyton, Cardington, St Athan 8884M, 612 GS, 613 GS, 623 GS, 123 GS, BGA.572	10-13
❑ WP270	EoN Eton TX.1	51	ex Manchester Henlow, Hendon, 8598M, 27 MU, 61 GCF	10-13
❑ WT619	Hawker Hunter F.1	54	ex Manchester, Henlow, St Athan, Weeton 7525M (22-11-57), 233 OCU, 222, 43. Sectioned	10-13
❑ XK781	ML Utility Mk.1	57	ex Cardington, Middle Wallop. Nacelle and other bits	8-13
❑ XL824	Bristol Sycamore HR.14	57	ex Manchester, Henlow, 8021M (2-7-68), Wroughton, CFS, 1564 Flt, 103, 284	10-13
❑ XM555	Saro Skeeter AOP.12	59	ex Hendon, Cosford, Shawbury 8027M, Ternhill, CFS, HQ BAOR, 654. SOC 25-7-68	10-13
❑ XN185	Slingsby Sedbergh TX.1 HNS	56	BGA.4077, ex Syerston 8942M, CGS, 643 VGS, 4 MGSP, 633 VGS, 635 VGS. CoA 12-4-04. Stored	8-13
❑ ZJ493	GAF Jindivik Mk.4A	c79	ex Llanbedr, QinetiQ/DERA, ATA, A92-814. Last flight 26-10-84	10-13
❑ –	Lakes Waterbird	1911	ex Cardington, Henlow, Windermere. Damaged 17-2-12. Avro-built. Centre section, float and other parts. [1]	10-13
❑ –*	Bleriot XI	c10	fuselage frame	10-13
❑ –*	Curtiss JN-4 'Jenny'	c22	fuselage frame	10-13
❑ –	Fairchild Cornell II	c42	ex Cosford, Wyton, Cardington, Henlow, Canada [2]	10-13
❑ –*	Eurofighter Typhoon FSM	03	BAPC.292, ex Hendon, BAE Systems. Dismantled	10-13

❑ J-1172		DH Vampire FB.6	52	ex Cosford, Wyton, Cardington, Manchester, Cosford, 8487M, Colerne, Swiss AF		10-13
❑ '20'		S-D Demoiselle replica	64	BAPC.194, ex Wyton, Cardington, Brooklands, Henlow, Gatow		10-13
❑ –*		Fieseler Fi 103 (V-1)	c44	BAPC.237, ex Soesterberg. Arrived 11-13		11-13

■ **[1]** See under Wickenby, Lincs, for details of a flyable Waterbird project. **[2]** A Fleet-built PT-26A Cornell II with parts coming from at least three identifiable machines. The port wing is from RCAF 15195 - the identity that has been quoted for the *whole* airframe in many previous editions. Starboard wing comes from 14590. Fuselage had a plate stamped 'FAL Ser No FV351, BAC Ser No FV351, Eng No R007174'. The RAF serial FV351 corresponds to RCAF 15252. These three machines all served with 24 EFTS at Abbotsford, British Columbia. These and several other Cornell 'elements' were acquired from/via Canadian Warplane Heritage as part of an exchange.

MoD Stafford: **12 Signal Group, 22nd Signal Regiment**: The Evans VP-2 is with the **Staffordshire Wing, Air Cadets**.

❑ G-BCVE		Evans VP-2	r75	ex Barton. Fuselage, unfinished. De-reg 9-6-93		10-08
❑ XT672	'WE'	Westland Wessex HC.2	66	ex Shawbury, Hixon, Shawbury, 2 FTS, Benson SF, 72. SOC 12-5-99. *Aries*	[1]	4-11
❑ XZ287		HS Nimrod AEW.3	77	ex 9140M(10-6-92), Abingdon, Waddington, JTU, Woodford, MR.2. Fuselage. *Fly Suki Airways*		4-11
❑ XZ987	'C'	HS Harrier GR.3	81	9185M, ex St Athan, 1417 Flt, 3, 4. Gate		4-13

■ **[1]** XT672 is on loan from Air and Ground Aviation.

Also: Vampire T.11 XE993 was reduced to spares on 28th November 2013.

STOKE-ON-TRENT

The Potteries Museum and Art Gallery:

◆ **Open:** *Mon-Sat 10:00 to 17:00, Sun 14:00 to 17:00. Closed Xmas and New Year.* **Contact:** *Bethesda Street, Cultural Quarter, Hanley, Stoke ST1 3DW* | **01782 232323** | **museums@stoke.gov.uk** | **www.stokemuseums.org.uk**

❑ RW388	'U4-U'	Supermarine Spitfire XVI	45	ex Kemble, 'AB917', 71 MU 6946M (30-9-52), 19 MU, 5 MU, Andover, Benson, Colerne, FC&RS, 612, 667. 667 Sqn colours	1-14

STONE on the A34 north of Stafford

Alan Simpson:

❑ XG629	'668'	DH Sea Venom FAW.22	56	ex Long Marston, Fleetlands, Higher Blagdon, Culdrose, ADS, 831, Yeovilton SF, 893, FAW.21, 893. SOC 3-9-70	4-12

TAMWORTH

Martyn Morgan: Martyn also has the envelope of Cameron O-77 G-BPYI. *Visits by prior arrangement* **only**

❑ XE793		Slingsby Cadet TX.3	53	ex Doncaster, Ringmer, St Athan 8666M (5-1-81), 626 GS, 621 GS, 625 GS, 622 GS, 89 GS, 87 GS	3-08

TATENHILL AERODROME south of the B5234, west of Burton-on-Trent EGBM

❑ G-BGAG	Cessna F.172N	78	Reims-built. CoA 25-5-07, stored	12-11
❑ G-BHIR	Piper Cherokee Arrow	69	ex SE-FHP. Crashed 21-8-03, de-reg 30-1-04. Fuselage, dump	4-08
❑ G-BNFS	Cessna 152	79	ex N5545B. CoA 14-7-08, de-reg 11-5-09	12-11
❑ G-BTGH	Cessna 152	78	ex 48919. CoA 25-4-07, de-reg 11-5-09	12-11
❑ G-BXGE	Cessna 152 II	79	ex N89283. Crashed 4-8-97, de-reg 22-3-02. Fuselage	10-06

WOLVERHAMPTON AERODROME or Halfpenny Green, east of Bridgnorth EGBO

The 'JP' has taken on the role of 'guardian' for the Halfpenny Green Flying Centre. The cockpit of Tomahawk G-BYMC, lasted noted in June 2010, had moved on by March 2013. Rallye G-AZMZ was flying again by 2012. Last noted in March 2008, Robinson R22 G-HERA had moved to the paintball site near Cosford, Shropshire, by May 2012.

❑ G-ATFF	'53'	Piper Aztec 250C	65	ex N5769Y. CoA 15-5-05	4-12
❑ G-PLAJ		BAe Jetstream 3102	87	ex N2274C, C-GJPH, N331QB, G-31-738. CoA 30-11-10	4-11
❑ G-SENE		Piper Seneca II 200T	81	ex N797WA, N8314P. CoA 26-11-06	3-12
❑ –		Slingsby Tandem Tutor	~	BGA.1346, ex Bidford, RAFGSA.297. CoA 24-1-79. Air Scouts	6-10
❑ XW434*	'MY'	BAC Jet Provost T.5A	72	ex Selby, Cosford 9091M (1-3-91), Halton, 1 FTS, 7 FTS, 3 FTS, CFS. Arrived 29-5-13. 'Gate guardian'	1-14

SUFFOLK

BECCLES AERODROME south of the A146 west of Lowestoft

EGSM

❑	G-ASMY	Piper Apache 160H	62	ex N4309Y. CoA 25-11-95	5-12
❑	G-ATHZ	Cessna 150F	65	ex EI-AOP ntu, N6286R. CoA 27-3-98	5-12
❑	G-AVPH	Cessna F.150G	67	ex Blackpool, Woodvale. Reims-built. CoA 9-4-86, de-reg 26-3-02. Fuselage	3-12
❑	G-BAOP	Cessna FRA.150L	73	Reims-built. Crashed 22-6-01, CoA 11-4-02. Fuselage	3-12

BECK ROW on the A1101 north of Mildenhall

The Hunter is kept on a *private* farm in the area.

❑	XG210	Hawker Hunter F.6	56	ex DRA Bedford, BAe Hatfield, CFE, 19, 14. SOC 11-9-85. RAE colours	10-13

■ **[1]** XG210 has the starboard wing of XL572 and XL623 to port.

BENTWATERS AIRFIELD south of the A1152, north-east of Woodbridge

Bentwaters Cold War Museum: Run by the **Bentwaters Aviation Society** with support of the landowners, **Bentwaters Parks Ltd**. Centred on the Wing Command Post this incredible museum includes the 'Battle Cabin' and the War Operations rooms. The Phantoms are very welcome, both acquired from Everett Aero (see Ipswich, Suffolk). Restoration of the Jaguar was completed in July 2013; the Meteor will return to F.8 status. Most airframes are in a HAS on the opposite side of the airfield.

◆ **Access:** *Follow signs for Bentwaters Park off the A1152 at Rendlesham*. **Open:** *1st and 3rd Sun of each month, Easter to Oct, 10:00 to 16:00 - check on the website*. **Contact:** *Building 134, Bentwaters Parks, Rendelsham, Woodbridge, IP12 2TW* | **07588 877020** | **info@bcwm.org.uk** | **www.bcwm.org.uk** and **www.bentwaters-as.org.uk**

❑	WH453	'L'	Gloster Meteor D.16		51	ex Llanbedr, 5 CAACU, 72, 222. Arrived 18-1-05	[1]	1-14
❑	XE707	'865'	Hawker Hunter GA.11	N707XE	55	ex Ashbourne, USA, Exeter, G-BVYH, FRADU, 764, 738, RAF F.4, 118, 98, 93. Last flown 21-4-94, arr 1-7-10	[2]	1-14
❑	XN629	'49'	Hunting Jet Provost T.3A	G-KNOT	61	ex North Weald, G-BVEG, XN629, 1 FTS, 7 FTS, 1 FTS, CFS, RAFC, 3 FTS. CoA 10-10-07, de-reg 21-6-07. Arrived 14-2-10. Fuselage	[3]	1-14
❑	XV401*	'I'	McD Phantom FGR.2		68	ex Boscombe Down, BDAC, DERA, Wattisham, 74, 228 OCU, 19, 56, 23, 56, 29, 228 OCU, 56, 111, 41, 228 OCU. Arrived 8-13	[4]	1-14
❑	XV497*	'D'	McD Phantom FGR.2		69	ex Waddington, Coningsby 9295M, 74, 1435 Flt, 23, 228 OCU, 92, 19, 92, 29, 19, 228 OCU, 92, 23, 56, 228 OCU, 17, 228 OCU, 41, 6. Last flown 31-10-92. Arrived 24-11-12	[5]	1-14
❑	XX741	'EJ'	SEPECAT Jaguar GR.1A		74	ex Ipswich, Shawbury. 226 OCU, 6, 54, 226 OCU. Acquired 16-8-09. Repainted in 6 Sqn colours by 6-13	[6]	1-14
❑	ZD667*		HS Harrier GR.3		86	ex Predannack, Culdrose 'DD67', A2684[2], 9201M, 1417 Flt, 233 OCU. 4 Sqn colours. Arrived 2-13	[4]	1-14
❑	ZF581		EE Lightning F.53		67	ex Rochester, Portsmouth, *Wing Commander*, Portsmouth, Warton, R Saudi AF 206, 53-675, G-27-45. Last flown 14-1-86, arrived 22-5-11. 56 Sqn colours		1-14
❑	E18-2	'42-71'	Piper Navajo		~	ex ?, Fownhope, Spanish Air Force, N7314L. Arrived 2004. Fuselage, stored		1-14

■ **[1]** Meteor was donated to BCWM Bentwaters Parks in 2012 and will appear in 72 Sqn colours. **[2]** GA.11 was exported to the USA and flown there in 1995; returning in 2005. **[3]** The 'JP' is on loan from Allan Dewhurst. **[4]** XV401 and ZD667 acquired from Everett Aero using donation from Brian Smee. **[5]** Purchased from Everett Aero by a private collector and placed on loan to BCWM. **[6]** Jaguar factoids: First flown 4-10-74, taken on charge 18-11-74; last flight 31-1-94; total flying time 4,260 hours; disposed of 18-11-05; joined BCWM 16-8-09 thanks to a donation from Brian Smee.

BROME on the A140 south of Diss

A 'JP' is stored in a yard.

❑	XW304	'MD'	BAC Jet Provost T.5	70	ex Colsterworth, Cosford 9172M (17-12-92), 6 FTS, CFS, 1 FTS. Dismantled	6-13

BURY ST EDMUNDS on the A140 south of Diss

Blenheim Camp: At the TA Centre in Newmarket Road is an instructional Lynx.

❑	ZD273*	'E'	Westland Lynx AH.7	83	ex Middle Wallop, 2 Rgt. Cabin. Arrived by 2-13		6-13

DEBACH south of the B1078, west of Wickham Market

493rd Bomb Group 'Helton's Hellcats' Museum: Centred on USAAF Station 152's former control tower, the museum has been painstakingly put together. As has the website, which includes a vast amount of material: for example, the locals pronounce it 'Deb-idge', while Americans call it 'Dee-bark'.

◆ **Open:** *Last Sun of Apr, May, Jun, Jul, Aug and Sep, 11:00 to 16:00pm - see the website for other times. Groups welcome by prior appointment.* **Contact:** *Richard Taylor, Grove Farm, Clopton, Woodbridge, IP13 6QS* | **01473 737236** | **richardfgt@btconnect.com** | **www.493bgdebach.co.uk**

FELIXSTOWE at the end of the A14, south-east of Ipswich

Glenn Cattermole: Restoration of the Buccaneer is well in hand; Glenn is keen to hear of facts and photos of XT284.

◆ **Access:** *Private location, visits possible* **only** *by prior arrangement*

❑	XT284	'H'	HS Buccaneer S.2A	65	ex Stock, St Athan, Abingdon 8855M (21-5-85), St Athan, 237 OCU, 15, 208, 809, 803, 736. Cockpit		6-13

Steve Williams: Has a Motor Cadet and Grasshopper in the *general* area.

❑	G-BVFS	Slingsby Motor Cadet III	93	ex Southend. Unflown. Stored, dismantled		2-10
❑	'WZ784'	Slingsby Grasshopper TX.1	c52	ex Southend, Thurrock	[1]	2-10

■ **[1]** The Grasshopper is a composite (aren't they all!); see also under Carlisle, Cumbria, and Dirleton, Scotland, for more.

FLIXTON on the B1062 west of Bungay

Norfolk and Suffolk Aviation Museum (N&SAM): Museum president since 1976, **Wg Cdr Ken Wallis** died on 1st September 2013, aged 97 - more details under Reymerston, Norfolk. 'Stearman' N62842 is the first of its type in 'captivity' outside of the IWM at Duxford (and that machine is 'under review') and is a major coup; thanks to the support of Black Barn Aviation. Two airframes previously on loan from the IWM have been signed over to N&SAM: the Colditz Cock and the MiG-15. N&SAM has no less than *four* Link Trainers, all of which are in use. Two work; the other two are statics with computer screens and interactive software. A Redifon simulator is also being restored.

◆ **Open:** *Apr to Oct, Sun to Thu 10:00 to 17:00; Nov to Mar, Tue, Wed and Sun 10:00 to 16:00. (Last admission 15:00) Closed Dec to Feb. Groups at other times by prior appointment.* **Contact:** *The Street, Flixton, near Bungay, NR35 1NZ* | **01986 896644** | **nsam.flixton@tesco.net** | **www.aviationmuseum.net**

Thinx: *The former airfield, home of the Liberator-equipped 446th BG lies just to the east, though there is little to see these days. The oak gates to St Mary's Church were installed in 1986 by 446th veterans, replacing an original set given in 1945. Close by is the 'Flixton Buck' public house, dating from the 16th century* | **01986 892382**

❑	G-ANLW	Westland Widgeon 2		54	ex Northampton, Blackpool, 'MD497', Wellingborough, Little Staughton, Tattershall Thorpe, *When Eight Bells Toll*, *Eye of the Needle*, Southend. CoA 27-5-81, de-reg 15-11-02. Arrived 1-5-02	[1]	1-14
❑	G-APUG	Luton Major		64	ex Wattisham. De-reg 5-8-87. Arrived 17-10-06		1-14
❑	'G-ARZB'	Wallis WA-116	G-AVDH	67	ex Reymerston, London, Reymerston. *Little Nellie II*. De-reg 19-2-69. Arrived 15-5-11	[2]	1-14
❑	G-ASRF	Gowland Jenny Wren		66	ex Brookmans Park, Panshanger, Brookmans Park. CoA 4-6-71, de-reg 11-12-96. Arrived 11-9-04	[3]	1-14
❑	G-BABY	Taylor Titch		75	CoA 10-10-91, de-reg 4-12-96. Arrived 28-7-03		1-14
❑	G-BDVS	Fokker Friendship 200		63	ex Norwich, Air UK, S2-ABK, PH-FEX, PH-EXC, 9M-AMM, PH-EXC, PH-FEX. *Eric Gander Dower*. CoA 5-6-00, de-reg 19-12-96. Arrived 17-12-96. Cockpit		1-14
❑	G-BFIP	Wallbro Mono replica		78	ex Shipdham, Swanton Morley. CoA 22-4-82, de-reg 28-3-01. Arrived 28-7-98	[4]	1-14
❑	G-BJZC	Thunder Ax7-65Z balloon		82	ex Lancing. CoA 17-6-94, de-reg 8-7-98. *Greenpeace*	[1]	1-14
❑	G-CDFW	Lovegrove Sheffy gyro		04	ex Didcot. De-reg 17-5-10. Arrived 3-4-10. *The Sheffy*		1-14
❑	G-MBUD	Skycraft Scout 2		r82	de-reg 6-9-94. Arrived 11-11-07		1-14
❑	G-MJSU	MBA Tiger Cub		r83	ex Swanton Morley. CoA 31-1-86, de-reg 23-6-93. Arr 8-8-02		1-14
❑	G-MJVI	Lightwing Rooster 1		r83	ex Littlehampton. De-reg 13-6-90. Arrived 24-2-04	[5]	1-14

❑ G-MMWL		Eurowing Goldwing	83	CoA 20-11-06, de-reg 19-4-10. Arrived 15-7-07		1-14
❑ G-MTFK		Flexiform Striker	r87	de-reg 13-6-90. Arrived 6-94	[1] [6]	1-14
❑ CDN		EoN Primary	r68	BGA.1461, ex Tibenham area. CoA 29-5-69. Arr 27-4-97		1-14
❑ -*		EoN Primary	48	ex Shipdham, Air Scouts. Arrived 29-10-13	[7]	1-14
❑ DUD		Grunau Baby III	54	BGA.2384, ex Bristol, BGA.2074, RAFGSA.374, D-9142. CoA 29-3-92. Arrived 2002		1-14
❑ HCG		Maupin Woodstock	r92	BGA.3833, ex Happisburgh. CoA 23-3-11. Arrived 25-9-10		1-14
❑ HKJ		Penrose Pegasus 2 replica	r93	BGA.4002, ex Littlehampton. CoA 15-9-98. Arr 24-2-02	[5] [8]	1-14
❑ JTA		Colditz Cock replica	00	BGA.4757, ex Duxford. *Spirit of Colditz*. CoA 20-2-00		1-14
❑ –	'LHS-1'	Bensen B.7	66	BAPC.147, ex Loddon, Marham, Coltishall. Arrived 1978		1-14
❑ –		Mignet HM.14 'Flea'	c70	BAPC.115, ex Earls Colne, Andrewsfield, Balham, S Wales	[9]	1-14
❑ –		Goldfinch Amphibian 161	c80	BAPC.303, ex Old Sarum. Arrived 23-9-08	[10]	1-14
❑ –		Wasp Falcon 4 hang-glider	c76	-		1-14
❑ –		Antonov C.14 hang-glider	92	-		1-14
❑ –		UFM Icarus II	74	arrived 6-11-05. Biplane, tail-less, hang-glider		1-14
❑ –		Lovegrove Discord gyro	~	BAPC.306, ex Didcot. Arrived 4-10. *The Discord*		1-14
❑ N16676		Fairchild 24C8F	c36	ex Tibenham, USA, CAP, NC16676. Arrived 18-3-03. Civil Air Patrol colours	[11]	1-14
❑ N62842*		Boeing PT-27 Kaydet	42	ex Tibenham, USA, FJ801, USAAF 42-15662. Arr 26-6-12	[12]	1-14
❑ –		Felixstowe F.5	18	ex Felixstowe. Nose section	[13]	1-14
❑ 'P3708'		Hawker Hurricane I	09	fuselage, under completion. Arrived 23-5-10	[14]	1-14
❑ 'P8140'	'ZP-K'	Supermarine Spitfire FSM	68	BAPC.71, ex Chilham Castle, 'P9390' and 'N3317', *Battle of Britain*. *Nuflier*. 74 Sqn colours		1-14
❑ 'TD248'	'8Q-T'	Supermarine Spitfire XVI	45	fuselage recreation. 695 Sqn colours	[9] [15]	1-14
❑ VL349	'V7-Q'	Avro Anson C.19 G-AWSA	47	ex Norwich, N5054, G-AWSA, SCS, NCS, North Coates SF, WSF, FCCS, HCCS, HCEU, 116, CSE, 1 FU. SOC 5-3-68. Arrived 1-74		1-14
❑ VX580		Vickers Valetta C.2	50	ex Norwich, MCS, MEAFCS, 114, HS. SOC 12-12-68. Arrived 27-5-83		1-14
❑ 'WE168'		EE Canberra PR.3	~	cockpit recreation. Arrived 2002	[16]	1-14
❑ WF128	'676'	Percival Sea Prince T.1	52	ex Honington 8611M (5-2-79), Kemble, Sydenham SF, A&AEE, 750. Arrived 25-9-81		1-14
❑ WF643	'F'	Gloster Meteor F(TT).8	51	ex Coltishall, Kemble, 29, Nicosia SF, 611, 1, 56. AWA-built. SOC 29-11-71. Arrived 10-5-75. 611 Sqn colours		1-14
❑ WG789		EE Canberra B.2/6	52	ex Mendlesham, Wycombe, Kew, Burgess Hill, RAE Bedford, RRE, 231 OCU. SOC 23-2-82. Arrived 6-3-02. Cockpit	[1]	1-14
❑ WH840		EE Canberra T.4	54	ex Seighford, Locking 8350M, St Athan, Geilenkirchen SF, A&AEE, 97, 151, 245, 88, 231 OCU, CFS. SOC 3-4-74. Arrived 3-94	[9]	1-14
❑ WV605	'T-B'	Percival Provost T.1	54	ex Henlow, Higher Blagdon, Macclesfield, 6 FTS, 3 FTS, 22 FTS. SOC 31-10-66		1-14
❑ WV838	'182'	Hawker Sea Hawk FGA.6	54	ex Warrington, Liverpool, Bruntingthorpe, Chippenham, Fleetlands, 736, 738, 806, 802. Crashed 9-2-59. Arrived 23-8-11. 806 Sqn colours. Cockpit	[1]	1-14
❑ XA226		Slingsby Grasshopper TX.1	53	ex Milton Keynes, Turweston, Ipswich, Halton, Sutton. Arrived 21-4-04		1-14
❑ XD857		Vickers Valiant BK.1	57	ex Manston, Rayleigh, Foulness, 49. SOC 6-3-65. Arrived 18-10-05. Flightdeck	[1]	1-14
❑ XG254	'A'	Hawker Hunter FGA.9	56	ex Clacton, Coltishall, Weybourne, Coltishall 8881M (9-12-85), St Athan, 1 TWU, 2 TWU, TWU, 229 OCU, 54, HS, 54. Arrived 19-2-02. 54 Sqn colours	[9]	1-14
❑ XG329		EE Lightning F.1	59	ex Swinderby, Cranwell 8050M (8-7-69), A&AEE, Warton. Arrived 1993	[9]	1-14
❑ XG518		Bristol Sycamore HR.14	55	ex Sunderland, Balloch, Halton 8009M (7-5-68), Wroughton, Khormaksar SF, El Adem SF, Habbiniya SF, CFS, Amman SF. Arrived 24-2-97	[9]	1-14
❑ XG523	'V'	Bristol Sycamore HR.14	55	ex Sunderland, Hayes, Middle Wallop, Ternhill 7793M, CFS, JEHU. Crashed 25-9-62. Arrived 25-1-97. Cockpit	[9]	1-14
❑ XH892	'J'	Gloster Javelin FAW.9R	57	ex Duxford, Colerne 7982M, Shawbury, 29, 64, 23. AWA-built		1-14

❑	XJ482	'713'	DH Sea Vixen FAW.1	58	ex Wimborne Minster, A2598 (3-8-69), 766, 700Y. Arrived 27-11-79		1-14
❑	XK624	'32'	DH Vampire T.11	56	ex Lytham St Annes, Blackpool, CFS, 3 FTS, 7 FTS, 1 FTS, 23 GCF, CFS, 7 FTS. SOC 14-12-71. Arrived 11-4-80		1-14
❑	XL160		HP Victor K.2	61	ex Walpole, Marham 8910M (2-7-86), 57, 55, 57, 55, Witt Wing, 100, MoA. Arrived 29-7-05. Cockpit	[1]	1-14
❑	XL445		Avro Vulcan K.2	62	ex Walpole, Lyneham 8811M (5-4-84), 50, 44, 35, 230 OCU, Wadd Wing, Akrotiri Wing, Wadd Wing, 27. Arrived 29-7-05. Cockpit	[1]	1-14
❑	XM279		EE Canberra B(I).8	59	ex Firbeck, Nostell Priory, Cambridge, 16, 3. SOC 19-3-74. Arrived 3-94. Cockpit	[9]	1-14
❑	XN304	'W'	Westland Whirlwind HAS.7	59	ex Bedford, Henlow, Wroughton, Shrivenham, Wroughton, 705, JHDU, 848. SOC 7-1-76. Arrived 19-7-82. 848 Sqn c/s		1-14
❑	XN500		Hunting Jet Provost T.3A	60	ex Southampton, Farnborough, East Midlands, Ipswich, Oxford, 7 FTS, RAFC, 3 FTS, RAFC, 3 FTS, RAFC. SOC 26-1-93. Arrived 7-10-07	[9]	1-14
❑	XR485	'Q'	W'land Whirlwind HAR.10	63	ex Wroughton, 2 FTS, CFS. SOC 29-1-81. Arrived 19-2-81		1-14
❑	ZA175		HS Sea Harrier FA.2	81	ex Yeovilton, 899, 800, 899, 800, 899, 801, 800, 899, 800, 801, 899. Arrived 27-7-04	[1]	1-14
❑	A-528		FMA Pucará	c80	ex Sunderland, Middle Wallop, Cosford, Abingdon 8769M, Stanley, Argentine AF, 9th AB, 3rd AB. Arrived 24-7-94. *Toto Juan*	[9]	1-14
❑	79	'2-EG'	Dassault Mystère IVA	c59	ex Sculthorpe, FAF, ET.2/8, 314 GE, EC.1/5. Last flown 3-5-78, arrived 18-11-78. Suez stripes	[17]	1-14
❑	'694'		Fokker D.VIII	c84	BAPC.239, ex Lowestoft. Arrived 1991. 5-eighths scale rep		1-14
❑	3794		MiG-15*bis* (S-103)	56	ex Duxford, Czech AF. Letov-built S-103. Arr 14-8-07		1-14
❑	42196		NAA F-100D-11-NA Super Sabre	54	ex Sculthorpe, French AF. EC.4/11, EC.2/11, USAF 48th FBW, 45th FS, USAF 54-2196. Last flown 22-2-77, arrived 18-3-78. 'Skyblazers' colours	[17]	1-14
❑	55-4433	'TR-433'	Lockheed T-33A-5-LO	55	ex Sculthorpe, French AF, 328 CIFAS, 338 CEVSV, USAF 803rd ABG. Last flown 25-1-78, arrived 21-7-78. 20th FBG colours	[17]	1-14
❑	146289		NAA T-28C Trojan	c54	ex East Ham, France, N99153, Zaire AF FG-289, Congolese AF FA-289, USN VT-3, VT-5, NABTC 146289. Crashed 14-12-77. Arrived 28-5-81. Fuselage		1-14

■ **[1]** Airframes on loan: Widgeon G-ANLW (from Sloane Helicopters); Friendship G-BDVS; Thunder balloon G-BJZC; Striker G-MTFK; EoN Primary (Norfolk Gliding Club); Canberra WG789 (Steve Pickup); Sea Hawk WV838, Valiant XD857 and Vulcan XL445 cockpits all from same individual; Victor XL160 (Victor Association); Sea Harrier ZA175 (IWM, Duxford). **[2]** WA-116 G-AVDH on loan from the estate of Wg Cdr Ken Wallis. It was turned into a clone of G-ARZB for the 1967 Bond movie *You Only Live Twice* and unofficially called *Little Nellie II*. Used for studio shots, it was later a source of spares for G-AXAS. (See notes under Reymerston, Norfolk.) **[3]** Jenny Wren built using the wings of Luton Minor G-AGEP. **[4]** Replica of the original built by brothers H S Wallis and G Wallis (hence Wallbro), respectively the father and uncle of the late Wg Cdr Ken Wallis, and flown at Reymerston, Norfolk, in 1910 powered by a 25hp JAP. *India-Papa* first flew 10-8-78 at Swanton Morley. **[5]** Rooster and Pegasus donated by the widow of the late John M Lee, who built the wings of the museum's Colditz Cock. **[6]** Striker was the last aircraft to fly from Flixton before the runways were broken up. **[7]** See under Shipdham, Norfolk, for more; being the museum's second Eon Primary, it *may* be used for onward exchange. **[8]** Penrose Pegasus 2 is a reproduction of the original Harald Penrose example. **[9]** Airframes on loan from Ian Hancock. **[10]** Goldfinch Amphibian 161 was built by the late Flt Lt Leslie 'Bill' Goldfinch at his home in Wiltshire. His illustrious career included the designing of the Colditz Cock glider during his time 'banged up' - the museum has a replica on show. Unfinished, the Goldfinch was intended as a scale taxiable aircraft, inspired by the Loening OA-1 Air Yacht, using Jodel D.11 wings and other components. The '161' bit comes from the plans number for the D.11 that 'donated' its wings. **[11]** Fairchild 24 (pre-Argus) was the second C8F built and served with the Civil Air Patrol, fitted with bomb racks and flare chutes as a sub 'scarer'. **[12]** PT-27 is a composite largely based on 42-15662 and was donated by Tibenham-based Black Barn Aviation. **[13]** The extreme nose section (10ft long) of a Felixstowe flying-boat, once a potting shed, while not fitting our criteria totally, represents a singular survivor. Another section of Felixstowe, about 8ft long, is on hand from the RAF Museum. **[14]** On 18-8-40, Sgt A G Girdwood flying 257 Sqn Hurricane I P3708 got the worst end of a combat with a Bf 110. Wounded, he took to his parachute and eventually went back into the fray, but was killed in a dogfight 29-10-40. Geoff Rayner is busy completing a fuselage based upon the salvaged remains of P3708 and reckons some 50% will come from this Battle of Britain veteran. **[15]** Spitfire XVI fuselage is centred on the original skin of TD248 acquired from Historic Flying. The skin, coupled with an original frame No.19, and a fibreglass tail section has created a fuselage that will, ultimately, contain as many original fittings as possible. (See under Humberside, Lincs, for the airworthy TD248.) After much thought, this is best termed a 'recreation'. **[16]** Canberra PR.3 WE168 was vandalised during its time with its previous owner. Exceptionally well equipped inside, it was emptied and the battered 'outer' airframe disposed of. N&SAM purchased all of the 'innards' and a completely new cockpit, including outer skin, was created in wood and metal. Like TD248, this is best termed a 'recreation'. **[17]** Airframes from the National Museum of the USAF's Loan Program.

FOXHALL west of the A12, south of Kesgrave

Suffolk Aviation Heritage Centre: Previously listed under 'Ipswich'. On the southern edge of the former Martlesham Heath airfield, indeed, a section of the threshold of the SW-NE runway is to be found a short distance to the east. Run by the Suffolk Aviation Heritage Group the cavernous building has great potential. Known to the USAF as 'The Roc', the building was last used by the 2164th Communications Squadron USAFE in the early 1990s.

◆ **Access:** *In Foxhall Road, east of Ipswich and west of the A12 at Brightwell. Follow the signs on the A12 for the waste management site, go past this and the massive aerial array of 'The Roc' will be seen on the right hand side.* **Open:** *Sun and Bank Hols 11:00 to 16:00.* **Contact:** *Old Communications Station, Foxhall Road, Ipswich, IP10 0AH* | **01473 711275** | **chairman@suffolkaviationheritage.org.uk** | **www.suffolkaviationheritage.org.uk**

❑ WH798		EE Canberra PR.7	54	ex Canterbury, Cardiff-Wales, WAM, CTTS St Athan 8130M, 31, 17, 13, 80, 17, 100, 542. SOC 30-11-81. Cockpit	1-14

FRAMLINGHAM AERODROME or Parham, on the B1116 north of Woodbridge

Parham Airfield Museum: incorporating the **390th Bomb Group Memorial Air Museum** and the **Museum of British Resistance**. The tower here houses a superb museum dedicated to the 390th and USAAF Station No.153. Within can be found a wide array of engines and many other artefacts. The Resistance Museum is dedicated to the work of the Auxiliary Units - the so-called 'Stay Behind' cells in the event of an invasion.

◆ **Access:** *'Brown signed' from the A12.* **Open:** *Sun and Bank Hols Apr to Oct 11:00 to 17:00. Also Wed 11:00 to 16:00 in Jun to Aug. Other times by arrangement.* **Contact:** *Parham, Framlingham, IP13 9AF* | **01728 621373** | **parhamairfield@yahoo.co.uk** | **www.parhamairfieldmuseum.co.uk**

Aerodrome: Baby Great Lakes G-BGLS had moved on by June 2010, probably staying in the county.

HADLEIGH on the A1071 west of Ipswich

Gunsmoke Paintball: Access: *By prior arrangement* **only** | **www.gunsmoke.co.uk**

❑ XN554		Hunting Jet Provost T.3	61	ex Ipswich, North Luffenham, Halton 8436M (16-1-75), St Athan, Shawbury, CFS	8-12
❑ XN579		Hunting Jet Provost T.3A	61	ex Ipswich, North Luffenham 9137M (5-3-92), Shawbury, 1 FTS, 7 FTS, 1 FTS, RAFC,TWU, RAFC	8-12
❑ XP629		Hunting Jet Provost T.4	62	ex Ipswich, North Luffenham, Halton 9026M (15-2-90), Shawbury, CATCS, SoRF, CAW, 2 FTS	8-12
❑ XP686		Hunting Jet Provost T.4	62	ex Ipswich, North Luffenham, Halton 8502M (31-8-76), 8401M, CATCS, 6 FTS, CAW, CATCS, CAW, 3 FTS	8-12
❑ XT467	'BF'	Westland Wessex HU.5	65	ex Ipswich, Bramley, Odiham, Laarbruch, Brüggen, Gütersloh, 'XR504' 8922M (8-1-87), Wroughton, 848, 771, Wroughton, 707, 781, 845	8-12
❑ XW796	'X'	Westland Scout AH.1	65	ex Ipswich, Wattisham, M' Wallop, Wroughton, 660, 659	8-12

HALESWORTH on the A144 south of Bungay

Halesworth Airfield Memorial Museum and the **56th Fighter Group Museum**: Established on the former 8th Air Force airfield (also known as Holton); this museum includes a wide range of exhibits.

Open: *Apr to Oct, Sun and Bank Hols 14:00 to 17:00.* **Contact:** *Sparrowhawk Way, Upper Holton, Halesworth, IP19 8NH* | **01986 875084** | **mail@halesworthairfieldmuseum.org.uk** | **www.halesworthairfieldmuseum.org.uk**

John Flanagan: Keeps his Carvair cockpit section nearby.

❑ CF-EPV		ATEL Carvair	43	ex Beccles, Thorpe Abbotts, Fritton Lake, Woodbridge, Southend, EI-AMR, N88819, C-54D 42-72343. *Larfhlaith*. Broken up 9-78. Cockpit [1]	1-14

■ **[1]** The name carried on the Carvair cockpit comes from its time with Aer Lingus (*St Jarlaith* in English) 1963-1968. C-54 N88819 re-flew as an ATL.98 Carvair on 19-4-63.

HONINGTON AIRFIELD on the A1088 south-east of Thetford EGXH

RAF Regiment: The Buccaneer was dedicated as a memorial in 1994 on hand-over of the base to the Regiment.

❑ XK526		HS Buccaneer S.2	60	8648M (10-3-80), ex RAE Bedford, RRE, A&AEE, RAE, A&AEE, RAE, A&AEE	9-13

HORHAM on the B1117 east of Eye

The Red Feather Club: The official museum of 95th Bomb Group, is operated and managed by the **95th Bomb Group Heritage Association.** It has brought back to life the former NCOs' club at USAAF Station 119, once home to the B-17s of the 95th. Included in the exhibits are the famous murals painted by S/Sgt Nathan Bindler.

◆ **Access:** *Located near Denham Corner and Whitehouse Farm on the former airfield site, access off the B1117.* **Open:** *Last Sun of each month, May to Oct, 10:00 to 16:00. Also often on Sat - usually when the flag is flying. Or by prior application.* **Contact: 01728 860930 | jamesmutton@suffolkonline.net| www.95thbg-horham.com**
Thinx: *At Horham Church and in nearby Redlingfield there are striking memorials to the 95th*

IPSWICH

Suffolk Aviation Heritage Centre: Is more precisely listed under Foxhall - which see.

Everett Aero: There are several storage sites and the location 'Ipswich' is generic - ***none*** are available for public inspection. *W&R23* (p207) noted Jaguar GR.3 XZ361 as departing for Greece, this was not the case, it remains in store.

Departures: **Harrier** GR.3 XV783 arrived 10-12 from Predannack, Cornwall, moving to Corley Moor, Warks, by 10-13; ZD667 from Predannack, Cornwall 8-12-12, moved on to Bentwaters, Suffolk, 2-13; GR.7 ZD462 to Malmesbury, Wilts, by 4-12; T.8 ZD992 to Knutsford, Cheshire, 11-12; **Sea Harrier** FA.2 ZD614 to Bournemouth, Dorset, 23-4-13 before settling upon Lymington, Hants, 24-11-13; FA.2 ZE693 to Greece, by 11-11; **Jaguar** T.2A XX832 departed 24-7-13 bound for the USA; **Jet Provost** T.3A XM473 moved to Wethersfield, Essex, by 11-12; **Jetstream** T.2 ZA110 to Aberdeen, Scotland, 14-9-12. **Also**: *W&R23* (p207) noted Scout AH.1 XV124 as 'exported to Greece by 11-10', this did not transpire, it moved briefly to Tattershall, Lincs, then to Godstone, Surrey. The wreck of Harrier T.12 ZH656 was listed in *W&R23*, this is a badly damaged fuselage, *less* cockpit and accordingly has been deleted. Phantom FGR.2s XV401 arrived in 8-13 from Boscombe Down and XV497 on 24-11-12 from Waddington; both were snapped up by BCWM and can be found under Bentwaters, Suffolk.

◆ **Access: Strictly** *private locations - by prior arrangement* **only | www.everettaero.com**

❑ 5X-UUX		Westland Scout Srs 1	~ G-BKLJ	ex East Dereham, Tattershall Thorpe, Heysham, Panshanger, G-BKLJ de-reg 7-2-91), Uganda Police Air Wing	7-13
❑ XP888		Westland Scout AH.1	63	ex Arborfield, Middle Wallop, Wroughton, 651, 652, 14 Flt. Cabin	7-13
❑ XP905		Westland Scout AH.1	63	ex Arborfield, Middle Wallop, Wroughton, 656, 655, 652, 654, 652	7-13
❑ XS726	'T'	HS Dominie T.1	65	ex Cosford 9273M (24-6-97), Cranwell, 3 FTS, 6 FTS, CAW	7-13
❑ XS733	'Q'	HS Dominie T.1	66	ex Cosford 9276M (20-6-97), Cranwell, 3 FTS, 6 FTS, RAFC, CAW	7-13
❑ XS734	'N'	HS Dominie T.1	66	ex Cosford 9260M (7-10-96), Cranwell, 3 FTS, 6 FTS	7-13
❑ XT597*		McD Phantom FG.1	66	ex Boscombe Down, BDAC, DERA, A&AEE, Bedford, NATC Patuxent River, USN. Arrived 17-9-13	11-13
❑ XT631	'D'	Westland Scout AH.1	64	ex Bolenda Eng, Boscombe Down.	2-04
❑ XT640		Westland Scout AH.1	64	ex Arborfield, Lee-on-Solent, Middle Wallop, 654, 666, 663	7-13
❑ XT905*	'P'	McD Phantom FGR.2	68	ex North Luffenham, Coningsby 9286M (7-5-00), 74, 228 OCU, 31, 17, 31, 14, 17, 228 OCU. Arrived 16-5-13	11-13
❑ XV460*	'R'	McD Phantom FGR.2	69	ex Sunderland, Coningsby, Wattisham, 74, 56, 19, 92, 29, 228 OCU, 92, 228 OCU, 19, 56, 228 OCU, 31. Cockpit. Arr 3-13	11-13
❑ XV497*	'D'	Phantom FGR.2		ex Waddington, Coningsby 9295M, 56, 92, 19, 92, 23, 56, 228 OCU, 17. Arrived 24-11-12	11-13
❑ XV804*	'O'	HS Harrier GR.3	70	ex North Luffenham 9280M (17-12-97), Winterbourne Gunner, 4, 3, 1, 3, 4, 233 OCU, 1417 Flt, 233 OCU. Arr 6-3-13	7-13
❑ XW267*	'SA'	HS Harrier T.4	70	ex Toton 9263M (23-10-96), Boscombe Down, SAOEU, RAE, A&AEE, RAE, 233 OCU, 1, 233 OCU, T.2, 233 OCU. Arr 1-14	1-14
❑ XW271*		HS Harrier T.4	71	ex Predannack, Culdrose A2692[2] (3-11-94), Cosford, 4, 1, 233 OCU. Arrived 28-9-12	7-13
❑ XW321*	'MH'	BAC Jet Provost T.5A	70	ex Cosford, 9154M (8-7-92), Shawbury, 1 FTS, 7 FTS, RAFC, 3 FTS. Arrived 16-10-13	10-13
❑ XW328*	'MI'	BAC Jet Provost T.5A	70	ex Cosford 9177M (20-1-93), 1 FTS, RAFC, CFS, RAFC. Arrived 16-10-13	10-13
❑ XW330*	'MJ'	BAC Jet Provost T.5A	70	ex Cosford, 9195M (7-6-93), 1 FTS, 7 FTS, 3 FTS, Leeming SF, CFS, RAFC, 3 FTS. Arrived 16-10-13	10-13
❑ XW367*	'MO'	BAC Jet Provost T.5A	71	ex Cosford 9193M (7-6-93), 1 FTS, RAFC. Arrived 9-10-13	10-13
❑ XW370*	'MP'	BAC Jet Provost T.5A	71	ex Cosford, 9196M (7-6-93), 1 FTS, 3 FTS. Arrived 9-10-13	10-13

	Serial	Code	Type	Year	History	Date
❑	XW416*	'MS'	BAC Jet Provost T.5A	71	ex Cosford 9191M (7-6-93), 1 FTS, RAFC. Arrived 9-10-13	10-13
❑	XW432*	'MX'	BAC Jet Provost T.5A	72	ex Cosford 9127M (14-10-91), Halton, 1 FTS, Leeming SF, 3 FTS. Arrived 9-10-13	10-13
❑	XX139	'PT'	SEPECAT Jaguar T.4	73	ex St Athan, 16, T.2, 226 OCU, 6, 226 OCU, JOCU. Last flown 12-4-05	7-13
❑	XX144	'U'	SEPECAT Jaguar T.2A	74	ex Shawbury, 16, 226 OCU, 6, 54, 226 OCU, JOCU	7-13
❑	XX146	'GT'	SEPECAT Jaguar T.2	74	ex St Athan, 54, T.2, SAOEU, 54, 16, 41, Shawbury, 54, 41, 6, Coltishall SF, 6, 226 OCU, JOCU. Last flown 7-3-05	7-13
❑	XX150	'FY'	SEPECAT Jaguar T.4	74	ex St Athan, 41, DERA, T.2, 16, 226 OCU, Shawbury, 14, 31, 14, 31, 20, 6	7-13
❑	XX478	'564'	HP Jetstream T.2 G-AXXT	73	ex Culdrose, 750, RAF T.1 CFS, G-AXXT, de-reg 5-12-83. Last flown 31-3-11	7-13
❑	XX481	'560'	HP Jetstream T.2 G-AXUP	76	ex Culdrose, 750, RAF T.1 5 FTS, G-AXUP, de-reg 7-1-74. Last flown 14-3-11	7-13
❑	XX486	'567'	HP Jetstream T.2	74	ex Culdrose, 750, RAF T.1 CFS, 5 FTS	12-13
❑	XX720	'FL'	SEPECAT Jaguar GR.3A	74	ex Shawbury, 41, 54, GR.1, 54, 6, A&AEE, 54, Indian AF JI003, G-27-319, Abingdon, A&AEE	7-13
❑	XX836	'ER'	SEPECAT Jaguar T.2A	75	ex Shawbury, 6, 17, 14, 54	11-13
❑	XX838	'FZ'	SEPECAT Jaguar T.4	75	ex St Athan, 41, 16, T.2, Shawbury, 226 OCU, 17, 226 OCU	7-13
❑	XX842	'FX'	SEPECAT Jaguar T.2A	75	ex St Athan, 41, 16, Warton, T.2, 16, 41, Shawbury, ETPS/RAE, 6, 2, 41, 54, 226 OCU	7-13
❑	XZ107	'FH'	SEPECAT Jaguar GR.3A	76	ex St Athan, 41, GR.1, 41, 6, 2	11-13
❑	XZ113	'FD'	SEPECAT Jaguar GR.3A	76	ex St Athan, 41, SAOEU, GR.1, Granby Det, 41, 54, 2, 41	11-13
❑	XZ360	'FN'	SEPECAT Jaguar GR.3	76	ex St Athan, 41, GR.1, 41	11-13
❑	XZ361	'FT'	SEPECAT Jaguar GR.3	76	ex Shawbury, St Athan, GR.1A, 41, 2, GR.1, 2. SOC 26-5-05 See notes above	11-13
❑	XZ366	'FC'	SEPECAT Jaguar GR.3A	76	ex St Athan, 41, GR.1, 41, Shawbury, 2	11-13
❑	XZ369	'EU'	SEPECAT Jaguar GR.3A	76	ex St Athan, 6, GR.1, 6, Shawbury, 17, 14	11-13
❑	XZ385		SEPECAT Jaguar GR.3A	77	ex St Athan, 41, 16, GR.1, 16, 6, 16, 54, 6, Gib Det, 41, 17, 14	11-13
❑	XZ394	'FG'	SEPECAT Jaguar GR.3	77	ex St Athan, 41, GR.1, 54, 6, Shawbury, 17, 20	11-13
❑	XZ396	'EQ'	SEPECAT Jaguar GR.3A	77	ex St Athan, 6, GR.1, 6, 226 OCU, 6, Warton	11-13
❑	XZ400	'FQ'	SEPECAT Jaguar GR.3A	78	ex St Athan, 41, GR.1, 54, Shawbury, 6, 54, Warton. Last flown 6-7-05	11-13
❑	XZ996*	'DD96'	HS Harrier GR.3	82	ex Predannack, Culdrose, A2685[2] (19-7-93), 1417 Flt, 4, 1417 Flt, 233 OCU, 1417 Flt, 233 OCU. Arrived 12-12	11-13
❑	ZD353*	'H'	BAe Harrier GR.5	88	ex Warton, Brough, Dunsfold, Brough, Wittering, 233 OCU, 1. Damaged 29-7-91. First noted 5-12	7-13
❑	ZD408	'37A'	BAe Harrier GR.7A	89	ex Cottesmore, crashed 16-6-08, wreckage	12-12
❑	'ZD993'*		HS Harrier T.4 XZ145	76	ex Predannack, Culdrose A2610[4], 9270M (25-3-97), Shawbury, 20, 233 OCU, 3. Arrived 14-9-12 and repainted in 899 Sqn colours as a T.8	7-13
❑	ZG478		BAe Harrier GR.9	90	ex Yeovilton, Cottesmore. Crashed Khandahar 14-5-09	7-13
❑	ZG509	'80'	BAe Harrier GR.7A	91	ex Cottesmore, Wittering, St Athan. Overstressed 31-7-01	7-13
❑	ZH658		BAe Harrier T.10	94	ex Cottesmore, St Athan, Wittering, 20. Crashed 16-4-03	7-13
❑	ZH806	'730'	HS Sea Harrier FA.2	98	ex Shawbury, 899, 800, 801, 899. SOC 28-7-05	11-13
❑	ZH810	'125'	HS Sea Harrier FA.2	98	ex Shawbury, 899, 801	11-13
❑	ZH812	'005'	HS Sea Harrier FA.2	98	ex Shawbury, Yeovilton, 801, 899, 801. SOC 29-3-06	7-13
❑	ZK534*		HS Hawk T.53	c80	ex Brough, Indonesian AF LL-5319. First noted 4-13	7-13
❑	-		BAE AV-8B Harrier II	~	ex Cottesmore, USMC. Fuselage	2-12

Locally: *W&R23* (p208) dealt with Skeeter AOP.12 XN351 here, and in a wider context, under Saxmundham, Suffolk, (p209). It was noted as departing to 'Norfolk' circa 2012. This was not bad going - see under Norwich, Norfolk.

IPSWICH (MONEWDEN) **AERODROME** south of the A1120, north of Ipswich

Not noted since February 2006, Cessna T.210L G-BENF has been deleted. Ercoupe G-AVTT moved to Doncaster, S Yorks on 21st February 2014.

❑	G-ARDZ	Jodel D.140A Mosquetaire	61	CoA 29-11-91, de-reg 26-2-99. SAN-built	2-10

KESGRAVE on the A12 east of Ipswich

❑ MM54-2372	Piper L-21B	54	ex Embry-Riddle, Woodbridge, Italian Army 'EI-184', I-EIXM, USAF 54-2372. Derelict	2-14

LAKENHEATH AIRFIELD on the A1065 south of Brandon EGUL

USAF Lakenheath, 48th FW – Wings of Liberty Memorial Park: *Viewable* **only** *by prior permission*

❑ 'BM631'	'XR-C'	Supermarine Spitfire V FSM	99	BAPC.269, 71 'Eagle' Sqn, Chesley Peterson colours	3-12
❑ '65-777'	'LN'	McD F-4C-15-MC Phantom 63-7419	63	ex Alconbury, Texas ANG. 48th TFW colours	3-12
❑ 74-0131	'LN'	McDD F-15A-12-MC Eagle	74	ex 122 TFS / Louisiana ANG	3-12
❑ 68-011	'LN'	GD F-111E-CF Aardvark	68	ex Upper Heyford, 20 TFW. 48th TFW colours, *Miss Liberty*	3-12

Airfield:

❑ 76-0124		McDD F-15B-15-MC Eagle	76	BDR	5-10
❑ '63319'	'FW-319'	NAA F-100D-16-NA Super Sabre 54-2269	54	ex '54048', French AF. Main gate Marked 'A2' on the fin	10-13

LAVENHAM AERODROME on the A1141 north of Sudbury

Terry Dann's Tiger Moth G-AIDS moved to Southend by road on 3rd August 2012 for fitting out prior to flight test. It took to the air again on 21st July 2013, returning to its base at Laindon, bringing to an end a four-year project. Isaacs Fury G-BKFK departed in 2012 and was flying shortly afterwards.

◆ **Access:** *Private airfield, visits by prior permission* **only**

❑ G-AIRK	DH Tiger Moth	39	ex Mk.II N9241, 8 EFTS, 10 FIS, TTU, 2 CPF, 224. CoA 1-8-07	6-13
❑ G-AOAA*	DH Tiger Moth	42	ex Spanhoe, Manston, Thruxton, Chilbolton, Mk.II DF159, 24 GCF, 1 RS, 1 GTS, 20 PAFU, 5 GTS. Morris-built. Crashed 4-6-89. 'Super Tiger' variant. Arrived 10-13	10-13
❑ G-BHYI	Stampe SV-4A	46	ex F-BAAF, French AF 18. Nord-built. CoA 25-7-07	6-13

◆ **Thinx:** *You really* **must** *visit the 'The Swan' in Lavenham - inside is the 'Old Bar' filled with photos of the 457th BG that flew from the airfield and the walls carry a bewildering array of signatures* | **www.theswanatlavenham.co.uk**

LOWESTOFT on the A12 south of Great Yarmouth

Simply Spitfire: Terry Arlow completed a full-scale Spitfire IX replica to very high standards in May 2010; it is available for hire for special events, films etc. *Visits available by prior arrangement* **only** | **www.simplyspitfire.com**

❑ 'MK805'	'SH-B'	Spitfire IX FSM	10	64 Sqn colours	[1] 12-13

■ **[1]** The *real* MK805 (once MM4084) is preserved in Italy.

MARTLESHAM HEATH south-east of Woodbridge, the A12 runs through the site

Martlesham Heath Control Tower Museum: The vista of a control tower, complete with its signals square, amid a housing estate is quite surreal. Run by the Martlesham Heath Aviation Society, the museum, opened in September 2000, contains a vast amount of material on an exceptional airfield with an incredible heritage. Take the time to browse through the series of albums charting the astounding *555 types* evaluated by the Aeroplane & Armament Experimental Establishment during the unit's extensive tenure at the airfield. The car park for the museum was once a series of revetments where the P-47s and P-51s of the USAAF's 356th FG used to park. Concrete sandbags that made the walls were revealed during 2012.

◆ **Access:** *On the west side of the A12, turn off at the roundabout with 'brown signs' for the Douglas Bader public house then look for Eagle Way, then Parkers Place and the museum signs.* **Open:** *Every Sun, Apr to Oct 14:00 to 17:00. Other times by appointment.* **Contact:** *c/o 341 Main Road, Martlesham, IP5 3UZ* | **01473 624510** or **01473 435104** | **control.tower@mhas.org.uk** | **www.mhas.org.uk**

Thinx : *Impressive former RAF buildings, including the guardroom and the huge red-brick barrack blocks, dominate the eastern side of the A12 in an extensive industrial estate called Adastral Park; they are publicly accessible and a series of memorials can be found.* **The Douglas Bader** *public house is well signed; a modern building, opened by the well-known fighter pilot in 1980, it contains a large number of images of the airfield, and not a bad selection of ales. Open concrete space to the east of the pub is* not *a car park; this is the remains of one of the runways, the pub being situated close to the intersection of the three wartime runways.* **www.thedouglasbader.co.uk**

Suffolk continues to wend its way beyond the photo-spread, to page 257

NORFOLK

Handley Page Victor K.2 XH673
Marham, July 2013
Terry Dann

English Electric Lightning F.53
(Saudi 53-686 to port and G-AWON to starboard)
Norwich Airport, August 2013
Both Terry Dann

NORFOLK

Hawker Siddeley 146 RJ85 EI-WXB
Norwich Airport, August 2013
Terry Dann

NORTHAMPTONSHIRE

Oldfield Baby Great Lakes G-BGEI
Kettering, July 2013
Ken Ellis

Hawker Hunter F.2 WN904
Northampton, May 2013
Ken Ellis

NORTHAMPTONSHIRE

De Havilland Vampire T.11 XD599
Northampton, May 2013
Ken Ellis

NORTHUMBERLAND & TYNESIDE

Hawker Siddeley Trident 1C G-ARPO
Sunderland, July 2012
David S Johnstone

North American F-86D Sabre 16171
Sunderland, July 2012
David S Johnstone

NOTTINGHAMSHIRE

Taylor Monoplane G-APRT
Newark, arriving 10th April 2012
Howard Heeley-NAM

Lee-Richards Annular biplane replica
Newark, June 2013
Ken Ellis

Scottish Aviation Bulldog T.1 XX634
and procedures trainer
Newark, June 2013
Ken Ellis

NOTTINGHAMSHIRE

SEPECAT Jaguar T.2A XX829
Newark, June 2013
Ian Haskell

SAAB AJSH.37 Viggen 37918
Newark, June 2013
Howard Heeley-NAM

Meteor T.7 VZ634, Canberra PR.7
'WH792', Dove 1 G-AHRI and
Vulcan B.2 XM594
Newark, September 2012
Ian Haskell

NEWARK AIR MUSEUM

21
FARA

OXFORDSHIRE

Panavia Tornado GR.1 ZA319
Bicester, August 2012
Les Woodward

SHROPSHIRE

British Aerospace EAP ZF534
Cosford, November 2013
Ken Ellis

Focke-Wulf Fw 190A-8 733682
Cosford, November 2013
Ken Ellis

SHROPSHIRE

Farman F.141 F-HMFI
Cosford, November 2012
Alf Jenks

Hawker Typhoon Ib MN235
Cosford, November 2013
Ken Ellis

Hawker Siddeley Kestrel FGA.1 XS695
Cosford, November 2013
Ken Ellis

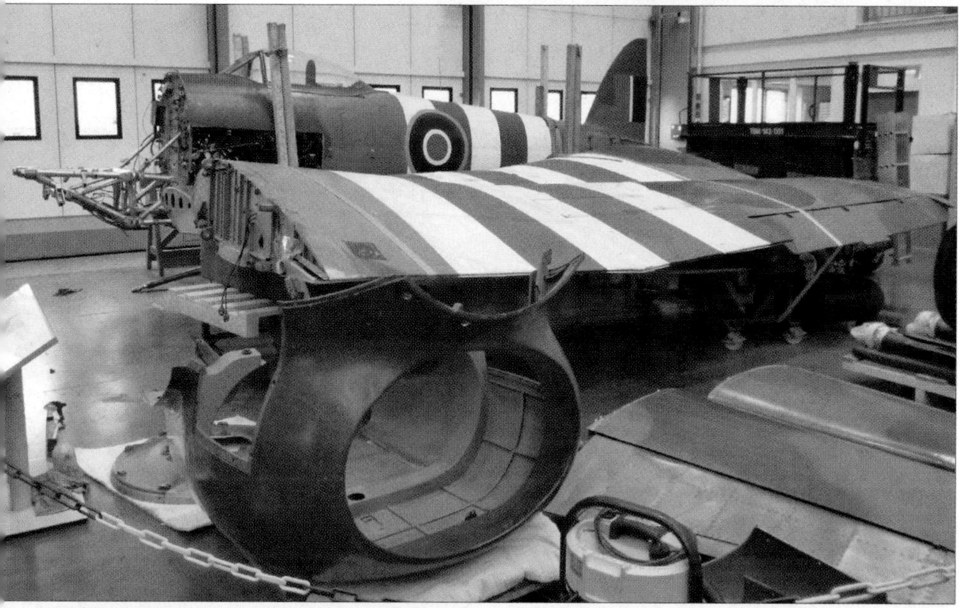

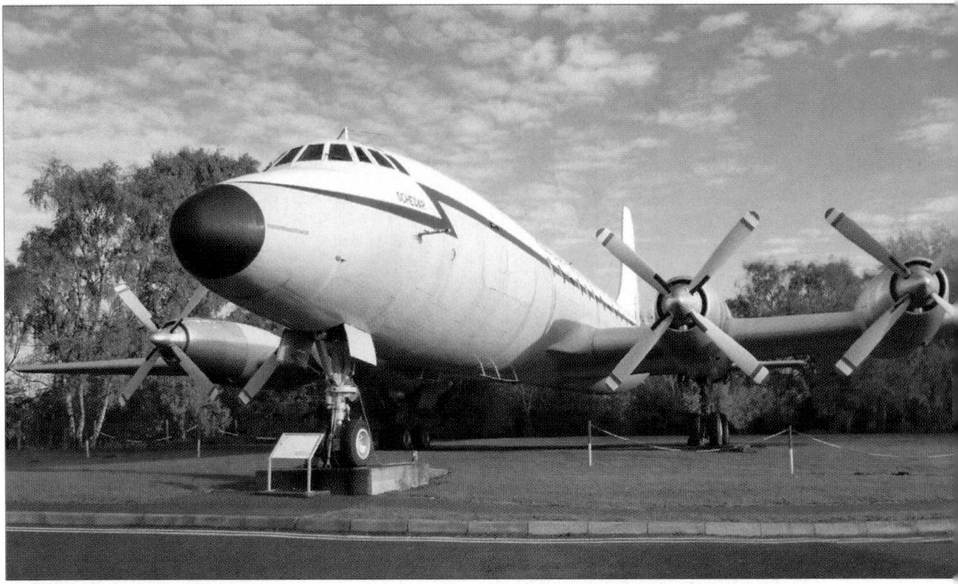

SHROPSHIRE

Bristol Britannia 312F 'XM497'
Cosford, November 2013
Ken Ellis

Hawker Siddeley Nimrod R.1 XV249
Cosford, November 2013
Ken Ellis

Hunting Jet Provost T.3 XM362
Cosford, May 2012
Mike Cain

SHROPSHIRE

Panavia Tornado F.3 ZE340 (foreground), Tornado GR.1s ZA450 and ZA357, Jaguar GR.3A XX112 Cosford, October 2013
Phil Adkin

Westland Wessex HU.5 XT480 Rednall, June 2012
Ken Ellis

Airspeed Horsa replica Shawbury, September 2013
Mike Cain

SOMERSET

Westland WG.30-200 G-ELEC
Weston-super-Mare, October 2013
David S Johnstone

Julian Wombat G-WBAT
Weston-super-Mare, October 2013
David S Johnstone

Kamov Ka-26 DDR-SPY
Weston-super-Mare, October 2013
David S Johnstone

SOMERSET

Short 184 8359
Yeovilton, July 2012
Mike Cain

Sopwith Pup replica 'N6452'
Yeovilton, November 2012
Ken Ellis

Grumman Martlet I AL246
Yeovilton, June 2012
Bob Turner

SOMERSET

Agusta 109A AE-331
Yeovilton, November 2012
Ken Ellis

Hawker Sea Hawk FGA.6 WV856 and
Fairey Gannet AEW.3 XL503
Yeovilton, November 2012
Mike Cain

Supermarine Scimitar F.1 XD312
Yeovilton, January 2013
Bob Turner

SOMERSET

Hawker Siddeley Sea Harrier FRS.1 XZ493
Yeovilton, November 2012
Richard Hall

Hiller HT.1 XB480
Yeovilton, November 2012
Mike Cain

McDonnell Phantom FG.1 XV586
Yeovilton, August 2013
Ian Humphreys

STAFFORDSHIRE

Lockheed Hercules C.3 XV221
Hixon, November 2013
Geoff Eastham

McDonnell Phantom FGR.2 XV499
Hixon, November 2013
Geoff Eastham

Westland Lynx line-up
Hixon, November 2013
Geoff Eastham

STAFFORDSHIRE

BAC Jet Provost T.5A XW434
Wolverhampton Aerodrome,
September 2013
David S Johnstone

SUFFOLK

Hawker Hunter F.6 XG210
Beck Row, March 2012
Jon Wickenden

McDonnell Phantom FGR.2 XV497
Bentwaters, July 2013
Graham Haynes-BCWM

78

RESCUE

676
HF
ROYAL NAV

U.S. AIR FORCE
42196

SUFFOLK

SEPECAT Jaguar GR.1 XX741
Bentwaters, July 2013
Graham Haynes-BCWM

Percival Sea Prince T.1 WF128
Flixton, August 2013
Tom Singfield

North American F-100D Super Sabre 42196
Flixton, August 2013
Tom Singfield

SUFFOLK

Hawker Hunter FGA.9 XG194
Wattisham, June 2013
Phil Adkin

SURREY

Supermarine Spitfire IIa P8088
Brooklands, January 2012
Ian Haskell

Supermarine Swift F.4 WK198
Brooklands, October 2012
Ian Haskell

N437

SURREY

Vickers VC-10 K.3 ZA150
Dunsfold, 24th September 2013
Both Jon Wickenden

Handley Page Jetstream T.3 N437UH
Dunsfold, August 2013
Richard Hall

EAST SUSSEX

Westland Wessex HAS.1 XS886
Ditchling, April 2013
Jon Wickenden

WEST SUSSEX

Handley Page Jetstream T.2 G-AWVJ
Shoreham, September 2012
Phil Whalley

WARWICKSHIRE

Miles Gemini 1A G-AKDK
Coventry, November 2013
Tim R Badham

WARWICKSHIRE

De Havilland Venom FB.50 'WR470'
Coventry, June 2012
Ian Humphreys

Westland Scout AH.1 XR635
Coventry, September 2012
Tim R Badham

Beagle 206-1 8449M
Coventry, March 2013
Tim R Badham

WARWICKSHIRE

McDonnell F-4C Phantom 37414
Coventry, July 2013
Dave Harding

British Aerospace ATP G-BTPJ
Coventry, February 2013
Ian Humphries

British Aerospace ATPs G-OBWP and G-MANC
Coventry, October 2013
Jon Wickenden

USAF
37414
USA

G-BTPJ
PJ

First Flight

WARWICKSHIRE

Percival Sea Prince T.1 G-RACA
Long Marston, August 2013
Roger Richards

WILTSHIRE

Sud Gazelle HT.3 ZA804
Boscombe Down, July 2012
Ken Ellis

De Havilland Devon C.2/2 VP955
Cricklade, May 2013
Les Woodward

WILTSHIRE

Royal Aircraft Factory BE.2c replica '2783'
Old Sarum, July 2012
Ken Ellis

Gloster Meteor D.16 WK800
Old Sarum, August 2012
Roger Richards

Hawker Hunter F.6A XF375
Old Sarum, October 2013
Richard Hall

AVIATION
COLLECTION
XF375
6

SAGITTARIUS

ROYAL NAVY

TSHIRE

ıavilland Comet C.2 XK699
Sarum, November 2013
Haskell

ʻker Siddeley Sea Harrier FA.2 XZ457
Sarum, July 2012
Ellis

avia Tornado F.3 ZD936 and
111-402 XX919
Sarum, July 2012
Ellis

.TSHIRE

Havilland Comet 4B G-APYD and
net 1A G-ANAV
ɔughton, July 2013
Woodward

Z37 Cmelak G-AVZB
ɔughton, July 2013
Woodward

egrove Four-Runner G-BXXR
ɔughton, July 2013
Woodward

EAST YORKSHIRE

Ward Gnome G-AXEI and Ward Elf G-MMUL
Breighton, January 2013
Andy Wood

Aero L29 Delfin 'Red 51'
Breighton, January 2013
Andy Wood

Blackburn Buccaneer S.2B XV168
Brough, 18th August 2013 - last 'Bucc' to leave
Francis Wallace

NORTH YORKSHIRE

Handley Page Halifax *Friday the 13th*
Elvington, June 2012
Richard Hall

Handley Page Victor K.2 XL231
Elvington, September 2012
Tony McCarthy

BAC Jet Provost T.5A XW410 and friend
Selby, January 2013
Jet Art Aviation

81
78
61
63
60
80
1 FTS
MB
MR

SOUTH YORKSHIRE

American AA-1B Trainer G-BCLW
Doncaster, May 2013
Andy Wood

SCOTLAND

Scottish Aviation Bulldog T.1 XX612
Ayr, September 2013
David S Johnstone

Lockheed T-33A FT-36
Dumfries, August 2013
Gemma Wilkinson

SCOTLAND

North American F-100D Super Sabre 54-2163
Dumfries, August 2013
Richard Flagg

Boeing 707-436 G-APFJ
East Fortune, April 2012
Ian Haskell

SEPECAT Jaguar GR.1A XZ119
East Fortune, April 2012
Ian Haskell

SCOTLAND

Scottish Aviation Bulldog 104 G-AXIG
Edinburgh, April 2012
Ian Haskell

Gloster Meteor T.7 WF825
Montrose, May 2013
Tony McCarthy

Beagle Pup 100 G-AXSD
Prestwick, July 2013
David S Johnstone

WALES

Antonov An-2R CCCP-40748
Hawarden, November 2013
Brian Downs

Sukhoi Su-17B 'Red 54'
Hawarden, November 2013
Brian Downs

Watkins CHW
Swansea, August 2012
Alf Jenks

NORTHERN IRELAND

CGS Hawk Arrow N216HK
Causeway, September 2013
Andy Wood

Fokker F.27-500 Friendship G-ECAT
Sligo, September 2013
Rowland Benbrook

Blackburn Buccaneer S.2B XV863
Weston, November 2013
Jon Wickenden

MILDENHALL AIRFIELD on the A1304 east of Cambridge

USAF Mildenhall, 100th ARW: You have to travel back as far as *W&R14* (p181) for the last reference at this massive base. During April 1993 the battle damage repair training T-33A 16769 and tow-training C-130A 70524 were both scrapped. A Cayuse has arrived, perhaps as an instructional airframe for the 7th and 67th Special Operations Squadrons.

❑ 69-15979*		Hughes OH-6A Cayuse	69	ex Hulburt Field, USA. Arrived 9-9-12	10-13

NEWMARKET on the A1304 east of Cambridge

A *private* collector has a Hunter in the area.

❑ XG274	'71'	Hawker Hunter F.6	56	ex Ipswich, Halton 8710M (30-11-81), 4 FTS, 229 OCU, 66, 14	4-08

ROUGHAM, or Bury St Edmunds, north of the A14 east of Bury St Edmunds

Rougham Tower Association: A surprising amount of the former B-17 airfield survives, including the superbly-preserved tower. The displays are dedicated to the men and the memories of the 322nd and 94th BGs and there are poignant memorials and expanding museum facilities - a great place of pilgrimage.

Access: *Turn off A14 east of 'Bury', follow signs for Rougham Industrial Estate, then signs for the tower/aerodrome.* **Open:** *May to Oct, Sun 11:00 to 16:00.* **Contact:** *Rougham Industrial Estate, Bury St Edmunds, IP30 9XA* | **07581 860674** | **roughamcontroltowermuseum@gmail.com** | **www.rougham.org**

Thinx: *Off the Bury St Edmunds to Thurston road is the 'Flying Fortress' pub at Mount Road. The building was part of the technical site for Station 468 and has lots of memorabilia on show* | **www.theflyingfortress.co.uk**

STOWMARKET on the A14 east of Bury St Edmunds

Giles Howell: The EE P.1B is in the *general* area for restoration and eventual display.

❑ XA847		EE P.1B	57	ex Portsmouth, Southampton, Hendon 8371M, Farnborough, A&AEE, EE. Last flight 21-4-66	7-12

SUDBURY on the A134 north-west of Colchester

AJD Engineering / Hawker Restorations Ltd: **Private** *workshop, access* **strictly** *by prior arrangement*

❑ P2902	'DX-R'	Hawker Hurricane I	G-ROBT	40	ex Dunkirk, P2902, 245. Crashed 31-5-40 245 Sqn colours	[1]	3-13
❑ P3717	'SW-P'	Hawker Hurricane II	G-HITT	40	ex Hinckley, Russia, Mk IIA DR348, 8 FTS, 55 OTU, 43, 257, 253, 238. 253 Sqn colours	[2]	3-13
❑ V7497		Hawker Hurricane I	G-HRLI	40	ex 501. Crashed 28-9-40	[3]	6-11
❑ A2-25		RAF SE.5a	G-ECAE	18	ex Australia, RAAF, C8996. Austin-built. Crashed 15-7-27		6-11

■ **[1]** G-ROBT is being restored for Rick Roberts. It was taken on charge by 245 Sqn at Hawkinge, Kent, on 19-5-40 and force-landed on the beach at Dunkirk 13 days later, piloted by Ken McGlashan. **[2]** G-HITT is for Hugh Taylor. **[3]** G-HRLI is a 'pending' project.

WALPOLE on the B1117 south-east of Halesworth

Former **Blyth Valley Aviation Collection** airframes are **not** available for public inspection.

❑ WE122	'845'	EE Canberra TT.18	52	ex North Weald, Stock, Llanbedr, St Athan, Llanbedr, FRADU, 7, B.2, 98, 245, 231 OCU. Cockpit	2-12
❑ WE192		EE Canberra T.4	54	ex Long Marston, Firbeck, Winsford, Samlesbury, St Athan, 231 OCU, 360, 231 OCU, 39, 231 OCU, 3, 231 OCU. SOC 26-11-81. Cockpit	2-12
❑ WH953		EE Canberra B.6(mod)	55	ex Lowestoft, Stock, Farnborough, RAE. Short-built. Cockpit	2-12
❑ XH165		EE Canberra PR.9	60	ex Stock, St Athan, 1 PRU, 39, 13, 58. Short-built. SOC 10-4-94. Cockpit	2-12

WATTISHAM AIRFIELD north of the B1078, south of Stowmarket EGUW

Wattisham Station Heritage: Run by the Wattisham Museum Society. Situated in what was the Station Chapel during the airfield's USAAF days, the displays are dedicated to every aspect of Wattisham's incredible history from 1937 to date. The team has the use of a 'Cold War' hardened aircraft shelter which serves both as a workshop and storage site for the airframes. Visitors have the opportunity to visit this as well as the museum. The Lynx was deployed to Iraq in 2003 and is another example of the loyal support and enthusiasm the Army Air Corps has for the museum.

◆ **Access:** *Located within a busy Army base, personal identification - a passport or* photo *driving licence - is required.* ***Visits must be pre-booked****, at least one week in advance via email or two weeks by post.* **Open:** *1st Sun of every month, Feb to Nov 13:00 to 16:30.* **Contact:** *Heritage Visits, c/o The Curator, Force Headquarters, Wattisham Flying Station, Ipswich, IP7 7RA* | **email via website** | **www.wattishamstationheritage.org**
Thinx: *Airfield memorial on the northern boundary at Charles Tye*

❑ XG194	'N'	Hawker Hunter FGA.9	56	ex North Luffenham, Cosford 8839M (25-10-84), 1 TWU, TWU, 229 OCU, 1, F.6, 92, 111, 43. Arrived 28-11-09 111 Sqn 'Black Arrows' colours	[1]	1-14
❑ XP743		EE Lightning F.3	64	ex Burton-upon-Trent, Stafford, Pendine, Leconfield, 29, 56, 29, 56, Wattisham TFF, 56. SOC 16-10-75. Arrived 6-09. 56 Sqn colours. Cockpit	[2]	1-14
❑ XT914	'Z'	McD Phantom FGR.2	68	ex Brampton, Leeming 9269M (5-10-92), 74, 228 OCU, 92, 56, 228 OCU, 92, 228 OCU, 56, 228 OCU, 17, 14, 228 OCU. Damaged 22-5-92. Arrived 8-3-12. 74 Sqn colours		1-14
❑ XZ605*		Westland Lynx AH.7	79	ex Middle Wallop		1-14

■ **[1]** Restored to F.6 status and 'Black Arrows' colours when it was flown by Sqn Ldr (now Air Cdre) Roger Topp, callsign *Blackjack Red 1*, from the famed 22-ship formations flown at Farnborough and Odiham in 1958. **[2]** XP743 owned by Ken Hayward.

No.**3 Regiment, Army Air Corps / 24 Air Mobile Brigade / 7 Battalion, REME**: The cabin of Scout AH.1 XP852, last noted on the dump in February 1998, has been deleted. Also long-in-the-tooth, not noted since June 2004, Slingsby T.21B AYK has been deleted. Stored in a HAS during 2009 were Skeeter AOP.12 XL739 and Scout AH.1 XP907 (G-SROE); both had moved on by late 2011.

❑ XT617	Westland Scout AH.1	65	ex Almondbank, Wroughton, 653, 660. Displayed	11-13
❑ XX380	Sud Gazelle AH.1	74	ex Sunderland, Shawbury, Fleetlands. Westland-built	3-11
❑ XX444	Sud Gazelle AH.1	76	ex Fleetlands, 25 Flt, 662, 663, 656, 663, 656, 658, 656, 658, ARWS, ARWF. Westland-built. For the gate	3-11
❑ XZ330	Sud Gazelle AH.1	77	ex Middle Wallop. Westland-built. Instructional	9-11
❑ ZA729	Sud Gazelle AH.1	80	ex Gütersloh, Shawbury, Fleetlands, 658, 1 Regt. 4 Regt, 661, 652. Westland-built. Instructional	6-13
❑ ZJ177*	McDD Apache AH.1	77	ex Middle Wallop, 9 Rgt. Westland-built. Crashed 4-9-08 Spares. First noted 12-09	4-13

Locally: Last noted in January 2004, Evans VP-1 G-BICT has been deleted.

SURREY

BROOKLANDS or Weybridge, on the B374 south of Weybridge

Brooklands Museum: In February 2013 the museum announced that it was pitching for Heritage Lottery funding to put some more of the hallowed motor racing circuit back to its original use and to improve the accommodation for airframes. Under a £4.8m bid, the 'Brooklands Aircraft Factory and Race Track Revival Project' will move the Grade 2-listed 'Wellington Hangar', add a new annexe to it and create a factory-themed display. The latter, emphasizing aircraft manufacture, ploughs new ground and, of course, acknowledges the hallowed names that have called Brooklands home, including A V Roe, Sopwith, Hawker, Vickers. Alongside this will be built a 'Flight Shed' for the museum's 'live' airframes; underneath this will be workshops. As the 'Wellington Hangar' was built on part of the race track, the circuit will be able to boast a continuous piece of track, including a straight and banked turn. Development work is in hand, it will be 2015 before the project goes to the next stage. See under Dunsfold, Surrey, for the museum's 'in steam' VC-10.

Two building projects are due to finish during 2014. Thanks to a major grant from the Association of Independent Museums, the 1947 Barnes Wallis Stratosphere Climatic Test Chamber has been refurbished and was due to re-open by the time *W&R24* appears. Next door to the 'Strat Chamber', the 1958-1959 Supersonic Balloon Hangar and Wind Tunnel is due to be completed in the summer and will house a new simulator and flexible space for temporary exhibitions and events.

Within the site is the **London Bus Museum** in Cobham Hall at Brooklands. This museum was previously housed in the former Vickers 'Skunk Works' at Foxwarren and contains around 35 buses and a vast amount of support material. Entry is included with the site ticket - expand your interests! **www.londonbusmuseum.com**

There is a very active **Brooklands Trust Members** organisation with plenty of benefits for regular visitors.

See under Farnborough, Hants, for Beagle 206 G-ARRM. One that slipped the net was 'Flea' 'G-ADRY' which moved to Langley, Berks, on loan in August 2010. Blériot XI replica G-LOTI moved to Halton, Bucks, on 30th April 2013. Roe Biplane replica G-ROEI moved to Filton, Glos, in January 2014, for storage. The museum has vigorously supported the newly-established Gliding Heritage Centre at Lasham, Hants, by loaning: Drone G-AEKV (leaving 1st September 2013, Willow Wren BGA.162, Gull III ATH and Scud I HFZ (all leaving 18th July 2013). Arriving on 12th December 2011 was the cockpit section of Spitfire II P8088 from Oxford in readiness for an auction staged at the museum on 18th February 2012. It failed to reach its reserve and remained on display until moving to Knutsford, Cheshire, on 18th February 2013.

◆ **Access:** *On the B374 south of Weybridge, access from Junctions 10 or 11 of the M25 - well signed.* **Open:** *Daily 10:00 to 17:00 (last entry 16:00), Easter to Oct. Winter, 10:00 to 16:00, last entry 15:00. Normally closed Xmas. Lots of special events - see the website. For the* ***'Concorde Experience'*** *places are limited and visitors are best to acquire tickets upon arrival.* **Contact:** *Brooklands Road, Weybridge, Surrey, KT13 0QN* | **01932 857381** | **info@brooklandsmuseum.com** | **www.brooklandsmuseum.com**

Flooding at Brooklands on 26th December 2013; plenty more where that came from in January and February 2014! The fly-by-wire BAC One-Eleven 475 G-ASYD. *Julian Temple*

❑	'G-EBED'	Vickers Viking replica	74	BAPC.114, ex 'R4', Chertsey, *The Land Time Forgot.* Arr 1988	1-14
❑	'G-AACA'	Avro 504K replica	68	BAPC.177, ex 'G1381', Henlow. Arrived 29-1-87	1-14
❑	G-AGRU	Vickers Viking 1	46	ex Cosford, Soesterberg, Channel, Kuwait Oil, BWIA, VP-TAX, G-AGRU, BEA. CoA 9-1-64, de-reg 9-6-64. Arrived 27-6-91. BEA colours, *Vagrant*	1-14
❑	G-APEJ	Vickers Merchantman	61	ex Hunting, ABC, BEA. *Ajax*. CoA 29-1-93, de-reg 15-11-96. Arrived 26-8-95. Cockpit, in 'Stat Chamber'	1-14
❑	G-APEP	Vickers Merchantman	61	ex Hunting, ABC, BEA. *Superb.* CoA 1-10-98, de-reg 28-3-97. Flew in 17-10-96	1-14
❑	G-APIM	Vickers Viscount 806	58	ex Southend, BAF, BA, BEA. Damaged 11-1-88, de-reg 1-3-91. Arrived 11-2-90. *Viscount Stephen Piercey*	1-14
❑	G-ARVM	Vickers VC-10 Srs 1101	64	ex Cosford, BA, BOAC. CoA 5-8-80, de-reg 9-11-79. Arrived 19-10-06. BA colours. Fuselage	1-14
❑	G-ASYD	BAC 111-475AM	65	ex Filton, BAe, BAC. CoA 13-7-94, de-reg 25-7-94. Flew 14-7-94. 'Fly By Light Technology'.	1-14

❑	G-AZLP*		Vickers Viscount 813	58	ex Sunderland, Middleton St George, BMA, SAA ZS-CDT. CoA 3-4-82; de-reg 19-12-86. Cockpit. Arrived by 9-13		1-14
❑	G-BBDG		BAC/Sud Concorde 100	74	ex Filton. CoA 1-3-82, de-reg 10-8-84. Arrived 5-6-04	[1]	1-14
❑	G-BJHV		Voisin scale replica	r81	ex Old Warden. De-reg 4-7-91. Arr 1987. Stored off-site from28-11-13		1-14
❑	G-CHOI		White Monoplane replica	12	1912 replica, completed early 2013	[2]	1-14
❑	G-MJPB		Manuel Ladybird	r82	de-reg 13-6-90. Arrived 1985. Stored	[3]	1-14
❑	G-VTOL		HS Harrier T.52	71	ex ZA250, Dunsfold. CoA 2-11-86, de-reg 13-3-90. Arrived 11-89	[3]	1-14
❑	–		Roe I Biplane replica	85	BAPC.187, displayed in reproduction of Roe's shed		1-14
❑	–		S-D Demoiselle 1909 rep	95	BAPC.256. Arrived 1997. Taxiable	[4]	1-14
❑	–*	'3'	Sopwith Tabloid rep	13	floatplane, partially covered. Handed over 27-11-13	[5]	1-14
❑	–		Vickers Vimy replica	97	cockpit section, centre section, engine nacelles		1-14
❑	–		Vickers VC-10 EMU	~	test shell, cockpit. BOAC colours		1-14
❑	–		BAC/Sud Concorde SIM	~	ex Filton		1-14
❑	–		Rogallo hang-glider	73	*Aerial.* On loan, stored		1-14
❑	–*		hang-glider	~	stored	[6]	1-14
❑	F-BGEQ		DH Tiger Moth	44	ex Hungerford, Brooklands, Chessington, Brooklands, French mil, Mk.I NL846, n/s. Morris-built. Stored, off site	[3]	1-14
❑	A40-AB		Vickers VC-10 1103	64	ex Sultan of Oman, G-ASIX, BCAL, BUA. Flew in 6-7-87		1-14
❑	NX71MY		Vickers Vimy replica	94	ex Dunsfold. Flew in 15-11-09	[7]	1-14
❑	'B7270'		Sopwith Camel F1 replica G-BFCZ	77	ex Land's End, Duxford, Chertsey. CoA 23-2-89, de-reg 23-1-03. Arrived 1988. 209 Sqn c/s. Ground-runs		1-14
❑	'F5475'	'A'	RAF SE.5a replica	94	BAPC.250, *1st Battalion Honourable Artillery Company*	[8]	1-14
❑	'K5673'		Hawker Fury I replica	94	BAPC.249, 1 Sqn 'A' Flt colours	[8]	1-14
❑	N2980	'R'	Vickers Wellington Ia	39	ex 20 OTU, 37, 149. Ditched in Loch Ness 31-12-40. Arrived 27-9-85	[9]	1-14
❑	-		Vickers Wellington rep	11	forward fuselage, reconstruction		1-14
❑	Z2389	'XR-T'	Hawker Hurricane II	40	ex Murmansk, 767 IAP, IA PVO, Sov AF, RAF 253, 136, 247, 71, 249. Shot down 23-6-42. 71 Sqn colours	[10]	1-14
❑	WF372	'A'	Vickers Varsity T.1	52	ex Sibson, 6 FTS, 1 ANS, RAFC, 201 AFS. SOC 25-3-76. Arrived 13-11-88		1-14
❑	WK198		Supermarine Swift F.4	53	ex Millom, Sunderland, Failsworth, Kirkham 7428M (23-7-57), Aldergrove, MoS. Fuselage. Arrived 3-2-11	[11]	1-14
❑	WP921		DHC Chipmunk T.10 PAX	52	ex Croydon, Henley-on-Thames, Benson, CoAT, G-ATJJ, WP921, Colerne SF, Ox UAS, HCMSU, 10 RFS. SOC 16-7-73. Arrived 1995. Stored	[3]	1-14
❑	XD816		Vickers Valiant BK.1	56	ex Henlow, Abingdon, BAC, 214, 148. SOC 21-9-64. Arrived 9-88. Cockpit	[3]	1-14
❑	'XF314'	'N'	Hawker Hunter F.51	56	ex Wycombe Air Park, Sandown, Tangmere, Dunsfold, G-9-439 (27-3-76), Danish AF E-412, Esk.724. Acquired 18-3-89. 43 Sqn colours		1-14
❑	XP984		Hawker P.1127	64	ex Dunsfold, Lee-on-Solent, Manadon A2658 (12-2-76), RAE. Arrived 28-9-00	[3] [12]	1-14
❑	XT575		Vickers Viscount 837	60	ex Bruntingthorpe, DRA Bedford, OE-LAG. SOC 10-7-93 Arrived 14-1-96. Cockpit		1-14
❑	XX499	'G'	HP Jetstream T.1	76	ex Ipswich, Shawbury, Cranwell, 45, 3 FTS, 45, 6 FTS, METS. SAL-built. Arrived 21-5-08	[13]	1-14
❑	–		BAC TSR-2 EMU	~	ex Farnborough. Arrived 8-92. Cockpit		1-14
❑	'976'	'K'	Avro Lancaster replica	~	ex East Kirkby, *Night Flight*, . Arrived 25-4-08. Cockpit reconstruction	[14]	1-14
❑	E-421		Hawker Hunter F.51	56	ex Brooklands Tech, Kingston, Dunsfold, G-9-443 (16-5-76), Aalborg, Esk.724, RDanAF		1-14

■ **[1]** *Delta-Golf* factoids: total hours 1,282, landings 633. **[2]** Canard Pusher of 1912, being built by Julian Aubert - see Demoiselle BAPC.256. **[3]** Airframes on loan, as follows: Ladybird from the estate of the late Bill Manuel; P.1127 and Harrier from BAE Systems; Chipmunk PAX from Peter Smith (see under Hawkinge, Kent); Valiant cockpit from the RAF Museum. **[4]** Demoiselle was built by Julian Aubert and friends with wing-warping and the original method of construction, bamboo - see also G-CHOI. **[5]** Replica built by Ken Gillett and Steve Green; representing the Schneider Trophy winner, flown by Howard 'Picky' Pixton at Monaco, April 1914, at 86mph. **[6]** Unidentified hang-glider, previously held in the 'Balloon' Hangar. **[7]** Vimy was officially handed over to the museum by Peter McMillan on 26-8-06. **[8]** SE.5A and Fury replicas were built on site. **[9]** *R-for-Robert* factoids: First flown, at Brooklands, by 'Mutt' Summers 16-11-39; with 149 Sqn took part in the ill-fated 'Battle of Heligoland Bight' 18-12-39; total time 330:20.

[10] Hurricane was shot down by a Bf 109F of JG5, near Murmansk. **[11]** Swift is on loan from Unimetals Industries Ltd. **[12]** P.1127 - the 6th prototype - is fitted with the wing of an earlier P.1127. **[13]** Jetstream, owned by Brooklands College, is used as an instructional airframe and exhibit. (See also Weybridge, Surrey.) **[14]** The Lancaster cockpit was created for the TV drama *Night Flight*. It includes the *extreme* nose section of the unfortunate KB976 (G-BCOH) and carries its 'last-three'. (The rear of KB976 can be found at Doncaster, S Yorks.)

CAMBERLEY on the M3 south of Bracknell

Parkhouse Aviation: A Gannet cockpit is at a *private* location in the general area. (See also Wycombe Air Park, Bucks.)

❑	XL449	'044'	Fairey Gannet AEW.3	58	ex Booker, Camberley, Cardiff, Yeovilton, Lossiemouth, GSU, 849, A&AEE. SOC 2-10-78. Cockpit	12-13

CHARLWOOD west of the A23/A217 junction, north of Gatwick Airport

Gatwick Aviation Museum: Turn to p212 of *W&R23* for the long-running planning dispute relating to the museum. During July 2012 an appeal against the decision refusing development of land occupied presently by chicken sheds and the creation of an exhibition hangar-cum-education centre was again refused. Peter Vallance told a local newspaper: "The only way they're going to take me out of here is feet first in a hearse."

Tragically, these were prophetic words: **Peter Vallance** died on 14th January 2013. Never the diplomat, often cantankerous and constantly out-spoken, in his eyes you were either 'with' him or 'agin' him. Despite this, it was hard not to have admiration for his enthusiasm and drive. Thankfully, provisions had been made and most of the collection passed into a trust fund. The trustees and volunteers are determined to carry Peter's vision through to completion. The watchword for the future is to drop the confrontational stance and to work *with* the authorities. To this end, a slimming-down of the collection was initiated from the spring of 2013 and is on-going.

Disposals: Privately owned, the cockpit of Victor K.2 XL164 was put up for sale in late 2011; it moved to Bournemouth, Dorset, 24-5-13. From the collection: Sea Prince T.1 WF118 to St Athan, Wales, 5-9-13; Provost T.1 WW442 to East Midlands, Leics, by 9-13; Pembroke C.1 XK885 to St Athan, Wales 19-9-13, via Wycombe AP, Bucks, arriving 25-9-13; Gannet AEW.3 XL472 to St Athan, Wales, 31-8-13; Jet Provost T.3A XN494 to Bruntingthorpe, Leics, 19-8-13; Wasp HAS.1 XS463 to Bournemouth, Dorset, 21-12-13; Jaguar GR.1 XX734 moved to Old Sarum, Wilts, on 15-5-13.

◆ **Access:** *South-east of Charlwood, on the minor road to Lowfield Heath*. **Open:** *Mar to Oct, Sat, 10:00 to 16:00. Otherwise by prior appointment*. **Contact:** *Lowfield Heath Road, Charlwood, RH6 0BT* | **01293 862915** | **gpvgat@aol.com** | **www.gatwick-aviation-museum.co.uk**

❑	VZ638		Gloster Meteor T.7 G-JETM	49	ex North Weald, Bournemouth, Southampton, Southend, Kemble, CAW, RAFC, 237 OCU, 501, Biggin Hill SF, FCCS, 85, 54, 25, 500. SOC 12-1-72, de-reg 15-12-09		3-13
❑	WH773		EE Canberra PR.7	53	ex Wyton 8696M (9-6-81), 13, 58, 80, 31, 82, 540		3-13
❑	WK146		EE Canberra B.2	54	ex Hull, Wroughton, Abingdon, Bicester, 59, 102. Avro-built. SOC 12-5-67. Cockpit		3-12
❑	WP308	'572'	Percival Sea Prince T.1 G-GACA	52	ex Staverton, Kemble, 750, Sydenham, 750, Lossiemouth, 750. SOC 16-9-80, de-reg 15-12-09		3-13
❑	WR974	'K'	Avro Shackleton MR.3/3	57	ex Cosford 8117M (9-12-70), Kinloss W, 203, 42, 203, SWDU, ASWDU		3-13
❑	WR982	'J'	Avro Shackleton MR.3/3	58	ex Cosford 8106M (28-9-70), 201, 206, MoA, 205, 203, 206		3-13
❑	'XE489'	'485'	Hawker Sea Hawk FB.3 G-JETH	54	ex Jet Heritage, Bournemouth, WM983, Chilton Cantelo, Culdrose, 'SAH-6', A2511, FRU, 806, 811. SOC 1-9-61, de-reg 15-12-09	[1]	3-13
❑	XL591		Hawker Hunter T.7	58	ex Kemble, Ipswich, Colsterworth, Shawbury, 237 OCU, 208, 237 OCU, 208, 237 OCU, 4 FTS, RAE, 4 FTS, 229 OCU, FCS		3-13
❑	XN923		Blackburn Buccaneer S.1	62	ex Boscombe Down, West Freugh, A&AEE, RAE, A&AEE, RAE, A&AEE, RAE, A&AEE, 700Z. SOC 17-5-54. Ground-runs		3-13
❑	XP351	'Z'	Westland Whirlwind HAR.10	62	ex Shawbury 8672M (9-2-81), 2 FTS, SAR Wing, 22		3-13
❑	XP398		Westland Whirlwind HAR.10	62	ex Peckham Rye, Shawbury 8794M (2-9-83), 22, 1563 Flt, 202, 103, 110, 225		3-13
❑	XS587		DH Sea Vixen FAW.2(TT) G-VIXN	65	ex Bournemouth, FRL, 8828M, RAE, FRADU, FRU, 899, 893. SOC 4-2-85, de-reg 15-12-09		3-13
❑	XV751	'AU'	HS Harrier GR.3	69	ex Bruntingthorpe, Charlwood, Lee-on-Solent A2672, A2760, 3, 1, 3, 20, 233 OCU. Grey colours, RN titles		3-13
❑	ZF579		EE Lightning F.53	67	ex Portsmouth, Luxembourg, *Wing Commander*, Stretton, Warton, R Saudi AF 203, 53-671, G-27-41. Last flown 14-1-86		3-13

❑ E-430		Hawker Hunter F.51		56	ex Faygate, Chertsey, Dunsfold, G-9-448, Esk.724, Dan AF. FAA colours, GA.11-style	3-13
❑ J-1605		DH Venom FB.50	G-BLID	52	ex Duxford, Swiss AF. F+W built. De-reg 15-12-09	3-13

■ **[1]** When Jet Heritage was restoring FGA.6 XE489 (G-JETH) to flight it was found that the spar attachments had been cut - very probably when it was moved by road to Southend, Essex, 5-67. To get around this FB.3 WM983 was borrowed from the Sea Scouts at Chilton Cantelo, Somerset, 8-85 and its *entire* fuselage was used in G-JETH, along with the wings of XE489. This is the status of the airframe acquired by Peter Vallance from auction at Bournemouth on 1-10-87 for £1,500 and delivered to this site on 10-10-87. By 3-87 the Sea Scouts got 'their' Sea Hawk back. It constituted the fuselage of XE489 plus the wings of 'WM983', which came from FGA.4 WV909 which had been fitted as far back as the mid-1960s when it was in service on the 'deck' at SAH Culdrose. Chilton Cantelo disposed of 'WM983' (but in the majority XE489) on 8-8-89 when it was sold in the Netherlands.

Aerospace Logistics: in Glovers Road. **Access:** *Visits possible* **only** *by prior arrangement* | **www.aerospace-logistics.co.uk**

❑ XX121	'EQ'	SEPECAT Jaguar GR.1	73	ex Cosford, Shawbury, Warton, Shawbury, 6, 54, 226 OCU	1-13
❑ XX140		SEPECAT Jaguar T.2	73	ex Faygate, Brough, Cosford 9008M, 226 OCU, 54, 226 OCU, JOCU. Cockpit	1-13
❑ XX223		HS Hawk T.1	78	ex Henlow, 4 FTS. Crashed 7-7-86. Cockpit	5-09
❑ XX257		HS Hawk T.1A	79	ex St Athan, Red Arrows. Crashed 17-11-98	8-11
❑ XZ497	'126'	HS Sea Harrier FA.2	82	ex St Athan, 801, AEE, FRS.1, 899, 801	1-13
❑ ZD412		BAe Harrier GR.5	89	ex St Athan, Dunsfold, Brough, 3. Crashed 30-9-01. Cockpit	5-10
❑ ZE698	'123'	HS Sea Harrier FA.2	88	ex St Athan, 800, FRS.1, 800, 801,899, 801	1-13

Also:

❑ G-AYLZ	Aero 45-04	57	ex 9M-AOF, F-BILP. CoA 11-6-76, de-reg 12-12-10	11-06

CHERTSEY north-east of Junction 12 of the M25 and Junction 2 of the M3

Thorpe Park: This 'adventure experience' was last covered in *W&R11* (1988) when the auction of the World War One and 'maritime' replicas was charted. The awesome 'Swarm' offers "a death-defying flight for your life through apocalyptic devastation [including a tasteful airliner crash scene a mere 4 miles from Heathrow] on the UK's first winged roller-coaster" with "nothing above or below you but air..." **www.thorpepark.com**

❑ 'G-SARD'*	Agusta A.109A	~	'Coast Guard' colours, first noted 7-12	[1]	8-13

■ **[1]** The real G-SARD is an AW.139 operating out of Aberdeen.

DUNSFOLD AERODROME or even Dunsfold Park, on the A281 south of Guildford EGTD

Dunsfold Airfield Museum: Within two portable buildings a small volunteer crew maintain a fascinating museum devoted to the airfield's wartime and Hawker heritage.

◆ **Access:** *Open every Wed. Note that the museum is within the security compound and that* **no** *access to other areas of the airfield is permitted* | **www.dunsfoldpark.com**

Aces High: The 747 is kept 'live' and available for film and TV 'set' work. At North Weald, Essex, are the company's DC-4 and C-54. R4D-1 Skytrain ZS-MRU *Jean Batten Clipper* flew out in April 2012 to Lympne and from there departed for New Zealand in October 2012. Sea Harrier FA.2 ZD610 moved to Bruntingthorpe, Leics, on 2nd May 2012.

◆ **Access:** *All visits by prior arrangement* **only** | **www.aceshigh-aviation.com**

❑ G-BDXJ		Boeing 747-236B	N88892	80	ex Air Atlanta Europe, BA G-BDXJ, N1792B. De-reg 12-1-11. Flew in 25-5-05		2-12
❑ WV795		Hawker Sea Hawk ...FGA.6		54	ex Farnborough, Bruntingthorpe, Cranfield, Bruntingthorpe, Bournemouth, Bath, Cardiff-Wales, Culdrose A2661, Halton 8151M, Sydenham, 738, 806, 700. SOC 17-3-71 806 'Ace of Diamonds' c/s		6-13
❑ XL621		Hawker Hunter T.7	G-BNCX	59	ex Brooklands, Bournemouth, G-BNCX, RAE, 238 OCU, RAE. SOC 10-12-86, de-reg 1-3-93. ETPS colours		6-13
❑ '337'		Mil Mi-24 *Hind-D*		~	ex Leavesden, '03 red', North Weald, Chester, Latvia, USSR. (3532461715415)	[1]	6-13
❑ 2100884	'L4-D'	Douglas Dakota 3 ✈	N147DC	42	ex North Weald, Dunsfold, North Weald, G-DAKS (de-reg 5-3-98), , Duxford, '10884', 'KG374', *Airline* 'G-AGHY', TS423, RAE, Ferranti, Airwork, Gatow SF, 436, 1 HGSU, 42-100884. 439th TCG, 91st TCS colours by 6-12		9-13

■ **[1]** The *Hind* was moved to the Bond, James Bond set at Leavesden, Herts, in late 2012, It returned in Hungarian colours.

Brooklands Museum: Thanks to the co-operation of Dunsfold Park, the museum was able to secure one of the last RAF VC-10 K.3s and there are plans to keep it in taxiable condition. When Super VC-10 Series 1154 5H-MOG first flew on 16th February 1970 from Brooklands, it was the last of 54 built; it was delivered to East African Airways 13 days later. Acquired by the RAF in 1977 it was converted to a K.3 tanker and made its final touch-down at Dunsfold on 24th September 2013.

◆ **Access:** *While it is planned to keep ZA150 'live' and stage events around this, at present visits can* **only** *be made by prior arrangement | Full contact details under Brooklands, Surrey* | **www.brooklandsmuseum.com**

❑ ZA150*	'J'	Vickers VC-10 K.3	70	ex Brize Norton, 101, 5H-MOG East African AW. Arrived 24-9-13	9-13

Also: Jetstream T.3 N437SS was broken up and left by road on 15th February 2012. See also Woodmancote, W Sussex.

❑ N437TH	'79'	BAe Jetstream T.3	85	ex Manston, Cranwell, ZE441, Culdrose, 750, *Heron* Flt, 750, *Heron* Flt, 750, G-31-667. SAL-built	9-13
❑ N437UH	'76'	BAe Jetstream T.3	84	ex Manston, Cranwell, ZE438, Culdrose, 750, *Heron* Flt, 750, *Heron* Flt, 750, G-31-647. SAL-built. Fuselage	9-13

EGHAM on the A30 west of Staines

Air Forces Memorial: "He is not missing, he is here." This is a quote from Field Marshal Lord Plumer when he opened the memorial at Ypres in 1927, but it sums up beautifully the role of the famed Runnymede memorial. Here is a tribute to the aircrew of RAF, Commonwealth and allied forces that have no known grave. Currently 20,331 souls are commemorated.

◆ **Access:** *'Brown signed' off the A30/M25 junction to the north of Egham. Access off the A308 Windsor road.* **Open:** *Daily except for Christmas Day and New Year's Day. 1st Nov to 31st Mar: weekdays 09:00 to 16:00, weekends and public holidays 10:00 to 16:00; 1st Apr to 31st Oct: weekdays 09:00 to 18:00, weekends and public holidays 10:00 to 118:00. Note, closing times in each case are as given, or dusk, if earlier.* **Contact:** *Commonwealth War Graves Commission, Cooper's Hill Lane, Englefield Green, Egham, TW20 0LB* | **01784 433329** | **www.cwgc.org**

Jeremy Hall: Using as many original parts as possible, Jeremy has created the forward fuselage (all 21ft of it) of a Lancaster. It 'does the rounds' of shows and events.

❑ –	Avro Lancaster replica	~	*Hi Ho!, Hi Ho!* to port and *Maggie's Murderous Mission* to stb. Forward fuselage	2-09

FAIROAKS AERODROME off the A319, east of Chobham

EGTF

Last noted in February 2008 in use with the rescue crews, the fuselage of Arrow 200 'G-DOAT' (G-BDKV) had moved on, or expired, by early 2013. Gazelle HT.2 XW863 departed on 11th June 2013 for Farnborough, Hampshire.

FARNHAM on the A31 south-west of Aldershot

Dave Hills and **Sue Bush**: Are restoring a Terrier 2 in the neighbourhood.

◆ **Access:** ***Private*** *location, access by prior arrangement* **only** | **hillsdav@googlemail.com**

❑ G-ASYN	Beagle Terrier 2	47	ex Doncaster, Bruntingthorpe, Derby, Southend, Sibson, Auster AOP.6 VF519, 661. Damaged 2-1-76, de-reg 26-10-78	2-12

A collector in the general area has a Lightning cockpit at a *private* location.

❑ XS933	EE Lightning F.6	67	ex Langport, Terrington St Clement, Narborough, Binbrook, 5, 11, BAC, 5, 56, 11. SOC 21-6-88. Cockpit	[1]	2-10

■ **[1]** See under Sunderland, T&W, for *another* 'XS933'.

FRENSHAM on the A287 south of Farnham

A *private* strip in the area holds a couple of 'resting' airframes.

❑ G-ATAG	Jodel DR.1050	61	ex F-BKGG. CEA-built. CoA 4-10-02	9-10
❑ G-AZEY	Beagle Pup 150	69	ex HB-NAK, G-AZEY, VH-EPP, G-35-136. CoA 8-7-08	9-10

GODALMING on the A3100, south west of Guildford

A *private* collector has a Spitfire IX in the *general* area.

❑ SM639	Supermarine Spitfire IX	44	ex Norwich, Russia, USSR, Sov AF, RAF no service	3-06

GODSTONE junction of the A22/A25 east of Redhill

A *private* collector has a Scout in the *general* area.

❑ XV124*	'W'	Westland Scout AH.1	67	ex Tattershall, Ipswich, Arborfield, Middle Wallop, Arborfield, Middle Wallop, Wroughton, 656, 653, 654. First noted 2-13	2-13

HASLEMERE on the A286 south-west of Godalming

Sea Vixen Preservation Group / 1268 Squadron Air Cadets: In Wey Hill, just off the B2131.

❑ XP925		DH Sea Vixen FAW.2	63	ex Farnborough, Tarrant Rushton, FRADU, FRU, 899. SOC 19-11-81. Cockpit	4-11

HORLEY on the A23 north of Crawley

A *private* owner keeps a Tomahawk locally.

❑ G-BRML*		Piper Tomahawk 112	79	ex Wellesbourne Mountford, N2510P. CoA 3-6-02	1-14

MERSTHAM south of the M25, west of the M23 junction

In the grounds of a *private* house in the general area is a much-travelled sort-of Sopwith 1½ Stutter.

❑ 'N5177'		'Sopwith 1½' FSM	~	ex Locks Heath, Bolton, Chorley, Barton, 'B9708', Chelford, Coventry	8-08

MYTCHETT on the B3411 south of Camberley

Defence Medical Services Training Centre and **Keogh Barracks**: are co-located off Mytchett Place Road. Within the complex is a Hunter, set on a circular concrete base. The Wessex is on another parade area, a short distance away. The complex is believed to be up for closure.

❑ XG196	'31'	Hawker Hunter F.6A	56	ex Bracknell 8702M (24-11-81), Kemble, 1 TWU, TWU, 229 OCU, 19	5-13
❑ XR501		Westland Wessex HC.2	63	ex Gosport, Shawbury, 22, 72, 18, 1 FTU, A&AEE. SAR c/s	5-13

REDHILL AERODROME south of South Nutfield, south-east of Redhill EGKR

The remains of Scion II G-AEZF moved to Rochester, Kent, on 12th June 2013. Grasshopper TX.1 WZ816 was exported to Malta by November 2013. Two deletions: Cessna 152 G-BNYN (last noted Mar 2008) and Warrior G-BVIH (Sep 2005).

❑ G-ATBH		Aero 145	65	CoA 26-10-81	1-06

SUNBURY-ON-THAMES south of J1 of the M3

In Fordbridge Road, the B375, **J and C Motor Spares** displays an Adams-Wilson Hobbycopter.

❑ –		A-W Hobbycopter	~	–	7-13

SUTTON

Simon Balch: Is restoring a Scout in the *general* area. Simon's web-site is a shrine to all things P.531, Scout and Wasp.

◆ **Access:** *Private location, visitors by prior arrangement* **only | www.westlandscout.com**

❑ XP853		Westland Scout AH.1	61	ex Dunkeswell, Bramley, Arborfield, Middle Wallop, 655	1-14

WALTON ON THAMES

Adrian Windsor: Has a Hunter cockpit.

❑ E-420		Hawker Hunter F.51	56	ex Marlow, Ascot, Dunsfold G-9-442 (1-5-76), RDanAF E-421. Cockpit	1-14

WARLINGHAM on the B269 east of Coulsdon

A Navajo is stored at a *private* location in the area.

❑ N131MP		Piper Navajo P	74	ex Shoreham, G-BWDE, G-HWKN, HB-LIR, D-IAIR, N7304L. Stored, dismantled	1-11

WEYBRIDGE on the B374 south of the town

Brooklands College: Church Road, Ashford. See also Brooklands, Surrey, for the college Jetstream.

◆ **Access:** *By prior application* ***only*** | **www.brooklands.ac.uk**

❑ XN586 '91' Hunting Jet Provost T.3A 61 ex Cosford 9039M (10-5-90), 7 FTS, 1 FTS, CFS, 2 FTS, RAFC 10-08

WHYTELEAFE on the A22 south-east of Croydon

Gary Brown: The airframe is being completed as a *Battle of Britain* film 'extra'.

◆ **Access: Private** *location, access by prior application* **only** | **messerschmitt.109@btinterent.com**

❑ - Hispano Buchón FSM ~ ex Lingfield, Bf 109G 'FM+BB', Germany 3-12

WOKING on the A320 north of Guildford

Big Apple: The centre in Crown Square is guarded by a pole-mounted Hunter. **www.thebigapple.co.uk**

❑ XL623 Hawker Hunter T.7 59 ex Newton, Cosford 8770M (31-12-82), 1 TWU, 74, 19, 1, 43, 92, 208, 65. Overall 'aluminium' colours [1] 5-13

■ **[1]** See under Poole, Dorset, and Beck Row, Suffolk, for Hunters fitted with XL623's wings.

EAST SUSSEX

Includes the unitary authority of Brighton and Hove

BEXHILL on the A259 west of Hastings

❑ G-ACXE Klemm L25cl Swallow 34 ex 'Hastings', Bagshot, Birmingham. CoA 7-4-40 12-09

BRIGHTON

No.**225 Squadron Air Cadets**: Lewes Road

❑ WD370 DHC Chipmunk T.10 PAX 51 ex Hove, 3 AEF, 2 SoTT, 1 AEF, Hull UAS, 2 BTFS. SOC 12-3-75 5-05

CHAILEY on the A275 north of Lewes

A pair of cockpits are with a *private* collector in the area.

❑ WH964 EE Canberra E.15 55 ex Bruntingthorpe, Cosford 8870M, St Athan, 100, 98, B.15, 98, Akrotiri Wing, 32, B.6, 12. Short-built. Cockpit 12-11

❑ XG195 Hawker Hunter FGA.9 56 ex Sleap, Seighford, Macclesfield, Bitteswell, G-9-453 (12-2-76), 208, F.6, 1, 19. Cockpit 12-11

CROWBOROUGH on the A26 south west of Royal Tunbridge Wells

No.1414 Squadron Air Cadets:

❑ XS510 '626' Westland Wessex HU.5 64 ex Gosport, A2676 [2], A2765 (24-3-88), Lee-on-Solent, 772, Lee SAR Flt, 707, 848 3-13

DEANLAND Last reported in August 2001, Viking Dragonfly II G-BRKY has been deleted.

DITCHLING on the B2112 east of Hassocks

Blackberry Wood: The Wessex has a pair of double beds within and is marketed as the 'Holicopter' in a variety of 'dwellings' offered at the venue. **Access** *By prior arrangement* **only** | **www.blackberrywood.com**

❑ XS886 '27' Westland Wessex HAS.1 66 ex Ipswich, Evesham, Birmingham, Lee-on-Solent A2685 (2-4-80), Wroughton, 771, 706, *Hermes* SAR Flt, 706, 826 1-14

HASTINGS

The former Afghan Hawker Hinds co-ordinated by Patrick Chriswick are stored in a location in this *general* area.

◆ **Access: Strictly private** *location,* **not** *available for inspection*

❑ K5409	Hawker Hind	36	ex Kabul, Afghan AF, RAF, 211, 218, 57, 52	7-10
❑ K5462	Hawker Hind	36	ex Kabul, Afghan AF, India, RAF 113, 15	7-10
❑ K5554	Hawker Hind	36	ex Kabul, Afghan AF, RAF 211, 113, 12	7-10
❑ K6618	Hawker Hind	36	ex Kabul, Afghan AF, India, RAF 211, 98	7-10
❑ K6833	Hawker Hind	37	ex Kabul, Afghan AF, India, RAF 211, 82	7-10
❑ L7191	Hawker Hind	37	ex Kabul, Afghan AF, RAF ME, 21	7-10

HOLLINGTON on the B2159 west of Hastings

St Leonard's Motors: WL345 Meteor came down off its pole on 11th November 2012 and had moved to Wycombe Air Park, Bucks, by the following month.

LEWES on the A27 north-east of Brighton

Airframes are held in *several* locations within the *general* area.

❑ G-AMYL	Piper Vagabond	49	ex N4613H, NC4613H. CoA 20-6-89, de-reg 27-4-06		8-00
❑ G-APNS	Fairtravel Linnet	58	ex Chessington. CoA 6-10-78, de-reg 5-2-09	[1]	8-00
❑ G-AYMU	Jodel D.112	60	ex F-BJPB. Wassmer-built. Damaged 7-1-92, CoA 5-6-92		8-00

■ **[1]** British-built version of the Piel Emeraude.

NEWHAVEN east of Brighton on the A259

Newhaven Fort: Robertsbridge Aviation Society (see below) has a display here. Also within the Fort (but not RAS originated) is a feature on the much-missed Royal Observer Corps and much else on World War Two.

◆ **Open:** *Mar to Oct, daily 10:30 to 18:00 (17:00 in Oct), last entry one hour before closing.* **Contact:** *Fort Road, Newhaven, BN9 9DS* | **01273 517622** | **info@newhavenfort.org.uk** | **www.newhavenfort.org.uk**

ROBERTSBRIDGE on the A21 north-west of Hastings

Robertsbridge Aviation Centre: Run by the Robertsbridge Aviation Society, the museum is a barrage of artefacts covering many aspects of aviation. RAS has a close relationship with Newhaven Fort, East Sussex - qv. A recent 'dig' has produced a substantial amount of remains of 44 Squadron Lancaster III LM650, which crashed near Battle on 1st November 1944 on return from a raid on Dusseldorf.

◆ **Open:** *During the afternoon of the last Sun of the month, Mar to Nov. Plus an annual open day in August.* **Contact:** *Trevor Woodgate, 77 Mongeham Road, Great Mongeham, Deal, CT14 9PD* | **trevorwoodgate@hotmail.co.uk**

❑ WA630	Gloster Meteor T.7	49	ex Newhaven, Robertsbridge, Oakington SF, 4 FTS, 205 AFS, RAFC. SOC 16-11-62. Cockpit	12-13
❑ WE173	EE Canberra PR.3	53	ex Stock, Coltishall, Farnborough, RAE, 39, 69, Upwood SF, 58, 82. SOC 31-3-81. Cockpit	12-13
❑ WN907	Hawker Hunter F.2	54	ex Walpole, Ascot, St Athan, Colerne, Melksham 7416M (1-8-57), 257. Cockpit	12-13
❑ XJ488	DH Sea Vixen FAW.1	58	ex Nottingham, New Milton, Portsmouth, Boscombe Down, A&AEE, 22 JSTU, A&AEE, DH, RRE, A&AEE, RAE, DH. SOC 23-3-72. Cockpit	12-13
❑ XP701	EE Lightning F.3	63	ex High Halden, Hawkinge, Binbrook 8924M (9-2-86), LTF, 5, 11, 56, 29, 111, 29, A&AEE. Cockpit	12-13
❑ XR681	Hunting Jet Provost T.4	63	ex Newhaven, Odiham, Abingdon 8588M, RAFEF, CATCS, 6 FTS, RAFC. SOC 1-10-71. Cockpit	12-13

ST LEONARDS-ON-SEA west of Hastings

Retrotec: The **Historic Aircraft Collection of Jersey** is closely associated – and see under Duxford, Cambs. When restored, the former Swedish Hart will be quite an eye-opener as the sleek looks of the breed's RR Kestrel-engined variants were totally neutered by the radial engined versions. Four Hawker-built Harts were supplied in 1934, followed by 42 licence-built by ASJA and fitted with Nohab-built Bristol Mercury radials. The substantial wreckage was discovered in Sweden in the late 1980s and is *believed* to be an ASJA-built version. The Hart is being rebuilt for Swede Joakin Westh.

◆ **Access: Strictly private** *location,* **not** *available for inspection* | **www.retrotec-ltd.co.uk**

❑ E8894	Airco DH.9	G-CDLI	18	ex India, 47, 30. Vulcan Motor-built		9-13
❑ K5600	Hawker Audax I	G-BVVI	37	ex Kirkham 2015M (18-6-40), SAC, 226. Avro-built. Off-site		4-10
❑ K5674	Hawker Fury I ✈	G-CBZP	35	ex Duxford, St Leonards-on-Sea, SAAF 215, 13, RAF 43. 43 Sqn colours, *Queen of North and South*. First flight 30-7-12. Off-site	[1]	8-12
❑ EF545	Supermarine Spitfire V	G-CDGY	43	ex New Zealand, ZK-MKV, RAAF A58-149, EF545 n/s Westland-built		1-08
❑ -*	Hawker Hart		c36	ex Sweden, RSwAF. See note above		9-13
❑ 1342	Yakovlev Yak-1	G-BTZD	41	ex Sudbury, Audley End, Paddock Wood, USSR		4-10

■ [1] In its original colours, as flown by Fg Off Frederick Rosier, OC 'B' Flight, 43 Sqn, Tangmere, 12-36 to 2-39.

SEDLESCOMBE AERODROME on the B2244 north of Hastings

❑ G-AWFT	Jodel D.9 Bebe		68	CoA 22-7-69	3-07
❑ G-AXPG	Mignet HM.293		71	CoA 20-1-77	10-10
❑ G-BLUL	Jodel DR.1051M		64	ex F-BMPJ. CEA-built. CoA 24-10-91, de-reg 27-6-06	11-01
❑ G-BUNS	Cessna F.150K		70	ex F-BSIL. Reims-built. De-reg 13-5-02	11-01

In the *general* area is a Spitfire restoration project.

❑ BM539	Supermarine Spitfire V	G-SSVB	42	ex G-CGBI, BM539, 19, 485, 610, 411, 242. Crashed 9-7-43	10-13

UCKFIELD Cessna 140 G-BTYX, and a spare fuselage, moved to Spanhoe, Northants, by December 2012.

WANNOCK west of the A22, north of Eastbourne

Foulkes-Halbard Collection: ***Private*** collection ***not*** available for public inspection

❑ G-BHNG	Piper Aztec 250E	74	ex Seaford, Shoreham, N54125. Crashed 19-12-81, de-reg 12-12-86. Fuselage	2-04
❑ –	Halton Jupiter MPA	72	BAPC.127, ex Old Warden, Cranwell, Halton	2-04
❑ –	Aldritt Mono replica	~	IAHC.2,ex Portlaoise	2-04

WEST SUSSEX

BALCOMBE on the B2036, south of Crawley

Wings World War Two Remembrance Museum: Run by Daniel and Kevin Hunt and friends. The quality of displays is excellent, ranging from parts of Hampden I P1273 'PL-Q' salvaged at Petsamo on the Russo-Finnish border, to crash-site relics of a 51 Squadron Halifax and a Chalgrove-based USAAF F-5B Lightning. The museum's previous home of Redhill is not forgotten, and a series of displays are devoted to the wartime history of that airfield.

By mid-2013, the cockpit of C-119F N2700 had moved to Ingatestone, Essex. The stored cockpit of C-47B 'FL586' was disposed of, believed ending up in France.

◆ **Access:** *At Brantridge Lane, off High Beeches Lane. Close to High Beeches Gardens and Nursery and Nymans Garden - both 'brown signed'.* **Please note** *that not all of the airframes listed below will be on public display.* **Open:** *Every Sat and Sun, 10:00 to 17:00, Mar to Oct - see web-site for details. Other times by prior arrangement.* **Contact:** **info@wingsmuseum.co.uk | www.wingsmuseum.co.uk**

❑ G-AIUA	Miles Hawk Trainer III	40	ex Redhill, King's Lynn, West Chiltington, Benington, Bushey, Old Warden, Duxford, Felthorpe, T9768, 10 AGS, 7 FIS, 15 EFTS, Wyton SF. CoA 13-7-67. Fuselage	1-14
❑ G-OJAS	Auster J/1U Workmaster	52	ex Redhill, F-BJAS, F-WJAS, F-OBHT ntu. Frame	1-14
❑ BD731	Hawker Hurricane II	41	ex Redhill, Murmansk, 605, 135. SOC in USSR 16-2-42. Remains, plus other parts	1-14
❑ 339	Nakajima B5N2 *Kate*	c44	ex Redhill, Kurile Island. Front fuselage	1-14
❑ -*	Nakajima Ki-43 Hyabusa	c44	ex Redhill, Kurile Island. Cockpit and wing sections	1-14

❑ -*	Nakajima Ki-43 Hyabusa	c44	ex Redhill, Kurile Island. Cockpit and wing sections		1-14
❑ 200611 '4U-D'	Douglas C-47A-65-DL Skytrain	42	ex North Weald, Woodley, Kew, Cranfield, 6W-SAF, F-GEFU, Le Bourget, Senegalese AF, USAF MAAG Brussels, USAAF 42-100611. *Lilly Bell II*. Cockpit and fuselage	[1]	1-14
❑ 43-11137	Bell P-63C Kingcobra	43	ex Redhill, Kurile Island. Acquired 2003. Cockpit, *LIttle Toots*		1-14
❑ 43-21664	Douglas A-20G Havoc	43	ex Redhill, Russia. Acquired 3-06. Substantial airframe	[2]	1-14
❑ 43-36140	NAA B-25J Mitchell	43	ex Redhill, Kurile Island. Front fuselage		1-14
❑ 44-4315	Bell P-63C Kingcobra	44	ex Redhill, Kurile Island. Remains, acquired 2003		1-14
❑ 64-17657	Douglas B-26K Invader N99218	64	ex Redhill, South Molton, Canterbury, Norwich, Ludham, Booker, Canterbury, Southend, Chino, USAF, USAAF 43-22649. Arrived 2-10. Cockpit	[3]	1-14

■ **[1]** The cockpit of C-47A 6W-SAF has been grafted to the fuselage of C-47B 'FL586' (ex OO-SMA, N99346, Belgian AF K-1 / OT-CWA, 43-49240 - and see notes above) to produce a 'walk-in' exhibit. **[2]** Also with the collection are the 'tail feathers' of A-20C 41-19393, one time BZ501. **[3]** Heavily rebuilt B-26 Invader by On Mark Engineering at Van Nuys, California, given new USAF serial.

BOGNOR REGIS

'Prom Bar': On the Esplanade, has a Bandeirante cockpit above the bar.

❑ G-OHIG	EMBRAER Bandeirante	79	ex Stock, Alton, G-OPPP, XC-DAI, PT-SAB. CoA 30-4-96, de-reg 11-4-01. Cockpit	1-14

BRIGHTON SHOREHAM AIRPORT or, just good old, historic, Shoreham EGKA

Airport Visitor Centre: A wide array of archives and artefacts concerning the incredible history of this aerodrome are on show. 'Flea' BAPC.277 moved on several years back; its place being by an example built by Tony Short.

◆ **Access:** *Near the entrance to the 1930s terminal building.* **Open:** *Weekdays 10:00 to 16:00, weekends 10:00 to 15:00. Guided tours by prior arrangement – see the website.* **Contact:** *Shoreham Airport, BN43 5FF* | **01273 441061** | **visitorcentre@gmail.com** | **www.visitorcentre.info**

❑ ASR	EoN Baby G-ALRU	49	BGA.628, ex Aston Down, G-ALRU. Cr 28-5-71	12-13
❑ –*	Mignet HM.14 'Flea'	c05	see above	12-13

Northbrook College: Last recorded in March 2000 the fuselage of Archer 181 G-OBUS has been deleted.

❑ G-AVKL	Piper Twin Comanche	66	ex OY-DHL, G-AVKL, N8284Y. CoA 27-6-08, de-reg 28-9-07	10-09
❑ G-AWKX	Beech Queen Air A65	68	CoA 25-10-89, de-reg 19-12-90	7-10
❑ G-AWVJ	HP Jetstream T.2 XX475	68	ex Boscombe Down, 750, A&AEE, XX475, N1036S, G-AWVJ. Arrived 20-11-05	5-11
❑ G-BOIU	SOCATA TB-10 Tobago	88	crashed 28-8-04, de-reg 16-2-05. Cockpit	9-06
❑ G-SACD	Cessna F.172H	67	ex G-AVCD. Reims-built. CoA 27-7-00, de-reg 29-11-10	10-09
❑ G-TOBY	Cessna 172B	60	ex Sandown, G-ARCM, N6952X. Crashed 15-10-83. De-reg 27-2-90. Cockpit	6-09
❑ XX491 'K'	HP Jetstream T.1	76	ex Ipswich, Culdrose, Cranwell, 45, 3 FTS, 45, 6 FTS, METS. Arrived 10-11-05	3-12

Also: The Tornado proudly 'guards' the **Transair** shop. The fire dump on the northern perimeter has gained a synthetic burning rig and been tidied up. The following have been deleted: Aztec G-BAUA, Cessna 310G G-BHEH, MD 600N G-THUG and the unidentified Cessna 150.

❑ 'WV514' 'CN'	Percival Provost T.1 G-BLIW	54	ex Irish Air Corps 177. Crashed 16-9-10	6-11
❑ WW447	Percival Provost T.1	55	ex Reading, Exeter, CATCS, CNCS, RAFC. SOC 24-1-69	7-13
❑ XX947	Panavia Tornado P.03	75	ex Ipswich, Cosford, St Athan 8979M, Marham, Warton	7-13

Locally:

❑ XZ459 '126'	HS Sea Harrier FA.2	80	ex Queensbury, Charlwood, St Athan, 809, 800, 801, 899, 800, 801, 800, 801, 800, A&AEE, 801, 899, 801, 899, 809, 800	4-08

CHICHESTER

Chichester College: Westgate Fields, the Department of Travel and Tourism has a 737 fuselage for cabin crew training.

◆ **Access:** *Busy campus, access by prior arrangement* **only** / **www.chichester.ac.uk**

❑ F-GCSL	Boeing 737-222	68	ex Chateauroux, Air Mediterranee, Euralair, United N9028U. Forward fuse. 'Chichester Airways' titles: *Spirit of Chichester*	7-11

Others: An MB.50 is under long-term restoration in the general area.

❑ G-AVKB		Brochet MB.50	48	ex Goodwood, F-PFAL. CoA 30-10-96, de-reg 24-2-09	8-06

CHICHESTER AERODROME The hulk of Tomahawk 112 G-BGRN was cleared from the dump prior to 2010.

COOLHAM on the A272 south of Horsham

Flightdeck Technology, Virtual Flight Centre: Has a 737-800 simulator available for flight training and 'joy-riding'.

◆ **Access:** *By prior arrangement* **only | 08456 800737 | www.virtualflight.co.uk**

❑ EI-CJE		Boeing 737-204	82	ex Prestwick, Ryanair, G-BJCU, EC-DVE, G-BJCU. Cockpit	7-11

FORD north of the A259 west of Littlehampton

Peter Hague: Perched atop a lofty plinth on the appropriately-named *Hunter*ford site on the edge of the former entrance of what was HMS *Peregrine*, the famed FAA station, is Peter's Hunter.

❑ WW654	'834'	Hawker Hunter GA.11	55	ex Oving, Portsmouth, Culdrose A2664, A2753, (11-2-87) FRADU, 738, F.4, 229 OCU, 98, 4, 98. SOC 11-2-87	1-14

HAYWARD'S HEATH on the A272 north of Brighton

No.**172 Squadron, Air Cadets**: Inside the TAVR centre in Eastern Road.

❑ XX520	'A'	SAL Bulldog T.1	73	ex Newton 9288M (1-9-00), EM UAS, CFS, RNEFTS, 2 FTS	9-12

HORSHAM Former Chilean Puma 255 was scrapped during 2012.

LANCING on the A27 east of Worthing

Fw 189 2100 (formerly G-BZKY) was exported to the USA by 2009. Bf 109G-2 13605 restoration project was acquired by M R Oliver in January 2013 and is listed under Knutsford, Cheshire.

LITTLEHAMPTON L-4H Cub G-LFOR was up for sale in 2011 and was sold in Malta in June 2013.

LONDON GATWICK AIRPORT EGKK

❑ G-ARWG	Druine Condor	r61	uncompleted project. De-reg 15-9-62. Fuselage	6-05
❑ G-AXGU	Druine Condor	69	crashed 31-3-75, de-reg 8-3-88. Rollason-built. Fuselage	6-05
❑ G-CEXP	HP Herald 209	68	ex Skyview, ChanEx, I-ZERC, G-BFRJ, 4X-AHO. CoA 7-11-96, de-reg 22-3-96. Skyview colours. Towing training	8-13
❑ I-DAVA*	McDD MD82	86	ex ItAli Airlines. Arrived 10-10, enginelss by 7-13	8-13

SHOREHAM AIRPORT Succumbed to the trends and is now officially Brighton Shoreham Airport - see above.

TANGMERE south of the A27, east of Chichester

Tangmere Military Aviation Museum: The Spitfire prototype full-scale model, previously on loan from the Spitfire Society, was handed over on a permanent basis to the museum on 27th April 2013. In return Spitfire FSM 'BL924' (BAPC.242) was presented to the Spitfire Society that day and by June 2103 had moved to Perranporth, Cornwall. Whirlwind HAS.7 XN299, long suffering from heavy corrosion, was broken up during late 2011, with parts going on to help several other airframes.

◆ **Open:** *Daily 10:00 to 17:30 (10:00 to 16:30 in Feb and Nov). Last admission one hour before closing. Closed Dec and Jan. Parties at other times by arrangement.* **Contact**: *Gamecock Terrace, Tangmere, Chichester, PO20 2ES* | **01243 790090 | info@tangmere-museum.org.uk | www.tangmere-museum.org.uk**

Thinx: *Take in a trip to St Andrew's Church in the village. Close by in Church Lane is a commemorative stone to the airfield and within the churchyard are Commonwealth War Graves Commission graves - Allied and German.*

❑ 'K5054'	Supermarine Spitfire prototype FSM	92	BAPC.214, ex Southampton, Hendon, Thruxton, Middle Wallop, Thruxton, Andover. Arr 1997 - see above	1-14

❑ 'L1679'	'JX-G'	Hawker Hurricane I FSM		92	BAPC.241, ex Chilbolton, Middle Wallop, Thruxton. Arrived 8-94. 1 Sqn colours	[1]	1-14
❑ P3179		Hawker Hurricane I		40	ex Hove, 43. Shot down 30-8-40. Arrived 2003. Cockpit		1-14
❑ EE549		Gloster Meteor IV Special		46	ex Cosford, St Athan, Abingdon, Hendon, St Athan, Innsworth, Fulbeck 7008M, Cranwell, CFE, FCCS, RAFHSF. SOC 10-6-52. Arrived 19-9-92	[2]	1-14
❑ 'VZ440'	'X'	Gloster Meteor F.8	WA984	51	ex 'WA829', Southampton, Wimborne, Tarrant Rushton, 211 AFS, 19. SOC 4-12-61. Arrived 12-90	[3]	1-14
❑ WB188		Hawker Hunter Mk.3		51	ex Cosford, St Athan, Colerne, Melksham, Halton 7154M (10-11-54), Hawker P.1067. Arrived 19-9-92	[2] [4]	1-14
❑ WE113		EE Canberra B.2		52	ex Woodhurst, Wyton, 231 OCU, 100, 85, 98, 231 OCU. Arrived 6-11. Cockpit	[5]	1-14
❑ WK281	'S'	Supermarine Swift FR.5		56	ex Hendon, St Athan, Swinderby, Finningley, Colerne, Northolt 7712M (7-3-61), 79. 79 Sqn colours	[2]	1-14
❑ WP190	'K'	Hunter Hunter F.5		55	ex Quedgeley, Hucclecote, Stanbridge 8473M, Upwood, Finningley, Bircham Newton 7582M (10-9-58), Nicosia, 1. AWA-built. Arrived 2-6-02. 1 Sqn colours, Suez stripes	[6]	1-14
❑ WV332		Hawker Hunter F.4		55	ex Godalming, Dunsfold G-9-406, Halton 7673M (17-1-61), 234, 112, 67. 234 Squadron colours. Cockpit	[7]	1-14
❑ XH313	'E'	DH Vampire T.11	G-BZRD	56	ex Godstone, Booker, Sandtoft, North Coates, St Albans, Hatfield, CATCS, Wattisham SF, 111. SOC 17-12-70. De-reg 22-2-05. Arrived 22-10-08		1-14
❑ XJ580	'131'	DH Sea Vixen FAW.2		60	ex Christchurch, Bournemouth FRL, RAE Farnborough, Llanbedr, 899, 766, FAW.1, 899, 893, 892. SOC 17-12-84. Arrived 27-6-00. 899 Sqn colours		1-14
❑ 'XR753'	'A'	EE Lightning F.53	ZF578	67	ex Quedgeley, Cardiff-Wales, Warton, R Saudi AF 53-670, G-27-40. Last flown 14-1-86. Arrived 6-02. 23 Sqn colours	[6]	1-14
❑ XS511	'M'	Westland Wessex HU.5		64	ex Gosport, A2660 [2], A2750 (18-9-86), Lee-on-Solent, 845. Arrived 2004	[8]	1-14
❑ XV408	'P'	McD Phantom FGR.2		68	ex Fairford, Halton 9165M, Cranwell, Wattisham, 19, 92, 19, 92, 29, 23, 228 OCU, 54, 228 OCU, 6. Arr 30-11-05	[2]	1-14
❑ XV744*		HS Harrier GR.3		69	ex Shrivenham, St Athan 9167M (10-4-93), 233 OCU, GR.1, 1, 233 OCU. Arrived 14-3-13		1-14
❑ ZA195	'002'	HS Sea Harrier FA.2		83	ex Farnborough, Booker, Yeovilton, St Athan, Warton, BAE, 899. Arrived 21-2-08	[9]	1-14
❑ -		EE Lightning CIM		~	ex Haslemere, Farnborough. Arrived 12-08. Cockpit, fully fledged simulator		1-14
❑ 51-9252		Lockheed T-33A-1-LO		51	ex Hailsham, Sculthorpe, French AF. Last flown 25-1-78. Arrived 1985. USAF colours		1-14

■ **[1]** Hurricane 'L1679' built by AeroFab at Thruxton, Hants. **[2]** On loan from the RAF Museum. **[3]** The F.8 is a composite, including items from VZ530. **[4]** Hunter prototype and, as the one-off Mk.3, world airspeed record breaker. See under Coventry, Warks, and Melksham, Wilts, for 'other' 'WB188s'. **[5]** WE113 is on loan from S/L Joe and Pam Marsden. **[6]** The Hunter F.5 and Lightning were donated by Raymond and Meryl Hansed and are located in the Meryl Hansed Memorial Hall. The Lightning is in the markings of F.6 XR753 'A', 23 Squadron. The *real* XR753 can be found at Coningsby, Lincs. **[7]** The Hunter F.4 cockpit is on loan from 1254 Sqn ATC, Godalming, Surrey. The rest became T.68 J-4201 of the Swiss Air Force and is still extant. **[8]** XS511 in on loan from 2464 Sqn ATC, Storrington, W Sussex. **[9]** The 'SHAR' is on loan from GJD Aviation Services - see Basingstoke, Hants.

TURNER'S HILL on the B2110 east of Crawley

At a farm in the general area is a long-retired ST-10.

❑ G-AYKG	SOCATA ST-10 Diplomate	70	ex Somerford, Turner's Hill. Crashed 4-3-75, de-reg 27-6-75	5-11

WEST CHILTINGTON on the B2139 south of Horsham

❑ G-AGOY	Miles Messenger 3	43	ex Hatch, Southill, Castletown, EI-AGE, HB-EIP, G-AGOY, U-0247. CoA 25-11-53, de-reg 20-12-06	1-00

WOODMANCOTE on the A281 east of Henfield

Aviation Trading Ltd: Jaguar GR.1 XX763 is on loan to the Bournemouth Aviation Museum at Bournemouth, Dorset. See also Dunsfold, Surrey. **Access**: *Busy facility, visitors by prior arrangement* **only** | **www.aviationtrading.co.uk**

❑ XX764	'13'	SEPECAT Jaguar GR.1	75	ex Small Dole, St Athan 9010M, ex Shawbury, 226 OCU, 6, 226 OCU, 14. Last flown 3-9-84	7-13
❑ ZE440		BAe Jetstream T.3 N437ZZ	85	ex Shawbury, Yeovilton, 750, Heron Flt, 750, Heron Flt, 750, G-31-659	4-11

WORTHING on the A281 east of Henfield

Saywell International: At the well-known spares and product support specialist's impressive Aviation Centre a 'heritage area' has been established with a Taylorcraft Plus D centre stage as a reminder of the organisation's Auster pedigree.

Access *By prior arrangement **only**.* | **www.saywell.co.uk**

❑ G-AHWJ*		Taylorcraft Plus D	42	ex LB294, West Raynham SF, Milfield SF, 43 OTU, 653. De-reg 11-11-11	10-12

WARWICKSHIRE

BAXTERLEY south of the A5 near Atherstone

The fuselage of Tiger Moth G-AOES moved to Northampton, Northants, during March 2013.

❑ G-ADPC		DH Tiger Moth	35	ex BB852, BRNC, Lossiemouth SF, BRNC, 7 EFTS. CoA 2-8-06	2-12
❑ G-APGL		DH Tiger Moth	44	ex Fairoaks, Mk.II NM140, LAS, AOPS, 14 RFS, 8 RFS, 8 EFTS, 3 EFTS, 22 EFTS, 3 EFTS, ORTU, Tarrant Rushton SF. Morris-built. De-reg 15-3-10	3-00

Staffordshire Aircraft Recovery Team: See also Abbots Bromley and Penkridge, Staffs, and Newport, Shropshire.

❑ G-MMFS		MBA Tiger Cub 440	83	ex Abbots Bromley, Wolverhampton, Otherton. *Black Adder*. CoA 27-7-01, de-reg 11-3-10. Travelling exhibit		3-12
❑ RA-01641	'3'	Antonov An-2 *Colt*	~	ex Wolverhampton. Forward fuselage. Crashed 9-99		1-10
❑ WJ576*		EE Canberra T.17	53	ex Wolverhampton, Bruntingthorpe, Cardiff, St Athan, 360, *Swifter* Flight, 231 OCU. HP-built. SOC 9-3-83. Cockpit		4-13
❑ WN516		BP Balliol T.2	53	ex Haverigg, Sunderland, Failsworth, RAFC. Blackburn-built. SOC 26-6-57. Cockpit		3-12
❑ WN534*		BP Balliol T.2	54	ex Wolverhampton, Bacup, Salford, Failsworth, Silloth, RAFC. Blackburn-built. SOC 26-6-57. Cockpit. Arrived by 4-13		4-13
❑ WZ755	FSC	Slingsby Grasshopper TX.1	52	BGA.3481, ex Wolverhampton, Gallows Hill, Brunton, Barnstaple. CoA 30-4-93	[1]	3-12
❑ XD445*	'51'	DH Vampire T.11	54	ex Abbots Bromley, Hemswell, Cleethorpes, Hatfield, Woodford, Chester, St Athan, 4 FTS, 5 FTS, Bückeburg SF. SOC 18-3-63. 79 Sqn colours. Arrived 5-13	[2]	7-13
❑ XP494*		Slingsby Grasshopper TX.1	61	ex Wolverhampton, Rattlesden, Breighton, Stoke-on-Trent, Syerston, Stamford, Cosford, Ratcliffe, Syerston		4-13
❑ XR662*	'25'	Hunting Jet Provost T.4	63	ex Wolverhampton, Bicester, Kemble, Finningley, Halton 8410M (6-6-74), SoRF, CAW, CATCS, RAFC, CAW, 6 FTS, CAW. Arrived by 4-13	[3]	4-13

■ **[1]** Grasshopper is owned by Peter Alcock. **[2]** Vampire flew in 79 Squadron colours when it served as a 'hack' with the Bückeburg Station Flight. **[3]** 'JP' is owned by Peter Alcock and Vaughan K Meers.

CORLEY MOOR on minor roads south west of the M6's Corley Services,

A farm in the area took delivery of a Wessex during mid-2013.

❑ XR506*	'V'	Westland Wessex HC.2	63	ex Selby, Greatham, Gosport, Cosford 9343M, Shawbury, 72, 60, 72, 18. Arrived 19-6-13	6-13
❑ XV783*	'DD83'	HS Harrier GR.3	70	ex Ipswich, Predannack, Culdrose A2609[3] (16-3-90), Lee-on-Solent, Culdrose SAH, Cosford, 233 OCU, 4, 3, 233 OCU, 1, 233 OCU, 1, 233 OCU, 1417 Flt, 233 OCU, 4, 20, 4. Arrived by 10-13	10-13

COVENTRY AIRPORT or Baginton

EGBE

Resident Percival Prentice G-APJB took to the air from Coventry for a special sortie on 15th April 2011. It was saluting a previous owner/operator, **John Coggins**, a name synonymous with Coventry Airport in the 1960s, 1970s and 1980s. John died that March, aged 74. A former BOAC engineering apprentice, he established Ravenstar Engineering and its off-shoot, City Airways, at Coventry. *Juliet-Bravo* was one of three Prentices he operated; in this case 1973 to 1984. The commute to work was minimal as he lived in Baginton village and there he turned his fascination and expertise in radios into the Aircraft Radio Museum in the former butcher's shop. In 1967 he was a founder-member of the Midland Aircraft Preservation Society (MAPS) - the organisation that established the Midland Air Museum (see below). John was a unique and kindly character, who made his mark on aviation heritage in many ways.

Let's move from commemoration to congratulation. In the autumn of 2013 another founder-member of MAPS and a leading light in the establishment of the Midland Air Museum, **Roger Smith**, had his unstinting pioneering and dedication to the UK's aviation heritage recognised. In what the author considers an unprecedented civic ceremony the Lord Mayor presented Roger with a well-deserved Good Citizen award on behalf of the people of Coventry. (There's plenty of scope for other townships or counties to pat an ALE - see the *Preface* - on the back!)

AIRBASE: The **Classic Aircraft Trust** was formed to look after the caucus of what the author, along with loads of other die-hards, will forever refer to as **Air Atlantique**. Not long after this, it was announced that most of the collection was de-camping to Newquay, Cornwall, under the stunningly unimaginative name of **Classic Air Force**. AIRBASE closed its doors on 30th September 2012. The migration to Newquay has proven to be a major undertaking and by late 2013 the decision was made to keep the Coventry facility as a maintenance centre. **But...** with the infrastructure in place, it made sense to open it up to the public, and from 5th April 2014 it is available for inspection at weekends.

Proctor V G-AKIU first flew following restoration on 28th September 2012 - just two days before the closure. On 2nd May 2013 Vampire T.55 U-1229 flew in from France for work to put it on a UK permit after which it will be ferried to Newquay.

With Dakotas G-ANAF and 'KK116' (G-AMPY) decamped to East Midlands, Leics, by mid-2012, on contract to sister operator Reconnaissance Ventures, it fell to G-AMRA to become the last 'Dak' out of Coventry. *Romeo-Alpha* had been resident since late 1981. Departing for Germany, on 30th July 2013, G-AMRA joined Air Service Berlin, becoming D-CXXX. That said, an organisation called Dakotair, the **RAF Transport Command Memorial**, announced during 2013 its intention to operate *Romeo-Alpha* and *Alpha-Fox* in a passenger-carrying capacity, with North Weald, Essex, as the intended base. As *W&R* closed for press, plans were still in the formative stages: **www.raftransportcommandmemorial.co.uk**

Departures: To Newquay, Cornwall: Dragon Rapide G-AGTM 25-3-13; Proctor V G-AKIU by 4-13; Chipmunk T.10 G-APLO by 4-13; Jet Provost T.3A G-BWDS 4-3-13; Autocrat G-JAYI 5-1-13; Dragon Rapide TX310 (G-AIDL) 14-3-13; Canberra T.4 'VN799' (G-CDSX) by 6-13; Prentice T.1 VR259 (G-APJB) 25-3-13; Meteor T.7 WA591 (G-BWMF) 30-4-13; Hunter GA.11 'WB188' (G-BZPB) 13-7-12; Anson C.21 WD413 (G-VROE) 20-3-13; Terrier 2 WE569 (G-ASAJ) by 7-13; Venom FB.50 'WK436' (G-VENM) by 4-13; Meteor TT.20 WM167 (G-LOSM) 18-5-13; Hunter T.8C WT722 9-7-12; Vampire T.55 'XJ771' 7-2-13; Sea Devon C.20 XK895 13-2-13; Jet Provost T.5A XW433 (G-JPRO) by 7-13; Venom FB.50 cockpit J-1629 by 4-13; Venom FB.50 cockpit J-1649 by 4-13. J/1 Autocrat G-AJRE was de-registered 11-12 and exported to the United Arab Emirates by 9-13. Yak C-11 G-BZMY and Yak-50 G-YKSO were based within the AIRBASE complex, but can now been deleted.

The **Shackleton Trust**, with AEW.2 WR963, and **DC-6 Diner** (G-SIXC) are now listed separately - see below.

◆ **Access:** *Airport well signed from the A45/A423 junction.* **Open:** *Weekends 10:00 to 17:00* ***from 5th April 2014****. Other times by appointment.* **Contact:** *Coventry Airport West, Coventry CV8 3AZ* | **www.classicairforce.com**

❑ G-AKRP		DH Dragon Rapide ✈	45	ex Eaglescott, Sywell, Little Gransden, Germany, CN-TTO, Senegal, F-DAFS, G-AKRP, RL958. CoA 6-1-08	[1]	10-13
❑ G-AKVF		Chrislea Super Ace ✈	48	ex Dunsfold, AP-ADT, G-AKVF	[2] [3]	1-14
❑ G-AORG		DH Sea Heron C.1 ✈	56	ex XR441, *Heron* Flt, 781, G-AORG, G-5-16. Jersey Airlines c/s, *Duchess of Brittany*. CoA 26-6-07	[4]	1-14
❑ G-APRS		SAL Twin Pioneer 3 ✈	59	ex Staverton, G-BCWF, XT610, G-APRS, PI-C430 ntu. *Primrose*. 'Raspberry Ripple' colours. CoA 15-7-08	[2] [3]	1-14
❑ G-APSA	'21'	Douglas DC-6A ✈	58	ex 4W-ABQ, HZ-ADA, G-APSA, CF-MCK, CF-CZY. British Eagle colours. CoA 23-5-09	[5]	1-14
❑ G-ARHW		DH Dove 8 ✈	61	CoA 19-5-06	[2]	10-13
❑ G-AZHJ		SAL Twin Pioneer 3	59	ex Prestwick, Staverton, Prestwick, G-31-16, XP295, Odiham SF, MoA, 1310F, Odiham SF, 230. CoA 23-8-90, de-reg 23-7-97. Off-site	[6]	3-02
❑ G-FLCA		Fleet Canuck	46	ex Turweston, Warwick, Baxterley, Chilbolton, Coventry, Rochester, Blackbushe, CS-ACQ, CF-DQP	[7]	10-13
❑ TX226		Avro Anson C.19	46	ex Duxford, Little Staughton, East Dereham, Colerne 7865M (22-1-65), Shawbury, FTCCF, OCTU Jurby, 187, Hemswell SF, Coningsby CF, CBE. Spares, stored off-site		3-02

❑ TX235		Avro Anson C.19/2	46	ex Caernarfon, Higher Blagdon, Andover, Shawbury, SCS, FCCS, CTFU, OCTU, 64 GCS, 2 GCS. SOC 11-10-65. Stored, off-site		3-02
❑ VP293	'X'	Avro Shackleton T.4	51	ex Duxford, Coltishall, Winthorpe, Coventry, Woodford, Coventry, East Kirkby, Strathallan, RAE, MOTU, A&AEE, MR.1, 206, 42, 224, 236 OCU. SOC 23-5-75. Cockpit, on loan		10-13
❑ VP959	'L'	DH Devon C.2 N959VP	48	ex Wellesbourne, Biggin Hill, N959VP ntu, G-BWFB, VP959, RAE. Stored, off-site		3-02
❑ VP981		DH Devon C.2/2 ✈ G-DHDV	54	ex BBMF VP981, Northolt, 207, 21, WCS, Wildenrath CF, AAFCE, MinTech, AAFCE, Paris Attaché, Hendon SF, AFWE	[8]	3-12
❑ WK163		EE Canberra B.2/6 G-BVWC	55	ex DRA Farnborough, Bedford, RAE, Napier, ASM, MoA. CoA 29-6-08, 617 Sqn colours.	[3] [9]	10-13
❑ 'WR470'		DH Venom FB.50 ✈ G-DHVM	54	ex G-GONE, Bournemouth, Chester, Bournemouth, Swiss AF J-1542. 'Ace of Clubs'	[2] [3]	6-12
❑ XL929		Percival Pembroke C.1 G-BNPU	56	ex Shoreham, Sandown, Shawbury, 60, Kemble, 207, SCCS, TCCS, FCCS, BCCS. De-reg 11-8-88. Stored, off-site		4-06
❑ XL954		Percival Pembroke C.1 G-BXES	57	ex N4234C, Tatenhill, White Waltham, 9042M, Northolt, 60, RAFG CS, 2 TAF CS. CoA 9-5-07	[3] [8]	10-13
❑ XM223		DH Dove 7 G-BWWC	57	ex Cumbernauld, West Freugh, DGTE, T&EE, RAE. Wings from Dove 5 G-APSO. Stored, off-site	[8]	4-10
❑ XV232		HS Nimrod MR.2	69	ex Kinloss, Kin Wing, Kin & St M Wing, Kinloss, 203 Flew in 11-5-10		1-14
❑ XM370*		Hunting Jet Provost T.3A G-BVSP	59	ex Binbrook, XM370, 1 FTS, 7 FTS, Kemble, 2 FTS. CoA 7-10-11. First noted 1-12	[9]	10-13
❑ U-1229*		DH Vampire T.55 G-HATD	59	ex F-AZGU, Swiss Air Force. Federal A/c Factory-built. Arrived 2-5-13	[2]	1-14

■ **[1]** Rapide registered to Eaglescott Dominie Group. **[2]** Registered to Aviation Heritage Ltd. **[3]** Ear-marked for the Classic Aircraft Trust. **[4]** Heron registered to Duchess of Brittany Ltd. **[5]** Registered to Grand Cayman-based G-APSA Ltd. An organisation entitled Cloudmaster plans to operate Sierra-Alpha - more details at **www.cloudmaster.aero**. **[6]** Last registered to the Prestwick Pioneer Preservation Society. **[7]** Fleet registered to Tamyco-Oag. **[8]** Registered to Air Atlantique. **[9]** Canberra registered to Classic Aviation Projects and was operated under the title Canberra Display Team. **[9]** 'JP' registered as H G Hodges and Son.

DC-6 Diner: The restaurant/coffee bar/bar is a popular venue; booking is the best bet!

◆ **Open:** *Wed to Sun - see website for details.* **Contact: 02476 882604 | www.dc6diner.com**

❑ G-SIXC	Douglas DC-6A/B	58	ex Transcontinental, Southern Air Transport, N93459, N90645, CAT B-1006, Royal Air Lao XW-PFZ, CAT B-1006. CoA 4-4-05, de-reg 2-8-11	2-14

Midland Air Museum (MAM), incorporating the **Sir Frank Whittle Jet Heritage Centre**: The Viscount has been fully assembled - no mean achievement - and from the spring of 2013 available for public inspection. The Tornado was acquired from the Leeming-based reduce to produce programme. Several airframes are held in deep store and not available for public inspection; the opportunity has been taken to list these machines separately - see below.

◆ **Access:** *Airport well signed from the A45/A423 junction.* **Open:** *Mon to Sat Apr to Oct 10:00 to 17:00, Sun and Bank Hols 10:00 to 18:00. Nov to Mar daily 10:00 to 16:30. Closed Dec 24-26. Other times by appointment.* **Contact:** *Coventry Airport, Rowley Road, Baginton, Coventry CV8 3AZ* | **02476 301033** | **midlandairmuseum@btconnect.com** | **www.midlandairmuseum.co.uk**

❑ G-AEGV	Mignet HM.14 'Flea'	36	ex Coventry, Knowle, Northampton, Sywell. De-reg 12-37		1-14
❑ 'G-ALVD'	DH Dove 2 G-ALCU	47	ex airfield, VT-CEH. CoA 16-3-73, de-reg 8-9-78. Dunlop c/s		1-14
❑ G-APJJ	Fairey Ultra Light Helicopter	57	ex Heaton Chapel, Coventry, Cranfield, White Waltham, RAE Bedford, RN trials. CoA 1-4-59, de-reg 2-3-73	[1]	1-14
❑ G-APRL	AW Argosy 101	59	ex ABC/Elan, Sagittair, N890U, N602Z, N6507R, G-APRL. *Edna*. CoA 23-3-87, de-reg 19-11-87, flew in 20-1-87		1-14
❑ G-APWN	Westland Whirlwind Srs 3	59	ex Cranfield, Redhill, VR-BER, G-APWN, 5N-AGI, G-APWN. CoA 17-5-78, de-reg 25-6-81, arrived 1984. Bristows colours		1-14
❑ G-ARYB	HS.125 Srs 1	62	ex Hatfield. CoA 22-1-68, de-reg 4-3-69, arrived 2-12-93		1-14
❑ G-BRNM	CMC Leopard	89	ex Bournemouth, Old Sarum. De-reg 31-1-05, arrived 26-3-08		1-14
❑ G-CHNX*	Lockheed Electra 188AF	59	ex Pershore, Bournemouth, Channel Express, EI-CHO, G-CHNX, N5535. CoA 31-10-01, de-reg 12-5-03. First noted 5-13. Cockpit, Evergeen colours		1-14
❑ G-MJWH	Vortex 120 hang-glider	r83	former microlight. Arrived 1989		1-14

❑ ANW		EoN Olympia 2	47	ex BGA.538, G-ALNE, BGA.538. CoA 9-3-04		1-14
❑ –		Slingsby Cadet TX.1	~	'BGA.804'	[2]	1-14
❑ –		Humber-Blériot Monoplane replica	c10	BAPC.9, ex Birmingham, Yeovilton, Wroughton, Yeovilton, Coventry, *Those Magnificent Men*, Old Warden. Arrived 12-91	[3]	1-14
❑ –		Druine Turbulent	c58	BAPC.126, ex Shoreham, Croydon. Rollason-built non-flyer		1-14
❑ F-BGNR		Vickers Viscount 708	54	ex Hatch, Perth, Air Inter. Last flown 8-10-73. Arrived 6-9-07		1-14
❑ EE531		Gloster Meteor F.4	46	ex Bentham, Coventry , Birmingham, Weston Park, Birmingham 7090M, RAE Lasham, A&AEE. SOC 25-8-53. Arrived 1977		1-14
❑ VF301	'RAL-G'	DH Vampire F.1	46	ex Stoneleigh, Debden 7060M (10-8-53), 208 AFS, 595, 226 OCU. EE-built. 605 Sqn colours		1-14
❑ VS623		Percival Prentice T.1 G-AOKZ	49	ex Shoreham, Redhill, Southend, VS623, CFS, 2 FTS, 22 FTS. SOC 11-5-56. De-reg 4-10-61, arrived 26-7-82	[4]	1-14
❑ VT935		Boulton Paul P. 111A	50	ex Cranfield, RAE Bedford. Arrived 13-7-75	[1]	1-14
❑ VZ477		Gloster Meteor F.8	50	ex Kimbolton 7741M, APS, 245. SOC 22-6-62. Cockpit		1-14
❑ WF922		EE Canberra PR.3	52	ex Cambridge, A&AEE, RRE, A&AEE, Wroughton, BP, 39, 69, 58, 1323 Flt, 82. SOC 23-5-75, arrived 24-6-84		1-14
❑ WH646		EE Canberra T.17A	52	ex Wyton, 360, B.2 45, RNZAF, 45, 10, 50. Arr 1995. Cockpit		1-14
❑ WS838	'D'	Gloster Meteor NF.14	54	ex Cosford, Manchester, Cosford, Shawbury, Colerne, RAE Bedford, RRE, MoS, 64, 238 OCU. AWA-built. SOC 9-2-72	[5]	1-14
❑ WV797	'491'	Hawker Sea Hawk FGA.6	54	ex Perth, Culdrose A2627, Halton 8155M (12-3-71), Sydenham, 738, 898, 899, Fleetlands, 787. AWA-built. Arrived 6-2-86		1-14
❑ XA508	'627'	Fairey Gannet T.2	55	ex Yeovilton, Manadon A2472 (12-4-57), 737. Arrived 26-9-82. 737 Sqn colours	[6]	1-14
❑ XA699		Gloster Javelin FAW.5	57	ex Cosford, Locking 7809M (14-2-64), Shawbury, Kemble, Shawbury, 5, 151. AWA-built. Arrived 9-81. 5 Squadron colours		1-14
❑ XE855		DH Vampire T.11	54	ex Upton-by-Chester, Woodford, Chester, 27 MU, 22 MU, 10 MU, AWOCU. SOC 30-10-67, arrived 28-8-82. Pod		1-14
❑ XF382	'15'	Hawker Hunter F.6A	56	ex Brawdy, 1 TWU, TWU, 229 OCU, FCS, 65, 63, 92. AWA-built. SOC 10-7-84. Arrived 1-12-86	[7]	1-14
❑ XJ579		DH Sea Vixen FAW.2	60	ex Farnborough, A&AEE, Llanbedr, 899, 766. Arrived 18-8-92. Cockpit		1-14
❑ XK789		Slingsby Grasshopper TX.1	55	ex Warwick, Cosford, Stamford		1-14
❑ XL360		Avro Vulcan B.2	62	ex 44, 101, 35, 617, 230 OCU, Wadd Wing, 230 OCU, Scamp W, 617. Flew in 4-2-83. *City of Coventry*. 617 Sqn colours		1-14
❑ XN685	'703'	DH Sea Vixen FAW.2	61	ex Chester, Cosford, Cranwell 8173M (3-8-71), 890, 766, 893, HSA. Arrived 14-9-92		1-14
❑ XR635*		Westland Scout AH.1	65	ex Coventry, Ipswich, Arborfield, Yeovilton, Middle Wallop, 653, 660. Arrived 10-9-12	[8]	5-13
❑ XR771	'BF'	EE Lightning F.6	66	ex Binbrook, 5, 11, 5, 56, 74. SOC 21-6-88, arrived 15-7-88		1-14
❑ XX899		HS Buccaneer S.2B	76	ex Kidlington, Stock, St Athan, Lossiemouth, 208, 12, Gulf Det, 237 OCU, 12, 237 OCU, 12, 237 OCU, 16, 15, 12, 208. SOC 10-10-94. Arrived 4-96. Cockpit	[9]	1-14
❑ ZA452*	'021'	Panavia Tornado GR.4	83	ex Leeming, 2, GR.1, 31, 15. Gutted fuselage. Arrived 9-13	[10]	1-14
❑ ZE694		HS Sea Harrier FA.2	88	ex Yeovilton, 801, 800, 801, 800, 801, 899, 800, 801, 800. Arrived 16-2-05		1-14
❑ –		Bristol Beaufighter	~	ex Birmingham, Coventry. Arrived 10-89. Cockpit	[11]	1-14
❑ –		Hunting Jet Provost SIM	~	procedure trainer		1-14
❑ –		BAe Harrier GR.5	~	procedure trainer		1-14
❑ 8449M*		Beagle 206-1 G-ASWJ	65	ex Bristol, Halton 8449M (9-8-76), Rolls-Royce. CoA 30-1-75, de-reg 9-9-75. First noted 2-13		1-14
❑ 17473		Lockheed T-33A-1-LO	51	ex Cosford, Sculthorpe, French AF, USAF 51-7473. Last flown 30-5-78, arrived 26-10-93. CAF colours	[8]	1-14

❑ R-756		Lockheed F-104G Starfighter		64	ex Aalborg, Danish AF, 64-17756. Arrived 30-4-87, air freight by RDanAF C-130H	[8]	1-14
❑ 'GN-101'		Folland Gnat F.1	XK741	57	ex Leamington Spa, Fordhouses, Dunsfold, Hamble, Boscombe Down, Dunsfold. SOC 10-11-61 *Kreivi von Rosen*, Finnish AF colours. Fuselage		1-14
❑ 70		Dassault Mystère IVA		c59	ex Sculthorpe, French AF. Last flown 3-5-78, arrived 1979. Patrouille de France colours	[8]	1-14
❑ 280020		Flettner Fl 282B V-20 Kolibri		44	ex Coventry, Cranfield, Brize Norton, Travemünde 'CJ+SN'. Frame	[1]	1-14
❑ 0-82062		DHC U-6A Beaver		58	ex Mannheim, US Army, 58-2062. Arrived 10-7-81	[8]	1-14
❑ 51-4419		Lockheed T-33A-1-LO		51	ex Sculthorpe, French AF. Last flown 25-1-78, arrived 1979. USAF colours	[8]	1-14
❑ 54-2174		NAA F-100D-16-NA		54	ex Sculthorpe, French AF, USAF 54-2174. Last flown 22-2-77. Arrived 27-4-78. *Carol Anne*. USAF c/s	[8]	1-14
❑ '1706'		PZL Iskra 100	408	~	ex airfield, Scampton, Duxford, Polish AF 408. On loan		1-14
❑ 55-713	'C'	EE Lightning T.55	ZF598	67	ex Warton, ZF598, R Saudi AF 55-713, G-27-72. Last flown 14-1-86. Saudi colours		1-14
❑ 29640	'08'	SAAB J29F 'Tunnen'		c54	ex Southend, R Swedish AF. Arrived 27-4-85		1-14
❑ 0242	'FU-242'	NAA F-86A-5-NA Sabre		48	N196B, ex Duxford, Chino, 48-0242. Arrived 22-4-05	[12]	1-14
❑ 37699		McD F-4C-21-MC Phantom		63	ex Upper Heyford, Fairford, Illinois ANG, 55th7 TFS, 356th TFS, 480th TFS, USAF 63-7699. Arrived 7-10-93. 366th TFW colours, MiG 'killer'	[8]	1-14
❑ 60312		McD F-101B-80 Voodoo		56	ex Alconbury, Davis-Monthan, Kentucky ANG, USAF 56-0312. Arrived 4-92	[8]	1-14
❑ 62-4535		Kaman HH-43B Huskie		52	ex Woodbridge, 40 ARRS, Det 2. Arrived 6-3-81	[8] [13]	1-14
❑ -	'06 red'	Mil Mi-24 *Hind-D*	3532464505029	c77	ex Rochester, Chester, Latvia, USSR. Arrived 15-9-05. BAE Systems colours	[14]	1-14
❑ 959		MiG-21SPS *Fishbed*		c66	ex Duxford, Cottbus, East German AF		1-14

■ **[1]** Airframes on loan from Cranfield University, Beds. **[2]** See under Keevil, Wilts, for the real BGA.804. **[3]** Humber on loan from the Shuttleworth Collection, Beds. It was assembled from the Goldsmith cache of Blériot parts/airframes at Old Warden in 1959. At Coventry, it was fitted with an original Humber engine, loaned from Coventry Museum, to represent a 1911 Humber-Blériot. **[4]** VS623 is fitted with the wings from G-AONB (VR244). **[5]** WS838 is on loan from the RAF Museum, Hendon. **[6]** Gannet T.2 is on loan from FAAM, Yeovilton. **[7]** Airframes from the National Museum of the USAF's Loan Program - a large number of RAF Hunters were MDAP funded. **[8]** The Scout is on loan from Coventry University - see Coventry, W Mids) and used as a teaching aid. **[9]** Buccaneer cockpit, a Gulf War veteran, is on loan from Robin Phipps - see also under Steventon, Oxfordshire. **[10]** Tornado credited with 32 'ops' during the 1st Gulf War, deployed to Tabuk, Saudi Arabia, from 8-90; carrying the code 'GK', this gave rise to one of the two names it carried on the nose, *Gulf Killer*; the other being *I Luv Gaynor XX*. **[11]** Beaufighter cockpit is *possibly* Mk.I T5298. In which case it was previously 4552M and TFU Defford. **[12]** The Sabre is on loan from the IWM, Duxford. **[13]** HH-43B uses parts from 24538, including the fins. **[14]** *Hind* on loan from BAE Systems.

Deep store: The following are *not* available for public inspection.

❑ G-EBJG	Parnall Pixie III		24	ex Coventry, Stratford. CoA 2-10-36, de-reg 1-12-46. Remains		1-14
❑ G-ABOI	Wheeler Slymph		r31	ex Coventry, Old Warden. De-reg 1-12-46	[1]	1-14
❑ –	Crossley Tom Thumb		37	BAPC.32, ex Coventry, Bewdley, Coventry, Banbury	[2]	1-14
❑ XD626	DH Vampire T.11		54	ex Bitteswell, Shawbury, CATCS, CNCS, 5 FTS, RAFC, CFS. SOC 19-7-67, arrived 10-8-82. Spares recovered		1-14
❑ XK907	Westland Whirlwind HAS.7		57	ex Bubbenhall, Panshanger, Elstree, G-AYXT ntu, Luton, ETPS, RRE Pershore, Alvis. Last flown 30-10-68. Arrived 8-3-81. Cockpit, spares recovered	[3]	1-14
❑ 37414	McD F-4C-15-MC Phantom		63	ex Woodbridge, New York ANG, USAF 63-7414. Arrived 15-92	[4]	1-14
❑ 70270*	McD F-101B-80-MC Voodoo		57	ex fire crews, MAM, Woodbridge, Davis-Monthan, Texas ANG, USAF 57-0270. Forward fuselage. Returned 5-13		1-14

■ **[1]** On loan from the estate of the late Air Cdre Alan Wheeler. **[2]** The Crossley is an unfinished 1930s homebuild, from Banbury. **[3]** See Weston-super-Mare, Somerset, for the *real* G-AYXT. **[4]** F-4C from the National Museum of the USAF's Loan Program.

Shackleton Preservation Trust: On 15th December 2012 the trustees decided to work towards putting WR963 back into the air; and it was placed on the UK civil register in February 2013. This does *not* mean that it *will*; the work is to assess what is needed, especially in terms of 'paperwork'. Stay tuned! This is a good place to also 'plug' the **Shackleton Association** which serves to unite air and ground crew and all interested in the 'Shack' and produce the magazine, *The Growler*. (Peter Dunn, *Meadow View*, Parks Lane, Prestwood, Great Missenden, Bucks HP16 0JH.) | **admin@shackleton963.co.uk** | **www.shackleton963.co.uk** **Access:** *visits by prior appointment* **only**

❑ WR963	'B-M'	Avro Shackleton AEW.2 G-SKTN	54	ex N953WR ntu, Waddington, Lossiemouth, 8 *Ermintrude*, 205, 28, 210, 224. *Gp Capt Dave Hencken*	1-14

Also: ATP G-BTPG had returned to service by late 2011. The magnificent Electras have been culled: G-LOFA and G-OFRT were scrapped before the end of 2008; G-FIJV was scrapped during May 2013; N4HG was ferried to Canada, leaving 30-6-11 and becoming C-FIJV. Not recorded since March 2000, AA-5 G-BDCL has been deleted. The cockpit of F-101B 70270 returned to MAM (above) in early May 2013.

❑ G-AVDB	Cessna 310L	67	ex Popham, Perth, N2279F. CoA 8-7-79, de-reg 6-8-79. Cockpit [1]	11-08
❑ G-BPJF	Piper Tomahawk 112	78	ex N9312T. Crashed 20-6-98, de-reg 2-10-98. Fire crews	3-02
❑ G-BTPJ	BAe ATP	89	ex Southend, EC-HFR, G-BTPJ, N386AE ntu. CoA 9-7-99	8-13
❑ G-BTPL	BAe ATP	91	ex Southend, EC-HES, G-BTPG, PH-MJK ntu, EC-GLH, G-BTPL, G-11-042. CoA 1-6-08	8-13
❑ G-BWPG	Robin HR.200	96	ex Inverness. Crashed 29-10-97, de-reg 26-1-98. Off-site	3-02
❑ G-JEMC*	BAe ATP	90	ex N856AW, G-11-032. CoA 14-4-10. First noted 4-10	8-13
❑ G-LOFB	Lockheed L.188CF Electra	61	ex Atlantic, N667F, N133AJ, CF-IJW, N131US. CoA 8-2-11	2-13
❑ G-LOFF	Lockheed L.188CF Electra	61	ex Fred Olsen LN-FON, N342HA, N417MA, OB-R-1138, HP-684, N417MA, CF-ZST, N7142C. De-reg 2-6-08	11-11
❑ G-MANC*	BAe ATP	92	ex VT-FFA, G-MANC, G-LOGF, G-11-054. CoA 20-10-03	10-13
❑ G-OAAF	BAe ATP	90	ex Atlantic, G-JEMB, N855AW, G-11-029. CoA 12-7-11	9-11
❑ G-OBWP*	BAe ATP	92	ex VT-FFC, G-OBWP, G-BTPO, G-5-051. First noted 4-10	10-13
❑ LZ-BPS*	BAe ATP	88	ex SX-BPS, SE-MAM, G-MANM, SX-BTK, G-MANM, G-OATP, G-BZWW, N375AE. First noted 1-12	8-13

■ [1] The cockpit of *Delta-Bravo* is with Aviation Optical and Medical and used as a rig to assess pilots' eyesight.

KENILWORTH west of the A46, south west of Coventry

Midland Aircraft Recovery Group: The group also has a wing, centre section and cockpit floor, parts of the tail and a rear turret for a long-term AW Whitley project. Much of this is currently on show by the Wartime Aircraft Recovery Group at Sleap, Shropshire. See under Bruntingthorpe, Leics, for MARG's Harvard cockpit.

◆ **Access:** *Visits by prior appointment* **only**. **Contact:** *Mark J Evans, Spring View, Crackley Lane, Kenilworth, CV8 2JS* | **mark.evans@couplandbell.com**

❑ Z1206	Vickers Wellington IV	41	ex Isle of Lewis, 104 OTU, 142. Cr 26-1-44. Forward fuselage	1-14
❑ AT605	Airspeed Oxford I	41	ex Canada, 36 SFTS. DH-built. Stored	1-14
❑ EB518	Airspeed Oxford V	42	ex Canada, RAF. Under restoration, off-site	1-14

KING'S COUGHTON Note recorded since April 2009, Whittaker MW-6S G-MZDI has been deleted.

LONG MARSTON AERODROME on the B4632, south-west of Stratford-upon-Avon

❑ G-MMUD*		Willmott Junior Cub	r84	de-reg 23-4-90	6-12
❑ G-MNBR		Mainair Gemini Flash	85	CoA 5-2-94, de-reg 31-5-00	7-05
❑ G-MYBZ		Solar Wings Pegasus XL-Q	92	CoA 27-9-97	7-05
❑ G-RACA	'571'	Percival Sea Prince T.1	52	ex Staverton, Kemble, WM735, 750, BTU, A&AEE. SOC 16-9-80, de-reg 28-11-95. Shark's mouth artwork	8-13
❑ WL332		Gloster Meteor T.7	52	ex Cardiff-Wales, Croston, Moston, FRU, Lossiemouth SF, Ford SF. SOC 11-3-69	8-13
❑ WR985	'H'	Avro Shackleton MR.3/3	58	ex Cosford 8103M (8-9-70), 201, 120, 206, 203, 206, A&AEE, 206	8-13
❑ XP346		Westland Whirlwind HAR.10	62	ex Tattershall Thorpe, Shawbury, Lee-on-Solent, Akrotiri 8793M (2-9-83), 84, 22, 225	8-13

RUGBY

The airframes are stored at a *private* location in the *general* area.

❑ '5964'	Airco DH.2 replica	77	BAPC.112, ex Middle Wallop, Chertsey. Wreck	5-05
❑ XP244	Auster AOP.9	61	ex Middle Wallop,'M7922', Arborfield 7864M (13-5-65), St Athan, 653, 8 Ind Recce Flt. Fuselage	5-05
❑ XR239	Auster AOP.9	61	ex Popham, Middle Wallop. SOC 8-6-64. Frame	5-05

STOCKTON east of the A426 north of Southam

Richard Adams: Has a Vampire T.11 pod for conversion to a simulator.

❑ WZ553	'40'	DH Vampire T.11 G-DHYY	53	ex Coventry, G-DHYY, Bournemouth, Bruntingthorpe, Cranfield, Lichfield, Winthorpe, South Wigston, Bruntingthorpe, Loughborough, E Midlands, Speke, Woodford, Chester, St Athan, 4 FTS, 7 FTS, 202 AFS. SOC 2-12-68, de-reg 7-11-02. Pod	3-10

STRATFORD-UPON-AVON

Peter Turner: Stored off-site, Gemini 1A G-AKDK was moved to Coventry on 1st November 2013 en route to Seaton Ross, E Yorks, for restoration on behalf of the Classic Air Force. It may well be than another of the breed is in the pipeline!

◆ **Access:** *Strictly* **private** *workshop, visits* **not** *possible*

❑ G-AKDF	Miles Messenger 4A	47	ex Hadlow Down, Rush Green, Fyfield, White Waltham, Shoreham. Sections and outer wings	[1]	2-14
❑ VH-BOB	Miles Gemini 1A G-AKHU	47	ex Australia, VH-BMV, G-AKHU		2-14
❑ VH-GBB	Miles Gemini 1A G-AKEN	47	ex Australia, VH-BTP, G-AKEN		2-14
❑ VP-KJL	Miles Messenger 4A G-ALAR	48	ex Redhill, Woodley, Stoke-on-Trent, Coventry, G-ALAR, RH371, BAFO CW, AEAF CS		2-14

■ **[1]** For *Delta-Fox*, see also Hooton Park, Cheshire. This was cancelled as permanently withdrawn from use 27-4-73; but is made of sterner stuff! Peter also has the tail sections of Messenger 2As G-AILL and G-AKAV. For *Lima-Lima*, see also Hooton Park, Cheshire.

WARWICK

At a *private* airstrip in the *general* area are a number of restoration projects. Also listed under the heading in editions long since gone by were a pair of gliders, an anonymous Hutter H.17 and the Nyborg TGN.II. Last physically noted in January 1992, it is best these are deleted.

❑ G-AAOR*	DH Moth	29	ex EC-AAO. CoA 17-11-05	4-13
❑ G-AFSV*	Chilton DW.1A	39	ex 'Coventry'. CoA 12-7-72	4-13
❑ G-AVPJ*	DH Tiger Moth	43	ex Mk.I NL879, RAFC, Yeovilton SF, BRNC, Arbroath SF, 727, 780, 798, 4 EFTS. Morris-built. Crashed 13-4-09, CoA 5-9-10	4-13
❑ G-PFAR*	Isaacs Fury II	84	CoA 9-6-07	4-13

WELLESBOURNE MOUNTFORD AERODROME south of the B4086, E of Stratford EGBW

Wellesbourne Wartime Museum: Operated by the **Wellesbourne Aviation Group**, the Museum charts the history of the airfield centred on the restored underground Battle Headquarters. Steve Austin re-located to Stranraer, Scotland, and took with him his Vulcan B.1 cockpit XA903, on 11th April 2011.

◆ **Open:** *Every Sun and Bank Hols 10:00 to 16:00*. **Contact:** *Derek Powell, 167 Colebourne Road, Kingsheath, B13 0HB*

❑ RA-01378	'14'	Yakovlev Yak-52	83	ex Sov AF	9-13
❑ WV679	'O-J'	Percival Provost T.1	54	ex Dunkeswell, H' Blagdon, Halton 7615M (13-10-59), 2 FTS	5-13
❑ XJ575	'SAH-13'	DH Sea Vixen FAW.2	60	ex Long Marston, Helston, Culdrose SAH, A2611, 766, 890, 893, FAW.1, 766. SOC 24-3-71. Cockpit	5-13
❑ XK590	'V'	DH Vampire T.11	56	ex Witney, Brize Norton, CATCS, 4 FTS, 7 FTS. SOC 6-2-70	5-13

XM655 Maintenance and Preservation Society: XM655 is owned by John Littler of Radarmoor, the airfield owners. There will be a big 'bash' in June 2014, celebrating XM655's 50th birthday and her 30th year at Wellesbourne.

◆ **Access:** *Safety considerations excepted, open for visits almost every Saturday. Large groups should make prior arrangements. Occasional ground-running days.* **Contact:** *Wellesbourne Aerodrome, Loxley Lane, Warwick, CV35 9EH* | **email via website** | **www.xm655.com**

❑ XM655	Avro Vulcan B.2 G-VULC	64	ex N655AV ntu, 44, 101, 50, 12, 35, 9. SOC 11-2-84, de-reg 25-3-02	1-14

Also: Chipmunk G-APPA moved to Cotswold, Glos, by May 2012. Last noted in May 2009, Luton Minor G-ASXJ has been deleted. Cessna 152 G-BNIV was flying again by 2012. By late 2010 Tomahawk G-BSYM had been removed from the dump.

WILTSHIRE

Includes the unitary authority of Swindon

AMESBURY on the A303 west of Andover

Gary Dean: For several years, Gary has been developing an exceptionally detailed P-51D cockpit procedure trainer. This fine creation easily merits its own listing. It is kept at a *private* location.

❑ '44-11175'*		NAA P-51D Mustang SIM	10	see above	6-12

BOSCOMBE DOWN AIRFIELD south of the A303 at Amesbury EGDM

Boscombe Down Aviation Collection: In April 2012, when *W&R23* was closing for press, the prognosis for BDAC was dire; it looked as the collection was heading for fragmentation. A search for a relevant, affordable, publically-accessible and practical venue was rewarded when the agreement to lease a World War One hangar at delightful Old Sarum, was secured in early June 2012 - perilously close to BDAC's 'sell by' date at Boscombe. Not content with the prospect of moving lock, stock and barrel, the BDAC team started handing out cards announcing it was open to the public at the new location from 1st July! This they achieved, with just a few airframes unmoved by that date.

Departures: To Old Sarum, Wilts, by 1-7-12 were the following (cockpits marked #): BE.2b FSM '2783'; Canberra B.2# WH876; Canberra T.4# WJ865; Supermarine 544# WT859; Sea Hawk FGA.4 WV910#; Swift F.7# XF113; Hunter F.6A XF375; Hunter F.6 XG290#; Sea Vixen FAW.1# XJ476; Jet Provost T.3A# XN503; Jet Provost T.4 XR650; Jet Provost T.5# XS231; Andover CC.2# XS790; Wasp HAS.1 XT437; Harrier GR.3# XV784; Jaguar S.06# XW560; Hawk T.1# XX343; Jaguar GR.1A# XX761; BAC 111-402# XX919; Sea Harrier FA.2 XZ457; Tornado F.2# ZD936; Jindivik 3A A92-664. And by 8-12: Chipmunk 22 G-BDCC, Meteor D.16 WK800, Lightning F.2A# XN726 and the final move was made by Sycamore HR.14 XJ380 on 22-8-12.

Air Defence Collection: Tony Dyer's superb work has previously been listed under this heading. As Tony has a close co-operation with BDAC, with some airframes on loan to that collection, the opportunity has been taken to list ADC under Old Sarum as well. Accordingly, the cockpits of Hurricane I P3554 and Hunters F.1 WT648 and F.2 WN890 can be found under Old Sarum, Wilts.

MoD Boscombe Down: Home of the **Aircraft Test and Evaluation Centre** and the privately-owned defence technology and security specialists **QinetiQ Group plc**, plus a 'lodger' unit, the **Joint Aircraft Recovery and Transport Squadron** (JARTS) previously at St Athan, Wales. The bread and butter of JARTS work is the moving of airframes by road and loads-in-transit can be found 'over-nighting' or staying for longer periods; only long-termers are given here. Within Hangar 104 is the **Apprentice Training Centre** (ATC).

W&R23 (p262) reported the scrapping of BAC 111 XX105 on 18th December 2011. That was close, the deed was actually done on the 17th and the aircraft left in skips on the 19th. BAC 111 ZE432 was *not* scrapped at the same time - see below. Basset CC.1 XS770 (G-HRHI), last noted July 2009, was reduced to spares, for the 'fly-by-wire' XS743. Last noted as far back as June 2001 the Scout hulk on the dump has long since gone.

Departures: **BAC 111**-479 ZE433 was scrapped 1-6-13; **Harrier** GR.3 XW917 moved to Swanwick, Hants, 7-8-12; **Phantom** FG.1 XT597 and FGR.2 XV401 were 'stay behinds' when BDAC moved to Old Sarum (see above), they left for Ipswich, Suffolk on 17-09-13 and during 8-13 respectively; **Tornado** GR.1 ZA326 to Bruntingthorpe, Leics, 1-10-13. *W&R23* (p263) recorded the arrival of Jindivik 3 A92-255 from Aberporth, Wales, by 2011; this was not so, it moved to Selby, N Yorks, in 6-11.

❑ XL629		EE Lightning T.4	59	ex ETPS, A&AEE. Last flight 3-11-75. Gate guardian		7-13
❑ XS180	'21'	Hunting Jet Provost T.4	63	ex '8238M', St Athan 8338M (6-8-73), Lyneham, St Athan, Halton, Kemble, CAW, 6 FTS. Travels, rescue exercises. JARTS		5-13
❑ XS596		HS Andover C.1PR	67	ex DERA etc, A&AEE, 60, 115, 46, Thorney Island SF, Abingdon SF, Andover Tng Sqn, 46, A&AEE. 'UK Open Skies' colours. Stored		5-13
❑ XS646*		HS Andover C.1	68	ex DERA etc, RAE, 84, 46. Stored, first noted 4-12		12-13
❑ XS765*		Beagle Basset CC.1 G-BSET	64	ex Cranfield ETPS, 26, 207, 32, MCS, SCS, NCS, HS. CoA 28-7-98, de-reg 25-3-04. Spares for XS743, f/n 8-04		6-12
❑ XW175*		HS Harrier T.2(mod)	69	RAE, HSA. VAAC test-bed. wfu 19-11-10. ATC		5-13
❑ XW299*	'MB'	BAC Jet Provost T.5A	70	ex Selby, Cosford, Halton, 9146M (18-5-92), 1 FTS, RAFC, 1 FTS. Arrived 24-1-14		1-14
❑ XW906	'J'	Sud Gazelle HT.3	74	ex Shawbury, 2 FTS, CFS. Westland-built. Pod, ATC	[1]	2-13
❑ XX705	'5'	SAL Bulldog T.1	75	ex Southampton UAS, Birm UAS. ATC		2-13
❑ XZ209		Westland Lynx AH.7	79	ex St Athan, Fleetlands, Middle Wallop, 655, 656, 4 Rgt, 3 Rgt, 662, 659. JARTS		4-13

❑ XZ646		Westland Lynx AH.7	80	ex St Athan, Fleetlands, Yeovilton, 847, 657, 656, 664, 656, 3 Rgt, 1 Rgt, 4 Rgt, 669, 654, 4 Rgt, 654. Crashed 21-2-05. Cabin, JARTS		9-12
❑ ZA144		Vickers VC-10 K.2	63	ex St Athan, 101, A40-VC, G-ARVC. Forward fuselage, JARTS		10-13
❑ ZD285*		Westland Lynx AH.5X	85	ex A&AEE, RAE Farnborough. Stored	[2]	2-13
❑ ZD559*		Westland Lynx AH.5X	85	ex ETPS, RAE Bedford. Retired by 2-13. ATC	[2]	2-13
❑ ZD560*		Westland Lynx AH.5X	87	last flown 28-3-12. Stored	[2]	2-13
❑ ZD899		Panavia Tornado F.2	84	ex Warton trials fleet. Stored, camouflaged		2-13
❑ ZD902*		Panavia Tornado F.2A	84	ex DERA. Ground rig	[3]	5-13
❑ ZD993	'723'	HS Harrier T.8	87	ex Yeovilton, 899, 233 OCU. ATC		5-13
❑ ZE432*		BAC 111-479	73	ex ETPS, DQ-FBV. Stored, engineless		12-13
❑ ZJ652		Dassault Alpha Jet	~	ex Furstenfeldbruck, Luftwaffe 41+09. Spares		9-08
❑ ZJ653		Dassault Alpha Jet	~	ex Furstenfeldbruck, Luftwaffe 40+22. Spares		9-08
❑ ZJ654		Dassault Alpha Jet	~	ex Furstenfeldbruck, Luftwaffe 41+02. Spares		9-08
❑ ZJ655		Dassault Alpha Jet	~	ex Furstenfeldbruck, Luftwaffe 41+19. Spares		9-08
❑ ZJ656		Dassault Alpha Jet	~	ex Furstenfeldbruck, Luftwaffe 41+40. Spares		9-08

■ **[1]** XW906 is fitted with the boom of ZA804 - see below. [2] The Lynx AH.5X were interim airframes prior to the AH.7. ZD285 has a substantially modified nose section. **[3]** The one-off F.2A was heavily modified to TIARA status - Tornado Integrated Avionics Research Aircraft. While grounded, it is kept 'live' for trials.

Solstice Business Park: Just off the A303, at the end of the westbound sliproad to the services, within sight of the airfield.

❑ ZA804	'I'	Sud Gazelle HT.3	ex airfield, Shawbury, 2 FTS, CFS. Westland-built	[1]	12-13

■ **[1]** Much-altered, but very effective, the Gazelle forms a 'sculpture' that is part helicopter, part dragonfly. It was officially unveiled 11-6-07. The original boom of ZA804 is fitted to XW906 - see above.

CLYFFE PYPARD on minor roads south-east of Lyneham

Imperial Airways Museum: Neil Farley launched this tribute to an iconic airline in early 2013 with a view to opening to the public during the summer of 2014. Central to the displays, backed by an impressive archive, will be a replica of the Croydon Airport booking office and a replica HP.42 forward fuselage cabin section. Set in the grounds of the 'Goddard Arms', the pub itself also holds other aviation artefacts.

◆ **Access:** *Planned opening, summer 2014; by prior application* **only**| **Contact:** c/o Goddard Arms, Wood Street, Clyffe Pypard, SN4 7PY | **01793 731386** | **info@imperial-airways.co.uk** | **www.imperial-airways.gb.com**

CRICKLADE south of the A419 between Cirencester and Swindon

A yard that borders the A419 near the town holds four Little Rissington 'refugees'.

❑ G-ARJB*	DH Dove 8		ex Little Rissington, Kemble, Cumbernauld, Carlisle, Rocester, East Midlands. CoA 10-12-73. *Exporter*	3-13
❑ G-DDCD*	DH Dove 8		ex Little Rissington, Kemble, Staverton, Biggin Hill, G-OEWA, G-DDCD, G-ARUM. CoA 7-10-91, de-reg 24-5-05	3-13
❑ VP955*	DH Devon C.2/2	G-DVON	ex Little Rissington, Kemble, Little Staughton, Cranfield, G-BLPD, VP955, 207, 21, C.1 WCS, MCS, 31, Upavon SF, Hendon SF, MEAF, Malta CF. CoA 29-5-96	3-13
❑ XA880*	DH Devon C.2	G-BVXR	ex Little Rissington, Kemble, RAE, RRE, TRE	3-13

DINTON By late 2013 Lightning F.6 XS919 had moved to Henstridge, Somerset.

HULLAVINGTON AIRFIELD north of junction 17 of the M4, on the A429 north of Chippenham

❑ WZ798*		Slingsby Grasshopper TX.1	52	ex Bournemouth. First noted 7-11	6-13
❑ ZE681	'YR'	Grob Viking T.1	84	ex Syerston, 615, BGA.3094. Crashed 27-6-03, Cat 5 12-5-06. Cockpit	7-12

KEEVIL AERODROME south of the A361, south-west of Devizes

Bannerdown Gliding Club: A pair of Grasshoppers have moved on by early 2013, XA225 to Odiham, Hants, and XA244 to Tavistock, Devon. | **www.bannerdown.co.uk**

❑ AXD	Slingsby Skylark 3	55	BGA.735, ex Aston Down. Crashed 11-7-03, CoA 5-6-04	2-10
❑ AXE	Slingsby Skylark 3	55	BGA.736, ex Ullenhall. CoA 21-8-01	2-10

❑ BAA		Slingsby Tutor	54	BGA.804,ex XE761, RAFC, VM589. CoA 9-3-97	[1]	1-12
❑ BJJ		Slingsby Swallow	61	BGA.1003, ex Lasham. CoA 30-8-82		2-10
❑ BPA		Slingsby Skylark 4	63	BGA.1115,ex Spalding. Crashed 9-6-05, CoA 3-1-06		2-10
❑ BVJ		Slingsby Dart 17R	66	BGA.1266,ex Usk. Damaged 5-5-07, CoA 14-6-07		6-11
❑ BYA		Slingsby Skylark 3	66	BGA.1330, ex Spalding. Crashed 15-8-04, CoA 18-5-05. Fuselage		2-10
❑ CFZ*		Slingsby Tutor	c69	BGA.1759, ex Wolverhampton, Dowty G/C, Pershore, RAFGSA.178. CoA 15-7-77		2-13
❑ CPL		Slingsby Tutor	r72	BGA.1698,ex Lasham, RAFGSA 183. *Mistress Tutor*. CoA 17-3-08		6-11
❑ EPZ		Scheibe Bergfalke	~	BGA.2855,ex Upavon, D-4012. COA 11-8-96. Stored		2-10
❑ FEZ		EoN Eton TX.1	c55	BGA.3214,ex RAFGSA R.13, WP269. CoA 3-6-01. Stored		1-12
❑ GDL		Eichelsdorfer SB-5E	~	BGA.3749, ex D-0307, Chatham, Gutersloh. CoA 12-6-94		2-10
❑ WB981	FFZ	Slingsby Sedbergh TX.1	50	BGA.3238, ex Oakhill, Aston Down, Sealand, 635 VGS, 611 GS, CGS, 1 GC, GIS, 125 GS, 42 GS. CoA 19-5-09		7-12
❑ WZ793		Slingsby Grasshopper TX.1	52	ex Croydon, Basingstoke, Taunton		1-12
❑ XP488		Slingsby Grasshopper TX.1	61	ex Cranwell, West Walton Highway, Long Sutton, Halton, West Malling		1-12

■ **[1]** See under Coventry, Warks, for 'another' BGA.804.

LYNEHAM AIRFIELD west of the A3102, south-west of Wooton Bassett EGDL

RAF Lyneham: The base closed officially on the last day of December 2012 and was handed over to the care of the horrendously-named MoD Defence Infrastructure Organisation. Dakota IV 'FZ626' (G-AMPO) moved to Brize Norton, Oxfordshire, on 15th September 2012. With the closure of the base - in its present form - the inevitable cloud settled over the 'gate guardian', Comet C.2 XK699. Long intended for the RAF Museum, its 46-plus years outside mitigated strongly against long-term preservation, not to mention the cost of removal and the existence of Mk.1XB G-APAS already at Cosford. It was offered to interested parties and it is reported that only BDAC responded. Wisely, the team appreciated that only the forward fuselage could be practically saved and the remainder was scrapped. The nose made the journey to Old Sarum, Wilts, on 12th November 2013.

Planning permission for what will become the £230m **Combined Defence Technical Training Establishment** was granted in mid-2013 and work commenced to transform the base for its new role. Included in the application was the note that aircraft would be taxied up and down the runway, so some of the role carried out at Cosford is expected to continue? The first phase of opening is expected to be 2015, while the long-term plan is that by 2020 all technical training will be centred here. (See under Arborfield, Berks, for the first casualty and under Cosford, Shropshire, and Gosport, Hants.)

MALMESBURY

Dyson Ltd: The company acquired a Lightning and Harrier, potentially for display, but presently stored off-site.

◆ **Access: Private** *location, visits by prior arrangement* **only**

❑ XM173*	'A'	EE Lightning F.1A	60	ex Old Sodbury, Preston, Bentley Priory, Binbrook 8414M (28-5-74), Binbrook TFF, Leuchars TFF, 226 OCU, 56. Arrived 11-2-13, off-site	8-13
❑ ZD462*		BAe Harrier GR.7	89	ex Ipswich, Cosford, St Athan, Cosford 9302M, St Athan, 1. Ditched 25-1-97. First noted 4-12, off-site	8-13

Martin Painter: Comet and Nimrod specialist Martin describes his work on the prototype Nimrod cockpit as keeping it "safe, warm and dry". The flight deck is 'live' and restoration continues. **Private** *location, visits by prior arrangement* **only**

❑ XV148	HS Nimrod proto	67	ex Guildford, Woodford, Bedford, Pershore, A&AEE. Cockpit	7-12

MELKSHAM on the A350 south of Chippenham

Adrian Brimson and **John Phillips**: Restoration of the Skeeter continues apace.

◆ **Access**, *viewing by prior permission* ***only*** | **01380 871956** | **john.sandie723@yahoo.co.uk**

❑ XL765	Saro Skeeter AOP.12	58	ex 'Northants', Clapham, Leverstock Green, Leamington Spa, Leeds, Rotherham, Wroughton, 17F, 654, 651, Saro. SOC 27-5-68	1-14

Riverside MoT Centre: On the B3107 Bradford-on-Avon road, close to the junction with the A350.

❑ 'WB188'	Hawker Hunter GA.11 G-BZPC	55	ex Kemble, Exeter, Shawbury XF300, Yeovilton, FRADU, F.4, 130, 234, 71. De-reg 16-3-11. Red scheme. Arrived 1-11-11	1-14

■ **[1]** See under Coventry, Warks, for another 'WB188' and Tangmere, W Sussex, for the *real* one.

No.**2385 Squadron Air Cadets**: Lancaster Road, Bowerhill.

❑ WP863	DHC Chipmunk T.10 PAX		55	ex Boscombe Down, Bournemouth, Marlborough, Chippenham 8360M, Shawbury, CoAT G-ATJI (de-reg 3-1-68), RAFC, 664, RAFC. SOC 4-4-73	1-14

NETHERAVON AIRFIELD on the A345 north of Amesbury EGDN

No.**7 Regiment, AAC**:

❑ XV136 'X'	Westland Scout AH.1		68	ex Almondbank, Wroughton. Gate	9-13
❑ XZ346	Sud Gazelle AH.1		78	ex Shawbury, Middle Wallop, 665, A&AEE, Yeovil, 3 CBAS, ARWS, 656, 655. Displayed	9-13

Also:

❑ TJ672	Auster 5D	G-ANIJ	44	ex Eggesford, Bournemouth, 227 OCU, 657. CoA 5-5-71	2-13

OAKSEY PARK AERODROME south of Cirencester, east of the A429 EGTW

Last noted in July 2009, Cherokee 140 G-BDGY has been deleted. Slingsby T.67 G-BLLR had moved on by December 2012, perhaps for Kent.

❑ G-BCLL	Piper Cherokee 180C	65	ex SE-EON. CoA 14-11-07	7-11
❑ G-BDFX	Auster 5	45	ex Kemble, Oaksey Park, F-BGXG, TW517, 661. Crashed 10-10-93	8-11

OLD SARUM AERODROME east of the A345 north of Salisbury EGLS

Boscombe Down Aviation Collection - **BDAC**: Take a look under Boscombe Down, Wilts, for some of the background on the re-establishment of BDAC at historic Old Sarum. The collection opened to the public on 1st July 2012. And 'opened' is a very appropriate word; the superb team has worked miracles to achieve this impressive new museum, with the emphasis on open cockpits, open for special events and a warm welcome. To avoid geographic confusion, the museum was referring to itself as initials only - ie BDAC - to prevent visitors turning up at a venue a little further to the north! A name change would be prudent. Unless noted, all of the airframes listed below arrived in June 2012. Last to arrive at the end of a momentous achievement was the Sycamore.

◆ **Access**: *Aerodrome is south of the minor road running from the Old Sarum fort on the A345 north of Salisbury to Old Sarum village and Winterbourne Gunner on the A338 north-east of Salisbury.* **Open**: *Feb to Nov 10:00 to 17:00 Tue to Sun - ie* not *open Mon; Nov to Feb Sat, Sun 10:00 to 15:00.* **Contact**: *Hangar 1 South, Old Sarum Airfield, Salisbury, SP4 6DZ* | **email** via website | **www.boscombedownaviationcollection.co.uk**

❑ '2783'*	RAF BE.2c replica		07	ex Boscombe Down, *Virgo Intacta*	[1]	1-14
❑ WD321*	DHC Chipmunk 22	G-BDCC	51	ex Boscombe Down, Husbands Bosworth, WD321, A&AEE, DH. Crashed 29-8-99, de-reg 8-4-04. Arrived by 8-12		1-14
❑ WH876*	EE Canberra B.2(mod)		53	ex Boscombe Down, Aberporth, Boscombe Down, A&AEE, 73, 207, 115. Short-built. Probe-equipped. Cockpit		1-14
❑ WJ865*	EE Canberra T.4		54	ex Boscombe Down, Bromsgrove, Stamford, Stock, Farnborough, ETPS, A&AEE. SOC 6-1-82. Cockpit		1-14
❑ WK800*	Gloster Meteor D.16		52	ex Boscombe Down, Llanbedr, DS&TL, RAE, RAAF A77-876, U.21A, 23, 77 RAAF, F.8, RAF. Arrived 23-7-12	[2]	1-14
❑ WN890*	Hawker Hunter F.2		54	ex Boscombe Down, Doncaster, Firbeck, Robertsbridge, Stamford, Hedge End, Boscombe Down, A&AEE, AWA. AWA-built. SOC 21-1-63. Cockpit	[3]	1-14
❑ WT648*	Hawker Hunter F.1		54	ex Boscombe Down, Salisbury, Kexborough, Stock, St Athan, Weeton 7530M (22-11-57), DFLS. Cockpit	[3]	1-14
❑ WT859*	Supermarine 544		56	ex Boscombe Down, Long Marston, Brooklands, Ruislip, Foulness, Culdrose, Fleetlands, Culdrose, Lee-on-Solent A2499, RAE, A&AEE. SOC 29-11-60. Cockpit		1-14
❑ WV910*	Hawker Sea Hawk FGA.4		55	ex Boscombe Down, DERA, DRA, ETPS, 806. Damaged 2-5-58. ETPS colours. Cockpit		1-14
❑ XF113*	Supermarine Swift F.7		56	ex Boscombe Down, Salisbury, Bath, Frome, Farnborough, ETPS, A&AEE, Handling Sqn. SOC 31-10-61. Cockpit	[4]	1-14

❑ XF375*	'6'	Hawker Hunter F.6A G-BUEZ	55	ex Boscombe Down, Spanhoe, Duxford, Cranwell 8736M (10-1-82), ETPS, English Electric, Rolls-Royce. AWA-built. De-reg 28-8-01. Acquired 12-07. ETPS colours by 8-13		1-14
❑ XG290*		Hawker Hunter F.6	56	ex Boscombe Down, Salisbury, Bournemouth, Bruntingthorpe, Swanton Morley, Bentley Priory, Halton 8711M (20-10-81), Laarbruch SF, A&AEE. Cockpit	[4] [5]	1-14
❑ XJ380*		Bristol Sycamore HR.14	56	ex Boscombe Down, Crowland, Montrose, New Byth, Drighlington, Finningley 8628M, Catterick, CFS, MoA, HS, 275. SOC 22-3-68		1-14
❑ XJ476*		DH Sea Vixen FAW.1	57	ex Boscombe Down, Southampton, Boscombe Down, A&AEE, HSD, ATU Woomera, DH, A&AEE, RRE. Cockpit	[6]	1-14
❑ XK699*		DH Comet C.2	57	ex Lyneham, Henlow 7971M (last flight 13-6-67), 216. *Saggitarius*. Forward fuselage. Arrived 12-11-13		1-14
❑ XN503*		Hunting Jet Provost T.3A	60	ex Boscombe Down, Haverfordwest, Milford Haven, Salisbury, Firbeck, Coventry, Bicester, Kemble, RAFEF, 4 FTS, 2 FTS, 6 FTS, A&AEE. SOC 28-5-76. Cockpit		1-14
❑ XN726*		EE Lightning F.2A	61	ex Boscombe Down, Rayleigh, Foulness, Farnborough, 8545M, Gütersloh, 92, 19. Cockpit. SOC 1-4-77. Arrived by 8-12	[7]	1-14
❑ XR650*	'28'	Hunting Jet Provost T.4	63	ex Boscombe Down, DERA, Halton 8459M (19-12-75), SoRF, CAW, CATCS, 3 FTS, CAW, 7 FTS		1-14
❑ XS231*		BAC Jet Provost T.5 G-ATAJ	65	ex Boscombe Down, South Molton, Barnstaple, Ipswich, Bruntingthorpe, Bournemouth, Scampton, Shawbury, A&AEE, G-ATAJ, de-reg 10-3-65. Cockpit	[4]	1-14
❑ XS790*		HS Andover CC.2	64	ex Boscombe Down, DERA, DRA, RAE, Queen's Flight. Much-modified nose. Cockpit		1-14
❑ XT437*	'423'	Westland Wasp HAS.1	65	ex Boscombe Down, Lee-on-Solent A2721[2] (23-3-88), A2641[2]. 829, *Diomede* Flt, 829. *Del Boy*		1-14
❑ XV784*		HS Harrier GR.3	70	ex Boscombe Down, DS&TL, Wittering 8909M (10-6-86), 233 OCU, 4, 1, 4. Damaged 2-4-86. Cockpit	[8]	1-14
❑ XW560*		SEPECAT Jaguar S.06	69	ex Boscombe Down, East Grinstead, Farnborough, A&AEE. Damaged 11-8-72. Cockpit	[4] [9]	1-14
❑ XX343*		HS Hawk T.1	81	ex Boscombe Down, DERA, ETPS. Crashed 8-4-97. ETPS colours. Cockpit	[4]	1-14
❑ XX734*		SEPECAT Jaguar GR.1	74	ex Charlwood, Coltishall 8816M (21-11-84), Abingdon, Indian AF JI014, G-27-328, 6. Arrived 15-5-13	[10]	1-14
❑ XX761*		SEPECAT Jaguar GR.1A	75	ex Boscombe Down, DERA, DRA, Warton, 226 OCU, 14. *Pudsey*. Damaged 6-6-78. Cockpit	[10]	1-14
❑ XX919*		BAC 111-402	66	ex Boscombe Down, DERA, RAE, D-AFWC ntu, PI-C-1121. Cockpit		1-14
❑ XZ457*	'104'	HS Sea Harrier FA.2	79	ex Boscombe Down, Yeovilton, 899, 800, 801, 800, 899, 800, 899, 700A. Crashed 20-10-95. *The Sharp End*	[11]	1-14
❑ ZD936*	'AO'	Panavia Tornado F.2	85	ex Boscombe Down, 'Manchester', Bedford, St Athan, 229 OCU. 229 OCU colours. Cockpit		1-14
❑ 3150*		TTL Banshee 400 UAV	c99	ex Sawnsea, Manorbier. Arrived 30-11-13		1-14
❑ A92-664*		GAF Jindivik 3A	~	ex Boscombe Down, Welshpool, Llanbedr, DRA, RAE	[12]	1-14

■ **[1]** BE.2b was built by a BDAC team at Boscombe Down over a period of 4½ years, it represents one built by Joncques Aviation in 1914 that served with 66 and 58 Sqns, 52 Reserve Sqn and came to Boscombe Down in 11-17 and is known to have also operated from Old Sarum. **[2]** Drone Meteor is on loan from Trevor Stone. Last flown 11-10-04. **[3]** Cockpits on loan from the Air Defence Collection / Tony Dyer - see below. **[4]** Airframes co-owned by John Sharpe and BDAC. **[5]** Rear fuselage of XG290 can be found at Woodhall Spa, Lincs. **[6]** Sea Vixen on loan from Solent Sky - see Southampton, Hants. **[7]** Lightning cockpit is on loan from Hugh Trevor. **[8]** GR.3 co-owned by Kim Fulton and BDAC. **[9]** UK prototype Jaguar, first flown by Jimmy Dell 12-10-69. **[10]** XX734 and XX761 co-owned by Ron Fulton and BDAC. **[11]** XZ457 is a Falklands veteran: operating from *Hermes* two separate pilots accounted for two A-4 Skyhawks on 21-5-82 and two Daggers on 24-5-82. **[12]** Jindivik was lost on 8-7-69 after 25 flights. It is a composite, including parts from A92-244, -442, -466 and -490. The intention is to restore it as A92-466 which is the serial discovered under layers of paint on the rear fuselage.

Air Defence Collection: Tony Dyer's projects were previously listed under Boscombe Down as a 'flag of convenience' and it makes sense to now list ADC under this location. Two of his cockpits, Hunters F.1 WT648 and F.2 WN890, are on loan to BDAC - see above.

Other projects include: a Spitfire V cockpit project which is a two-time *CockpitFest* award-winner and originally centred around the instrument panel and windscreen but now 'growing' towards the tail and destined for a formal listing before too long; a long-term project based upon a substantial chunk of the cockpit area of Seafire F.46 LA546 (acquired in 2006, see also Colchester, Essex) and parts from the cockpit of P-51D Mustang 44-13835 *Damm Yankee*. (crashed 8th February 1945, remains recovered in the early 1980s).

◆ **Access:** ***Not*** *open to the public, some airframes with BDAC - see above* | **www.airdefencecollection.co.uk**

❑ P3554	Hawker Hurricane I	40	ex Salisbury, Swanage, 607, 213, 56, 32. Shot down 5-10-40. *Jessamy*	[1]	3-12

■ **[1]** Project started in 1978 and the intention is to create an airframe that is 85-percent composed of wartime Hurricane material. To date over 60 Hurricanes have 'provided' parts. Main cockpit items come from P3554 - Plt Off D Evans of 607 Sqn baled out from it over Swanage after combat with a Bf 109.

Aerodrome: Shadow G-MYCM was flying again by 2013.

❑ G-BRZZ	CFM Streak Shadow	90	CoA 13-5-08	12-11
❑ G-CDYA	Gippsland Airvan	06	ex VH-IMI. Crashed 28-11-10. Spares	8-12
❑ G-MTXR	CFM Shadow CD	88	CoA 6-10-08	12-11

SALISBURY PLAIN

Within the vast exercise are at a site called Copehill is a pair of Lynx cabins.

❑ XZ171*	Westland Lynx AH.1	77	ex 4 Rgt, 3 Rgt, 9 Rgt, 4 Rgt, 3 Rgt, 1 Rgt, 9 Rgt, 664, 671, RR, A&AEE. First noted 5-07	3-13
❑ XZ203*	Westland Lynx AH.7	79	ex Middle Wallop, 671, 1 Rgt, 9 Rgt, 3 Rgt, 4 Rgt, 671, 3 Rgt, 671, LCF. First noted 7-12	3-13

SWINDON

Two projects are with restorers in *separate*, private, locations.

❑ G-AYMP	Currie Wot	72	CoA 4-10-94	2-12
❑ KF435	NAA Harvard IIB	44	ex Guildford, Duxford, Ottershaw, Wycombe AP, Camberley, Sandhurst, 1 FTS, 2 FTS, 22 SFTS, 20 FTS, 11 (P)AFU. Noorduyn-built. SOC 24-9-57	2-12

UPAVON AIRFIELD Last reported in January 2004, Bergfalke II D-4019 has been deleted.

WARMINSTER

Warminster Skirmish Paintball Park: In Bath road. Access by prior arrangement ***only*** | **www.skirmishpaintballgames.co.uk**

❑ G-BOZU	Sparrow Hawk II	r88	de-reg 9-6-10	5-10

WINTERBOURNE GUNNER east of the A338 north-east of Salisbury

Defence Chemical, Biological, Radiological and Nuclear [Event] **Centre** and the **Defence Science and Technology Laboratory**-run Porton Down DANGER AREA are included under this heading. The Dominie is used by the Health Authority Response Team.

❑ XS736	'S'	HS Dominie T.1	66	ex Ipswich, Cranwell, 55, 3 FTS, 6 FTS, RAFC, CAW	5-12
❑ XV201		Lockheed Hercules C.1K	67	ex Cambridge, Sri Lanka AF CR-882 ntu, 1312F, LTW, USAF 66-8551. Flight deck	5-09

WROUGHTON AIRFIELD on the A4361 south of Swindon

Science Museum: In December 2013 it was announced that planning permission had been granted for a giant solar farm of 150,000 panels to be built on the 170 acre airfield site. As well as electricity it will generate a steady income for ScM.

◆ **Access:** *Visits by prior arrangement* **only**. **Contact:** *Wroughton Airfield, Swindon, SN4 9LT* | **01793 846200** | **wroughton.enquiries@nmsi.ac.uk** | **www.sciencemuseum.org.uk/wroughton**

❑ G-AACN	HP Gugnunc	29	ex Hayes, K1908 RAE, Air Ministry. Acquired 7-34	7-13
❑ G-ACIT	DH Dragon	33	ex Southend, Beagle, ANT Blackpool, BEA, Scottish, Highland. CoA 25-5-74, acquired 8-83, de-reg 26-4-02	7-13

❑ G-ALXT		DH Dragon Rapide	43	ex Strathallan, Staverton, 4R-AAI, CY-AAI, G-ALXT, NF865, 5 MU, 18 MU, MCS. Arrived 12-81		7-13
❑ G-ANAV		DH Comet 1A	52	ex South Kensington, Farnborough, BOAC G-ANAV, CPA CF-CUM, G-ALZA ntu. De-reg 1-7-53, acquired 21-5-62. Arrived 16-12-94. Cockpit		7-13
❑ G-APWY		Piaggio P.166	59	ex Southend, Marconi. CoA 14-3-81, last flown 1-6-83, de-reg 20-10-00		7-13
❑ G-APYD		DH Comet 4B	60	ex Dan-Air, Channel G-APYD, Olympic SX-DAL, BEA, G-APYD. CoA 3-8-79, last flown 1-11-79, de-reg 23-11-79		7-13
❑ G-ATTN		Piccard HAB	66	ex South Kensington, Hayes, South Ken'. Acquired circa 1978		7-13
❑ G-AVZB		LET Z37 Cmelak	67	ex Southend, OK-WKQ. CoA 5-4-84, last flew 25-6-88, de-reg 21-12-88		7-13
❑ G-AWZM		HS Trident 3B-101	71	ex Heathrow, BA, BEA. CoA 13-12-85, last flew 28-2-86, de-reg 18-3-86		7-13
❑ G-BBGN		Cameron A-375	74	ex South Kensington, Hayes, South Kensington. *Daffodil II*. Gondola, acquired 1989		7-13
❑ G-BGLB		Bede BD-5B Micro	c79	ex Booker. CoA 4-8-81, de-reg 21-11-91. Arrived 11-93		7-13
❑ G-BXXR*		Lovegrove Four-Runner	98	de-reg 3-11-09		7-13
❑ G-IPSY*		Rutan Vari-Eze	82	CoA 6-8-09, de-reg 16-7-09		7-13
❑ G-MMCB		Huntair Pathfinder II	r83	de-reg 23-11-88, acquired 9-85		7-13
❑ G-RBOS		Colt AS-105 hot air airship	82	CoA 6-3-87, acquired 9-87		7-13
❑ –		Lilienthal Glider	c1894	BAPC.52, ex South Kensington, Hayes, South Kensington, Oxford, Berlin. Acquired 1920	[1]	7-13
❑ –		Newbury Manflier MPA	76	BAPC.162, major elements, acquired 9-81		7-13
❑ –		Chargus Midas	78	BAPC.172. acquired 1981		7-13
❑ –		Birdman Grasshopper hg-g	77	BAPC.173, acquired 1980		7-13
❑ –		Bensen B.7 gyroglider	c74	BAPC.174, acquired 1980		7-13
❑ –		McBroom Cobra 88 h-g	76	BAPC.188, acquired 10-85		7-13
❑ –		Hartman Ornithopter	59	BAPC.276, ex Cranfield. Acquired 1993		7-13
❑ EI-AYO		Douglas DC-3A-197	36	ex Shannon, N655GP, N65556, N225JB, N8695SE, N333H, NC16071. Last flown 25-12-78		7-13
❑ N18E		Boeing 247	33	ex Wings and Wheels, Orlando, Sky Tours, NC18E, NC18, NC13340 CAA, United/National A/T. Last flown 3-8-82		7-13
❑ N7777G		Lockheed L-749A-79 Constellation G-CONI	47	ex Dublin, Lanzair, KLM PH-LDT, PH-TET. Arrived 12-8-83, de-reg 13-6-84		7-13
❑ OO-BFH		Piccard gas balloon	32	ex South Kensington, Hayes, South Kensington. Gondola, acquired circa 1937		7-13
❑ VP975	'M'	DH Devon C.2/2	49	ex RAE Farnborough, A&AEE, CCCF, 19 GCF, CPE. Last flew 2-86		7-13
❑ XP505		Folland Gnat T.1	62	ex South Kensington, RAE, MinTech, Dunsfold, CFS. Last flew 18-11-84		7-13
❑ ZJ452*		GEC Phoenix UAV	~	Army titles		7-13
❑ 100509		Focke-Achgelis Fa 330A-1	44	ex South Kensington, Farnborough. Acquired 2-46		7-13

■ **[1]** Type XI hang-glider built by Otto Lilienthal and brought to the UK in March 1895.

WORCESTERSHIRE

BEWDLEY on the A456, west of Kidderminster

Ross McNeill: **Access:** *Visits possible* **only** *by prior arrangement*

❑ XH175	'AR'	EE Canberra PR.9	60	ex Stock, St Athan, 1 PRU, 39, 58. Short-built. Cockpit	6-10
❑ -		Avro Anson II	~	ex Canada, RCAF,. Cockpit	6-10
❑ 'Z5663'		Hawker Hurricane II	~	fuselage, complex composite	6-10

BIRLINGHAM on the A4104, east of the B4080 to the west of Evesham

During 2013 the cockpit of Vampire T.11 XE979 was removed and moved to Cantley, Norfolk. The remainder was still to be found on site here in late 2013, but was likely to be disposed of.

◆ **Access:** *Private* collection, visits possible by prior appointment **only**

❑ WF299		Hawker Sea Hawk FB.3		54	ex 'WN105', Helston, St Agnes, Topcliffe, Catterick 8164M, Lee-on-Solent, Culdrose SAH-8 A2662, A2509 (21-7-61), 802, 738, 736. AWA-built	1-14
❑ WH166		Gloster Meteor T.7		51	ex Digby 8052M (9-9-69), CFS, 5 CAACU, CAW, 4 FTS, 205 AFS, 210 AFS, 208 AFS	1-14
❑ WZ425		DH Vampire T.11		52	ex Cardiff-Wales, Woodford, Chester, St Athan, 5 FTS, RAFC, 229 OCU, CGS. SOC 24-11-67	1-14
❑ XF526	'78' *and* 'E'	Hawker Hunter F.6		56	ex St Athan, Halton 8679M (9-11-81), Laarbruch SF, 4 FTS, 229 OCU, 56, 43, 56, 63, 66	1-14
❑ 'XN623'		Hunting Jet Provost T.3	XN632	61	ex Eaglescott, Chivenor, St Athan 8352M (16-7-73), Kemble, Shawbury, 3 FTS	1-14

BROMSGROVE on the A448 north-west of Redditch

Jason Allen, Brian Barrett and Bob Dunn of the **Wolverhampton Aviation Group** keep their Hunter cockpit locally.

❑ XE597		Hawker Hunter FGA.9		56	ex Moreton-in-Marsh, Halton, Bentley Priory 8874M (4-10-85), Brawdy, 1 TWU, 2 TWU, TWU, 229 OCU, West Raynham SF, 1, 54, MoA, 208, 56, 63, 66. Cockpit. 1 Squadron colours	9-13

DEFFORD on the A4104 south-west of Pershore

Defford Airfield Heritage Group: Working closely with the National Trust, the wartime buildings on the wartime airfield are being conserved and work is in hand to open the **Defford Airfield Heritage Museum**, possibly during 2014. For more details take a look at **http://deffordairfieldheritagegroup.wordpress.com**

Also: The two 150s are used by **Mission Aviation Fellowship** (MAF) for fund-raising and travel considerably. Last noted in April 1998, Air Command 503 G-BPAO and Pegasus XL-R G-MNAF had moved on by June 2013 at the latest.

❑ G-ATMN		Cessna F.150F		66	ex ?, Shobdon, Billericay, Andrewsfield, Southend. Reims-built. Crashed 11-5-84, de-reg 21-10-04.	4-12
❑ 'G-BMAF'		Cessna 150J	G-BOWC	69	ex N60626. De-reg 16-9-94. 'Taildragger'	12-05
❑ G-MYYZ*		Medway Raven X		96	CoA 27-6-04	6-13

ECKINGTON Last reported in December 2003, Cherokee Arrow II G-TOBE has been deleted.

KIDDERMINSTER

A *private* owner keeps a Hunter in the area.

❑ 'XF324'		Hawker Hunter F.51	E-427	56	ex Bruntingthorpe, Brough, Holme-on-Spalding Moor, Brough, Dunsfold, G-9-447 (28-2-76), Danish AF, Esk.724. 92 Sqn 'Blue Diamonds' colours	4-05

PERSHORE on the A44 west of Evesham

John S Morgan: During 2013, the cockpit of Electra G-CHNX moved to Coventry, Warks. Olympia AMV moved to the Newbury/Basingstoke area in April 2013 and is under restoration. T.34A Sky DPZ moved in July 2013 to Lasham, Hants.

◆ **Access:** *Viewable by prior arrangement* **only** | **jsmorgan@btconnect.com**

❑ G-ANAP		DH Dove 6		53	ex Bristol, CAFU Stansted. CoA 6-9-73, de-reg 31-8-73. Cockpit	2-14
❑ G-APFG		Boeing 707-436		60	ex Cove, Bruntingthorpe, Cardington, Stansted, British Airtours, BOAC. CoA 24-5-81, de-reg 24-4-81. Cockpit	2-14
❑ G-AVFM		HS Trident 2E		69	ex Cove, Bristol, BA and BEA. CoA 2-6-84, de-reg 20-3-84. Cockpit	2-14
❑ G-AXDM		HS.125-400B		69	ex Farnborough, Edinburgh, BAE Systems, GEC-Marconi. CoA 7-6-03, de-reg 13-11-03. Cockpit	2-14
❑ G-BNCY		Fokker F.27-500F		77	ex Bournemouth, Guernsey, Air UK, VH-FCE, PH-EXH. *Friendship Lilly Langtree*. Damaged 7-12-97, de-reg 19-2-98. Cockpit	2-14
❑ BVF		Slingsby Swallow		65	BGA.1263, ex Bidford. *Monica*. CoA 13-8-03	2-14

❑	CWV	Schleicher Rhonlerche II	~	BGA.1873, ex Lasham, D-8226. CoA 26-5-94	[1]	2-14
❑	WK128	EE Canberra B.2	54	ex Llanbedr, FRL. Avro-built. Cockpit		2-14
❑	–	HS Hawk SIM	~	ex Farnborough		2-14

■ **[1]** Type and pedigree amended from *W&R23*.

No.**233 Squadron Air Cadets**: Have a Tomahawk, care of John Morgan.

❑	–	Piper Tomahawk 112	~	cockpit	2-14

REDDITCH Chipmunks G-ARMD and 'WZ868' (G-ARMF) had moved to K..Kem... Cotswold Airport, Glos, by May 2012.

WORCESTER

John Hancock: *W&R22*, in all innocence, wrote this TT.18 cockpit out (p253) and moved it to the general area of Scampton, Lincs, by June 2006. Not so. It remained resolutely here among John's incredible, *private*, collection of all things militaria.

❑	WK118 'CQ'	EE Canberra TT.18	54	ex Worcester, Stock, Wyton, 100, 7, B.2. 59, 103. Avro-built. Cockpit	10-12

EAST YORKSHIRE

Includes the unitary authority of Kingston-upon-Hull

BEVERLEY Last noted in August 2008, Vampire T.11 XD542 has long since moved on.

BREIGHTON AERODROME in between Bubwith and Breighton, east of Selby

Real Aeroplane Company: Aircraft owned and operated by Tony 'Taff' Smith or Rob Fleming plus the collection assembled by Nigel Ponsford and any other aircraft under long-term restoration are the only ones listed here. (See also under Wigan, Gtr Man, and Selby, N Yorks, for other elements of Nigel's collection.) '

Mew Gull G-AEXF flew to its former home at Shuttleworth, Beds, on 6th October 2013. Jungmeister U-99 (G-AXMT) left by road during July 2013 for Italy. Texan 52-8543 (G-BUKY) departed on 8th March 2012 for Duxford, Cambs. Nigel Ponsford's EoN Olympia AMW was listed under this heading in *W&R23* (p268); it did *not* come here, going direct to his workshop, listed under Selby, N Yorks.

◆ **Access:** *Attendance at events and entry to the aerodrome is restricted to RAC members* **only**. *Fear not, membership is very reasonable and a couple of visits during the year will easily see 'break even'! Other visits by prior arrangement.* **Contacts:** *The Aerodrome, Breighton, Selby, YO8 6DS* | **01757 289065** | **dav@realaero.co.uk** | **www.realaero.com**

❑	G-ABVE	Arrow Active II ✈	32	ex Old Warden, Tiger Club	[1]	1-14
❑	G-ADXS	Mignet HM.14 'Flea'	35	ex Cambridge, East Tilbury, Andrewsfield, Southend, Staverton, Southend. CoA 1-12-36. *The Fleeing Flea*		1-14
❑	G-AEVS	Aeronca 100 ✈	37	*Jeeves*	[1] [2]	1-14
❑	G-AEXT*	Dart Kitten II ✈	37	-	[1]	1-14
❑	G-AMAW	Luton Minor	48	ex Batley, Old Warden, Hitchin. CoA 6-8-88. Dismantled in container	[1] [3]	1-14
❑	G-ATCN	Luton Minor ✈	65	ex Wickenby, Colchester	[1]	1-14
❑	G-AXEI	Ward Gnome	67	ex East Kirkby, Tattershall. De-reg 30-5-84	[4]	1-14
❑	G-AYDV	Coates Swalesong SA.2	74	CoA 8-8-07	[1] [3]	1-14
❑	GBAAD*I	Evans VP-1	73	CoA 20-9-11. First noted 10-12; off-site 11-13		11-13
❑	G-BDTB	Evans VP-1	81	CoA 29-10-04		1-14
❑	G-LCGL	Comper Swift replica ✈	93	-	[1]	1-14
❑	G-MJLK	Dragonfly 250	r82	de-reg 18-4-90. Dismantled in container		1-14
❑	G-MMUL	Ward Elf	r84	ex Newark area. Citroen Ami. De-reg 12-4-89	[4]	1-14
❑	G-RLWG	Ryan PT-22 Recruit ✈	42	ex N58612, 41-15687	[1]	1-14
❑	G-RPAX*	Bücker Jungmeister	40	ex Spain, Span AF ES1-31. CASA-built. Arrived 13-10-12, off-site	[5]	10-12
❑	G-TAFF	Bücker Jungmann ✈	57	ex Sherburn, Breighton, G-BFNE, SpanAF E3B-148. CASA-built 1-131E	[1]	1-14

❑ -		Mignet HM.14 'Flea'	~	ex 'F50', Harrogate.	[6]	1-14
❑ T9738		Miles Magister I ✈ G-AKAT	40	ex F-AZOR, Winthorpe, Leicester, G-AKAT, T9738, 24 EFTS, 15 EFTS	[1]	1-14
❑ XT434	'455'	Westland Wasp HAS.1 G-CGGK	65	ex Ipswich, Fleetlands, A2643 [2], A2723 (2-3-880, Lee-on-Solent, 829, 703	[1]	1-14
❑ 255*	'5-ML'	MH Broussard ✈ F-GGKL	~	ex France, ALAT. Arrived 26-5-13	[5]	1-14
❑ 152/17		Fokker Dr.I rep ✈ G-BVGZ	94	ex Netheravon	[1]	1-14
❑ 'CG+EV'		Gomhouria Mk.6 G-CGEV	70	ex Gainsborough, Egyptian AF. On site from 8-6-13	[7]	1-14
❑ 491273	'51'	Aero L29 Delfin	~	ex Chester, YL-PAG, SovAF. 'Gate'		1-14
❑ -	'03'	Yakovlev Yak-18A ✈ G-CEIB	58	ex RA-3336K. Soviet colours	[1]	1-14

■ **[1]** Aircraft registered to Rob Fleming. **[2]** Aeronca G-AEVS is a composite, including parts from G-AEXD which is under restoration to fly, see Northampton, Northants. **[3]** G-AMAW was built by J A Coates and was also known as the Coates SA.1 Swalesong. Original design G-AYDV was also built by John. **[4]** Airframes on loan from Nigel Ponsford - see also Wigan, Lancs, and Selby, N Yorks. **[5]** Aircraft registered to Tony 'Taff' Smith. **[6]** The 'Flea' was built by Mick Ward and is fitted with a Citroen Ami. **[7]** *Echo-Victor* ready for flight test, see under Tony Brier below for details of what a Gomhouria is.

Also:

❑ G-BDDF	Jodel D.120 Paris-Nice	57	ex F-BIKZ. Wassmer-built. CoA 10-11-03	1-14
❑ G-BMDS*	Jodel D.120 Paris-Nice	65	ex F-BMOS. Wassmer-built. CoA 27-9-11	1-14
❑ G-MOTW*	Myers OTW-145	41	ex N34301, NC34301. Arrived 8-13	1-14
❑ WG458	DHC Chipmunk T.10	51	N458BG, ex 1 AEF, 5 AEF, Cam UAS, 3 BFTS	1-14

Tony Brier: Has a workshop in the general area. Gomhouria 'CG+EV' (G-CGEV) moved to the aerodrome for flight test.

❑ 356	Gomhouria Mk.6	~	ex Gainsborough, Egyptian AF. Spares	[1]	1-14

■ **[1]** The Gomhouria is a licence-built Zlin Z.381, powered by a Continental O-300A. The Z.381 was itself a version of the Bücker Bü 181 Bestmann. Gomhourias were built by the Heliopolis Aircraft Works. *Echo-Victor* is fitted with a Walter Minor 4-III.

BROUGH AIRFIELD south of the A63 west of Hull

BAE Systems Military Air Solutions: Many of the airframes listed here are with the **Structural and Dynamic Test** facility. Bruntingthorpe-based The Buccaneer Aviation Group (T-BAG) were contracted to prepare S.2B XV168 to Elvington, Yorks. All Buccaneers were roaded out of Brough for flight test, the prototype (XK486) to Thurleigh, Beds, all others to Holme-on-Spalding Moor. Francis Wallace notes: "...being a part of the last ever Buccaneers road movement out of Brough was not only an historic moment but a very proud one for T-BAG!"

Departures: **Buccaneer** S.2B XV168 to Elvington, N Yorks, 18-8-13 - see above; **Hawk** 200 ZH200 to Loughborough, Leics, by May 2012; Mk.102D ZJ100 flew again at Warton, Lancs, on 22-8-12, starting trials as part of the ASTREA drone programme. These were completed by 12-11-13 when it moved by road to Doncaster Sheffield (pronounced 'Finningley'), S Yorks; T.53s ZK531 and ZK532 to Warton, Lancs, by 1-13;. T.53 ZK534 to Ipswich, Suffolk, by 4-13; static test **F-35** AG-1 completed its trials and returned to the USA by 8-12. Of the other test rigs, all were last noted in 1-09 and are believed to have moved on or been scrapped: Nimrod AEW.3 XV263 and both the single and two-seat Eurofighter EMUs. That leaves:

❑ LL-5313	HS Hawk T.53	c80	ex Bournemouth, Indonesian AF. Gate, BAE colours	12-13

FLINTON on the B1238, north-east of Hull

At a strip in the *general* area, the fuselage of a Cherokee is stored.

❑ G-RECK	Piper Cherokee 140	69	ex G-AXJW, N11C. CoA 10-1-11, de-reg 17-2-11. Fuselage	1-14

FULL SUTTON AERODROME south of the A166, east of Stamford Bridge

Air Camper G-BWVB moved to Bagby, N Yorks, by June 2012. Rallye G-AOACI and Shadow G-MYON were flying by 2013.

❑ G-BOOE	American GA-7 Cougar	79	ex N718G. CoA 6-8-08	10-11
❑ G-BSED*	Piper Tri-Pacer 160(Mod)	57	ex Perth, Portmoak, N9494D. Crashed 21-6-02. F/n 5-12	5-12

HULL

Streetlife Museum of Transport: Five extensive galleries ranging from bicycles, cars, carriages and railways.

◆ **Open:** *Mon to Sat 10:00 to 17:00; Sun 13:30pm to 16:30; open Bank Hols. Last admission 30 mins before closing. Closed Xmas, New Year and Good Friday.* **Contact:** *36 High Street, Hull, HU1 1PS* | **01482 613902** | **www.hullcc.gov.uk**

❑ 'G-EBVO'	Blackburn Lincock FSM	99	BAPC.287, ex Brough	6-13

LECONFIELD east of the A164, north of Beverley

Defence School of Transport and **RAF enclave**: The Meteor is held within the RAF enclave; although 'E' Flight 202 Squadron is due to leave during the period 2015 to 2017.

❑ WH132	'J'	Gloster Meteor T.7	51	ex Chelmsford 7906M (17-7-66), Kemble, CAW, CFS, CAW, 8 FTS, 207 AFS. Assembled by 9-13		9-13

PAULL on minor road south of Hedon

Fort Paull Armouries: The fort itself may have been around for 500-odd years, but for *W&R* readers, it is the 'support act' to the Beverley. A conservation programme is on-going and visitors can inspect its interior.

◆ **Open:** *Nov to Mar, Tues to Sun, 11:00 to 16:00. Apr to Oct, all week 10:00 to 18:00.* **Contact:** *Battery Road, Paull, HU12 8FP* | **01482 896236** | **fortpaull@aol.com** | **www.fortpaull.com**

❑ -		Blackburn Triplane replica	07	ex Brough	[1]	5-11
❑ XB259		Blackburn Beverley C.1	55	ex Beverley, Paull, Luton, RAE, G-AOAI. De-reg 30-3-55. Last flown 30-3-74	[2]	12-13
❑ XF509		Hawker Hunter F.6	56	ex Marfleet, Chivenor 8708M (21-12-81), Thurleigh, 4 FTS, AFDS, 54		12-13
❑ XX557		SAL Bulldog T.1	73	ex Topcliffe, Linton-on-Ouse, St Athan, Gla UAS, CFS. Crashed 11-9-75. Cockpit, stored		12-13

■ **[1]** A replica of the 1916 model built and donated by the Brough Heritage Group and presented to Fort Paull by Prof Robert Blackburn - grandson of Robert Blackburn. **[2]** 'Paull' in XB259's history is the now long-defunct aerodrome not far from its current resting place.

POCKLINGTON AERODROME east of the A1079, west of the village

Wolds Gliding Club: *Active airfield, access by prior arrangement only* | **www.wolds-gliding.org**

❑ OY-MUB		Short 330-200	81	ex Alton, B'mouth, Muk Air, G-BITX, G-14-3069. Fuselage		7-13

Locally:

❑ '29'		Aero L29 Delfin 893046	~	ex '142', Market Drayton, Romanian AF	[1]	2-14

■ **[1]** The L29 is a composite, with outer wings and tailplane from another, or other, aircraft.

PRESTON on the B1239 north of Hedon

Wright's Garage: Staithes Road.

❑ WL627		Vickers Varsity T.1	53	ex Hull, Newton 8488M (3-3-76), 6 FTS, 2 ANS, 1 ANS, BCBS. Cockpit, poor state		10-13

SEATON ROSS north-west of Holme-on-Spalding Moor

Hornet Aviation: David and Pat Fenton continue to work their magic. Messenger 2A G-AKBO moved to Sherburn in May 2012 and was in the air by December 2013. Gemini G-AKDK is being restored for the Classic Air Force of Newquay, Cornwall.

❑ G-AKDK*		Miles Gemini 1A	47	ex 'Stratford', Denmark, G-AKDK. Arrived 1-11-13		1-14
❑ G-AYZI		Stampe SV-4C	45	ex F-BBAA, French mil. Nord-built. Damaged 13-6-04		8-10

STORWOOD on a minor road south of Elvington

In the general area is a store of helicopters.

❑ XL763		Saro Skeeter AOP.12	58	ex Leeds, Ivybridge, Ottershaw, Southall, Wroughton, 15/19 Hussars, 2 Div, 654, 1 Wing. SOC 23-5-68		11-12
❑ XM565		Saro Skeeter AOP.12	59	ex Leeds, Ivybridge, Middle Wallop, Fleetlands, Middle Wallop, Southampton, M' Wallop 7861M (17-9-64), 651.	[1]	7-13
❑ XR627*	'X'	Westland Scout AH.1	64	ex Townhill, Ipswich, Wattisham, Arborfield, Dishforth, Middle Wallop, Wroughton, Garrison Air Sqn, 3 CBAS. First noted 6-12		7-13
❑ XT788	'316'	Westland Wasp HAS.1 G-BMIR	67	ex Dunkeswell, Faygate, Tattershall Thorpe, Wroughton, 829. SOC 19-12-85. De-reg 22-12-95		11-13

■ **[1]** Long since thought to be XL738 fitted with the *boom* of XM565; sleuthing by Alan Allen has proved that this is *all* of XM565. The pedigree has been altered accordingly.

NORTH YORKSHIRE

Includes the unitary authority of York

BAGBY (THIRSK) AERODROME on the A19 south-east of Thirsk — EGNG

Last noted in August 2013, the fuselage of Cessna 152 G-BRBF had gone by February 2014.

❑ G-ARLR	Beagle Terrier 2	48	ex Auster AOP.6, VW996, AAC, 663. CoA 9-9-01	2-14
❑ G-AXHS	MS Rallye Club	69	CoA 14-7-06. Off-site	5-11
❑ G-AXHT	MS Rallye Club	69	CoA 19-4-07	2-14
❑ G-AZSW	Beagle Pup 100	69	ex PH-VRT, G-35-140. Damaged 3-9-06, CoA 15-6-09, de-reg 15-2-11	2-14
❑ G-BGGG	Piper Tomahawk 112	78	CoA 28-6-04, de-reg 3-10-11	2-12
❑ G-BSSE	Piper Cherokee 140	75	ex N33440. CoA 14-11-07, de-reg 19-11-10	2-14
❑ G-BWVB*	Pietenpol Air Camper	97	ex Full Sutton. CoA 11--07	2-14
❑ G-HMES	Piper Warrior 161	81	ex OY-CSN. CoA 20-8-01, de-reg 5-5-04	2-14
❑ G-SOOZ*	Rans Coyote II	01	CoA 27-11-09, de-reg 5-8-11	8-13

BIRKIN east of the A162 and north of the A645, north-east of Knottingley

Paintball Commando: **Access:** *by prior arrangement* **only | 01924 252123 | www.paintballcommando.co.uk**

❑ XE874 '61'	DH Vampire T.11	54	ex Montrose, New Byth, Valley 8582M, Woodford, Chester, Shawbury,1 FTS, 4 FTS, 8 FTS, 4 FTS, 1 FTS, 4 FTS, 7 FTS. SOC 30-10-67	[1]	2-11

■ **[1]** Fitted with the booms of XD528.

BURN AERODROME between the A19 and A1041 south of Selby

Burn Gliding Club: **Access:** *by prior arrangement* **only** | **www.burnglidingclub.co.uk**

❑ JDW*	PZL PW-5 Smyk	r97	BGA.4440. Stored, first noted 6-10	10-13

CARTHORPE west of the A1, south-east of Bedale

Camp Hill Activity Centre | **Access**, *by prior arrangement* **only** | **01845 567788** | **www.camphill.co.uk**

❑ G-BHXJ	Nord Norecrin II	48	ex 'London', F-BEMX. CoA 28-7-89, de-reg 15-6-89	4-10

DINSDALE on a minor road south of Middleton St George

Anthony Harker: Keeps a Lightning at a *private* location in the general area.

❑ XR718 'DA'	EE Lightning F.3	64	ex Walpole, Wattisham 8932M (9-2-87), ABDR, LTF, 11, LTF, 11, 5, LTF, 5, 11, LTF, 5, LTF, 5, 226 OCU, 29, 56	2-14

Also: A North Yorks-based collector stores cockpits locally.

❑ WM145	Gloster Meteor NF.11	52	ex Gatenby, Great Ayton, Rotherham, Finningley, 5, 29, 151, 219. AWA-built. SOC 30-10-63. Cockpit	2-14
❑ WZ557	DH Vampire T.11	53	ex Gatenby, Great Ayton, Huntingdon, Acaster Malbis, Woodford, Chester, St Athan, 5 FTS, 16. SOC 13-11-67	2-14
❑ XH563	Avro Vulcan B.2MRR	60	ex Bruntingthorpe, Banchory, Rotherham, Scampton 8744M (31-3-82) 27, 230 OCU, MoA, 230 OCU, Wadd W, 230 OCU, 12, 83. Cockpit	2-14

DISHFORTH AIRFIELD alongside the A1(M), east of Ripon — EGXD

No.**9 Regiment AAC**: The regiment is due to move to Yeovilton, Somerset, in 2016.

❑ XX384	Sud Gazelle AH.1	74	ex Shawbury, Fleetlands, 7 AAB, 661, 652, 669, 1 Regt, 3 Regt, 2 Flt,652, 661, 652, 661, 657, 16th/5th Lancers	1-13
❑ ZB670	Sud Gazelle AH.1	84	ex Arborfield, 665. Westland-built. 'Gate'	2-14
❑ ZE379	Westland Lynx AH.7	86	ex Arborfield, 655, 657, 655. Cabin	8-13

ELVINGTON off the B1228 south-east of York

Yorkshire Air Museum and Allied Air Forces Memorial: As well as the watch tower and other World War Two buildings, the famed 'NAAFI' remains a 'must do' at this atmospheric site.

The *third* Buccaneer on site was donated by BAE Systems, Brough, and was moved with the assistance of Bruntingthorpe-based T-BAG (for more, see under Brough, E Yorks). On 18th August 2013, XV168 was dedicated to the memory of Blackburn and HSA aircrew who gave their lives during the Buccaneer development programme. For the record, they were: John Joyce flight test observer (FTO) in S.1 XK490 12th October 1959 (NASA pilot W A Alford also killed); Trevor Dunn FTO in S.1 XK529 31st August 1961 (A&AEE pilot 'Ozzie' Brown also killed); pilot 'Sailor' Parker and FTO Gordon Copeman in S.1 XN952 19th February 1962.

Victor *Lusty Lindy* stormed down Elvington's runway on 25th November 2013 to celebrate the 20th anniversary of its arrival. Typical of the team headed by André Tempest, this was timed not to the day, hour, or minute, but to the *second!* The continued operation of this beauty is a tribute to all involved. All being well, 2014 will see the number of taxiable aircraft at YAM come to seven, with regular 'Thunder Day' running sessions planned into the event calendar.

On 24th July 2013 a new building containing the **Aircrew Association Archive Trust** (or A3T) collection was officially unveiled as the final act of the wound-down Aircrew Association.. A vast amount of reference matter, with plenty more to come, is available for researchers on a prior arrangement basis.

◆ **Access:** *'Brown signed' from the A64 southern York ring, at the A64/A166/A1079 junction.* **Open:** *Late Oct to late Mar 10:00 to 16:00 daily, summer 10:00 to 17:00 daily.* **Contact:** *Elvington, York, YO41 4AU* | **01904 608595** | **museum@yorkshireairmuseum.org** | **www.yorkshireairmuseum.org**

❑	'G-AAAH'		DH Moth FSM	97	BAPC.270. Arrived 1997. *Jason*		1-14
❑	'G-AFFI'		Mignet HM.14 'Flea'	75	BAPC.76, ex Hemswell, Cleethorpes, Nostell, Rawdon. Arrived 1989	[1]	1-14
❑	G-AVPN		HP Herald 213	64	ex Channel Express, I-TIVB, G-AVPN, D-BIBI, HB-AAK ntu. CoA 14-12-99, de-reg 8-12-97. Flew in 20-10-97		1-14
❑	G-MJRA		Mainair Tri-Flyer	r82	ex Wetherby. (Demon 175 wing) De-reg 24-1-95		1-14
❑	G-TFRB		Air Command 532	90	ex Hartlepool. CoA 6-8-98, de-reg 7-6-01		1-14
❑	G-YURO		Shaw Europa 001	92	ex Wombleton. CoA 9-6-95, de-reg 22-4-98.		1-14
❑	–		Wright Flyer replica	66	BAPC.28, ex Leeds, Eccleston, Cardington, Finningley. Arrived 11-99		1-14
❑	–		Cayley glider rep	72	BAPC.89, ex Manchester, Hendon, Lasham. Unveiled 12-8-99		1-14
❑	–		Blackburn 1911 replica	78	BAPC.130, ex Stoke, Helston, *Flambards.* Arrived 10-1-95. *Mercury*		1-14
❑	'6232'		RAF BE.2c replica	62	BAPC.41, ex St Athan, Halton. Arrived 10-94		1-14
❑	'F943'	'S'	RAF SE.5a rep	r82	ex Selby, Elvington, Selby, G-BKDT. De-reg 11-7-91. Arrived 1987. Taxiable		1-14
❑	'H1968'		Avro 504K replica	68	BAPC.42, ex St Athan, Halton. Arrived 10-94		1-14
❑	N540		Port Victoria Kitten rep	~	ex Selby. Arrived 1996. Taxiable	[2]	1-14
❑	'P3873'	'YO-H'	Hawker Hurricane I FSM	99	BAPC.265, 1 Sqn RCAF colours		1-14
❑	'R6690'	'PR-A'	Sup' Spitfire I FSM	96	BAPC.254. Unveiled 9-96. 609 Sqn colours	[3]	1-14
❑	FK338		Fairchild Argus II	42	ex Woodhall Spa, Tattershall, Wigan, Mkt Drayton, Wigan, Southend, Southend, Sywell, G-AJOZ, FK338, Kemble, ATA 2 FP, 42-32142. Cr 16-8-62, de-reg 27-2-67. Arrived 2000		1-14
❑	HJ711	'VI-C'	DH Mosquito NF.II		ex Huntington, Squires Gate, Enfield, Chingford, 169, 14. Arrived 1988. 169 Sqn colours. *Spirit of Val*	[4]	1-14
❑	KN353		Douglas Dakota IV	44	ex 'KG427', Coventry, Air Atlantique, SU-AZF, G-AMYJ, XF747, G-AMYJ, KN353, 110, 96, 243, 44-76384. CoA 4-4-97, de-reg 12-12-01. Engine runs 2013		1-14
❑	'LV907' *and* 'NP763'		HP Halifax II	44	*Friday 13th*, 158 Sqn colours, Mk.III 'NP-F', to port, Mk.VII 'H7-N', 346 Sqn colours to starboard	[5]	1-14
❑	RA854		Slingsby Cadet TX.1	44	ex Wigan, Woodford, RAFGSA, Woodvale, 41 GS. Arr 6-4-00		1-14
❑	VP967		DH Devon C.2/2 G-KOOL	48	ex Redhill, Goodwood, Redhill, East Surrey Tech G-KOOL, 'G-DOVE', Biggin Hill, VP967, Kemble, Culdrose SF, 21, 207, SCCS, SCS, WCS, SCS, NCS, SCS, MCS, MoA, MCS, CCCF, 38 GCF, TTCCF, FCCS, 2 TAF CS, MCCS, RAFG CS, 2 TAF CS, Wahn SF, RCCF. SOC 1-4-82, de-reg 13-1-12. 207 Sqn colours. Taxiable		1-14
❑	VV901		Avro Anson T.21	49	ex Bacup, Burtonwood, Cosford, Irton Holme, Leconfield, CFCCU, Dur UAS, 1 RFS. Arrived 8-6-93. Dismantled		1-14

❑	VW993	'JA'	Beagle Terrier 2	48	ex 'TJ704', Holme-on Spalding Moor, Nympsfield, Blackbushe, PH-SFT,G-ASCD, Auster AOP.6 VW993, 651, 663. CoA 26-9-71, de-reg 5-10-89. Arrived 1988		1-14
❑	WH846		EE Canberra T.4	54	ex Samlesbury, St Athan, Laarbruch SF, 231 OCU. SOC 29-1-82. Arrived 19-5-88		1-14
❑	WH903		EE Canberra B.2	54	ex 100, 85, MoA, 85, W Raynham TFF, 228 OCU, 102, 617. Cockpit		1-14
❑	WH991		Westland Dragonfly HR.5	53	ex Storwood, Tattershall Thorpe, Tattershall, Wisbech, Taunton, Fleetlands, Culdrose SF, 705, 700, Eglinton SF, *Centaur* Flt, 705, *Illustrious* Flt. SOC 8-6-70. Arrived 10-94		1-14
❑	'WK864'	'C'	Gloster Meteor F.8 WL168	54	ex Finningley, 'WH456', St Athan, Swinderby, Finningley, Heywood 7750M (10-5-62), Sylt, 604, 111. Arrived 12-4-96. 616 colours		1-14
❑	WS788	'Z'	Gloster Meteor NF.14	54	ex Leeming 'WS844', Patrington 7967M (5-9-67), 1 ANS, 2 ANS, 152. AWA-built. Arrived 17-3-92		1-14
❑	XH278	'42'	DH Vampire T.11	55	ex Felton, Henlow 8595M, Upwood 7866M (9-11-64), 27 MU, RAFC. RAFC colours		1-14
❑	XH767	'L'	Gloster Javelin FAW.9	57	ex Leeming, Norwich, Monkton Farleigh, Worcester 7955M (10-7-67), Shawbury, 228 OCU, 11, 25, FAW.7. Arrived 4-2-01. 11 Sqn colours		1-14
❑	XL231		HP Victor K.2	62	ex 55, 57, Witt Wing, Victor TF, Witt Wing, 139. Flew in 25-11-93. *Lusty Lindy*. Taxiable	[6]	1-14
❑	XL502		Fairey Gannet AEW.3 G-BMYP	61	ex Sandtoft, Carlisle, G-BMYP, Leuchars 8610M (1-12-78), 849, MinTech, Pershore, 849. CoA 29-9-89, de-reg 22-2-05. Arrived 11-3-05		1-14
❑	'XL571'	'V'	Hawker Hunter T.7 XL572	58	ex Brough, Bournemouth G-HNTR (de-reg 11-10-91), Cosford 8834M (23-8-84), XL572, 1 TWU, 2 TWU, TWU, 229 OCU. Arrived 12-1-95. 92 Sqn, 'Blue Diamonds' colours		1-14
❑	XM553		Saro Skeeter AOP.12	59	ex Wattisham, Saxmundham, Middle Wallop, G-AWSV (de-reg 23-5-95), 15 MU, 5 Flt, 1 Wg. SOC 25-11-68		1-14
❑	XN974		HS Buccaneer S.2A	64	ex Warton, HoSM, RAE Bedford, HoSM, A&AEE, Driffield, HoSM, A&AEE, RAE Bedford, A&AEE, Holme on Spalding Moor. Flew in 19-8-91. Taxiable	[1]	1-14
❑	XP640	'M'	Hunting Jet Provost T.4	62	ex Halton 8501M (13-9-76), CATCS, 6 FTS, CAW, CFS, 3 FTS. Arrived 10-93		1-14
❑	XS903	'BA'	EE Lightning F.6	66	ex Binbrook, 11, 5-11 pool. SOC 18-5-88. Flew in 18-5-88. 11 Sqn colours	[1]	1-14
❑	XV168*	'AF'	HS Buccaneer S.2B	66	ex Brough, Lossiemouth, 12, 208, 12, 801. SOC 15-10-93. 12 Sqn colours. Arrived 18-8-13, see notes above	[7]	1-14
❑	XV250		HS Nimrod MR.2	71	ex Kinloss, Kin Wing, Kin & St M Wing, MR.1, 42, Kinloss, 202, Kinloss. Flew in 13-4-10. Taxiable		1-14
❑	XV748	'3D'	HS Harrier GR.3	69	ex Cranfield, Bedford, 233 OCU, 1, GR.1, 233 OCU, 1. Arrived 21-10-00	[8]	1-14
❑	XX901		HS Buccaneer S.2B	77	ex Kemble, St Athan, Lossiemouth, 208, 12, 237 OCU, 208. SOC 10-1-95. Arrived 26-5-96. *Kathryn - The Flying Mermaid / Glen Elgin*. Pink colours	[1]	1-14
❑	XZ631		Panavia Tornado GR.4	78	ex Warton, Panavia, A&AEE. Arrived 22-3-05		1-14
❑	ZA354		Panavia Tornado GR.1	82	ex Warton. Arrived 29-4-05		1-14
❑	–	'1'	Hunting Jet Provost T.3	~	ex Linton-on-Ouse. Procedure trainer, stored. Arrived 10-92		1-14
❑	–	'2'	Hunting Jet Provost T.3	~	ex Linton-on-Ouse. Procedure trainer, 1 FTS badge	[9]	1-14
❑	21417		Lockheed CT-133 Silver Star	54	ex Sollingen, 414 Sqn, CAF 133417, RCAF 21417. Canadair-built		1-14
❑	538	'3-QH'	Dassault Mirage IIIE	~	ex Chateaudun, 3 Esc, French AF. Arrived 1995		1-14
❑	'15919'	'1'	M'schmitt Bf 109G FSM	94	BAPC.240, ex Garforth. Arrived 5-94	[10]	1-14
❑	'N-2'		Hawker Hunter FGA.78	68	ex Bournemouth, Qatar AF QA-10, G-9-286, Dutch AF N-268. Arrived 25-4-92		1-14
❑	'319764'		Waco CG-4A Hadrian	~	BAPC.157, ex '237123', Bacup, Ormskirk		1-14

■ **[1]** Airframes on loan: the 'Flea' from Dave Allan; Buccaneer XN974 from Ollie Suckling; Lightning from Peter Chambers; Buccaneer XX901 from Buccaneer Aircrew Association. **[2]** Kitten was built by Bill Sneesby; it has been fitted with a Citroen 2CV and was due to make its taxying debut in 2014. **[3]** Spitfire FSM 'guards' the memorial room of the 609 (West Riding) Squadron Association.

[4] Mosquito is on loan from Tony Agar and is a complex composite, using the cockpit of HJ711 (and the history of HJ711 is charted above), the rear fuselage of TT.35 RS715 from Elstree; the centre section from Mk XVI PF498 from Leyland; and the outer wings of T.3 VA878 from St Davids. Work is in hand to get is ground-running. **[5]** Halifax re-creation is a complex composite: using a rear fuselage section from former 58 Squadron Mk.II HR792 which came to grief in a take-off accident at Stornoway on 13th January 1945; the centre section and inner wings from Hastings C.1 TG536 from Catterick; unused outer wings from a Hastings C.1; myriad Halifax detail parts; Hercules engines courtesy of the French Air Force and ex-Noratlas, plus new-build cockpit and rear section and other elements. **[6]** Victor was acquired on behalf of YAM by André Tempest and his late father, Gerry; as noted above, it regularly taxies. **[7]** XV168 was donated by BAE Systems and dedicated 18-8-13 to the company aircrew who gave their lives during the development of the Buccaneer. **[8]** Harrier XV748 - see also Coventry, W Mids, for at least one set of its wings. **[9]** 'JP' '2' is *very likely* XM373, ex Cranwell 7726M before Linton, it crashed 29-6-61 with 2 FTS. **[10]** Bf 109G was built by Danny Thornton of Garforth, W Yorks.

FELIXKIRK AERODROME between the A19 and A170 north-east of Thirsk

By October 2013 Isaacs Fury 'S1579' (G-BBVO) was flying from a strip in Northamptonshire.

❑ G-AIPR		Auster J/4 Archer	47	ex Popham. CoA 27-9-07		7-13

Aircraft Restoration Group: By the summer of 2013, the workshop established in the general area moved to Pickhill, N Yorks. 'Flea' 'G-ADRZ' arrived in this area from South Molton, Devon, and made the move to the new location. Auster Alpha G-APRF is believed to have gone to France in mid-2011 for restoration. Soko Kraguj 30151 was available for sale in July 2012 and moved on, perhaps also bound for France. Vampire T.11 XD547 arrived at an off-site location from Dumfries, Scotland, by February 2012, but it moved north o' the border again by December 2012, to Elgin, Scotland.

INGLEBY ARNCLIFFE between the A19 and A172 north-east of Northallerton

❑ G-BHNV		Bell 47G-3B1 XW180	68	ex F-GHNM, G-BHNV, XW180. Westland-built. CoA 28-5-89		1-14
❑ G-MMKM		Flexiform Dual Striker	83	CoA 11-6-99		1-14

LEEMING AIRFIELD east of the A1, west of Bedale EGXE

RAF Leeming: BAE Systems and the RAF use the station for the **Tornado Reduce To Produce Programme**; stripping for spares and then moved on apace to a Midlands scrapyard. On 9th July 2012 three F.3s (ZE203, ZE794 and ZE961) were ferried in from QinetiQ at Boscombe Down, representing the last flights of the variant. During 2012 work started on GR.4s, in similar manner but by later 2013 some GR.4s were arriving purely for scrapping, being declared beyond 're-cycling'. The Tornado RTP contract is due to run until 2017. Last noted in January 2004 for BDR training, the cockpit of Tornado F.2 ZD934 has been scrapped. Phantom FGR.2 XV499 moved to Hixon, Staffs, 13th February 2013.

Opened on 3rd June 2010 as part of the base's 70 anniversary celebrations, the **RAF Leeming Historical Training Facility** is housed in an original World War Two-era Nissen hut, once used as the station chapel. It is currently organised as a force facility and not available for public inspection.

❑ XA634	'L'	Gloster Javelin FAW.4	56	ex Shawbury, Colerne, Melksham 7641M (2-6-60), Gloster. 228 OCU colours	[1]	6-13

■ **[1]** Displayed outside the Bernard Building, HQ for 90 Signals Unit.

LINTON-ON-OUSE AIRFIELD west of the A19, north-west of York EGXU

RAF Linton-on-Ouse Memorial Room: Curator W/C Alan Mawby and his volunteers have created a detailed and moving tribute to the 2,009 personnel from Linton and its satellites at East Moor and Tholthorpe that were killed during World War Two. Exhibits also include Linton's post-war history through to the Tucano.

◆ **Access:** *Tours staged on a number of Sundays, 14:00 to 17:00. All must be booked in advance* | **01347 8477660**

RAF Linton-on-Ouse: The 'JP' is outside Cheshire Hall, the HQ Flying Wing, while the Tucano is adjacent to the Officers' Mess. 'JP' XN492 is kept by 2434 (Church Fenton) Squadron ATC. A number of Tucanos are held in store, but as most are short/medium term, do not merit an entry. Tucano T.1s ZF344 and ZF409 moved to Church Fenton, N Yorks, by July 2012 where they were readied for sale. Both moved to Ipswich, Suffolk, in October 2013 for export to the USA. UTVA-66 YU-DLG arrived from Biggin Hill, Gtr Lon, by December 2012, but moved to Morpeth, N&T, 9th February 2013.

❑ G-RADA*		Soko Kraguj	76	ex Biggin Hill, Yugoslav AF 30140. CoA 5-9-05. Arr by 12-12		11-13
❑ XN492		Hunting Jet Provost T.3	60	ex Redhill, Haydock, Levenshulme, Firbeck, Stock, Odiham, Cosford, Halton 8079M (18-3-70), 6 FTS, RAFC. Cockpit, moved off-site by 2-13		2-13
❑ XN589	'46'	Hunting Jet Provost T.3A	61	9143M, ex 1 FTS, RAFC. 1 FTS colours. Displayed		11-13
❑ ZF202		Short Tucano T.1	89	ex Shawbury, 72, 1 FTS, 3 FTS, CFS. Displayed	[1]	11-13

■ **[1]** Erected to mark the 90th anniversary of 1 FTS which was formed on 23rd December 1919 at Netheravon.

MALTON north-east of York

Eden Camp Modern History Theme Museum: Each hut in this former prisoner of war camp has a different theme and the level of presentation is breath-taking. There is much to fascinate the aviation follower, including a Link trainer display, plotting room, items on 617 Squadron, the Comete escape line and much more.

◆ **Access:** *'Brown signed' off the A64 north of Malton at the A169 junction.* **Open:** *Daily 10:00 to 17:00, last admission 16:00. (Extended closure Xmas and New Year, call or click for details.)* **Contact:** *Malton, YO17 6RT* | **01653 697777** | **admin@edencamp.co.uk** | **www.edencamp.co.uk**

❑ 'P2793'	'SD-M'	Hawker Hurricane FSM	93	BAPC.236, 501 Sqn colours	[2]	3-12
❑ 'AB550'	'GE-P'	Supermarine Spitfire FSM	91	BAPC.230, ex 'AA908'. 349 Sqn colours	[1]	3-12
❑ –		Fieseler Fi 103 (V-1) FSM	93	BAPC.235, -	[1]	3-12

■ **[1]** The Spitfire and V-1 were built by TDL Replicas of Lowestoft. **[2]** The Hurricane by G B Mouldings of Norfolk.

NEWBY WISKE north-west of Thirsk, near South Otterington

Falke G-AYZU had moved out by July 2013.

❑ G-BBBW	Clutton FRED 2	78	CoA 19-6-08. Dismantled	7-13
❑ G-BWSI*	K&S Cavalier SA.102-5	87	CoA 19-4-08. First noted 1-12	7-13
❑ G-BGFK	Evans VP-1	r92	de-reg 7-4-99. Dismantled	7-13
❑ E3B.369	Bücker Jungmann G-BPDM	54	ex Spanish AF. CASA-built 1-131E Srs 2000. CoA 22-6-96. Off-site	7-13

NORTHALLERTON on the A168/A684 east of Leeming Bar

'The Standard': A consortium, the **XN458 Club**, is working on the 'JP' in the grounds of the pub in the High Street.

◆ **Access:** *Viewable during opening hours* | **www.xn458.co.uk** | **www.thestandard-pub.co.uk**

❑ XN458	Hunting Jet Provost T.3	60	ex Ashington, 'XN594' WAM Cardiff, St Athan, Halton 8334M (21-3-73), Shawbury, 1 FTS. Black colour scheme	1-14

Also:

❑ G-AGYH*	Auster J/1N Alpha	46	ex Barrow	1-14

NORTH DUFFIELD on the A163 north-east of Selby

Modifly: Set up by Condor Holdings, Modifly is established a flying centre specifically for disabled pilots and is funding the design of a twin boom type specifically for such aviators. An aerodrome, called Birchwood, has been set up and the forward fuselage of a HS.125 acquired for use on site.

◆ **Access:** *Viewable by prior arrangement* **only** | **hello@modifly.co.uk** | **www.modifly**

❑ VP-CFI*	HS 125-700B	~	ex Bournemouth. Forward fuselage	1-14

NORTH STAINLEY on the A6109 north-west of Ripon

Lightwater Valley Theme Park / Lightwater Village:

◆ **Contact: 0870 4580040** | **leisure@lightwatervalley.co.uk** | **www.lightwatervalley.co.uk**

❑ –	Sopwith Baby replica	78	BAPC.137, ex Land's End, Chertsey	5-09

PICKHILL between the A1 and A167 west of Thirsk

Aircraft Restoration Group: Has settled on a small workshop locally, with storage sites in the general area. The Tawney Owl was written out of *W&R18* (p61) as having left Stondon, Essex, by mid-2001. The twin-boom, pusher, light aircraft crashed on its first flight. During the last couple of years it is reported to have received some restorative treatment.

◆ **Access:** *Not available for inspection* | **http://aircraftrestorationgroup.webs.com**

❑ 'G-ADRZ'*		Mignet HM.14 'Flea'	~	ex South Molton, Dunstable, South Molton. Citroen 2CV, stored, off site	7-13
❑ G-APWU*		Thurston Tawney Owl	59	ex Leamington Spa, 'Herefordshire', Stondon, Stapleford Tawney. Crashed 22-4-60. De-reg 15-9-86. Arrived 9-13. Stored - see notes above	9-13
❑ 'BR954'*	'JP-A'	Supermarine Spitfire FSM	~	stored	7-13
❑ XG743*	'597'	DH Sea Vampire T.22	54	ex Duxford (issued to IWM 15-6-72), Wymondham, Duxford, Brawdy SF, A&AEE, Brawdy SF, 766, 736, 764. F/n 5-13	2-14

PICTON on a minor road west of the A19, south of Yarm

Battlezone Paintball: **Access:** *busy venue, by prior permission* **only** | **www.battlezonepaintball.co.uk**

❑ G-BFGS*	MS Rallye 180GT	75	ex Spalding, F-BXYK. CoA 23-12-11, de-reg 24-1-12	1-14
❑ XN385	Westland Whirlwind HAS.7	60	ex Bolton, Chorley, Bruntingthorpe, Bournemouth, Wroughton, Culdrose, Wroughton, HS, A&AEE, 771, 824, 825, 824. SOC 18-9-92	1-14

RIPON on the A61 south west of Thirsk

Ripon Flight Simulators: Has a trailer-mounted L29 cockpit.

❑ -	Aero L29 Delfin	~	ex Prague. Cockpit	8-11

RUFFORTH AERODROME south of the A1237, west of York

Two** flying areas exist on the former RAF station. Rufforth West is operated by the Yorkshire Gliding Centre -* ***www.yorkglidingcentre.co.uk *- and Rufforth East is run by the Yorkshire Microlight Centre -* ***www.yorkflyingclub.com***

Gyrocopter Experience and Academy: On the 'East' Site have established a small visitor centre with a couple of gyros at the shop. Also on this site is 'Chocs Away' a cafe which is open daily March to end of October.

◆ **Access:** *Busy operation, viewing by prior arrangement* | **www.gyrocopterexperience.com**

❑ G-ARTJ*	Bensen B.8M	62	ex Leven, Cupar, East Fortune, Cupar, Currie, Cupar. De-reg 6-6-75. First noted 9-13	9-13
❑ G-BXCJ*	Campbell Cricket	97	CoA 28-4-09. First noted 10-12	9-13
❑ G-CDBE*	Bensen B.8M	05	CoA 7-9-04. First noted 10-12	9-13
❑ G-CEUI*	Rotorsport MT-03	07	CoA 25-10-08, de-reg 23-9-08. Used as simulator	9-13
❑ 'PCL-132'*	PFA Gyroglider 001	~	first noted 10-12	9-13

'East' site:

❑ G-MJFK*	Flexiform Tri-Flyer	r82	de-reg 10-5-00. Stored in roof	10-12
❑ G-MJGK	Eurowing Goldwing	r82	de-reg 13-6-90. Stored	2-10

McLean's Sailplanes: On the 'West' site

◆ **Access:** *Busy workshop; when conditions permit, a charity donation allows a look inside* | **www.mclean-aviation.co.uk**

❑ G-ATSY		Wassmer Baladou IV	66	ex Newcastle. CoA 23-11-91	11-13
❑ G-BCHX		Scheibe SF-23A Sperling	59	ex Netherthorpe, D-EGIZ. Damaged 7-8-82, de-reg 22-3-02	11-13
❑ G-BSPC		Jodel D.140C	65	ex Lashenden, F-BMFN. CoA 31-10-85, de-reg 5-8-94	11-13
❑ G-DEJD	EJD	Slingsby T.65D Vega	81	ex BGA.2715, RAFGSA	8-10
❑ DPT		Schiebe L-Spatz 55	~	BGA.2278, ex RAFGGA.510. Dam 28-3-97, CoA 12-7-98	11-13
❑ EGQ*		Schleicher K.7	~	BGA.2678, ex Bicester, D-4114. CoA 22-6-96	11-13
❑ GAC		Schleicher Ka 6	~	BGA.3670, ex RAFGGA.510. Cr 25-11-98, CoA 2-2-99	8-10

SCARBOROUGH

Three projects are located in the (very!) general area within *private* workshops. Work on Geoff New's three-seater 504L continues apace. At another location, the reference for the Austers is getting long-in-the-tooth.

❑ S-AHAA*	Avro 504L	G-EASD	20	ex Woodford, Richmond, Sudbury, S-AAP, G-EASD	[1]	6-12
❑ G-AHCK	Auster J/1N Alpha		46	ex Thwing, Spilsby, Croft, Skegness. Damaged 14-9-91, de-reg 22-4-94		12-03
❑ G-AJRC	Auster J/1 Autocrat		47	ex Thwing. CoA 14-7-02, de-reg 22-2-08		12-03

SELBY on the A19 south of York

Jet Art Aviation Ltd: Chris Wilson's family-run business specialises in the restoration, supply and transportation of static display or museum airframes - with a decided penchant for Harriers and Tornados - as well as cockpits, engines, Martin-Baker seats, spares and collectibles. A veritable 'fleet' of Jet Provost T.5s arrived from Cosford early in 2013, most moving on quickly. Several of the Tornado RTP programme F.3 cockpits listed within this edition were supplied courtesy of Jet Art; the last of the kind being ZE695. Having brought the first whole Tornado F.3 into private hands, the former Warton GR.1 is a similar coup, RB.199s and all! The Jindivik arrived on site in June 2011 and has been in storage; the plan is to turn it into Jet Art's 'gate guard'. **Gentle reminder** - with a blunter one below - this is a commercial premise and non-customer visitors *cannot* be admitted.

Departures: **Buccaneer** S.2B cockpit XZ431 to an owner in the Nottingham area, circa 2013; **F-104G Starfighter** 22+57 exported to Taiwan during 2012; **Harrier** T.4 XW269 moved to Caernarfon, Wales, on 2-10-122; **Jet Provost** T.5A XW299 arrived from Cosford, Shropshire, 31-1-13, departing to Boscombe Down, Wilts, 24-1-14; XW301, XW318 and XW361 arrived on site 31-1-13, 16-1-13 and 16-1-13 respectively from Cosford, Shropshire, and were despatched to the Netherlands 17-1-14; XW410 arrived from Cosford, Shropshire, 31-1-13, was reduced to spares, while the cockpit moved to a owner in Norfolk 1-14; XW434 arrived from Cosford, Shropshire, 16-1-13 departing for Wolverhampton, Staffs, 29-5-13; **Tornado** GR.1 ZA399 arrived from Cosford, Shropshire, 29-5-13, it was refurbished and delivered to Knutsford, Cheshire, 15-8-13; F.2 cockpit ZD932 was exported to Germany during 2013; an unflown Tornado IDS cockpit, build number GS.400, was delivered to Marham, Norfolk, during 10-13; **Wessex** HC.2 XR506 arrived from Greatham, Hants, 19-11-12, but moved to Corley Moor, Warks, 19-6-13.

◆ **Access:** ***PRIVATE** location, access* ***STRICTLY by prior appointment***
Contact: 01757 290962 | jetartaviation@gmail.com | www.jetartaviation.co.uk

❑ WK275		Supermarine Swift F.4	55	ex Upper Hill Hatfield, Filton, C(A). SOC 25-5-59. Restoration project		2-14
❑ XM191*		EE Lightning F.1A	61	ex North Scarle, EP&TU Cranwell 8590M, St Athan, Abingdon 7854M, Wattisham, 111. Crashed 9-6-64. Shark's mouth. Cockpit. First noted 10-13		2-14
❑ XR751		EE Lightning F.3	65	ex Queensbury, Ipswich, Tremar, Binbrook, 11, LTF, 29, 226 OCU, EE. SOC 21-6-88. Cockpit		2-14
❑ XV741*	'DD41'	HS Harrier GR.3	69	ex Gosport, Culdrose, A2608[3], A2607, Cosford, 233 OCU, 3, 233 OCU, 3. 25th anniversary Transatlantic air race c/s Arrived 13-9-12		2-14
❑ XW358*	'MK'	BAC Jet Provost T.5A	71	ex Cosford 9181M (11-3-93), Shawbury, 1 FTS, RAFC. Arrived 16-1-13		2-14
❑ XW360*	'ML'	BAC Jet Provost T.5A	71	ex Cosford 9153M (8-7-92), Shawbury, 1 FTS, RAFC, 7 FTS. Arrived 16-1-13		2-14
❑ XW425*	'MV'	BAC Jet Provost T.5A	71	ex Cosford 9200M (6-7-93), CFS, 6 FTS, CFS, 3 FTS, Leeming SF, CFS. Arrived 16-1-13		2-14
❑ XZ132*	'C'	HS Harrier GR.3	76	ex Cranwell 9168M, St Athan, 4, 1, 1351 Flt, 1, 233 OCU, 1, 3. Arrived 13-11-13		2-14
❑ XZ455		HS Sea Harrier FA.2	79	ex Queensbury, Ipswich, Yeovilton, FSAIU, 801, 899, 800, 899, 801, 899, 700A. Crashed 14-2-96	[1]	2-14
❑ XZ993*	'M'	HS Harrier GR.3	81	ex Welshpool, St Athan 9240M (25-7-94), Laarbruch, St Athan, 4, 1, 1453 Flt, 3. Cockpit. Arrived 14-11-13		2-14
❑ ZA353		Panavia Tornado GR.1	80	ex Boscombe Down, TTTE. Spares source		2-14
❑ ZA359*	'B-55'	Panavia Tornado GR.1	81	ex Warton, TTTE. Arrived 24-1-14		2-14
❑ ZE256	'TP'	Panavia Tornado F.3	87	ex Leuchars, 56, 29, 111, 56, 5. 11 Sqn colours, one side painted as 'ZE343' 'DZ'	[2]	2-14
❑ ZE965*		Panavia Tornado F.3	89	ex Leeming, 111, 111. Cockpit		2-14
❑ ZH807*		HS Sea Harrier FA.2	98	ex East Cowes, Newport, Basingstoke, St Athan, accident 1-5-02, 899. Cockpit. Arrived by 12-12		2-14
❑ –*		Supermarine Swift CIM	~	ex Newark, Hemswell. Arrived by 6-13		2-14
❑ –		HS Harrier GR.1 or 3	~	ex Ruthin. Cockpit, flying control rig		2-14
❑ A92-255*		GAF Jindivik 3	~	ex Aberporth, DRA, RAE. Arrived 6-10. See notes above		2-14
❑ 163205		HS AV-8B Harrier II	~	ex Queensbury, St Athan, USMC. Forward fuselage		2-14

■ **[1]** XZ455 flew 58 combat sorties during the Falklands conflict, scoring two air-to-air 'kills' and dropping 28 bombs. Then in, in its *second* war, crashed on return from a patrol over Bosnia; the pilot ejecting safely. **[2]** Tornado ZE256 was last flown on 27-3-03 and was the first whole example of the breed in private hands.

Anne and **Nigel Ponsford / Ponsford Collection**: See also under Breighton, E Yorks and Wigan, Gtr Man.

◆ **Access:** *Airframes listed held in deep storage or restoration in and around the area and visits are* **not** *possible*

❑ G-AEFG	Mignet HM.14 'Flea'	36	BAPC.75, ex Breighton, Leeds, Harrogate, Kirkby Overblow, Accrington	1-14
❑ G-APXZ	Payne Knight Twister	r60	ex Breighton, Tumby Woodside, Loughborough, Biggin Hill. De-reg 26-3-73. Frame	1-14
❑ ALX	Hawkridge Dagling	47	BGA.491, ex Leeds, Great Hucklow	1-14
❑ AMW*	EoN Olympia 2B	47	BGA.514, ex Millom, G-ALKM. CoA 16-4-03. Arrived 1-10-11	1-14
❑ AQY	EoN Primary	48	BGA.588, ex Breighton, Hemel Hempstead. Stored	1-14
❑ BVM	Slingsby Dart 17R	66	BGA.1269, ex Breighton, Rufforth. CoA 25-7-90	1-14
❑ –	Hutter H.17a	36	ex Leeds, Accrington	1-14

❑	–	Dickson Primary	31	ex Leeds, Harrogate		1-14
❑	–	Addyman STG	34	BAPC.14, ex Leeds, Harrogate, Wigan		1-14
❑	–	Addyman Ultralight	36	BAPC.16, ex Leeds, Harrogate, Wigan		1-14
❑	–	Killick Gyroplane	c63	BAPC.18, ex Leeds, Harrogate, Irlam		1-14
❑	–	Addyman Zephyr	33	BAPC.39, ex Leeds, Harrogate. Substantial parts		1-14
❑	F-CALY*	Nord 2000	47	ex Rufforth, Belgium, France. Arrived 19-1-14	[1]	1-14
❑	XK819	Slingsby Grasshopper TX.1	55	ex Breighton, Warmingham, Stoke-on-Trent, Cosford, Malvern, 2 MGSP, Kimbolton		1-14

■ **[1]** Nord 2000 was a licence-built DFS Olympia Meise; which was also built post-war in the UK as the EoN Olympia. Acquired for spares for the restoration of BGA.514 and for Meise BGA.449 at a location near Rufforth, N Yorks. Initially imported to Rufforth, but is best listed under this heading as it will 'settle' here.

SHERBURN-IN-ELMET AERODROME on the B1222 east of the town, east of Leeds EGCJ

❑	G-BDFZ*	Cessna F.150M	75	Reims-built. CoA 9-7-10, de-reg 8-4-10	8-12
❑	G-BNOE	Piper Warrior II	87	ex N9121X, N9568N. Crashed 28-1-11	8-11
❑	G-BRJN	Pitts S-1C Special	64	ex N6A. Crashed 10-7-03, CoA 20-5-04	8-12
❑	G-OBMW*	American AA-5 Traveler	75	CoA 16-7-12, de-reg 18-6-12	8-12
❑	G-SACU	Piper Cadet 161	88	ex N9162X. Crashed 29-6-96, de-reg 7-6-01	8-12

THIRSK on the A19 north-east of Ripon

Evans VP-2 G-BFFB had moved on by July 2012, perhaps ending up in Scotland.

❑	G-BEKM	Evans VP-1	86	ex Eaton Bray. CoA 23-3-95	2-10

TOPCLIFFE on the A168 south west of Thirsk EGXZ

Allanbrook Barracks: Home of **645 VGS**.

❑	XE797	Slingsby Cadet TX.3	53	ex Dishforth, Catterick, Dishforth, 645 GS, 2 GC, 641 GS, 27 GS. SOC 28-9-78. Cockpit	9-10

WOMERSLEY south of the M62, west of the A19

Blue Lagoon Diving and Leisure Centre: As well as the Hunter on show on the surface, in the depths is F.6A XJ639, sunk in July 2006. **www.divebluelagoon.co.uk**

❑	WT799	'879'	Hawker Hunter T.8C	55	ex Exeter, North Weald, Ipswich, Shawbury, FRADU, FRU, 759, RAE, F.4, 4, 11. SOC 3-4-95. Displayed	10-13

YORK

A Chipmunk and a Robin are in a workshop in the *general* area. After spares reclamation Chipmunk T.10 WB555 was scrapped by mid-2013.

❑	G-BICP	Robin DR.360 Chevalier	71	ex F-BSPH. CoA 28-7-08	1-12
❑	WK622	DHC Chipmunk T.10 G-BCZH	52	ex Breighton, Yeovilton, 2 FTS, Wattisham TFF, Bri UAS, 3 AEF, Bri UAS, Leeds UAS, 24 GCF, Ox UAS, 18 RFS, 22 RFS. Crashed 6-9-87, de-reg 14-12-06	1-14

SOUTH YORKSHIRE

Includes the unitary authorities of Doncaster, Rotherham and Sheffield

BAWTRY on the A638 south of Doncaster

Bawtry Paintball and Laser Fields: *Busy site - by prior arrangement* **only | www.bawtrypaintballfields.co.uk**

❑	XL840	Westland Whirlwind HAS.7	57	ex Long Marston, Norwich, Sibson, Blackpool, Fleetwood, Wroughton, 705, Brawdy SF, Culdrose SF, 705, 820. SOC 26-6-76	12-11

DONCASTER

South Yorkshire Aircraft Museum: The diversity here, particularly into 'people-friendly' light aviation, continues to delight. Latest is this category is the AA-1B Trainer *Lima-Whisky*. Perhaps an unremarkable machine in terms of UK heritage, it is a great example of how 'Joe Public' could learn to fly in such a modest machine. It has a more specific provenance, having been resident at Doncaster 1974 to 1975 with Flight-Line and was last with a Sheffield-based owner.

Working with SYAM and co-based is the **Yorkshire Helicopter Preservation Group** - see separate entry. SYAM curator Naylan Moore bases his **Classic Aircraft Collection** here. As well as *two* Typhoon projects, Naylan has other Hawker types under way although they are not yet at the stage of a formal listing: a Hurricane and a Tempest II.

As might be expected by such an extensive collection, there are many airframes that are in store or under restoration and not available for public inspection - but there occasionally there are 'back lot' tours.

The cockpit of Lightning F.6 XR754 moved to Upwood, Cambs, on 17th December 2013.

◆ **Access:** *Within Doncaster Lakeside Leisure Park. Access off the A638 beyond 'The Dome' or follow signs off the M18/ A6182 for 'Lakeside'.* **Open:** *Apr to Oct Tue to Sun, 10:00 to 17:00; Nov to Mar, Tue to Sun 10:00 to 16:00 and daily during school summer holidays. SYAM is happy to offer 'back lot' tours of the storage area - applications in advance* **only**. *Regular special events - see the website.* **Contact:** *Dakota Way, Airborne Road, Doncaster Leisure Park, Doncaster, DN4 7FB* | **01302 761616 | via website | www.southyorkshireaircraftmuseum.org.uk**
Thinks: *Within the Lakeside complex, is a memorial to those who served at RAF Doncaster and Doncaster Airport, co-ordinated by the Doncaster Lakeside team with input from SYAM and the Airfield Research Group.*

❑ 'K-158'		Austin Whippet replica	90	BAPC.207, ex Sunderland, Stoke-on-Trent		1-14
❑ G-ACBH		Blackburn B-2	32	ex Redhill, 'Kent', Ingatestone, West Hanningfield, Wickham Bishops, Downham, Ramsden Heath, Brentwood 2895M. CoA 27-11-41, de-reg 14-7-42. Arrived 21-2-12. Fuselage		1-14
❑ G-AEJZ		Mignet HM.14 'Flea'	36	BAPC.120, ex Hemswell, Cleethorpes, Brough. De-reg 31-12-38. Arrived 2004		1-14
❑ G-APMY		Piper Apache 160	58	ex Firbeck, Connah's Quay, Halfpenny Green, EI-AJT. CoA 1-11-81, de-reg 25-11-81. Acquired 4-96. United Steel c/s		1-14
❑ G-ATXH		HP Jetstream 200	67	ex Cranwell, Finningley, Prestwick, Filton. De-reg 22-4-71. Cockpit	[1]	1-14
❑ G-AVAA		Cessna F.150G	67	ex Firbeck, Shobdon, Bournemouth. Reims-built. CoA 5-7-96, de-reg 16-4-96. Arrived 26-11-97		1-14
❑ G-AVTT*		Erco Ercoupe 415D	47	ex Monewden, SE-BFZ, NC3774H. CoA 20-1-86, de-reg 12-4-02. Arrived 21-2-14		2-14
❑ G-BCLW*		American AA-1B Trainer	74	ex Doncaster-Sheffield. Damaged 12-2-13, CoA 9-6-13 Arrived 27-4-13		1-14
❑ G-BOCB		HS.125-1B/522	66	ex Cardiff, Hatfield, G-OMCA, G-DJMJ, G-AWUF, 5N-ALY, G-AWUF, HZ-BIN. CoA 16-10-90, de-reg 22-2-95. Arrived 2001. Cockpit	[2]	1-14
❑ G-DELB		Robinson R22B	88	ex Firbeck, Sherburn, Retford, N26461. Crashed 27-12-94, de-reg 20-4-95. Acquired 11-97		1-14
❑ G-MJKP		Hiway Skytrike	r82	CoA 31-12-86, de-reg 9-12-94. Arrived 2001		1-14
❑ G-MMDK		Mainair Tri-Flyer	83	CoA 30-5-99, de-reg 2-12-10. Arrived 2009		1-14
❑ G-MVNT		Whittaker MW.5-K	90	CoA 5-5-07, de-reg 27-5-11. Arrived 2009		1-14
❑ G-MYJX		Whittaker MW.8	93	de-reg 31-7-01. Arrived 2007	[3]	1-14
❑ G-OPFW		HS.748-2A/266	72	ex Haverigg, Emerald, G-BMFT, VR-BFT, G-BMFT, 5W-FAO, G-11-10. CoA 16-2-07, de-reg 15-6-09. Arrived 4-9-10 Parcel Force colours, cockpit		1-14
❑ G-RAYE		Piper Cherokee Six	66	ex Stamford, Tatenhill, G-ATTY, N11C. CoA 27-9-08, de-reg 2-6-08. Arrived 2009. Fuselage	[2]	1-14
❑ -		Blériot XI replica	09	BAPC.307	[4]	1-14
❑ -		hot-air balloon	~	envelope and basket		1-14
❑ -*		Bensen B.8	~	-	[5]	1-14
❑ EI-JWM		Robinson R22	90	ex G-BSLB. Arrived 2004		1-14
❑ HB-NAV	'A'	Beagle Pup 150	71	ex Dover, Stock, Henley-on-Thames, Henlow, Redhill, G-AZCM. Forward fuselage, trailer mounted	[2]	1-14
❑ N4565L		Douglas DC-3-201A	39	ex Framlingham, Ipswich, Dublin, LV-GYP, LV-PCV, N129H, N512, N51D, N80C, NC21744. Arrived 6-8-03. *Aisling*		1-14
❑ –		Hawker Typhoon	~	ex Boscombe Down, Salisbury. Cockpit project	[6]	1-14
❑ –		Hawker Typhoon Ia or 'b	~	ex Staverton. Cockpit	[6]	1-14

❑ FX322		NAA Harvard II		44	ex Bruntingthorpe, Stoke, ?, French AF, FX322, n/s. Arrived 2006. Cockpit	[7]	1-14
❑ RT520		Auster 5	G-ALYB	44	ex Firbeck, Bristol, White Waltham, RT520, 85 GCS, 84 GCS. CoA 26-5-63, de-reg 29-2-84. Acq 1983. Frame		1-14
❑ SN280		Hawker Tempest V			ex Napier. SOC 30-12-49. Cockpit/firewall	[6] [8]	1-14
❑ VP519		Avro Anson C.19/2		47	ex Wolverhampton, 'Manchester', Dukinfield, Hadfield, Stockport, Peel Green, Cosford, Wigan, Irlam, Halfpenny Green, TAT, G-AVVR (de-reg 16-9-72), Shawbury, FCCS, 11 GCF, MCS, 31, Malta CF, TCDU. SOC 19-2-68. Arrived 2011. Cockpit, on loan		1-14
❑ WA662		Gloster Meteor T.7		50	ex Firbeck, Willington, Chalgrove, Llanbedr, Farnborough, FCCS, 3, Wildenrath SF, Gütersloh SF, 3. Acquired 1994	[9]	1-14
❑ WB733		DHC Chipmunk T.10		50	ex Firbeck, Sevenoaks, Shawbury SF, Hamble CoAT G-ATDE (de-reg 19-1-68), Marham SF, 4 SoTT 'hack', Lyneham SF, Upavon SF, Hull UAS, 11 RFS. SOC 12-9-73		1-14
❑ WB969		Slingsby Sedbergh TX.1		50	BGA.2036, ex Wroot, WB969, CGIS, 168 GS. Crashed 24-8-80, CoA 8-10-80. Arrived 10-01		1-14
❑ WD935		EE Canberra B.2		51	ex Birdlip, Bridgnorth, Ottershaw, Egham, St Athan 8440M (17-4-75), 360, 97, 151, CSE, EE, BCDU, RAAF A84-1 ntu. Arrived 2003. Cockpit	[6]	1-14
❑ WE987	DZX	Slingsby Prefect TX.1		50	BGA.2517, ex Newport Pagnell, ACCGS, CGS, 633 GS, 642 GS, 2 GS. CoA 17-7-89. Arrived 12-01. Stored, off-site		1-14
❑ WF122	'575'	Percival Sea Prince T.1		51	ex Bruntingthorpe, Helston, Culdrose A2673 (5-2-79), 750, Sydenham SF, Arbroath SF, Lossiemouth SF, 700Z Flt, Lossie' SF, FOFT, 750, Eglinton SF, 744. Arrived 29-8-03		1-14
❑ WJ565		EE Canberra T.17		53	ex Harrington, North Coates, Coventry, North Coates, Binbrook, Bruntingthorpe, Cosford 8871M, St Athan, 360, B.2, A&AEE. HP-built. Arrived 22-3-03. Cockpit		1-14
❑ WJ903		Vickers Varsity T.1		52	ex Firbeck, Dumfries, Glasgow Airport, 6 FTS, AE&AEOS, 1 ANS, 2 ANS, 3 ANS. SOC 5-2-75. Acquired 14-3-97. Cockpit		1-14
❑ WJ975	'S'	EE Canberra T.19		53	ex Hemswell, Cleethorpes, Cambridge, 100, 7, 100, 85, West Raynham TFF, 228 OCU, B.2, 44, 35, 231 OCU. Avro-built. SOC 21-5-80. Arrived 2005. Cockpit	[2]	1-14
❑ WL131		Gloster Meteor F.8		53	ex Firbeck, Guernsey 7751M, APS Sylt, 601, 111. SOC 16-11-62. Acquired 9-95. Cockpit	[2]	1-14
❑ WT741	'791'	Hawker Hunter GA.11		55	ex Hemswell, Macclesfield, Bitteswell, HAS, 738, F.4, 118. SOC 13-7-71. Cockpit. 738 Sqn colours	[6]	1-14
❑ –		Vickers Valetta		~	ex Cardington, Henlow (?), ATC unit (?). Cockpit	[10]	1-14
❑ XE935	'30'	DH Vampire T.11		55	ex Firbeck, Sibson, Hitchin, Woodford, Chester, St Athan, 8 FTS. SOC 8-11-67. Acquired 1966		1-14
❑ XG297	'Y'	Hawker Hunter FGA.9		56	ex Firbeck, Newton-le-Willows, Bacup, Macclesfield, Bitteswell, HSA, 20, 28, 20, F.6, 4. SOC 12-2-76. 20 Sqn colours. Cockpit	[2]	1-14
❑ XH584		EE Canberra T.4		55	ex Firbeck, Sunderland, Marham, 231 OCU. SOC 12-7-66. Acquired 1993. Cockpit	[2]	1-14
❑ XL149		Blackburn Beverley C.1		57	ex Winthorpe, Finningley 7988M (7-11-67), 84, 30, 84, 242 OCU. Arrived 2005. Cockpit. 84 Sqn colours		1-14
❑ XL388		Avro Vulcan B.2		62	ex Walpole, Honington 8750M (2-4-82), 50, Wadd Wing, Scampton Wing, 9. Arrived 7-4-03. *Mayflower III*. Cockpit		1-14
❑ XM350	'89'	Hunting Jet Provost T.3A		58	ex Firbeck, Church Fenton 9036M (10-11-89), 7 FTS, 1 FTS, RAFC, A&AEE. Acquired 1995		1-14
❑ XM411	'X'	Hunting Jet Provost T.3		60	ex Firbeck, Otterburn, Halton 8434M (10-11-74), St Athan, Shawbury, Kemble, CFS. Acquired 1999. Cockpit		1-14
❑ 'XM651'		Saro Skeeter AOP.12	XM561	59	ex Firbeck, East Kirkby, Tattershall, Moston, Middle Wallop, Arborfield 7980M (4-8-67), 15 MU, HQ 1 Wg, HQ 2 Wg, 651. Acquired 1993		1-14
❑ XN238		Slingsby Cadet TX.3		59	ex Firbeck, Robertsbridge, St Athan, 622 VGS, ACCGS, 1 GC, 626 GS, 634 GS, 614 GS, 662 GS. SOC 20-10-83. Acquired 5-97. Cockpit		1-14

❑ XN386	'35'	Westland Whirlwind HAR.9	60	ex Lancaster, Blackpool, Heysham, Wroughton A2713 (10-8-76), Fleetlands, *Endurance* Flt, HAS.7, 846, 814. Arrived 1999		1-14
❑ XN511	'12'	Hunting Jet Provost T.3	60	ex Firbeck, Robertsbridge, 'XM426', Lutterworth, Liversedge, Blackpool, Kemble, CFS, 1 FTS, CFS. SOC 28-5-76. Acquired 1997. Cockpit	[2]	1-14
❑ XN979		HS Buccaneer S.2	64	ex Stamford, Croydon, Popham, Stanbridge, Henlow, Cranfield, Fleetlands, 801 700B. Ditched 9-6-66. Cockpit	[2]	1-14
❑ XP190		Saro P.531-2	61	ex Firbeck, Wroughton, Arborfield, Middle Wallop, BSE Filton, A&AEE. SOC 1-5-72. Acquired 27-8-92		1-14
❑ XP706		EE Lightning F.3	63	ex Hemswell, Strubby, Binbrook 8925M (9-2-87), LTF, 11, 5, LTF, 23, 111, 74. Arrived 19-11-02		1-14
❑ XP902	'DT'	Westland Scout AH.1	63	ex Firbeck, Otterburn, Edinburgh, Dishforth, Netheravon, Wroughton, Garrison Air Sqn, 3 CBAS. Acquired 1999. Cockpit		1-14
❑ XS216		Hunting Jet Provost T.4	64	ex Goole, Finningley, 6 FTS, CAW. Damaged 7-5-73. Cockpit. Arrived 2003. Marked 'CRAN22/1'		1-14
❑ XS481		Westland Wessex HU.5	63	ex Firbeck, Dishforth, Wroughton, Yeovilton, Culdrose, Yeovilton, 771, 707. SOC 21-7-92. Acquired 6-98		1-14
❑ XV139		Westland Scout AH.1	67	ex Wattisham, 'XV137', Yeovil, Arborfield, Wroughton, 657, 656, 662, 653. Arrived 6-09		1-14
❑ XV677	'269'	Westland Sea King HAS.6	70	ex Gosport A2619 [3] (7-6-99), Fleetlands, 814, 810, 819, 706, 814, 820. Arrived 25-7-06	[11]	1-14
❑ XV752	'B'	HS Harrier GR.3	69	ex Bletchley, Cosford 9078M, 4, 3, 1, 233 OCU, GR.1, 1, 233 OCU. Arrived 5-12-11	[12]	1-14
❑ XW666		HS Nimrod R.1	73	ex Long Marston, Warton, Woodford, Kinloss, 51. Crashed 16-5-95. Arrived 2001. Cockpit		1-14
❑ XX411	'X'	Sud Gazelle AH.1	75	ex Chichester, 3 CBAS. Shot down 21-5-82, San Carlos. Westland-built. Arrived 5-02		1-14
❑ XX477		HP Jetstream T.1	73	ex Askern, Finningley 8462M, Little Rissington, CFS, G-AXXS (de-reg 2-5-73). Crashed 1-11-74. Arrived 1-11-08. Fuselage		1-14
❑ XX669	'B'	SAL Bulldog T.1	75	ex Halton, Andover, Llantrisant, Bruntingthorpe, Cosford 8997M, 2 FTS, Birm UAS, Man UAS. Damaged 6-9-88. Arrived 2006. Fuselage		1-14
❑ XX736		SEPECAT Jaguar GR.1	74	ex Brough, 9110M, Coltishall, Shawbury, Warton, Indian AF JI013, G-27-327, 6, 226 OCU. Cockpit. 54 Sqn c/s	[2]	1-14
❑ ZD938	'AR'	Panavia Tornado F.2	85	ex Chester, Market Drayton, Shawbury, St Athan, 229 OCU. Arrived 28-6-11. Forward fuselage. 229 OCU colours	[13]	1-14
❑ –		Avro Vulcan B.1 EMU	~	ex Reigate, East Kirkby, Tattershall, Waddington. Arrived 2011. Cockpit, stored	[14]	1-14
❑ 0767*		Aermacchi MB.339AA	81	ex Derby, Mickleover, Filton, Yeovilton, Stanley, Argentine Navy. First noted 11-13	[15]	1-14
❑ N-302		Hawker Hunter T.53	58	ex Firbeck, Chelford, Macclesfield, Leavesden, Elstree, Hatfield, RDanAF Esk.724 ET-273, RNethAF N-302. RNethAF colours. Cockpit	[2]	1-14
❑ –		Waco CG-4 Hadrian rep	~	ex Hatfield, *Saving Private Ryan*. Arrived 2003. Cockpit	[2]	1-14

■ **[1]** Prototype Jetstream, first flown at Radlett 18-8-67. **[2]** Airframes on loan from Bill Fern. **[3]** MW.8 prototype, built by the designer, Mike Whittaker. **[4]** Full-size replica Blériot XI commissioned from Ken Fern to celebrate the 100th anniversary of the first aviation meeting in the UK - at Doncaster racecourse 15/18-10-09 - built using original drawings. **[5]** SYAM has had a locally-built B.8 for around a *decade*; it is being restored and starting to look like a Bensen! **[6]** Airframes on loan from Naylan Moore's Classic Aircraft Collection. **[7]** Naylan Moore is restoring Harvard FX322 for Phil Jarvis - 1944 airframe, no RAF service. For more on Phil see note 11. **[8]** SN280 served exclusively with Napier and was SOC 30-12-49. **[9]** Cockpit of WA662 has finished restoration and is on display; the remainder is elsewhere being worked on. **[10]** Valetta cockpit came from Cardington and Henlow and is said to have been with an ATC unit before joining the museum. The 'smart-money' is on this being WJ476. **[11]** Previously listed under YHPG, the Sea King is owned by Nigel Porembski and Phil Jarvis and known as 'Project 677' - more gen on **www.project677.co.uk** See also Worksop, Notts, and note 7 for more on Phil Jarvis. **[12]** Harrier is on loan from 1053 Sqn ATC, Armthorpe, S Yorks. **[13]** Tornado is owned by Simon Pulford - see Chester, Cheshire, and **www.airpulford.com** **[14]** Vulcan cockpit is an 'unplumbed' B.1 with a B.2 'hood' and is held on behalf of Vulcan to the Sky Trust - see under Doncaster Sheffield, S Yorks. **[15]** MB.339 was last used as a static demonstrator/installation mock-up for the US Navy JPATS programme, which was won by the Beech T-6 Texan (aka rethought Pilatus PC-9) in 1995.

A Gazelle's eye view of a part of the SYAM site, May 2013. *Andy Wood*

Deep Store and **Workshop**: Not available for inspection without **prior arrangement**. Vampire T.11 XD459 moved to East Midlands, Leics.

❑ G-AOKO		Percival Prentice 1	49	ex Coventry, Southend, VS621, CFS, 2 FTS, 22 FTS. CoA 23-10-72, de-reg 9-10-84. Arrived 9-5-00		1-14
❑ G-ARGI		Auster 6A	46	ex Newark-on-Trent, Chirk, Heathfield, VF530, 661. CoA 4-7-76, de-reg 23-8-77. Arrived 1-00. Frame		1-14
❑ G-BAML		Bell JetRanger	67	ex Walton Wood, N7844S. Crashed 30-5-03, de-reg 7-7-03. Arrived 2004		1-14
❑ G-BDIN*		SAL Bulldog 125	76	ex Popham, R Jordan AF 408, JY-BAI. Spares for XX669. First noted 12-12		1-14
❑ G-BECE		AD Skyship 500	76	ex Cardington, Old Warden, Cardington, Kirkbymoorside. Gondola, damaged 9-3-79, de-reg 30-5-84. Arrived 1-08		1-14
❑ G-MJPO		Eurowing Goldwing	82	de-reg 9-4-02		1-14
❑ WK393		DH Venom FB.1	53	ex CGS, FWS, Silloth, Firbeck, Dumfries, Silloth. SOC 28-2-58. Pod	[1]	1-14
❑ WK626		DHC Chipmunk T.10	52	ex Firbeck, Salisbury, Welling, White Waltham 8123M (4-8-72), Bicester SF, Odiham SF, Ox UAS, South Cerney SF, 1 FTS, Bicester SF, Odiham SF, FTCCS, Lon UAS, Cam UAS, Colerne SF, Leeds UAS, Nott UAS, 16 FRS, 18 RFS. Acquired 1997. Fuselage	[1]	1-14
❑ WP255		DH Vampire NF.10	51	ex Haverigg, Firbeck, Ecclesfield, Bingley, Church Fenton, 27 MU, CNCS, 1 ANS, CNCS, 23. SOC 30-11-59. Acquired 1991. Cockpit	[2]	1-14
❑ WT913	FGA	Slingsby Cadet TX.1	52	BGA.3239, ex Strubby, 614 GS, 618 GS, 613 GS, 618 GS, 671 GS, 203 GS, 183 GS. CoA 21-7-96. Arrived 2003	[2] [3]	1-14
❑ WX788		DH Venom NF.3	54	ex Elvington, Kenilworth, Long Marston, Cardiff, Bledlow Ridge, Connah's Quay, DH. SOC 25-11-57. Arrived 2-02	[4]	1-14
❑ WZ822		Slingsby Grasshopper TX.1	52	ex Firbeck, Robertsbridge, Halton, London. Acquired 5-97		1-14
❑ XD377	'A'	DH Vampire T.11	53	ex Firbeck, Barton, Elvington, Cosford, Birmingham, Shawbury 8203M (28-7-72), Hawarden, 66. Arr 1999. Pod	[2]	1-14
❑ XE317	'S-N'	Bristol Sycamore HR.14	54	ex Firbeck, Winthorpe, Portsmouth, CFS, 275, G-AMWO (de-reg 30-9-53). SOC 6-5-72		1-14
❑ XT236		Bell Sioux AH.1	66	ex Sunderland, Middle Wallop, MoAF, Sek Kong. Westland-built. Stored		1-14

❑ XX655	'V'	SAL Bulldog T.1		74	ex Manston, Colerne 9294M (10-6-00), Bri UAS, 2 FTS. Cockpit		1-14
❑ E-424		Hawker Hunter F.51		56	ex Firbeck, East Kirkby, Tattershall, Cosford, Dunsfold, G-9-445 (20-2-76), Aalborg, RDanAF, Esk.724. Acquired 1988		1-14
❑ 333		DH Vampire T.55		53	ex Barton, Chelford, Hadfield, Dukinfield, New Brighton, Chester, Iraqi AF. Arrived 2-03. Pod	[1]	1-14

■ **[1]** Airframes on loan from Naylan Moore's Classic Aircraft Collection. **[2]** Airframes on loan from Bill Fern. **[3]** Bill Fern's Cadet is fitted with the wings of WT917. **[4]** Venom NF.3 WX788 is on loan from the Night Fighter Preservation Group.

Yorkshire Helicopter Preservation Group: Heartiest congratulations to **Charlotte and Chelsea Dresser** who were presented with the Transport Trust's 'Young Preservationist of the Year' award for 2013. The sisters started helping their grandfather, YHPG's Mike Fitch, on a variety of projects, in 2009 when they were 12 and 14 respectively. This was the first time that two people had been selected; the first time for females and at 16, Charlotte was the Trust's youngest recipient. Female ALEs - see the *Preface* - brilliant!

As well as the airframes, the group has a wealth of artefacts and documentation. Not suitable for a 'formal' listing is a Whirlwind hydraulic system training aid constructed from gearbox, rotor head and tail rotor components by Bristow Helicopters trainees at Redhill. This carries the fictitious registration 'G-YHPG'.

◆ **Access:** *Most airframes on display within SYAM, as above. Workshop and at other times by appointment.* **Contact:** *Alan Beattie, 18 Marshall Drive, Pickering, YO18 7JT* | **info@yhpg.co.uk** | **www.helicopter-preservation-yhpg.org.uk**

❑ WN499	'Y'	Westland Dragonfly HR.5		53	ex Caernarfon, Higher Blagdon, Blackbushe, Culdrose SF, 705. SOC 1-6-44. Arrived 3-6-06. Dismantled	[1]	1-14
❑ XA862		Westland Whirlwind HAR.1		53	ex Colerne, Weston-super-Mare, Coventry, Wroughton, Lee-on-Solent A2542 (20-5-66), Seafield Park, Haslar, Lee-on-Solent, Fleetlands, 781, 771, 700, 705, G-AMJT ntu. Arrived 13-7-05. Cockpit area	[2]	1-14
❑ XA870	'911'	Westland Whirlwind HAR.1		54	ex Helston, Predannack, Lee-on-Solent A2543 (18-5-66), 705, 155, 848. Arrived 1-12-02. Sectioned		1-14
❑ XJ398		Westland Whirlwind HAR.3	G-BDBZ	57	ex Elvington, Oxford, Luton G-BDBZ, XJ398, Culdrose, RAE, ETPS, Weston-super-Mare, DH Engines, A&AEE, XD768 ntu. De-reg 28-3-85. Arrived 27-603. 202 Sqn colours		1-14
❑ XP345		Westland Whirlwind HAR.10		62	ex Elvington, Storwood, Tattershall Thorpe, Lee-on-Solent Cyprus 8792M (2-9-83), 84 'B' Flt, 1563 Flt, 202, CFS. Arrived 6-7-02. 84 Sqn UN colours		1-14
❑ XS887	'403'	Westland Wessex HAS.1		66	ex Helston, Culdrose A2690 (29-5-80), Wroughton, 772, Yeovilton SAR Flt, 829. Arrived 9-12-07		1-14
❑ XT150		Bell Sioux AH.1		65	ex Netheravon, Middle Wallop 7883M, Wimbourne, Andover, Arborfield, Seletar, 6 Lt Regt, 28 Brig, 42 Cdo, 45 Lt Regt, 6 Lt Regt. Arrived 7-8-08. Off-site	[3]	1-14
❑ XT242	'12'	Bell Sioux AH.1		66	ex Firbeck, Hooton Park, Warmingham, Long Marston, Wimborne, Middle Wallop, 'Blue Eagles'. Acquired 13-2-03. 'Blue Eagles' colours	[4]	1-14

■ **[1]** In due course, WN499 will be restored to represent an HC.4 used in Operation FIREDOG, in Malaya. **[2]** The remainder of XA862 - well battered - is in the fire training area at Colerne, Wilts. **[3]** XT150 is a composite airframe, incorporating elements of the purely instructional 7884M. **[4]** Owned by YHPG's Alan Beattie and is a composite, with parts of XW179 included.

Museum and Art Gallery: The 'Flea' and the Bensen are displayed on the first floor.

◆ **Open:** *Mon-Sat 10:00 to 17:00, last entry 16:45* - **NB** *closed Sun. Closed Xmas and New Year.* **Contact:** *Chequer Road, Doncaster, DN1 2AE* | **01302 734293** | **museum@doncaster.gov.uk** | **www.doncaster.gov.uk/museums**

❑ 'G-AEKR'	Mignet HM.14 'Flea'	72	BAPC.121, ex Breighton, Firbeck, Nostell Priory, Crowle, Oakington. *This is the 'Flea' that Claybourne's Built*	[1]	3-12
❑ –	Bensen B.7	c61	BAPC.275		3-12

■ **[1]** Original G-AEKR, first flew at Doncaster 28-5-36. It became part of the RAF Finningley 'Station Museum' in the 1960s but was burnt out in a hangar fire 5-9-70. Some metal parts incorporated in this 'replacement' built largely at Oakington. [2] Bensen built by S J R Wood of Warmsworth.

DONCASTER SHEFFIELD AIRPORT (ROBIN HOOD) or Finningley, east of A638, north of Bawtry EGCN

Vulcan to the Sky Trust and **Vulcan Operating Company**: A double engine failure while running up on 28th May 2012 looked set to keep G-VLCN out of the air for at least the season. After major efforts it was back in the skies on 3rd July 2012.

The latest in a stream of gun-to-the-head appeals to keep the big delta flying was launched during 2013; this time to meet a modifications to leading edge and winter overhaul. The 2013 flying season was cut short in August by a fuel tank problem. By November £420,000 had been pledged by supporters and 'Joe Public' and work was in hand. See under Doncaster, S Yorks, for a Vulcan cockpit held for VTST.

◆ **Access:** *90-minute tours of XH558 available on Wed, Thu, Fri and* **some** *weekends, between 10:00 and 15:00 by prior booking* **only** | **1302 776411**. **Contact:** *Units 1 and 2, Venture Court, Dodwells Road, Hinckley, LE10 3BT* | **0845 5046558** | **enquiries@vulcantothesky.org** | **www.vulcantothesky.org**

❑ XH558	Avro Vulcan B.2(MRR) ✈ G-VLCN	60	ex Lyneham, Bruntingthorpe, Waddington, VDF, Marham, Waddington, 50, Wadd Wing, A&AEE, Wadd Wing, 27, 230 OCU, 27, Wadd Wing, 230 OCU. *Spirit of Great Britain*	1-14

Directions Finningley CIC | **The National Aviation Academy**: Centred upon Hangars 2 and 3; run in association with BAE Systems and Lufthansa Resource Technical Training (for the latter, see also Cotswold, Glos).

◆ **Access:** *Visits by prior arrangement* ***only*** | **www.directionscic.co.uk**

❑ EC-DDX	Boeing 727-256	79	ex Oakley, Bournemouth, Iberia. Forward fuselage	5-12
❑ ZJ100*	HS Hawk Mk.102D	92	ex Warton, Brough, BAE. Arrived 12-11-13	11-13
❑ ZK533	HS Hawk T.53	c80	ex Brough, Warton, Indonesian AF LL-5317. RAF colours	11-13
❑ ZK535	HS Hawk T.53	c80	ex Brough, Warton, Indonesian AF LL-5320. RAF colours	11-13

NETHERTHORPE AERODROME north of the A619, west of Worksop EGNF

Taylor Titch G-BABE was airworthy again by late 2012.

❑ G-AJIU	J/1 Autocrat	47	CoA 20-6-03	6-13
❑ G-ARJT	Piper Apache 160G	62	ex N10F. CoA 18-8-07	6-13
❑ G-AYXW	Evans VP-1	72	CoA 15-8-01, de-reg 7-6-02	6-13

SHEFFIELD

Brimpex Metal Treatments: *Visits by prior arrangement* ***only*** | **brimpex@demon.co.uk**

❑ –	Mignet HM.14 'Flea'	c35	BAPC.13, ex Kirk Langley, Wigan, Peel Green, Styal, Urmston, Berrington, Tenbury Wells, Knutsford		3-02
❑ –	Bensen B.7	~	–	[1]	3-02

■ **[1]** Is a Campbell-Bensen and known to have been involved in blade-tip propulsion experiments.

WEST YORKSHIRE

Includes the unitary authorities of Barnsley, Bradford, Calderdale, Kirklees, Leeds and Wakefield

BATLEY on the A652 north of Dewsbury

Northern Aeroplane Workshops (NAW): Skeletal Sopwith Camel G-BZSC made the road journey to Shuttleworth, Beds, on 28th August 2013. With that NAW disbanded; its three superb creations at Old Warden, the Camel, the Sopwith Triplane and the Bristol M.1C serving as shining examples of craftsmanship and dogged determination since the workshop was founded in 1973.

BIRD'S EDGE on the A629 north-west of Penistone

❑ G-BKIR	Jodel D.117	56	ex F-BIOC. SAN-built. CoA 28-8-92	1-12

BIRKENSHAW north of the M62, south-east of Bradford

West Yorkshire Fire Service: Have the cockpit of an 748 at the headquarters.

❑ G-OTBA	HS 748-2A/242	73	ex Emerald, A3-MCA, ZK-MCA, G-11-7. CoA 3-5-07, de-reg 15-6-09. Cockpit	11-09

BRADFORD

International Food and Travel Studio / Bradford College: The facility in Thornton Road took delivery of a 32ft forward fuselage section - cockpit and nine seat rows - of a Boeing 737 for instructional use on 2nd November 2012. Reported to have cost £25k, it is being fitted out to teach cabin staff. *Busy campus - by prior permission* **only | www.iftstudio.co.uk**

❑ -*	Boeing 737	~	ex Germania. Forward fuselage. 'IFT Airways' titles. Arrived 2-11-12	1-13

HALIFAX

❑ G-AIBY	Auster J/1 Autocrat	46	ex Sherburn, 'Halifax'. CoA 13-4-81	8-12

HUDDERSFIELD AERODROME or Crosland Moor, south of the A670 west of the city

Noted as 'off-site' since October 2008, Tiger Moth G-ANZU certainly is, believed in a Cambridgeshire workshop.

❑ G-AYKK	Jodel D.117	55	ex F-BHGM. SAN-built	5-11
❑ G-GREG	Jodel DR.220	67	ex Eversden, F-BOKR. CEA-built. CoA 19-2-91, de-reg 1-4-97	5-11
❑ G-MVZR	Aviasud Mistral 582	89	de-reg 14-3-05	5-11

LEEDS

Coney Park Heliport: Bell UH-1L N116HS left by road on 19th October 2011.

❑ G-BTOC*	Robinson R22 Beta	91	ex N23004. CoA 20-9-09	10-13
❑ 80+39	Bölkow Bö 105M	~	ex Heer. Spares, yellow scheme	10-13
❑ 80+40	Bölkow Bö 105M	~	ex Heer. Spares	10-13

Hesco Bastion: Cross Green Industrial Estate, Knowsthorpe Way. The SHAR is kept on the roof of this *private* location.

❑ ZD613 '122'	HS Sea Harrier FA.2	85	ex Shawbury, 800, 899, 801, 899, 801, 800, 899, 801, 899, 801, 899	8-12

Others: Not noted since November 1993, Bensen B.7 BAPC.200 has been deleted.

LEEDS-BRADFORD AIRPORT or Yeadon

EGNM

❑ G-ATND	Cessna F.150F	66	Reims-built. Cr 9-12-72, de-reg 24-8-73. Engine test-rig	10-13
❑ G-PROG*	Robinson R44 II	06	crashed 2-5-06, de-reg 29-9-07, CoA 8-3-08. Fire crews, first noted 4-13	10-13
❑ EI-BPD	Short 360-100	84	ex Southend, Aer Arran, Gill, G-RMCT, Aer Lingus EI-BPD, G-BLPU, G-14-3656. Dam 4-2-01. Fire crews, poor state	10-13

Locally:

❑ G-ACGT	Avro Avian IIIA	28	ex Linthwaite, EI-AAB. CoA 21-7-39, de-reg 1-1-39	12-06

LIVERSEDGE on the A62 north-east of Huddersfield

❑ AMK	EoN Olympia 1	G-ALJP 47	BGA.503, ex Shennington, Booker, Camphill, G-ALJP, BGA.503. CoA 28-5-95	3-08

PART TWO
SCOTLAND

Scotland comprises 32 unitary authorities ranging from Orkney, Shetland to Dumfries and Galloway and Borders

ABERDEEN AIRPORT or Dyce
EGPD

Instructional Sikorsky S-76A G-BIBG was roaded out on 13th August 2013, bound for K-K-Kemb... Cotswold, Glos. Also heading that way in April 2012 was Super Puma G-TIGG.

❑ G-BHIC		Cessna F.182Q Skylane	80	ex Kemble, Alton, Kidlington. Reims-built. Damaged 9-06, CoA 3-8-08, de-reg 4-5-07. Fuselage, fire crews		11-11
❑ G-BKXD*		Sud SA.365N Dauphin II	83	ex CHC Scotia, F-WMHD. De-reg 8-4-13	[1]	10-11
❑ ZA110*	'563'	HP Jetstream T.2	81	ex Ipswich, Culdrose, 750, F-BTMI. SAL-built. Fire crews. Arrived 14-9-12		4-13
❑ XZ372	'FV'	SEPECAT Jaguar GR.3A	76	ex Ipswich, St Athan, 41, 6, GR.1, 6, 226 OCU, 20, 14. Last flown 5-7-05. Fire crews, non-destructive		4-13
❑ -		Westland Lynx	~	forward fuselage, red scheme	[2]	12-11

■ **[1]** The Dauphin is in use with **Survivex** on the western perimeter and is a composite, largely based upon X-Ray-Delta. Survivex also has a purpose-built helicopter training aid for HUET - Helicopter Underwater Escape Training. **[2]** The anonymous Lynx is a fire-trainer with **Falck NUTEC** on the eastern perimeter.

ABOYNE south of the A93 west of Banchory

Deeside Activity Park: Restaurant, farm shop and a barrage of "corporate teambuilding opportunities". The original fuselage of the rebuilt Zodiac G-OANN is used in a 'crash' scene.

◆ **Access:** *Busy centre, by prior arrangement* ***only*** | **www.deesideactivitypark.com**

❑ G-OANN	Zenair CH.601 Zodiac	00	ex airstrip, crashed 23-4-06	4-11

Also: Locally a Stampe is being worked on.

❑ G-BKRK	Stampe SV-4C	47	ex Aéronavale 57. Nord-built. CoA 28-6-98	3-08

ABOYNE AERODROME south of the A93 west of Banchory

❑ G-BAHP	Volmer Sportsman	73	CoA 18-10-93	4-11

ALEXANDRIA Bücker Bestmann G-CBKB moved to Perth, Scotland, during the spring of 2013

ARBROATH AIRFIELD

No.**662 VGS**: Stored inside the hangar is a Cadet.

❑ XE786	HLR	Slingsby Cadet TX.3	53	BGA.4033, ex Syerston, 662 VGS, 615 GS, 612 GS, 106 GS. CoA 15-4-04	11-12

AYR east of the A77 south west of Kilmarnock

Ayr College: Campus at Dam Park, off the A79. **Access:** *Busy campus, by prior arrangement* **only** | **www.ayrcoll.ac.uk**

❑ XX612	'03' *and* 'A'	SAL Bulldog T.1	74 G-BZXC	ex Prestwick, Dunfermline, Dundee, Wales UAS, S'ton UAS, RNEFTS, QUAS, CFS. CoA 15-1-09, de-reg 5-3-08	9-13

BALADO PARK or Balado Bridge, on the A91 west of Milnathort

❑ XM412	'41' *and* '49'	Hunting Jet Provost T.3A	60	ex Ipswich, North Weald, Binbrook, Colsterworth, Halton 9011M (10-8-89), 1 FTS, 3 FTS, 2 FTS	10-13

BANCHORY on the A93 west of Aberdeen

As store of aircraft in the *general* area is believed to be extant.

❑ G-ARXD	Beagle Airedale	62	ex Netherley. CoA 13-6-86	2-02
❑ G-ASAI	Beagle Airedale	62	ex Dundee, Islay. CoA 20-5-77	2-02
❑ G-TUGS	Piper Pawnee 235D	77	ex G-BFEW, N82553. CoA 26-4-07	4-07

BORGUE on the B727 west of Kirkcudbright

Brighouse Bay Caravan Park: Displayed inside the camp is the former Carlisle Meteor.

❑ WS792	'K'	Gloster Meteor NF.14	54	ex Carlisle, Cosford 7965M (19-6-67), 5 MU, 1 ANS, 2 ANS. AWA-built	7-12

BRIDGE OF WEIR on the A761 north-west of Paisley

Neil Geddes: Has a *private* store/workshop in the general area.

❑ G-CDUW	Aeronca C.3	35	ex F-AZKE ntu, N64765, NC14631		5-09
❑ WZ824	Slingsby Grasshopper TX.1	52	ex Dirleton, Strathaven, Ringmer, Dishforth, St Bees	[1]	5-09
❑ XK820	Slingsby Grasshopper TX.1	56	ex Strathallan, Aberdeen, Lancing, Locking	[2]	6-09

■ **[1]** For WZ824 refer to notes under Carlisle, Cumbria, and further headaches! **[2]** XK820 has wings from WZ754 and WZ778 and its *own* wings are at Kirton-in-Lindsey, Lincs.

BROADFORD AERODROME Isle of Skye, on the A87 west of Kyle of Lochalsh

❑ G-MVIP*	AMF Chevvron	88	CoA 19-6-07. Spares Arrived by 4-13	7-13
❑ G-MWST*	Medway Hybred	91	ex Inverness. CoA 3-8-05	7-13

CARLUKE on the A73 south-east of Motherwell and Wishaw

Reynard Nursery: *Visitors welcome during open hours, but best to check before* | **www.reynardnursery.co.uk**

❑ G-CONV		Convair CV-440-54		57	ex Coventry, CS-TML, N357SA, N28KE, N4402. De-reg 20-12-06	8-13
❑ XM697	'S'	Folland Gnat T.1	G-NAAT	61	ex Market Drayton, Exeter, Bournemouth, Dunsfold, Hurn, Woking, HSA, A&AEE, HSA. SOC 23-9-68, de-reg 10-4-95. 'Reds' colours	8-13

COALSNAUGHTON on the B9140 between Tillicoultry and Alloa

❑ G-MMBE	MBA Tiger Cub 440	83	ex Wick, Kirknewton, East Fortune, Edinburgh	12-11

CROSSHILL on the B7023 south of Maybole

❑ G-BVOD	Montgomerie Two-Place	r94	de-reg 23-11-00. Stored in rafters	9-06
❑ CKJ	Slingsby Prefect	~	BGA.1601, ex PH-197. CoA 14-4-90. Stored in trailer	7-08

CULLEN on the A98 east of Elgin

A *private* collector has the forward fuselage of a Nimrod at a location in the general area.

❑ XV252	HS Nimrod MR.2	71	ex Kinloss, Kinloss Wing, MR.1, Kinloss, 51 (loan), 203, 42, St Mawgan. Forward fuselage	2-14

CULLODEN north-east of Inverness

❑ G-APOD	Tipsy Belfair	58	ex Dundee, OO-TIF ntu. CoA 23-8-88, de-reg 6-9-00	2-01

CUMBERNAULD AERODROME north of the A80, north of Cumbernauld EGPG

Turnover of BN hardware with Cormack Islander Aircraft is steady and relatively swift; only long-termers are given here.

❑ G-BEVV	BN Trislander		77	ex Bembridge, Cumbernauld, 6Y-JQK, G-BNZD, G-BEVV. De-reg 20-3-03. Fuselage	5-09
❑ XV268	DHC Beaver 1	G-BVER	66	ex G-BTDM, XV268, Middle Wallop. CoA 23-4-95	10-13

CUPAR on the A91 west of St Andrews

With almost an anagram of a registration, Bensen G-BOTZ, mentioned in *W&R23*, was never here; while *Oscar-Zulu* remains. At *another* location, an enthusiast keeps a Victor cockpit in the *general* area.

❑ G-ATOZ	Bensen B.8M	65	CoA 9-12-05	11-12

❑ XA917		HP Victor B.1	56	ex Crowland, Barnham, Marham, Wittering 7827M (13-12-63), A&AEE, HP. Cockpit	[1]	4-13

■ **[1]** XA917 hit the headlines on a sortie out of Radlett 1-6-57 with John Allam at the helm; in a shallow dive at around 40,000ft, it clocked 675mph - Mach 1.02 - becoming the largest aircraft at the time to go supersonic.

CURRIE on the A98 east of Elgin

Robert Whitton: At a private location, Robert is building a Spitfire FSM fuselage which will wear 602 Squadron markings.

❑ 'L1018'*		Supermarine Spitfire FSM	12	fuselage		9-12

DIRLETON on A198 between Gullane and North Berwick

A *private* strip in the area.

❑ G-BBBO		SIPA 903	51	ex Eggington, F-BGBQ. CoA 9-9-09, de-reg 3-6-11. Off-site		10-11
❑ XX690*	'A'	SAL Bulldog T.1	75	ex Greenock, Shawbury, Liv UAS, 3 FTS, CFS, York UAS, RNEFTS, EL UAS, RNEFTS, 2 FTS. Arrived 14-9-12		9-12

DRUMSHADE AERODROME on the A928 south of Kirriemuir

❑ FTG		Schleicher K7	~	BGA.3509, ex D-8321. CoA 26-3-00		10-10

DUMFRIES off the A701 north-east of Dumfries on the former airfield

Dumfries and Galloway Aviation Museum: All smiles on 3rd April 2013 as the team at D&G announced they had secured the future of the site, including the control tower. For a long time the worry about having to re-locate hung over the heads of the Dumfries and Galloway Aviation Group but a 'Save our Museum' appeal raised a total of £40,000 over seven years. Grants from Solway Heritage, the Robertson Trust and the Holywood Trust also contributed. Not content with this incredible effort, the team then pledged they would get on with a host of improvements to the site!

The restored watch tower that forms the centrepiece of the museum contains a huge array of artefacts, all well presented. The ground floor includes an impressive engine collection.

Work on the Loch Doon Spitfire continues at an off-site location. The DGAM team hope to have the restored machine back at Dumfries in 2014 when it will move to a local workshop for fitting out and painting. The plan is it will return to the museum site in 2015 for display in a new Romney shed.

Turn back to page 278 in *W&R21* when the departure of Chipmunk T.10 WD386 in2007 was noted; anticipated destination was 'Northern Ireland'. All things must pass, this was so; see under Upper Ballinderry, NI.

◆ **Access:** *Follow 'brown signs' from A75 at the A701 roundabout.* **Open:** *Sat and Sun 10:00 to 17:00 and Wed 10:00 to 16:00 Apr (or Easter, if earlier) to Oct inclusive. Also Thu and Fri in Jul and Aug, 11:00 to 16:00. Also open* **most** *Bank Hols. Special visits by prior arrangement.* **Contact:** *Former Control Tower, Heathfield Industrial Estate, Dumfries, DG1 3PH* | **01387 251623** | **info@dumfriesaviationmuseum.com** | **www.dumfriesaviationmuseum.com**

❑ G-AWZJ		HS Trident 3B-101	71	ex Prestwick, BA, BEA. CoA 12-9-85, de-reg 7-3-86. Arrived 1999. Forward fuselage	[1]	1-14
❑ G-AYFA*		SAL Twin Pioneer 3	58	ex Hooton Park, Morecambe, Mold, Carlisle, Hooton Park, Warmingham, Sandbach, Shobdon, Prestwick, G-31-5, XM285, SRCU, 225, Odiham SF, 230. De-reg 16-5-91. Cockpit. Arrived 9-13	[2]	1-14
❑ -*		HS 748	~	ex Perth, Woodford. Cockpit	[3]	1-14
❑ P7540		Supermarine Spitfire IIa	40	ex off-site, Loch Doon, 312, 266, 609, 66. Crashed 25-10-41 See notes above	[4]	**due**
❑ WA576		Bristol Sycamore 3	51	ex East Fortune, Strathallan, Halton 7900M (5-1-66), RAE, A&AEE, G-ALSS. Arrived 7-6-87		1-14
❑ WJ880		EE Canberra T.4	55	ex Firbeck, North Weald, Halton 8491M (2-4-76), 7, 85, 100, 56, Laarbruch SF, RAE, 16, Laarbruch SF, Gütersloh SF, 104. Cockpit, travelling exhibit		1-14
❑ WL375		Gloster Meteor T.7(mod)	52	ex West Freugh, RAE. SOC 16-6-69, arrived 1978	[5]	1-14
❑ WT746	'A'	Hawker Hunter F.4	55	ex 'XF506', Saighton, Halton 7770M (28-11-62), St Athan, AFDS. 43 Sqn colour scheme, *Clara*		1-14
❑ XL497	'041'	Fairey Gannet AEW.3	61	ex Prestwick, Lossiemouth, 849, A&AEE, 849. SOC 7-12-78		1-14
❑ XP557	'72'	Hunting Jet Provost T.4	62	ex Hemswell, Firbeck, Bruntingthorpe, Halton 8494M (30-6-76), 6 FTS, RAFC. Arrived 25-3-05		1-14

❑ XT280		HS Buccaneer S.2B	65	ex Dundonald, Birtley, East Fortune, Lossiemouth, 208, 12, 208, 12, 16, 809, A&AEE, 809. SOC 10-4-94, arrived 2-03. Cockpit	1-14
❑ XT486		Westland Wessex HU.5	66	ex Altcar, Brize Norton 8919M (3-2-87), Wroughton, 848, 847, 772, 707, 781. Arrived 13-6-07	8-13
❑ XW363	'36'	BAC Jet Provost T.5A	71	ex Haverigg, Swinton, Warton, Samlesbury, Preston, Warton, RAFC, 6 FTS, 1 FTS. SOC 11-1-91, arrived 2010. Off-site	1-14
❑ XX483	'562'	HP Jetstream T.1	74	ex Welshpool, Weston-on-Trent, Shawbury, 750, CFS, 5 FTS. Arrived 2002. Cockpit, travelling exhibit	1-14
❑ ZF584		EE Lightning F.53	68	ex Edinburgh, Turnhouse, Warton, R Saudi AF 53-682, G-27-52. Last flown 22-1-86, arrived 22-5-06. 111 Sqn c/s	1-14
❑ FT-36		Lockheed T-33A-1-LO	55	ex Sculthorpe, Belg AF, USAF 55-3047. Last flew 26-11-79, arrived 8-9-81. *Little Miss Laura*	1-14
❑ 318	'8-NY'	Dassault Mystère IVA	c58	ex Sculthorpe, French Air Force. Last flown 15-5-79, arr 1981	1-14
❑ Fv 35075	'40'	SAAB J35A Draken	c61	ex Duxford, RSwAF F16. Arrived 19-8-05 [6]	1-14
❑ 54-2163	'005'	NAA F-100D-11-NA Super Sabre	54	ex Sculthorpe, FAF. Last flown 24-5-77, arrived 11-1-79. USAF colours, *Shillelagh*	1-14
❑ 68-0060		General Dynamics F-111E	68	ex 20 TFW. Escape pod. Crashed 5-11-75	1-14

■ **[1]** *Zulu-Juliet*'s fuselage is open to the public and includes an extensive interior display and 30-seat lecture hall. **[2]** 'Twin Pin' on loan from Mike Davey (see Liverpool, Merseyside, and Newark, Notts); Jon Howard (see Hooton Park and Warrington, Cheshire); Terry Parker (see Connah's Quay, Wales) and Simon Pulford (see Chester, Cheshire, and Doncaster, S Yorks). **[3]** The HS.748 cockpit *might* be from the uncompleted HS.748-2B c/n 1808, or a jigs-built cockpit for training/outfitting trials. **[4]** Based at Ayr with 312 (Czechoslovak) Sqn, P7540 was flying ultra-low over Loch Doon, near Craigmalloch, 25-10-41, when a wing tip hit the water and it crashed. **[5]** Meteor fitted with an FR.9 or PR.10 nose cone. **[6]** Draken was signed over to the museum from the IWM during 2012.

Also: Stored briefly by DGAM (see above) during early 2014 an unfinished CoZy project joined **1153 (Dumfries) Squadron Air Cadets** and its cockpit will be turned into a simulator. At another site in the *general* area, a glider under restoration.

❑ G-CESP*		Puffer CoZy Mk.4	07	ex Perth. Unfinished project, de-reg 5-11-10. Stored	1-14
❑ '113'	BJU	Slingsby Skylark 3G	61	BGA.1013, CoA 7-77	4-10

DUNDEE AIRPORT

EGPN

Super Cub 135 floatplane G-BWUB departed by road on 28th April 2012, sold in France.

❑ G-BXET*	Piper Tomahawk 112	80	ex N25089. CoA 26-8-11, de-reg 23-6-11. Fire crews	6-13

EAST FORTUNE AERODROME north of the A1, west of East Linton

National Museum of Flight Scotland: Part of National Museums Scotland - see under Edinburgh. During 2013, the museum was granted a £1.3m towards a £3.6m restoration of the World War Two hangars and new exhibitions.

There are four hangars with exhibits roughly grouped as follows: 1 military, 2 civil, 3 restoration and storage and 4 Concorde and the 'Jet Age'. A major inter-active 'zone' - 'Fantastic Flight' - is designed to show kids of all ages how aircraft fly; it also includes Sheila Scott's Comanche *Myth Too*. Many of the wartime buildings have been restored and serve a new purpose for the museum. Meanwhile, large parts of the once iconic and nationally pioneering light aircraft collection, and others, remain in long-term store. These are listed separately.

Working in support of all aspects of the museum is the **Aviation Preservation Society of Scotland** (APSS) which was founded in 1973. APSS also operate Slingsby T.53B G-DDHE from Portmoak, Scotland. The team is busy at work on a flyable Sopwith 1½ Strutter, but it is too early yet to give it a 'formal' reference. Among many benefits APSS members receive copies of the excellent journal, *The Fortune Teller*. Contact: **contact@apss.org.uk** | **www.apss.org.uk**

Not noted since October 2009, Tomahawk G-BGXB, has been deleted.

◆ **Access:** *Since the A1 has been improved, it is* not *possible to turn off it immediately south of the airfield. You need to be on the 'old' A1 - the A199 - and from Edinburgh that means following the brown signs and coming off the A1 at Haddington or from Dunbar, come off at East Linton.* **Open:** *Daily Apr to Oct 10:00 to 17:00. Weekends only Nov to Mar 10:00 to 16:00. Closed Xmas and New Year. Parties by appointment. Guided tours of Hangar 3 (storage and restoration), but* not *the 'deep' store, are available, enquire prior to arrival. Regular tours of the airfield also available.* **Contact:** *East Fortune Airfield, near Haddington, East Lothian, EH39 5LF* | **0300 1236789** | **www.nms.ac.uk/flight**

❑ G-ACYK	Spartan Cruiser III	35	ex Hill of Stake, Largs. Crashed 14-1-38, de-reg 86-38. Arrived 1973. Fuselage	1-14
❑ G-AGBN	GAL Cygnet II	41	ex Strathallan, Biggin Hill, ES915, MCCS, 52 OTU, 51 OTU, 23, G-AGBN. CoA 28-11-80, de-reg 15-11-88. Arrived 11-8-81	1-14

❑ G-AHKY		Miles M.18-2	40	ex Perth, Strathallan, Blackbushe, HM545, U-0224, U-8. CoA 20-9-89, de-reg 19-3-92. Arrived 1991		1-14
❑ G-AMOG		Vickers Viscount 701	53	ex Cosford, Cardiff, BOAC, Cambrian, BEA G-AMNZ ntu. CoA 14-6-77, de-reg 17-5-76. Arrived 17-8-06. BEA colours, *Robert Falcon Scott*		1-14
❑ G-ANOV		DH Dove 6	54	ex CAFU Stansted, G-5-16. CoA 31-5-75, de-reg 6-7-81. Arrived 10-78		1-14
❑ G-AOEL		DH Tiger Moth	40	ex Strathallan, Dunstable, Mk. II N9510, 7 FTS, 2 GU,11 RFS, 1 RFS, 7 RFS, 7 EFTS. CoA 18-7-72, de-reg 21-1-82. Arr 1980		1-14
❑ G-APFJ		Boeing 707-436	60	ex Cosford, British Airtours, BOAC. CoA 16-2-82, de-reg 30-5-84. Arrived 4-06. BOAC colours. Forward fuselage, 'Jet Age' exhibition		1-14
❑ G-ARCX		Gloster Meteor NF.14	53	ex Ferranti, WM261. CoA 20-2-69, de-reg 25-10-73. AWA-built. Arrived 8-75	[1]	1-14
❑ G-ARPH		HS Trident 1C	64	ex Cosford, BA, BEA. CoA 8-9-82, de-reg 24-5-82. Arr 2006. BA colours. Cockpit. 'Jet Age' exhibition		1-14
❑ G-ASUG		Beech E.18S	56	ex Loganair, N575C, N555CB, N24R. CoA 23-7-75, de-reg 12-5-75. Arrived 1976		1-14
❑ G-ATOY		Piper Comanche 260B	66	ex Elstree, N8893P. Crashed 6-3-79; de-reg 14-5-79. Arrived 1979. *Myth Too*. Fuselage	[2]	1-14
❑ G-AVMO		BAC 111-510ED	68	ex Cosford, Bournemouth, BA, BEA. *Lothian Region*. CoA 3-2-95, de-reg 12-7-93. Arrived 9-9-06		1-14
❑ G-AVPC		Druine Turbulent	73	CoA 28-9-99, de-reg 13-9-02. Arrived 4-03. Stored		1-14
❑ G-AXEH		SAL Bulldog Srs 1	69	ex Prestwick, Shoreham. CoA 15-1-77, de-reg 19-6-78. Arrived 23-12-84. Beagle-built. Stored	[3]	1-14
❑ G-BBVF		SAL Twin Pioneer 2	59	ex Shobdon, XM961/7978M, SRCU, Odiham SF, 230, 21. Damaged 11-3-82, de-reg 8-8-83. Arrived 19-8-82		1-14
❑ G-BDIX		DH Comet 4C	62	ex Lasham, Dan-Air, XR399, 216. CoA 11-10-81, de-reg 13-6-83. Arrived 30-9-81		1-14
❑ G-BELF		BN-2A-26 Islander G-HEBZ	77	ex Cumbernauld, D-IBRA, G-BELF. CoA 12-3-01, de-reg 21-3-09. Arrived 7-7-05. Scottish Ambulance c/s	[4]	1-14
❑ G-BOAA		BAC/Sud Concorde 102	75	ex London, BA, G-N94AA (1-79 to 7-80), G-BOAA. CoA 24-2-01, de-reg 4-5-04. Arrived 19-4-04	[5]	1-14
❑ G-BVWK		Air & Space 18A	65	ex Kinnettles, SE-HID, N6108S. De-reg 18-10-00. Arr 10-04		1-14
❑ G-JSSD		HP Jetstream 3100	69	ex Prestwick, N510F, N510E, N12227, G-AXJZ. CoA 9-10-90. De-reg 4-1-96. Arrived 2-96		1-14
❑ G-SJEN		Icarus C42 FB80	04	ex Strathaven. De-reg 10-8-10. Arrived 7-11		1-14
❑ G-UNIV*		Montgomerie Two-Place	96	ex Glasgow, G-BWTP. CoA 18-1-05. First noted 12-13	[6]	1-14
❑ –		HP Jetstream 1 (Super 31 EMU)	69	ex Hatfield, East Midlands, N14234, N102SC, N200SC ntu, N1BE, G-BBBV, G-8-12. Arrived 5-94. Fuselage		1-14
❑ VH-SNB		DH Dragon I	42	ex Strathallan, VH-ASK, RAAF A34-13. Arrived 1981	[7]	1-14
❑ VH-UQB		DH Puss Moth	30	ex Strathallan, Bankstown, G-ABDW. Arrived 1981		1-14
❑ TE462		Supermarine Spitfire XVI	45	ex Ouston 7243M (14-12-54), 101 FRS, Finningley SF. Arrived 19-2-71		1-14
❑ VM360		Avro Anson C.19	47	ex Strathallan, Thruxton, Kemps, G-APHV (de-reg 21-1-82), TRE, A&AEE. SOC 18-11-57. Arrived 8-77		1-14
❑ VX185		EE Canberra B.5	52	ex Wroughton, South Kensington, EE. Arrived 10-97. *The Record-Breaking Canberra*. Cockpit	[8]	1-14
❑ WF259	'171'	Hawker Sea Hawk F.2	54	ex Lossiemouth A2483 (24-6-59), Lossiemouth SF, 736. AWA-built. Arrived 10-7-72		1-14
❑ WV493	'29'	Percival Provost T.1	53	ex Strathallan, G-BDYG, Halton 7696M, 6 FTS. CoA 28-11-80, De-reg 4-11-91. Arrived 11-8-81		1-14
❑ WW145	'680'	DH Sea Venom FAW.22	55	ex Lossiemouth, 750, 891. SOC 13-2-70. Arrived 1972		1-14
❑ XL762		Saro Skeeter AOP.12	58	ex Middle Wallop, Halton 8017M, 2 RTR, 9 Flt, 652, 22 Flt, 654, 651. SOC 27-5-68. Arrived 1-11-75		1-14
❑ XM597		Avro Vulcan B.2	63	ex Waddington, 50, 35, 101, 9, 50, 35, Wadd W, 12. Arrived 12-4-84		1-14
❑ XN776	'C'	EE Lightning F.2A	62	ex Leuchars 8535M (1-4-77), 92, 19. Arrived 8-5-82		1-14
❑ XT288		HS Buccaneer S.2B	66	ex Lossiemouth 9134M (10-4-91), A&AEE, 208, 12, FAA 800. Arrived 7-94		1-14

❑ XV241		HS Nimrod MR.2	70	ex Kinloss, Kinloss Wing, Kin & St M Wing, 42, MR.1, A&AEE, Kinloss Wing, 203, Kinloss. Arrived 10-2-11. Forward fuselage		1-14
❑ XV277		HS Harrier GR.1	66	ex Ipswich, Yeovilton A2602[2], A2600[2] (28-11-88), Filton, HSA. Arrived 4-00		1-14
❑ XZ119	'FG'	SEPECAT Jaguar GR.1A	76	ex Cranwell, Coltishall, 41, Warden Det, 41, Gulf Det, ETPS, 41. Arrived 27-4-09. *Katrina Jane*		1-14
❑ ZE934	'TA'	Panavia Tornado F.3	89	ex St Athan, 56, 111, 11, 43, 11, 111, 5. Arrived 13-9-05		1-14
❑ -		GEC Phoenix UAV	~	-		1-14
❑ 9940		Bristol Bolingbroke IVT	42	ex Strathallan, RCAF 5 B&GS. SOC 21-8-46. Fairchild Canada-built. Arrived 8-8-81		1-14
❑ 3677	613677	MiG MiG-15*bis* SB	53	ex Cáslav, Ostravian Air Regt, Czech AF. Letov-built	[9]	1-14
❑ –	'FI+S'	MS.505 Criquet	47	ex Duxford, G-BIRW, OO-FIS, F-BDQS. CoA 3-6-83, de-reg 15-11-88. Arrived 9-11-82		1-14
❑ 191659	'15'	Me 163B-1a Komet	44	ex Cambridge, Cranfield, Brize Norton, RAE, Husum, II/JG400. Arrived 1976		1-14
❑ BF-10		Bristol Beaufighter TF.10	44	ex South Africa, Portugal, Port AF BF-10, RD220 n/s. Arrived 9-12-00		1-14
❑ 155848	'WT'	McD F-4S-MC Phantom II	68	ex Yeovilton, VMFA-232, USMC, F-4J US Navy. Arrived 13-5-99. VMFA-232 colours	[10]	1-14

■ **[1]** *Charlie-Xray* factoids: Built as an NF.11, it was fitted with the NF.14 clear canopy and was the prototype for that variant, first-flying at Bitteswell 15-7-53 and despatched to Boscombe Down for trials 13 days later. With the Ferranti test fleet its colour scheme gave it the nickname *Mentadent*, after a toothpaste of the time! Retired in 1969 with just 346 hours 'on the clock'. **[2]** The unrestored Comanche fuselage, was flown solo around the world by Sheila Scott in 1966. **[3]** Built by Beagle, *Echo-Hotel* was the prototype Bulldog, first flying from Shoreham on 19-5-69; it was SAL that brought the type through certification and production **[4]** Although wearing G-BELF, this registration was cancelled 21-3-07 and on that day it was re-registered as G-HEBZ. **[5]** *Alpha-Alpha* factoids: Withdrawn from BA service 12-8-00, total hours 22,769, landings 8,064. It is on long-term loan from British Airways. **[6]** Donated by Glasgow University's Department of Aerospace Engineering. **[7]** Built by DH Australia at Bankstown, NSW, for the RAAF; *believed* no active service. **[8]** Canberra B.5 VX185 has been quoted in previous editions as 7631M. This 'M' number was indeed allocated to VX185, in 1959. But this was *after* it had lost *this* cockpit, and it was converted to the prototype B(I).8 in 1954; it was broken up at Filton 30-4-64. *With* this cockpit, the crew of Beamont, Hillwood and Wilson made the first-ever out-and-back crossing of the North Atlantic in VX185 on 26-8-52 in an elapsed time of 10 hours 3½ mins, hence the lettering on the nose. **[9]** Built as an S-103 by Letov in Czechoslovakia. **[10]** Previously noted as on loan from the Fleet Air Arm Museum, the F-4 is more precisely on loan from the US DoD / US Navy.

Deep store: Stored away from public gaze are the following; including the UK's oldest 'flying machine', the Pilcher.

❑ G-BDFU		Dragonfly MPA	81	ex Blackpool Airport, Warton, Prestwick. De-reg 15-12-83. Arrived 1981		3-12
❑ G-MBJX		Hiway Super Scorpion	r82	ex Halton. De-reg 13-6-90. Arrived 1998		3-12
❑ G-MBPM		Eurowing Goldwing	80	CoA 21-8-98, de-reg 3-8-00. Arrived 4-99		3-12
❑ G-MMLI		Solar Tri-Flyer / Typhoon	r84	BAPC.244, ex Glasgow. De-reg 7-9-94. Arrived 1998		3-12
❑ BED		Slingsby Gull I	38	BGA.902, ex Edinburgh, Newbattle, 'G-ALPHA'. Arr 1968	[1]	3-12
❑ BJV		Slingsby T.21A	49	BGA.1014, ex Feshiebridge, SE-SHK. CoA 30-4-81. Arr 28-5-82		3-12
❑ –		Pilcher Hawk	1896	BAPC.49, ex Edinburgh. Crashed 30-9-1899. Off-site	[2]	3-12
❑ –		Chargus 18/50 h-glider	75	BAPC.160, ex Tranent. Arrived 1975, ie from new		3-12
❑ –		Birdman Moonraker h-g	77	BAPC.195, ex Edinburgh. Arrived 1987		3-12
❑ –		Southdown Sigma II h-g	c80	BAPC.196, ex Penicuik. Arrived 1987		3-12
❑ –		Scotkites Cirrus III hang-g	c82	BAPC.197, ex Edinburgh. Arrived 1987		3-12
❑ –		Electra Floater h-g	79	BAPC.245, ex Edinburgh. Arrived 1995		3-12
❑ –		Hiway Cloudbase h-g	79	BAPC.246, ex Edinburgh. Arrived 1995		3-12
❑ –		Albatros ASG.21 h-g	77	BAPC.247, ex Edinburgh. Arrived 1995		3-12
❑ –		Catto CA-16	c81	BAPC.262, ex Gifford. Arrived 1983	[3]	3-12
❑ –		Firebird Sierra h-glider	c83	ex Huntly. Arrived 2002		3-12
❑ –		Goldmarque Gyr	c82	ex Huntly. Arrived 2002		3-12
❑ –		Airwave Magic Kiss h-glider	89	ex Biggar. Arrived 2005		3-12
❑ TS291	BCB	Slingsby Cadet TX.2	44	BGA.852, ex Portmoak, TS291. CoA 12-66. Arrived 1980		3-12
❑ XA228		Slingsby Grasshopper TX.1	53	ex Glenalmond School. Arrived 6-00		3-12
❑ XK533		Blackburn Buccaneer S.1	61	ex Arbroath, Lossiemouth, 809, 700Z, A&AEE, 700Z. Crashed 10-10-63. Arrived 1972. Cockpit		3-12
❑ 309	3309	MiG MiG-15UTI *Midget*	53	ex Polish AF. WSK-built SBLim-2. Cockpit		3-12
❑ 591		Schleicher Rhönlerche II	56	ex D-0359. Arrived 1987		3-12
❑ –		Waco CG-4A Hadrian	44	ex Aberlady. Arrived 1980. Nose section. *The Bunhouse*		3-12

■ **[1]** Gull I BED is *possibly* the former VW912. **[2]** Built by Percy Pilcher with help from his sister Ella, the Hawk was first flown in 1896 and is the UK's oldest heavier-than-air craft and therefore exceptionally iconic. It should be on national show - *somewhere*. Pilcher crashed this machine while flying at Stanford Hall, Leics, on 30-9-1899 and he died of his injuries two days later. (There is a Hawk replica at Stanford Hall - qv.) The Hawk was repaired by the RAeS in 1909 and put *on loan* to the Royal Scottish Museum that year; ownership was transferred to the RSM on 24-3-20. **[3]** The Catto CA-16 microlight 'trike' has the wing of G-MJEN.

Microlight strip: Kitfox G-BSNO was scrapped during 2013.

EAST KILBRIDE on the A726 south of Glasgow

Rolls-Royce Heritage Trust Scotland Branch: The facility carries out major jet engine repairs and overhauls. The Scotland Branch has a collection of engines and artefacts, including material on the Hillington plant that built Merlins 1939 to 1947.

◆ **Access:** *By prior appointment* only. **Contact:** *Mavor Avenue, Nerston Industrial Estate, Nerston, East Kilbride, Glasgow, G74 4PY* | **01355 277113** | **www.rolls-royce.com/about/heritage**

EDDERTON on the A9 north of Tain

❑ G-BVCO	Clutton FRED Srs 2	98	CoA 21-6-06		10-10

EDINBURGH

National Museum of Scotland: The National Museum of Flight at East Fortune (above) is a part of the group.

◆ **Open:** *Daily 10:00 to 17:00. Closed Xmas and New Year.* **Contact:** *Chambers Street, Edinburgh, EH1 1JF* | **0131 2257534** | **info@nms.ac.uk** | **www.nms.ac.uk**

❑ G-ACVA	Kay Gyroplane	35	ex Edinburgh, Glasgow, Strathallan, Perth, Glasgow, Perth. De-reg 5-5-59. Acquired 1998, arrived mid-2009		9-12
❑ G-AXIG	SAL Bulldog 104	71	ex Dirleton, Compton Abbas, Blackbushe, SAL. CoA 12-11-11, de-reg 21-4-11. Acquired 7-11	[1]	9-12
❑ W-2	Weir W-2	34	BAPC.85, ex East Fortune, Glasgow, East Fortune, Hayes, Knockholt, Hanworth, Cathcart. Arrived 2005	[2]	9-12

■ **[1]** Built by Beagle at Shoreham, India-Golf was completed at Prestwick as the second prototype and first flew 14-2-71. **[2]** Co-incidently has the 'B Condition' ('B Class' or 'trade-plate') identity W-2, used by G & J Weir Ltd of Cathcart. Previously recorded as on loan from the Science Museum, this was the case until 1986 when it was donated to NMS by Viscount Weir.

Edinburgh Academy: In Kinnear Road, close to the Botanic Gardens, a Grasshopper is stored.

❑ WZ773	Slingsby Grasshopper TX.1	52	stored		6-12

Also: Last noted in June 2009, Robinson R22 G-BSIT has been deleted.

EDINBURGH AIRPORT or Turnhouse

EGPH

❑ G-BMXD	Fokker F.27-500	69	ex BAC Express, TF-FLR, HL5210, HL5206 ntu, PH-FOR. CoA 12-12-05, de-reg 10-10-08. Fire crews		9-12
❑ G-MALK	Cessna F.172N	79	ex PH-SVF, PH-AXF. Reims-built. Crashed 23-7-97, de-reg 23-12-97. Fire crews		6-08
❑ EI-SLC*	ATR 42-300F	88	ex Air Contractors, OY-CIE, D-BATB. Last flown 19-8-11. Dismantled by 4-12		2-13
❑ TC-MBG	Fokker F.27-600	71	ex G-CEXG, G-JEAP, 9Q-CBI, OY-APF, PH-RUA, VH-EWR. Damaged 1-2-08. Fire crews		9-12
❑ 'L1067' 'XT-D'	Supermarine Spitfire FSM	89	BAPC.227, ex 'L1070', 'XT-A', 603 Sqn colours. *Blue Peter*. Plinth-mounted near entrance	[1]	2-10

■ **[1]** The **603 (City of Edinburgh) Squadron Association** look after the Spitfire FSM.

ELGIN on the A941 south of Lossiemouth and north of Elgin

Buccaneer Service Station: Ian Aitkenhead keeps the 'Brick' in excellent condition on the forecourt.

❑ XW530	HS Buccaneer S.2B	70	ex Lossiemouth, 208, 12, 208, 216, 16, 15, 16		4-13

Morayvia - Moray's Aviation Experience: The group hopes to establish a "temporary centre" before instigating ambitious plans for a museum. See under Kinloss, Scotland for XV244. Vampire T.11 XD547 came here from Felixkirk, N Yorks, but had moved to Cantley, Norfolk, by September 2013.

◆ **Access:** *In formative stages; by prior appointment* **only. Contact: admin@morayvia.org.uk | www.morayvia.org.uk**

❑ XS176*	'N'	Hunting Jet Provost T.4	63	ex Inverness, Stamford, Luton, Solihull, Bruntingthorpe, Salford, Halton 8514M (24-3-77), CATCS, 3 FTS, 2 FTS. Cockpit. Arrived 11-11-12	[1]	9-13
❑ XV240		HS Nimrod MR.2	70	ex Kinloss, Kin Wing, St M, 42, Kin, MR.1, Kin, 42, Kin, 203, Kin. Forward fuselage		9-13

■ **[1]** The 'JP' in on loan from Peter Westley and is used as a travelling display.

ERROL south of the A90, east of Perth

The trio is kept by a *private* collector locally.

❑ 'XE897'		DH Vampire T.11	XD403 54	ex Leuchars, Errol, Strathallan, Woodford, Chester, 4 FTS, 1 FTS, 7 FTS, 8 FTS, 5 FTS, 4 FTS. SOC 2-12-68	[1]	11-12
❑ XG882	'771'	Fairey Gannet T.5	57	ex Lossiemouth 8754M (21-7-82), 845.	[2]	4-13
❑ XN981		HS Buccaneer S.2B	65	ex Lossiemouth, 12, 208, 12, 809, 12, 900, 801, 700B. Stored, off-site		11-12

■ **[1]** See under Bournemouth, Dorset, for *another* 'XE897'. **[2]** The Gannet is a composite, including parts from XA463.

Also:

❑ G-AVID	Cessna 182K	67	ex N2534Q. CoA 18-4-06, de-reg 25-2-10. Dismantled	6-13

FALGUNZEON on the A711 south-west of Dumfries

Dumfries and Galloway Gliding Club: The EoN is used as a travelling 'roadshow'.

❑ BRQ	EoN 460 Srs 1C	r61	BGA.1177, ex G-ARFU. CoA 4-8-96	7-08

FENWICK north of Kilmarnock on the A77

Rowallan Activity Centre: West of the town, on the B751 at Meikle Mosside. A Cherokee Six fuselage is in use with the paintball sector of this varied centre. **Access**, *busy site, by prior arrangement* **only | www.rowallanac.co.uk**

❑ G-BAXJ	Piper Cherokee Six 300	70	ex Old Buckenham, N1362Z, G-BAXJ, 4X-ANY, N5224S. Damaged 3-07, CoA 29-6-08, de-reg 26-11-07. Fuselage	1-12

FIFE AERODROME or Glenrothes, on the A92 north of Kircaldy EGPJ

Kitfox G-LOST departed early in 2013 with no 'forwarding address'. To quote a correspondent, it's really lost now!

❑ G-AREH	DH Tiger Moth	41	ex Bridge of Weir, Lochwinnoch, Kilkerran, G-APYV ntu, 6746M, Mk. II DE241, 22 RFS, 22 EFTS. Morris-built. CoA 19-4-66. Off-site	3-08
❑ G-BHJK	Maule M-5-235C	80	ex N56359. CoA 23-6-08	8-11

FORT WILLIAM It is thought that Carlson Sparrow II G-BVVB had moved to England by late 2010.

GAIRLOCH west of Loch Maree, on the A832

No.**832 Squadron, Air Cadets**: (Formerly 2405 Detached Flight.) The cockpit is owned by civilian instructor Bruce Hudson.

❑ WJ721	EE Canberra TT.18	53	ex Oban, Dundonald, Bacup, Samlesbury, 7, B.2, 50, 40. SOC 19-11-81. Cockpit	5-12

GLASGOW

Kelvingrove Art Gallery and Museum: There is a huge amount going on within this superb building, but from the *W&R* point of view, it is the Spitfire which 'flies' in the main hall.

◆ **Access:** *In Kelvin Park in the West End of the city - the Riverside Museum - see below - is a short distance away.* **Open:** *Mon to Thu and Sat 10:00 to 17:00; Fri and Sun 11:00 to 17:00.* **Contact:** *Argyle Street, Glasgow G3 8AG* | **0141 2769599 | museums@glasgowlife.org.uk | www.glasgowmuseums.com**

❑ LA198	'RAI-G'	Supermarine Spitfire F.21	44	ex Kelvin Hall, East Fortune, Cardington, St Athan, Leuchars, Locking, Worcester, 7118M (19-2-54), 3 CAACU, 602, 1. 602 Sqn colours	1-14

Riverside Museum: Sub-titled 'Scotland's Museum of Transport and Travel' and in a whiz-bang new building with many more exhibits than the previous Museum of Transport, there is, however, little in the way of aeronautical content.

◆ **Access:** *North shore of the Clyde off the A814 in Pointhouse Place - the Kelvingrove - see above - is close by.* **Open:** *Mon to Thu and Sat 10:00 to 17:00; Fri and Sun 11:00 to 17:00.* **Contact:** *100 Pointhouse Place, Glasgow G3 8RS* | **0141 2872720** | **museums@glasgowlife.org.uk** | **www.glasgowmuseums.com**

❑		Pilcher Hawk replica	66	BAPC.48, stored	[1]	3-10
❑	-	Pilcher Bat replica	07	ex Prestwick	[2]	3-12

■ **[1]** The Hawk was built by 2175 Squadron ATC, Glasgow, and awaits restoration. **[2]** The Bat, built by volunteers from BAE Systems at Prestwick, Scotland, was unveiled 23-11-07.

Locally: All at *different* locations. Last noted in December 2001, Nipper G-AWJF has been deleted. Glasgow University's Department of Aerospace Engineering donated Montgomerie Two-Place G-UNIV to East Fortune, Scotland, by December 2013. Last recorded in May 2009, the anonymous BD-5J noted inside the Clydeside Antiques Centre had migrated to Shannon, Ireland, by late 2013.

❑	G-BKSE	QAC Quickie 1	84	CoA 8-5-89	5-09
❑	G-BRGO	Air Command 532	89	ex Kingsmuir. CoA 13-2-91, de-reg 22-2-10	10-10

GRANGEMOUTH

No.1333 Squadron Air Cadets' memorial to the site of the former RAF Grangemouth, on Bo'Ness Road

❑	'X4859'	'PQ-N'	Supermarine Spitfire FSM	08	2 TEU colours	6-13

■ **[1]** 2 Tactical Exercise Unit was resident at Grangemouth 1943 to 1944.

GREENOCK Bulldog T.1 XX690 moved to Dirleton, Scotland, on 14th September 2012.

HADDINGTON east of Edinburgh, south of the A1

Ian Sheffield | **Access**, *viewable by prior appointment* ***only*** | **ian.sheffield@tesco.net**

❑	G-BXEE	Enstrom 280C	77	ex OH-HAN, N336AT. Damaged 13-4-06, de-reg 31-5-06	2-08

HAMILTON on the A72 south-east of Glasgow

Strathclyde Fire and Rescue HQ: In Bothwell Road. A Cessna hulk arrived by April 2012 for use as a training aid. This was 'written out' of *W&R22* (p280) at Kirknewton, Scotland.

❑	G-BRTC*	Cessna 150G	67	ex ?, Kirknewton, N3296J. Damaged 23-12-91. de-reg 3-2-99	4-12

INSCH AERODROME west of the B992 at Auchleve

❑	G-BALK	Stampe SV-4C		46	ex Aboyne, 'Cheshire', Liverpool, Littleborough, F-BBAN, French mil No.387. Nord-built. De-reg 4-12-96. Fuselage	10-12
❑	479781	Piper L-4H Cub	G-AISS	44	ex D-ECAV, SL-AAA, 44-79781. CoA 25-6-97	10-12

INVERNESS

Highland Aviation Museum:

The cockpit of Jet Provost T.4 XS176 moved to Elgin, Scotland, on 11th November 2012.

◆ **Access:** *On the Dalcross Industrial Estate alongside the airport.* **Note**: *no direct access from the airport site.* **Open:** *Apr to Nov Sat and Sun 10:00 to 16:30. Other times by appointment.* **Contact:** *9 Dalcross Industrial Estate, by Inverness Airport, IV2 7XB* | **01667 461100** | **ham254@hotmail.co.uk** | **www.highlandaviationmuseum.org.uk**

❑	G-ASVO		HP Herald 214	64	ex Glenrothes, Perth, Shoreham, Alto, Bournemouth, Channel Express, PP-SDG, G-ASVO, G-8-3. Damaged 8-4-97, de-reg 25-9-01. Forward fuselage	[1]	1-12
❑	WT660	'C'	Hawker Hunter F.1	54	ex Inverness, Cullen, New Byth, Carlisle, 71 MU 7421M (11-4-57), 229 OCU, DFLS. 43 Sqn colours		4-13
❑	XD875		Vickers Valiant B.1	57	ex Winthorpe, Bruntingthorpe, Marham, Firbeck, Coventry, Cosford, 7, 138, 207, 49, 207. SOC 9-11-62. Cockpit	[2]	4-13
❑	XK532	'632'	Blackburn Buccaneer S.1	61	ex airport, Lossiemouth 8867M, Manadon A2581 (22-2-68), Arbroath, Lossiemouth, 736. Arrived 23-12-02		4-13

❑ XM169		EE Lightning F.1A	60	ex Great Ayton, Thirsk, Leuchars 8422M (13-6-74), Leuchars TFF, 23, Binbrook TFF, 111, A&AEE. Arrived 23-6-04. Cockpit	[2]	4-13
❑ XN607		Hunting Jet Provost T.3	61	ex Great Ayton, Leeds, 3 FTS. SOC 28-5-76, arr 23-6-04. Grey colours. Cockpit	[2]	4-13
❑ XV254		HS Nimrod MR.2	71	ex Kinloss, Kinloss Wing, A&AEE, Kin W, St Mawgan W, 42. Arrived 20-7-10. Forward fuselage		4-13
❑ XV867		HS Buccaneer S.2B	68	ex Great Ayton, Leeming, 208, 12, 208, 237 OCU, FAA, 809, 736, 803. Crashed 10-9-93. Arrived 2005. Cockpit	[2]	7-12
❑ ZA362	'TR'	Panavia Tornado GR.1	81	ex Lossiemouth, 15, TTTE. Arrived 9-6-05		4-13

■ **[1]** The Herald is owned by Peter Westley. **[2]** On loan from a N Yorks-based collector; XD875 was the last of 107 - including the prototypes - Valiants, delivered to the RAF on 27-8-57.

Also: Last noted in August 2003, Campbell Cricket G-AYHI is thought to be well south of the border. The Jetstream cockpit is with a *private* collector at a location close to the airport.

❑ G-BRJY	Rand KR-2	90	CoA 23-5-96	6-09
❑ G-UIST*	BAe Jetstream 3102	87	ex *Batman*, Iver Heath, Inverness, Highland Airways, N190PC, N331QH, N840JS, G-31-750. CoA 4-6-10, de-reg 5-5-11. Cockpit. Arrived 2012	9-12

INVERNESS AIRPORT or Dalcross — EGPE

❑ G-BTCI	Piper Vagabond	48	ex N4839H, NC4839H. CoA 9-8-05	3-11
❑ G-JXTA	BAe Jetstream 3103	83	ex D-CNRY, SE-KHC, OY-EDB, SE-KHC, D-CONI, G-31-50. CoA 15-9-09. Spares	1-14

KILKERRAN AERODROME south of the B7023, north-east of Girvan

❑ G-BBCY*	Luton Minor	77	CoA 29-9-11	3-12
❑ G-MYAZ*	Renegade Spirit	94	CoA 10-10-03	3-12

KINGSMUIR or Sorbie, on the B9131 south-east of St Andrews

❑ G-BRFW	Bensen B.8	89	CoA 7-9-06	3-11

KINLOSS AIRFIELD

RAF Kinloss was handed over to the Army on 26th July 2012, becoming **Kinloss Barracks**. *W&R23* (p291) reported the forward fuselage of Nimrod MR.2 XV235 possibly moving to Scampton, Lincs, for onward delivery to Germany. As of March 2012, it was to be found stored at the Lincolnshire airfield. LongEz G-BMUG moved to Inverness, Scotland, by mid-2012.

❑ XV244		HS Nimrod MR.2		71	ex Kin Wing, 42, Kinloss, 203, 42, Kinloss. Displayed	[1]	1-14
❑ 'XX530'	'F'	SAL Bulldog T.1	XX637	74	ex Cranwell, St Athan 9197M, North UAS, 2 FTS	[2]	11-08

■ **[1]** Held by Morayvia, see Elgin, Scotland - see also Elgin, Scotland. **[2]** The Bulldog was/is with the Glasgow Wing Air Cadets.

KIRKNEWTON on the B7031 west of Currie

This location was last mentioned in *W&R22* (p280), noting the departure of G-BTVG and 150s G-BRTC and EI-APF. In mid-2013 *Victor-Golf* returned for continued storage. For G-BRTC, see Hamilton, and EI-APF, Perth, both Scotland.

❑ G-BTVG*	Cessna 140	46	ex -?-, N2114N, NC2114N. CoA 15-4-99, de-reg 18-5-01	6-13

LEUCHARS AIRFIELD on the A919, north-west of St Andrews — EGQL

RAF Leuchars: 1 Squadron stood up on Typhoons on 15th September 2012 but got little time to adapt to its new machines and base. Leuchars will close in the autumn of 2014 with the Typhoons migrating north to Lossiemouth. Leuchars will live on with the Army and it will act as a relief landing ground for Lossiemouth. Phantom FG.1 XV586 moved by road to Yeovilton, Somerset, arriving on 16th May 2012. Not noted since September 2001, the cockpit of Tornado F.2 ZD906 has been deleted.

❑ LA255*	'JX-U'	Supermarine Spitfire F.21	45	ex Coningsby, Cottesmore, Wittering 6490M (14-12-47), West Raynham, Cardington, Tangmere, 1. Arrived 20-8-12	[1]	9-12
❑ XR713	'C'	EE Lightning F.3	64	8935M (9-3-87), ex LTF, 5, 11, 5, LTF, 11, LTF, 5, 111, Wattisham TFF, 111. Displayed		9-13

❑ XT864	'A' *and* 'BJ'	McD Phantom FG.1	68	8998M, ex 111, 892, 767, 700P. Joint 43 / 111 Sqn colours, displayed		12-13
❑ XV582	'M'	McD Phantom FG.1	69	9066M, ex WLT, 43. *Black Mike*. All black colours		9-13
❑ XW265	'W'	HS Harrier T.4A	70	ex ??, St Athan, Cosford 9258M (3-10-96), Shawbury, 20, 233 OCU, A&AEE. Cockpit	[2]	12-13
❑ ZE967	'UT'	Panavia Tornado F.3	89	ex 56, 43, 111, 43, 25, 23, 25, 43, 11, 111. Displayed	[3]	12-13

■ **[1]** LA255 is owned by the 1 Squadron Association - will it move to Lossie??. **[2]** Harrier cockpit with 2345 Sqn ATC. **[3]** Tornado on the gate is multi-faceted: 43 Squadron colours to port, 111 Squadron on the starboard side and 56 Squadron on both sides of the tail.

LEVEN By September 2013 Bensen G-ARTJ had moved to Rufforth, N Yorks.

LIMERIGG on the B8022 south of Falkirk

Not recorded since January 2008, Bensen G-BVMG has been deleted.

❑ G-BRFJ	Aeronca 11AC	46	ex N9163E, NC9163E. CoA 11-9-02	1-08

LONGSIDE AERODROME on the A950 between Peterhead and Mintlaw

❑ G-BLDC*	K&S Jungster	r83	de-reg 6-3-99	5-12
❑ G-BYRE*	Rans S10 Sakota	r91	de-reg 8-5-99	5-12

LOSSIEMOUTH AIRFIELD south of the B4090, west of Lossiemouth EGQS

RAF Lossiemouth: The sensitively-named 'Base Estates and Transformation' paper was released on 18th July 2011 and it was announced that 'Lossie' would become the new home for the northern Typhoon force - with Leuchars defecting to the Army. The resident Tornado force is due to apply for visas and depart to Marham, Norfolk, during 2013.

❑ ZA355	'TAA'	Panavia Tornado GR.1	80	9310M, ex 15, TTTE. WLT		4-12
❑ ZA474	'AJ-F'	Panavia Tornado GR.1	83	9312M, ex 617, 12, 27, 20, 16. Spares		4-12
❑ ZA475	'FH'	Panavia Tornado GR.1B	83	9311M, ex 12, 27, 20, 17, 9, 16. Gate	[1]	9-13
❑ ZD793*	'101'	Panavia Tornado GR.4	84	ex Marham, 15. Arrived 22-6-11. WLT	[2]	6-13

■ **[1]** ZA475 was refurbished and put back on the gate in 12-11; it wears 15 Sqn colours to port as 'FH' and 617 Sqn as 'AJ-G' to starboard. [2] ZD793 carries 'Engineering and Logistics Wing' titles.

MAYBOLE Not noted since July 2005 the hulk of Rallye OO-NAT has been deleted.

MINTLAW Not noted since January 2001, Goldwing G-MBFZ and Tiger Cub G-MJUF have been deleted.

MOFFAT east of the A74(M) north of Lockerbie

Dr Hamish Macleod: The Spitfire is in a *private* garden. It is hoped it will be displayed at Dowding House in Well Street.

❑ 'PT462'	'SW-A'	Sup' Spitfire Tr.9 FSM	~	-	[1]	3-09

■ **[1]** The real PT462 is operated by Anthony Hodgson (as G-CTIX) from his strip in North Wales.

MONTROSE on the A92 north of Arbroath

Montrose Air Station Heritage Centre:

◆ **Open:** *Wed to Sat 10:00 to 16:00, 1st Apr to 30th Sep. Sun 12:00 to 16:00 all year. Other times by prior arrangement.*
Contact: *Waldron Road, Broomfield, Montrose, DD10 9BB* | **01674 678222** | **via the website** | **www.rafmontrose.org.uk**

❑ G-MMLM*		MBA Tiger Cub 40	84	ex Dundee. De-reg 22-5-00. Red colours and German crosses, *Red Baron*	3-12
❑ 'B5577'	'W'	Sopwith Camel replica	c72	BAPC.59, ex East Fortune, Cosford, St Athan 'D3419', St Mawgan, 'F1921', St Athan, Colerne	7-12
❑ 'EP121'*	'LO-D'	Sup' Spitfire V FSM	~	602 Sqn colours, *Red Lichtie*. Arrived 17-7-13	7-13
❑ WF825	'A'	Gloster Meteor T.7	51	ex Redhill, Yatesbury, Malmesbury, Monkton Farleigh, Lyneham 8359M, Kemble, CAW, 33, 603. SOC 6-2-69	7-12
❑ XA109		DH Sea Vampire T.22	53	ex Leuchars, East Fortune, Lossiemouth, Lossiemouth SF, 831, Culdrose SF, 781. SOC 17-3-67	7-12

Neil Butler: Neil has a workshop locally.

❑ G-AWSS		Druine Condor	69	ex Fordoun. CoA 19-10-94. Rollason-built	4-07
❑ VS356		Percival Prentice T.1 G-AOLU	50	ex Stonehaven, Perth, Strathallan, Biggin Hill, EI-ASP, G-AOLU, VS356, CFS, 2 FTS. Blackburn-built. CoA 8-5-76	4-07
❑ VS610*	'K-L'	Percival Prentice T.1 G-AOKL	49	ex Old Warden, Bassingbourn, VS610, 1 FTS, 22 FTS, RAFC, 22 FTS. CoA 20-9-96	3-13

Robert Gordon Institute of Technology: *Visits by prior application* **only | www.rgitmontroseltd.co.uk**

❑ N116WG	Westland WG.30-160	85	ex Weston-super-Mare, Yeovil, PanAm, G-BLLG ntu, G-17-20	12-09

MUSSELBURGH on the A199 east of Edinburgh

No.**297 Squadron Air Cadets**: Goose Green Place

❑ G-BEYN	Evans VP-1	77	ex East Fortune. Unfinished project. De-reg 2-9-91	6-06

NETHERLEY on the B979 north of Stonehaven

Alba Power: Rolls-Royce Avon and Olympus specialists have a 'guardian' at the Mill of Monquich. **www.albapower.co.uk**

❑ N-315	Hawker Hunter T.7	58	ex Long Marston, Hucclecote, Batley, Amsterdam, and NLS spares, XM121, n/s	3-12

NORTH ROE on the A970 north of Lerwick, 'Mainland' Shetland Islands

Duncan Feather: After an epic recovery from Sumburgh, Duncan keeps the Potez locally.

❑ F-BMCY	Potez 840	62	ex Sumburgh, N840HP, F-BJSU, F-WJSU. Damaged 29-3-81	3-10

ORPHIR near Kirkwall, Orkney Islands

❑ G-ASRP	Jodel DR.1050	59	ex F-BITI. SAN-built. Ditched 17-3-86, de-reg 20-1-99	10-94
❑ G-BXBC	Anderson EA-1 Kingfisher	96	unflown, de-reg 29-1-10	9-04

PALNACKIE on the A711 south of Dalbeattie, south west of Dumfries

James Halliday: Keeps the cockpit of a 737 in the general area. **Access**, *visits by prior arrangement* **only**

❑ EI-CJF	Boeing 737-204	83	ex Prestwick, Ryanair, G-BTZF, G-BKHF,G-BKGV ntu. Cockpit	7-07

PERTH

BlueSky Experiences: Within the grounds is a Buccaneer cockpit used for team-building exercises.

◆ **Access:** *Busy venue, visitors* **strictly** *by prior arrangement* | **www.blueskyexperiences.com**

❑ XX892	HS Buccaneer S.2B	75	ex Forres, Lossiemouth, 208, 237 OCU, 16. Cockpit	12-12

Also: Bensen G-BSMG, last noted in June 2009, has been deleted.

PERTH (SCONE) AIRPORT EGPT

Air Service Training - Perth College: By August 2013 the anonymous HS.748 cockpit had moved to Dumfries, Scotland.

◆ **Access:** *Busy campus, visitors* **strictly** *by prior arrangement* | **www.airservicetraining.co.uk**

❑ G-AYGB	Cessna 310Q	70	ex N7611Q. CoA 23-10-87, de-reg 23-6-94	5-12
❑ G-BEWP	Cessna F.150M	77	Reims-built. Crashed 4-10-83, de-reg 5-12-83	5-12
❑ G-BTIN	Cessna 150C	63	ex N7805Z. Damaged 12-98, de-reg 10-5-01	5-12
❑ G-BWYE	Cessna 310R II	79	ex F-GBPE, N26369. CoA 10-9-09, de-reg 7-7-11	5-12
❑ G-NFLC	HP Jetstream 1	69	ex Cranfield, G-AXUI, G-8-9. CoA 3-6-05, de-reg 3-8-04	5-12
❑ XL875	W'land Whirlwind HAR.9	58	ex Wroughton, Lee SAR Flt, Culdrose SAR Flt, 847, 848, 815	7-13
❑ XT140	Bell Sioux AH.1	65	ex Middle Wallop	7-13
❑ –	BAe ATP	~	ex Prestwick. Cockpit, simulator	6-09

Also: Sundown 180 G-BBSB had gone by April 2013.

❑ G-BKTV*	Cessna F.152	81	ex OY-BJB. Reims-built. CoA 3-11-10	3-13
❑ G-CBKB*	Bücker Bü 181C Bestmann	44	ex Alexandria, F-PCRL, F-BCRU. Arrived by 4-13	7-13

❑ G-MPBH*	Cessna FA.152	81	Reims-built. crashed 28-4-12, CoA 3-9-12, de-reg 7-2-13		3-132
❑ EI-APF	Cessna F.150G	66	ex Anstruther, Kirknewton, Perth, Sligo. Reims-built. CoA 8-98		5-12
❑ N310WT	Cessna 310R	78	ex G-BGXK, N6070X. De-reg 17-10-01		5-12

PETERHEAD on the A90 south of Fraserburgh

Score Energy Ltd: The Lightning 'guards' the GLEN Test Facility, which handles industrial R-R Avons, among other types.

◆ **Access:** *Private site, entrance* **strictly** *by prior arrangement* | **www.score-group.com**

❑ XR749 'DA'	EE Lightning F.3	65	ex Tees-side, Chop Gate, Leuchars 8934M, 11, LTF, 11, LTF, Binbrook pool, 29, 226 OCU, 56. Overstressed 17-2-87. LTF c/s		4-13

PORTMOAK (KINROSS) AERODROME, west of Glenrothes

W&R23 (p294) noted that Tri-Pacer 160 G-BSED had moved on to Perth and then in 2010 went 'down south', probably to Lincolnshire. That was a little too much 'down south' as it settled upon Full Sutton, E Yorks.

❑ BCS	Slingsby Skylark 3	58	BGA.867, ex Keevil, Rattlesden. CoA 16-4-05		2-10

PRESTWICK AIRPORT EGPK

Last noted in February 2008, Aztec 250D N250TB has been deleted.

❑ G-ATDB	Nord Noralpha	48	ex Edinburgh, Skelmorie, Prestwick, F-OTAN-6, Fr mil 186. CoA 22-11-78, de-reg 11-10-10		4-11
❑ G-AXSD	Beagle Pup 100	69	G-35-139. CoA 10-5-08, de-reg 2-2-11		7-13
❑ G-BCNZ*	Fuji FA-200-160	74	CoA 23-2-08		11-12
❑ G-ORJX	HS 146 RJX85 T1	01	ex Woodford, de-reg 12-12-02	[1]	6-11
❑ N852FT	Boeing 747-122	70	ex Polar Air Cargo, N4712U. Fire crews		4-12
❑ –	BAe ATP/J61	~	c/n 2068, fuselage. Fire crews		4-11

■ **[1]** The prototype RJX (first flown 28-4-01) is used as an engineering design aid by Spirit AeroSystems and comprises fuselage, starboard wing and tail. It arrived on site 8-6-11. It last flew 10-1-02 and clocked 321:59 hours.

Locally: The Wagtail Flying Group is *believed* to keep its Tipsy in the area.

❑ G-AISC	Tipsy B	48	ex Cumbernauld, Henstridge, Yeovil. CoA 23-5-79		12-06

ROTHESAY Island of Bute

❑ G-BUTE	Anderson EA-1 Kingfisher	90	ex Cumbernauld, G-BRCK. CoA 15-10-99. de-reg 23-1-14		12-07
❑ G-CCUB	Piper J3C-65	46	ex N33528, NC33528		12-07

SHOTTS on the B717, north of the A71 east of Glasgow

Scottish Adventure Centre: Within the multi-function centre paintballing meets 4x4, an 'alien hunt' and even 'airsofting'.

◆ **Access:** *Busy site, by prior arrangement* **only** | **www.scottishadventurecentre.co.uk**

❑ G-OLIZ	Robinson R22	88	CoA 16-8-07, de-reg 25-1-07		6-09

STONEHAVEN on the A90 north of Montrose

❑ G-ASBU	Beagle Terrier 2	50	ex Netherley, Auster T.7 WE570, LAS, CFS, 2 FTS, CFS. Crashed 12-8-80, de-reg 16-10-85		9-07

STRANRAER

Steve Austin: **Access:** *Visits by prior arrangement* ***only*** | **www.2av8.co.uk**

❑ XA903	Avro Vulcan B.1	57	ex Wellesbourne Mountford, Sidcup, Cardiff, Farnborough, RB.199 and Olympus test-bed, Blue Steel trials, Avro. Cockpit		6-13
❑ XP558 '20'	Hunting Jet Provost T.4	62	ex Sheffield, Ipswich, Norwich, Honington 8627M, St Athan, Culdrose, A2628 (13-5-74), CAW, 3 CAACU, RAFC. Cockpit		6-13
❑ Q497	EE Canberra T.4 WE191	54	ex Dumfries, Warton, Samlesbury, Bracebridge Heath, Samlesbury, Kemble, WE191, 231 OCU, 237 OCU, 231 OCU, 245. SOC 1-2-78. Cockpit	[1]	6-13

■ **[1]** WE191 was acquired by BAC in February 1978 and was intended for conversion to B.52 status for the Indian Air Force. Frustrated, it never made it and was stored at various locations before disposal.

STRATHALLAN AERODROME west of the B8062, north of Auchterarder

Skydive Strathallan | www.skydivestrathallan

❑ G-ATRO*	Piper Cherokee 140	66	CoA 24-8-10, de-reg 28-11-11. First noted 2-12	9-12
❑ G-BAGV	Cessna U.206F	72	ex N9667G. Crashed 5-5-02, CoA 14-5-04, de-reg 19-9-11. Para-trainer	6-07
❑ R1914	Miles Magister I G-AHUJ	40	ex Aboyne, Balado Bridge, Kemble, 137, 604, Middle Wallop SF, 604. CoA 9-7-98, de-reg 19-11-09	7-13

STRATHAVEN AERODROME on the A71 south-east of East Kilbride

By June 2013 the following had moved on, perhaps broken up: Weedhoppers G-MBPW and G-MMNV, Eagle G-MBRS and the unflown fuselage of a Skycraft Scout.

❑ G-MBZH	Eurowing Goldwing	82	CoA 31-3-03, de-reg 28-8-09 [1]	6-13

■ **[1]** Goldwing G-MBZH first flew in 1983 and was the first to be built on the East Kilbride 'production line'.

TAIN north Inverness

❑ G-ATWS	Luton Minor	68	CoA 26-3-69, de-reg 8-2-82	5-13

TOWNHILL By June 2012 Scout AH.1 XR627 had travelled to Storwood, E Yorks.

YARROW on the A708 west of Selkirk

❑ G-ANOK	SAAB Safir	r54	ex Strathallan, East Fortune, SE-CAH ntu. De Schelde-built. CoA 5-2-73, de-reg 15-10-81	6-03

***Will Scotland be in the 'international' section by the time of* W&R25?**

PART THREE

WALES

Comprises 22 unitary authorities ranging from Anglesey and Flintshire to Pembrokeshire and Rhondda, Cynon and even Taff

ABERGAVENNY on the A40 west of Monmouth

❑ N9191		DH Tiger Moth	G-ALND	39	ex Shobdon, Shipdham, Mk. II N9191, 5 SoTT, 19 EFTS, Duxford CF, 6 CPF. Crashed 8-3-81		8-12

AMMANFORD on the A483 north of Swansea

No.**2475 Squadron Air Cadets**: Penybanc Road.

❑ WH739		EE Canberra B.2		53	ex St Athan, 100, 85, 45, 75 RNZAF, Upwood SF, 50, 101. SOC 27-7-76. Cockpit		7-11

CAERNARFON AERODROME or Llandwrog north of the A499, south-west of Caernarfon EGCK

Caernarfon Airport Airworld Museum: The museum tells the story of aviation in general and aviation in North Wales in particular. The mountain rescue exhibit is a graphic story of wartime crashes, both Allied and Luftwaffe, and includes a large amount of salvaged wreck items. Among the many interesting exhibits is a 'Turtle' narrow-gauge railway shunting engine, salvaged from what was RAF Hell's Mouth (west of Abersoch on the Lleyn Peninsula).

The cockpit of the anonymous Gannet moved to Hooton Park, Cheshire, on 20th July 2012.

◆ **Open:** *Mar 1 to Oct 31, 10:00 to 17:00.* **Contact:** *Caernarfon Airport, Dinas Dinlle, Caernarfon, LL54 5TP* | **01286 832154 | info@airworldmuseum.co.uk | www.airworldmuseum.co.uk**

❑ 'G-EGCK'		Mignet HM.14 'Flea'		~	BAPC.286, ex St Athan, 'local area'. Arrived 12-02	[1]	1-14
❑ G-BSMX		Bensen B.8MR		90	de-reg 17-5-10		1-14
❑ G-MBBB		Skycraft Scout 2		79	-		1-14
❑ G-MBEP		Aerolights Eagle 215B		80	CoA 8-4-96, de-reg 16-5-96. Arrived 1996	[2]	1-14
❑ –		Blériot XI replica		~	stored		1-14
❑ –		Chotia Weedhopper		~	arrived 1995	[3]	1-14
❑ -		Skycraft Scout 2		~	spares for the above		1-14
❑ 'N5137'		DH Tiger Moth	G-BNDW	~	ex Shobdon, Fownhope, N6638, Fairford SF, 27 GCF, St Mawgan SF, Prestwick SF, 25 EFTS, 22 EFTS, 22 ERFTS. Arrived 26-11-97. Fuselage and mocked-up port wings		1-14
❑ WL756		Avro Shackleton AEW.2		53	ex St Austell, St Mawgan 9101M, 8, 204, 205, 37, 38. SOC 23-2-88. Arrived 10-2-06. Cockpit	[4]	9-13
❑ WM961	'J'	Hawker Sea Hawk FB.5		54	ex Higher Blagdon, Culdrose A2517, FRU, 802, FB.3, 811. SOC 17-1-62. Arrived 1988		1-14
❑ WT694		Hawker Hunter F.1		54	ex Newton, Debden 7510M (22-11-57), 229 OCU, DFLS, 54. Arrived 9-95. 245 Sqn colours		1-14
❑ WV781		Bristol Sycamore HR.12		52	ex Finningley, Odiham, Digby 7839M (16-3-61), HDU, CFS, ASWDU, G-ALTD. Arrived 1986. Forward fuselage		1-14
❑ XA282		Slingsby Cadet TX.3		52	ex Syerston, 635 VGS, 617 GS, 1 GC, CGIS, 105 GS. SOC 19-8-86. Arrived 1986		1-14
❑ XH837		Gloster Javelin FAW.7		57	ex Northolt, Ruislip 8032M (21-2-62), 33. Arrived 1987 Forward fuselage		1-14
❑ XJ726		Westland Whirlwind HAR.10		55	ex Sibson, Wroughton, 2 FTS, CFS, ME SAR Flt, 22. SOC 4-2-81. Arrived 1986		1-14
❑ XK623	'56'	DH Vampire T.11		56	ex Bournemouth 'G-VAMP', Moston, Woodford, Chester, St Athan, 5 FTS. SOC 6-12-68. Arrived 1986		1-14
❑ XL618		Hawker Hunter T.7		59	ex Cottesmore 8892M (3-4-86), Shawbury, Kemble, 1 TWU, 229 OCU, Jever SF, Gütersloh SF. Arrived 9-95		1-14
❑ XW269*	'BD'	HS Harrier T.4		71	ex Selby, Queensbury, Boscombe Down, QinetiQ, Wittering, SAOEU, 233 OCU, 3, 1, 233 OCU, 4. 4 Sqn colours, T.2 era. Arrived 2-10-12		1-14
❑ –		Vickers Varsity T.1 EMU		~	ex Higher Blagdon, Oakington. Arrived 1988	[5]	1-14
❑ A92-740	'A'	GAF Jindivik 3		~	ex Llanbedr. Arrived 2006		1-14
❑ A92-808		GAF Jindivik 3		~	ex Llanbedr, ZJ489. Arrived 2006. Stored	[6]	1-14

■ **[1]** The former University of Wales Air Sqn St Athan 'Flea' is *believed* to be largely new-build, but with Scott A2S engine. From circa 2006 it incorporated the metal elements - including the unique undercarriage - from the Idwal Jones-built example BAPC.201 acquired from nearby Talysarn. The wings and tail 'feathers' are uncovered and it is part of a 'workshop' scene. The 'registration' is derived from the aerodrome's ICAO Location Indicator. **[2]** Eagle microlight is on loan from R W Lavender **[3]** Weedhopper *may* be G-MJSM and is on loan from Ray Bancroft, Prestatyn. **[4]** The Shackleton cockpit is privately owned and was put up for sale 9-13. **[5]** Varsity cockpit - within the 'Astra' cinema area *underneath* the mountain rescue display - carries a Marshall of Cambridge mod plate and is *very* substantial. **[6]** Jindivik A92-808 has been transformed in a bizarre 'manned' version designed for use by children as a 'sit in' exhibit. It has been reported elsewhere as a GAF Pika reproduction - not so!

Others:

❑ G-AWUK		Cessna F.150H	68	ex Shobdon, Stansted, Oaksey Park, Bristol, Biggin Hill. Reims-built. Crashed 4-9-71, de-reg 13-4-73. Cockpit, fire dump	6-13
❑ G-AYPJ		Piper Cherokee 180E	70	ex Mona, N11C. CoA 1-10-04. Fuselage, stored	10-07
❑ XD165	'B'	Westland Whirlwind HAR.10	54	ex Doncaster, Storwood, Wattisham, Netheravon, Halton 8673M (2-2-81), SARTS, 202, 228, 22, 225, 155. Dump	6-13

CARDIFF AIRPORT or Rhoose

EGFF

Airport: In their compound on the south-west side, the fire crews have a synthetic trainer and a BAC 111. Last noted in 2001 Cherokee G-AVGH is believed to have expired. By June 2012 it had been replaced with an inverted Cessna 172.

❑ G-AVMT	BAC 111-510ED	68	ex Hurn, European, BA, BEA. CoA 5-12-03, de-reg 17-12-04	11-12
❑ -*	Cessna 172	~	fire crews, inverted. See notes above	6-12

International Centre for Aerospace Training: In a very high-tech campus on the main access road to the terminal.

◆ **Access:** *By prior application* **only** | **www.part66.com**

❑ G-BDAX		Piper Aztec 250C	67	ex 5B-CAO, N6399Y. CoA 12-11-93, de-reg 13-3-92	9-09
❑ D-AGEG*		Boeing 737-35B	88	ex Kemble, Germania, UR-GAF, D-AGEG, G-EURP. Forward fuselage. Arrived 14-12-12	2-12
❑ XX487	'568'	HP Jetstream T.2	74	ex Culdrose, 750, T.1 n/s. Arrived 17-6-11	3-13
❑ XX687	'F'	SAL Bulldog T.1	75	ex Shawbury, EM UAS, Liv UAS. Arrived 18-7-01	3-13

CAREW CHERITON on the A477 east of Pembroke

Carew Control Tower Group: Based at the unique watch tower at the former airfield.

◆ **Access:** *On the edge of the Carew Cheriton Showground.* **Open:** *10:00 to 15:00 Sun and Mon over Bank Holiday weekends and every Sun in Jul to Sep.* **Contact:** *John Brock, Milton Bakery, Milton, near Tenby, SA70 8PH* | **01646 651356** | **info@carewcheritoncontroltower.co.uk** | **www.carewcheritoncontroltower.co.uk**

❑ VM325	Avro Anson C.19	47	ex Gloucestershire, Bentham, Staverton, Coventry, Halfpenny Green, WCS, NCS, WCS, TCCF, Upavon CF, 173, 4 FP. SOC 19-9-68	10-11

CHIRK on the A5 north of Oswestry

❑ G-AJBJ	DH Dragon Rapide		44	ex Coventry, Blackpool, NF894, 18 MU, HQ TCCF. Brush-built. CoA 14-9-61, de-reg 16-12-91	11-11
❑ 'G-AJCL'	DH Dragon Rapide	G-AIUL	45	ex Southend, British Westpoint G-AIUL, NR749, Kemble, 2 RS. Brush-built. CoA 29-9-67, de-reg 6-4-73	11-11
❑ G-AKOE	DH Dragon Rapide	X7484	42	ex Booker, X7484, PTS. CoA 25-2-82, de-reg 18-6-02	11-11
❑ G-ANFC	DH Tiger Moth		42	ex London Colney, Dunstable, Mk.II DE363, 22 EFTS, 4 FIS. Morris-built. CoA 9-10-03, de-reg 13-7-10	11-11
❑ G-AZMX	Piper Cherokee 140		68	ex Connah's Quay, Chester, Halfpenny Green, SE-FLL, LN-LMK. CoA 9-1-82, de-reg 9-1-84	9-11
❑ G-BAYL	Nord Norecrin VI		48	ex Ivychurch, Solihull, Bodmin, F-BEQV. De-reg 14-11-91	3-06
❑ G-BEDB	Nord Norecrin		48	ex Liverpool, Chirk, F-BEOB. CoA 11-6-80, de-reg 14-11-91	4-11
❑ G-MVBT	Thruster TST Mk.1		88	CoA 19-12-07. Wreck	9-11
❑ G-MYHR	Cyclone AX3/503		93	CoA 27-6-05. Stored	9-11

CONNAH'S QUAY on the A548 west of Chester

Deeside College: **Access**, *busy campus; visits by prior application* **only** | **enquiries@deeside.ac.uk** | **www.deeside.ac.uk**

❑ N66SW		Cessna 340	~	ex N5035Q	3-09
❑ XR658		Hunting Jet Provost T.4	63	ex Bournemouth, Wroughton, Abingdon 8192M (29-12-71), RAFEF, 6 FTS, CAW, 7 FTS. Crashed 26-10-71	6-12
❑ XW423	'14'	BAC Jet Provost T.5A G-BWUW	72	ex Little Snoring, RAF, Shawbury, 3 FTS, RAFC, 1 FTS, 3 FTS. CoA 14-2-02, de-reg 29-6-06	7-11

Terry Parker: Continues to work on his Venom. Terry also has a part-share in 'Twin Pin' G-AYFA - see Dumfries, Scotland.

❑ 'J-1712'	DH Venom FB.54	56	ex Charnock Richard, Hurn, Thayngen, Swiss AF. Pod [1]	12-13

■ **[1]** The Venom pod *could* be from J-1711.

During October 2013, the RAF Museum removed a cache of Handley Page O/400 wing spars that had been in use as roof trusses in a building from in the area. The substantial spars were taken to the store at Stafford, Staffs. The museum holds other O/400 elements - who knows?

COWBRIDGE on the A48 west of Cardiff

Task Force Paintball | Access, *busy venue; visits by prior application* **only | www.taskforcepaintball.co.uk**

❑ XG592	W'land Whirlwind HAS.7	57	ex Cardiff, Wroughton, 705, 846, 705, 700, HS. SOC 5-5-76	7-11

CWMBRAN on the A4051 north of Newport

Mark Gauntlett: **Access:** *Visits by prior application* **only | www.hawkerhunter.com**

❑ XE985	DH Vampire T.11	55	ex Exeter, Bridgend, Cwmbran, Bridgend, London Colney, Woodford, Chester, St Athan, 5 FTS. SOC 17-11-67. Pod	7-11
❑ QA-12	Hawker Hunter FGA.78	56	ex Woking, Bournemouth, Qatar AF, G-9-284, RNethAF N-222. Cockpit	7-11

HAVERFORDWEST AERODROME or Withybush, on the A40, north of Haverfordwest EGFE

Pembrokeshire Spitfire Aeroplane Company: *Visits possible* **only** *by prior arrangement* | **www.welshspitfire.com**

❑ JG668	Supermarine Spitfire VIII	G-CFGA	44	ex Oxford, Australia, Oakey, RAAF A58-441 (SOC 22-5-46), JG668 no service	7-13
❑ MA764*	Sup' Spitfire IX	G-MCDB	42	ex Ipswich, 122. Missing 2-11-43. First noted 4-12	7-13

Also: Stampe G-BMNV moved to Belgium by February 2012; Tri-Pacer G-BTWU (last noted Oct 1999), has been deleted.

HAWARDEN AIRFIELD or Broughton, on the B5129 west of Chester EGNR

Hawarden Air Services and **North Wales Military Aviation Services**: As well as the former Eastern bloc types, the restoration and operation of jet 'warbirds' is a speciality. Only those under long-term restoration and storage are listed. MiG-23ML '04' and MiG-27K '71' at the Newark Air Museum, Winthorpe, Notts, are on loan from HAS. The unfinished Tucano T.1 was registered as N312RS in October 2010 and was exported to the USA.

◆ **Access:** *Private location, visits possible* **only** *by prior arrangement* | **www.nwmas.com**

❑ XW409	'123'	BAC Jet Provost T.5A		71	ex St Athan 9047M (29-6-90), 7 FTS, 1 FTS.	8-11
❑ CCCP-07268		Antonov An-2R *Colt*	YL-LEV	~	ex Latvia, USSR	2-08
❑ CCCP-17939		Antonov An-2R *Colt*	YL-LFC	~	ex Latvia, USSR	11-13
❑ CCCP-19731		Antonov An-2R *Colt*	YL-LEU	~	ex Hooton Park, Chester, Latvia, USSR	2-08
❑ CCCP-19733		Antonov An-2R *Colt*	YL-LEZ	~	ex Latvia, USSR	2-08
❑ CCCP-20320		Mil Mi-2 *Hoplite*	YL-LHN	~	ex Latvia, Latvian AF 154, USSR	2-08
❑ CCCP-20619		Mil Mi-2 *Hoplite*	YL-LHO	~	ex Latvia, Latvian AF 153, USSR	2-08
❑ CCCP-40748		Antonov An-2R *Colt*	YL-LFA	~	ex Latvia, USSR	11-13
❑ CCCP-40749		Antonov An-2R *Colt*	YL-LFD	~	ex Latvia, USSR	2-08
❑ CCCP-40784		Antonov An-2R *Colt*	YL-LEY	~	ex Latvia, USSR	11-13
❑ CCCP-40785		Antonov An-2R *Colt*	YL-LFB	~	ex Latvia, USSR	2-08
❑ CCCP-54949		Antonov An-2R *Colt*	YL-LEX	~	ex Latvia, USSR	2-08
❑ CCCP-56471		Antonov An-2R *Colt*	YL-LEW	~	ex Latvia, USSR	2-08
❑ 323		BAC Strikemaster Mk.81	N21419	69	ex Singapore ADC, S Yemen AF 504, G-27-36, G-AXFX, G-27-36, S Yemen AF 504	11-13
❑ 1104		BAC S'master 80A	G-SMAS	68	ex N399WH, R Saudi AF 1104, G-27-23	1-14
❑ 1120		BAC S'master 80A	G-RSAF	74	ex R Saudi AF 1120, G-27-231	1-14

❑ '23' red		MiG MiG-27 *Flogger*	~	ex Latvia, USSR. (83712515040)	1-14
❑ '35' red		Sukhoi Su-17M-4 *Fitter*	~	ex Latvia, USSR. (25102)	1-14
❑ '54' red		Sukhoi Su-17M *Fitter*	~	ex Latvia, USSR. (69004/5)	1-14

No.**2247 Squadron Air Cadets**: In Manor Lane to the west of the airfield.

❑ XE852	'H'	DH Vampire T.11	54	ex Woodford, Chester, Shawbury, 1 FTS, 4 FTS . SOC 30-10-67	9-13

KENFIG HILL north of the B4281 east of Pyle

No.**2117 Squadron Air Cadets**: Off Main Street, and behind Pwll-y-Garth Street.

❑ WT569		Hawker Hunter F.1	55	ex St Athan 7491M (21-11-57), A&AEE, Hawker trials	12-13

LLANBEDR AIRFIELD west of Llanbedr and the A496 on the road to Shell Island

No.**2445 Squadron, Air Cadets**: HQ opposite the entrance to the airfield.

❑ ZJ503		GAF Jindivik A92-908	~	trolley-mounted	6-13

LLANGEINOR on the A4064 north of Bridgend

Irvin-GQ: The rescue equipment manufacturer has a former Swedish Draken on display within the grounds.

❑ 35515	'49'	SAAB J35F Draken	~	ex F10, RSweAF	7-11

MOLD The cockpit of Sea Hawk FGA.4 WV903 moved to Hooton Park, Cheshire, on 28th December 2012.

NANTGARW on the A470 north-west of Cardiff

The Collection Centre: The large object store for the National Museum of Wales.

◆ **Access:** *Visits by prior appointment* **only** | **www.museumwales.ac.uk**

❑ XM300		Westland Wessex HAS.1	59	ex Cardiff, Cardiff-Wales, RAE Farnborough, RAE Bedford, A&AEE, Westland. SOC 1-8-79. SAR colours	1-14

NEWBRIDGE-ON-WYE on the A470 north of Builth Wells

Quackers Indoor Play Centre: Has a 'JP' in the grounds, among the delights on offer to rugrats | **www.quackersnow.com**

❑ XM358		Hunting Jet Provost T.3A	59	ex Twyford, North Scarle, Colsterworth, Halton 8987M (10-1-89), 1 FTS, 3 FTS, 1 FTS, CFS, RAFC, CFS, 7 FTS, 2 FTS	3-13

PEMBREY FOREST west of the A484 and Llanelli

Two Jaguars act as targets on the range.

❑ XX962	'P'	SEPECAT Jaguar GR.1B	75	ex Cosford, Cranwell 9257M (2-10-96), Coltishall, 6, 17, 20, 17	7-12
❑ XX966	'JJ'	SEPECAT Jaguar GR.1A	75	ex Cosford, Halton 8904M (23-5-86), Shawbury, 6, 54, 20, A&AEE, 20, 17	7-12

PEMBROKE DOCK on the A477 north-west of Pembroke

Pembroke Dock Flying-Boat Visitor Centre: Administered by the **Pembroke Dock Sunderland Trust**, the centre displays many recovered parts, including two Pegasus radials, from 210 Squadron Sunderland I T9044 which sank in a gale and sank at Pembroke Dock on 21st November 1940. A campaign is underway to salvage the rest. Displays chart the history of this famous flying-boat haven.

◆ **Access:** *Signed from A477 - close to South Pembrokeshire Hospital.* **Open:** *Tue to Sat (***not** *Sun or Mon) 10:00 to 16:00. Closed Xmas through to New Year. Other times by appointment.* **Contact:** *Sunderland Trust, Royal Dockyard, Pembroke Dock, SA72 6YH* | **01646 684220** | **enquiries@sunderlandtrust.org.uk** | **www.sunderlandtrust.org.uk**

PENWYLLT Dominie T.1 XS735 departed on 15th August 2013 bound for Walcott, Lincs.

PYLE on the A48 west of Bridgend, north of junction 37, M4

AMSS Ltd: Aircraft Maintenance Support Services, specialists in the creation of ground support equipment, unveiled a Spitfire full-scale model outside of its factory at the Village Farm Industrial Estate on 6th December 2013. A generous number of 'EN398s' can be found elsewhere in this edition; the exact pedigree can await *W&R25*!

❑	'EN398'*	'JE-J'	Supermarine Spitfire IX FSM	~	unveiled 6-12-13	12-13

RUTHIN on the A494 south-west of Mold

Phantom Preservation Group: Mark A Jones keeps the cockpits in the locality.

◆ **Access:** *Visits by prior arrangement* **only**. **Contact:** *Mark A Jones, Tyn Yr Erw, Llanfair Road, Ruthin, LL15 1BY* | **mark3045@tesco.net**

❑	–		McD Phantom FGR.2	69	cockpit	9-13
❑	ZE788	'HV'	Panavia Tornado F.3	88	ex Selby, Leeming, 11. Cockpit	9-13

ST ATHAN AIRFIELD on the B4265 west of Barry EGDX

MoD Saint Athan: (Note the full-out spelling instead of 'St'; the ever-reactionary *W&R* will continue to call it St Athan!) Operating as an enclave is **71 Instruction and Repair Squadron**. As well as the Lynx, it has several Hawk rear fuselages. Tidying up this reference, the following are long-in-the-tooth and are assumed to have been scrapped in the wind-down of the RAF presence: Islander G-BCWR fuselage (last noted 1-10); Hawk T.1A XX326 front fuselage (1-04); Jaguar GR.1 XX722 cockpit (3-06); Tornado GR.1A ZG706 fuselage (1-07); AV-8B Harrier II 162737 cockpit (3-10).

The airfield took on some of the look of its past glories during 2013 as it started to 'collect' the final 'first generation' Hercules upon their retirement after incredible service with the RAF, latterly with 47 Squadron. The last C-130K flight took place on 29th October 2013 when C.3A XV214 arrived from Brize Norton. The 'Herks' are here on behalf of Marshall Aerospace hopefully to find a new operator. As they are regularly ground-run, a formal listing in *W&R* would seem to be premature. But, just in case they were/are: XV177 C.3A (arriving 29-10-13), C.3A XV188 (5-9-13), C.1 XV196 (4-9-13), C.1 XV200 (18-4-13), XV209 C.3A 25-4-13, XV214 C.3A (29-10-13), XV295 C.1 (22-10-13) and XV303 C.3A (22-10-13). Unlike the Hercules, the recently-arrived HS.125 is unlikely to return to service and is perhaps destined for instructional use after spares recovery.

❑	XZ183*	Westland Lynx AH.7	78	ex Fleetlands, 656, 661, 1 Rgt, 654, 657, 659, 663, 669, 4 Rgt, 654, 659, 654. Instructional. First noted 3-13		3-13
❑	ZD704*	HS 125 CC.3	83	ex 32. Damaged 23-4-13. Arrived 20-11-13	[1]	12-13
❑	'JP098'*	Eurofighter EF.2000 EMU	~	dumped out on the East Camp. First noted 7-11		7-13

■ **[1]** The '125 was badly damaged in a hailstorm at Kandahar, Afghanistan, and is almost certain to be declared a write-off.

Horizon Aircraft Services: To better portray its wide range of services, **Hunter Flying Ltd** was renamed as HAS during 2013. Operates jet warbirds and other types, on behalf of a series of owners: these are not given a formal listing here, only long term restoration projects or stored airframes are presented. Not content with the challenging return-to-flight project of the Gannet AEW and operating Pembroke C.1 WV740 (G-BNPH) since June 2012, **Mark Stott** has extended his Percival fleet, with the intention of putting Sea Prince T.1 G-BRFC back into the air.

Departures: **Delfin** G-BYCT was flying again by 6-12 and is based; G-DELF was also flying by 6-12 moving to Hungary (still UK registered) in 5-13; **Hunter** T.8M WV322 (G-BZSE) arrived from Exeter, Devon, 21-3-12, but moved to North Weald, Essex, 14-11-12. Spares-ship T.66B 801 does not constitute enough of an airframe for listing and has been deleted.

◆ **Access:** *Visits possible* **only** *by prior arrangement* | **www.horizonaircraft.co.uk**

❑	G-BRFC*		Percival Sea Prince T.1		53	ex Bournemouth, N7SY, G-BRFC, North Weald, Bourn, WP321, Kemble, 750, 744. Arrived 4-5-12	[1]	6-13
❑	G-BZNT	'51'	Aero L29 Delfin		68	ex Winkleigh, North Weald, Caernarfon, ES-YLG, Sov AF. CoA 10-11-04		11-12
❑	'VH-FDT'*		DHA Drover II	G-APXX	51	ex Booker, Lasham, Blackbushe, Southend, Blackpool, G-APXX, VH-EAS. De-reg 26-11-73. Arrived 5-8-13		8-13
❑	RA-01611*		Aero L29 Delfin		~	ex Germany, Sov AF. Arrived 12-4-12. 'Tiger' colours		6-13
❑	WF118*	'569'	Percival Sea Prince T.1	G-DACA	51	ex Charlwood, Staverton, Kemble, 750, A&AEE, 727, A&AEE, RAE. SOC 1-8-80, de-reg 15-12-09. Spares. Arrived 5-9-13	[1]	9-13
❑	WF137*		Percival Sea Prince C.1		50	ex Booker, Lasham, Yeovilton, Culdrose SF, Shorts FU, Arbroath SF, 781. SOC 25-4-69. 'Admiral's Barge' colours. Spares. Arrived 11-7-13	[1]	7-13
❑	XK885*		Percival Pembroke C.1	N46EA	56	ex Charlwood, Staverton, St Athan 8452M (22-8-75), 60, 21, WCS, Seletar SF, B&TTF, Seletar SF, S&TFF, 209, 267. Arrived 25-9-13	[1]	9-13

❑ XL472*	'044'	Fairey Gannet AEW.3	59	ex Charlwood, Boscombe Down, 849 'B', HQ, 'A' Flts. SOC 6-12-78. Spares. Arrived 1-9-13	[1]	9-13
❑ XL500		Fairey Gannet AEW.3 G-KAEW	61	ex Exeter, North Weald, Chatham, Culdrose, Fleetlands, Lee-on-Solent, Dowty-Rotol, Culdrose SAH A2701, A&AEE, 849. Last flown 28-2-85	[1]	6-13
❑ XL602		Hawker Hunter T.8M G-BWFT	58	ex Exeter, Shawbury, Yeovilton, FRADU, 759, 764. CoA 23-7-99	[2]	6-13
❑ J-4083		Hawker Hunter F.58 G-EGHH	59	ex Bicester, Bournemouth, Swiss AF. Last flown 16-6-95	[3]	3-13

■ **[1]** The Gannet and Percivals are with Mark Stott - see notes above. **[2]** XL602 is registered to a Ruthin-based owner. **[3]** J-4083 is registered to Milton Keynes-based Heritage Aviation Developments.

Aerospace Enterprise Zone: There other operators on the former RAF station: **Cardiff Aviation**, in the 'Twin Peaks' hangar complex and offering maintenance and storage for big jets; and **eCube Solutions** specialising in what the author would call scrapping, but recently became 'parting-out' and the new buzz-phrase is 'end-of-life solutions'. The latter activity is short-term and recently has included former Austrian and Donavia Boeing 737s and a variety of Airbus single-aisle twins.

❑ VN-A190*	Boeing 737-4H6	94	ex Kemble, Jet Star Pacific, Malaysian 9M-MQJ. Fuselage, cabin trainer. Arrived by 7-13	12-13

Locally: Stuart Carr and friends are working on a Chipmunk forward cockpit off site.

❑ WD293	DHC Chipmunk T.10	50	ex Cardiff, Newport, Caerleon, Cwmbran, 7645M (4-7-60), QuB UAS, StA UAS, G&S UAS, StA UAS, Chatham Flt, 1 BFTS	3-13

SWANSEA

National Waterfront Museum: Part of the National Museum of Wales.

◆ **Open:** *Daily, 10:00 to 17:00, closed Dec 24-26 and Jan 1.* **Contact:** *Oystermouth Road, Maritime Quarter, Swansea, SA1 3RD* | **01792 638950** | **www.museumwales.ac.uk/en/swansea**

❑ –	Watkins CHW	1909	BAPC.47, ex Nantgarw, Cardiff, St Athan, Cardiff. *Robin Goch*	[1]	1-12

■ **[1]** Single-seat monoplane designed and built by C H Watkins at Maendy, Cardiff, 1907-1909. Fitted with a 40hp three-cylinder also designed by Watkins. Claimed to have made its first hop in 1909, a cross-country in 1910 and flown extensively until 1916.

SWANSEA AIRPORT or Fairwood Common EGFH

Two airframes, not noted since June 2004, have been deleted: Ultravector 627 G-MJAZ and Schleicher K.8b EHA.

❑ XL612	Hawker Hunter T.7	58	ex Exeter, Boscombe Down, ETPS, 8, 1417 Flt, APS Sylt. Last flown 10-8-01. Arrived 8-1-12. ETPS colours.	8-13

TREFOREST on the A473 south-east of Pontypridd

University of Glamorgan: The purpose-built centre at the Faculty of Advanced Technology's **Aircraft Maintenance Training Centre** includes a hangar for the Jetstream. *Busy campus, access by prior arrangement* **only** | **www.glam.ac.uk**

❑ PH-KJG	BAe Jetstream 31	86	ex Eindhoven, G-JXTC, G-LOGT, G-BSFH, PH-KJG, G-31-690	1-10

VALLEY AIRFIELD south of the A5, south-east of Holyhead EGOV

RAF Valley: With the **Search and Rescue Training Unit** (SARTU), the 'Huey' plays the role of a Griffin. A 'synthetic' Hawk fire training aid serves on the dump. The **Hawk Composite Servicing School** *should* still have a Hawk cockpit for instruction. Hawk T.1A XX349 is thought to have been intended to replace the Hunter on the gate, but by February 2013 it had been cut up, with the cockpit section going to Scampton, Lincs. Not recorded since April 1998, the cockpit of Hawk T.1 XX300 has been deleted.

❑ WV396	'91'	Hawker Hunter T.8C	55	ex 9249M, Yeovilton, FRADU, 229 OCU, 20. SOC 16-5-95 4 FTS colours. Gate	9-13
❑ XV709	'263'	Westland Sea King HAS.6	71	ex St Mawgan 9303M, Gosport A2831 (29-8-00), 810, 706, 820, 826, 820, 814, 706. Inst airframe	9-12
❑ '998-8888'		Bell UH-1H Iroquois	72	ex Middle Wallop, Greenford, Middle Wallop, Fleetlands, Stanley, Arg Army AE-406, 72-21491. SARTU	3-13

WELSHPOOL on the A483 west of Shrewsbury

Military Aircraft Cockpit Collection: Run by Sue and Roy Jerman. Jaguar GR.1 cockpit XX826 moved to Market Drayton, Shropshire, on 30th February 2012. Harrier GR.3 cockpit XZ993 departed in mid-2013 to an owner in the Midlands, but moved to Selby, N Yorks, on 14th November 2013. **Private** *collection, visits possible by prior arrangement* **only**

❑ WH775		EE Canberra PR.7	54	ex Bruntingthorpe, Cosford 8868M/8128M (11-3-71), 100, 13, 31, 17, 31, 13, 82, makers. Nose		3-13
❑ WK102		EE Canberra T.17	54	ex Bruntingthorpe, Cosford 8780M, 360, B.2, 45, RNZAF, 207. SOC 18-2-83. Avro-built. Cockpit		3-13
❑ XF321		Hawker Hunter T.7	56	ex Crediton, Coltishall, Bruntingthorpe, Exeter, Yeovilton A2734, Manadon A2648, RAE, 8, 56, F.4, 130. SOC 24-4-85. Cockpit		3-13
❑ XJ758		Westland Whirlwind HAR.10	56	ex Oswestry, Shrewsbury, Shawbury 8464M (10-2-76), CFS, 230, CFS, HAR.2, 217, 1360F, 22. Cockpit	[1]	3-13
❑ XM652		Avro Vulcan B.2	64	ex Burntwood, Sheffield, Waddington, 50, Wadd Wing, Cott Wing. SOC 20-2-84. Cockpit		6-13
❑ XM692		Folland Gnat T.1	60	ex South Molton, East Tilbury, Boscombe Down, Robertsbridge, Salisbury, Southampton, Fareham, Foulness, A&AEE. SOC 28-3-69. Forward cockpit		3-13
❑ XP642		Hunting Jet Provost T.4	62	ex Lavendon, Luton, Bruntingthorpe, Nottingham, Finchampstead Ridges, Lasham, Shawbury, 2 FTS, CFS. SOC 14-8-72. Cockpit		6-13
❑ XS923	'BE'	EE Lightning F.6	66	ex Bruntingthorpe, Cranfield, Binbrook, 11, LTF, 5-11 pool. SOC 24-6-88. Cockpit		3-13
❑ XT277		HS Buccaneer S.2B	65	ex Bruntingthorpe, Cosford 8853M (21-5-85), Shawbury, 237 OCU, 12, 800, 809, 801. Cockpit		3-13
❑ XV281*		HS Harrier GR.1	67	ex Cannock, Preston, Samlesbury, Dunsfold, Boscombe Down, A&AEE, BSE, Dunsfold. First noted 6-13	[2]	6-13
❑ XZ356	'FU'	SEPECAT Jaguar GR.3A	76	ex Ipswich, St Athan, 41, SAOEU, 54, GR.1, Shawbury, 6, Gulf Det, 41, 14, 17, 41		6-13

■ **[1]** Whirlwind cockpit is on loan from Dave Higgins. **[2]** Harrier has the cockpit of XV281, the centre fuselage of XW272 and the rear of a P.1127 test-rig.

WEST WALES AERODROME or Aberporth, north of the A487, east of Cardigan EGFA

W&R23 (p302) recorded Jindivik 3 A92-255 leaving here bound for Boscombe Down, Wilts. This was not the case; it departed for Selby, N Yorks, during June 2011.

WHITSON Last noted in June 2005, the hulk of Rallye G-ATWE has been deleted.

WREXHAM

Glyndŵr University: In Mold Road. **Access**, *busy campus, visits possible by prior arrangement* **only** | **www.new.ac.uk**

❑ XP585	'24'	Hunting Jet Provost T.4	62	ex Halton 8407M (7-10-74), St Athan, RAFC, 6 FTS, RAFC	11-13

YSTRAD MYNACH on the A469 south of Pontllanfraith

The College Ystrad Mynach: **Access**, *busy campus, visits possible by prior arrangement* **only** | **www.ystrad-mynach.ac.uk**

❑ –	HP Jetstream 41 EMU	67	ex Rhoose, Wales Aircraft Museum, Luton, G-ATXJ, HP. CoA 8-2-71, de-reg 11-4-72. Fuselage. 'Ystrad Mynach Airways' titles	3-10

■ **[1]** Jetstream factoids: Based on G-ATXJ, the third prototype; first flying 28-12-67. Became the Srs 200/300 prototype; maiden flight 16-12-69. Last flight 5-3-70, total time 636 hours.

PART FOUR
CHANNEL ISLANDS

The Islands are self-governing British Crown Dependencies - part of the British Isles, but not part of the United Kingdom, or the European Union - so that's clear, then!

ALDERNEY AIRPORT

EGJA

Both of these references are very long-in-the-tooth...

❑ G-ASHV	Piper Aztec 250B		63	ex Guernsey, N5281Y ntu. CoA 22-7-85, de-reg 20-6-88. Dump	9-08
❑ G-BDTN	BN Trislander		76	ex Guernsey, Aurigny, S7-AAN, VQ-SAN, G-BDTN. CoA 10-6-98, de-reg 5-1-11	9-08

GUERNSEY

Reference to the EAA Biplane is well dated, but it is believed to be extant. **Lucas Harrison** has the forward fuselage of a former Bristow Helicopters JetRanger converted into a comprehensive flight simulator.

❑ G-ATEP	EAA Biplane		67	CoA 18-6-73, de-reg 14-7-86	5-03
❑ G-ATHN	Nord Noralpha		48	ex F-BFUZ, Fr mil No.84. CoA 27-6-75, de-reg 16-12-91	1-10
❑ 5N-AHN	Bell JetRanger	G-AWFV	68	ex Bristow, G-AWFV. Forward fuselage	5-11

GUERNSEY AIRPORT

EGJB

Trislander fuselage G-BBYO (last noted Oct 2011) and Seneca 200 N32625 (Oct 2006) have been deleted.

❑ G-BAZJ		HP Herald 209	74	ex Air UK, 4X-AHR, G-8-1. CoA 24-11-84, de-reg 4-1-85. Fire crews	1-13
❑ G-PCAM		BN Trislander	76	ex Aurigny, G-BEPH, S7-AAG, G-BEPH. CoA 14-6-04, de-reg 5-1-11. Fire crews	1-13
❑ N97121		EMBRAER Bandeirante	~	ex City-Link, PT-SDK. Fire crews	1-13
❑ XM409		Hunting Jet Provost T.3	60	ex Firbeck, Moreton-in-Marsh, Halton 8082M (13-5-70), Shawbury, 2 FTS. Cockpit	10-01
❑ XS888	'521'	Westland Wessex HAS.1	66	ex Lee-o-Solent, Wroughton, Fleetlands, 772, 771, *Eagle* SAR Flt, 820, 826. SOC 2-6-80. Dump	1-13
❑ XX466	'830'	Hawker Hunter T.7	59	ex ?, Predannack A2651 [2], Culdrose SAH A2738 (15-5-86), FRADU, 1 TWU, Jord AF, R Saudi AF 70-616, HSA, XL620, 74, 66. Cockpit	1-10

JERSEY AIRPORT

EGJJ

❑ XP573	Hunting Jet Provost T.4	62	ex Halton 8336M (21-3-73), '8236M', Kemble, Shawbury, R-R, 1 FTS, CFS. Fire crews	6-12

PART FIVE
NORTHERN IRELAND

ARMAGH on the A3 / A28 north-west of Newry

A private location to the north-east of the town holds a variety of out-of-use types.

❑ G-APXR*	Piper Tri-Pacer 160	60	CoA 31-3-11	10-13
❑ G-ARDO*	Jodel D.112	60	ex F-PBTE, F-BBTE, F-WBTE. CoA 30-5-07	10-13
❑ G-BWKJ*	Rans S.7 Courier	97	CoA 4-11-04, de-reg 17-2-10	10-13
❑ EI-CGT*	Cessna 152 II	79	ex G-BPBL, N16SU, N68715. De-reg 6-11-12	10-13

Also: Another location in the area holds a pair of microlights.

❑ G-MJYF*	Mainair Gemini Flash	85	CoA 15-6-01, de-reg 31-1-03	8-13
❑ G-MVRB*	Mainair Gemini Flash	89	CoA 13-5-06	8-13

AUGHNACLOY at the A5/A28 junction, north of Monaghan

AWOL Outdoor Adventure: Actively encouraging its 'punters' to go absent without leave; this paintball, rafting, trekking, and other forms of team-bonding nausea, has a battered Rallye.

◆ **Access:** *Busy site, visits* **not** *possible* **without** *prior arrangement* | **www.oakfirepaintball.com**

❑ EI-BDK*	MS Rallye Club 100ST		ex Abbeyshrule, F-BXMZ	1-14

BALLYKELLY on the A2 between Londonderry and Limavady

Shackleton Aviation Museum: On 1st March 2013 the museum had to vacate its display premises and the collection of artefacts was put into store in the locality, pending a new venue. **Contact**: Norman B Thorpe | **n.thorpe1@sky.com**

BALLYKINLER Last noted in April 2003, Wessex HAS.1 XS865 had moved to Saintfield, NI, by early 2013.

BALLYMAGORRY on the N14 north-west of Strabane

❑ G-MTCZ*	Solar Wings Tri-Pacer 250	r87	CoA 3-8-94	11-13

BALLYMENA on the A26/36 north of Antrim

❑ VR-HJB	Rotorway Scorpion 145	83	ex G-BMEB, VR-HJB	11-13

BALLYMONEY on the A26 south-east of Coleraine

A yard in the area holds a Sierra hulk.

❑ G-BBSC*	Beech Sierra 200	73	ex Aldergrove. Damaged 4-12-97, de-reg 27-7-01. Fuselage	12-13

BANGOR on the A2 east of Belfast

❑ G-MMZS*	Eipper Quicksilver MXI	r85	CoA 16-12-93	11-13

BANN FOOT north-west of Craigavon

❑ G-BDWA	MS Rallye 150ST	76	CoA 7-6-01, de-reg 12-2-09	7-10
❑ G-BFHI	Piper L-4J	44	ex F-BFBT, 44-80236. CoA 28-5-04	7-10
❑ G-PFAL	Clutton FRED II	81	CoA 27-7-88, de-reg 12-10-10	7-10

BELFAST AIRPORT, or Aldergrove

EGAA

Cherokee G-ATRR was flying again by 2012 but suffered an accident on 19th May 2013 and may well be a write-off. Last noted in January 2006, the fuselage of Sierra 200 G-BBSC was to be found at Ballymoney, N Ireland, by November 2013. Also last noted in January 2006, Warrior II G-KNAP was to be found at Randalstown, N Ireland, by December 2013. Not reported since April 2009, the battered Aztec on the fire dump, G-OSNI, has been deleted.

❑ G-AVFE		HS Trident 2E	67	ex BA, BEA. CoA 6-5-85, de-reg 20-3-85. Fire crews	2-14
❑ G-AVYP		Piper Cherokee 140	68	ex N11C. CoA 14-2-04, de-reg 3-7-03	11-11
❑ XT456	'XZ'	Westland Wessex HU.5	65	ex 8941M (11-11-87), Wroughton, Yeovilton, Wroughton, 845, 847, 846, 845, 707. Fire crews	2-14

Joint Helicopter Command Flying Station Aldergrove. The cockpits are used by RAF Careers and do 'the rounds'.

❑ XE643		Hawker Hunter FGA.9	56	ex Abingdon 8586M, 208, F.6, 56, 63, 66, 92. Crashed 9-12-61. Cockpit	8-13
❑ XR529	'E'	Westland Wessex HC.2	64	ex 9268M, 72, SARTU, 2 FTS, 18, 78, 72. Gate, since 2002	4-12
❑ XR700		Hunting Jet Provost T.4	63	ex Abingdon 8589M, Shawbury, CATCS, 3 FTS, 1 FTS. SOC 1-10-71. Cockpit	8-13

Also: Close to the airport, a *private* collector keeps a Vampire pod. This was written out of *W&R23* (p304) as reported scrapped at Campbell College, Belfast, but thankfully this was not the case.

❑ XD525*	DH Vampire T.11	54	ex Belfast, Holywood, Belfast, Aldergrove 7882M (8-4-65), 1 FTS, 4 FTS, 5 FTS, 7 FTS. Pod, camouflaged	2-14

BELFAST (GEORGE BEST) CITY AIRPORT, or Sydenham EGAC

❑ ZF167	Short Tucano T.1	89	ex Shawbury, 1 FTS, 7 FTS. Arrived 1-12-04. Stored, off-site	2-09

BELLARENA AERODROME north of Limavady

Ulster Gliding Club | www.ulsterglidingclub.org

❑ G-ARAP	Champion 7EC Traveler	60	ex Londonderry, Eglinton. Crashed 22-9-81, de-reg 30-5-84	9-13
❑ EVN	Monnett Monerai	r87	ex BGA.3190. CoA 6-11-88	9-12

BLACKHILL AERODROME, or Draperstown

Renegade G-MWAJ was flying again by 2011, becoming EI-EYN. Whittaker MW.5 G-MWEO was flying again by 2011.

❑ G-MTZA	Thruster TST Mk.1	88	CoA 13-5-06	7-10
❑ G-MZGB	Cyclone AX2000	97	CoA 19-5-08	7-10

CASTLEROCK Cessna 337s EI-AVC moved to Dungannon, N Ireland and G-RORO (last noted 1-06) has been deleted.

CAUSEWAY AERODROME near Aghadowey, south of Coleraine

❑ G-AWLF	Cessna 172H	68	CoA 5-1-07	8-12
❑ G-BASO	Lake LA-4-180	67	ex Londonderry, N2025L. CoA 19-6-06	8-12
❑ G-BVRY	Cyclone AX3/582	95	crashed 9-7-98. CoA 2-3-99, de-reg 21-11-02	9-12
❑ G-MYPM	Cyclone AX3/503	94	CoA 20-6-03, de-reg 22-5-09	9-12
❑ N216HK*	CGS Hawk Arrow	r92	G-MWYP, de-reg 9-2-93	9-12
❑ N217HK*	CGS Hawk Arrow	r92	G-MWYR, de-reg 9-2-93	9-12

COALISLAND Last noted in March 2008, Evans VP-2 G-BEHX has been deleted.

DROMORE By July 2012 Argus II G-AJSN had moved to Long Kesh, NI.

DUNGANNON on the A29 between Cookstown and Armagh

The Magister is with a *private* collector in the *general* area. It was air-freighted into Shannon in November 1988 and was last noted in *W&R16* (p327) as stored in Swords, outside of Dublin. The Cessna 337s are at two *separate* sites in the area.

❑ G-AVJG*	Cessna 337B	67	ex N2415S. CoA 31-5-92, de-reg 30-7-96	7-13
❑ EI-AVC*	Cessna F.337F	~	ex Castlerock, Abbeyshrule, N4757. Reims-built. De-reg 26-6-03. Dismantled, first noted 7-13	7-13
❑ EI-BXO*	Fouga CM-170-2 Magister	c62	ex Saggart, Swords, Shannon, N18FM, Finnish AF FM-28 Valmet-built. Dismantled, arrived circa 2010	7-13

ENNISKILLEN AERODROME, of St Angelo EGAB

❑ G-ORHE	Cessna Citation 1	74	ex N619EA, G-OBEL, G-BOGA, N932HA, N93WD, N5220J. CoA 24-7-08, de-reg 19-8-11		12-12

FIVEMILETOWN on the A4 east of Enniskillen

Blessingbourne Carriage and Costume Museum: Within the Blessingbourne Estate.

◆ **Open:** *Easter to Sep by prior appointment* **only**. **Contact:** *Fivemiletown, Co Tyrone, BT75 0QS* | **028 8952 1188** | **info@blessingbourne.com** | **www.blessingbourne.com**

❑ XT208	Bell Sioux AH.1	66	ex Sek Kong, 656. Ditched 16-3-72, cabin	[1]	2-14
❑ XW795	Westland Scout AH.1	72	ex Middle Wallop, Almondbank, Wroughton, 659, 655, 669		2-14

■ **[1]** A crew door opened in flight while flying low over Tolo Harbour, Hong Kong. Distracted while closing it, the chopper struck the water. Pilot rescued and learned to suffer draughts!

GILFORD on the A51 north of Newry

❑ G-BKAF	Clutton FRED Srs II	83	CoA 30-5-97	8-10
❑ EI-AUT	Forney F.1A Aircoupe	60	ex Bann Foot, Cork, G-ARXS, D-EBSA, N3037G. CoA 30-7-76	8-10

GORTIN on the B48 north of Omagh

Stored in a shed locally is a modified HM.14 'Flea' built circa 1973, taxied, but not flown.

❑ –	Mignet HM.14 'Flea'	c73	stored - see above	6-04

HOLYWOOD on the A2 east of Belfast

Ulster Folk and Transport Museum: (Part of National Museums Northern Ireland) The 'Folk' and 'Transport' elements - and you really should take the time to visit *both* - are on either side of the A2 Belfast to Bangor road. The Transport Museum is in extensive grounds on the banks of Belfast Lough and a series of halls take the visitor through railways, buses, trams, cars, horse-drawn vehicles, shipping models, a special *Titanic* exhibition and then to the small, but pleasing aviation section. The Sealand is being restored and its workshop has a large window allowing visitors to glimpse this rarity. At least two of the deep store airframes - the Nimbus and the Scion - really should get an 'airing'.

◆ **Access:** *On the A2 east of Belfast. The commuter rail system stops close by.* **Open:** *Oct to Feb Tue to Sun 10:00 to 16:00, Mar to Sep Tue to Sun 10:00 to 17:00, so* ***closed*** *Mondays. Check for details of closures over Xmas and New Year.* **Contact:** *Cultra Manor, Holywood, BT18 0EU* | **028 90428428** | **email via website** | **www.nmni.com/uftm**

❑ G-AKLW	Short Sealand 1	51	ex Connecticut, Jeddah, RSaudiAF, SU-AHY, G-AKLW. Acquired 8-86		1-14
❑ G-ATXX	McCandless M4	68	ex Killough. De-reg 9-9-70. Acquired 1987		1-14
❑ G-BKMW	Short Sherpa	82	ex Belfast City, CoA 14-9-90, de-reg 14-11-96. Cockpit, acquired 2000		1-14
❑ XG905	Short SC.1	57	ex Sydenham, Thurleigh, BLEU, RAE. Acquired 20-5-74	[1]	1-14
❑ –	Ferguson Mono replica	73	IAHC.6, ex Dublin. Acquired 4-5-76		1-14

■ **[1]** XG905 made the type's first full transition from vertical to horizontal flight at Thurleigh 6-4-60. It crashed following a autostabilsation failure at Sydenham 2-10-63, killing J R Green. It was rebuilt and flying again in 1966.

Deep store: *Not* available for inspection.

❑ G-AJOC	Miles Messenger 2A	47	ex East Fortune, Strathallan, Dunottar. CoA 18-5-72, de-reg 5-1-82		1-09
❑ G-AKEL	Miles Gemini 1A	47	ex Kilbrittain Castle. CoA 29-4-72, de-reg 30-5-84	[1]	1-09
❑ G-AKGE	Miles Gemini 3C	47	ex Kilbrittain Castle, EI-ALM, G-AKGE. CoA 7-6-74, de-reg 30-5-84	[1]	1-09
❑ G-AOUR	DH Tiger Moth	43	ex Belfast, Mk.I NL898, 15 EFTS. Morris-built. Crashed 6-6-65, de-reg 8-7-65		5-08
❑ G-ARTZ (1)	McCandless M2	66	ex Killough	[2]	1-09
❑ ALA	Short Nimbus I	47	BGA.470, ex Bishop's Stortford, Duxford. CoA 8-75		1-09
❑ –	Ferguson Mono replica	75	IAHC.9, ex Belfast Airport, Holywood		1-09
❑ VH-UUP	Short Scion I	34	ex East Fortune, Strathallan, G-ACUX, VH-UUP, G-ACUX		1-09

■ **[1]** See under Dromod, Ireland, for a possible insight into Gemini G-AKEL and G-AKGE. **[2]** The registration G-ARTZ has been used twice, both times on Rex McCandless' products. See under St Merryn, Corn, for the second use.

JENKINSTOWN on the R173 east of Dundalk

A Cessna 337 is under restoration at a *private* site in the *general* area; it has been here since 2008.

❑ F-BXIL*	Cessna FTB.337GA	~	ex Ostend. Reims-built. See notes above	11-13

KEADY on the A29 south of Armagh

A Cessna 150 had appeared in a scrapyard in the town by the summer of 2013.

❑ EI-COP*	Cessna F.150L	74	ex G-BCBY, PH-TGI. Reims-built	8-13

LARNE Last noted in April 2005, Kitfox 2 G-RWSS has been deleted.

LETTERKENNY on the N56, west of Londonderry

The Rallye is in a local scrapyard; the Goldwing is stored in the general area.

❑ EI-AWU	MS Rallye Club	67	ex Rosnakill, G-AVIM	10-11
❑ G-MJDG	Eurowing Goldwing	82	CoA 5-11-92, de-reg 18-4-11	5-11

LISBELLAW on the A4 east of Enniskillen

❑ G-BSPJ*	Campbell Cricket	00	CoA 8-10-04, de-reg 8-1-04	10-13
❑ G-BTEI*	Campbell Cricket	92	CoA 12-12-98, de-reg 25-5-01	10-13
❑ G-BUOA*	Whittaker MW6 Fatboy A	93	CoA 4-10-06	10-13

LISBURN

No.**817 Squadron Air Cadets** still has its Devon fuselage.

❑ VP957	DH Devon C.2/2	48	8822M, ex Bishop's Court, Belfast, Northolt, 207, 21, C.1, WCS, SCS, NCS, SCS, WCS, SCS, Andover SF, 38 GCF, AAFCE, 2 TAF CS, BAFO CS. Last flown 4-7-84. Cockpit	8-13

LONDONDERRY

Oakfire Paintball: west of the A6. *Busy site, visits* **not** *possible* **without** *prior arrangement* | **www.oakfirepaintball.com**

❑ G-BFWK	Piper Warrior 161	78	ex Belfast, N9589N. CoA 8-12-99, de-reg 26-5-98	8-13

LONDONDERRY AIRPORT or Eglinton, on the A2 east of Londonderry — EGAE

Last noted in August 2010, Sonerai IIL G-BGLK had moved on by November 2011, probably to deepest Somerset.

❑ G-BWWX	Yakovlev Yak-50	85	ex LY-AOI, Sov AF. CoA 11-6-09	11-13
❑ EI-DIF*	Piper Navajo 350	77	ex G-OAMT, G-BXKS, N350RC, EC-EBN, N27230. F/n 11-11	11-13

LONG KESH east of Moira, close to J9 of the M1

Ulster Aviation Collection, run by the **Ulster Aviation Society**. Within what is now known as the Maze Long Kesh Regeneration Site, the UAC is on the northern perimeter of the former Long Kesh airfield, and the hangar was once used by Shorts to assemble Stirlings and *very probably* was used by Miles immediately post-war for Messengers prior to settling upon Newtownards. During October 2012 negotiations with the Imperial War Museum bore fruit and ownership of Sherpa G-14-1 was transferred to UAS. As the first aircraft wholly designed and built by Shorts in Northern Ireland, it a very appropriate acquisition. A team led by Fred May is creating from scratch a set of wings for this aero-isolclinic test-bed.

UAS publishes an excellent monthly magazine, *Ulster Air Mail*, and stages a series of talks and other events, as well as running an excellent website.

◆ **Access:** *At the Maze Long Kesh Regeneration Site, off the A3 Moira Road between Mazetown and Lisburn, on Halftown Road* **but** *see below.* **Open:** *Presently* **only** *available on a pre-arranged basis (excluding Dec, Jan, Feb) Downloadable application form on the website.* **Contact: hangar@ulsteraviationsociety.org** | **www.ulsteraviationsociety.org**

❑ G-AJSN*	Fairchild Argus II	43	ex Dromore, Cork, HB612, ATA, 43-14885. Crashed 10-6-67, de-reg 12-3-73. *Barbara Ann*. Arrived 3-3-12	1-14
❑ G-BDBS	Short 330	75	ex Langford Lodge, Belfast City, Short, G-14-3001. CoA 2-9-92, de-reg 1-7-93. Acquired 7-4-93	1-14

❑ G-BNZR		Clutton FRED II	91	ex Belfast. CoA 25-5-99, de-reg 11-8-10. Acquired 31-5-10		1-14
❑ G-BTUC		EMBRAER Tucano	83	ex Langford Lodge, Belfast City, Short, G-14-007, PP-ZTC. CoA 20-8-91, de-reg 20-12-96. Acquired 16-1-01		1-14
❑ G-MBJV*		Rotec Rally 2B	r82	ex Armagh. De-reg 13-6-90. Arrived 12-10-13	[1]	1-14
❑ G-MJWS		Eurowing Goldwing	r83	ex Langford Lodge. De-reg 23-6-97. Acquired 29-7-00	[2]	1-14
❑ G-MZHM		Team Hi-Max 1700	97	CoA 26-10-06. Acquired 13-9-07	[3]	1-14
❑ G-RENT		Robinson R22 Beta	88	ex Langford Lodge, Newtownards, N2635M. Damaged 30-9-92, de-reg 11-12-03. Acquired 28-2-03	[4]	1-14
❑ G-14-1		Short SB.4 Sherpa	53	ex Flixton, Rochester, Duxford, Staverton, Bristol, G-36-1, Cranfield, G-14-1. Fuselage. Acquired 16-7-08	[5]	1-14
❑ –		Chargus Cyclone	79	BAPC.263, ex Langford Lodge, Ballyclare. Last flight 4-4-88, acquired 11-94		1-14
❑ –*		Quicksilver Ultralight	~	arrived 18-2-12		1-14
❑ –		Rogallo hang glider	77	BAPC.266, ex Langford Lodge. Last flown 1978, acquired 2-00		1-14
❑ -*		Aerosport Scamp	~	arrived 31-8-13	[6]	1-14
❑ -*		Hapi Sygnet SF-2A	~	arrived 31-8-13	[6]	1-14
❑ –		Short Tucano EMU	c86	ex Sydenham, Langford Lodge, Sydenham. Acquired 1-12		1-14
❑ EI-BUO		Aero Composites Sea Hawker	87	ex Langford Lodge, Newtownards. Ditched Strangford Lough 9-91. Acquired 1998		1-14
❑ EI-CNG*		Air & Space 18A	66	ex Sligo, Knock, G-BALB, N6170S. Last flown 11-2007. Arrived 17-11-12		1-14
❑ N80BA*		Pitts S-1A	~	ex Killinchy, Newtownards. Crashed 7-11-99. Arr by 9-13		1-14
❑ 'P7895'*	'RN-N'	Supermarine Spitfire FSM	13	ex Seaton Burn, Linton-on-Ouse. 72 Sqn colours Arrived 21-12-13	[7]	1-14
❑ JV482		Grumman Wildcat V	44	ex Langford Lodge, Newtownards, Castlereagh, Lough Beg, 882. Crashed 24-12-44. Acquired 30-4-84		1-14
❑ WF911*	'CO'	EE Canberra B.2	52	ex Alveley, Gloucester, Hooton Park, Charnock Richard, Bacup, Preston, Samlesbury, G-27-161, 231 OCU. SOC 21-5-69. Cockpit. Arrived 19-10-13		1-14
❑ WN108	'033'	Hawker Sea Hawk FB.3	54	ex Langford Lodge, Newtownards, Sydenham, Bournemouth, FRU, 806, 895, 897, 800. SOC 26-9-63, acquired 17-10-89		1-14
❑ WZ549	'F'	DH Vampire T.11	53	ex Langford Lodge, Newtownards, Coningsby, Tattershall, Coningsby 8118M (10-12-70), CATCS, 1 FTS, 8 FTS, FTU, C(A). Acquired 10-91		1-14
❑ XA460	'768'	Fairey Gannet AS.4	56	ex Doncaster, Connah's Quay, Brawdy, Gannet Support Unit, 849, AS.4, 831, ECM.6, 849, AS.4. SOC 10-2-71, last flight 22-1-71. Acquired 29-10-11		1-14
❑ XH131		EE Canberra PR.9	59	ex Kemble, Marham, 39, 1 PRU, 39, 13, 39, MoA. Short-built. Last flight 31-7-06, acquired 13-12-10		1-14
❑ XM414	'101'	Hunting Jet Provost T.3A	60	ex Langford Lodge, Dundonald, Binbrook, Colsterworth, Halton 8996M (10-4-89), 7 FTS, RAFC, 1 FTS, RAFC, 2 FTS. Acquired 23-12-04		1-14
❑ XR517	'N'	Westland Wessex HC.2	64	ex Langford Lodge, Shoreham, Ipswich, Fleetlands, 60, 72, 18. Acquired 3-12-05		1-14
❑ XV361		HS Buccaneer S.2B	68	ex Langford Lodge, Lossiemouth, 208, 15, 208, 12, 15, 809, 800. Last flight 18-4-94		1-14
❑ 202		Sud Alouette III	72	ex Baldonnel, IAC. Ditched 20-10-95. Acquired 27-5-09	[8]	1-14
❑ -		Fieseler Fi 103 (V-1) FSM	c09	acquired 1-10	[9]	1-14

■ **[1]** Rotec donated by Stuart Wilson. **[2]** Eurowing Goldwing donated by Jeff Salter. **[3]** Hi-Max built and donated by Maurice McKeown. **[4]** Robinson is on loan from Harold Hassard. **[5]** See narrative for more on the Sherpa. **[6]** Both the Scamp and the Cygnet were built by UAS member Don Chisholm. **[7]** Built by GB Replicas. The *real* P7895, a Mk.IIa, served with 72 Sqn during the Battle of Britain; it ended its days in a take-off accident at Westwood, 8-3-45. **[8]** Alouette taken on charge by the IAC 22-3-72, ditched on 20-10-95 and struck off charge 31-10-95, with 7,100 hours on the clock. **[9]** V-1 was built by member James Herron.

Also: In the *general* area are two airframes, both at different locations.

❑ G-AVCS	Beagle Terrier 1	52	ex Auster AOP.6 WJ363, Odiham SF, AAC, 1900 Flt. Crashed 18-10-81, de-reg 3-4-89	1-06
❑ EI-BGB	MS Rallye Club	72	ex Upper Ballinderry, Abbeyshrule, G-AZKB. CoA 18-5-91	2-14

LOUGH FOYLE
Sometimes visible just off shore is the hulk of Corsair II JT593 'R' of 1837 Flight, which crashed on 9th October 1944.

MIDDLETOWN on the A3 south west of Armagh
Perched on an ISO container at a scrapyard at Wards Cross is a much-modified Cessna hulk, once used for a charity push around Ulster. It has been there since at least 2008. It is no stranger to the book, having last been 'written out' of *W&R13* (p225), having been derelict at Shannon, Ireland. With many thanks to Ian Thompson for his sleuthing.

❑ G-AWUP*	Cessna F.150H	68	ex -?-, Shannon. Reims-built. Dam circa 1983, de-reg 9-1-89		8-13

MONEYMORE on the A29, north of Cookstown

❑ -	Mignet HM.14 'Flea'	37	fuselage, stored	[1]	8-04

■ [1] The 'Flea' was built by the late Robert Wilbert Harris in the town in 1937. It was powered by a converted Austin 7.

MULLAGHMORE AERODROME south-west of Ballymoney

❑ G-BWWG	MS Rallye 235E Gabier	79	damaged 28-6-06, CoA 28-7-06	6-10
❑ G-MYIU	Cyclone AX3/503	93	CoA 29-8-06, de-reg 13-5-10	6-10
❑ G-MZGU	Arrowflight Hawk II	97	CoA 3-5-02	6-10
❑ EI-BGA	MS Rallye 100ST	74	ex G-BCXC, F-OCZQ. CoA 7-01	6-10

NEWRY Last noted in March 2008, Tiger Cub G-MMJS and Cessna F.150F EI-BHW have been deleted.

NEWTOWNARDS AERODROME south of the town, between the A20 and A21 EGAD
Last noted in the locality in January 2006, the wreck of Pitts S-1A N80BA moved to Long Kesh, N Ireland, by September 2013. Super Cub 95 G-BPJH was re-registered as G-RCUB in December 2012 and restored to flying condition; sadly it was involved in an accident on 26th December 2013. Quad City Challenger G-MYDN had moved out by August 2012. The Canberra nose, an Air Cadet airframe, is stored.

❑ G-ARSX*	Piper Tri-Pacer 160	56	ex Rathfriland, N2907Z. CoA 19-5-02, de-reg 12-2-02, First noted 1-12	9-13
❑ G-BANF	Luton Minor	77	ex Moneymore. CoA 5-6-92	9-13
❑ G-CBDO*	Raj Hamsa X'Air	01	CoA 8-8-10. First noted 11-11	9-13
❑ G-MYCN	Mainair Mercury	92	CoA 14-9-06	9-13
❑ G-OHKS	Pegasus Quantum 15	01	CoA 26-5-08	8-12
❑ G-OLFB*	Pegasus Quantum 15	01	CoA 28-5-10. First noted 11-11	8-12
❑ WT486	EE Canberra T.4	55	ex Gilnahirk, Belfast, Aldergrove 8102M (20-8-70), Wildenrath, 14, 17, 88, Wildenrath SF. Short-built. Cockpit	9-13

Locally:

❑ G-BSNY	Bensen B.8M	94	CoA 6-9-01, de-reg 31-3-09	1-06
❑ G-BUON	Avid Aerobat	93	CoA 6-11-01	10-10

OMAGH

❑ G-MTHS	CFM Shadow CD	87	CoA 17-5-97, de-reg 11-6-99	5-11

PORTADOWN on the A3 south west of Belfast
Never leaving a stone unturned, Ian Thompson was following up a lead and trawling the web; he found an 'arty' shot of a sports car against a pile of industrial scrap. The pile included the fuselage of a Short 330. The photographer was from Portadown and the trail led to the yard of **Gerald Hamill and Sons** in the town. There was the majority of the prototype 330, which left Sydenham in 1999! **Access**: Busy yard, by prior arrangement ***only***.

❑ G-BSBH*	Short 330	74	ex Sydenham, G-14-3000. De-reg 8-12-88	[1]	11-13

■ [1] *Bravo-Hotel* was the prototype, first flown 22-8-74.

RANDALSTOWN at the end of the M22 west of Antrim

Escarmouche Paintball: ('Escarmouche' est 'skirmish' dans 'Anglais n'est pas...)

◆ **Access:** *Busy site, visits* **not** *possible* **without** *prior arrangement* | **www.escarmouche.com**

❑ G-KNAP*	Piper Warrior II	81	ex Aldergrove, G-BIUX, N9507N. Crashed 13-7-99, de-reg 12-1-10. First noted 12-13	12-13

RATHFRILAND on the A25 north-east of Newry

❑ EI-AVB	Aeronca 7AC Champion	~	ex Galway, N151JC, 7P-AXK, ZS-AXK. De-reg 18-10-12	9-10

SAINTFIELD on the A7 south west of Belfast

The former Ballykinler Wessex arrived in the *general* area.

❑ XS865*	Westland Wessex HAS.1	65	ex Ballykinler, Lee-on-Solent, A2694, Wroughton, 771, 820. SOC 10-10-80. Camouflaged. First noted 6-13	2-14

STRABANE on the A5 south of Londonderry

❑ G-BDRL	Stits Playboy	62	ex Londonderry, Coleraine, Mullaghmore, N730GF. CoA 17-6-98, de-reg 11-5-01	11-13

UPPER BALLINDERRY

A collector at a private location in the general area has two airframes.

❑ EI-BAG		Cessna 172A	60	ex Langford Lodge, Upper Ballinderry, Portadown, Enniskillen, Abbeyshrule, G-ARAV, N9771T. CoA 26-6-79		2-14
❑ WD386*	'O'	DHC Chipmunk T.10	51	ex Dumfries, Firbeck, Cranfield, Tenby, St Athan, 1 FTS, Ox UAS, 22 RFS , 2 BFTS. SOC 29-7-70	[1]	2-14

■ **[1]** WD386 has the rear fuselage of WD377 - see under Blackburn, Lancs. *May* have arrived in 2007 - see under Dumfries, Scotland.

Argus II G-AJSN in its long-term lofty perch at Dromore. It moved to Long Kesh in the summer of 2012, joining the thriving Ulster Aviation Collection. *Ken Ellis*

PART SIX
IRELAND

ABBEYSHRULE AERODROME Westmeagh, north-west of Mullingar EIAB

Cherokee 140 EI-ATK, last noted in April 2004, moved to Longford, Ireland, by November 2012. Cessna 140 G-BSUH, last noted in April 2009, moved to Limetree, Ireland, by December 2012. The following have been deleted; last noted dates in brackets: Cessna F.150L EI-AWE (4-03); Sedan EI-BJJ (6-97); American AA-5 EI-BNR (5-07) and Cessna 172N G-SKYH (4-03).

❑ EI-ANN	DH Tiger Moth	40	ex Dublin, Kilcock, G-ANEE, Mk.II T5418, 63 GCF, 24 EFTS, 19 EFTS, 12 EFTS. Morris-built Cr 18-10-64. Spares		11-93
❑ EI-AOP	DH Tiger Moth	40	ex Dublin, G-AIBN, Mk.II T7967, 18 EFTS, 1667 CU, 1 GCF, 16 PFTS. Morris-built. Crashed 5-5-74		11-93
❑ EI-ARN	Wren 460	~	ex N2096X. Crashed 16-5-80, de-reg 22-9-80. Wreck	[1]	8-11
❑ EI-AYT	MS Rallye Minerva	69	ex G-AXIU. Crashed 12-11-89		11-13
❑ EI-BDP	Cessna 182P	72	ex G-AZLC, N9327G. Damaged 1998		9-09
❑ EI-BFI	MS Rallye 100ST	~	ex F-BXDK. Crashed 14-12-85		9-09
❑ EI-BHB	MS Rallye 125	~	ex F-BUCH		9-09
❑ EI-BIC	Cessna F.172N	~	ex OO-HNZ ntu. Reims-built. Cr 13-4-95, de-reg 18-11-02		11-13
❑ EI-CAA	Cessna FR.172J	74	ex G-BHTW, 5Y-ATO. Reims-built. Dam 12-93, de-reg 27-11-98		11-13
❑ EI-WRN	Piper Warrior 151	76	ex G-BDZX, N9559N. Fuselage		9-10

■ **[1]** STOL conversion of a Cessna 182H.

Locally: During August 2013 **Gerald Lynch** was offering Plus C EI-AGD, two spare fuselages, three spare wings, two engines and "lots of tail spares" for sale. One of the spare fuselages is EI-ANA; see also under Ballyjamesduff, Ireland. *Golf-Delta* has very likely been in the Abbeyshrule area since the early 1990s.

❑ EI-AGD*	Taylorcraft Plus C	39	ex Charleville, Cork, G-AFUB, HL534 43 OTU, 651, G-AFUB. Damaged 2-1-76. See notes above	12-13
❑ EI-ANA*	Taylorcraft Plus D	42	ex Ballyjamesduff, G-AHCG, LB347, 657, 655	12-13

ASHBOURNE between the N2 and the N3 north-west of Dublin, Meath

Leo Murray: Has established a private collection, called the **Meath Aero Museum**, in the *general* area.

◆ **Access:** *Private location, visits are* **not** *possible* **without** *prior arrangement*

❑ 'EI-ABH'	Mignet HM.14 'Flea'		99	fuselage and rudder	[1]	1-09
❑ '176'	DH Dove 6	VP-YKF	50	ex Omagh, New Ross, Waterford, Cork, Dublin, 3D-AAI, VQ-ZJC, G-AMDD. Accident, Cork, 8-82		1-09
❑ VM657	Slingsby Tutor	IGA.6	47	ex Galway, Gort, Castlebridge, Cork, IGA,6, IAC.6, VM657, 126 GS, 146 GS. SOC 23-5-57	[2]	1-09

■ **[1]** Leo started construction of the 'Flea' in 1999. To quote him, "in best Pou tradition [work] stopped two years later with the wings being built!" The only HM.14 to aspire to the Irish civil register was EI-ABH. **[2]** In 1962 the Tutor had a 'bit part' in the film *The Running Man* (Laurence Harvey, Alan Bates, Lee Remick, et al) in yellow colours. This *could* well be VM659 as VM657 was reported stored in a farm in poor condition at Killiney, Co Dublin, in 1993 and destined for a private owner in/around Galway for restoration. In 1993 VM659 was being rebuilt at Salthill, having been found in "a former airfield" in Wexford.

Puddenhill Activity Centre: *Busy site, visits* **not** *possible* **without** *prior arrangement* | **www.puddenhill.com**

❑ EI-BHM*	Cessna F.337E	77	ex Dublin, Farranfore, Weston, OO-PDC, OO-PDG. CoA 9-7-82. First noted 10-13	10-13
❑ E-402	Hawker Hunter F.51	56	ex Farnborough, Bournemouth, Kemble, Bournemouth, Macclesfield, Dunsfold, G-9-433 (8-8-76), RDanAF Esk.724.	10-13

ASKEATON on theN69 west of Limerick

❑ N1CD	Cessna T.337D	~	dismantled	9-11
❑ N3119K	Cessna 337C	~	de-reg 18-2-97.fuselage	9-11

BALDONNEL AIRFIELD or Casement, west of Dublin, Co Dublin EIME

Irish Air Corps Museum and Heritage Centre:

◆ **Open:** *By prior arrangement* ***only,*** *Monday to Friday.* **Contact:** *Air Corps Museum and Heritage Centre, Baldonnel Aerodrome, Baldonnel, Dublin 22, Ireland*

❑ C-7	Avro Cadet ✈	34	ex New Zealand ZK-AVR, Southampton, Abbeyshrule, Terenure, EI-AGO, EI-AFO, IAC C-7		2-14
❑ 141	Avro XIX Srs 2	46	ex Dublin, Baldonnel		2-14
❑ 164	DHC Chipmunk T.20	52	-		2-14
❑ 168	DHC Chipmunk T.20	52	-		2-14
❑ 172	DHC Chipmunk T.20	52	stored		2-14
❑ 183	Percival Provost T.51	55	ex Dublin, Baldonnel		2-14
❑ 191	DH Vampire T.55	61	ex Gormanston, Dublin, Baldonnel		2-14
❑ 199	DHC Chipmunk T.20	51	ex Gormanston, G-APTF, WG320, TTCCF, Wyton SF, 18 RFS. Dismantled		2-14
❑ 216	Fouga CM-170-1 Magister	~	ex Cork, Baldonnel, Aust AF 4D-YK		2-14
❑ 219	Fouga CM-170-1 Magister	~	-		2-14
❑ 231	SIAI-M SF-260WE Warrior	77	-		2-14
❑ '98'	Cessna 172B	61	ex Southend, G-ARLU, N8002X. Damaged 30-10-77. Rig		2-09
❑ - c/no 1012	Sud Alouette III	~	instructional, non-flying, rig.	[1]	2-14
❑ - '3-KE'	Fouga CM-170-2 Magister	~	ex French Air Force No.79. 221 allocated		2-14
❑ -	Wright Flyer replica	03	-		9-08

■ **[1]** The Alouette airframe has the constructor's number 1153 painted on it.

Irish Air Corps Headquarters:

❑ 195	Sud Alouette III	63	ex F-WJDH. '30 Years' markings, instructional	11-13
❑ 218	Fouga CM-170-1 Magister	~	ex Austrian AF 4D-YU	6-04
❑ 237	Sud Gazelle	79	fire dump	2-09
❑ EI-BMM	Cessna F.152 II	~	ex Weston. Reims-built. De-reg 31-10-12. IAC roundels	10-05
❑ EI-BSF*	HS 748-1/105	62	ex Dublin, Ryanair, EC-DTP, G-BEKD, LV-HHF, LV-PUM. *Spirit of Tipperary.* CoA 21-5-87, de-reg 26-7-94. Fuselage, fire crews. Arrived 3-5-<u>05</u>	9-13
❑ G-ASNG	DH Dove 6	57	ex Waterford, Cork, (EI-BJW), Coventry, HB-LFF, G-ASNG, HB-LFF, G-ASNG, PH-IOM	2-14

BALLYBOGHIL on the R122 north of Dublin, Co Dublin

❑ EI-AGJ	Auster J/1 Autocrat	47	ex G-AIPZ. Fuselage	10-04
❑ EI-ALP	Avro Cadet	35	ex Weston, Castlebridge, G-ADIE. Dam 5-4-67. CoA 6-4-78	1-12

BALLYBOY east of the N52 south west of Tullamore

❑ EI-CUB	Piper J3C-65 Cub	46	ex G-BPPV, N88392, NC88392	4-11
❑ EI-ETC	Aeronca 15-AC Sedan	49	ex G-CETC, HB-ETC	4-11
❑ G-MWJS	Pagasus Quasar TC	90	CoA 14-3-05, de-reg 3-3-09	4-11

BALLYJAMESDUFF on the R194 south of Cavan, Cavan

Last noted under this heading in April 2006, Plus D EI-ANA moved to Abbeyshrule, Ireland. It might be that EI-ALH also made the trek.

❑ EI-ALH	Taylorcraft Plus D	39	ex G-AHLJ, HL534, 43 OTU, 651, G-AFTZ	8-04
❑ XE808	Slingsby Cadet TX.1	54	ex Syerston, 617 VGS, 645 VGS, 631 GS	8-04

BIRR AERODROME on the N62 south of the town

❑ EI-CMN*	Piper Super Cruiser	~	ex N2363M. Stored, first noted 8-13	8-13

CARLOW on the N9 south-west of Dublin, Carlow

Carlow Institute of Technology: Kilkenny Road. **Access**: *Busy campus: by prior arrangement* **only** | **www.itcarlow.ie**

❑ EI-AUE	MS Rallye Club	69	ex Kilkenny, G-AXHU	7-13
❑ EI-BGJ*	Cessna F.152 II	r79	ex Kilrush. Reims-built. First noted 7-13	7-13
❑ EI-CUP*	Cessna 335	80	ex Sligo, N2706X. First noted 7-13	7-13
❑ G-HUGS	Robinson R22 Beta	90	ex Enniskillen. CoA 23-3-11, de-reg 21-2-11	7-13
❑ 220	Fouga CM-170-1 Magister	~	ex Baldonnel, IAC	2-14

CLONBULLOGUE AERODROME on the R401 south of Kinnegad, Kildare EICL

❑	EI-BNK	Cessna U206F	71	ex G-HILL, PH-ADN, D-EEXY, N9506G. De-reg 31-10-12	4-12
❑	EI-HOG	Cessna U206G	~	ex N566N, N5429X. Crashed 10-3-09	4-12
❑	G-MWCJ	Powerchute Kestrel	90	CoA 17-7-07, de-reg 15-9-06	4-12

DELGANY east of the N11, south of Dublin, Wicklow.

Mick Donohoe: Is *thought* to still be at work on restoring the 'Flea'.

❑	-	Mignet HM.14 'Flea'	IAHC 3, ex Carbury	4-96

DROMOD on the N4, north of Longford, Leitrim

South East Aviation Enthusiasts Group (SEAEG): Thanks to the exceptional **Cavan and Leitrim Railway** has a great base. Contacts for SEAEG: Philip Bedford, 10 Walled Gardens, Castletown, Celbridge, Kildare, Ireland | **pbedford@tcd.ie** See under Dublin, Ireland, for Proctor G-AHWO which may also make the move in due course.

◆ **Access:** *On the L1600 out of Dromod, west of the new N4 Dublin-Sligo road and alongside the mainline railway station.* **Open:** *Sat 10:00 to 17:00, Sun 13:00 to 17:00, and Mon 10:00 to 17:00, all year except Christmas and St Stephens Day.* **Contact: Cavan and Leitrim Railway**: *Station Road, Dromod, Leitrim, Ireland* | **00 353 9638599** | **dromod@eircom.net** | **www.cavanandleitrim.com**

❑	EI-BDM	Piper Aztec 250D	69	ex New Ross, Waterford, Kildimo, G-AXIV, N6826Y	[1]	2-14
❑	EI-100	SZD Mucha	58	ex OY-XAN. CoA 1-7-97		2-14
❑	EI-139	Slingsby Cadet TX.3 EI-GMH	53	ex New Ross, Gowran Grange, BGA.3485, Falgunzeon, Motor Cadet III G-BOKG, TX.3 XE789, 553 GS, 662 GS, 663 GS, 661 GS, 31 GS. CoA 2-8-97	[1] [2]	2-14
❑	–	Mignet HM.14 'Flea'	35	IAHC.1, ex New Ross, Waterford, Dublin, Coonagh. *St Patrick.* Off-site	[3]	2-14
❑	G-AKGE	Miles Gemini 3C	47	ex New Ross, Waterford, Kilbritain. De-reg 30-5-84. Cockpit	[1] [4]	2-14
❑	G-ANIS	Auster 5	44	ex Longford, TJ375, 1952 Flt. CoA 19-9-76, de-reg 8-10-81		2-14
❑	G-AOGA	Miles Aries 1	55	ex New Ross, Baldonnel, Dublin, Kilbrittain Castle, EI-ANB, G-AOGA. Damaged 8-8-69, de-reg 3-5-84. Stored, off-site		2-14
❑	G-AOIE	Douglas DC-7C	56	ex 'EI-AWA', New Ross, Waterford, Shannon, PH-SAX, G-AOIE Caledonian. *County of Perth.* Forward fuselage	[1]	2-14
❑	G-BJMM	Cremer Toy HAB	81	cancelled 18-10-98	[1]	2-14
❑	G-OGGS*	Thunder Colt Ax-8 HAB	89	CoA 10-2-95, de-reg 12-12-01. Arrived 17-6-13		2-14
❑	CBK	DFS Grunau Baby III	c48	BGA.1410, ex New Ross, Naas, Breighton, Stoke-on-Trent, Firbeck, RAFGSA.378, D-4676. CoA 2-4-83	[1]	2-14
❑	CBZ	Slingsby Tutor	c44	BGA.1424, ex New Ross, Naas, Gowran Grange, Jurby, RAFGSA.214, RA877. CoA 4-4-78	[1] [5]	2-14
❑	VP-BDF	Boeing 707-321	61	ex New Ross, Waterford, Dublin, N435MA, G-14-372, G-AYAG, N759PA. *Spirit of 73.* Cockpit	[1]	2-14
❑	NC285RS	NAA Navion	46	ex New Ross, Naas, Abbeyshrule, N91488. Crashed 11-6-79. *My Way.* Cockpit, rear fuselage, tail	[1]	2-14
❑	173	DHC Chipmunk T.20	52	ex New Ross, Waterford, Gormanston, IAC	[6]	2-14
❑	184	Percival Provost T.51	55	ex New Ross, Waterford, Baldonnel, IAC	[6] [7]	2-14
❑	187	DH Vampire T.55	56	ex New Ross, Waterford, Baldonnel, IAC. Pod	[6] [8]	2-14
❑	192	DH Vampire T.55	61	ex New Ross, Waterford, Baldonnel, IAC. Dismantled	[6] [8]	2-14
❑	RA881	Slingsby Cadet TX.1	c44	ex New Ross, Breighton, Halfpenny Green, RAFGSA 163. Cockpit, stored	[1] [5]	2-14

■ **[1]** Airframes on loan from the leading light of the group, Philip Bedford. **[2]** EI-139 has been brought back to Cadet TX.3 status. It is hoped to fly it again and it has the registration EI-GMH reserved for it. **[3]** 'Flea' is on loan from the Aviation Society of Ireland Preservation Group. **[4]** See also Holywood, Northern Ireland for more on G-AKGE. **[5]** Phil Bedford is restoring T.8 Tutor CBZ to its original 1944 condition as a long-span Cadet TX.2. CBZ was converted into an enclosed cockpit motor glider and will use the cockpit of RA881 in the rebuild. Phil owns CBZ along with Damian Smyth. **[6]** Airframes on loan from the Ministry of Defence. **[7]** Provost 184 has the wings of 183 (see Baldonnel) Ireland. **[8]** Pod of Vampire 187 came on site 30-1-2011. Its wings are fitted to 192.

DUBLIN

National Museum of Ireland: Within the impressive Collins Barracks, the museum takes in a wide sweep of Irish life, including the section 'Soldiers and Chiefs'.

◆ **Open:** *Tue to Sat 10:00 to 17:00, Sun 14:00 to 17:00,* ***closed*** *Mondays, Xmas and Good Friday.* **Contact:** *Collins Barracks, Benburb Street, Dublin 7, Ireland* | **00 353 1 6777444** | **www.museum.ie**

❑ 34	Miles Magister	39	ex Baldonnel, Dublin, Baldonnel, RAF N5392 n/s	[1]	10-12
❑ 198	DH Vampire T.11	55	ex Baldonnel, XE977, 8 FTS	[2]	10-12

■ **[1]** Magister 34 was delivered from new 22-2-39 and became an instructional airframe 11-3-52. **[2]** Vampire 198 was never operated by the IAC, having been acquired ex-RAF as an instructional airframe 30-8-63.

Dublin Institute of Technology: By October 2013 the campus at Bolton Street had given up its airframes and the following had moved to the larger facility at Dublin Airport, Ireland: Robinson R22 EI-CGU and CM-170 Magister 215. Last noted in December 2011, Bölkow Bö 105S EI-LIT was scrapped, *perhaps* after making the move to the new site. By May 2013 Cessna F.337E EI-BHM had moved out; settling upon Ashbourne, Ireland, by October 2013. The Bonanza arrived at Bolton Street by late 2012, to be converted into a simulator; it *may* move to the Airport.

◆ **Access:** *Busy campus: by prior arrangement* **only** | **www.dit.ie**

❑ N7205R*	Beech A36 Bonanza	~	ex Ballingarry. Accident 9-8-02. Cockpit, simulator	9-12

Philip Bedford and **Paul Martin**: Keep their Auster locally, it is a long term restoration to fly project. Phil's Proctor project is also in the general area. (See also Dromod, Ireland.)

❑ EI-ACY	Auster J/1 Autocrat	46	ex Dromore, G-AIBK. Crashed 6-4-67	2-14
❑ G-AHWO	Percival Proctor V	46	ex Whitehall, Dublin, (EI-ALY). Crashed 5-5-59, de-reg 17-11-60	2-14

Others: *W&R21* (p304) wrote out the cockpit section of Viscount EI-AOH, as noted October 1997. It is made of sterner stuff!

❑ EI-AOH*	Vickers Viscount 808	67	ex Dublin Airport, Aer Lingus, PH-VII. Scrapped 12-72. *St Fiacre*. Cockpit	10-13

DUBLIN AIRPORT or Collinstown, Dublin

EIDW

The fuselage of HS 748-1 EI-BSF left the dump on 3rd May 2005 and moved to Baldonnel, Ireland.

❑ EI-ABI	DH Dragon ✈	36	ex EI-AFK, G-AECZ, AV982, EE, 7 AACU, 110 Wing, G-AECZ. *Iolar*	[1]	6-13
❑ EI-BEM	Short 360-100	84	ex ALT, East Midlands, G-BLGC, G-14-3642. *St Senan*. Crashed 31-1-86. Cabin trainer		9-93
❑ EI-CJD	Boeing 737-204	83	ex Ryanair, G-BKHE, G-BKGU ntu. Fire crews / tow-training		10-12

■ **[1]** EI-ABI is operated by the Aer Lingus Charitable Foundation and represents the first Aer Lingus aircraft in 1936. Factoid: The original EI-ABI was previously G-ACPY and returned to the UK in 1938. It was shot down by a Ju 88 off the Scilly Isles 3-6-41.

Dublin Institute of Technology: The new facility at the Dublin Airport Business Park was fully up and running by late 2013, with two airframes making the trek from Bolton Street, Dublin (which see). The Learjet came direct to the new location. Also here, is the rear fuselage of ATR 72-212 EI-SLM.

◆ **Access:** *Busy campus: by prior arrangement* **only** | **www.dit.ie**

❑ EI-CGU*	Robinson R22	81	ex Dublin, G-BSNH, N9065D. wfu 16-4-97. DIT titles. First noted 10-13	10-13
❑ N829AA*	Learjet 25B	72	ex N25TK, N741F, N741E, N262JE. Arrived 3-13	10-13
❑ 215*	Fouga CM-170-1 Magister	~	ex Dublin, Baldonnel, Katanga AF not delivered, Austrian AF 4D-YJ. First noted 10-13	2-14

Simtech Flight Crew Training: In the Airport Logistics Park. *By prior arrangement* **only** | **www.simtech.ie**

❑ G-NJIB	HS 146-300	90	ex B-1776, G-BSXZ, G-6-174. CoA 11-4-04, de-reg 27-1-07. Cockpit	8-11

DUBLIN WESTON AIRPORT near Leixlip, Kildare

EIWT

There have been many changes at the aerodrome, not least a re-branding. As the news spread, disbelief broke out, but the reality was that on 27th June 2012 PBY-5A Catalina VP-BPS was scrapped on site. Last noted in January 2012, Cessna F.337G G-BTVV, last noted January 2006, moved to Shannon, Ireland, on 5th March 2013. Cessna 401B N9146N was donated to a children's charity in County Kildare. There has been a major clear-out at the aerodrome and the opportunity has been taken to delete some long term light aviation hulks from the listing: Rallyes EI-BBG (last noted 1-02); EI-BBJ (1-06); EI-BCU (9-05); EI-BEA (1-02); EI-BKN (1-02); EI-BMB (5-09) and Diplomate EI-BUG (1-06).

❑	EI-CGG		Forney Aircoupe 415C		~	ex N2522H, NC2522H. CoA 10-00. de-reg 6-11-12	11-13
❑	N4575C		Grumman Goose ✈		45	ex Superior Oil, USAF OA-13B 45-49088, USN JRF-5 87726 National Flight Centre titles [1]	2-14
❑	XE982		DH Vampire T.11		55	ex Dunkeswell, Hereford, St Athan 7564M (15-5-58), RAFC	5-12
❑	XV863	'S'	HS Buccaneer S.2B		68	ex Lossiemouth 9145M, 9139M, 9115M, 16, 237 OCU, 208, 237 OCU, 208, 809. *Sea Witch*. Pink colours. National Flight Centre titles	2-14
❑	51-11701		Beech C-45H	G-BSZC	52	ex N9541Z, USAF 51-11701. CoA 4-6-06. USAF colours, *Southern Comfort*. Engine running 6-13	12-13

■ **[1]** The Goose was registered to Aerofloat G21A Inc but was cancelled from the US register 4-13.

EDGEWORTHSTOWN on the N4 between Longford and Mullingar

Midland Karting: *Busy centre, by prior arrangement* **only | www.midlandkarting.net**

❑	EI-CFV*	MS Rallye Club	71	ex Abbeyshrule, G-OLFS, G-AYYZ. First noted 3-12	3-12

FOYNES on the N69 west of Limerick, Limerick

Foynes Flying-Boat and Maritime Museum: Centred on the former transatlantic terminal for the flying-boat services. Expanded and slightly re-branded, the €1.5 million facelift was officially opened on 24th September 2013. There is now a maritime section to extend appeal and the control tower, which provides panoramic views of the Shannon, has been renovated. The fantastic Boeing 314 'Clipper' is a phenomenal 'walk-in' exhibit that has to be sampled to be believed.

◆ **Open:** *Mar to Oct, 09:00 to 17:00; Jun to Sep 09:00 to 18:00 – last admission 16:00. Other times by prior arrangement.*
Contact: *Foynes, Limerick, Ireland* | **00 353 69 65416 | info@flyingboatmuseum.com | www.flyingboatmuseum.com**

❑	-	Boeing 314 'Clipper' FSM	06	PanAm colours	1-14

GALWAY

❑	EI-CJR	Stampe SV-4A	63	ex G-BKBK, OO-CLR, F-BCLR. Nord-built. Crashed 9-8-09	4-11

GOWRAN GRANGE near Dublin, Kildare

Dublin Gliding Club: Last noted in August 2004, the following have been deleted: Kite EI-102, Phoebus EI-123, Ka 6 EI-128.

❑	EI-124	Grob G-102 Astir CS	~	ex Churchtown. Stored	9-11
❑	WZ762	Slingsby Grasshopper TX.1	~	EI-135, ex Cosford, Rugby [1]	11-13

■ **[1]** Grasshopper WZ762 is fitted with the wings of WZ756.

HACKETSTOWN Last noted in June 2004, Rallye EI-BFV has been deleted.

KILRUSH AERODROME on the N78 north-east of Athy, Kildare EIKH

By July 2013 Cessna F.152 EI-BGJ had moved to Carlow, Ireland. Two inmates have been deleted: Rallye EI-BIT (last noted in August 2004) and Snowbird G-MTXL.

LIMERICK

National Kart and Adventure Centre: *Busy site, by prior arrangement* **only | www.nationalkartcentre.ie**

❑	EI-BBO*	MS Rallye	~	ex F-BVNM	1-12
❑	EI-BPJ	Cessna 182A	58	ex Abbeyshrule, G-BAGA, N4849D. *The Hooker*	1-12
❑	-	MS Rallye	~	-	1-12

Also: A Luscombe is stored at a local strip.

❑	G-AFZK	Luscombe 8A Silvaire	39	ex N25118, NC25118. CoA 15-6-09	9-11

LIMETREE AERODROME north of Portlaoise, Laois

❑	EI-CTI*	Cessna FRA.150L	74	ex Abbeyshrule, G-BCRN. Reims-built. Fuselage	3-13
❑	G-BSUH*	Cessna 140	46	ex Abbeyshrule, N89088, NC89088. Damaged 6-93, de-reg 28-4-95. First noted 12-12	3-13

❑ G-BZJO*		Pegasus Quantum 15	00	CoA 29-9-05	3-13
❑ G-MMTJ*		Southdown Puma Sprint	85	CoA 16-4-00, de-reg 17-4-09	3-13
❑ G-MTBP*		Whittaker MW-5B	87	CoA 21-9-94, de-reg 6-3-13	3-13

LONGFORD on the N55 north of Edgeworthstown, east of Longford

Midland Paintballing and Karting: *Busy site, by prior arrangement* **only | http://midlandpaintballing.com**

❑ EI-ATK*		Piper Cherokee 140	67	ex Abbeyshrule, G-AVUP. Crashed 14-2-87. Fuselage	11-12
❑ EI-BKE*		MS Super Rallye	~	ex Abbeyshrule, F-WKUN. Cr 5-4-81, de-reg 16-9-86. Fuselage	11-12
❑ EI-CHN*		MS Rallye	67	ex Abbeyshrule, G-AVIO. Fuselage	11-12

MAYNOOTH, Dolly's Grove, Meath, north of the town, south of the R156

An airstrip here boasts some heavweight inmates.

❑ ES-YLK		Aero L29 Delfin		~	ex Cork	2-14
❑ LY-AFO		Antonov An-2 *Colt*		~	ex Cork	2-14
❑ XZ995	'3G'	HS Harrier GR.3	G-CBGK	86	ex Lowestoft, Shoreham, Ipswich, St Mawgan 9220M, Chivenor, 1417 Flt, 4, 3, 233 OCU, 3. De-reg 14-3-05	2-14

MULLINGAR on the N4 west of Dublin

W&R16 'wrote out' airworthy Whirlwind HAR.10 XJ729 (G-VBGE) from p229 - Cricklade, Wilts - as departing for Ireland on 7th August 1999. It routed from Kemble to Haverfordwest, Waterford and then Abbeyshrule; later settling at a location in this *general* location. Its permit expired on 17th June 2008 and it is presumed to have been in store since. On 11th July 2013 it was noted on the N11 heading south-east, very likely for the ferry at Rosslare. It was shown off in the static at Yeovilton's Air Day two days later. After that, it vanished again. It had been offered for sale since late 2010, the vendor then *perhaps* being Polish. Thanks to the continually exceptional *Irish Air Letter* for this.

NAAS south of the N7/M7, south west of Dublin

To the west of the town, near Junction 8 of the N7 is an EC120 advertising Kildare Helicopters.

❑ EI-PJW		Eurocopter EC120	~	fire damaged 4-06	12-11

NEWCASTLE AERODROME on the R671 north of Wicklow EINC

❑ G-MCCY		Yakovlev Yak-52	90	ex LY-AQF, UR-BBP, Ukraine AF 129, Sov AF 129. IAV Bacau-built. CoA 20-11-08	8-13

PORTARLINGTON north of the M7 and Portlaoise

A yard here took delivery of the Venoms from Bournemouth by February 2013. FB.50 'WR410' (G-DHUU) moved on quickly to Shannon, Ireland.

❑ 'VV612'*		DH Venom FB.50	G-VENI	55	ex Bournemouth, 'WE402'. Swiss AF J-1523. CoA 25-7-01, de-reg 5-3-13. Swiss-built. Silver colours. Arr by 2-13	11-13
❑ 'WR360'*	'K'	DH Venom FB.50	G-DHSS	56	ex Bournemouth, Swiss AF J-1626. CoA 22-4-03, de-reg 5-3-13. Swiss-built. White 60 Sqn c/s. Arr by 2-13	11-13
❑ 'WR421'*		DH Venom FB.50	G-DHTT	56	ex Bournemouth, G-BMOC ntu, ex Swiss AF J-1611. Swiss-built. CoA 17-7-99, de-reg 5-3-13. Red c/s. Arr by 2-13	11-13
❑ J-1573*		DH Venom FB.50	G-VICI	55	ex Bournemouth, HB-RVB, G-BMOB ntu, Swiss AF. Swiss-built. CoA 24-11-99, de-reg 5-3-13. Arrived by 2-13	8-13

POWERSCOURT, Wicklow

❑ EI-AUS		Auster J/5F Aiglet Tnr	52	ex G-AMRL. CoA 2-12-75, de-reg 18-10-12	4-95

RATHCOOLE, Cork EIRT

❑ EI-AFN		BA Swallow 2	38	ex G-AFGV. Off-site	4-03
❑ G-AXVV		Piper L-4H Cub	44	ex F-BBQB, 43-29572. CoA 16-6-73, de-reg 12-4-99	5-12

ROUNDWOOD, on the R765 west of Newtown Mount Kennedy, Wicklow

Skirmish Paintball: Within the 30-acres are six gaming sites, one of which holds a ubiquitous Rallye hulk.

◆ **Access:** *Busy site: by prior arrangement* **only** | **www.skirmish.ie**

❑ -*		MS Rallye	~	first noted 11-13	11-13

SHANNON AIRPORT, Clare EINN

Atlantic AirVenture: **Shannon Aviation Museum** and the Shannon Flight Simulation Centre.

◆ **Open:** *Mon to Sat 10am to 6pm; Sun in Jul and Aug 2pm to 6pm.* **Contact:** *Aviation Education Centre, Link Road, Shannon Airport* | **00 353 061363687** | **info@atlanticairventure.com** | **www.atlanticairventure.com**

❑ EI-CIA*		MS Rallye	~	ex Toomyvara. Arrived 23-8-12	8-13
❑ EI-COZ*		Piper Cherokee 140C	70	ex Abbeyshrule G-AYMZ, N11C. Arrived 1-3-13	8-13
❑ G-AVMZ		BAC 111-510ED	69	ex Alton, Bournemouth, European, BA, BEA. CoA 17-2-02, de-reg 10-6-03. Forward fuselage	8-13
❑ G-BAHI		Cessna F.150H	68	ex Little Staughton, PH-EHA. Reims-built. CoA 14-12-07. Fuselage	8-13
❑ G-BTVV*		Cessna F.337G	73	ex Weston, PH-RPD, N1876M. Reims-built. CoA 12-1-03. Arrived 5-3-13	8-13
❑ G-CDPF*		HS 146-300	89	ex Lasham, Southend, Air Wisconsin N614AW, G-5-132. Cockpit - simulator. De-reg 23-6-07. First noted 8-13	8-13
❑ G-GFCD*		Piper Seneca III	81	ex G-KIDS, N83745. CoA 20-5-12, de-reg 15-10-12. First noted 8-13	8-13
❑ -		Piper Cherokee	~	ex Cannock, cockpit	1-12
❑ -*		Monnett Monerai	~	on loan from Larry Kelly. Fuselage. First noted 8-12	8-13
❑ -*		Bede BD-5J Micro	~	ex Glasgow.	12-13
❑ C-GAPW		Boeing 737-275	74	ex Canadian, N127AW, C-GAPW. Simulator [1]	1-12
❑ D-3229		Scheibe Bergfalk 55/II	~	suspended in main building	8-13
❑ VS562*		Avro Anson T.21	48	ex Market Drayton, Coventry, Crowland, Llanbedr, Portsmouth, Llanbedr 8012M (9-4-65), A&AEE. Forward fuselage. First noted 7-13	11-13
❑ 'WR410'*		DH Venom FB.50 G-DHUU	54	ex Portarlington, Bournemouth, G-BMOD ntu, ex Swiss AF J-1539. Swiss-built. CoA 24-5-02, de-reg 5-3-13. 6 Sqn colours, Suez stripes. Arrived by 2-13	8-13
❑ XM144*		EE Lightning F.1	60	ex Spark Bridge, Pershore, Wycombe AP, Eaglescott, Burntwood, Leuchars 8417M (28-5-74), Leuchars TFF, 23, Leuchars TFF, 226 OCU, 74. 74 Sqn colours. Cockpit. Arrived 2-13	8-13
❑ XX826*	'JH'	SEPECAT Jaguar GR.1	75	ex Market Drayton, Welshpool, Ipswich, Cosford 9021M 10-1-90), Shawbury, 2, 20, 14. Cockpit. Arrived 7-13	8-13
❑ XX897*		HS Buccaneer S.2B(m)	76	ex Bournemouth, DRA Bedford, RAE, RRE. Tornado nose. Arrived 26-8-12	8-13
❑ -*		Supermarine Spitfire FSM	c98	ex Lytham St Annes. Cockpit, arrived 3-13	8-13

■ [1] *Papa-Whisky* factoids: 71,151 hours, 74,613 landings and is now a fixed-base trainer for a 737-800 series.

Airport:

❑ EC-CFA	Boeing 727-256	73	ex N907RF ntu, Iberia. *Jeres Xeres Sherry*. Arrived 9-01. Stored	8-13
❑ VP-BNA*	Boeing 727-21	67	ex N199AM, VR-BNA, N360PA. Arr 2-9-08. Poor state by 7-11	8-13

SLIGO, Sligo

Gerry O'Hara: Gerry's homegrown aircraft are *believed* to be still stored here.

❑ –	Sligo Concept	~	IAHC.7, single seat low wing monoplane. Unflown, stored.	8-91
❑ –	O'Hara Gyroplane	~	IAHC.8, on Bensen lines. Unflown. Stored.	8-91

Sligo Extreme Paintball: Took delivery of a Cessna 150 to add to the adrenaline-pumping ambience in mid-2013.

◆ **Access:** *Busy site: by prior arrangement* **only** | **www.sligoextremepaintball.com**

❑ EI-BYF*	Cessna 150M	~	ex Sligo Airport, N3924V. Arrived 29-5-13	5-13

SLIGO AIRPORT or Strandhill, Sligo EISG

❑ G-ECAT	Fokker F.27-500	86	ex G-JEAI, VH-EWY, PH-EXL. Damaged 2-11-02. CoA 16-12-02, de-reg 12-8-03. Fire crews	9-13
❑ G-OMDG	Hoffmann Dimona	83	ex OE-9215. CoA 9-1-05, de-reg 7-4-10	7-13

TRIM on the R154 north-west of Dublin, Meath

❑ EI-ASU	Beagle Terrier 2	51	ex Rathcoole, G-ASRG, Auster T.7 WE599, LAS, HCCS. Stored, dismantled in container	4-12
❑ EI-BFO	Piper L-4J Cub	44	ex F-BFQJ, N79856, NC79856, 44-80405. De-reg 18-10-12. Frame	8-12

TULLAMORE By June 2012 Omega 56 EI-ANP had left the Tullamore Dew Heritage Centre.

WATERFORD AIRPORT, Waterford EIWF

On 9th October 2013 MS Rallye EI-BGG was removed to a paintball site in the Kilkenny area. It had been on the fire dump here since 2004 and slipped the *W&R* net so far! Last noted in January 2005 Cessna F.150G EI-BFE had been deleted.

❑ EI-CIV	Piper Cherokee 140	77	ex G-BEXY, N9648N	12-11
❑ N80JN	Mitsubishi Mu-2B-36	~	ex EC-GLU, OY-ATZ, SE-GHY, N476MA. Derelict	4-09

WESTON AERODROME has been re-branded, see Dublin Weston Airport above

APPENDIX AND INDEX SECTION

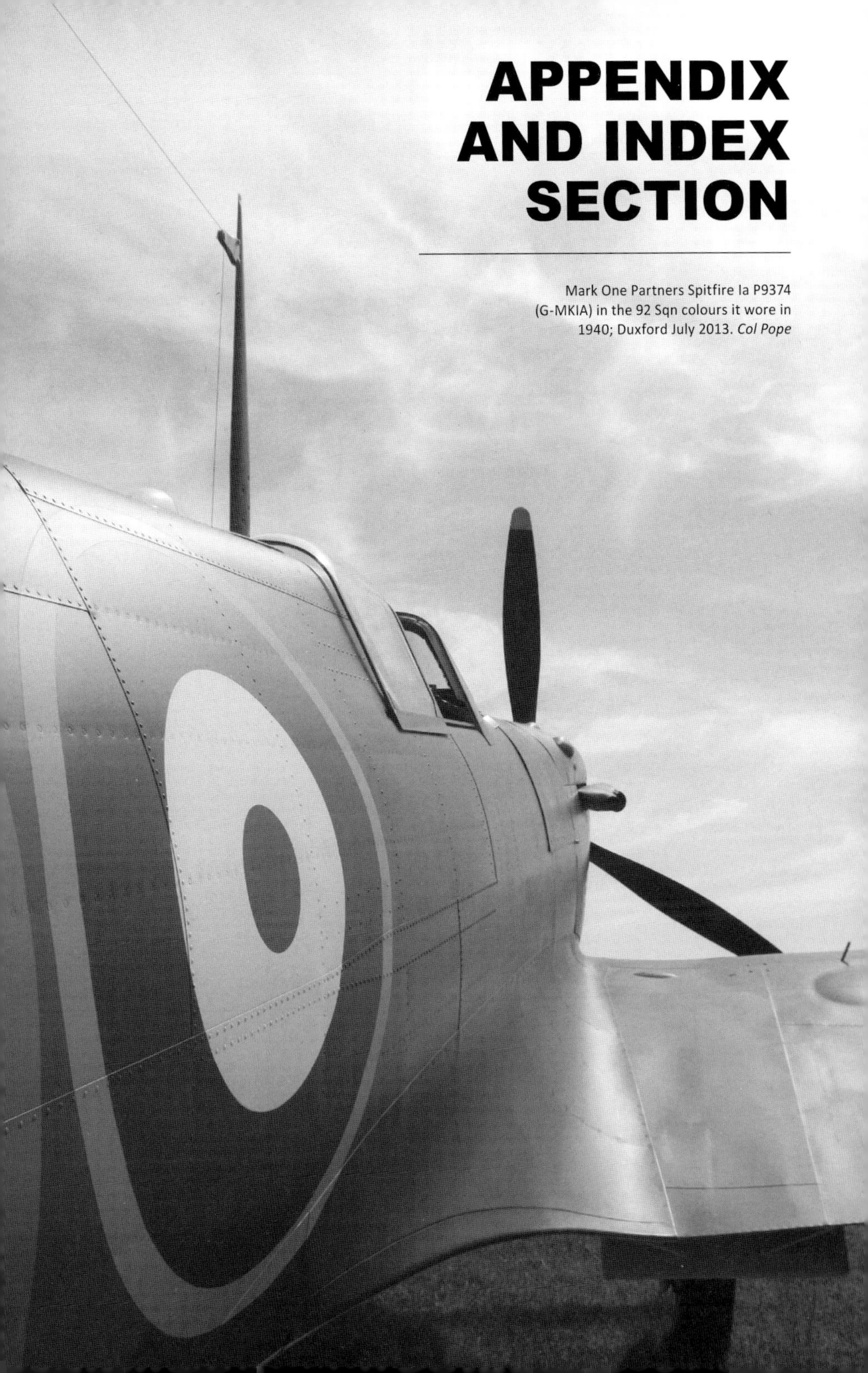

Mark One Partners Spitfire Ia P9374 (G-MKIA) in the 92 Sqn colours it wore in 1940; Duxford July 2013. *Col Pope*

Appendix A : RAF OVERSEAS

British military aircraft in the *W&R* categories to be found on *Crown* territory or property.

CYPRUS – AKROTIRI AIRFIELD

RAF Akrotiri:

❑ XD184		W'land Whirlwind HAR.10	54	ex 8787M (2-9-83), 84 'A' Flt, 1563F, 228, 155. SAR c/s. Gate	1-14
❑ XR504		Westland Wessex HC.2	63	ex 9327M, 84, 22, SARTS, 18, 1 FTU. Displayed	1-14
❑ XS929	'L'	EE Lightning F.6	67	ex 8970M (20-5-88), Binbrook, 11, LTF, 11, 56, 11. 56 Sqn colours. Gate	1-14
❑ XV470	'BD'	McD Phantom FGR.2	69	ex 9156M, 56, 228 OCU, 11, 43, 228 OCU, 56, 228 OCU, 18, 228 OCU, 29, 228 OCU, 92, 228 OCU, 92, 56, 228 OCU, 31, 17, 14. Stored	1-14

FALKLAND ISLANDS – MOUNT PLEASANT AIRPORT

As related in *W&R23*, Phantom FGR.2 XV409 was scrapped and its cockpit was due to be saved. This came to pass and it went into the care of the Falkland Islands Government Air Service, for treatment of corrosion and readying for display. Bigger museum premises in Port Stanley are due to open in June/July 2014. As such, XV409 leaves the remit of *W&R*.

GIBRALTAR

RAF North Front:

❑ XX956	'BE'	SEPECAT Jaguar GR.1	75	ex Ipswich, Halton 8950M (3-12-87), Shawbury, 17, 31, 17, 14, 17. Gate	10-12

GUTERSLOH - GERMANY

On 4th October 2013, the Army Air Corps moved out and the Lynxes of 1 Regiment came back to the UK; ending an era that traces its roots back to 1945.

Breaking up Phantom FGR.2 XV409 at Mount Pleasant, Falkland Islands, during January 2013. *Darrel Phillips*

Appendix B : EXPORTS

All known exports are of course listed in the text, but not highlighted as such. The table here should help to tie all of this activity together. Column 4 gives the location under which it was to be found within *W&R* and Column 5 the destination.

G-AJRE		J/1 Autocrat ✈	Coventry, Warks	United Arab Emirates by 9-13
G-AMRA		Dakota IV ✈	Coventry, Warks	Germany as D-CXXX 30-7-13
G-AZDA		Pup 100	Elstree, Herts	France 9-12
G-BPIL		Cessna 310B	Bourn, Cambs	Hungary, mid-2012
G-BMNV		Stampe SV-4L	Haverfordwest, Ws	Belgium, by 2-12
G-BWUB		Super Cub 135	Dundee, Scotland	France, 28-4-12
G-CCWB		L39ZA Albatros	Duxford, Cambs	South Africa, 9-13
G-CGYN		Tiger Moth ✈	Chalgrove, Oxfordshire	India as HU512 23-9-12
G-DINT		Beaufighter I	Hatch, Beds	Australia, 2012
G-FLTA		HS 146-200 ✈	Southend, Essex	USA as N147FF 26-8-12
G-OTAF		L39ZO Albatros	Duxford, Cambs	South Africa, 9-13
G-PIXS		Cessna 336	Lydd, Kent	Portugal by 4-09
G-TIGG		Sud Super Puma	Aberdeen, Scotland	USA 4-12
F-HMFI		Farman F.41	Cosford, Shropshire	New Zealand, 12-12
N4HG		Lockheed Electra ✈	Coventry, Warks	Canada as C-FIJV 30-6-11
N6210K		RC-3 Seabee	Nottingham, Notts	USA, circa 2009
N96240		Beech D.18S ✈	North Weald, Essex	France 29-7-12
SE-FGV	G-CGHX	Beagle Pup 100	Chester, Cheshire	France 9-8-12
ZS-MRU		Douglas R4D-1 ✈	Dunsfold, Surrey	New Zealand 4-12
'TJ398'	BAPC.70	Auster AOP.5	South Shields, N&T	Canada 30-9-13
WZ816		Grasshopper TX.1	Redhill, Surrey	Malta, by 11-13
XG252		Hunter FGA.9	Hereford, Herefordshire	France, circa 2010
XG613		Sea Venom FAW.21	Duxford, Cambs	Poland, 5-13
XS876		Wessex HAS.1	East Midlands, Leics	Greece, 12-12
XW301		Jet Provost T.5A	Selby, N Yorks	Netherlands, 17-1-14
XW318		Jet Provost T.5A	Selby, N Yorks	Netherlands, 17-1-14
XW361		Jet Provost T.5A	Selby, N Yorks	Netherlands, 17-1-14
XX832		Jaguar T.2A	Ipswich, Suffolk	USA 24-7-13
ZD932		Tornado F.2 cockpit	Selby, N Yorks	Germany, 2013
ZE693		Sea Harrier FA.2	Ipswich, Suffolk	Greece, 11-11
ZF344		Tucano T.1	Linton-on-Ouse, N Yorks	via Ipswich to USA 12-13
ZF409		Tucano T.1	Linton-on-Ouse, N Yorks	via Ipswich to USA 12-13
- (c/n S45/T42)		Tucano T.1	Hawarden, Ws	USA as N312RS, 10-10
HD-75		Hanriot HD.1	Hendon, London	New Zealand 12-12
'D.5397'		Albatros D.Va	Yeovilton, Somerset	USA as N428UT 11-12
'CF+HF'	EI-AUY	MS Criquet	Duxford, Cambs	Germany 8-10-12
'4V+GH'	6316	Ju 52/3mge (AAC.1)	Duxford, Cambs	Poland, 5-13
22+57		F-104G Starfighter	Selby, N Yorks	Taiwan, 2012
96+21		Mi-24D *Hind*	Duxford, Cambs	USA 21-9-12
HA557	MW404	Tempest II	Wycombe, Bucks	USA by 4-12
C4E-88		Bf 109E-1	Lambourn, Berks	Germany 12-12
221		Vampire T.55	Hemel Hempstead, Herts	South Africa, 13-6-12
U-99	G-AXMT	Jungmeister ✈	Breighton, E Yorks	Italy, 7-13
-		P-40 Warhawk	Duxford, Cambs	USA, 2013
225068	G-CDVX	P-47G Thunderbolt ✈	Duxford, Cambs	USA, 27-12-13

Appendix C : 'COCKPITFEST'

CockpitFest - occasionally imitated, never surpassed - is a unique occasion in the aviation 'year'. Staged at the Newark Air Museum, the event was pioneered by Bill O'Sullivan, who hosts each gathering, assisted by a host of staff and volunteers from the museum.

Awards are as follows: 'Grand Champion' (GC) as judged by the attending public; 'Cockpiters' Cockpit' (CC) voted for by the attending 'cockpiters'; and *Wrecks & Relics* 'Spirit of *CockpitFest*' (*W&R*) awarded by the author of this 'ere book! Presentations are also made for instrument clusters flying clothing etc, but these are not applicable here. The 2012 event had a handful of fuselages or similar turn up; these are *not* listed here as they were *not* eligible for judging - the clue is in the title of the event, folks!

Information is given as follows: Column 1 gives type and identity plus award (if applicable); Column 2 location at that time. Readers seeking more information should take a look at: **www.cockpitfest.co.uk** and **www.newarkairmuseum.org**

CockpitFest XIII Newark Showground, 16th-17th June 2012

Canberra PR.7 WH779		resident
Canberra B(I).6 WT319		Lavendon, Bucks
Canberra PR.9		resident
Chipmunk T.10 WZ869		Leicester, Leics
F-4F Phantom II 37+86	GC	Lutterworth, Leics
Harrier GR.3 XV806		Worksop, Notts
HS.125-3B/RA 5N-AAN		resident
Hunter F.1 WT684		Lavendon, Bucks
Hunter F.5 WN957		Stockport, Gtr Man
Hunter FGA.9 XE584		Hooton Park, Cheshire
Hunter FGA.9 XE597	CC	Bromsgrove, Worcs
Jaguar GR.1 XX736		Doncaster, S Yorks
Jaguar GR.1A XX761		Old Sarum, Wilts
Jet Provost T.3 XN549		Warrington, Cheshire
Jet Provost T.5 G-BYED		Sleaford, Lincs
Lightning F.6 XS922		Spark Bridge, Cumbria
Lightning F.3 XP757	*W&R*	Stamford, Lincs
Lightning F.6 XS932		Metheringham, Lincs
Lightning F.53 ZF590		Upwood, Cambs
Meteor T.7 WA662		Doncaster, S Yorks
Meteor T.7 WL405		Hooton Park, Cheshire
P-51D Mustang SIM	WA	Amesbury, Wilts
P-63C 43-11137	*W&R*	Balcombe, W Sussex
Phantom FGR.2 XV490		resident
Sea Hawk FGA.6 WV838		Flixton, Suffolk
Spitfire		Boscombe Down, Wilts
Twin Pioneer 3 G-AYFA		Hooton Park, Cheshire
Tempest V		Doncaster, S Yorks

Mike Davey's Phantom FGR.2 cockpit XV490 arrived during *CockpitFest XII* in June 2011 and has been a 'resident' entrant ever since. It is illustrated at the June 2012 event. *Ken Ellis*

CockpitFest XIV Newark Showground, 15th-16th June 2013

Avro XIX G-AGPG	*W&R*	Liverpool, Merseyside
Canberra B.6 WT319		Lavendon, Bucks
Canberra PR.7 WH779	CC	resident
Canberra PR.9 SIM		resident
Chipmunk T.10 WZ869		Leicester, Leics
Gannet T.2		Hooton Park, Cheshire
Harrier GR.3 XV806		Worksop, Notts
Harrier GR.3 XV810		Metheringham, Lincs
HS.125 5N-ANN		resident
Hunter F.1 WT684		Lavendon, Bucks
Hunter FGA.9 XE597		Bromsgrove, Worcs
Jaguar GR.1 XX736		Doncaster, S Yorks
Jet Provost T.3 XN549		Chester, Cheshire
Jet Provost T.5 G-BYED		Sleaford, Lincs
Jet Provost T.5A XW315		Preston, Lancs
Lightning F.3 XP757		Stamford, Lincs
Lightning F.6 XS922	*W&R*	Spark Bridge, Cumbria
Lightning F.6 XS932		Metheringham, Lincs
Lightning F.53 ZF590		Upwood, Cambs
Meteor T.7 WA662		Doncaster, S Yorks
Scimitar F.1 XD235	GC	Lavendon, Bucks
Sea Hawk		Hooton Park, Cheshire
Tornado F.3 SIM		Chester, Cheshire
Tornado GR.1 ZD710		Chester, Cheshire
Typhoon		Doncaster, S Yorks

Right: Tony Collins is a multi-award winner at *CockpitFest*, including his incredible Scimitar F.1 XD235, here at the June 2013 event. Tony has developed a display stand that allows a flat-bed trailer to be driven underneath, the legs are removed and it's ready to roll! *Ken Ellis*

Below: You will always be assured a warm welcome at the 'North-West Ghetto' display area-cum-encampment at *CockpitFest*. Left to right at the June 2013 event: Avro XIX G-AGPG, anonymous Gannet T.2, Jet Provost XN549 and the anonymous Sea Hawk. *Ken Ellis*

Appendix D : FURTHER READING

Magazines

Air-Britain News, Air-Britain, monthly | Howard Nash, The Haven, Blacklands Lane, Sudbourne, Woodbridge, IP12 2AX
membership@air-britain.co.uk | www.air-britain.co.uk

Air North, North-East Branch of Air-Britain, monthly | Andrew Murray, 12 Burnside, Cullercoats, North Shields, NE30 3LE
ajmurray1967@blueyonder.co.uk

Hawkeye, Gatwick Aviation Society, monthly | Mike Green, 144 The Crescent, Horley, RH6 7PA
membership@gatwickaviationsociety.org.uk | www.gatwickaviationsociety.org.uk

Humberside Air Review, Humberside Aviation Society, monthly, also publish is an excellent annual *Residents Review*
Pete Wild, 37 Church Drive, Leven, HU17 5LH | **pwild117@yahoo.com | www.focalplane.karoo.net/HAR/has/htm**

Irish Air Letter, published by Paul Cunniffe, Karl E Hayes and Eamon C Power, monthly (also available as an 'e-zine')
20 Kempton Way, Navan Road, Dublin 7, Ireland | **ial.magazine@upcmail.ie**

Military Aviation Review, Military Aircraft Photographs, monthly (also available as an 'e-zine') | Brian Pickering, MAP, Westfield Lodge, Aslackby, near Sleaford, Lincs, NG34 0HG | **brianmap@btinternet.com | www.mar.co.uk**

Scottish Air News, Central Scotland Aviation Group, monthly (also available as an 'e-zine') and also publishes a residents run-down, *The Scottish Register* | Martin Wilson, 17 Ardlair Terrace, Dyce, Aberdeen, AB21 7LA
info@scottishairshnews.co.uk | www.scottishairnews.co.uk

SWAG-Mag, South West Aviation Group, monthly, (also available as an 'e-zine') | Mike Screech, 4 West Meadow Road, Braunton, EX33 1EB | **michael.screech@talktalk.net | www http://beehive.thisisnorthdevon.co.uk/swagmag**

Ulster Air Mail, Ulster Aviation Society, monthly | Paul McMaster, 107 Culcavey Road, Hillsborough, Co Down, BT26 6HH
info@ulsteraviationsociety.org | www.ulsteraviationsociety.co.uk

Plus... of course (!):

FlyPast, monthly magazine published by Key Publishing Ltd. PO Box 300, Stamford, Lincs, PE9 1NA
01780 480404 | subs@keypublishing.com | www.flypast.com

Books

The following have been on and off the shelves with great speed and are regarded as trusted friends:

British Civil Aircraft Register 1919-1999, Michael Austin, Air-Britain, 1999

Category Five, RAF Aircraft Losses 1954 to 2009, Colin Cummings, Nimbus Publishing, 2010, plus ***Final Landings*** (2001) and ***Last Take-off*** (2000) in this exceptional series

Civil Aircraft Registers of United Kingdom, Ireland and IoM, Dave Reid and Barry Womersley, Air-Britain, 2011

Combat Codes, Vic Flintham and Andrew Thomas, Airlife, 2003 - the seminal work on the subject

Fleet Air Arm Fixed-Wing Aircraft since 1946, Ray Sturtivant with Mick Burrow and Lee Howard, Air-Britain, 2004 – a masterpiece!

Fleet Air Arm Helicopters since 1943, Lee Howard, Mick Burrow and Eric Myall, Air-Britain, 2010 - likewise!

Great Aviation Collections of Britain, Ken Ellis, Crécy Publishing, Manchester, 2013

Lost Aviation Collections of Britain, Ken Ellis, Crécy Publishing, Manchester, 2011

Military Airfields of the British Isles 1939-1945 *(Omnibus Edition)*, Steve Willis and Barry Holliss, self-published, 1987

Phillip's Navigator Road Atlas, Phillip's, 2011

Piston Airliner Production List, Tony Eastwood and John Roach, The Aviation Hobby Shop, 2002

Royal Air Force Aircraft XA100 to XZ999, Jim Halley, Air-Britain, 2001 – and others in the series

Royal Air Force Flying Training & Support Units since 1912, Ray Sturtivant, John Hamlin, James J Halley, Air-Britain, 2007

Royal Air Force Squadrons, Wg Cdr C G Jefford, Airlife, 1988

Royal Navy Instructional Airframes, Ray Sturtivant & Rod Burden, British Aviation Research Group/Air-Britain, 1997 - superb!

Squadrons of the Fleet Air Arm, Ray Sturtivant, Air-Britain, 1984

Warbirds Directory, 4th Edition, Geoff Goodall, published by Derek Macphail, 2003

Web sites

For the unwary, these can be a minefield. Many web sites are mentioned within the main narrative, but the following have been of great use and proven worth.

www.caa.co.uk - the excellent GINFO database run by the Civil Aviation Authority

www.demobbed.org.uk - great database on former military from the stalwarts of the Wolverhampton Aviation Group

www.landings.com - massive aviation database, including US civil registration 'N-numbers'

Appendix E : ABBREVIATIONS

Without the use of abbreviations for the 'potted' histories of the aircraft listed in *W&R*, the book would be twice the size. To save repetition, abbreviations that are clearly combinations of others are not listed in full, eg MEAFCS, breaks into MEAF and CS, ie Middle East Air Force Communications Squadron.

AA	Air Attaché
A&AEE	Aeroplane and Armament Experimental Establishment. From the late 1980s became the Aircraft and Armament Evaluation Establishment. Now QinetiQ!
AAC	Army Air Corps
AACU	Anti-Aircraft Co-operation Unit
AAFCE	Allied Air Forces Central Europe
AAIU	Air Accident Investigation Unit
ABDR	Aircraft Battle Damage Repair
ABG	Air Base Group (USAF)
ACC	Allied Control Commission
ACSEA	Allied Command, South East Asia- *see Note 1*
ACU	Andover Conversion Unit
ADS	Air Director School
AE&AEOS	Air Engineers and Air Electronic Operators School
AEF	Air Experience Flight
AES	Air Engineers School
AES	Air Engineering School
AETW	Air Engineering Training Wing
AFDS	Air Fighting Development Squadron,
AFDU	Air Fighting Development Unit
AFEE	Airborne Forces Experimental Establishment
AFN	Air Forces North
AFNE	Air Forces Near East
AFS	Advanced Flying School
AFTS	Advanced Flying Training School
AFU	Advanced Flying Unit
AFWF	Advanced Fixed Wing Flight
AIU	Accident Investigation Unit
ALAT	Aviation Legere de l'Armee de Terre
ALE	Aviation Legacy Enthusiast
AMARC	Aerospace Maintenance& Regeneration Center, Arizona, USA
AMIF	Aircraft Maintainance Instruction Flight
AMS	Air Movements School
ANG	Air National Guard
ANS	Air Navigation School
AONS	Air Observer and Navigator School
AOTS	Aircrew Officers Training School
APS	Aircraft Preservation Society
APS	Armament Practice Station
AR&TF	Aircraft Recovery and Transportation Flight, St Athan – tri-service 'mover' of fixed-wing airframes. (See MASU)
ARW	Air Refueling Wing (USAF)
ARWF	Advanced Rotary Wing Flight,
AS	Aggressor Squadron
AS&RU	Aircraft Salvage and Repair Unit
ASF	Aircraft Servicing Flight
ASS	Air Signals School
AST	Air Service Training
ASWDU	Air-Sea Warfare Development Unit
ATA	Air Transport Auxiliary
ATAIU	Allied Technical Air Intelligence Unit
ATC	Air Training Corps (Air Cadets)
ATDU	Air Torpedo Development Unit
ATF	Airframe Technology Flight
Att	Air Attache
AuxAF	Auxiliary Air Force
aw/cn	AWaiting CollectioN - *see Note 2*
AWFCS	All Weather Fighter Combat School
AWOCU	All Weather Operational Conversion Unit
AWRE	Atomic Weapons Research Establishment,
BA	British Airways
BAAT	British Airways Airtours
BAC	Bristol Aero Collection
BAC	British Aircraft Corporation
BAe	British Aerospace
BAE	BAE Systems - the 'B' 'A' and'E' apparently standing for nothing!
BAF	British Air Ferries
BAFO	British Air Forces of Occupation
BAH	British Airways Helicopters
BAM	Booker Aircraft Museum
BANS	Basic Air Navigation School
BAOR	British Army of the Rhine
BAPC	British Aviation Preservation Council
BATUS	British Army Training Unit, Suffield (Can)
BBMF	Battle of Britain Memorial Flight
BBML	British Balloon Museum and Library
BC	Bomber Command.
BCAL	British Cdonian Airlines
BCBS	Bomber Command Bombing School
BDRF	Battle Damage Repair Flight
BDTF	Bomber Defence Training Flight
BDU	Bomber Development Unit
BEA	British European Airways
BEAH	British European Helicopters
BEAS	British Executive Air Services
BFTS	Basic Flying Training School
BFWF	Basic Fixed Wing Flight
B&GS	Bombing & Gunnery School (RCAF)
BG	Bomb(ardment) Group (US)
BLEU	Blind Landing Experimental Unit
BMA	British Midland Airways now bmi
BOAC	British Overseas Airways Corporation
BPPU	Bristol Plane Preservation Unit
BRNC	Britannia Royal Naval College
BSE	Bristol Siddeley Engines
B&TTF	Bombing & Target Towing Flight
BTF	Beaver Training Flight
BTU	Bombing Trials Unit
BUA	British United Airlines
BW	Bomb(ardment) Wing (US)

C(A)	Controller (Aircraft) see also CS(A) - *see Note 3*
CAA	Civil Aviation Authority
CAACU	Civilian Anti-Aircraft Co-operation Unit
CACF	Coastal Artillery Co-operation Flight
CACU	Coastal Artillery Co-operation Unit
CAF	Canadian Armed Forces
CAFU	Civil Aviation Flying Unit
Cam Flt	Camouflage Flight
CATCS	Central Air Traffic Control School
CAW	College of Air Warfare
CBE	Central Bombing Establishment
CC	Coastal Command.
CCAS	Civilian Craft Apprentices School,
CCF	Combined Cadet Force
CF	Communications Flight as suffix with other unit, or for an airfield
CFCCU	Civilian Fighter Control and Co-op Unit
CFE	Central Fighter Establishment - see CFE-EAF.
CFE-EAF	Central Fighter Establishment - Enemy Aircraft Flight
CFS	Central Flying School
C&TTS	Communications and Target Towing Sqn
CGS	Central Gliding School
CGS	Central Gunnery School
CIFAS	Centre d'Instruction des Forces Aeriennes Strategiques
CIT	Cranfield Institute of Technology
CNCS	Central Navigation and Control School
CoA	Certificate (or Permit) of Airworthiness.
Cott	Cottesmore, in relation to V-Bomber wings
CPF	Coastal Patrol Flight
cr	crashed, or other form of accident
CR	Crash Rescue, training airframe.
CRD	Controller, Research and Development
C&RS	Control and Reporting School
CS	Communications Squadron, as a suffix with other units, or for an airfield.
CS(A)	Controller, Supplies (Air), see also CA - *Note 3*
CSDE	Central Servicing Development Establisment
CSE	Central Signals Establishment
CSF	Canberra Servicing Flight
CTE	Central Training Establishment
CTTS	Civilian Technical Training School
C&TTS	Communications & Target Towing Squadron
CU	Communications Unit, as suffix
CU	Conversion Unit, as suffix
DARA	Defence Aviation Repair Agency, Fleetlands, St Athan, Sealand
dbr	damaged beyond repair, to distinguish an aircraft that was written off but did not crash
deH	de Havilland
de-reg	de-registered (from a civilian identity)
DERA	Defence Evaluation and Research Agency — replaced DRA and DTEO.
Det	Detachment, flight or other unit detached from main base
DFLS	Day Fighter Leader School
dism	dismantled
DLO	Defence Logistics Organisation
DPA	Defence Procurement Agency replaced MoD(PE)
DRA	Defence Research Agency – see DERA
DSA	Disposal Ss Agency
DSDA	Defence Storage and Distribution Agency
DTEO	Defence Test and Evaluation Organisation – see DERA
DU	Development Unit, as suffix
EAAS	East Anglian Aviation Society
EASAMS	European avionics consortium
ECTT	Escadre de Chasse Tous Temps
EE	English Electric
EFTS	Elementary Flying Training School
EOD	Explosive Ordnance Disposal
EP&TU	Exhibition, Production and Transport Unit
ERFTS	Elementary & Reserve Flying Trng School
ERS	Empire Radio School
Esc	Escadre, French squadron
ETPS	Empire Test Pilots School
ETS	Engineering Training School
ETU	Experimental Trials Unit
EWAD	Electronic Warfare and Avionics Detachment
EWE&TU	Electronic Warfare Experimental & Training Unit
F / Flt	Flight, suffix to number
FAA	Fleet Air Arm
FAA	Fuerza Aerea Argentina
FAAHAF	Fleet Air Arm Historic Aircraft Flight
FAAM	Fleet Air Arm Museum
FAF	French Air Force.
FAH	Fuerza Aerea Hondurena
FC	Fighter Command.
FC&RS	Fighter Control and Reporting School
FCS	Fighter Control School
FCTU	Fighter Command Trials Unit
FEAF	Far East Air Forces - *see Note 1*
FECS	Far East Communications Flight
FF	Ferry Flight
FF&SS	Fire Fighting and Safety School
FGF	Flying Grading Flight
FLS	Fighter Leader School
f/n	first noted
FOAC	Flag Officer, Aircraft Carriers
FOCAS	Friends of Cardington Airship Station
FOFT	Flag Officer, Flying Training
FONA	Flag Officer, Naval Aviation
FONAC	Flag Officer, Naval Air Command
FP	Ferry Pool
FPP	Ferry Pilots Pool
FRADU	Fleet Requirements and Direction Unit
FRL	Flight Refuelling Ltd
FRS	Flying Refresher School
FRU	Fleet Requirements Unit
FS	Fighter Squadron (US)
FSM	Full Sc Model
FSS	Ferry Support Squadron
FSS	Flying Selection Squadron
FTC	Flying Training Command
FTS	Flying Training School
FTU	Ferry Training Unit

FU	Ferry Unit
FW	Fighter Wing (USAF)
FWS	Fighter Weapons School
GIA	Ground Instructional Airframe
GS	Glider School
GSU	Group Support Unit
GTS	Glider Training School
GU	Glider Unit
GWDS	Guided Weapons Development Squadron
HAB	Hot air balloon
HAM	Historic Aircraft Museum, Southend
HC	Home Command
HCEU	Home Command Examining Unit
HCF	Hornet Conversion Flight
HDU	Helicopter Development Unit
HGSU	Heavy Glider Servicing Unit
HHU	Helicopter Holding Unit
HMTS	Harrier Maintenance Training School
HQ	Headquarters
HS	Handling Squadron
HSA	Hawker Siddeley Aviation
HTF	Helicopter Training Flight
IAC	Irish Army Air Corps
IAF	Indian Air Force
IAM	Institute of Aviation Medicine
IAP	(Russian) Fighter Aviation Regiment
IA PVO	(Russian) Air Defence Fighter Force
IFTU	Intensive Flying Trials Unit
IGN	Institut Geographique National
IHM	International Helicopter Museum
ITF or 'S	Instrument Training Flight / Squadron
IWM	Imperial War Museum
JASS	Joint Anti-Submarine School
JADTEU	Joint Air Delivery Test and Evaluation Unit - replaced JATEU !!
JATE	Joint Air Transport Establishment - see JATEU
JATEU	Joint Air Transport Evaluation Unit – see JADTEU!
JCU	Javelin Conversion Unit
JEHU	Joint Experimental Helicopter Unit
JMU	Joint Maritime Unit
JOCU	Jaguar Operational Conversion Unit
JTU	Joint Trials Unit
JWE	Joint Warfare Establishment
LAS	Light Aircraft School
LC	Logistics Command
LCS & 'U	Lightning Conversion Squadron / Unit
l/n	last noted
LRWE	Long Range Weapons Research Est
LTF	Lightning Training Flight
LTW	Lyneham Tactical Wing (Hercules)
MAM	Midland Air Museum
MASL	Military Aircraft Spares Ltd
MASU	Mobile Aircraft Support Unit – DARA Fleetlands, tri-service 'mover' of helicopters See AR&TF
MBA	Museum of Berkshire Aviation
MC	Maintenance Command
MCS	Metropolitan Communications Squadron
MEAF	Middle East Air Force- *see Note 1*
MECS	Middle East Communications Squadron
METS	Multi-Engine Training School
MGSP	Mobile Glider Servicing Party
MinTech	Ministry of Technology, see also MoA, MoS - *see Note 3*
MoA	Ministry of Aviation, see also MinTech, MoS - *see Note 3*
MoD(PE)	Ministry of Defence (Procurement Executive) – see DPA
MoS	Ministry of Supply, see MinTech, MoA - *see Note 3*
MoTaT	Museum of Transport & Technology, NZ
MOTU	Maritime Operational Training Unit
MPA	Man-powered aircraft
MU	Maintenance Unit - *See Note 4*
NAAS	Navigator and Airman Aircrew School
NACDS	Naval Air Command Driving School
NASA	National Aeronautical and Space Admin
NASU	Naval Aircraft Servicing Unit
NBC	Nuclear, Bacteriological and Chemical
NCS	Northern Communications Squadron
nea	Non effective airframe - *See Note 2*
NECS	North Eastern Communications Squadron
NFLS	Night Fighter Leaders School
NGTE	National Gas Turbine Establishment
NIBF	Northern Ireland Beaver Flight
n/s	No service - UK military only
NSF	Northern Sector Flight
ntu	Not taken up, registration applied for, but not worn, or paperwork not concluded
(O)AFU	(Observers) Advanced Flying Unit
OCTU	Officer Cadet Training Unit
OCU	Operational Conversion Unit
OEU	Operational Evaluation Unit
OFU	Overseas Ferry Unit
OTU	Operational Training Unit
(P)AFU	(Pilot) Advanced Flying Unit
PAX	Passenger, as used in Chipmunk PAX trainer
PCSS	Protectorate Comms and Support Squadron
PEE	Proof & Experimental Establishment
PFA	Popular Flying Association
PFS	Primary Flying School
PFTS	Primary Flying Training School
PP	Pilots' Pool
PPS	Personal Plane Services
PRDU	Photo Reconnaissance Development Unit
PRU	Photographic Reconnaissance Unit
PTC	Personnel and Training Command
PTF	Phantom Training Flight
PTS	Primary Training School
PVO	(Russian) Air Defence Force
QF	Queen's Flight
RAAF	Royal Australian Air Force
RAE	Royal Aircraft / Aerospace Establishment
RAeS	Royal Aeronautical Society
RAF	Royal Air Force
RAFA	Royal Air Force Association
RAFC	Royal Air Force College
RAFEF	Royal Air Force Exhibition Flight
RAFFC	Royal Air Force Flying College
RAFG	Royal Air Force Germany
RAFGSA	Royal Air Force Gliding & Soaring Assoc

RAFHSF	Royal Air Force High Speed Flight
RAFM	Royal Air Force Museum
RAN	Royal Australian Navy
RC	Reserve Command
RCAF	Royal Canadian Air Force
RCN	Royal Canadian Navy
RCS	Rotary Conversion Squadron
Regt	Regiment
RFS	Reserve Flying School
RHK	Royal Hong Kong
RMAF	Royal Malaysian Air Force
RNAY	Royal Naval Aircraft Yard
RNEC	Royal Naval Engineering College
RNEFTS	Royal Navy Elementary Flying Training School
RNGSA	Royal Navy Gliding and Soaring Association
RNHF	Royal Navy Historic Flight
RNoAF	Royal Norwegian Air Force
RNZAF	Royal New Zealand Air Force
ROC	Royal Observer Corps
RPRE	Rocket Propulsion Research Establishment
RRAF	Royal Rhodesian Air Force
RRE	Royal Radar Establishment
RRF	Radar Reconnaissance Flight
RRHT	Rolls-Royce Heritage Trust
RS	Radio School
RSRE	Radar and Signals Research Establishment
RSS & 'U	Repair & Servicing Section / Unit
RTR	Royal Tank Regiment
RWE	Radio Warfare Establishment
SAAF	South African Air Force
SAC	School of Army Co-operation
SAF	School of Aerial Fighting
SAH	School of Aircraft Handling
SAOEU	Strike Attack Operational Evaluation Unit
SAR	Search and Rescue
SAREW	Search and Rescue Engineering Wing
SARTS	Search and Rescue Training Squadron
SARTU	Search and Rescue Training Unit
SC	Signals Command
Scamp	Scampton, to distinguish a V-Bomber wing
SCBS	Strike Command Bombing School
SCS	Southern Communications Squadron
SEAE	School of Electrical and Aeronautical Engineering
SF	Station Flight, usually with an airfield name
SFDO	School of Flight Deck Operations
SFTS	Service Flying Training School
ShF	Ship's Flight
SHQ	Station HQ
SKTU	Sea King Training Unit
SLAW	School of Land/Air Warfare
SMR	School of Maritime Reconnaissance
SOC	Struck off charge - *See Note 2*
SoRF	School of Refresher Flying
SoTT	School of Technical Training - *See Note 5*
SRCU	Short Range Conversion Unit
SRW	Strategic Reconnaissance Wing
SS	Signals Squadron
SS	Support Squadron
SU	Support Unit
SVAS	Shuttleworth Veteran Aeroplane Society
TAC	The Aeroplane Collection
TAF	Tactical Air Force
TAW	Tactical Airlift Wing
TC	Transport Command
TCS	Troop Carrier Squadron (USAAF)
TCW	Troop Carrier Wing (USAAF)
TEE	Trials and Experimental Establishment
TES	Tri-Partitie Evaluation Squadron
TEU	Tactical Exercise Unit
TF	Training Flight
TFF	Target Facilities Flight
TFS	Traget Facilities Squadron
TFS	Tactical Fighter Squadron
TFTAS	Tactical Fighter Training Aggressor Squadron
TFU	Telecommunications Flying Unit
TFW	Tactical Fighter Wing
TGDA	Training Group Defence Agency
Thum Flt	Temperature and HUMidity Flight
TMS	Tornado Maintenance School
TMTS	Trade Management Training School
TOC	Taken on charge - *See Note 2*
TOEU	Tornado Operational Evaluation Unit
TRE	Telecommunications Research Establishment
TS	Training Squadron
TTC	Technical Training Command
TTF	Tanker Training Flight
TTTE	Tri-National Tornado Training Establishment
TTTE	Thomas The Tank Engine
TTU	Torpedo Training Unit
TWDU	Tactical Weapons Development Unit
TWU	Tactical Weapons Unit
UAS	University Air Squadron - *See Note 6*
UNFICYP	United Nations Forces In Cyprus
USAAC	United States Army Air Corps
USAAF	United States Army Air Force
USAF	United States Air Force
USMC	United States Marine Corps
USN	United States Navy
VAFA	Vintage Aircraft Flying Association
VAT	Vintage Aircraft Team
VGS	Volunteer Gliding School – and, from 2005: Volunteer Gliding *Squadron*
VVS KA	(Russian) Soviet Army Air Force
VVS VMF	(Russian) Soviet Naval Air Force
Wadd	Waddington, denoting a V-Bomber wing
WAP	Wycombe Air Park
WCS	Western Communications Squadron
wfu	Withdrawn from use
Witt	Wittering, denoting a V-bomber wing.
WLT	Weapons Loading Trainer
WSF	Western Sector Flight

Notes on UK military airframes

1 **RAF 'Holding Units'**: For administrative purposes, the history cards of some RAF aircraft become fairly vague when transferred to either Middle East or Far East theatres of operations. Accordingly, the following abbreviations denote the 'operator' for the segment of an aircraft's life in that theatre, even though it may have been used by several front-line units: ACSEA, FEAF, MEAF.

2 **History Card 'milestones'**: There are several RAF aircraft history card 'milestones' referred to in the main text. Essentially an aircraft starts off as AWaiting Collection (Aw/cn) - a signal from the manufacturer that the aircraft is ready for issue to service; it is then taken on charge (toc) and becomes a part of the RAF; after service life, it may eventually to be declared a non-effective airframe (nea) and down-graded to instructional or fire-training use; the final act is for it to be struck off charge (SOC), either being written-off in an accident, scrapped, sold to another user etc etc.

3 **Government 'owning' bodies**: Technical 'owner' of UK military machines is the C(A) or CS(A) and at times these are noted within the aircraft history cards instead of a unit, although it may well be a pointer to the aircraft being operated at that time of its life by a test or trials unit. In similar manner, MinTech, MoA or MoS can appear, frequently meaning operation by the RAE, or DRA.

4 **Maintenance Unit** (MU): Frequently mentioned in the text are: 2 - Sealand, 5 - Kemble, 6 - Brize Norton, 7 - Quedgeley, 8 - Little Rissington, 9 - Cosford, 10 - Hullavington, 12 - Kirkbride, 13 - Henlow, 14 - Carlisle, 15 - Wroughton, 16 - Stafford, 18 - Dumfries, 19 - St Athan, 20- Aston Down, 22 - Silloth, 23 - Aldergrove, 24 - Tern Hill, 25 - Hartlebury, 27 - Shawbury, 29 - High Ercall, 32 - St Athan, 33 - Lyneham, 34 - Montford Bridge, 36 - Sealand, 37 - Burtonwood, 38 - Llandow, 39 - Colerne, 44 - Edzell, 45 - Kinloss, 46 - Lossiemouth, 47 - Sealand, 48 - Hawarden, 51 - Lichfield, 52 - Cardiff, 54 - Cambridge, 57 - Wig Bay, 60 - Leconfield, 71 - Bicester. Note that several locations had more than one MU, eg Sealand, St Athan.

5 **School of Technical Training** (SoTT): The following are mentioned in the main text: 1 - Halton, 2 - Cosford, 3 - Manston, 4 - St Athan, 5 - Locking, 6 - Hednesford, 7 - Innsworth, 8 - Weeton, 9 - Newton, 10 - Kirkham, 11 - Credenhill, 12 - Melksham, 14 - Henlow, 21 - Burtonwood.

6 **University Air Squadron** (UAS): Prefixed with a university name: Abn - Aberdeen, Dundee and St Andrews, Bir - Birmingham, Bri - Bristol, Cam - Cambridge, Dur - Durham, Edn - Edinburgh, Elo - East Lowlands, Ems - East Midlands, G&S - Glasgow & Strathclyde, Lee - Leeds, Liv - Liverpool, Lon - London, Man - Manchester and Salford, Nor - Northumbrian, Not - Nottingham, Oxf - Oxford, QUB - Queens University Belfast, Sotn - Southampton, Wal - Ws, Yor - Yorkshire.

Index I : BY TYPE

For the purposes of this index, no distinction is made for replicas.

Index II : LOCATIONS

This index also includes a decode of alternative names to help you find Robin Hood!

Thoughts on 40 years...
Time is an illusion
Lunchtime doubly so

Douglas Adams, *The Book*
The Hitch Hiker's Guide to the Galaxy, 1979

Also by Ken Ellis

Lost Aviation Collections of Britain

A tribute to the UK's bygone aviation museums and collections

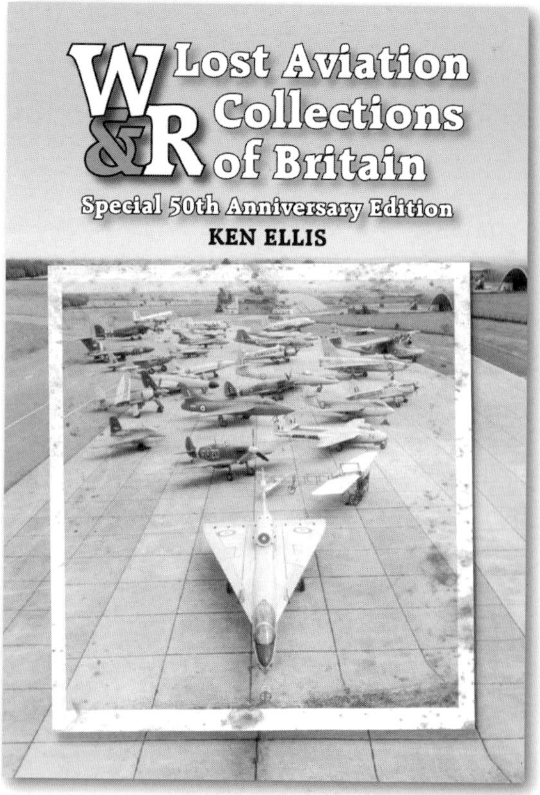

Britain's diverse aviation heritage owes much to the pioneer museums and collections that preserved irreplaceable aircraft from the 1930s onwards and to celebrate the 50th anniversary of the first publication of *Wrecks & Relics*, this special edition of 'W&R' commemorates the most important of these collections.

Warbird pioneers such as Richard Nash, Spencer Flack and Charles Church feature together with important institutions, such as Cranfield and Loughborough, that helped kick-start the aircraft preservation 'booms' of the 1960s and 1970s. Additionally, many much-loved museums that are no more are described, including Colerne, Skyfame, Southend, Strathallan and Torbay. Over 40 such organisations, large and small, are covered.

Lost Aviation Collections of Britain also examines 'Ones that Got Away' – important types that slipped through the preservation 'net' and into extinction, such as the ATEL Carvair, Miles Marathon and the Westland Whirlwind fighter.

Lavishly illustrated with over 200 period images, 96 in full colour, *Lost Aviation Collections of Britain* provides a wonderful record of the UK's aircraft preservation movement, a unique reference book from the author who knows its history better than anybody else.

224 pages | hardback
234mm x 156mm
Over 100 b/w and 96 colour photos
ISBN 9 780859 791595
£16.95

Great Aviation Collections of Britain

The UK's National Treasures and Where to Find Them

A century ago the Cody Biplane was presented to the Science Museum, putting Britain at the forefront of the worldwide aviation heritage movement. This special edition of *Wrecks & Relics* celebrates the centenary and the development of the UK's aviation museums. It tells the story of the national icons - Science Museum, Imperial War Museum, RAF Museum, Fleet Air Arm Museum, Museum of Army Aviation and the Shuttleworth Collection including how they developed and their exhibits, past and present. *Great Aviation Collections of Britain* also pays tribute to provincial, regional and local collections, large and small, revealing the story of the UK's diverse aviation achievements and providing details of nearly 100 venues open to the public.

Over 200 of the most important exhibits are profiled in detail, with their backgrounds described, their significance explained and the exploits of the pilots that flew them revealed. From Roe's Triplane, Amy Johnson's Moth, a Battle of Britain veteran Spitfire and the very first Mosquito to Concorde and Eurofighter, each has its biography outlined and a cross-reference of aircraft allows the reader to visit the 'must see' exhibits across Britain.

Lavishly illustrated with over 250 illustrations including 96 in full colour, archive imagery stretches back over 100 years to graphically show the UK's treasures when they were in service, or found disused and decaying.

A vital addition to the *Wrecks & Relics* series and the perfect companion to *Lost Aviation Collections of Britain*.

272 pages | hardback
234mm x 156mm
Over 250 photographs and illustrations
ISBN 9 780859 791748
£17.95

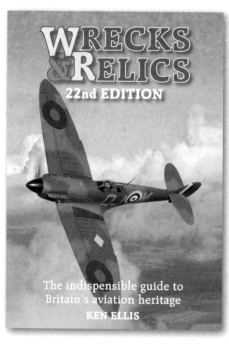